Sylvia Beach
and
the Lost Generation

Sylvia Beach

and

the Lost Generation

*A History of Literary Paris
in the Twenties and Thirties*

NOEL RILEY FITCH

W·W·NORTON & COMPANY · *NEW YORK · LONDON*

The text of this book is composed in photocomposition Times Roman, with display type set in Baskerville. Composition and manufacturing by The Maple-Vail Book Manufacturing Group. Book design by Marjorie J. Flock.

First published as a Norton paperback 1985

Library of Congress Cataloging in Publication Data
Fitch, Noel Riley.
    Sylvia Beach and the lost generation.
    Includes index.
    1. Beach, Sylvia.   2. Booksellers and bookselling —
France — Paris — Biography — Shakespeare and Company.   3. Paris (France) —
Intellectual life.   4. American literature — France —
Paris — History.   5. English literature — France — Paris —
History and criticism.   I. Title.
Z305.B33F57   1983   070.5'0944'36   82-24621

ISBN 0-393-30231-8

W. W. Norton & Company, Inc.
500 Fifth Avenue, New York, N.Y. 10110
www.wwnorton.com

W. W. Norton & Company Ltd.
Castle House, 75/76 Wells Street, London W1T 3QT

6 7 8 9 0

To Philip and Gailyn
Dorcas and John

CONTENTS

An illustration section appears following page 204

Sylvia Beach
and
the Lost Generation

The only real voyage is not an approach to landscape but a viewing of the universe with the eyes of a hundred other people.

— Marcel Proust

INTRODUCTION

MY LOVES WERE Adrienne Monnier and James Joyce and Shakespeare and Company," proclaims Sylvia Beach. This book is the story of these three loves.

The first is the story of the love between two women. The details were and still are little known. The story began in Paris on a cold, gusty March afternoon in 1917. A shy young American woman named Sylvia Beach hesitated at the door of a Left Bank bookshop and lending library. The owner, a self-assured young French writer and publisher named Adrienne Monnier, got up quickly from her desk and drew her visitor into the shop, greeting her warmly. The two talked the afternoon away, each declaring love for the language and literature of the other. As Sylvia Beach left with a library membership card, a gust of wind blew her broad Spanish hat from her head and set it down in the middle of the rue de l'Odéon. Adrienne Monnier ran to retrieve it, brushed it off, and returned it to her new friend. When their eyes met, they broke into laughter. They sensed clearly that this meeting was to be the first of many meetings. It proved to be more than that: the opening chapter of a literary life together, a life that for thirty-eight years nurtured two generations of American, English, and French writers.

The second story is that of the love of a woman for a man's genius. Like the first, it began in Paris—but on a hot summer afternoon three years later. At a dinner party, Sylvia Beach spied the author of *A Portrait of the Artist as a Young Man* drooping in the corner between two bookcases. Trembling, she approached and asked, "Is this the great James Joyce?" "James Joyce," he replied. They shook hands and, as she tells it, "he put his limp, boneless hand in my tough little paw—if you can call that a handshake." With this simple exchange, Sylvia Beach, since 1919 the owner of her own bookshop and lending library—Shakespeare and Company—met her literary god. "I worshiped James Joyce," she confesses. Like most gods, he did not return her love. Even so, she published *Ulysses,* one of the longest modern novels, and devoted twelve trying years to his often selfish wants and needs. The loyal supplicant worked feverishly to publish and promote the genius of her remote beloved, whom Tom Stoppard (in *Travesties*) ironically but accurately characterizes as an "essentially private man who wishes his total indifference to public notice to be universally recognized." Together, he plotting each move from backstage and she working openly in the public arena, they fiercely peddled his epic novel. They were the most successful clandestine promotional team in the history of high art.

The story of Sylvia Beach's love for Shakespeare and Company supplies the lifeblood of this book. It began in Paris in November of 1919. For more than two protean decades, the Company there forgathered altered the course of modern literature. Sylvia Beach created a literary center that magnetically attracted artists from all over the world during what Archibald MacLeish calls the "greatest period of literary and artistic innovation since the Renaissance." This Company, no less than that of Chaucer, comprised a diverse array of modern pilgrims—T. S. Eliot, André Gide, Ernest Hemingway, Ezra Pound, Gertrude Stein, Paul Valéry, and most of the other men and women who made the Paris of the twenties and thirties the cultural capital of the world. Many of the Company—including Samuel Beckett, Elizabeth Bishop, André Chamson, Malcolm Cowley, Leon Edel, Janet Flanner, Archibald MacLeish, Virgil Thomson, Glenway Wescott, and Thornton Wilder—generously tapped their memories so that these tales might be told in full. I am deeply grateful for their assistance.

These literary pilgrims (the term was Sylvia's) were not, in a personal or artistic sense, a "lost" generation. Sylvia and Adrienne and Joyce—and the Company they kept—were not wanderers but seekers. Like true pilgrims, they were in quest of salvation. Shakespeare and Company was their house of worship, consecrated to the cult of Art which was their uncommon bond of faith.

CHAPTER 1

A Gift of Tongues

1922

Paris rawly waking, crude sunlight on her lemon streets . . .

—*Ulysses*

Sylvia beach paced the platform of the Gare de Lyon, waiting alone in the chill morning air for the arrival of the train from Dijon. The date was 2 February 1922. Since the day, eleven months earlier, when she had naively suggested to James Joyce that she publish his novel *Ulysses,* she had not had a moment's rest. She had solicited subscriptions, written hundreds of letters, hired typists, corrected proofs, and taken care of the family needs of the Joyces. But her shrewdest acts she had reserved for the printer, M. Maurice Darantière, of Dijon. She had time and again persuaded Darantière to allow Joyce to add to his manuscript—Joyce had written nearly a third more on the page proofs, which were repeatedly reset to accommodate a quarter of a million words. Now she was demanding the impossible. Although she had returned the last of the page proofs only two days earlier, she wanted two copies for Joyce's fortieth birthday: being superstitious in an Irish way, Joyce attached significance to birthdays, dates, and numbers. She knew the present that would please him most. And she knew Darantière.

The express train arrived at 7 A.M. "I was on the platform," Sylvia remembered, "my heart going like the locomotive, as the train from Dijon came slowly to a standstill and I saw the conductor getting off, holding a parcel and looking around for someone—me." She raced to his side and claimed the first two copies of *Ulysses,* then hurried out to the street and hailed a taxi for the ride across the Seine to 9 rue de l'Université, where the Joyces lived. After leaving the taxi, Sylvia rang the Joyces' bell. The door was opened by a thin and bespectacled Joyce. This momentous occasion was shaped by their natural restraint and marked only with a simple gesture. She handed the frail and partially blind Irishman his first copy of *Ulysses.* His epic novel—begun eight years earlier and, in early partial publication, condemned by the New York Court of Special Sessions as "unintelligible" and "obscene"—was finally to be published. Fortunately the typesetters could not read the English manuscript. But for the next ten years—during which time eleven printings appeared—it would have to be smuggled into the United States, sometimes wrapped as the *Complete Works of William Shakespeare*.

Sylvia returned that morning to her lending library and bookshop just a few streets away, on the rue de l'Odéon. Shakespeare and Company was her primary concern, but for the next few months she was to devote all her energies to the sale and distribution of *Ulysses*. Although days would pass before the regular copies of the novel were ready to be distributed to the subscribers, she placed her own copy—with its Greek blue cover and white lettering—in the window. There it was "unfurled," cheered one English resident of Paris, "like the flag of freedom on the Left Bank." Sylvia and her subscribers, who had been coaxed to pay for the book in advance of publication, knew that this was a book that would change the course of fiction. "In Sylvia Beach's bookshop," claims Cyril Connolly, "*Ulysses* lay stacked like dynamite in a revolutionary cellar." One young American in Paris confessed, "It bursted over us like an explosion in print[,] whose words and phrases fell upon us like a gift of tongues, like a less than holy Pentecostal experience."

Not long after Sylvia opened the shop that morning, she was deluged with visits by friends and patrons. First came her young French assistant, Myrsine Moschos, daughter of a Greek physician. Then came Adrienne Monnier, owner of the French bookshop across the street, La Maison des Amis des Livres. It was to Adrienne, her life companion, that Sylvia had first turned for help with the publication of *Ulysses*. Although they had agreed to divide French and English literature between them, they shared all publishing secrets and also Darantière, who had for several years been Adrienne's printer. After Adrienne came the Paris subscribers. By that afternoon, she had to remove *Ulysses* from the window because many of them could not understand why their copies were unavailable. Joyce described the bookshop as being "in a state of siege." For over a week, she had to put off the small group of French, American, and English writers who were eager to get their copies.

Meanwhile that first day, Joyce was busy sending telegrams and letters to his friends and supporters. Chief among these was Harriet Weaver, an Englishwoman who for years had been financially supporting the Joyce family. For the record, he also wrote Sylvia; "I cannot let today pass without thanking you for all the trouble and worry you have given yourself about my book during the last year." That evening he brought to the bookshop a poem he had written, in the manner of Shakespeare, in tribute to his publisher:

> Who is Sylvia, what is she
> That all our scribes commend her?
> Yankee, young and brave is she
> The West this grace did lend her
> That all books might published be.
>
> Is she rich as she is brave
> For wealth oft daring misses?
> Those about her rant and rave

To subscribe for *Ulysses*
But, having signed, they ponder grave.

Then to Sylvia let us sing.
Her daring lies in selling.
She can sell each mortal thing
That's boring beyond telling.
To her let us buyers bring.

                    J.J.
                    after
                    W.S. [*The Two Gentlemen of Verona*]*

When the regular copies began arriving from Dijon, Sylvia and Myrsine spent two hours packaging them for mailing to foreign subscribers in two dozen countries. The slightly built women carried the heavy books—*Ulysses* was 732 pages long and weighed two pounds four ounces—to the post office, a few blocks away. Joyce, who was unable to stay away from the excitement, hurried each day to the bookshop.

I loved to see Joyce walking up the street twirling his ashplant stick, his hat on the back of his head. "Melancholy Jesus," Adrienne and I used to call him. It was from Joyce himself that I learned this expression. Also "Crooked Jesus" (he pronounced it "croo-ked").

Afraid of missing something, he busied himself with every detail of distribution. Concerning publicity he was astute. Deliver a copy to Miss Natalie Barney on Friday, he suggested; "as this is her reception day it would arrive at a good moment." But when it came to the physical chores, such as packaging and mailing, he was a hindrance. Trying to keep up with the furious pace, Joyce put more glue in his hair and on the floor than on the mailing labels. Sylvia removed the stray glue with alcohol and completed the mailing of this first printing. Before port authorities had been alerted, the first shipments were received by subscribers in Dublin and London. But soon the New York Port Authority (under Section 211 of the Federal Criminal Code) began seizing shipments, and Sylvia vowed to mail no more. Instead she planned surreptitious means of getting copies of the book into the hands of its remaining American subscribers.

Inserted in each book was a little slip of paper with the publisher's apology:

The publisher asks the reader's indulgence for typographical errors unavoidable in the exceptional circumstances.

Few persons knew how exceptional the circumstances had been. Nor did they know how many errors there really were. Sylvia estimated from one to six per page. It was not just that the printers did not read English. They set the book by hand! There were twenty-six typesetters to make errors. One, for example, swung away from a capital *W* on *Weight,* gathered up his tray of new letters, and returned

*The word *grace* in the fourth line was mistakenly printed as *pace* in Sylvia Beach's memoirs, *Shakespeare and Company,* although both pace and grace were certainly needed for her dealings with Joyce.

to the *W* on *Wonder,* leaving out ten words: "or size of it, something blacker than the dark. Wonder."*

This flurry in the spring of 1922 in the rue de l'Odéon was but the physical aftermath of a profound, unseen artistic revolution, which had for several years been fermenting in Paris. For a decade Paris had been the center of a gravitational pull of international artistic talent. In the years immediately following the First World War, when the revolution of the arts was peaking, Paris still guarded its intimacy and remained much as it had been in the late nineteenth century. Most of the streets remained quiet and tranquil, especially in the sixth arrondissement, one of the oldest parts of Paris, between the boulevard du Montparnasse and the Seine. The rue de l'Odéon is in a neighborhood of bookshops and publishing houses north of the Luxembourg Garden. The neighborhood's quaint little courtyards, its narrow cobbled streets, not yet encumbered by lines of vehicles, and its bistros, not yet replaced by espresso cafés, make it the very picture of tranquillity. Here, as in the almost provincial rue de l'Odéon, most people still walked, some rode bicycles, and an early riser could hear the sound of wooden carts and horse hoofs. Here, away from the noisy centers of social revolution, was a quiet center of artistic revolution.

Behind the storefront facade of Shakespeare and Company met French, Irish, English, and American writers such as James Joyce, Paul Valéry, André Gide, T. S. Eliot, Ernest Hemingway, and Ezra Pound. From 1919 until 1941 this bookshop was meeting place, clubhouse, post office, money exchange, and reading room for the famous and soon-to-be-famous of the avant-garde. More grandly, it was a literary center for the cross-fertilization of cultures. Its opening in the fall of 1919 signaled the beginning of a new French zeal for American literature. Its opening also preceded by two years the arrival in Paris of American artists such as Thornton Wilder, Stephen Vincent Benét, Hemingway, and Archibald MacLeish. Within a few years of its opening, the bookshop became, in the words of Morrill Cody, the "cradle of postwar American literature."

The hand that rocked this cradle—that presided over this literary exchange—was the hand of a petite and energetic American. Sylvia fed and cared for young artists. She fussed over Hemingway's eating habits and raised money for the composer George Antheil; yet, in the main, she was more sister than mother to them. She was a near contemporary of the artists she served—twelve years older than Hemingway, five years younger than Joyce. Hemingway describes her with admiration:

Sylvia had a lively, sharply sculptured face, brown eyes that were as alive as a small animal's and as gay as a young girl's, and wavy brown hair that was brushed back from her fine forehead and cut thick below her ears and at the line of the collar of the brown velvet jacket she wore. She had pretty legs and she was kind, cheerful and interested, and loved to make jokes and gossip. No one that I ever knew was nicer to me.

*Lest history blame only the Dijon printers, one must take into account all other points of error: Joyce's occasionally illegible handwriting, the crossword puzzle additions (30 percent of the novel), Joyce's occasionally inaccurate recopying, the errors by a variety of typists who had tried to follow all the arrows into Joyce's margins, and the "corrections" by helpful friends and copy editors.

Sylvia went to France accompanied only by her sister Cyprian, worked in the First World War for the Red Cross, studied French poetry in Paris, opened her own bookshop as a foreigner and a single woman, edited a book the world and especially her friends in America would consider erotic and shocking, and acted like a free and independent woman—bobbing her hair, smoking continually, walking about Paris unaccompanied, and bartering with sign makers, window washers, and booksellers. Her adventurousness and daring, as well as the freedom her foreign citizenship allowed, made her one of this century's first generation of liberated women.

Yet for all her freewheeling and independence, Sylvia Beach was a woman for others. She inherited her sense of service and morality from her family. Her nurturing skills were doubly inbred: she was a woman born in a parsonage. She was the daughter and granddaughter of Presbyterian ministers; indeed, she claimed nine clerical generations. Yet her choice was not for the traditional service of wife and mother and church worker. Her service was, rather, to art and especially to those artists who were changing the world of letters. A girl reared in the first decade of the twentieth century—especially the daughter of a parson—learned zeal for service. But without minimizing the service, even sacrifice, she gave Joyce, one must be careful to avoid patronizing references to female self-effacement. She chose service—it did not choose her. She was gritty, visionary, and self-assured. Leaving proper and Presbyterian Princeton, she moved to Paris as an agnostic, a friend of the avant-garde, a woman who would choose never to marry. She served the muses religiously. "She never allowed logic to regret over-charity to a beneficiary," recalls Marianne Moore. Although she had no pretensions to literary talent herself, she lived her life among books, trusted her own literary judgment, and helped those artists she believed in. Indeed, she vicariously shared the joy of their success. She possessed an outgoing and vivacious personality; a nervous, restive energy; and a witty, unsentimental intelligence. Occasionally she used the flattery and disarming diplomacy of the parson's daughter, but was as wise as Machiavelli. She retained her identity in a crowd of dominant personalities.

Although she was hostess, publisher, booklender, and bookseller, her greatest achievement was as a "pump-primer" who provided access to current and experimental literature; made American works available to the French for reading, translation, and criticism; brought artist and public together; and united artists from a dozen countries. She encouraged young writers to write critical essays, influenced their reading, found them printers and translators, rooms, and protectors, received their mail, lent them money, collected money due them, and solicited funds for their support. The line between personal and professional aid was never drawn. In addition to giving exhibitions and readings, she was an agent for the little magazines and publishing firms, and was herself a translator and publisher. The English author Winifred Ellerman, who called herself Bryher, questions whether "a citizen has ever done more to spread knowledge of America abroad."

As a rule, the publisher of a new great book does not become famous, but she was an exception. She was quickly bombarded by other requests and could undoubtedly have built a flourishing publishing house. But she preferred to remain a port of call for writers, where for twenty-two years artists met for tea, tips, and the sound of their native tongue.

Of little bookshops operated by booklovers, of little magazines founded by young writers and sustained for three issues, of manuscripts published privately by those who believe in their worth—of all of these Sylvia Beach, heir of nine ecclesiastical generations, has become patron saint. But it was a perilous road that led her from the churchly respectability of Princeton to bohemian sainthood in Paris.

CHAPTER 2

Who Is Sylvia?
1887–1919

. . . for Who is silvier—

— James Joyce, *Anna Livia Plurabelle*

I was twenty-five . . . when I went away
Thousands of miles away, to another climate
To another language, other standards of behavior
To fabricate for myself another personality
And to take another name. Think what that means—
To take another name.

— Gomez to Lord Claverton, in T. S. Eliot, *The Elder Statesman*

So you're the little woman who made the book that made this great war.

— Abraham Lincoln to Harriet Beecher Stowe

TWENTY YEARS before the publication of *Ulysses,* a tall and stately fifty-year-old American minister, his thirty-eight-year-old wife, Eleanor, and their three teenage daughters arrived by ship in Le Havre. In 1902, France was enjoying *la belle époque*—a lull of peace between the political turbulence of the 1890s (with the Dreyfus Affair and the deaths of the anarchists of Clichy) and the First World War. The family took the train to Paris, the cultural nerve center of Europe. Art nouveau decorated homes, posters, and books. Their stay abroad was a romantic and impressionable interlude for the members of this rather conventional family from Bridgeton, New Jersey. The Reverend Sylvester Beach had come to assist a Reverend Thurber with the Presbyterian ministry to Americans in Paris. Sylvester's three-year ministry in Paris was to have a profound effect on his three daughters, particularly his fifteen-year-old middle daughter, Nancy— now called, at her own choosing, Sylvia. In her twenties she would leave home and country to live the rest of her life in Paris, enduring two world wars with the French and dying in her apartment on the Left Bank in her seventy-sixth year. Sylvia's love for France began to grow during this first trip. Or perhaps the origins of her affection were rooted in family decisions made twenty years earlier.

The family's love for Europe and the arts probably began when Eleanor,

Sylvia's mother, was at an early age sent to live with wealthy cousins who were well traveled and cultured. Eleanor (called Nellie), the second of four children of Nancy Dunlap Harris and James Henry Orbison, was born in 1864 in Rawalpindi, India, where her parents were Presbyterian missionaries. But soon after her fourth birthday the family moved to Bellefonte, Pennsylvania, where her father died, leaving his wife, Nancy, a pious and hardworking woman, with the burden of rearing four children alone. To ease the burden, she sent her youngest child, Eleanor, to live for several years with her wealthy cousin Mary Harris Morris (Mrs. Wistar Morris) of Greenhill Farm in Overbrook, Pennsylvania. The Morrises' only child, Holly, was Eleanor's age and needed a companion. The Morris home was a happy, Quaker home housed in a three-story stone mansion, with all the material privileges that Eleanor's widowed mother could not provide. At the Morris home, Eleanor learned to paint and to play the piano. Her head soon teemed with stories of foreign lands where the Morrises had traveled. Years later, Eleanor told her daughters of those glorious years at Greenhill Farm. Sylvia remembered that

we knew the story by heart, but always begged her to tell it again, about the two little girls dressed alike and sharing together the pony rides, the dogs whose teeth Holly brushed every day, each with his own brush . . . the Quaker Meeting on Sunday . . . the Japanese girls at Bryn Mawr on Cousin Wistar's scholarships . . . riding horses instead of ponies and wearing long broadcloth riding habits, high hats with feathers and high boots. . . .

This idyllic and romanticized childhood ended abruptly when Eleanor's mother insisted she return to Bellefonte. Eleanor and her cousin Holly Morris were torn apart and inconsolable. Leaving music, drawing, and riding behind, she learned mending, sewing, and cooking, which she hated. Eleanor's mother, Nancy, was zealous and widely revered by the citizens of Bellefonte. Many years later her granddaughter Sylvia, who inherited her looks and energy but not her piety, characterized Nancy:

I admired Granny very much. She taught us to knit, and taught herself Greek so as to be able to read the Greek Testament at 6 a.m. before rising. Granny planned to go to Heaven when she died, and was determined to get all her relatives and friends past the gate of it.

The discipline and piety of her home estranged the fragile and impulsive Eleanor, whose mind was not bent toward heaven. When she had daughters of her own, Eleanor would determine that they should taste the pleasures that she had enjoyed during those years at Greenhill Farm. She would, for example, send Sylvia to live several years at the farm. And she would see that the three girls studied and traveled in Europe even at the embarrassment of borrowing money from her cousin—money which a minister's salary could not provide.

With her mother's encouragement, Eleanor—then just sixteen—became engaged to marry her Latin teacher at Bellefonte Academy. Sylvester Woodbridge Beach, a descendant of the colonial governor William Bradford, was a recent graduate of Princeton College and of Princeton Theological Seminary. He was twelve years her senior. After a two-year wait, during which she assembled her trousseau, they married. But with her marriage to Sylvester, the eighth of nine generations of ministers, she moved even further from the life of leisure and religious freedom that she craved. The sexual realities of marriage to Sylvester were a burden to Eleanor, who confided to her daughters that soon after her third daughter was born, she chose to sleep apart from him. The life in a parsonage was at times alien to her spirit; so that, after the girls had become teenagers, she spent more and more time in Europe. She was creative. She sang, played the piano well, and painted still lifes and European landscapes. Even as an adolescent she had dressed herself in her own artistic dress designs. Gliding around the dining room table at Greenhill Farm, touching each family member with a dab of the perfume she always carried with her, Eleanor exclaimed that the Orbisons (her father's family) were "slow" and needed coffee to stimulate them into action. She never did learn to deal with the discipline and responsibility that organized religion, especially in the parsonage, demanded.

During Sylvester's first pastorate, in Baltimore, Maryland, Mary Hollingsworth Morris (17 June 1884) and Nancy Woodbridge (14 March 1887) were born. Eleanor named her oldest daughter for her beloved cousin Holly Morris and her second daughter for her mother, Nancy Orbison. In the second pastorate in Bridgeton, New Jersey, where the Beaches moved when Nancy was six months old, Eleanor Elliot, their third daughter, was born on 23 April 1893. Bridgeton was an American small town, with winter wood fires and summer fireflies. The two-story parsonage with its high wooden porch and banging screen door was on Commerce Street, across from the church. Holly and Nancy played jacks on the porch and attended Ivy Hall Seminary during the day and Mrs. Leonidas Coyle's sewing class each week at the church. Part of each summer was spent with the girls' "Granny" (Nancy Orbison) in Bellefonte. It was the mauve decade, when horses and women drew buggies and skirts through the same dust of the streets. Sylvia was later to recall the itchy long flannel drawers, the large gummy black elm trees, the smell of gingerbread, and their unsuccessful prayers for a pony. She did not speak of long church services, lulled by lugubrious Presbyterian hymns. This religious world she would forget through escape, when she was old enough. Instead, the sisters gave amateur theatrical productions and loved the outdoors, particularly surrey rides and ice-skating. On this same pond in the summer, the girls chaperoned their mother and the Episcopal minister, who rowed and recited poetry.

Eleanor encouraged the imagination of her three girls. In her adolescent years, Nancy changed her name to Sylvia, probably a variant of the name of her father, Sylvester. Years later her youngest sister, Eleanor, after having experimented with several stage names in Paris, changed her name to Cyprian. Only Holly, the namesake of Mary Hollingsworth Morris (who died at twenty-seven, when Holly was seven), kept her given name.

Sylvia was born into the Victorian era, grew up in the era of emerging literary honesty, and matured with the blossoming of modern literary experimentation. She was born two years before William Dean Howells shifted the American literary center of influence from Boston to New York. When she was a teenager and a young woman, Howells was the pre-eminent man of letters: an editor for *Harper's;* a friend of Henry James; an adviser to Twain, Garland, Crane, and Norris; a champion of polite realism. The modernist patrons of Shakespeare and Company, such as Ezra Pound, would later scorn Howells as a "fusty old crock." Pound was to snap that Howells could "never be sufficiently ridiculed," for his was a "wholly contemptible generation of male American matrons." The influence of the "matrons" would be fading when Sylvia moved to Paris. Her maturity would coincide with a modernist revolution she herself would foster.

The early influences of her pious grandmother Nancy Orbison, the staidly orthodox Sylvester Beach, and the briskly heterodox Eleanor Beach presented conflicting values to Sylvia—contradictions that were later to find expression in the severe migraine headaches she chronically suffered. From Eleanor she learned to love Europe, particularly France, to seek pleasure and individual freedom, to admire bold and creative artists above all others, and to shun sexual contact with men. From Sylvester—whose ministry was less a devout call to service than a prestigious profession—she learned social respectability and congenial good manners. From her grandmother Nancy Orbison and her missionary heritage, she learned dedication to a cause beyond self-gratification. Prudence and good taste would temper the personal freedom she enjoyed by living in Paris. Though her manners were an integral part of her Victorian childhood, she rejected the religious beliefs of that heritage. Her parents—her father with his concern for social status and her mother with her love of the arts—had already moved far from the stern heritage of those generations of ministers called to a life of self-denial. Sylvia's abandonment of religious faith was the final and logical step. As an adult she had nothing to do with organized religion. And yet she also repudiated the comfortable bourgeois life of her parents. Fashionable clothes and household possessions meant nothing to her. Her choice of a simple, almost ascetic, life was an implicit rejection of their worldly values. Sylvia never needed a new suit of clothes. And for many years she lived without kitchen or shower facilities. Her life, then, was a secular version of that of her namesake missionary grandmother—Nancy Dunlap Harris Orbison. Sylvia served the arts with missionary zeal. If it is true that, in reacting against a shaping force in one's life, one reflects both that force and its opposite, Sylvia was perhaps both puritan and libertarian. She rejected material comfort for a life of service to literature, yet she was also a freethinker open to socialism and sexual liberty.

Sylvia was a frail and unhealthy child who suffered from headaches and eczema, which often kept her home from school and church. As a consequence, she had little formal schooling. She had learned to read when she was four and found her society in books. Years later she testified to the importance of books:

In Bridgetown, owing to my headaches, I spent many hours on the divan in the back parlor; in the bookcase beside me was a little set of Shakespeare's works: excepting the volume containing *Hamlet,* in which Granny had come across a passage that "wasn't nice": so she had burnt the book. What would Granny have thought of *Ulysses?*

She studied no mathematics and no Latin or Greek, she remembered, but only spent her "time on unimportant things such as poetry, philosophy, languages, and a little history." Later she concluded, by observing the French students who patronized her store and seemed to need annotated editions and biographies in order to understand a work, that hers was the best education: she had discovered for herself every book she read. This untutored taste perhaps allowed her to be open to the power of Joyce and other experimental writers whom she met in the twenties. Her early escape into books yielded an education and a vocation.

As a middle child, Sylvia found her role in the family early. She suffered neither the pressure of responsibility of the eldest child nor the temptation to narcissism of the youngest. To avoid being overlooked in this sibling sandwich, she cultivated what the family needed—a sense of humor. Her father called her the "jolly joker." According to her playmate Mary Streets, Sylvia had a quick wit and a flair for mime, traits she used in neighborhood theatricals. In her adult years, she continued the mimicry with close friends at the bookshop. Her quick wit made her a welcome guest at social occasions. As the middle child, negotiating between older and younger sisters, she also learned to serve, with skill and humor, as a link. The role was central to her adult success uniting French, American, and British writers with one another and with potential publishers.

Sylvia and her sisters were free of the overshadowing presence of male siblings. A recent biography of the French novelist George Sand claims that Sand's childhood was happy "perhaps because she was the center of it, since there was no brother (the case of so many remarkable women) to share it or automatically claim it." A family without brothers may not definitely have secured the happiness of the sisters, but it did secure careers for all of them. Concerned that they become educated through study and travel, their parents borrowed money from relatives and friends in order to help them. Holly studied business and secretarial skills; Sylvia, the violin and languages; Cyprian, voice. Holly became a Red Cross administrator in Italy; Sylvia, the owner of a bookshop in Paris; Cyprian, a popular film actress in France.

Although the Beach family had a rather limited income, it associated with people of wealth and fame. Like the college professor, the minister often shares the education and culture of the upper class, without having its economic advantages. Thus, the minister all too often depends upon the goodwill and generosity of others: the clothier who sends a modest bill, the dentist who sends no bill at all, the wealthy parishioners who entertain the pastor's family, enjoying the posture of benevolence. From the wealth and goodwill of the Morrises, who for decades gave money to the Beach family, to the power and influence of Woodrow Wilson, the Reverend Beach's most famous Princeton parishioner, the Beaches learned to accept and appreciate what could be done for them by others. Sylvia would learn to use to advantage such association with wealth.

In an early draft of her memoirs, Sylvia describes an example of Beach association with the wealthy. When the children were quite young, the girls spent several Christmases in the home of the hat manufacturer John B. Stetson, near Philadelphia. Their aunt Emma was governess for John, Jr., who was Holly's age, and for Henry, who was Sylvia's age. Mr. Stetson, who loved children, insisted that the Beach girls call him papa. According to Sylvia, he was a benevolent man:

Spending Christmas there was a joyful event and everything so strange and wonderful for us. On Christmas Eve we hung up our stockings in front of the enormous fireplace in the hall, and when we came down next morning we found them crowded to overflowing with presents and in the toe a new twenty dollar gold piece from our Papa.

Sylvia was impressed when Papa Stetson took the girls to his factory, where he showed them "how hats grow"; to the hospital, "where everything was free for the workers and their families"; and to the Christmas ceremony, where he called each employee by name as he gave him a gift. Her reaction—albeit a naive response to benevolent capitalism—reveals her earliest belief that the rich should share with the poor. Several years later, while visiting Sweden, she would express horror at the lack of benevolence for tenant farmers who lived in "wretched" living conditions. These immature emotional responses to poverty, tested during her father's pastoring of wealthy congregations and her own service in war-wrecked Serbia, would mature into firmly held socialist views.

It was in 1902, after fourteen years in Bridgeton, New Jersey, that the family made the move to Paris, where Sylvester became an associate pastor of the American Church of Paris, serving the American students of the Latin Quarter. This was the same year that James Joyce concluded his education at University College, Dublin, broke with the Catholic Church, and lived briefly in Paris. Although five years younger and protected by her family environment, Sylvia also was drawn to the arts at this time. Her most vivid memories of these years were to be of creative and charismatic artists who performed at the student atelier reunions, supervised by her father. The students met at Vitti's, which served as a studio during the week. According to Sylvia,

Every Sunday evening, in a big studio in Montparnasse, American students came under home influence. That is, Father gave a sensible talk, and some of the most brilliant singers of the time, such as Mary Garden and Charles Clark, the great cellist Pablo Casals, and other artists gave their services to this work. Even Löie Fuller. She came not to dance but to talk about her dancing.

Löie Fuller danced at the Moulin Rouge. For the Beach girls, her appearance at the Sabbath evening gathering bestowed Christian sanction on the artistic life of Paris. "We were exceedingly fond of Paris, my sisters and I," claimed Sylvia, "and this was the fault of my parents who took us there and gave us a taste of it when we were very young."

Sylvester and Eleanor loved France and the French—Sylvia thought "he was a Latin at heart"—though his French acquaintances were limited mostly to Protestant ministers and politicians. He made a great effort to learn the language, but did not have a good ear. In contrast, Eleanor Beach, according to Sylvia, knew the language: "Paris was paradise to Mother; an Impressionist painting. She enjoyed getting up the programs for the student reunions; that was her job. And she liked the company of the artists."

In the *Independent: A Weekly Magazine,* the Reverend Beach energetically defended "The American Student in Paris." Misrepresented as "unconscionable Bohemians," the young people were, on the contrary, "soberminded" lovers of truth and beauty, who lived exemplary lives of "privation and unselfish devotion to work." He concludes his defense with a description of his church services, which these students attended at the atelier on Sunday evenings. Twenty years later, another group of Americans in Paris (not all "lovers of truth and beauty" or Sunday-evening churchgoers) would be similarly attacked—but not as well defended.

Despite Sylvia's introduction to some of the charismatic artists in Paris, she remained sheltered. She lived in Paris from the fifteenth through the seventeenth years of her life—years that intensified her chafing against parental protection. "I was not interested in what I could see of Paris through the bars of my family cage," she complained in a suppressed early version of her memoirs. "I never seemed to get anywhere near the living Paris. This was not my life but Father's." She felt even more restricted in a school she and Holly attended in Lausanne. She suffered from headaches and rebelled against the discipline, which she described as "more suitable to a bunch of incorrigibles in a reformatory than a lot of weak maidens." With her parents' consent, she soon left her more stoic sister at the school and returned to France. Though she had learned French grammar, her schooling was unavailing. "About my education," she later informed her editor with deliberate error, "the less said the better: I ain't had none: never went to school and wouldn't have learned anything if I had went. You will have to copy what goes for T. S. Eliot: say I have degrees from all those places, same as him." And so she received, instead of the formal Swiss education then fashionable for the offspring of expatriate Americans, a sporadic and informal tutoring. She was sent to live with a family that belonged to the American Church of Paris. Mr. Francis (Frank) Welles, a representative of Western Electric in Europe, lived in La Touraine, on the river Cher near the town of Bourré. His sixteen-year-old daughter Carlotta, who was ordered by her doctor from school to the outdoors, was soon Sylvia's best friend. They spent their days reading and watching birds from the trees. In the early part of the century, Touraine was a picturesque little region where horse-drawn carts full of mushrooms (the local industry) lumbered along the dirt roads. The old Welles home, built partially in caves, featured red-brick chimneys whose smoke seemed to puff up from the fields themselves. Sylvia loved this country, much as her mother had loved Greenhill Farms. During the years when she owned her bookshop in Paris, Sylvia would spend many holidays here. At the outbreak of World War II, she would use the safety of the half-buried old home to hide from the Nazis.

While Sylvia was absorbing the rustic pleasures at Bourré, James Joyce, who had abandoned his medical studies, was living the bohemian life in Paris. The illness of his mother took him back to Ireland, where he lived in 1904—the year of the action of *Ulysses*—with Oliver St. John Gogarty outside Dublin in the Martello Tower, which is one of the novel's settings. This same year was Sylvia's last full year as a teenager in France before her father was called to pastor

the First Presbyterian Church of Princeton, New Jersey. Sylvia left to spend
Christmas of 1904 in Hogstad, Sweden, and then went home to the United States
early with an elderly lady, Mrs. Grundy, who thought sulfuric acid baths would
help Sylvia's headaches.

The Beach family moved to Princeton in 1905. Several months earlier, during a brief visit to Princeton for the thirtieth reunion of the class of 1875, Sylvester had learned of the vacant pastorate at the First Presbyterian Church. He was
immensely proud to be in Princeton, a prestigious Presbyterian center. And
Eleanor Beach loved the pastoral setting and university climate of the small town.
They settled down in the parsonage on a street named Library Place. In her
memoirs, Sylvia remembers the parklike setting of the town and her excursions
by horse cart with Annis Stockton—a descendant of Richard Stockton, a signer
of the Declaration of Independence—who gave her historical tours of colonial
Princeton. After she had lived over thirty years in Paris, Sylvia would still look
at New Jersey, where she had spent fourteen years in Bridgeton and about ten
years in Princeton, as her home. In a letter to Bryher many years later, Sylvia
would loyally claim, "That's my state, and though there are dreary spaces and
it's far too flat, I can't help being quite fond of it—the country-side, of course."

The intellectual and liberal Presbyterianism of the Beaches, reinforced by the
cultural influence of Paris, had brought them far from their provincial and pious
ancestors. The comfort and wealth of Princeton sanctioned, even rewarded, the
secular drift. John Peale Bishop, in a 1921 essay entitled "Princeton," explains,
at once, the failure of a "Presbyterian" Princeton College and the betrayal of
the devotion and piety of the earlier generations. The establishment of a Presbyterian college was "doomed to failure," Bishop argues, because of its climate
and geography. "Calvinism required a clear mountainous air; Princeton is set
near slow streams, and the air is always either softly damp or suave with sunlight." But perhaps it was, more than damp sunlight, the climate of wealth and
social prestige that doomed the last ministerial Beach generation. Among their
close friends and parishioners were the wealthy and influential: Mrs. James Gar-
field, Grover Cleveland (who was president of the United States when Sylvia
was born), and Woodrow Wilson, president of Princeton University (1902–1910).
Sylvester Beach's friendship with Woodrow Wilson was one of the most important in his life. And, after Wilson's election in 1913, he would become known
in the American press as the "president's pastor."

The Beaches were close to the Wilsons not only because they shared religious
and cultural ideals but as well because each family had three daughters of roughly
the same ages: Margaret (nineteen), Jessie (eighteen), and Eleanor (sixteen) Wilson; and Holly (twenty-one), Sylvia (eighteen), and Cyprian (twelve) Beach.
Because the Wilsons had no piano, Margaret came to the parsonage to have
Cyprian accompany her voice practice.

One sultry Sunday morning at the First Presbyterian Church, Cyprian sat
herself on the front pew and began stirring the air with a large fan decorated with
a black cat and the name of a famous cabaret in Paris: *Au Chat Noir*. Some of

the parishioners were dismayed. But Margaret Sloane, Sylvia's friend and a daughter of the French historian Prof. William Sloane, smiled with delight, for she shared the Beach sisters' passion for France. The passion grew, and the Beach girls repeatedly after 1910 left Princeton for Europe, particularly France. They often stayed for months at a visit.

The first adult trip to Europe for Sylvia was in 1907, the year Lucia was born to Nora Barnacle and James Joyce, who was then teaching English in Trieste and beginning his long campaign to have *Dubliners,* his collection of short stories, published. Eleanor Beach took Sylvia, for her health, to Paris, where Eleanor met another American woman, named Mrs. Mason, whose young daughter Marian was planning to spend the year in Florence. With the blessing of the two mothers, Sylvia and Marian (both twenty), left Paris by train for Italy, where for a year they stayed together at a pension. Sylvia read, toured Italy, learned her third language, and occasionally bought antiques for her mother, who had returned to Princeton, to sell.

In the year Sylvia spent in Florence, her best friend, Carlotta Welles, sailed to England after a visit to the United States. Also traveling on the ship, the *Minneapolis,* on the way to receive an honorary degree from Oxford, was Mark Twain. Twain became infatuated with Carlotta (whom he called "Charley"), penning her notes and regaling her with tall tales. He autographed one of his books for her, and a cartoonist on board drew a caricature of the two of them. Carlotta, who reportedly looked like his daughter Susy, soon became restless with the older man's fatherly attentions and stayed in her room. Finally, Twain grew disgruntled at her indifference. Bored though she may have been, sitting with Twain for hours, Carlotta was flattered. When next she met Sylvia, she proudly showed her the Twain inscription.

The Beach women sailed again to Europe in the first days of 1911, six months after Sylvester Beach had been named to the board of directors of Princeton Theological Seminary. While Sylvia attended the opera and the theater, a future friend and patron studied literature and philosophy at the Sorbonne. T. S. Eliot, who would later choose the English life and tradition, was in the midst of his first romance with Europe.

Sylvia returned to the United States while Eleanor remained in Paris with Cyprian, who began to study music with Jean Alexis Perier. Mary Morris paid for her lessons until she learned that Cyprian was studying opera, whereupon the conservative and pious cousin Mary cut off her support for this worldly endeavor. During those years when Cyprian was studying opera and secretly beginning a film career in Paris, Holly learned secretarial skills and Sylvia assisted Prof. Charles Osgood of the Department of English at Princeton in preparing his *Concordance to the Poems of Edmund Spenser* (1915). Sylvia next found a job near Greenhill Farm, where she lived for several months, commuting to Philadelphia for medical treatment of her headaches. Unlike her mother, Sylvia was lonely at Greenhill Farm and not well. She "sticks it out," her father confided to Cyprian, only "because she wants to be independent." Sylvester Beach was proud that his three "girls—all of them—are determined to be independent, and make their own way." This spirit was manifested in their concern for the women's suffrage movement, especially for the suffragettes fasting in English prisons. During the winter of 1913–1914 Sylvia wrote to Cyprian,

And you have identified yourself with votes for Women. That's right. I have too except for the Forcebal [sic] Feeding. . . . I have made Cousin Mary decide to subscribe to the *Suffragette*. . . . [She] keeps saying "oh those dreadful men in England to treat the Women so!!" . . . Wasn't it disgraceful in England the way those tedious Bishops treated the women! Pretending they didn't see any harmful torture at the prison and that Miss Rachel Peace had a "nice round face." Huh!

One day in 1914, while in New York City to check out books from the public library, Sylvia visited the publisher Ben W. Huebsch—who in 1916 would publish James Joyce's *Portrait of the Artist as a Young Man**—to talk about a career. Later, she would claim that they had talked about a bookshop. The discussion may also have touched on journalism, a profession she mentioned occasionally in family letters of this time. Although Sylvia later remembered that she had visited Mr. Huebsch in 1917, this visit had probably occurred in 1914. After this stagnant time† of living at Greenhill Farm and wondering about a career, she left, despite the war, in the closing days of 1914 for Europe. This fourth extended trip would be her last one to Europe. When Eleanor, who accompanied her daughter, wrote confidentially to her cousin Mary that she would leave Sylvia in Spain, she regretted only that Sylvia would be "lost to this country." Prophetic words. Sylvia lived for nearly two years in Spain, chiefly in Madrid, where she learned her fourth language. Eleanor spent most of 1915 and 1916 with her. While Eleanor and Sylvia were absent from Princeton, the following scandalous gossip appeared in New York's *Town Topics:*

The clerical garb of a well-known Princeton clergyman is not protecting him from some very severe verbal castigation by his indignant flock and others. Dominies who wander into the by-paths trodden, or supposed to be trodden, only by the unregenerate who are *arcades ambo* with Satan must expect criticism and this particular dominie has strayed very far and they say the time has come to call a halt. Princeton has been scandalized for years by his neglect of his wife and family; and his open attentions to a fair, fat and fifty member of his congregation, is causing no little comment and setting a very bad example for the young gentlemen of the University who probably are looking forward to receiving their diplomas under a wedding veil—so to speak. The philandering dominie and his fair companion were seen much at the Opera and theatre in New York last season, when they

* No record establishes Sylvia's having read by late 1914 any early work by James Joyce. She could have been familiar with *Dubliners;* but because it had been published so recently (London, June 1914) and because it had sold so few volumes, it is safe to assume that she was not familiar with it. Probably before she left for Spain late in 1914 she had seen some of the installments of *Portrait,* which appeared in 1914–1915 in the *Egoist,* a publication she could have read in the New York Public Library or in a New York bookshop.
† This year had been, in contrast, one of the best for the thirty-two-year-old Joyce: *Portrait* was finished and appearing in serial form; *Dubliners* was finally published; *Exiles* was written; and, most significant for the later Beach-Joyce association, *Ulysses* was begun.

specialized in first nights and holidays. The sudden departure of his wife and daughter to Europe a few months ago, despite the danger of sea voyaging under the present uncertain war conditions, together with the almost immediate ensconcement of himself at the woman's Summer home in New Jersey, where he still remains, indulging in numerous gay automobile trips, sometimes with, more often without, a chaperon, has and is causing much comment in the exclusive little Summer colony, as well as New York and Princeton.

> When common mortals trip the light fantastic ways of sin,
>   'Tis bad enough,
> But when the mouthing preachers stroll that way the devils grin,
>   'Tis overrough,
>   The arch-fiend Eblis chuckles to behold his sway,
>   Full well he knows there'll be hell to pay.

Holly, who was working in New York City, responded immediately with a letter to her mother urging her to return home and kill the gossip. In the meantime, Holly appeared each weekend in Princeton. Her mother returned from Madrid fully a year later, a delay that tends to invalidate the implication of the gossip-column portrait of a neglectful husband and father. But the Reverend Beach had to call a special meeting of the church board to clear himself. What he and the "fair, fat and fifty" parishioner undoubtedly knew—but the press did not know—was that Eleanor Beach preferred to live apart from her husband. In letters to his family, he justified their absence on grounds of health and education. The following passage from a letter to Sylvia suggests the defense he took with his church board and his anger at their interference in his affairs:

Since we went to Paris 15 years ago, it has not been possible for the family to be together much of the time. Our first duty is to the children. We owe them the best possible chance in life. In lieu of money, which we have not, we can give them a little travel and experience to fit them for the career they may choose . . . I wish people would understand that, and LET US ALONE.

From Madrid, Eleanor and Sylvia went to Paris, which William Butler Yeats had recently called the center of experimental poetry and criticism. Although she had yet to meet a French poet, Sylvia was eager to study experimental poetry. As soon as she was settled with Cyprian in the late summer of 1916, her mother went back to Princeton. But her letters to her daughters reveal a recurrent desire to return to Europe and be with them. Eleanor found living in Princeton especially difficult after 1917, when Holly sailed on the S.S. *Lapland* to work for the Red Cross in France. Now all three daughters were in Europe.

The arrival of Sylvia in Paris at the end of August 1916 marked the beginning of her long resident life as an American in Paris. The passport for "Mlle. Woodbridge Beach," stamped 29 July and 15 August, lists her age as twenty-nine, and her profession as *"journaliste littéraire."* But it would be nearly three years before she would find a profession in Paris. Her long delay in selecting a profession was due in large part to the war in Europe. She had gone to Paris in order to read—specifically French poetry—and to be away from home. Uneasy with

Presbyterian theology and uneasy in a divided home, she sought in Paris a tradition with which she could be comfortable.

While absorbing the tradition of European literature, Sylvia watched each development of the war and enjoyed life with her sister Cyprian, whom she called "the Babe." Cyprian was at the height of her film career—portraying Belle-Mirette in *Judex,* a film directed by Louis Feuillade and appearing serially in theaters. Children recognized her on the street, and the young poet Louis Aragon enjoyed following her. Cyprian and Sylvia lived in the Palais Royal, where in 1823 John Howard Payne had written "Home, Sweet Home."

Sylvia was inevitably drawn into the war. From their balcony by night, she and Cyprian watched air raids; by day she was frightened to hear the Germans' "Big Bertha" shell the streets. On Good Friday, while she attended at the Palace of Justice the trial of a militant pacifist schoolteacher friend, a large bomb exploded nearby. "Rushing out," she exclaimed, "we saw that the church of Saint Gervais, just across the river, had been hit. A lot of people who had come from all over town to hear the famous choir were killed and a very interesting old church was sadly damaged." The bombing was a catalyst for action. She must do something to help the French. Holly had joined the war effort as secretary to Major Peck, chief surgeon in the Roosevelt Hospital unit in France. And the letters from their father, who had gone to Washington for Wilson's inauguration, teemed with the idealism of war. "In Princeton we are all for war," he proclaimed, adding that at every service he hung a silk flag from the pulpit and the congregation sang "America." He described Princeton as being "on a military footing." Many wore khaki, and the young men were training at the Schenck farm outside Princeton. For several years American young men from colleges and high schools had been arriving in Paris to join the ambulance corps; the students were the first conspicuous invasion of Americans in France. For these young drivers, wealthy Americans in London donated vehicles. Earlier, Henry James had written one of the first pamphlets to appeal for volunteers. Such enterprises were at once patriotic and literary; scores of battle memoirs and diaries quote the poetry of Alan Seeger, Robert Service, and Rudyard Kipling. Scores of undergraduates who had time, idealism, and French were recruited from campuses. The American Ambulance Field Service recruited 181 young men from Princeton alone. Because each ambulance section billeted and took mess with a French division, many became Francophiles. Among the future American writers who served, chiefly in the ambulance corps, were Ernest Hemingway, E. E. Cummings, Harry Crosby, Slater Brown, John Peale Bishop, Dashiell Hammett, Sidney Howard, Louis Bromfield, Malcolm Cowley, and John Dos Passos. Cowley was later to call the ambulance service a "college-extension course for a generation of writers." After the war, many of these men remained in France. Others returned on completing their university degrees. They found jobs with the Paris *Herald,* with banks, or with import firms and became early customers of Shakespeare and Company.

No women drove ambulances. Instead, Sylvia joined the *Volontaires Agri-*

coles for two months of hard work with the peasant women of Touraine: picking grapes, bundling wheat, and grafting trees. So that the men could fight the war, they worked twelve hours a day. And Sylvia, who had been treated as a semi-invalid by her parents, wrote home that her health had never been better. In a picture taken at this time, she is standing on her tiptoes, head held proudly high, dressed in calf-length khaki culottes, a pith helmet under her arm. Her clothes attracted attention wherever she went. She told a reporter ten years later that her "riding breeches" had amused the peasants. "A woman in pants!" they gasped. "Ah! the eccentric Americans!" they sighed. Also, the bobbed hair curled about her face contrasted sharply with the long, straight hair and skirts of the peasant women. The picture shows a woman who is brave, free, and proud of the work she has been doing. But the farm work was short-term; and, of course, the need for a genuine career persisted.

Both the war and her particular circumstances as a woman delayed a decision concerning a career. She was limited by the options that tradition dictated to her. Journalism interested her, as her passport testifies. She had talked of it with Ben Huebsch and had even written several essays for publication, including one (with her father) on Cubism. She sent "The Neutrality of Spain," "Even the Beggars," and "Spanish Feminism in 1916" to Holly for typing. In the first of what would become her lifetime role as unofficial U.S. "agent" for her sister, Holly retyped the essays and mailed them (with negative results) to magazines such as the *Woman's Home Companion*.

When Sylvia sent an essay on the Rodin Museum to her parents, her father offered to type it and make corrections. "You wouldn't have known it!" Mrs. Beach protested to her daughter. "All your Sylviaesque touches were changed into ministerial style. It *was* funny. I never said a word but took it to Miss McLenagham and had her type it over." Thinking she would "strike high," Mrs. Beach sent the essay, with two museum pictures from Sylvia, to a prestigious art magazine, which immediately sent a check for $15 and a request for more articles. When the essay appeared, her father read it, glanced suspiciously at his wife, but said nothing. "A Musée Rodin in Paris" appeared in the July 1917 edition of the *International Studio: An Illustrated Magazine of Fine and Applied Art*. In this beautifully printed essay she tells of the founding of the Rodin Museum in the Hotel Biron and of the honors that she believes are due the seventy-five-year-old sculptor. The three-page, illustrated article concludes that when men "return from the preoccupations of the war to the eternal beauty of art, many will be the pilgrims from all the countries of the world to this shrine of beauty, the Musée Rodin." The author of this lofty prose would establish her own "shrine" to art less than two miles from the Rodin Museum.

But one publication did not make a career. And job opportunities for women, even in journalism, were not available in wartime France. Therefore, while Hemingway was beginning his literary education with the *Kansas City Star,* Sylvia was abandoning talk of journalism and trying to get a job as a wartime translator. Even with an American Red Cross troupe of women, who had come to France to aid the war effort, she was unsuccessful. In a letter to her mother, she expresses annoyance that the Finley unit, called "a triumph for feminism," is "full up" and, therefore, not interested in her services as a translator. With characteristic irony she exclaims, "I don't see what the dickens they would want with a mere interpreter [translator] around the place; none of the units keep such an article. If I was qualified for a secretaryship, it would be different." Although she is untrained as a secretary and uninterested in becoming one, she confesses to her mother, "It's urgent, très urgent besides! I *must* get at something profitable. My uselessness utterly depresses me." And then she declares for the first time her keenest hope: "As for a business, when the war is over, if I'm not old and buried by that time, I must have a bookstore, I must." She has talked to Brentano, she informs her mother, about getting a job in New York to learn the trade: "I'm sure, positively, I could make a nice little bookshop in New York go, working up a certain regular clientele. Good English and American books and a supply of French and others. I should love it, (all but being in N.Y.)." The response of her mother was typically protective:

Dearest little Mack, why *do* you worry about making money? It isn't worthwhile. And to call yourself useless! You're worth a dollar a minute to us! I only mention different schemes for you to go into because I know how every normal person wants to be doing something and because I am afraid writing is bad for you. But don't *don't* worry, my dearest child. We must just go easily along trying different things and enjoying the varied experiences but not getting intense over it. . . . I am quite doubtful about the bookshop idea. I don't believe it would pay—and would be such hard indoor work. And there are some shops now of that kind in New York. However, we can decide after the war is over.

Two events at this time changed her life. The first was her decision, despite strong pressure to the contrary from her mother, not to return to the United States. The second was meeting Adrienne Monnier, who would become her life companion. All during 1918 Mrs. Beach, ill and unhappy with her marriage and life in Princeton, poured out her anguish to her daughters in Europe: in April she longed for Paris; in June the doctor declared nothing would cure her illness but the return of her children; in October she could not "live without" them, and Holly decided that one of them must return; by December she was "morbid and desperate" listening to her husband complain about their daughters' expenditures and ingratitude, while she secretly sold the lamps she had bought in Europe and sent them money. In a very significant decision by the oldest sister, Holly urged Sylvia to stay in Europe and Cyprian to return to their parents. Even while Cyprian, who would never again find success in a career, sailed home, Mrs. Beach begged the forgiveness of her three daughters for hurting them with her pressuring and complaining. This unhappiness at home and the happy meeting of Adrienne many months before moved Sylvia closer to a permanent residency in France.

It was a windy and cold day, and Sylvia held her cape tightly about her with one hand and held on to her round Spanish hat with the other. As she turned in to the rue de l'Odéon, she saw the shop a few doors up on the left at No. 7: "A.

Monnier.'' This was the bookshop that was supposed to carry the Paul Fort review *Vers et Prose* that she was seeking. A note found in one of the books of poetry in the Bibliothèque Nationale had led her here. She looked at the books in the window and hesitated timidly at the door because there were no other customers in sight. But her Spanish cloak and hat did not disguise her origin, and a young woman who had been seated at a table came swiftly to the door to welcome the American. This Frenchwoman had what she called an ''immediate and intuitive understanding,'' a ''private fixing of the soul,'' when a passerby crossed her threshold:

A shop seems to us to be a magic chamber: at that instant when the passer-by crosses the threshold of the door that everyone can open . . . nothing disguises the look of his face, the tone of his words . . . and if we know how to observe him at that instant when he is only a stranger, we are able now and forever, to know him in his truth. . . . This immediate and intuitive understanding, this private fixing of the soul, how easy they are in a shop, a place of transition between street and house!

The warm greeting of this Frenchwoman surprised Sylvia. But she soon learned that Adrienne Monnier liked Americans very much. She had read all the American literature that had been translated, beginning with her favorite, Ben Franklin. Very little modern American literature was available at that time in France. It would become available later, as a result of this meeting between the American woman and Frenchwoman, each of whom this day expressed an enthusiasm for the country of the other:

"*J'aime beaucoup l'Amérique.*"
"*J'aime beaucoup la France.*"

Their future collaboration would prove these sentiments true.

Sylvia surveyed the book-lined walls of the library, which she later learned was called ''the Monnier Chapel.'' She noticed the few volumes of eighteenth- and nineteenth-century American literature in translation and the shelves of French books in their crystal-paper overcoats, waiting to be bound. And, finally, she spotted the entire stock of Paul Fort's *Vers et Prose* review, which featured the symbolist poetry she had been studying. Adrienne also had all eighteen volumes of his *Ballades Françaises*. Sylvia was delighted and impressed with the selection of books and the walls lined with portraits of writers whose works she had been reading.

The two women sat down at the table to discuss Paris, food, and books. Adrienne named the American literature she had read, and Sylvia recommended other works, specifically *Moby-Dick*. Later, when Melville's novel appeared in French, it became a favorite of Adrienne's. When the discussion shifted to French literature, Sylvia, much to Adrienne's pleasure, expressed her enthusiasm for Paul Valéry. And she said she had read Jules Romains's work in America but wanted help with further studies of French literature. Adrienne suggested that Sylvia read more Romains and then the poetry of Paul Claudel. With keen anticipation, Sylvia joined the library. Adrienne signed the *carte de sociétaire* on 15 March 1917, the month of Sylvia's thirtieth birthday. Sylvia declared it a momentous occasion: "So I was enrolled as a member of A. Monnier's library for a year—that never ran out."

As they sat talking, Sylvia looked carefully at the chubby Adrienne, nearly twenty-six years old, whose straight hair was brushed back from her round face. Her complexion was fair, her cheeks rosy. Later Sylvia described Adrienne's appearance that day:

Most striking were her eyes. They were blue-gray and slightly bulging, and reminded me of William Blake's. She looked extremely alive. Her dress, of a style that suited her perfectly, somebody once described as a cross between a nun's and a peasant's: a long, full skirt down to her feet, and a sort of tight-fitting velvet waistcoat over a white silk blouse. She was in gray and white like her bookshop. Her voice was rather high; she descended from mountaineers who must have hailed each other from peak to peak.

With her high voice, she attempted a few English phrases that she had learned during a nine-month stay in England. At seventeen she had gone to England to be near Suzanne Bonnierre, her classmate and later a partner in her bookshop. But Sylvia and Adrienne always spoke French together.

An observer of this meeting would have been struck with their physical differences. One was plump and matronly, and the other slim and wiry. Adrienne has often been described as looking like a nun or a monk, but those who knew her well describe her in Rabelaisian terms. She was a gourmet cook who sucked on the last chicken bones of her famous chicken dinners and talked to friends about the squeals of pigs as they were slaughtered. She had earthy appetites, exclaimed William Carlos Williams, and she seemed "to stand up to her very knees in heavy loam."

Sylvia was not Rabelaisian, but collegiate. Five feet two inches tall, small as a teenager, with bobbed hair, she looked like an English schoolboy or, more accurately, a Pre-Raphaelite figure in velvet jacket and necktie ribbon. Malcolm Cowley describes her as "a wisp of a woman with a determined chin." She always held a cigarette in her long, delicate fingers. Janet Flanner (Genêt) thought she looked like one of Colette's young heroines. Although Sylvia was five years older than Adrienne, she seemed, because of her petite size and manner of dress, the younger of the two. Adrienne, because she was plump and wore long skirts, looked prematurely matronly. She had a face, Sisley Huddleston exclaims, "at once virginal as that of a nun, and indulgent as that of a mother." Adrienne's round face and clear, creamy skin contrasted with the sharply sculptured features of Sylvia. Adrienne was "all curves and placidity"; Sylvia, "angular and brisk."

Sylvia and Adrienne contrasted sharply not only in appearance but also in personality and philosophical outlook. Adrienne had a religious temperament— her ancestors were Catholic, she was drawn to Buddhism, her mother to Theosophy. Sylvia, though reared in an established church, was agnostic. If Adrienne was French and mystical, Sylvia was American and pragmatic. Sylvia bobbed her hair, never wore makeup, and insisted that her skirts be made short for ease of movement and built with pockets—a working person always needed pockets, she insisted. Whereas Adrienne spoke deliberately and philosophically, Sylvia was gifted with an understated and swift wit. She delighted in inventing puns, quoting comic verse, and playing practical jokes. If Adrienne was contemplative, Sylvia had a nervous, restless energy. The French poet Yves Bonnefoy has said that Sylvia walked briskly through life, looking curiously about her "as if she would be writing it all in a school notebook."

During the months that Sylvia continued to read French literature and worry about a future career, she attended the poetry readings that Adrienne held in her library. "Crowded into the little shop and almost on top of the reader at his table," she later exclaimed, "we listened breathlessly." She listened as André Gide read his own work and, later, the poetry of his friend Paul Valéry. Jean Schlumberger, Valery Larbaud, and Léon-Paul Fargue read their work. And she listened to a musical program by Erik Satie and Francis Poulenc. A uniformed Jules Romains read his peace poem, *Europe,* and Valéry lectured on Poe's *Eureka.* These were the most eminent French men of letters and she was the only American to have the pleasure of meeting and hearing them. In the coming months, Adrienne's bookshop and library—soon named La Maison des Amis des Livres (The House of the Friends of Books)—proved the only spiritual refuge from the explosions of the Germans' Big Bertha.

Adrienne had taught school and worked as a literary secretary, first for the *Université des Annales* lecture series and then at the *Mercure de France.* Finally, she had been able to open her bookshop with the indemnity money her father had received for a crippling injury he had incurred during a train accident. She had opened her bookshop and lending library on 15 November 1915, at a time when a wintry, war-weary Paris needed the warmth and peace of art. In the uncertain years during and immediately after the war, when writers were unsure of where they stood, Adrienne offered sympathy and contact with other writers. Soon she became, according to Samuel Putnam, the "strong woman of Gallic letters."

"Because of my inexperience," Adrienne later admitted, "I knew many struggles and trials. But if I had been able to foresee the dangers, I would never have ventured forth." To save money, she had lived for several years in the back room of the shop. Suzanne Bonnierre was her partner for a short time. Sylvia met both Suzanne and the second partner, Pierre Haour, a wealthy man with whom Adrienne published a series of small editions entitled Les Cahiers des Amis des Livres. Following the sudden illness and death of both partners, Adrienne would run the business alone and turn increasingly to the friendship of Sylvia.

Despite their physical differences, Sylvia and Adrienne shared a love of literature and independence. Although Clovis Monnier financed Adrienne's shop and Eleanor Beach financed Sylvia's shop, each woman remained friendly with but independent of her family. They had sisters, no brothers: Adrienne was the older of two sisters and Sylvia the middle of three sisters. The girls received the moral and financial encouragement that ordinarily would have gone to sons.

On the day they met, their lives began slowly to change. In a poetic salute to Sylvia, Adrienne acknowledges what she believed was their mutual destiny:

> I salute you my sister born beyond the seas!
> Behold my star has found your own . . .

While their transatlantic sisterhood grew during the final months of the war, Sylvia again took a war-related job. She had been spending her days in libraries and in Adrienne's bookshop absorbing French literature and attending readings by French writers. But her father's letters were full of talk of "Woodrow" and the war. In one particularly offensive letter, signed "Daddy" and full of capitalized words, he exclaims that he regrets having "NO SONS TO DIE fighting FOR LIBERTY" and urges his daughters to continue their work for the cause. She was unable to fulfill the masculine role of hero for her father. And she was not willing to consider the traditional role of wife, unlike Marian Peter, her good friend from the Florence days, who had married a wealthy Lake Forest, Illinois, lawyer. Frustrated by her other options, Sylvia yielded to her sister Holly's enthusiasm for secretarial skills. In June—the month Marian Peter gave birth to her first child, named Sylvia—the Reverend Beach's middle daughter began typing and French-shorthand lessons at the Remington School in rue Édouard-VII. Her secretarial training earned her a job with the Balkan commission of the Red Cross, which Holly had joined at the end of 1918.

On 11 November, Sylvia listened to the bells toll the armistice. A month later she joined two million people cheering Woodrow Wilson, the most admired man in the world, who rode in triumph through Napoleon's victory arch and down the Champs-Élysées. He had arrived for negotiations that would culminate in the Treaty of Versailles. Although he would be deserted by the U.S. Senate and the public, Europe now welcomed the idealistic Wilson as its savior. Some of the French burned candles in front of his photograph. Nearly ten thousand persons poured into Paris for the peace negotiations; a few, such as the reporter Lincoln Steffens, were to stay on in Paris to become members of Shakespeare and Company.

With their own brand of postwar idealism, and the promise of a full-time job, Holly and Sylvia went to Serbia for the Red Cross. "A deserter from the literary front" is the way she describes herself in an early draft of her memoirs. But her experiences in Serbia—her end of innocence—were a necessary interval before Shakespeare and Company. She would return six months later with firm social views, an urgent purpose for her life, and the knowledge that she had to live in Europe. She would go to Serbia because she needed money. Once there, she would experience the horror of the aftermath of war. Serbia had been ravaged by years of fighting. Thousands were homeless, and thousands more died in the epidemics that had swept the country. Her social and political awakening would disillusion her. War was the worst insanity, she would realize. It was, as Henry James predicted on the day Britain entered World War I, "the plunge of civilization into the abyss of blood and darkness." This disillusionment was shared by the friends she made a few years later—Eliot and Joyce and Lawrence. Although she occasionally describes the suffering of the peasants, she did not share her political views in her family letters. Her letters to her father, always written in the tone of the little girl, are less frequent and more formally affectionate. But she was able to express her feminism in her letters to her mother and Cyprian, who had returned to Princeton with hopes for a career in American films. In fact, she always penned her most expressive family letters to the only kindred spirit among her kin—Cyprian.

Two months after the armistice bells had tolled throughout France, Holly and Sylvia rode by train to Rome and then to Belgrade. Together they traveled five days "during a blinding snowstorm in a carriage with no panes in the window." During the first six months of 1919, the two sisters worked in Serbia as secretaries and translators—"very few of the others [Red Cross employees] speak any languages but American," she remarked. But Holly and Sylvia both knew French and Italian; Holly knew German as well, and Sylvia, Spanish. They continued their language studies, Sylvia informed Cyprian:

We are busy all day and of an evening take a Serbian lesson with the young lady of the house who is ONE OF US where the Emancipation of the Sex is concerned. She claims there are 14 Suffragettes in Serbia alone not counting Albania, Makedonia (see correct spelling of this name) and female Croats.

Feminist remarks, expressed with equal parts of humor and resolve, appear often in Sylvia's letters to Princeton. She notes that women have no voice in the decisions of the Red Cross. Her beliefs were doubtless quickened by the quasi-military environment in which she worked, with many male doctors. The Red Cross, she explains angrily, "has made a regular feminist of me." The men held the highest rank; the women corrected their errors and did all the work. "These creatures are in the dark ages as regards women—but what can you expect." She is almost as critical of the helpless women as of the domineering men. She contrasts the frivolous American women in their high-heeled shoes with the self-sufficient British women who wear "real uniforms" and sleep "right along the road-side! And do a man's work." Sylvia's social and political views are also revealed by her friendship with Hélène Brion, who organized in the same year in Paris a group of feminists. Brion edited *La Lutte Féministe*. The first eight numbers—one of which included a letter from Sylvia in Serbia—were handwritten and circulated to nine women (Sylvia was seventh on the list). By the time *Féministe* was printed, it bore the subtitle "Pour le communisme." These feminist and socialist views evident in her friendship with Brion were fortified in Serbia.

Most of Sylvia's family letters from Serbia describe gypsy violins, ox carts, the deep snow, the weekend trips by boat with the Serbian peasants and their geese and pigs. She also describes the returning prisoners and the desolation of the war. Looking to the future, she informs her father, "I should like to get into a publishing house or newspaper office over here and perhaps sometime a little book business of my own." Occasionally she mentions the "Books Tore" she wants to open in New York, where the French writers she admires can "be introduced to my country." By the summer she had decided that she could not go home again and abandoned the plans for a New York bookstore. Later she justified the decision by contending that New York rents were so high that "only a pushcart was within my means . . . that is my mother's means." But at this time she knew nothing of New York expenses, because her family had never done the scouting around for her that she had asked them to do. By July, then, she was talking about a London bookshop: "There is so much more interest in that sort of thing over there than there is anywhere at home, and besides that I like living on this side [of the Atlantic] so much better. It's near Paris and I could keep in touch with the Situation." The "situation" is both Paris and Adrienne. She justifies her decision to Cyprian by insisting that Americans seem interested only in sports and business, while she, on the other hand, has "been cursed with a preference" for books "instead of good, practical horse sense. . . . All the same someone has to do their thinking for them and I must have some books for these someones."

On 21 July, Holly and Sylvia left on the Orient Express from Belgrade, via Trieste, Milan, Geneva, and Dijon, arriving in Paris forty-eight hours later. Sylvia hurried first to Adrienne with an engraved silver cigarette case from Sarajevo and the news of her plans for a London bookshop. In their spring correspondence, Sylvia and Adrienne had planned the Paris–New York connection. Now Sylvia was worried, she confesses in a letter to her mother, that Adrienne, who "doesn't like English things," would disapprove of her plans for a London shop: "Still it can't be helped. I've decided to stay on this side and if one scheme doesn't work another will." Serbia had given Sylvia, in her own words, a "perspective of life," the money to stay in Europe, and a sense of vocation.

On 26 July, Sylvia, zealous to open a shop in London, asked her mother for additional finances. Her mother, she conjectured in an early draft of her memoirs, wished to finance the opening of the bookshop because it was "an enterprise that was after her own heart"and because"she believed in daughters having careers." Her sixty-seven-year-old father, however, was skeptical and wanted his daughters around him now that the war was over. Mrs. Beach had been working quietly since April with her broker, Alex Hudmet, to get the capital needed for Sylvia. In this same 26 July letter to her mother, Sylvia reports that Adrienne had "greeted the bookshop-in-London scheme enthusiastically—said we would be sort of partners and she would help me start my place in London and would send me the books from Paris as they came out. . . ." But she needs $3,000 for the venture, and, she concludes, "I'm sure you would approve of my wanting to make a supreme effort to take up something interesting and worthwhile for a life work instead of working under someone at an uninspiring task—with ideas and art taboo and you might as well be a squirrel in a wheel. But I would hate to risk your money mother—that would be awful, if I failed!!!"

Sylvia spent the first week of August 1919 in London. She went directly upon arrival to the Poetry Book Shop to talk to Harold Monro, who "walked right down his winding stair in his velvet jacket to advise me strongly against" a French bookshop in London. He told her that there was no market there for a French bookshop and that, moreover, rent was too high. She abandoned her project for a shop in London "right on the doorstep of Poetry Book Shop," she admits, and spent the remaining days sightseeing.

Soon after Sylvia returned to Paris, Adrienne found a small shop, around the corner and across the rue Monsieur-le-Prince from her own, at 8 rue Dupuytren. Sylvia would open a "poetry center" in English—to complement Adrienne's French center. Sylvia describes the day Adrienne showed her the empty shop:

We hurried to the rue Dupuytren, where, at No. 8—there were only about ten numbers on this hilly little street—was a shop with the shutters up and a sign saying *Boutique à louer*. It had once been a laundry, said Adrienne, pointing to the words *"gros"* and *"fin"* on either side of the door, meaning they did up both sheets and fine linen. Adrienne, who was rather plump, placed herself under the *"gros"* and told me to stand under the *"fin."* "That's you and me," she said.

Two obstacles threatened their hopes: there was a housing shortage, and "La Mère Garrouste," the old concierge in a black lace cap, was not fond of renting to foreigners. When Mme Garrouste reluctantly agreed to her request, Sylvia's heart leaped. She signed the lease and rushed to the well-stocked English secondhand bookstores in Paris to search for library classics. She was particularly fond of the booksellers Boiveau and Chevillet, where she excavated the basement, candle in hand, looking by the hour for treasured books. From the catacombs of M. Chevillet's bookshop, she built up her library—for Shakespeare and Company would be chiefly a lending library—from *Beowulf* through the nineteenth century. She found here all of Henry James. Cyprian, who was working at Brentano's in New York City, sent her the most recent American books. Later, to avoid paying full price, she negotiated directly with publishers for a bookseller's discount. And finally, her mother sent her large photographs of Whitman, Poe, and Emerson for the walls.

The late summer and the fall of 1919 were full of brave anticipation and hard work in preparation for her new life. With the daily advice of Adrienne and the daily assistance of Holly, she met each challenge boldly. She matched her business daring with a feat of physical daring one day when she jumped into the Seine to save Cyprian's green parrot.

She and Holly, tired after numerous errands to the end of preparing the shop, were resting in their room at the Hotel du Quai Voltaire. Their window was open to the late summer day. Guapo, the parrot Cyprian had left, liked to sit on Sylvia's shoulder and drink tea and lemon from her cup. But on this day he flew out the window. Sylvia, hastily donning her Touraine farming pants, pursued him to a nearby tree on the quai. When a passing street-lamp cleaner could not rescue the parrot from the top of the tree, Sylvia climbed on his shoulders and reached for Guapo, who gave her a sly look and flew toward the river. Halfway across, his wings failed and he fell into the water and was swept to a ledge under the bridge. The waves from an approaching barge would soon have dislodged him if Sylvia, pulling off her shoes, had not jumped in and swum toward him. He hung on; she "grabbed the miserable little bunch of feathers" and was swimming back to the shore when the river brigade approached in a boat. She was certain they would arrest her. But their attention was soon diverted by the cheering spectators on the bridge. When she landed, a group of small boys fought over who would carry Sylvia's shoes as they all accompanied the dripping heroine back to her hotel. Her impetuosity and pluck—which impelled her to plunge into the Seine, work in the fields with French peasants, and take the Orient Express to Serbia—would be put to its keenest test in Shakespeare and Company.

Her mother's 19 August 1919 check for $3,000 (changed at Lloyd's bank for 24,810 francs) arrived on 2 September, and on the following day Sylvia paid six months rent for her shop. Before Holly left France for Italy, where she was to direct the Junior Red Cross for the next three years, she helped Sylvia choose drawing paper and arrange for carpenters, electricians, and painters. The two sisters also went to London, where they purchased two trunks of English books, mostly poetry, and met publishers. She visited Alida Monro at the Poetry Book Shop, the showcase of the Georgian poets, who, according to Sylvia, "gave me a great deal of information on the subject of poetry publications and how to procure them." She also stopped on Cork Street at the bookshop of Elkin Mathews, who "was sitting in a sort of gallery, with books surging around and creeping up almost to his feet." For the shelves of Shakespeare and Company, she ordered books by Yeats, Joyce, and Pound. For the walls, she purchased two Blake drawings and portraits of various writers. She planned to hang the drawings and portraits on the bookshop walls alongside a few Whitman papers that her aunt Agnes Orbison had given her. After this intoxicating buying spree, she left London, as she later put it, "drunk with joy" and a bona fide "member of the book trade."

Less than four months after her return from Serbia, she opened the doors of Shakespeare and Company for business on Monday, 17 November 1919—a year after the armistice and eight months before the arrival of Joyce in Paris. She was busy from the first days, she declares: "From that moment on, for over twenty years, they [the patrons] never gave me time to meditate." For a woman who "liked to be left alone in a corner to dream and read and meditate," she had chosen an odd career. For, as she soon realized, she had exchanged a life of musing for one of bustling.

She did not know on that cold November morning how many Americans—she would call them "pilgrims"—would, in succeeding years, flood Paris and her door. She had been counting on only Adrienne's French patrons for support. Nor could she know that the man who would radically change her bookshop was then teaching English in Trieste and working persistently on a book he was to call *Ulysses*. Nor could she have known, this severe November morning, that her deepest personal and professional fulfillment lay around the corner—as a full partner in the life of Adrienne Monnier.

If Sylvia had met and married a man the year before, when she was reading literature in Paris, her name might not be known to us today. But instead she had met Adrienne Monnier, who would mean as much to her as any parent or husband might have meant. Adrienne's gentle friendship allowed her to cultivate her true career. Before that meeting, her life had lacked focus and vocation. She had studied French, Spanish, and Italian; traveled a great deal; supported herself as a secretary; tried her hand at journalism; and worked as a farmhand and a Red Cross secretary. But the two years in which the lives of Sylvia and Adrienne began to flow together channeled Sylvia's life both personally and professionally. Personally, she left her wandering for a home in Paris. Professionally, she chose a career in literature and service to art. Within months of the November 1919 opening of her bookshop, she would become a personality. Within two years she would be a literary leader. And within six years she would be, in the words of Eugene Jolas, "probably the best known woman in Paris"—the "Sylvia Beach" of modern letters. As Shakespeare and Company grew financially and culturally, Sylvia grew intellectually and spiritually. A richer person in her own right, she would give of herself in greater measure.

CHAPTER 3

... and Company
1919–1920

WHEN SHAKESPEARE AND COMPANY opened, on 17 November 1919, the era of Stravinsky, Picasso, and Cubism was passing. Gertrude Stein and Alice B. Toklas had returned in May from their war retreat in Palma de Mallorca to find that "friends were gone, an era had passed: Matisse had moved south; Picasso . . . was playing the successful, suave husband; Apollinaire was dead." A new era began with the appearance of Shakespeare and Company on a tiny street the size of a cobblestone alley, near the school of medicine. Within eight months Pound and Joyce would arrive in Paris, and the influence of American and British literature be felt across the Left Bank. In the following year, 1921, Malcolm Cowley, Ernest Hemingway, Thornton Wilder, Robert McAlmon, and Sherwood Anderson would arrive. And following them would be the crowds overflowing the café terraces on the boulevard du Montparnasse.

The opening of the shop made quite an impression on the French. Not only was it the first combination English-language bookshop and lending library in Paris; it was unlike any other shop, particularly in its décor and the appearance of its owner. "Everybody was staggered if I do say it," Sylvia confided to her mother. Her velvet smoking jacket charmed the French, as did the black-and-white woolen Serbian rugs on the hardwood floor. The room was softened by the beige sackcloth that covered the old walls and the bright-colored paint on the baseboard. Adrienne had suggested that she paint her walls "battleship gray," as Sylvia called the color, but she preferred brighter colors. The only dark objects in the room were the pieces of antique furniture that, except for the gate-legged table, she and Adrienne had bought at the flea market. She had racks on one wall for the English and American reviews: *Dial, Nation, Chapbook, New Republic, New Masses, Poetry, Egoist,* and *New English Review*. She also lent *Playboy,* a pre-Hefner literary magazine published in New York (1919–1921, 1923–1924). On another wall with Blake drawings and Whitman manuscripts were pictures of Whitman, Poe, and Oscar Wilde. Beyond this first room was a small storage room and a kitchenette with gas stove, running water, and space for one person. It was the "quintessence of the literary bookshop," remembers one visitor, "picturesque beyond the imagination of any designer of stage or movie sets, and of an authentic homeyness that thousands of art booksellers have [since] tried and failed to attain."

She watched with excitement as the name "Shakespeare and Company" was painted across the front. Fortunately she abandoned an earlier plan to call it "The Little Book Club." The name Shakespeare and Company, she reports, "came to me one night as I lay in bed. My 'Partner Bill,' as my friend Penny O'Leary called him, was always, I felt, well disposed toward my undertaking; and, besides, he was a best seller." A portrait of Shakespeare—painted by Adrienne's friend Charles Winzer and depicting Shakespeare with an egg-shaped bald head, slanting eyes, and a gold chain around his neck—was hung from an iron finger over the door. The perpendicular signboard, typically English, was not common for Paris shops, and Adrienne disapproved. On the outer sides of the front windows were painted "Lending Library" and "Bookhop," the latter a spelling that she felt was oddly appropriate and did not hurry to correct. Occasionally the sign caused some confusion. One day, a Frenchman with no knowledge of English literature studied the painted picture of Shakespeare on the signboard and solemnly walked in to inquire about the business. *"Est-ce que vous êtes M. Shakespeare?"* he asked a bearded customer seated at the desk.

"No, I am not Mr. Shakespeare," the customer replied. "I am only one of the Company."

"But the portrait outside then—it is of M. Company, not of M. Shakespeare?" the puzzled Frenchman asked. The man seated at the table pointed to Sylvia and introduced her as Mlle Shakespeare. The Frenchman left, seemingly pleased.

Adrienne's French customers, whether they knew English or not, were her first visitors. They came with flowers and encouragement. Whereas Adrienne had required months and years to gain these customers, Sylvia inherited an instant clientele from Adrienne. Shakespeare and Company, she supposed at the time, would be an English-language bookshop and lending library primarily for the French.

There was no formal announcement of the opening, but the throng of artisans in and out of the shop and the talk at Adrienne's shop brought readers' interest to a peak. A helpful waiter at a nearby café had no sooner taken the shutters from Shakespeare and Company's windows than the first customer, Thérèse Bertrand, a student at the school of medicine and a friend of Adrienne's, walked in to join the lending library. Among the many students who patronized the lending library thereafter, Bertrand was Sylvia's favorite because she exemplified the qualities she admired in a woman—intellect, curiosity, and independence. According to Sylvia, she played a good game of tennis, was well-read (she borrowed every new American book for the next twenty-two years), and went to the top of her profession, becoming médecin des hôpitaux. She would become the physician of Sylvia, Adrienne, and Joyce.

Students, their professors, and members of Adrienne's lending library received a 20 percent discount. Many students from the Sorbonne needed English books and could afford only a lending library in this era before the "paperback revolution." Some read English well; others hesitated at the window, peering in at the first display of works by Thomas Hardy, George Bernard Shaw, Ezra Pound, William Blake, Henry James, and Ralph Waldo Emerson. During the first year, when a student asked her to recommend a book, she suggested James, Hardy, Shaw, or Masters, who were among her own personal favorites at that time. Inasmuch as the French knew little of American literature beyond Whitman and Twain, she often gave short lectures on American literature. By 1921, her recommended reading would include the experimental writers, especially Joyce.

Sylvia awakened on the second day (18 November) with enthusiasm and hurried to the shop, which was fragrant with the flowers her French friends had brought. She was certain that her opening had been a success. Her high spirits were sustained by a visit from Louis Aragon, the handsome twenty-two-year-old Dada poet and devoted admirer of Cyprian. He had once followed Cyprian to the bird market, declaring his passion for her and his wish to rescue her from a burning building. When he asked for Cyprian on this day, Sylvia told him that she had been in New York City since February, working at Brentano's and looking for film roles. The disappointed Aragon, who would return many times in search of Cyprian, stayed to talk and amuse Sylvia. He spoke excellent English, without an accent, and was known as an eloquent and tireless talker. He recited his poetry for her—poetry that would be collected for publication the following year in *Feu de Joie* (*Fire of Joy* or *Bonfire*). His poem "La Table" consisted only of *la table* repeated over and over again. "The Alphabet" was just that: "A,b,c,d,e. . . ."

In March 1919, Aragon had founded, with his friends André Breton and Philippe Soupault, a review satirically entitled *Littérature*. This review would by the following year become the organ of the French Dada movement. "Any work of art that can be understood," the Dadaists proclaimed, "is a product of a journalist." These men would soon become the founders of French Surrealism. The English journalist and editor Sisley Huddleston claims that Dada and Surrealism began in the rue de l'Odéon: "Adrienne received the first copies of *Dada*, printed in Zurich, and lent them to Jean Paulhan. They were read by Louis Aragon, André Breton, Philippe Soupault; and thus Dadaism spread to Paris, and was transformed into Surrealism, and certainly began a revolution in literature."

In those first, November days of the bookshop, Sylvia was visited by many other French writers—Léon-Paul Fargue, Valery Larbaud, André Gide, Georges Duhamel, and Jules Romains. The first week, indeed, brought customers who, over the next twenty-two years, would be her most faithful patrons and friends. For example, a young music student named Jacques Benoist-Méchin, who joined nine days after she opened the library, would play a key role in dramatic events of the rue de l'Odéon. They brought a flurry of trade that quickened the need for both more books and more money. She wrote to her mother urgently and humbly for an additional thousand dollars. In the letter she also asked for half a dozen inexpensive editions of the poetry of Whitman, which she could not get from England. One unwanted package she received from England was from Elkin Mathews, who had taken advantage of her commercial inexperience and sent dozens of "nightingales" (*rossignols*), as the French call unsalable volumes. She returned most of them with a stern letter.

According to Sylvia, the "baptism of the infant" Shakespeare and Company took place at 4 P.M. on the second Wednesday after it had opened. Sylvia had been the mother. The godfather, Valery Larbaud, brought the port. The godmother, Adrienne, brought sugared almonds, *dragées* for the *nouveau né*. The guests drank to the health of the baby. No godparents were more faithful in supporting a child. Adrienne, of course, had served as midwife. But the thirty-eight-year-old Larbaud, who was the most respected French critic of foreign literature, became her steadiest customer. In fact, Brentano's of Paris, where as a student Larbaud had spent all his pocket money on American literature, complained that Sylvia had stolen their best customer. He devoured English and American literature. He shared Sylvia's enthusiasm for Whitman, his favorite American author. Larbaud had written essays on Whitman's poetry, praising him as the "poet of a nation in the making." Though most readers today remember Larbaud for *A. O. Barnabooth,* a novel that was popular among the young of France and South America, it was for his work as a scholar and translator that Larbaud depended on the two lending libraries. Few have introduced French literature more effectively to England and America or translated English and American literature more handsomely into French. His chief translation challenge would be to supervise the translation of Joyce's work, to which he would be introduced by Sylvia, who also, with Adrienne, presented him to Joyce in person.

Larbaud was stout, with a short neck and a rather large, square head. Although he thought he looked like a rhinoceros, Sylvia declares in her memoirs that he

was one of the most attractive men I have ever known. Personally, Larbaud was charming. His large eyes were beautiful and had the kindest expression in them. He was of heavy build; his head was set close to the shoulders. His hands were one of his chief beauties, and he was proud of them. Also, he was proud of his feet, which he crowded into shoes a size smaller than was comfortable. One of his charms was his way of laughing—shaking soundlessly, and blushing. And in quoting a line from some poem he liked, he would turn pale, his eyes fill with tears.

The son of a wealthy farmer-chemist who owned one of the springs that make the Vichy region famous, Larbaud as a young man translated and published at his own expense Coleridge's *Rime of the Ancient Mariner,* earned his degree at the Sorbonne in languages, and traveled extensively. He was fluent in Italian,

Spanish, and English, which he loved best after French. Sylvia recalls that "he knew English so well that he could get into a discussion over Shakespeare's use of the word 'motley' with Shakespeare scholars in the *Times Literary Supplement*."

Larbaud first met Adrienne after returning from Spain in 1919, where he had spent the war years translating several volumes of Samuel Butler, the English novelist and essayist. Although Sylvia had herself spent two of those years in Spain, they did not meet until they both became members of Adrienne's library, where Larbaud read his poetry aloud. He was involved in the plans for Shakespeare and Company. "What brought Larbaud and me together was his love of American literature," claims Sylvia. "It was my job to introduce him to our new writers, and every time he left the bookshop, he carried away another armful of their books. He met there, too, live specimens of the new generation." On the day of the baptism of the bookshop, Larbaud gave Sylvia a small china Shakespeare's house which he had owned since he was a child. Several months later, Larbaud brought a large box to the bookshop and invited Sylvia to tea. As godfather of the bookshop, he announced, he was ensuring the protection of the premises. Inside the box was a collection of toy soldiers: George Washington and his troops mounted on prancing horses and a company of West Point cadets. Larbaud, who was a zealous collector of toy soldiers, had consulted documents at the Bibliothèque Nationale, supervised their making, and painted each by hand. "I always kept our armed forces in a small cabinet near the door as you entered the shop," reports Sylvia. "Its glass window was fastened by a secret spring to guard these irresistible little men from rape by my children and animal customers." She, Adrienne, Larbaud, and Fargue celebrated the arrival of the troops with a dinner party that Friday night.

Larbaud's closest friend was the forty-three-year-old poet Léon-Paul Fargue, who had introduced him to Adrienne. He was one of the most famous figures in Paris literary life—the last of his generation of bohemians. He was a poet of the streets, invoking the sounds of night, the smell of alleys, the shadows of buildings. He went about Paris in taxis, which he always kept waiting for him. His brow figures prominently in the numerous pictures of the bookshop crowd of these early years: bald on the top of his head since adolescence, he arranged a lock of hair across the top of his high brow. These pictures taken during the first years of the bookshop indicate that the relationship of Sylvia, Larbaud, Fargue, and Adrienne was both professional and social. In a rough draft of her memoirs, Sylvia compares her two dissimilar friends Larbaud and Fargue:

One of them, Larbaud very polite: a dandy in dress, methodical in his work, a Seigneur but not a "grand seigneur," not a talker, altruistic and a great admirer of other people's talents: the other, Fargue an egoist, a bohemian, no sense of time, unaware of the existence of anyone but himself, but a genius in poetry.

Unlike the multilingual Larbaud, Fargue spoke not a word of English. Nevertheless, he was at the bookshop on the day of its opening and visited often thereafter, as a friend rather than as a customer. He felt quite at home there, amid hundreds of books in a language he could not read. Because he was a daily visitor at Adrienne's bookshop and an intimate friend of Marie Monnier, Adrienne's sister, he was, in a sense, a member of the Odéon family. Every afternoon at Adrienne's he told stories to a circle of his delighted friends, whom he called *les potassons,* a word of his own invention meaning, roughly, "buddies." Larbaud was his most appreciative listener, laughing silently, his body shaking; he "would say, 'Oh!' in his Larbaldian manner." According to Sylvia, who found him fascinating, Fargue's "verbal inventions were unimaginably obscene . . . and nothing in *Ulysses . . .* could shock me after Fargue." Whenever he came in, he took over the conversation, which then became a witty monologue. She shared with him, as well as with Larbaud, a love of puns and jokes. There was a spirit of play in their relationship: "Love for the game of language and play itself was an element of the *esprit* of the citizens of Odéonia." Joyce would never participate in this *esprit.* He would save all his language inventions for the written page. Besides, his sense of bourgeois decorum would never allow such language in a lady's presence. Fargue's stories would make Joyce blush. Hemingway, by contrast, "liked Fargue the best" of all the French to whom Sylvia introduced him. Fargue had the ability to caricature friend and foe alike, an ability that, to a less biting extent, Sylvia shared. Two examples are recalled by friends. Adrienne claims that "before a photograph of such and such a great poet [Claudel] he said: 'He resembles an anemic gendarme, a swimming teacher.' " She admits, however, that "there was always an hallucinating resemblance. The person was transformed before your eyes, as if struck by the wand of a magician." A second testimony to Fargue's wit comes from Sisley Huddleston, who remembers when Fargue received from a count a haughty letter full of misspellings. Fargue replied: "Monsieur, I am the offended party. I have the choice of arms. I know my orthography. You are dead." Many of the humorous stories are told on Fargue himself. He had no sense of time and habitually appeared for an engagement hours late. Several of his friends, including Sylvia, claim that one day he rang a doorbell for a party and upon entering remarked that he was sorry to be so late that all the guests had left. "Yes," remarked the host, "a week ago."

On his first visit to Shakespeare and Company, Fargue was delighted with the appearance of the shop and thought it an improvement on the previous business. He tried to explain to Sylvia how it had once looked as a laundry. He drew a picture of the laundress's stove that had once stood in front on the fireplace. Carefully, he drew in the irons. Then he signed the drawing "Léon-Poil Fargue," a play on the French word for stove, *poêle.* His later visits would come at odd hours. To Fargue's delight and for the convenience of her customers, Sylvia worked long hours. The shop was open for business every day except Sunday and holidays from 9:00 to 12:00 (usually 12:30) and from 2:00 to 7:00. She tried to close Wednesday afternoons in order to run personal errands. Although she later reduced the hours, during these early years she spent many nights in the shop, occasionally working until midnight. Sometimes Fargue, who was a night wanderer, would find her alone at the close of a twelve-hour day. According to Sylvia, "he would drink a cup of tea, which I knew he disliked, and tell me woeful tales of love and treachery, his tears, all the while, falling into his teacup." He was paranoid, so that she believed much of what he told her was from a "rich imagination." But she listened with affectionate amusement to his tales, full of poetry and witty obscenity.

Late one night, Sylvia awakened with a sense that she was not alone in her room. She was sleeping on a daybed in the back room of her shop, where she had moved soon after opening day. It was a small room with an adjoining kitchenette; sleeping there saved her money and kept her, quite literally, close to her work. She had never been frightened before. There were bars on the window, to which her eyes now fixed. Squinting into the room, with his hand cupping his face, was Fargue. On one of his nocturnal prowlings—he called them his "ministry of the night"—he had found the front shutters up and the door locked. Having wandered round to the back courtyard, he was now peering in through to the iron-barred window. Her bed was below the window, and she could stare back at him. A curious man, "he always hoped to see something interesting." He also desired frequent contact with a *potasson,* especially when he could not sleep at night: "It was a positive necessity for him to follow his friends everywhere." He had been known even to climb a ladder to look into Larbaud's window. Whatever price his friends paid in loss of nightly privacy, they gained in the amusement of his daily company.

Raymonde Linossier, a law student, was an admirer of Fargue's poetry and one of the *potassons.* She possessed a copy of everything he wrote, including most of his manuscripts. Raymonde, an early member of Adrienne's library, soon became a close friend of Sylvia. Often Raymonde stayed in the shop if Sylvia had to run an errand, attend an afternoon literary reception, or swim on women's day at the local pool. A daily customer of Adrienne, Raymonde had gained the attention of French writers in 1918 when she published *Bibi-la-Bibiste* (which Sylvia loosely translated as "One's Self the One's Selfist"). This fourteen-page work was dedicated to her close friend the composer Francis Poulenc, who was a member of the music group called The Six. Sylvia gave a copy of the book to Ezra Pound, who sent it to the *Little Review,* proclaiming it a major work. Amused by his claim that the book had "absolute clarity, absolute form," Sylvia did not believe that "the French, nor particularly Raymonde herself, would have gone so far." As a writer she was gifted, but she neither cultivated nor acknowledged her gift. She published *Bibi* anonymously, attributing it to "the X Sisters" (her sister, Dr. Alice Linossier-Ardoin, merely paid for the publication). Her deceptions were protective, Sylvia believed, for her "very great unselfishness and warm heart were, like her writing, clandestine, camouflaged by paradox and the comical." As "the carefully brought-up daughter of a famous physician," she kept her writing as well as her literary associations secret. Sylvia thought these prim limitations on French women outrageous:

It was difficult for an American girl like myself who had always been free to do what I pleased to understand the necessity for Raymonde's secretiveness. I couldn't make out at all why a young woman who mixed with the company at the Law Courts, who once even defended a prostitute, and had, in fact, made a considerable study of prostitution, must not be found in the vicinity of a Fargue or a Joyce.

At the end of two weeks of business, the lending library of Shakespeare and Company had twenty-three subscribers. Several of these were Americans. Holly had written from Italy to all her friends at the Red Cross in Paris, urging them to drop by and patronize the new American bookshop. In a letter to her mother, Sylvia remarked that many of the American patrons seemed terrified, ignorant of what books to choose. A friend from childhood days of Sylvia and Holly visited during the first two weeks: John Stetson, Jr., who as a youngster had gone horseback riding with Holly, at the same time his younger brother had played dolls with Sylvia, who had felt cheated. Stetson, now an American diplomat in Warsaw, was surprised to find Shakespeare and Company with Holly's picture on the wall. And Sylvia was surprised to find Stetson, with whom she had once longed to ride, prosperously stout.

On the first of December, only two weeks after opening, Sylvia glanced out the window and saw Adrienne, in a long cape and knit cap, turn the corner, accompanied by a lean man in a cape and a broad-brimmed Stetson. "My, he looks like William S. Hart," she thought, recognizing André Gide, whom she had heard read several times at Adrienne's. She had always been timid in his presence, and she was excited now to see him approaching.

Adrienne was hurrying to keep pace with Gide's long stride as they walked down the street and into the warm bookshop, where the three sat down to talk. She filled out a small white card with his name and the amount of deposit, twenty-eight francs. He placed it in his large coat pocket. From time to time over the next ten years, he would carry one of her English books, such as *Moby-Dick,* which he bought in 1925. Then she took out a large borrower's card and wrote, "André Gide, 1, Villa Montmorency, Paris—XVI, 1 year, 1 volume." She was so intimidated by his presence that she quavered: "I was very scared of him and trembled as I made out his card." In her trembling she left a small puddle of ink on the card and hurried to blot it. Her timidity, unlike the blot, would later disappear, and Gide would become one of her most loyal supporters, leading the group that would save the shop in the late thirties. Gide was complex and proud; yet he was kind to her assistants. One of them recalls that "he was comfortable speaking to a small young girl." Gide had been a founder and the informing spirit of the *Nouvelle Revue Française* (1908) and, though a respected critic, he was the renegade of French literature. His writings until this time, the chief of which was *L'Immoraliste* (1902), emphasized his abhorrence of religious and moral restraints. His iconoclastic novel *Les Caves du Vatican (The Vatican Swindle* or *Lafcadio's Adventures,* 1914), whose chief character, Lafcadio, commits an apparently motiveless murder, was a favorite of French youth. Sylvia believed that French young people could not decide whether to model themselves after

Gide's Lafcadio or Larbaud's Barnabooth. By 1919, the fifty-year-old Gide had emerged as one of the foremost writers of the recent literature of introspection and self-confession. Five years later his *Corydon,* comprising dialogues on homosexuality, would arouse a storm of controversy. He was scornful of Proust's discreet concealment of his own homosexuality. Sylvia shared Gide's love of personal freedom and sympathy for homosexuals, but not his need to proclaim his sexual preferences publicly in his works.

The friends of Shakespeare and Company did not always approve of one another. One of Adrienne's great enthusiasms was the poetry of Paul Claudel, a devout Catholic mystic and distinguished sometime French ambassador to Japan. Adrienne described the fleshy-faced Claudel as a man who looked like a Chinese thunder god with "a little cyclone in his neck, in place of an Adam's apple." After the publication of Gide's *Les Caves du Vatican,* Claudel refused to collaborate on a translation of Whitman's poetry that they had planned as early as 1913. Claudel promptly denied the Whitman influence when Gide discovered in Whitman a kindred homoerotic spirit. Claudel tried unsuccessfully to convert Gide, who was a Huguenot (their correspondence, published in 1949, records Gide's flirtation with Catholicism). Adrienne tells us that one day Claudel, "brandishing a crêpe flambée on the end of a fork, declared to the son of Francis Jammes that Gide would burn that way in hell." French students gave Gide the last word in a gesture that illustrates the star status of French writers, around whom legends grow. On a bulletin board in the hall of the Sorbonne after Gide's death, in 1951, there appeared a telegram supposedly signed by Gide: *"L'enfer n'existe pas. Préviens Claudel."* ("Hell doesn't exist. Better notify Claudel.")

Among the other French writers who became patrons during the opening weeks of Shakespeare and Company were Georges Duhamel, a physician and writer; Luc Durtain, another physician, who had written poetry about trench warfare; André Maurois; and Jules Romains. Duhamel brought inscribed copies of his novels and essays about the hospital scenes during the First World War. On his motorbike, Durtain brought copies of his verse. Maurois, whose first subscription is dated 19 December 1919, was an enthusiastic admirer of English literature through his war experience as liaison contact officer with the British forces. He too brought a novel, *Les Silences du Colonel Bramble* (1918), which perceptively studies an English officers' mess hall. He later gave up fiction to write biographies of Sand, Proust, Hugo, Shelley, Balzac, Disraeli, and others.

These Frenchmen, all Sylvia's contemporaries, were more than patrons of her shop. With Sylvia and Adrienne, they formed a literary circle of friendship, socializing as well as working together. This friendship is illustrated in Sylvia's associations with Jules Romains, a handsome French novelist of stocky build, two years older than she. Romains was an early patron of Adrienne's library. Sylvia had first read his work in the New York Public Library in 1914 and had met him personally in 1917 after one of his readings at La Maison des Amis des Livres. He was one of the first to visit Shakespeare and Company but missed the baptism, much to Sylvia's regret, because he was in Barcelona. She soon became

a regular guest of Romains, an unrepentant practical joker whose evening entertainment usually revolved around some intrigue or mystery. For example, one
evening the *copains* (cronies)—as he called his friends, after the characters in a
book of his by that title—met, in disguise, at a bistro in a tough neighborhood
in Paris. Hat pulled down over one eye, Romains was best disguised and so last
recognized. The character of this group of *copains* exemplified Romains's doctrine of *unanimisme,* a sort of urban pantheism which held that the spirit of the
individual becomes a part of the spirit of the group or country—a doctrine similar
to Whitman's theory of universal brotherhood. In Romains's great novel *Mort
de Quelqu'un (Death of a Nobody,* 1911), Jacques Goddard, at his death, becomes
a part of the lives of his neighbors, whose procession winds through streets,
becoming part of the city. Adrienne was particularly attracted to the idea that
individual lives have their fullest value in the group. Unanimism appeared to her
"to be a great, fecund, truly inspired idea. It was the firmest and clearest answer
. . . to the religious question." When Adrienne, Romains, and Durtain had an
afternoon or Saturday *promenade des copains,* Sylvia asked a friend to keep the
shop open. They all walked arm in arm through the oldest streets of Paris, drinking white wine in *guinguettes* (taverns with singing and dancing) and exploring
fortifications.

One Sunday, Romains guided them by train to Beauvais to see the cathedral.
He also introduced them all to Copeau's creative acting troupe (1913–1924) at
the Théâtre du Vieux-Colombier–a troupe that included Blanche Albane, the
wife of Georges Duhamel. The group also attended Copeau's production of
Duhamel's great success *L'Oeuvre des Athlètes (The Action of Athletes),* which
takes its name from the literary club that the play satirizes. Blanche Albane was
in a cast of characters that closely resembles contemporary French writers. They
saw, as well, Romains's screenplay *Donogoo-Tonka,* a sequel to his novel *Les
Copains,* and Copeau's production of Romains's *Cromedeyre-le-vieil,* in which
an isolated mountain village, energetically displaying unanimism, reverts to
primitive customs.

Sylvia was taken into a milieu that, in her own words, was "as hermetically
walled in as a harem." She was the only "profane foreigner" in this select
group. But her membership in the *copains* was informed by her knowledge of
American literature. Indeed, her knowledge of and enthusiasm for Whitman's
poetry—as much as her friendship with Adrienne—was a passport to the unanimism spirit. This spirit would culminate in 1926 with her Whitman exhibition.

Despite her preference for Whitman, Sylvia was initially a seller and lender
of English literature. For example, in the few weeks that she was open in 1919,
she sold more English than American titles. She sold four titles by Alan Seeger;
three by Joseph Conrad; two by Shakespeare; two by William Butler Yeats;
Joyce's *Exiles, Chamber Music,* and *Portrait of the Artist;* two copies of Oscar
Wilde's *Picture of Dorian Gray;* as well as single titles by Kipling, Dickens,
Stevenson, and Rupert Brooke. Specifically, there were twenty-four English as
compared with six American titles. The American titles, with one exception all

from the nineteenth century, were as follows: Pound's *Cathay,* London's *Call of the Wild,* Poe's *Poems,* Whitman's *Leaves of Grass,* Emerson's *Essays,* and Hawthorne's *Scarlet Letter.* These same six American authors also sold in 1920, with the addition of a number of volumes by Henry James. Not until 1921–1922 would her sales reflect the arrival of Joyce and the avant-garde American writers.

As a librarian, Sylvia's only assets were her love of books and her interest in people. She had no card catalog, no reference numbers on her books, no card file. Adrienne referred to her lending operations as *le plan américain,* not because it followed a prescribed system, but precisely because it did not. No formal procedure spoiled the intimacy of her library. Later, according to an early draft of her memoirs, she began recording in a big looseleaf notebook the whereabouts of her library books. Her only record at first was a narrow, tall card with the borrower's name and address at the top and the book titles listed with dates borrowed and returned. To each new member—Holly called a member a "bunny," after the French word *abonné* (subscriber)—she gave a small card, which served as a receipt for the deposit and a reminder of the expiration date. These small identity cards would soon become an *emblème d'honneur,* a literary passport.

As a bookseller, Sylvia seemed indifferent. She had no prices marked on books, no placards announcing sales, and, of course, no great profits. She preferred to have a customer sit down and read a book before deciding to buy. One assistant in the shop thought she parted with each book reluctantly. Very carefully she matched customer and book, a challenge she thought as difficult as fitting shoes. Janet Flanner, in an essay entitled "The Great Amateur Publisher," asserts that Sylvia had a "vigorous clear mind, an excellent memory, a tremendous respect for books as civilizing objects and was a really remarkable librarian." She was certainly no ordinary bookseller. "The person who can bring

SHAKESPEARE AND COMPANY
— Sylvia Beach —
BOOKSHOP   LENDING LIBRARY
PUBLISHER
12, RUE DE L'ODÉON, 12
Tél. : Littré 33-76

PARIS VIᵉ

to an 'ordinary' profession a sense of dedicated vocation, restores to that profession its genius,'' testifies the publisher Leslie Katz years later. ''Lincoln was a politician, Melville a seaman, Thoreau a camper. She was a bookseller.''

The beginning of 1920 marked a turning point for Adrienne and Sylvia. At the end of 1919, Adrienne's closest personal friend, Suzanne Bonnierre, died. Adrienne had loved her passionately during their school years, had followed her to London to work, and had taken her as a partner briefly in 1915, when her library first opened. Before Sylvia opened Shakespeare and Company, Adrienne and Suzanne had resumed their partnership by jointly operating a French lending library and bookshop on the rue Dupuytren. In fact, Suzanne had accompanied Sylvia to the notary to secure her first lease and had helped her with the many administrative details of establishing Shakespeare and Company. At the end of September 1919, Suzanne had married Gustave Tronche, director of the *Nouvelle Revue Française*. She died soon after her marriage.

The shock of Suzanne's death quickened certain tensions between Sylvia and Adrienne. ''We always did hit it off all right,'' Sylvia confided to Holly, ''but she used to make me a little frantic you remember.'' Finally they had what Sylvia called ''a sort of set-to or climax effect one day'' and resolved their tensions, which were manifest in their arguments over the design of Sylvia's shop. ''Since then we have become the best of friends,'' she disclosed to Holly; ''Adrienne is the best friend in the world and we get along puffickly [*sic*] now.'' Sylvia continued to rely on their personal and professional friendship to maintain her bookshop. Although they were now two established bookshops, they were interdependent and sweetly uncompetitive.

Shortly before the confrontation between Sylvia and Adrienne early in 1920— a confrontation that led to their deeper friendship—Holly had visited Sylvia, encouraged her to spend a little money on herself, and lent her the money for a new dress. But on 30 January, just three months after France's ratification of the Versailles peace treaty and twelve days after Paul Deschanel was elected president of the Republic, the franc fell to the lowest exchange rate in French history. During the following months Sylvia sold few books and had to raise the rental fee for the lending library. Fortunately the raise did not cause her to lose customers. In fact, this fall in the value of the franc soon attracted many Americans.

The activities in the rue de l'Odéon in February 1920 indicate the growth of the friendship between Adrienne and Sylvia and the increased vitality of the bookshops in the literary life of the Left Bank. In two letters to Holly, Sylvia— who for months had been too busy with business and social life to write letters to her family—revealed that in this month alone they had attended several concerts; entertained lunch and dinner guests such as Fargue, Duhamel, Durtain, and Erik Satie; and were entertained by several editors, the London conductor Eric Clark, writers, and musicians. Sylvia was busy and happy. ''I am so lucky to be able to do something interesting the rest of my life,'' she joyfully exclaimed to Holly. The bookshop now had over eighty subscribers.

One of Shakespeare and Company's first English subscribers was Sisley Huddleston, who had lived in Paris for nearly thirteen years. A thirty-eight-year-old Englishman whose mother was of French descent, Huddleston was educated in Paris as well as in Manchester, worked for the *Christian Science Monitor* during the war, then became chief correspondent of the London *Times*. He was to write, over the next fifteen years, more than a dozen books on France: *Peace-Making at Paris* (1919), *France and the French* (1925), *In and about Paris* (1927), *Paris Salons, Cafés, Studios* (1928), and *Back to Montparnasse* (1931), to name but five. He had followed every mood of Paris and was regarded by French editors and publishers as one of the best-informed men who devote themselves to maintaining a liaison between the Anglo-Saxon countries and France. Four months after its opening, Huddleston, to his delight, discovered Shakespeare and Company and on 27 March paid the first of his yearly subscriptions. He liked Sylvia immediately because she "had a cultivated taste, but she was also immensely practical." "Her loyalty," he adds, "is only equalled by her courage." One of the most vivid and extended descriptions of the life of the two bookshops during these early years is in his *Paris Salons, Cafés, Studios*. After this book came out, Fargue humorously disparaged Adrienne's bookshop as a "saloon."

On 16 March 1920 Sylvia received her first visit from an American writer. Glancing up from her desk, she saw a short, fat woman "squeezed into my little shop." Her hair was pulled into a topknot and crowned with a top-of-the-basket hat. A long full skirt and robe concealed her 200-pound bulk. She had, one young visitor later noticed, "the face of a Roman emperor on the body of an Irish washerwoman." She looked matronly and Victorian and, until she laughed, showed a stern and masculine face. When she laughed she was beautiful. She had, as another young American noted, "a delectable voice, mannish but velvety." Shadowing her was a thin, birdlike woman. She had a large hooked nose, drooping eyelids, dark hair in bangs over her forehead, and a thin mustache above her upper lip. With her long, dangling earrings and black hair she reminded Sylvia of a gypsy. This pair was Gertrude Stein and Alice B. Toklas.

Gertrude was a forty-six-year-old American with a large collection of her mostly unpublished manuscripts. She had earned her reputation in Paris as an expert on modern art. She and her brother Leo had acquired some of the best work of the Cubist period. They had studied and bought paintings of Cézanne, Matisse, and Picasso. It would be several years, however, before Gertrude achieved her international reputation as the mothering director of a group of young American writers in Paris, and as an author in her own right. Sylvia claimed to be one of the few Parisians who had read her work: "Having been an early reader of *Tender Buttons* and *Three Lives*, I was, of course, very joyful over my new customers. And I enjoyed their continual banter. Gertrude was always teasing me about my bookselling, which appeared to amuse her considerably. It amused me, too."

Gertrude, the youngest of five children, was born in 1874. Before coming to Paris in 1903, she had studied psychology (with William James) at Harvard and medicine at Johns Hopkins. In Paris she lived with Leo at 27 rue de Fleurus. Alice, three years her junior, had moved from San Francisco to Paris in 1907, the year she met Stein. In 1910 Alice moved into the rue de Fleurus apartment, and in 1914 Leo moved out. He quarreled with Gertrude over her championing of Picasso, whose work he considered "god-almighty rubbish." He took all the Renoirs and half the Cézannes, and apparently all the Matisses, since Matisse later claimed that none of his work hung in Gertrude's apartment. Still, the apartment of "the Steins"—as Gertrude and Alice were known—was lined with paintings.

By 1920 Gertrude had gained, through her weekly open houses, a professional reputation. She collected admiring young men. Her first had been Picasso in 1906. In the twenties there would be Sherwood Anderson and Ernest Hemingway. Sympathetic with her craving for fame, Alice encouraged, even pressured for, Stein's success. By the time they met Sylvia in 1920, they had lived ten of their nearly forty years together. Alice was devoted to Gertrude, giving her what she needed most—love and praise. Alice also had the daily care and management of their lives. In the following passage from her memoirs, Sylvia intimates why Alice was a giver and Stein a taker:

[Gertrude's] remarks and those of Alice, which rounded them out, were inseparable. Obviously they saw things from the same angle, as people do when they are perfectly congenial. Their two characters, however, seemed to me quite independent of each other. Alice had a great deal more finesse than Gertrude. And she was grown up; Gertrude was a child, something of an infant prodigy.

Although Alice claimed that Stein was Sylvia's first annual member, the records reveal that by the time Stein joined, four months after the bookshop opened, Sylvia had acquired about ninety members, several of whom were annual subscribers. In March of 1920 Stein bought her first year's membership for fifty francs. She would renew it the following year, on 27 May 1921, and until March of 1922. But by 1922, when the second subscription expired, Sylvia had published Joyce's *Ulysses,* and, consequently, Stein, who regarded Joyce as her rival, snubbed the shop. But during the spring and summer of 1920, when the three women became friends, there still existed goodwill. They talked of bookselling, and Sylvia explained how few American and English patrons she had. Gertrude responded by writing "Rich and Poor in English" to encourage Left Bank residents to join the bookshop. Alice typed the manuscript, and they mailed it to their friends. Stein alleges in this poem, later published in *Painted Lace,* "I have almost a country there [at Shakespeare and Company]." And she characterizes the shop in the lines "The poor are remarkably represented . . . / In dealing with money we can be funny." As if to punctuate the poetry prosaically, she adds, finally, the prices for book rentals.

Sylvia was not misled by Stein's kindness. Emphatically, she declares, "Gertrude's subscription was merely a friendly gesture. She took little interest, of course, in any but her own books." Yet on her library cards are 70 titles she borrowed over the years. Her brother Leo, with 216 titles, was a more active member of the lending library. Gertrude and Alice would drive to the rue Dupuytren in their Ford, named Godiva, which they had used during the war to deliver

hospital supplies. Or Sylvia would walk across the northwest corner of the Luxembourg Garden to the rue de Fleurus, which began at the west gate of the
garden. She remembered that "Gertrude always lay stretched on a divan and
always joked and teased." Sylvia also went for rides with them in the old Ford.
Gertrude would climb down from high atop the car—not an easy feat for someone of her bulk—and crank the car until it jerked to a rolling start. Sylvia, being
unaccustomed to car travel, was quite shaken up by the chugging of the "under-
taker" car, as she called it. Sylvia remembers their pride in the acquisition of
headlights that worked from the inside and an electric cigarette lighter. She was
also impressed by Gertrude's efficiency in changing a flat tire:

I climbed up on the high seat beside Gertrude and Alice, and off we roared to Mildred
Aldrich's "hilltop on the Marne." Gertrude did the driving, and presently, when a tire
blew out, she did the mending. Very competently too, while Alice and I chatted by the
roadside.

Gertrude was less attracted to the books than to the atmosphere—the "country"—at Shakespeare and Company. She came for a taste of "American life,"
she claimed. Gertrude was singularly American in her independence and self-
love and, in Whitmanesque fashion, celebrated herself. Although she insisted
that "America is my country but France is my Home," she was never really at
home in France, at least not among the French. Unlike Sylvia, she had little to
do with the French and did not speak the language well. She wrote and read only
English and used expressions such as "You betcha." In an unpublished portion
of her memoirs, Sylvia contends, "Gertrude had a way of looking at the French
without seeing them, something like a tourist passing through their country,
glancing with amusement at the inhabitants as she passed. Her remarks were
those any traveller might make: she was the eternal tourist." Sylvia claims never
to have seen a French person at the rue de Fleurus apartment. Only twice did
Sylvia venture to take Adrienne there. Their visit is described in an early draft
of her memoirs, which Sylvia suppressed:

I had been urged to bring her. It was an opportunity for Gertrude to express an interesting
idea of hers on the subject of the value of French writings: turning to Adrienne she
declared the French had "no alps" in literature, nor in music either. "You have no
Shakespeare and no Beethoven . . . your genius is in those things that generals say: [such
as] *On ne passera pas* [they shall not pass] . . . yes, fanfare is what [the French] do best:
the bombastic."

Adrienne protested good-naturedly, mentioning a few contemporary French writers, whom Gertrude casually tossed aside.

Of course Gertrude didn't mean it: she only wanted to tease—she loved to tease. I didn't
see the joke, nor did Adrienne think it so very funny.

Sylvia suspected Gertrude of "a little spite against" some of the French writers
who "had not acknowledged her genius."

Adrienne may have returned only once. Late in 1921, she accompanied Sylvia and Valery Larbaud to dinner. Larbaud had read Stein's *Three Lives* in 1910 and, in a letter to André Gide, had conceded that it has a "great deal of life in it, and . . . seems true." Sylvia arranged the dinner (though she later falsely remembered that Gertrude "set out to catch him") in hopes that Larbaud would become interested in Stein's work and write an article on it. There is no record of Larbaud's response to Gertrude. But he never wrote such an article.

The writers who accompanied Sylvia to meet Gertrude, most of them Americans, enriched the life of the rue de Fleurus. The first American she introduced to Gertrude and Alice was Stephen Vincent Benét. She accompanied him to their apartment at the back of the courtyard at No. 27. Benét, who was the first young American writer to visit Shakespeare and Company, bought a student subscription on 12 November 1920. He renewed the subscription twice (21 March and 14 December) in the following year. He was twenty-two, a "quiet, solemn bespectacled young man" who had just graduated from Yale, where, as an undergraduate, he had published two books of poetry and one of dramatic monologues. While in Paris, he visited the shop often, for it was his home away from America. One day, soon after he appeared in one of the early *New York Times* press photos of the shop, standing shyly behind Sylvia and Holly, he asked Sylvia whether she knew Gertrude Stein. She suggested he write to her and request an audience, but he said he could not ask; for like many later young Americans, he was afraid to approach Gertrude alone. When these young writers begged Sylvia to take them to her, she felt as if she were "a guide from one of the tourist agencies." On this occasion, she alerted Gertrude by note and led the trembling young Stephen to the rue de Fleurus. She reports her first intermediary role as successful: "The visit to Gertrude went off pleasantly. I believe Stephen mentioned that he had some Spanish blood, and since Gertrude and Alice liked anything Spanish, that interested them. I don't think the meeting left any traces, however." The following year Benét published his first novel, *The Beginning of Wisdom*, a college story in the Fitzgerald vein. Neither the first novel nor his best-known works, *John Brown's Body* and *The Devil and Daniel Webster* (published eight and nineteen years later), show Stein influences.

April brought the yearly rise of the waters, which covered the meadows by the Seine, and the first enveloping visit from mother. Mrs. Beach was on her yearly visit to her three "chicks," as she called her daughters. From Paris—where she bought Sylvia clothes, a kitchen table, and books—she went on in May to Florence to visit Holly. In a letter to Holly dated 19 April, Sylvia reports that "poor little mother is flourishing." The daughters occasionally abbreviated this reference to their mother as "P.L.M."—this French abbreviation for the Paris-Lyon-Marseille railroad line was appropriate for their wandering "poor little mother." In this letter during her mother's first visit, Sylvia describes the first spring of the bookshop: the sun is streaming into the shop, and the birds are perched on the ledge of the facade heralding the arrival of spring. It has been a cold and busy first winter for Sylvia, but the library now has 103 subscribers.

The increased number of members demanded more time and energy. One

American visitor spent several hours interrogating Sylvia about names and addresses of every useful service: bus line, train schedule, apartment house, and restaurants. When the interrogation was over, Sylvia complained that "she left me flat as a punctured tire." Feature articles about the bookshop in *Publishers' Weekly* and in English-language newspapers of France brought piles of letters. For example, she received now, as she was to receive later, many letters from young people who, after reading an article about the bookshop, wanted to work for her. Increasingly, she complained, the work reminded her of her secretarial chores for the Red Cross. Finally, she bought a file to keep her letters organized. Sylvia declined several dinner invitations from Stein because the demands of her correspondence had become too great: "It's a miserable business and I am going to sell out . . . or something if this keeps on!" Increasingly, she used part-time helpers in the store. One night she became so busy that she forgot to take the sign in, and it was stolen. A second sign was stolen sometime later. A third and permanent sign, with a rather French-looking Shakespeare, was painted by Adrienne's sister, Marie.

If Howells's death in 1920 suggested the end of an era, certainly the arrival, in the summer of 1920, of James Joyce and Ezra Pound in Paris heralded a new literary era. Both men were to change the nature of Shakespeare and Company. Pound would move Sylvia into the vortex of little-magazine publications, and Joyce would make the bookshop a publishing company—bringing it fame and near bankruptcy.

Their move to Paris was Pound's idea. They had met only recently in Italy. Their correspondence had begun in December of 1913, after W. B. Yeats had introduced Pound to the work of Joyce, then an unknown thirty-two-year-old Irish writer teaching English in Trieste. Within days the American had written the Irishman, requesting to see more of his work and explaining his own connections with several little magazines—*Poetry, Egoist,* and *Blast.* When he asked for permission to reprint Joyce's poem "I hear an army charging upon the land," Joyce sent it to him, complaining about the difficulty he was having publishing his first novel, *A Portrait of the Artist as a Young Man.* Pound persuaded Harriet Weaver to publish *Portrait* serially in the *Egoist* (1914), thus beginning a promotional campaign that culminated in the Irish writer's arrival in Paris in 1920. Joyce had been, as Sylvia humorously remarks, "discovered by Ezra Pound, a great showman and the leader of a gang that hung around the *Egoist* [in London] and included such suspicious characters as Richard Aldington, H.D., T. S. Eliot, Wyndham Lewis, and others almost as bad." Later, Joyce had begun sending sections of *Ulysses,* his second novel, to Pound. When he received the first chapter on 19 December 1917, he responded by letter in one of his American dialects: "Wall, Mr. Joice, I recon' your a damn fine writer, that's what I recon'." When printers in England refused to set portions of *Ulysses* for Harriet Weaver, Pound persuaded Margaret Anderson to publish it in the *Little Review.* "Episode I" had begun appearing March 1918; five small selections had followed in 1919. Joyce and Pound had corresponded for seven years before they met in 1920.

Professionally, it was a perfect union of the inventive and persistent literary promoter and the seemingly shy writer who had to struggle for years to get anything at all published. Personally the two men were markedly different, and so their delay in meeting was probably fortunate. In a letter to Harriet Weaver several years later, Joyce expressed in musical metaphor these personal differences:

. . . the more I hear of the political, philosophical, ethical zeal and labours of the brilliant members of Pound's big brass band the more I wonder why I was ever let into it "with my magic flute."

After much cajoling, Pound had been able to get Joyce, accompanied by his son, George, to come from Trieste to Sirmione, Italy, for a two-day meeting and rest (8 and 9 June 1920). During this visit, Pound persuaded him to move from chaotic Italy to Paris, where the franc was weak and the possibility of publication strong. Although neither of them planned to stay long in Paris, their move proved to be a major one for both writers. Pound arrived in mid-June, the Joyces on 9 July. After introducing Joyce around and locating both funds and living quarters for him, Pound returned to London to write his "Island of Paris" reports for the new *Dial*. The physical and mental life of the "island"—"Paris . . . the Paradise of artists"—finally drew him back at the end of 1920 for four more years.

In June, when Pound first visited the bookshop, Sylvia thought she was looking at an Englishman. When he began to speak, she recognized a compatriot: "His costume—the velvet jacket and the open-road shirt—was that of the English aesthete of the period. There was a touch of Whistler about him; his language, on the other hand, was Huckleberry Finn's." Her allusion to Whistler fitted his bearded informality. Appropriately, the Pounds were soon to move to their permanent Paris address in the rue Notre-Dame-des-Champs—the same street where Whistler had once lived. Here, for almost four years, he would influence the writing and publishing of many young writers.

The tall and lanky Pound, who soon became one of the most colorful figures of the Left Bank, made a vivid first impression on Sylvia. Although she had no easy chairs in her library, "Ezra managed to perform the feat of lounging in a straightbacked one, sprawled on the end of his spine with his legs stretching from one end of the shop to the other. It was his tiger period and very feline he was[;] his eyes and hair and beard gave a tawny impression." His seemingly ever uncombed hair was golden red and stood several inches above his head. His beard, of the same color, was pointed. He spoke with a nasal drawl in elliptical sentences, peppering his speech with slang and dialects. He cultivated and projected a distinct literary persona. At thirty-five he was two years older than she. "I found the acknowledged leader of the modern movement not bumptious," asserts Sylvia. "In the course of conversations, he did boast, but of his carpentry. He asked me if there was anything around the shop that needed mending, and he mended a cigarette box and a chair. I praised his skill, and he invited me to his studio. . . ." In the courtyard pavilion apartment, she saw his art and admired both his furniture and the painting of the woodwork—"all the work of his hands.'' In an early draft of her memoirs, Sylvia confides that "everybody admired the furniture and the painting . . . except Joyce who wondered why Ezra wasted his time on labors that any competent workman could perform for him.'' For publication she declares that Joyce thought "a cobbler should stick to his last, but I'm sure a 'violon d'Ingres [hobby]' is a very good thing for a writer."

During the first visit of the Pounds to the bookshop, he saw his own work prominently displayed. Sylvia had read his work in the *Little Review,* in the *Egoist,* in *Poetry,* and in other magazines sold in her shop. Indeed, the first American title bought by a customer had been Pound's *Cathay* (1915), a thirty-two-page booklet of his translations of Ernest Fenollosa's translations of Chinese poetry. Pound's works sold slowly but consistently for years—his titles were sixth in sales among those by American authors.

Dorothy Pound, during one of her first visits to the bookshop, pointed out that customers might have difficulty locating the bookshop. Accordingly, she drew a map for the back of the library circular that Sylvia was preparing. Although Pound biographers claim that bookshop patrons were directed to the shop by Dorothy Pound's map, it was in fact far too small to be reproduced. Adrienne drew the map for Sylvia's flyer.

In the publication and distribution of modern literature, the association between Pound and Shakespeare and Company flourished. Although only one library card in Pound's name survives, with the title *Gentle Art* written on it, the correspondence between Pound and Sylvia suggests that he was an important member of the Company. Visitors often recall seeing the two huddled over a manuscript or magazine. One library member testifies that she "often came into the shop when she and Ezra (Pound) were together over a book—both unkempt, unpressed, eyes glowing, dedicated to the service of the printed word."

The presence of Pound helped to draw many younger writers to Paris. Although rather poor himself, he lent them money or solicited it from someone who had it. In tribute to his influence, Hugh Kenner named his literary history of the period 1910–1925 *The Pound Era.* Although the title may be excessive, considering the powerful presences of Eliot and Joyce, Pound was doubtless at the vortex of the literary activity. He certainly promoted literary publication more zealously than did the other two, whose works, however, were perhaps more influential than Pound's. The man—more than his work—influenced a generation of writers. He discovered talent, including to some extent that of Eliot and Joyce, and acted as their unpaid agent. He fathered new magazines; read and criticized poetry (he blue-penciled out a third of *The Waste Land*); cajoled editors into publishing Joyce, Eliot, Lewis, and many others; and dispatched letters against and collected signatures of protest against tariffs on books, censorship of literature, and diverse other nuisances and injustices prevalent in his era. Sparing no puns, he parodied commercial publications such as the "Ladies' Home Urinal" and "Vanity Puke." He was as stubborn and inflexible in his disdain for popular literature as he was in his possessive loyalty to the writers and magazines he admired.

Pound's greatest aid to artists was the work he did for various little literary magazines. A "little magazine" is defined by the historian Frederick Hoffman as one "designed to print artistic work which for commercial expediency is not acceptable to the money-minded periodicals or presses." A study of Pound's endeavors is essential to any thorough history of little or "serious" magazines. His name is linked to many of them as foreign correspondent, drama critic, music critic, or editor. Occasionally he planned the format for a magazine, conceived it in a flurry of passionate reform, then turned it over to others to publish while he moved on to other causes.

The little magazines of the twenties and thirties sponsored every literary movement—Dadaism, Vorticism, Surrealism, and the Revolution of the Word—and published the early work of the century's best writers. Some 80 percent of our most important poets, novelists, and critics since 1912 were first published in little magazines. These magazines served primarily as nurturers of art and secondarily as forums for the evaluation of this modern art. The readership was select. Thus, the magazines were relatively free from censorship. A mere $50 sufficed to start a little magazine; but not many could maintain their existence for more than a year. Because they shunned commercial appeal, they "died to make verse free," Stein swore. "If a manuscript was sold to an established publisher, its author was regarded as a black sheep," declares Bryher. In the twenties, she continues, "we were permitted to appear without loss of prestige in *Contact, Broom, transition,* the *transatlantic* and *This Quarter.*"

Because it was difficult and often impossible to distribute an avant-garde magazine in the larger stores or libraries, Sylvia was their major source of distribution in Paris. The kind of obstacles she overcame is illustrated in the banning of Mencken's *American Mercury* by the American Library on the Right Bank of Paris. Angrily, Pound wrote to Sylvia that although he is not "keen on" Mencken, he defends his right to publish and distribute: "DAMN the right bank pigs, anyway." Sylvia often kept the manuscripts of young writers and circulated them to the editors of little magazines and to the publishers of little presses.

Shakespeare and Company handled the little English and American magazines as well as exile magazines published in Europe. She distributed T. S. Eliot's *Criterion* (London), Harriet Monroe's *Poetry* (Chicago), Harriet Weaver's *Egoist* (London), Scofield Thayer's *Dial,* and Margaret Anderson's *Little Review* (New York), as well as a score of other, now forgotten, little publications from the United States. She always prominently displayed poetry issues. She never published a review of her own, she admits, because she "had enough to do taking care of those published by our friends."

In the three weeks before Joyce arrived in Paris on 9 July, Pound played John the Baptist to the "Crooked Jesus," as Sylvia and Adrienne were soon calling Joyce. By sending out clippings of news releases about Joyce and copies of his *Portrait,* Pound had quickened public curiosity about and personal commitments to Joyce. He convinced both Jenny Serruys and Ludmila Bloch-Savitsky of the greatness of Joyce and of his urgent need for swift and direct assistance. Mme Savitsky, who had become a member of Shakespeare and Company on 16 March

1920, was an essayist and translator and the mother-in-law of the English poet John Rodker. She promised her three-room flat in Passy free of rent until Joyce found housing of his own. Pound asked Serruys, who in November of 1921 was to marry William Bradley (the Paris agent for Harcourt, Brace), to translate *Portrait*. Serruys, although she eventually did translate Joyce's play *Exiles*, declined the offer. Mme Savitsky, when asked, accepted and during the next five years worked on *Dedalus*—the French title she chose for *Portrait*. By 9 July 1920, when Joyce made his triumphant entry into Paris, Pound had found a flat, a translator, and a band of future disciples.

On 4 July, Mme Savitsky had written to her friend André Spire, an influential French poet, to ask whether he would receive Pound's friend James Joyce, who would be arriving soon from Trieste. Spire responded to Pound, whom he knew only slightly, suggesting he bring Mr. and Mrs. Joyce on Sunday to a tea he had already planned. The Savitskys and the poet André Fontainas took the Joyces to Spire's apartment, on the second floor of 34 rue du Bois de Boulogne. It was a warm Sunday but pleasant enough for an afternoon tea and early supper.

The story of the July 1920 meeting of James Joyce and Sylvia Beach at the Spire party—which should be called Beachsday—is an oft-repeated but partially told one. They met at the Spire afternoon supper. Ironically, Sylvia had not been invited to the gathering. Though she had read and admired Spire's poetry, particularly *Le Secret* (1919), a long poem Pound was to call "uncompromising vers libre" in the next issue of *Dial*, she did not know Spire personally and so was reluctant to attend. Adrienne, who had been invited, insisted that she accompany her, saying that the Spires would be delighted.

The Spire house sat among shady trees, birds were singing, and the windows were open to the warm July day. Sylvia was reassured when Spire, "rather Blake-like in his Biblical beard and curly mane," greeted her with "great cordiality." Soon she saw her friends Mme Savitsky, Jenny Serruys, and Ezra Pound, and realized that she knew most of the people present. Pound was stretched out in a big armchair in his usual relaxed, bohemian manner, his blue shirt open at the neck. André Spire whispered in her ear, "The Irish writer James Joyce is here." Her response, remembered thirty years later, was fright: "I worshiped James Joyce, and on hearing the unexpected news that he was present, I was so frightened I wanted to run away. . . ." She admired the episodes of *Ulysses* being published in the *Little Review* and did not know that their author was in Paris. The humble, worshipful, awestruck response (recalled years later) is an unconvincing one from a woman who was friends with some of the leaders of French literature.

Because she could not get near enough to hear what Pound was disclosing to his circle of listeners, she wandered over to talk to Dorothy Pound, who introduced her to Nora Joyce and then left the two women alone. Sylvia thought the tall, attractive Mrs. Joyce, who would always occupy a backseat in her husband's literary world, "charming, with her reddish curly hair and eyelashes, her eyes with a twinkle in them, her voice with its Irish inflections, and a certain dignity that is so Irish also. She seemed glad to find that we could speak English together," Sylvia added, for she "couldn't understand a word" of the French being spoken around her. Nora confided to Sylvia that the Joyces, having lived many years in Trieste, spoke Italian at home.

"À table!" called Spire, interrupting all conversations. His guests sat down to a delicious cold supper of meats, chicken, fish, salad, pastries, and baguettes. Sylvia also remembers Spire's filling the glasses with wine. He filled all, she claimed, "except that of the guest sitting opposite him, Pound's friend James Joyce," who resisted every offer of wine, finally turning his glass upside down to show he meant it. After staring at the overturned glass for a few moments, the mischievous Ezra Pound collected all the bottles and lined them up in front of Joyce. Everyone enjoyed the joke, except Joyce, who blushed and appeared so embarrassed that Sylvia pitied him. Although she wanted to look at him during the meal, she considerately avoided glancing his way. Later, when Sylvia and Joyce became close, he confided why he had resisted the wine. He had resolved never to touch a drop before 8 P.M.

Following the meal, most diners gathered about Adrienne Monnier and Julien Benda, who were arguing about contemporary literature. With coffee cups in hand, the guests listened to Benda's attack on the romantic-sentimental-mystical-intuitive in literature, the thesis of his recent controversial book, *Belphégor*. His attack was on the writers Adrienne most admired: Valéry, Gide, Claudel. Leaving Adrienne to defend their friends, Sylvia wandered into the library, where she found Joyce drooped in a corner against one of the bookcases. He had perhaps taken refuge from the embarrassment of the dinner joke. In any event, it was not his practice to engage in group discussions of the writings of others.

"Is this the great James Joyce?" she asked timorously.

"James Joyce," he responded firmly, extending his frail hand. They shook hands; or, as she remembers, "he put his limp, boneless hand in my tough little paw—if you can call that a handshake." The limp handshake called her attention to his hands; on the left one he wore heavy rings on the middle fingers. He had fine, almost delicate, features. And he was thin, slightly stooped, and graceful. The "light of genius" shone in his eyes, she observed, despite the abnormal right eye behind the thicker right lens of his round glasses. She gazed at his thick, sandy-colored, wavy hair, which was brushed back from a high, lined forehead. "He gave an impression of sensitiveness exceeding any I had ever known," she confessed. "His skin was fair, with a few freckles, and rather flushed. On his chin was a sort of goatee." With "his well-shaped nose and narrow lips," he was subject for a portrait. "I thought he must have been very handsome as a young man."

Joyce looked with interest at the lively American with sympathetic brown eyes. When she grasped his hand, he was struck with her understated power and energy. But the characteristic that impressed him most was her voice. Joyce often remarked later to friends that she had a beautiful voice. Sylvia, in turn, was charmed by the marked Irish timbre of his voice and its "sweet tones pitched

like a tenor's.'' "His enunciation was exceptionally clear,'' she mused, probably
the result "both of his musical ear and of his years teaching foreigners to speak
English correctly. His pronunciation of certain words such as 'book' (bōō-k) and
'look' (lōō-k) and those beginning with 'th'—he almost left out the 'h'—was
Irish, and the voice particularly Irish.''

After telling her of his adventures in moving from Trieste to Paris and of
Pound's efforts on his behalf, he inquired, "And what do you do in Paris, Miss
Beach?'' A smile spread across his face when he heard the name Shakespeare
and Company. Both her name and the name of the shop delighted him. He loved
words, their sounds, and their correspondences. Instantly, he must have envisioned the Company of Shakespeare and Shakespeare's "who is Silvia,'' from
The Two Gentlemen of Verona. And his keen mind probably played with the
puns he would later use in *Finnegans Wake:* Sylvia , silver, and sylvan or sylva
(meaning wood or grove); Beach, the sea's beach, beech bark (on which the first
books were written). Taking out his notebook, he informed her that he would
soon visit her at the bookshop. Holding it close to his face, he wrote down
"Shakespeare and Company, 8, rue Dupuytren.'' When a dog suddenly barked
from across the road, he started and turned pale.

"Is it coming in? Is it feerrce?'' he asked, almost trembling.

She assured the apprehensive Joyce that the dog, which continued to bark
and startle him, would not come in. Joyce explained that "he had been afraid of
dogs since the age of five, when one of 'the animals' had bitten him on the chin.
Pointing to his goatee, he said that it was to hide the scar.'' The conversation
that wove together the first threads of friendship was simple, anecdotal, and
unpretentious. "Joyce's manner was so extremely simple,'' she later confessed,
"that . . . I somehow felt at ease with him. This first time, and afterwards, I
was always conscious of his genius, yet I know no one so easy to talk with.''

Adrienne entered the study, looking for Sylvia. The guests were beginning
to leave. Again Sylvia took the limp hand of her new friend and affirmed that
she would be awaiting his visit. In the living room the two women said their
good-byes to their friends.

"Thank you for your generous hospitality toward an uninvited guest,'' she
remarked to Spire.

"We are delighted that you came,'' he replied. "I only hope that you were
not bored.''

"Bored?'' she echoed incredulously, glancing in the direction of the study.
"I have just met James Joyce!''

CHAPTER 4

The Battle of *Ulysses*
1920–1921

Who ever anywhere will read these written words?
— *Ulysses*

She had wanted to have her modest little bookshop, her literary foyer modeled on
Adrienne's, but fame, in the figure of the tall, slouching Irishman with his cane and
his arrogance, thrust itself through her doorway.
— Leon Edel

Twirling his ashplant stick, in the manner of his character Stephen
Dedalus, Joyce strolled up the rue Dupuytren the following day. A black felt hat
was cocked at the back of his head, where he always placed it. When he entered
the bookshop, Sylvia glanced at the incongruous combination of his dark blue
serge suit and his dirty white tennis shoes. But beneath an appearance that might
be called shabby lay a manner that was graceful and dignified. One recent
acquaintance had remarked that he carried himself with the dignity of a bishop.
Certainly his manners were elegant, even old-fashioned. After careful scrutiny
of the walls, including the photographs of Whitman, Poe, and Wilde and the
Blake drawings, Joyce sat in the blue-cushioned chair they would later call "good
wife." Sylvia thought his way of sitting with his legs crossed, and his angle of
slouching, looked "broken up." Resting his ashplant stick on her table, he
explained that it was "the gift of an Irish officer on a British man-of-war that
had stopped at the Port of Trieste." It was one piece of the Ireland he had left.

On this their second meeting, Joyce poured out his troubles to his new American friend. Her openness and evident concern put him at ease. She had the
ability to become so involved in the conversation and needs of another that that
person dropped his reserve. Her sympathy would disarm Ernest Hemingway just
seventeen months later, allowing him the freedom, minutes after meeting her, to
pull up his pant leg and display his "battle scars."

Joyce told Sylvia about his activities of the last few years, explaining again
that Pound had encouraged him to come to Paris. He spoke of his problems,
Sylvia noticed, without using superlatives:

Even the worst happenings he described as "tiresome." Not even "very tiresome," just "tiresome." I think he disliked the word "very." "Why say 'very beautiful'?" I once heard him complain. " 'Beautiful' is enough."

Through the narrative of all of his problems emerged three needs: finding an apartment, feeding and clothing his family, and finishing *Ulysses*. When she told him she had no leads for an apartment, he said that he believed she could help him with the second problem. He had had years of teaching experience in Zurich and Trieste. If she heard of any people wanting lessons, would she send them to Professor Joyce?

"What languages do you teach?" she inquired.

"English," he responded. "This is the table. This is the pen." He could also teach German, Latin, French, Italian—and they counted nearly seven more languages he knew. "Languages apparently were Joyce's favorite sport," she observed.

When she asked about his eyes, he explained the operation he had had. "Glaucoma," he announced. She had never heard of this dreadful disease with the beautiful name. "The gray owl eyes of Athena," added Joyce. The teacher Joyce pulled a notebook and pencil from his pocket and drew a picture of the eye and his disease, noting (in a mystical parallel) that Homer had gone blind with glaucoma. The most serious attack had occurred on 18 August 1917 when he had collapsed in Zurich with an attack of iritis. A week later the doctors had operated.

"How do you write? Do you sometimes dictate?" she asked.

"Never," was his firm reply. He always wrote by hand, holding himself back, watching the work as he gave it shape word by word. Even when he became nearly blind, Joyce continued to write his words, using large sheets of colored paper and charcoal. When she inquired about the progress of *Ulysses,* Joyce claimed he would complete the novel as soon as he was settled in Paris.

Joyce had begun writing *Ulysses,* his second novel, in 1914. As early as 1906, in a letter to his brother Stanislaus, he had talked of a plan for a short story about a dark-complexioned Dublin Jew by the name of Hunter (Bloom). From that time until 1914, when he began the work, "it grew steadily more ambitious in scope and method," according to his biographer Richard Ellmann, "and represented a sudden outflinging of all he had learned as a writer up to 1914." Four of eighteen sections of the novel remained. John Quinn, the New York lawyer who supported the arts and listened to the advice of Pound, was sending him a small amount of money for what he believed was a "fair copy" of each section as it was finished. Margaret Anderson and Jane Heap published the first segment in March of 1918. With concern, Joyce told Sylvia about the confiscations and burnings of the January (Lestrygonians) and May (Scylla and Charybdis) 1919, and January (Cyclops) 1920 issues. "I hope I shall pass through the fires of purgatory as quickly," he had told Harriet Weaver. Sylvia expressed her admiration for the courage of the *Little Review* editors and asked for reports from the battlefield. Joyce promised to keep her informed.

Sylvia would soon learn from Joyce the full plot and interlocking motifs of the novel. *Ulysses* is the experience and consciousness of three persons: Stephen Dedalus, the young Irish hero of *The Portrait of the Artist as a Young Man;* Leopold Bloom, an Irish Jew who collects advertisements for a Dublin newspaper; and Molly Bloom, his wife. The time setting is one day: 16 June 1904. In a parallel to Homer's *Odyssey*—Joyce found an analogy for almost every detail of Homer—the novel is written in eighteen episodes, each with a different style to match the contents, as if eighteen different authors had written the book. Joyce disclosed to a friend, "It is an epic of two races (Israelite-Irish) and at the same time the cycle of the human body as well as a little story of a day (life)." The intelligence of the plan and the experimentation with language made it a revolutionary tour de force. The most innovative technique, for which Joyce credited Édouard Dujardin as his source, was the use of the interior monologue, or what Joyce called the "uninterrupted unrolling of thought."

Before Joyce left that 12 July day, he requested a membership in the lending library. Sylvia took out a long lending-library card and wrote down: "James Joyce: 5, rue de l'Assomption, Paris; subscription for one month; seven francs." He took from the shelf a copy of John Synge's *Riders to the Sea*—a play he had translated and staged in Zurich two years before. Several days after joining the library, when no bank would touch a three-party check from his agent James Pinker, Joyce went to Sylvia for help. He was to return many times during the coming weeks and months to borrow more books, to cash checks, and to keep her informed of the progress of *Ulysses*. Through the years of his association with the bookshop, he borrowed books by or about the Irish, the contemporary little magazines, books by Pound and Eliot, and an occasional American title such as Twain's *Huckleberry Finn* and Benjamin Franklin's *Autobiography*.

When Joyce left that day, Sylvia wrote a letter to Harriet Weaver, requesting as many Egoist Press books as she could buy with one pound. Miss Weaver replied on 29 July with an offer of a third off all purchases and post-free delivery. Thus began a long friendship between the two women who would do most for *Ulysses* and its author.

Joyce's move to Paris shifted him into the public eye, that is, the eye of the writers of the Left Bank. The attention was both pleasant and unpleasant. He enjoyed the long-awaited regard as the leader of a movement, and there were a number of people who gave him money and gifts. But he was ill at ease in the Paris literary world. One such occasion of discomfort was in the salon of Natalie Barney. In front of a large group of French writers, Joyce expressed his dislike of Racine and Corneille. Barney, embarrassed, said that such a remark reflected "something about the person who said it." This and other incidents, according to the biographer Richard Ellmann, created in Joyce a "peasant scorn of Parisian sophistication." He became more "somber." "While other writers practiced their *mots,* he measured his silences." A second defense was formality. "He was invariably courteous and extremely considerate of others," notes Sylvia. In her rough-and-tumble American shop he was "excessively" formal, addressing everyone with "Mr.," "Miss," or "Mrs.," and "let no one dare to call him anything but 'Mr. Joyce'!" "Politeness," says Ellmann, "had become one of Joyce's principal social defenses, and one he resorted to constantly in Paris."

The sobering of Joyce's public demeanor was also caused by his constant need of money and his dignified begging. He wrote at night and devoted part of many days to borrowing books, bedding, furniture, and money, which he spent faster than he could borrow it. From Jenny Serruys, he borrowed a bed for George, a desk, sheets and blankets, as well as money. From Mme Savitsky he had a free apartment where he stayed, not the two intended weeks, but more than four months. The aid he received from numerous people was an acknowledgment of his art. His great endeavor and commitment—a gift or calling, he believed—crowded out all other interests: the problems or work of others, political issues, economic independence. The concerns of daily life were important only as a means to the end of his art, to which he assumed anyone should be privileged to contribute. After a series of loans from Mlle Serruys, some of which were never returned, he thanked her in an unintentionally backhanded way: "You never attached any importance to small matters—a quality unusual in a woman."

Joyce succeeded in meeting the "small" matter of his daily bread, or cake, with an elaborate indirection that preserved his dignity and pride. A poignant but humorous example of a threat to his dignity occurred during his first meeting with T. S. Eliot and Wyndham Lewis, an incident told in Lewis's *Blasting and Bombardiering*. Joyce had sent Pound on 5 June 1920 a detailed description of his poverty; he was wearing his son's boots (two sizes too large) and cast-off suits. Pound, concerned for Joyce's needs, sent a brown paper package with his two friends Eliot and Lewis, who were coming to Paris from London. The three great men of letters met ceremoniously, and Joyce, after much pulling and cutting of knots, opened the bag to find used clothes and a pair of old brown shoes. A shocked and dismayed Joyce uttered only, "Oh!" and the men sat in silent embarrassment. Without touching the shoes, he sent the package home with his son and went to lunch with the two men from London, paying the tab and tipping lavishly. During the remainder of their visit to Paris, Joyce paid cab fare, bought the coffee at the café, and insisted on paying for the dinners. Lewis reports that Eliot believed that beneath Joyce's politeness was a burdensome arrogance.

Lewis and Eliot came to Shakespeare and Company, which they were to visit during each trip to Paris hereafter. Their works had been on sale in the library since its opening. Lewis, whose novel *Tarr* (1918) was in the library, "dressed like someone out of *La Bohème*," Hemingway later observed. Lewis had spent many years in Paris during his early adulthood and had been associated with Pound and the review *Blast* in London. Eliot would become a longtime friend of Sylvia and active in the literary life of the bookshop whenever he came to Paris. Tom Eliot and Sylvia were about the same age, and, though born in the United States, both had chosen a second country as home. She had admired his work before she met him and had sold his first volume of verse, *Prufrock and Other Observations* (1917), and the hand-printed *Poems,* published the year before their meeting. Occasionally during the next twenty years, she would feature his poetry in a display in the window. Her enthusiasm for his work affected sales; she sold more copies of his various titles than of those of any writer other than Joyce.

Meanwhile John Rodker, the English poet and a longtime friend of Pound and Lewis, arrived in Paris. In a meeting with Joyce, no doubt encouraged by Pound and by Rodker's mother-in-law, Mme Savitsky, Rodker said he would like to publish *Ulysses* when it was completed. He wanted to print it on his handpress at the expense of the *Egoist,* which had put out his own poetry. Rodker did not join the lending library for several months, though he was photographed there during one of Holly's visits.

Harriet Weaver was also working to find a publisher for *Ulysses.* Since 1916, in her role as editor of the *Egoist,* she had been fully involved in Joyce's problems, receiving almost daily letters from either Joyce or Pound or both. As Joyce's appointed English publisher, she had published portions of *Portrait* in the *Egoist* (1914–1915), succeeded in getting Huebsch to print the novel in New York, and then issued it in England, on 12 February 1917—all at her own expense. She began publishing portions of Joyce's *Ulysses;* when the printers and subscribers objected, she determinedly transformed her periodical into a press and announced that she would issue the novel in full. She had to abandon her plans, however, after rejections by all the printers. It was at this point that the *Little Review* stepped in. During those years when she was financing the *Egoist* herself and paying for the printing of *Portrait,* Miss Weaver sent him not only royalty checks but also anonymous gifts of money, which in the summer of 1918 she acknowledged as being from herself. The hundreds of letters Joyce wrote to her, now available in the British Library, document the years of support she gave him. The letters consist of equal portions of news about literary progress, his health, and his money problems.

Harriet Weaver was a shy Englishwoman of integrity, modesty, and breeding whose story, particularly her friendship and generous aid to James Joyce, is told in detail in *Dear Miss Weaver,* a biography by Jane Lidderdale and Mary Nicholson. The daughter of a wealthy and conservative Church of England family, she rejected her evangelical past and, taking with her its intrepid values and idealism, embraced socialism. She shared her family wealth with those who had less. Apparently preferring to give her money to a poor genius rather than to a poor fool, she supported Joyce.

As a person, Miss Weaver seemed a paradox. She "symbolized domestic rectitude," observed Leonard Woolf, after Miss Weaver's visit to the Hogarth Press in April of 1918 in an attempt to get *Ulysses* published. The Woolfs, who owned the press, turned her down. Virginia thought the book "indecent," and yet she described Miss Weaver as "spinsterly" and "buttoned up" as she walked in carrying in her gloved hands *Ulysses,* wrapped in brown paper. There was also some irony in her intentions. Obsessed with the dangers of alcohol, she supported unknowingly at first a man who drank, and occasionally drank to excess.

Frugal, she abhorred capital, and in giving away her filthy lucre she bestowed it on one who spent it freely on food and drink and the finest hotels. "Neither of them liked keeping money," note her biographers. "They both preferred to get rid of it, although in very different ways and for very different reasons." She learned to suffer in silence and yet gave her sympathy to a man who poured out every detail of his physical problems in hundreds of letters. She was tender-hearted, Sylvia observed, and incredibly kind to anyone in need. Joyce touched her sympathetic vein often.

Joyce had intended to come to Paris for only three months to "write the last adventure *Circe* in peace (?)," as he told Miss Weaver. This would be the last and longest of the twelve episodes of the central portion of *Ulysses*—the twelve episodes of Leopold Bloom's day, 16 June 1904—which paralleled the ten-year wandering of Homer's Ulysses after the Trojan War. Ulysses's encounter with Circe, who turns his men into swine, was set in Joyce's Dublin at midnight, in a brothel, "The Mabbot street entrance of nighttown." Unlike previous portions, this section was written in dialogue and in vaudevillian form. The drunken hallucinations of Stephen Dedalus and Leopold Bloom parallel the drunkenness and metamorphosis of Ulysses's men.

Sylvia was still just an interested friend to Joyce, listening during each of his visits to the latest news of the writing and publishing of *Ulysses*. Amid the bad news of the beleaguered ship *Ulysses* and the good fortune of a thriving business activity for the summer months, Sylvia took a vacation to Rapallo, the town Pound would make his permanent home by the end of 1924. Holly and Mrs. Beach met her for a relaxed vacation at the Hotel Regina. Sylvia swam in the sea and her mother painted. Holly had to return early to the Red Cross in Florence. Sylvia wrote her on 26 August, "The vacation has made me over and removed the extra ten years I took on last summer." After putting her mother on the train for Florence on the thirtieth, Sylvia boarded the train to Paris, her business, and a growing involvement with Joyce.

When she arrived in Paris, Joyce informed her that he had received a settlement from Harriet Weaver, who decided to place an inheritance from her aunts in his name. He would live off the interest. Once again Joyce was the beneficiary of her guilty conscience about the "exploitation of labour by capital." She "disapproved, on grounds of her socialist principles, of wealth not proportionate to personal need," reveal her biographers. Her needs were small; his were large. And because she "believed that her money, tainted by usury, was hers in trust," she did not want the money to be seen as a gift from her. In an August letter to Joyce, she expressed pleasure in the fact that now his "best and most powerful and productive years" will be free from financial worries. She had no idea how little this endowment would seem to Joyce or how steadily he would chip away at the principal. According to her biographers, the receipt of his endowment affirmed Joyce's belief in his calling:

From his boyhood, James Joyce had been convinced that he was one of the elect—indeed, the only one of his kind; and he needed, from time to time, the reassurance of the power that had elected him. Unlike the religious elect, however, he did not look to that power for guidance. As alone as the Creator, he wrote what he chose to write. Having thus arrogated to himself one of the prerogatives of his elective power, his attitude to it was ambivalent. That power was, nevertheless, important to him; and Harriet was there to personify the myth. She had singled him out. That in itself was enough. But, being extremely superstitious, he probably saw in this singling out something, if not mystical, certainly supernatural. She possessed, furthermore, an essential characteristic of an elective power: impartial judgment. Her obvious sincerity in commenting on his work had an immense appeal for him. She could not, would not, flatter. To Harriet, needless to say, it would have been inconceivable that she was performing an important symbolic function in lightening for him his double burden as Creator and Creature.

This sense of election was affirmed again the following year when Sylvia Beach dedicated the resources of her bookshop to him.

Joyce's trials seemed to confirm, not shake, his sense of election. The bad news that he shared with Sylvia on her return was the failure of all attempts to publish *Ulysses*. Storms of fear and censorship discouraged each attempt. In July the Pelican Press had refused Harriet Weaver's inquiry; in August Miss Weaver gave up her last hope of an English edition because printers, who were subject to prosecution for obscenity and certainly did not have the commitment to art that a publisher might, refused to take any chances on the printing of *Ulysses*. In September a complaint of obscenity was lodged against Margaret Anderson and Jane Heap for their publication of the July–August 1920 issue of the *Little Review,* which contained part of the Nausicaa or Gerty MacDowell episode. The complaint was lodged by the New York Society for the Suppression of Vice, whose secretary was John S. Sumner. Although John Quinn did not like the two women, and with Pound had advised against their continued printing of *Ulysses,* he represented them at the hearing on 22 October 1920. Unable to delay the case so that Joyce could finish the book and have it published complete in America, Quinn watched as the women were bound over to the Court of Special Sessions for trial.

When news of the court proceedings became known, John Rodker informed Joyce that he could not publish the book. Huebsch, who was visiting in Paris, was very reluctant to publish in America. Though Joyce was not ready, Miss Weaver considered Huebsch the last chance, and she sent him fourteen episodes and began gathering orders.

With the advent of cold fall weather, the pace of literary and social life increased. Sylvia told her family about the great "swarms of people" who come to the shop—"New Bunnies flock and old ones renew." One of the new bunnies, or subscribers, was Natalie Barney. One of the old customers was Gertrude Stein, who came to inform Sylvia that the American Library might have to close because of the economic crisis. Sylvia would not mourn the loss: *"Les petits n'ont pas peur des grands,"* she shrugged. ("The small do not have to fear the large.") Her letters to her family in America this fall are full of requests for books: the articles of John Reed, a book by Upton Sinclair that can be purchased only from the author in Pasadena, two copies of Fitzgerald's *This Side of Para-*

dise, for which customers are beginning to ask, and *Jurgen,* recently suppressed in America.

Natalie Clifford Barney, who became a library member on 11 October 1920, presided over the most famous salon in Paris—the only salon in the eighteenth-century sense of the word. Every Friday the famous and eccentric were drawn to her exotic, Persian-decorated rue Jacob rooms. In her garden stood a little temple of Eros, where she and her women friends danced by moonlight. But during the Friday afternoons of tea and cakes and ices, reputations were launched, diminished, or broken. No alcohol was served by the soft-shoed Chinese servants, but the chocolate cake was from Colombin's and was the best in Paris, Sylvia testifies. Morrill Cody attended for the food. Valéry, who was always welcomed as a "brilliant talker," attended for the "tinkle of teacups and the chatter," which, he confessed to Sylvia, he found "beneficial after his work." Samuel Putnam would love the heady atmosphere—the "grace, the wit, the dignified abandon—everything but the powdered perukes" of an eighteenth-century salon. William Carlos Williams would remember only the lesbian women dancing together.

Natalie Barney was called *Amazone* by Remy de Gourmont in his *Letters* because she rode horseback in the Bois de Boulogne each morning. When Gourmont, her platonic lover, died in 1915, she kept their salon going. It was a favorite of the *Mercure de France* crowd, Valéry, Gide, and the other leading French writers. Poetry readings there were common. Joyce could not ignore her importance, although he claimed that his first visit was to find someone to lend him four beds so that he could establish his family in Paris.

Beautiful women also gravitated to the rue Jacob, for Barney was openly bisexual. She was a lover of beautiful women. Talented men found her irresistible. As Stein collected art, so Barney collected dazzling people. She organized the Académie des Femmes, her counterpart to the male Académie Française. At her salon, exclaims Sylvia in a passage suppressed by her editor, one met lesbians, "Paris ones and those only passing through town." Williams would not be the only one shocked or titillated by the lesbians. One Englishwoman, obviously enlightened by her visit to the salon, asked Sylvia in the shop the next day whether she had any books about "those unfortunate creatures."

Natalie Barney was hardly unfortunate. Born in 1877 in Cincinnati, Ohio, she was wealthy, self-indulgent, charming, and attractive. Her white clothes and blond coloring made her beauty and her wit more seductive. Different though they were in many ways, Sylvia Beach and Barney both possessed epigrammatic wits that inspired social gatherings. "Write with one's life," Gourmont had decreed, and Barney did. She lived for seductions—even though by 1917, when they were both forty years of age, she and the painter Romaine Brooks became lifelong companions. They would live together into their nineties. Brooks was faithful to Barney for sixty years; Barney was openly unfaithful—into her eighties. Her life and loves inspired not only Gourmont's "Letters to the Amazone" (1912–1913 in *Mercure*) but also numerous fictional portraits by women, such as those by the French authors Rénee Vivien and Liane de Pougy and the American Djuna Barnes.

When work permitted, which was not often, Sylvia and Adrienne attended the Barney salon. According to their letters, they would attend more frequently in the thirties, when the work connected with publishing lessened. Records show that Barney took out her first library subscription on 11 October 1920 and renewed it yearly. In her memoirs, Sylvia testifies that Barney was "one of the people who always took a great interest in my bookshop." Although Barney was the author of more than a dozen books of memoirs, poetry, and fiction, she was best known as a personality. In an unpublished typescript of her memoirs, Sylvia voices her suspicion that the only time Barney opened books was when a writer was expected at her salon. So that she would at least "be familiar with the titles" of her invited guest, Barney would send a chauffeur to the bookshop at the last moment for all his works.

Perhaps Sylvia's uncharitable judgment of Barney's "detachment in literary matters" stemmed from an incident that occurred at Barney's home. When they could not find a particular title long overdue at the library, Barney insisted that Sylvia take a replacement. As she opened her bookcase, the signed, limited edition of Pound's *Instigations* fell out. Seeming not to value the book, Barney insisted that "she never read anything but poetry." This incident and Barney's public life of notorious sexual conquests probably triggered Sylvia's question "I wonder if she ever took literary things very seriously."

Mrs. Beach arrived from a visit with Holly in Florence to brave the dampness of Paris in order to see Sylvia before returning to the United States. "I'm devoting myself to mother while she is here," Sylvia complained to her sister. "It's a wretched business her having to go home but she seems not to be depressed at all over it, the thought of [seeing] Cyprian I know makes her wild with joy." In this letter, which suggests the unhappy nature of the Beach marriage, Sylvia expressed her concern about the amount of medication that their mother was taking for her heart trouble. Mrs. Beach left on 23 October with the flu. On 20 December Sylvia expressed fears to Holly that poor little mother would return: "I do hope she won't install herself in Paris in the spring. I shall go mad you know."

The major literary event of the fall season was Larbaud's lecture on Samuel Butler, which took place at La Maison des Amis des Livres on 3 November 1920. Sylvia and Adrienne had followed his translation work on Butler, and with Larbaud's direction Sylvia carefully ordered Butler's books for her library. Following the lecture, the nineteen-year-old music student Jacques Benoist-Méchin played several of Butler's musical compositions on the piano. After each day's work and the activities of the evening, Sylvia had little time for personal indulgences. She apologized to her mother, who had left specific instructions for the making of some clothes, that she had only had time to buy a dress at the Galeries Lafayette, a black velvet, "the whole thing is as simple as the Tubes," to wear to the "Larbaud-on-Butler" and to a Stein dinner. This letter, which catches the characteristic style of Sylvia, was written on 22 November at Adrienne's apartment. The letter reveals not only that Sylvia, much to her mother's concern, did not care for nice clothes and personal adornment, but also, and more important, that she had begun living with Adrienne. For the sake of privacy, since the whole Monnier family is visiting, Sylvia has retired "into my bedroom." This remark is the first indication that Sylvia, after eleven months of living in the back room of her shop, has begun the move in with Adrienne, with whom she would live happily until 1937.

Adrienne and Sylvia both loved the theater. During the holiday season, their friends invited them often to plays, ballets, and operas. They were taken to the Ballet Russe several times in December. One evening after attending the Comédie-Française nearby, she walked through the galleries and garden of the Palais Royal, homesick for Cyprian and their years together there. During these weeks of the early winter of 1920, Sylvia sent the theater news to her young sister, who eventually abandoned any hope of a successful career with the stage or movies.

Joyce in the meantime had spent weeks looking for an apartment. He must have a large one to accommodate his family and his need for privacy. By December he had moved his family to an expensive (£300 a year) flat in 5 boulevard Raspail. In a letter to Frank Budgen, he expressed a certain amused satisfaction in his panhandling and good fortune: "By the way, is it not extraordinary the way I enter a city barefoot and end up in a luxurious flat?" The other residents of Paris were not so fortunate, according to Sylvia:

My business is maintaining itself in spite of crashes all about. The Bon Marché, the Louvre, the Printemps, different automobile manufacturers and other goods are tottering on the brink. The Galeries are very low indeed they do say. No one will buy anything till the prices drop and the manufacturers and shops are left with floods of stuff on their hands which they'd rather hold onto than sell at a sacrifice—*naturellement*.

By 20 December, after many rewrites, Joyce had pronounced the Circe section of *Ulysses* complete. He thought it was the best of his writing. In the final portion of Circe, Bloom is supporting a drunken Stephen, holding his hat and ashplant stick: "A dog barks in the distance. Bloom tightens and loosens his grip on the ashplant. He looks down on Stephen's face and form." Then Bloom has a vision of his own dead son, Rudy, holding a book, reading "inaudibly, smiling, kissing the page."

Four days later, Joyce met Valery Larbaud, who would present his work to the French artistic world. Sylvia, who had talked often of the importance of Joyce's achievement to Adrienne, believed that Larbaud, of all their French friends, would best appreciate it. Adrienne agreed, and accordingly the two women arranged to bring the writers together. According to the following account, Sylvia introduced them at Shakespeare and Company. Larbaud was already familiar with Joyce's earlier work. "When he visited the bookshop," Sylvia says, he

always asked me what he should read in English, and one time when he came I asked him if he had seen any of the writings of the Irishman James Joyce. He said that he had not, so I gave him *A Portrait of the Artist as a Young Man*. He brought it back soon, saying that it interested him very much, and that he would like to meet the author.

I arranged a meeting between the two writers at Shakespeare and Company on Christmas Eve, 1920. They immediately became great friends. Perhaps I realize more than anyone what the friendship of Valery Larbaud meant to Joyce. Such generosity and unselfishness toward a fellow writer as Larbaud showed to Joyce is indeed rare.

Before another year had passed, this Christmas meeting would prove fortunate for Joyce.

One of Sylvia's Christmas gifts this year gave her honor. Georges Duhamel dedicated his *Confession de Minuit* to Sylvia: *"pour notre amie Sylvia Beach qui à elle toute seule ferait aimer l'Amérique"* ["for our friend Sylvia Beach who, all by herself, would make America lovable"]. With Larbaud, Fargue, the Durtains, and other friends, Sylvia and Adrienne attended a midnight Christmas party that lasted until 5 A.M. If the extremity of the New Year's resolutions matched holiday excesses, she had great fun. She resolved to begin this new year by giving up cigarettes, coffee, and tea—"nothing but verbena, so as to grow stolid and unstimulated and stouter."

On 14 February 1921, after several postponements, Margaret Anderson and Jane Heap faced the charges of obscenity for publishing the Nausicaa portion of Joyce's novel in the July–August 1920 issue of the *Little Review*. Three judges presided; the courtroom was packed; and John Quinn advised his clients they would be found guilty. Nevertheless he tried several defenses: questioning the authority of the court to try such a case, using witnesses to testify to the novel's literary value, and arguing that an incomprehensible work, as they called it, cannot corrupt anyone. This latter defense, which Quinn himself thought "brilliant," came after the judges heard portions of the novel read and declared it "unintelligible." Before the reading one white-haired judge, who had slept through most of the proceedings, awakened and insisted with paternal protectiveness that the "ladies" must be excused from hearing the language. With amusement, Quinn pointed to Miss Anderson and replied, "But she is the publisher!" "I am sure she didn't know the significance of what she was publishing," was the judge's gallant reply. The ladies remained. After a discussion of the lack of punctuation—not unlike the style of American writers to whom they did not object—and Joyce's poor eyesight, the trial was adjourned for a week so that the judges could read the entire Nausicaa section.

The Nausicaa portion, the thirteenth chapter of *Ulysses*, is written in a style that parodies romantic fiction and corresponds in Homer to the story of the king's daughter by that name who finds Ulysses washed ashore. Bloom is walking on the Sandymount Street at 8 P.M. when he spots the young Gerty MacDowell with a group of her friends. When she takes off her hat to arrange her hair, she catches the "swift answering flush of admiration" in Bloom's eyes and it sets "her tingling in every nerve. . . . He was eying her as a snake eyes its prey. Her woman's instinct told her that she had raised the devil in him and at the thought a burning scarlet swept from throat to brow till the lovely colour of her face became a glorious rose." The power of the scene that follows lies in Joyce's language—he implies Bloom's act through the metaphor of the fireworks—and the fact that Bloom and Gerty never meet or touch but remain yards apart on the beach. When her friends rush off down the strand to see the display, Gerty remains where she is. For she has seen the "whitehot passion" in the stranger's face and the working of his hands and face. Catching one knee in her hands, she leans back to watch the fireworks, exposing her ankles and calves. What certainly must have offended the Society for the Suppression of Vice was her knowledge. Knowing he is watching and yielding, yet not looking his way, she leans farther and farther back at each call from her friends.

> . . . she knew about the passion of men like that, hotblooded, because Bertha Supple told her once in dead secret and made her swear she'd never tell about the gentleman lodger that was staying with them . . . [who] used to do something not very nice that you could imagine sometimes in the bed. But this was altogether different from a thing like that. . . . Besides there was absolution so long as you didn't do the other thing before being married. . . .

When the young people shout to look high in the sky at the Roman candle going up, up, up,

> she had to lean back more and more to look up after, high, high, almost out of sight, her face suffused with a divine, an entrancing blush from straining back and he could see her other things too, nainsook knickers, the fabric that caresses the skin, better than those other pettiwidth, the green, four and eleven, on account of being white and she let him and she saw that he saw and then it went so high it went out of sight a moment and she was trembling in every limb from being bent so far back and he had a full view high up above her knee where no-one ever not even on the swing or wading and she wasn't ashamed and he wasn't either to look in that immodest way like that because he couldn't resist the sight of the wondrous revealment. . . . And then a rocket sprang and bang shot blind and O! then the Roman candle burst and it was like a sigh of O! and everyone cried O! O! in raptures and it gushed out of it a stream of rain gold hair threads and they shed and ah! they were all green dewy stars falling with golden, O so lovely! O so soft, sweet, soft!

Quinn's final argument was given when the trial resumed on 21 February: he compared Joyce's technique to that of Cubism and concluded that the work was disgusting but not indecent. "There may be found more impropriety in the displays in some Fifth Avenue show windows or in a theatrical show," declared the *New York Times*, "than is contained in Gerty MacDowell's display of her drawers." When the prosecuting attorney began shouting angrily, Quinn pointed at him and declared that the novel obviously provoked anger, not lust. When the judges laughed, he thought he had won the case.

According to the *New York Times* the following morning, the main objection to the novel was stated by Assistant District Attorney Joseph Forrester as the "too frank expression concerning woman's dress when the woman was in the clothes described." The defendants, who "were accompanied to court by several Greenwich Village artists and writers," were fined $50 each. The judges decreed that *Ulysses* must not appear again in the *Little Review*. The decision's most important consequence was that henceforth publishers would not wish to touch it. Soon Huebsch reluctantly withdrew his offer. Boni and Liveright also declined.

Apparently Quinn failed to notify Joyce immediately about the trial, for it was several weeks before the news of the trial and conviction reached Paris. In the meantime, Joyce had sent the Eumaeus section to the typist and was planning the last two portions of his novel. He kept Sylvia informed of his progress in frequent visits to the bookshop, which was thriving, despite a deflated economy and an obscure location. Sylvia introduced him to her sister Holly, who was making more frequent visits to Paris from Italy, where she still directed the Junior Red Cross. Cyprian arrived in March, much to the delight of Fargue, who renewed his declarations of love. When she was not looking for an apartment, Cyprian helped in the bookshop. With their mother's encouragement, Cousin Mary, Mrs. Wistar Morris of Overbrook, Pennsylvania, gave Eleanor $50 a month for the bookshop, which the family viewed as a kind of missionary work. With this money Sylvia planned to buy a typewriter and move to a larger shop:

I am putting by Cousin Mary's money for the day when a shop in the rue de l'Odéon is free. We have our eye on Wermelinger's boots-made-to-order. He is an old man and ought to retire soon and his place is just beyond Adrienne's. . . . I could sell quantities of books if I were on that street and the exchange improved. . . . What could I not do in the rue de l'Odéon and with the exchange as improved as it will some day be.

Late in March, Joyce heard the results of the trial from Sylvia, who showed him a news clipping from New York. Probably on the next day, Harriet Weaver informed him that Huebsch could not publish *Ulysses*. He went to inform Sylvia, who says in her memoirs:

It was a heavy blow for him, and I felt, too, that his pride was hurt. In a tone of complete discouragement, he said, "My book will never come out now."

All hope of publication in the English-speaking countries, at least for a long time to come, was gone. And here in my little bookshop sat James Joyce, sighing deeply.

It occurred to me that something might be done, and I asked: "Would you let Shakespeare and Company have the honor of bringing out your *Ulysses?*"

He accepted my offer immediately and joyfully. I thought it rash of him to entrust his great *Ulysses* to such a funny little publisher. But he seemed delighted, and so was I. We parted, both of us, I think, very much moved. He was to come back next day to hear what Adrienne Monnier, "Shakespeare and Company's Adviser," as Joyce called her, thought of my plan. I always consulted her before taking an important step. She was such a wise counselor, and she was, besides, a sort of partner in the firm.

Modesty and humor aside, it was hardly "rash" of Joyce to accept her offer. England and America were closed to him, and he had watched too many long battles for publication of his works, beginning with the twenty-two publishers who refused *Dubliners*. Although Sylvia had no experience as a publisher, he recognized what his biographer Herbert Gorman calls her "great courage and definite conviction . . . to think with her was to act." It is also possible that Joyce went to see Sylvia with just such a plan in mind: to have Sylvia or Adrienne publish his novel. For nearly two years Adrienne had been publishing Les Cahiers des Amis des Livres, volumes by Claudel, Valéry, and Larbaud and translations by Auguste Morel, who would become Joyce's translator. Most recently Adrienne had published the Larbaud lecture on Butler. Could not her friend and partner, the owner of an English-speaking bookshop in a land of foreign printers, become a publisher also? It is difficult to believe that Joyce, who had considerable insight into people and knew very well the type of help he could get from each, had not thought of this possibility. That he had is supported in an early draft of Sylvia's memoirs: "I accepted with enthusiasm Joyce's suggestion that I publish his book," she reveals.

Leaving the shop with Cyprian, Sylvia walked around the corner to confer with Adrienne, who "thoroughly approved" of the idea. "She had heard a great deal about Joyce from me," claims Sylvia, "and I had no trouble convincing her of the importance of rescuing *Ulysses*." They talked of the number of copies to be printed, the varying qualities of the printed books, and the profit terms for publisher and author. They would use Darantière, the printer of Adrienne's Cahiers editions. While Sylvia and Adrienne were talking, Joyce went to see his new friend and supporter, Valery Larbaud, who apparently gave Sylvia his highest recommendation.

The next day, 1 April, Sylvia wrote, "Mother dear it's more of a success every day and soon you may hear of us as regular Publishers and of the most important book of the age . . . shhhhhh . . . it's a secret, all to be revealed to you in my next letter and it's going to make us famous rah rah!" As Sylvia was finishing the letter, a happy Joyce walked in, laid his ashplant stick across the desk, and placed his hat on top of it. Sylvia thought the "Melancholy Jesus" looked particularly cheerful. She told him that she would make immediate arrangements for the publishing. For the second time, they agreed to the deal. She shared a few of the plans with him, including the name of the printer they wished to use and the decision to publish a limited edition of 1,000. They signed no contract. When Joyce left, she hurried to add a note to the letter to her mother and to mail it: "P.S. It's decided. I'm going to publish 'Ulysses' of James Joyce in October—!! Subscriptions to be sent to Shakespeare and Company at once. Don't spend any of Cousin Mary's money on a typewriter." And then in the margin, to the woman who had given, begged, and borrowed the most money for Shakespeare and Company, she scribbled: "Ulysses means thousands of dollars in publicity for me." "Ulysses is going to make my place famous," she cheered three weeks later. "Already the publicity is beginning and swarms of people visit the shop on hearing the news. I'm getting out a bulletin . . . and if all goes well I hope to make money out of it, not only for Joyce but for me. Aren't you excited?"

Many writers have conjectured about the reasons for Sylvia Beach's decision to publish *Ulysses* and her devotion to his professional needs for over ten years. Their reasons include a desire for fame, perceptiveness, eros, motherly love, blind faith, compassion, and inability to say no. First, she believed he was a great writer. When she found that her faith in his work and her compassion for his plight could be demonstrated in a way that would bring fame to Shakespeare and Company, she was delighted. What kept her working for Joyce—and this is a more complex motivation than her initial decision—was her sense of commitment and the inevitable result of linking the fame of the man and the shop. However, despite the whispers of some, there was no erotic motive involved, though in an unpublished draft of her memoirs she says, "Probably I was strongly attracted to Joyce as well as to his work, but unconsciously. My only love was really Adrienne."

The delight of Joyce no doubt exceeded that of his future publisher. Arthur Power reports that the writer was in a jovial mood the evening of the day that he and Sylvia talked over their publishing arrangements. As they passed the son of his concierge, Joyce declared to Sylvia, "One day that boy will be a reader of *Ulysses.*" They went first to a dance hall, where Sylvia proposed a toast to *Ulysses,* and later to the Closerie des Lilas, at the corner of the boulevards Montparnasse and Saint-Michel. Throughout the evening he talked about literature: the importance of being an Irish (national) writer before being an international writer and the superior power of the English over the French language.

On 10 April, Joyce, with his own particular business emphasis, informed Harriet Weaver of the plan for publication of *Ulysses:*

. . . I arranged for a Paris publication to replace the American one—or rather I accepted a proposal made to me by *Shakespeare and Co,* a bookseller's here, at the instance of Mr Larbaud.

The proposal is to publish here in October an edition (complete) of the book . . . 1000 copies with 20 copies extra for libraries and press. A prospectus will be sent out next week. . . . They offer me 66% of the net profit. . . . The actual printing will begin as soon as the number of orders covers approximately the cost of printing.

In a curious way, Joyce first takes credit, then claims it was Sylvia's idea, then confers outside authority on the decision by invoking Larbaud, whom he undoubtedly consulted, as Sylvia had consulted Adrienne. This first explanation is probably the truest. But the most astonishing element in the letter to Miss Weaver was his 66 percent take of the profits. Until the profits arrive, he pleads to Miss Weaver, "I need absolutely an advance."

Two days later, Miss Weaver wrote to Sylvia, "I am very glad to hear that you are to take over the American publication of *Ulysses.*" She inquired whether there would be one edition or whether the Paris sheets were to be sent to England for Miss Weaver to publish an English edition. Without awaiting a response, she drew up a written agreement for the English edition; when Joyce saw the generous advance (90 percent after expenses and an immediate advance of £200), he telegrammed immediate acceptance. Miss Weaver, who had independent means, could do even better than the outstanding percentage that Sylvia offered. In actuality, Sylvia would rarely manage to rescue any publisher's profit. She and Miss Weaver began a frequent correspondence about the list of persons and shops who wanted the book, the sending of 750 prospectuses to England, the including of reviews of *Portrait* on the prospectus, and the percentage that should be given to bookshops and wholesalers. Sylvia profited by Miss Weaver's knowledge of the English and American publishing and bookshop trade. From Adrienne she learned about French publishing. "Undeterred by lack of capital, experience, and all the other requisites of a publisher," Sylvia testifies, "I went right ahead with *Ulysses.*"

The first of many crises involved the typing of *Ulysses,* which was a precarious effort. Several typists refused to type the Circe episode, the bawdiest in the book. Finally, the eighth "threatened in her despair to throw herself out the window." The ninth rang Joyce's doorbell and threw the manuscript on the floor, leaving before he could even pay her. Joyce brought the manuscript to Sylvia, who took charge. Cyprian began the typing, which progressed slowly because of the lines and circles and almost undecipherable handwriting. Because Cyprian awakened at 4 A.M., she typed before going to work at the studio. But when her film took her away, Sylvia asked her friend Raymonde Linossier. When Raymonde's father became ill, she had to stop typing, but found a friend to take her place: Mrs. Harrison, who was the wife of an employee of the British embassy. One evening he picked up the manuscript from the table where she had left it and began reading. Angered at what he read, he tore some of the pages and threw them into the fire. Embarrassed and dismayed, Mrs. Harrison told Raymonde what had happened. Sylvia, who was immediately informed, went to Joyce to give him the bad news. Fortunately, Mrs. Harrison had hidden the remaining portion of the manuscript from her husband, but to recover the burned six or seven pages, they had to appeal to John Quinn in New York. At Joyce's suggestion, Sylvia cabled, then wrote, Quinn. Quinn flatly refused all wires and letters from her and from Joyce as well. Mrs. Beach, who was to sail for France on 4 May, interceded with a call from Princeton, but was also rudely turned down. "He flew into a rage," exclaims Sylvia, "and used language unfit for a lady like my mother." After numerous letters of entreaty, Quinn finally agreed to have the particular pages of his copy photographed and sent with Mrs. Beach. Joyce concluded that all the trials of the typists were a result of the numbers of the year adding up to thirteen ($1 + 9 + 2 + 1 = 13$). Fortunately, Sylvia's relations with her printer ran smoothly.

Darantière, who had printed her bookshop stationery and prospectus, came from Dijon, a town 150 miles southeast of Paris. According to Sylvia, the Darantière men "were good, old fashioned provincials and styled themselves 'Master Printers.' The recent 'Master' was M. Maurice Darantière, the son of Huysmans' printer." He was not deterred when he heard that portions of the book had been banned in America or that the book would probably be large or that she wished it printed in English, with installment payments after subscriptions were obtained. Although Joyce occasionally expressed doubt that *Ulysses* would sell, Sylvia and Adrienne insisted on 1,000 copies, choosing the best Dutch paper for 100, *vergé d'Arches* for 150, and ordinary "good paper" for

750 numbered copies. With Joyce's revolutionary use of language, these French printers, who could not understand English words or punctuation, were an advantageous choice that ensured French publication. In turn, Darantière, Sylvia believed, shared the glory: "So the dignified printing house of M. Maurice Darantière was in a bustle. The quiet town of Dijon, which produced mustard, 'Glory' roses, and candied black currants [*cassis*] in liqueur, had now another speciality—*Ulysses*."

The prospectus, announcing the "Autumn of 1921" publication of Joyce's *Ulysses*, "complete as written," was probably designed by Adrienne. It was paid for at the beginning of May and mailed to people all over the world, including Miss Weaver's subscribers and members of the two Paris bookshops. Friends in journalism publicized her plans. May and June were frantic. Mailings were sent out by the score. Cyprian helped "cope with the crowds." Bookshop business increased daily and Joyce's needs with them. Joyce, who spent his social time with Valery Larbaud, Wyndham Lewis, and Sisley Huddleston, haunted the bookshop every day waiting for the orders to arrive.

Very few American writers had visited the bookshop before 1921. They began arriving in May at the height of the gathering of subscriptions for *Ulysses*. Among the first of this early group from America was Florence Gilliam, who arrived in Paris in 1921 and joined the Shakespeare and Company library in April. With her husband, Arthur Moss, she published the first English-language expatriate magazine on the Continent: *Gargoyle* (1921–1922). Gilliam and Moss were located only a few steps from the bookshop at 15 carrefour de l'Odéon. *Gargoyle* was distributed at the bookshop, although Sylvia pointed out that the *chimère* on the cover was a very different animal from a gargoyle and that the "French don't like the identity of their pets to be confused." The short-lived *Gargoyle* contained comments on European life as well as the achievements of the Paris Crowd in art and life. Malcolm Cowley called *Gargoyle* "Greenwich Village in Montparnasse." Later in the decade, Gilliam would become Paris correspondent for the *Theatre Magazine* and *Theatre Arts* and write reviews for the Paris *Tribune*. She, like Sylvia, Gertrude and Alice, Natalie Barney, and many other American women, would never leave Paris.

The shy twenty-four-year-old Thornton Niven Wilder arrived in Paris in the late spring of 1921 from the American Academy in Rome, where he had spent the year studying archaeology and languages after his graduation from Yale. When his father telegrammed that he had found Thornton a job teaching French at a boarding school near Princeton, Wilder had rushed from Rome to Paris to improve his knowledge of the language. Wilder later claimed that he had come on the bookshop "by accident." By June he and his sister Isabel had become regular members of the lending library, "stealing quietly" in and out of the bookshop, as Sylvia describes him in her memoirs:

His manners were the best of any of my friends': he was rather shy and a little like a young curate; his background seemed quite different from that of others of his generation in Paris. . . . [He] didn't wear cowboy shirts and corduroy pants, [was] shy, never boastful, [and] came quietly in and out of the bookshop. . . . Adrienne and I were very fond of Wilder and liked to think of him as a member of the family.

Sylvia told Gertrude Stein that he reminded her of "a man taking everyone in the whole world on a Sunday school picnic and trying to get them all on the train at the same time."

Wilder's "old fashioned American manners" call attention to the diversity of her friends and patrons. They were not of a single literary school or social cadre. Sylvia was a close friend of both Hemingway and Gide. The sociable Robert McAlmon and the retiring Thornton Wilder were both at home at the bookshop. Her patrons included a variety of personalities and literary groups, and the famous as well as the unknown. Wilder was so shy that he never attempted to approach James Joyce, whom he saw in the bookshop. "Sylvia offered to introduce me," Wilder divulged, but as he "appeared to wish to avoid interruption I refused." During this first visit to Paris, Wilder was a bashful and serious student, attending museums, libraries, and the theater. He would not publish his first novel, which he had begun in Rome, for five more years. Only later, during his professorships, would he return often to Paris to meet Anderson, Hemingway, Fitzgerald, and Stein, and to visit again in the rue de l'Odéon.

A contrast to the young and retiring Wilder was Sherwood Anderson, who came to Paris in June to see all he could and meet the writers he admired, including Gertrude Stein. Anderson, then in his middle forties, was making a name for himself as a short-story writer. Anderson was the most English of the American visitors, Sisley Huddleston remembers, because he was "rich" and "suave," was not shrill, and cared about the past. He was on his grand tour of Europe in 1920–1921, "to fill in the sense of history that he felt lacking in his own and in the American past." While making the rounds of the bookshops, which were as numerous (he confided to his Paris notebook) as Chicago saloons before Prohibition, he found Shakespeare and Company. Sylvia describes his approach:

One day I noticed an interesting-looking man lingering on the doorstep, his eye caught by a book in the window. The book was *Winesburg, Ohio,* which had recently been published in the United States. Presently he came in and introduced himself as the author. He said he hadn't seen another copy of his book in Paris.

Anderson was a warm, romantic, effusive man, given to hyperbole. Sylvia thought him most interesting, "a man of great charm . . . a mixture of poet and evangelist (without the preaching), with perhaps a touch of the actor." He had soft brown eyes set in a square face, with a shock of hair often falling down his broad forehead. She listened attentively to the story of his new life. When he had neared middle age in Ohio, he had suddenly walked out of his paint factory and, leaving wife and family, respectability and security, moved to Chicago. There he wrote advertising copy and published his first book, *Windy McPherson's Son* (1916), a novel with autobiographical elements: a man suddenly rejects a dull Iowa childhood and success as a manufacturer in order to "find truth." But his great success was *Winesburg, Ohio* (1919), short stories about small-town life and the instinctive forces that govern human behavior.

Sylvia introduced Anderson to Adrienne, who invited him to a supper made from her famous chicken recipe.

Anderson and Adrienne got on very well together, she speaking pidgin American, he pidgin French. They discovered that there was a great similarity of ideas between them. In spite of the language barrier, Adrienne understood Sherwood better than I did. Describing him to me afterward, she said he resembled an old woman, an Indian squaw, smoking her pipe at the fireside. Adrienne had seen squaws at Buffalo Bill's show in Paris.

Because Anderson could not speak French, Sylvia accompanied him to his French publisher, Gallimard, for a conference concerning the French translation of *Winesburg*. But the introduction that has become a part of literary history by virtue of its many retellings is that of Anderson and Stein. According to Sylvia, "He admired her immensely, and asked me if I would introduce him to her." Immediately Sylvia made the contact for him:

Dear Miss Gertrude Stein:
   Would you let me bring around Mr. Sherwood Anderson of Poor White and Winesburg, Ohio to see you say tomorrow evening Friday? He is so anxious to know you for he says you have influenced him ever so much and that you stand as such a great master of words.

Yours Affectionately,
Sylvia Beach

After an exchange of several letters Sylvia arranged a meeting time and accompanied Sherwood and his second wife, Tennessee, a music teacher, to the rue de Fleurus. The meeting was a great success: "Sherwood's deference and the admiration he expressed for her writing pleased Gertrude immensely. She was visibly touched." (Sylvia's note repeats the same disarming flattery.) Later, in his notebook, Anderson recorded that he saw Stein as "a strong woman with legs like stone pillars sitting in a room with Picassos." That fall Stein asked him to write the introduction for her first major anthology, *Geography and Plays*.

Tennessee Anderson did not fare as well. Alice had strict orders to keep wives out of the way while Gertrude conversed with the husbands. Wives could not be prevented from coming, but they were to be kept across the room or in another room. Sylvia, who knew the rules well, watched uncomfortably as Tennessee tried in vain to take part in the interesting conversation. She tried in vain to resist Alice's efforts to take her across the room to see something interesting. Sylvia, like other unmarried women, was never treated with this cruelty:

This was not the way Adrienne and I treated wives. Not only did we always make a point of inviting Mrs. Writer with her husband, but we found them quite as interesting. Many a time a wife will be more enlightening on the subject of writers than all the professors in the classrooms.

Sylvia also introduced Anderson to Joyce, with whom he had several meetings. On this first visit, Anderson thought that when Joyce "said a good thing," his infrequent smile lighted up his "gloomy face." Later he described Joyce's

attitude of the respectable burgher as "Burjoice." In a letter to Adrienne after a
later visit, Anderson said that Paris means Adrienne's shop, Sylvia's house, and
the Bécats' apartment more than anything else: "I am a bit afraid of Miss Sylvia—alas—I did not like Joyce so much as I saw him clearer—don't tell him."

In return for Sylvia's introductions and hospitality, Anderson helped her gather
subscriptions for *Ulysses*. He compiled a list of American names with as many
addresses as he knew. He even sent a personal note with the prospectuses, a
gesture that greatly increased the publicity for *Ulysses* among Americans. When
he returned from this first trip to Paris, he told Ernest Hemingway that he must
go to Paris if he considered himself a serious writer. For Hemingway he wrote
letters of introduction to Sylvia, Stein, Joyce, Pound, and Lewis Galantière.
Though Hemingway would become a resident of Paris, Anderson wandered in
and out of the city in later years, always the spectator or tourist.

Increasing numbers of visitors and the announcement of her *Ulysses* publication brought Sylvia recognition. The Paris *Tribune,* the European edition of
the *Chicago Tribune,* carried an article about her in its 28 May 1921 edition:
"American Girl Conducts Novel Bookstore Here." In commenting on her coming publication of *Ulysses,* the article states, "It is said that its present publication may mean that Miss Beach will not be allowed to return to America." Such
publicity added to the drama of publication. Following a description of the bookshop and an introduction to Sylvia's life, it concluded with an ink sketch by Fred
Pye of Sylvia, "an attractive as well as a successful pioneer."

That same month two of her longest and most important friendships began.
Bryher, an English woman named Annie Winifred Ellerman, had met the American Robert McAlmon while she was traveling in the United States with the poet
H.D. (Hilda Doolittle), the one true and lasting love of her life. (Bryher had met
McAlmon, Marianne Moore, Edna St. Vincent Millay, and other artists in
Greenwich Village.) McAlmon was publishing a little magazine named *Contact*
with the New Jersey physician and poet William Carlos Williams. To escape the
strictures of her parents—her father was Sir John Ellerman, a shipping magnate
and the wealthiest man in England—Bryher arranged marriage, a marriage never
consummated, with McAlmon. He wanted, in turn, to go to Paris and meet
Joyce. Although most of their acquaintances assumed that he was hoodwinked
concerning either the nature of the marriage or her true identity, a letter that he
wrote to Williams this year proves otherwise: "The marriage is legal only, unro-
mantic, and strictly an agreement," McAlmon admits. "Bryher could not travel,
and be away from home, unmarried. . . . She thought I understood her mind, as
I do somewhat, and faced me with the proposition." They married on 14 February 1921, within hours of meeting, and sailed for England, where they met her
parents, and Harriet Weaver, Eliot, Lewis, and the *Egoist* group, who took in
McAlmon. The *Egoist* later published his first book of poems, *Explorations.*
During this visit, Bryher paid for the Egoist Press's publication of Marianne
Moore's *Poems* and subscribed for 300 copies of H.D.'s *Hymen.* This gesture
toward Moore was typical of Bryher's quiet helping of those she cared for and
believed in. Bryher was a major support for the Egoist Press (whose debts had

always been underwritten by Harriet Weaver herself) and, eventually, for Shakespeare and Company.

When he arrived in Paris, McAlmon immediately became involved in the
café life. According to his arrangement with Bryher, he was free to do as he
wished as long as he visited her parents with her several times a year. McAlmon
also became a member of Shakespeare and Company, on 6 May 1921, and thereafter dropped in every day to get his mail. Sylvia was curious to meet his wife,
with the unusual name Bryher (after one of the Scilly Islands, which she had
visited as a child). In her chapter devoted to Bryher in her memoirs, Sylvia
recalls thirty-eight years later the day they met:

> Then, one day, a great day for Shakespeare and Company, Robert McAlmon brought her
> in—a shy young English girl in a tailor-made suit and a hat with a couple of streamers
> that reminded me of a sailor's. I couldn't keep my eyes off Bryher's: they were so blue—
> bluer than the sea or sky or even the Blue Grotto in Capri. More beautiful still was the
> expression in Bryher's eyes. I'm afraid that to this day I stare at her eyes.

Bryher was "practically soundless . . . quietly observing everything," Sylvia
adds. "This was so different from the way most people blew in and out, wrapped
up in themselves like parcels for the post." Only twenty-seven when she met
Sylvia, Bryher was slight, short, and plain, deliberately plain. She never wore
makeup or curled her hair or wore anything but nondescript clothes, rejecting an
ultrafeminine role and the awkward petticoats. Her chief interests were archaeology, history, and adventure. She had published a novel, *Development* (1919),
and was soon to begin writing her first historical novel. Pictures of Bryher invariably show her hands clenched in what Adrienne calls "little energetic fists from
which her thumbs thrust out like thick buds."

Bryher was reared with Victorian restraint in an environment that she found
uncongenial. To escape it, she made a marriage of convenience. Her love was
given to talented women. Yet she was discreet, "the most perfectly discreet
person whom I know," declared Adrienne, "as much in her appearance as in
her words and in her writings." Although she loved France, and particularly the
poetry of Stéphane Mallarmé, she was not comfortable in Paris or any big city.
As a shy teetotaler, she was uneasy with the Paris literary crowd and fled to
Switzerland.

Bryher was, however, at home in the bookshop, in which she took a protective interest, and with Sylvia, whom she called "my life-long friend." Noticing
that mail was stacked on the mantelpiece to be rummaged through by the patrons,
she had a pigeonhole box made for Sylvia. Three large boxes were for Bryher,
McAlmon, and Joyce; the others were alphabetically arranged. Shakespeare and
Company was now a more organized mail distributor—a veritable American
Express of the Left Bank. Bryher was particularly interested in Sylvia's mails
because for years she sent to Sylvia her letters to her mother. Sylvia then mailed
on the letters with a Paris stamp, which kept Lady Ellerman from knowing that
Bryher was not living in Paris with McAlmon.

Lady Ellerman later sent Sylvia a beautiful nine-inch Staffordshire bust of

William Shakespeare, which adorned her mantel thereafter. Sylvia remained
Bryher's confidante and correspondent for forty years. Their correspondence is
a candid record of the literary and personal lives of the two women. They talk
most of other women writers: H.D., Virginia Woolf, Adrienne, Dorothy Richardson. Bryher visited Paris regularly and gave financial assistance to Sylvia and
Adrienne, who sent her the best books each year. In her memoirs, Bryher pays
tribute to Sylvia:

There was only one street in Paris for me, the rue d l'Odéon. It is association, I suppose,
but I have always considered it one of the most beautiful streets in the world. It meant
naturally Sylvia and Adrienne and the happy hours that I spent in their libraries. Has there
ever been another bookshop like Shakespeare and Company? It was not just the crowded
shelves, the little bust of Shakespeare nor the many informal photographs of her friends,
it was Sylvia herself, standing like a passenger from the *Mayflower* with the wind still
blowing through her hair and a thorough command of French slang, waiting to help us
and be our guide. She found us printers, translators and rooms, she was busy all those
years with the problem of publishing *Ulysses,* yet she never lost her detachment nor
identified herself with any particular group. If there could be such a thing, she was the
perfect Ambassador and I doubt if a citizen has ever done more to spread knowledge of
America abroad.

McAlmon appeared in numerous photos of the twenties artistic life in Paris,
with his intense and serious eyes (Williams called them "icily cold blue") set
close together, and his Roman nose. He had a long face, a lean and prominent
jaw, narrow lips, and a handsome profile. Occasionally he wore a turquoise
earring in one ear. Sylvia thought he was attractive, especially his "Irish sea
blue eyes," and "a mystic in drink the way Adrienne was in food." The picture
that emerges from those who knew him best highlights his personal magnetism
and his compulsion to write. Sylvia, like the others, was moved by this magnetism. At one point, according to a suppressed portion of her memoirs, she was
romantically infatuated:

Both men and women were strongly attracted to McAlmon. At one time I felt myself
falling in love with him and even wrote him a letter mentioning the matter. I was at the
seaside and probably had nothing much to think of. Receiving no reply, I felt quite relieved
and when I returned to Paris a fortnight later I was completely cured of the attack. When
McAlmon sneaked into the shop looking very apprehensive I assured him he had nothing
to fear. It didn't take much to discourage me from love affairs anyway.

She notes that his "ample means, unique to his Bohemian world, contributed
not a little to his popularity. The drinks were always on him, and alas! often in
him." He was the most popular, and has since become the most neglected,
American writer in Paris between the wars.

Like Sylvia's father, McAlmon's father was a Presbyterian minister, an itin-
erant Minnesota preacher; McAlmon was the youngest of his many children.
Sylvia later noted that he must have inherited the roving quality from his father.
Although they shared similar parsonage backgrounds, an interest in helping oth-

ers, and a talent for introducing people to each other, Sylvia and McAlmon were quite dissimilar in other ways. McAlmon was a gregarious traveler and drinker, whose social life at the Dôme and the Dingo inevitably led to the neglect of his talent.

Sylvia introduced Joyce to McAlmon, who soon began giving Joyce $150 a month to "tide him over." They became good friends. Both Joyce and Larbaud found McAlmon amusing, and the three of them, under McAlmon's guidance, sometimes made the rounds of the nightclubs together. In a suppressed portion of her memoirs written years later, Sylvia says that the three men enjoyed drinking at a dance hall (frequented by prostitutes), called Gipsy's, off the Boul' Mich: "A quarter of an hour was a long time in this place, it seemed to me. But our friends had been known to stay till they were thrown out in the morning early." One morning McAlmon and Larbaud brought Joyce home in a wheelbarrow. But McAlmon's association with Joyce was more than frivolous. He became an untiring collector of subscriptions for *Ulysses*—seeking them everywhere, as Sylvia soon discovered:

He combed the night clubs for subscribers, and every morning, early, on his way home, left another "Hasty Bunch" of the signed forms, the signatures slightly zigzag, some of them. When *Ulysses* came out, I met people who were surprised to find themselves subscribers, but they always took it cheerfully when McAlmon explained it to them.

Furthermore, he typed forty pages of *Ulysses* when Sylvia could not find a typist. McAlmon describes the shortcut he took with the tedious work of typing from a "hen-scrawly" handwritten script and four notebooks of insertions marked in red, yellow, blue, purple, and green:

For about three pages I was painstaking and actually retyped one page to get the insertions in the right place. After that I thought, "Molly might just as well think this or that a page or two later, or not at all," and made the insertions wherever I happened to be typing. Years later I asked Joyce if he had noticed that I'd altered the mystic arrangement of Molly's thought, and he said that he had, but agreed with my viewpoint. Molly's thoughts were irregular in several ways at best.

Subscriptions for *Ulysses* were kept in separate record books for orders from Europe, Great Britain, and the United States. The bulk of the orders came from Great Britain, and the list includes Winston Churchill and almost every leading English person of letters. Fewer came from the United States: publishers such as Huebsch and Knopf, Quinn (fourteen copies) and several bookshops, and individuals, including Wallace Stevens, William Carlos Williams, and Yvor Winters. The Washington Square Book Shop placed the largest order, for twenty-five copies. Even the Michigan Booksellers Circulating Library wanted five. One wonders how widely they were allowed to circulate. Jane Heap asked for "as many circulars" as Sylvia thought fit, promising to distribute them to people who were interested. She graciously expressed the excitement and happiness that she and Margaret Anderson felt about the *Ulysses* publication: "We had plans all laid to ask him to let us bring it out but in book form here when we heard of your adventure.'' The price of the book ($12 for the cheapest copy and $28 for the signed copy) is a tribute to Joyce's reputation and to the persistence of the American subscription collectors. The list of French orders was headed by Gide, who brought his order in personally, largely as a gesture of support for another of Sylvia's enterprises. Sylvia laughed when the Frenchmen would admit that their English vocabulary was limited and that they were "pinning their hopes on *Ulysses* to enlarge it.'' Subscriptions began lagging during June because many people were waiting for a cheap English edition to be published by Harriet Weaver. After a brief correspondence, Miss Weaver agreed to "postpone indefinitely'' the publishing of an edition in England. Subscriptions resumed.

While Sylvia was busy collecting subscriptions, Joyce was writing the Ithaca and Penelope sections of *Ulysses,* the last two sections. The third and final part of *Ulysses,* the Nostos (sections 16–18) consists of three sections: Eumaeus (narrative), Ithaca (catechism), and Penelope (monologue), all written in 1921. Eumaeus was in the typist's hands, and Joyce had begun writing the Ithaca section when the New York trial occurred. Ithaca, which he continued to write while the publishing was initiated, consists chiefly of a question-and-answer catechism between Dedalus and Bloom concerning the past life of Bloom. They have returned to Bloom's house in No. 7 Eccles Street, and Bloom talks of his wife's past suitors. The chapter corresponds to Ulysses' return and his slaying of Penelope's suitors. It was a difficult chapter for Joyce, who created it in the "form of a mathematical catechism.'' He wanted this seventeenth section, written in cold, astronomical, and "heavenly'' style and tone, to counterpoint the very human and earthy final (Penelope) section.

In the writing and rewriting of *Ulysses,* Joyce was using the names and characteristics of the people around the bookshop. When Raymonde Linossier helped with the typing of the manuscript, Joyce included her as a wax model in a shoe shop. In the list of "fashionable international world'' guests at the wedding of the high chief ranger of the Irish National Foresters (Cyclops section), he included the Beach women: Lady Sylvester Elmshade, Mrs. Holly Hazeleyes, Mrs. Liana Forrest (Cyprian), and Mrs. Gladys Beech (the Beaches had considered naming Sylvia "Gladys''). The "very reverend Dr Forrest, Dean of Worcester'' performs a wedding reported in the *Irish Independent.* Adding notes that he had accumulated in Trieste and Zurich and incorporating persons and incidents of Paris, he expanded the mosaic of previously written chapters in a manner that one Joyce scholar calls "continual embroidery upon a fixed idea.''

Working hours for Sylvia were long and demanding. In addition to conducting her own bookkeeping and banking activities, she conducted Joyce's personal and business affairs and assisted in a small way with the banking needs of many of her compatriots. Joyce "had no bank account,'' says T. S. Eliot. "It was Sylvia who acted as his banker. When he needed money he wrote to Sylvia, who promptly sent a banker's draft.'' Because she did so much cashing of checks and lending and exchanging of money, she sometimes referred to the shop as "the Left Bank.'' It was a time before universities and foundations supported artists to the extent they do today, and she would spend a great deal of time finding financial backers for the artists—"literary welfare work," she calls it.

As a banker and bookkeeper she was not efficient. Jessie Sayre, Woodrow Wilson's second daughter and an old Princeton friend of Sylvia, visited in the course of this year and attempted to teach her an arithmetic system that had been very successful with a class of backward children Jessie had taught. Sylvia abandoned the plan when she left. Her chief difficulty was the fluctuation of exchange of tuppence, centimes, and pennies. Despite the cumbersome bookkeeping and the lack of a careful system of selling and lending books, Shakespeare and Company's operating costs, which included Sylvia's scant personal expenses and the small wages of an assistant, were quite small. The shop records show a few francs spent each month for the boy who raised and lowered the shutters each day, for the bimonthly window cleaning, and for customs, taxi, stamps, and coal. She operated with a minimum of overhead. Extra expenses were met by loans from members of her family. The major expense of the shop was books, primarily books that had to be paid for in English and American currency. As the library fees barely covered regular expenses, the shop's only profit came from book sales.

In addition to its banking activities, the bookshop served as a post office; it served as the mailing address of McAlmon, Joyce, and many of the other customers. According to Sylvia, they "would inform me that they had given Shakespeare and Company as their address, and they hoped I didn't mind. I didn't, especially since it was too late to do anything about it except try to run an important mailing office as efficiently as possible." She had her own mailing, of course—the mailing of *Ulysses* all over the world and the mailing of library books to her customers who were skiing in Austria or vacationing on the Riviera. She used an old-fashioned copper balance to determine weight and postage. Her experience as a postmistress would be called into use years later when she served as postmistress for her hotel in a German internment camp.

"When Joyce's affairs came to swell the stream at Shakespeare and Company," asserts Sylvia, "it was more than rushing, it overflowed its banks." All this was too much to cope with alone, and Sylvia looked for a regular assistant. Probably during May of 1921, a twenty-five-year-old Frenchwoman of Greek descent joined the lending library. Mrs. Beach took the membership fee of Myrsine Moschos, who had studied at the University of London and was now living with her family in Paris. Her father was a physician who had traveled widely. Noticing the heavy workload at the shop, Myrsine asked whether she could assist, adding that she would love to work in the bookshop environment. Later in the day, after she had returned home, she received a *pneumatique* (local telegram) from Sylvia accepting her offer of assistance. When they talked the following day, her employer tried to warn her that the pay would be small. Myrsine did not care. Sylvia, who was going south to Hyères with Adrienne, gave her the keys to the shop and Adrienne's apartment, where she could prepare herself a lunch. She left her new employee with simple instructions: "If someone really wants a book, he will find it. If it can be found, lend or sell it." Using her initiative, Myrsine managed well until a man ordered several books. She took the order and then spent a sleepless night looking through publishers' books, attempting to decipher the publishers of each book and the ordering instructions.

Joyce considered the hiring of a Greek a good omen. Myrsine was more than that. She shared the physical labor of wrapping boxes and was "not afraid of manual work." She was also personable, talkative, and an immediate favorite of the members. And, very important, she spoke several languages. Her openness and her contagious laughter fit the "American" atmosphere of the bookshop. She loved to gossip. Joyce thought her gossip was a match for Fargue's: "If she and Fargue want to make a million quickly all they have to do is to sit down and collaborate and print their recollections."

Luckily, Myrsine had a large family of sisters to draw on when extra help was needed. The youngest, Hélène, who was mentally retarded and had never before taken the metro alone, became a messenger between the bookshop and the Joyce apartment. As Joyce's one or two daily visits to the shop were not enough, Hélène delivered proofs, front-row tickets to the theater, messages, mail, and later, books to be signed and press clippings. The Joyces were kind to her, often keeping her for tea, and Joyce wrote her a poem, which she lost. Myrsine remembers that it began "Little Miss Moschos / Soft as a mouse goes. . . ." According to Sylvia, her step was never soft:

Joyce awaited what he called her "t'undering step"—she had rather a heavy step for such a small person. When all her messenger business was done, he would perhaps detain her to read something in a magazine aloud to him, and he was probably more interested in Hélène's pronunciation, for instance, of "Doublevé Vé Yats" (W. B. Yeats), than in the article itself.

Once, when Sylvia was gone, Joyce found three Moschos sisters working in the shop. One was wrapping books to be sent to members on vacation, another was helping a customer, and the third was behind the desk. He observed their activity for a few minutes and suggested that the shop should be renamed "Les Soeurs Moschos," like some provincial sewing shop run by "The Moschos Sisters."

The Moschos family took an interest in Cambodian medical students. One of these young men, whom Dr. Moschos had brought to Paris to study medicine, was the heir to the Cambodian throne. He enjoyed spending time in the bookshop, where there was so much talk about *Ulysses*. When he planned to change his name to Westernize it, he asked Sylvia and Myrsine about the name "Ulysses." A very famous and distinguished name, they assured him, and a name that suited him, they added, glancing at each other. He, like the book, was fat. He legally changed his name from Ritarasi to R. Ulysses (with the *s* at the end). He declared he was now "born again." Joyce was pleased.

When the wealthy Irish-American lawyer John Quinn finally came to Paris to meet the publisher of *Ulysses*, he pronounced the shop in the rue Dupuytren a hovel. The tall and distinguished-looking New Yorker, whom Sylvia thought "testy and explosive," paced about, lecturing her on her responsibilities and grumbling about the work of art he had been lured into buying, particularly the "stuff of Wyndham Lewis" and "this rubbish of Yeats—a ragpicker wouldn't look at it." He had been buying Joyce's manuscripts (on Pound's advice) since 1916, had purchased Joseph Conrad manuscripts, and had made a fine collection of French Impressionist paintings. He would soon pay Eliot for *The Waste Land* and finance the *transatlantic review*. His specialty was finance law, and he was disciplined, methodical, and energetic. Gruff and insulting as he could be, Sylvia thought that beneath his burliness was a good heart. Pound had assured her of this. Quinn obviously enjoyed his involvement with the world of literature. But he was patronizing of Sylvia because she was an amateur and a woman—"another woman," as he referred to her. He looked on *Ulysses* as "his" book and acted the part of the fussy parent. She found his visits "brief but impressive." His letters, on the other hand, were lengthy, repetitious, patronizing, and full of advice on punctuation, typing, and printing. He would also go into minute detail about shipping his many copies. One needed a thick skin to be on the receiving end of Quinn correspondence.

Within days of Quinn's first visit, Adrienne noticed that an antiques dealer on her street was looking for someone to take over her lease. Sylvia and Adrienne had talked of this possible move to 12 rue de l'Odéon, and when the chance came Sylvia moved fast. In the heat of midsummer, wanting to be settled before taking a brief vacation with Adrienne, she and Myrsine moved all the books, magazines, photographs, and baskets of unanswered "urgent" mail to 12 rue de l'Odéon, across the street from La Maison des Amis des Livres. On her left were a shoemaker, a corset maker, and an appraiser of libraries and book auctions; on her right was a well-known orthopedic shoemaker, a music shop, a nose-spray manufacturer, and, at No. 18, Adrienne's apartment. A few steps beyond the apartment was the wide Place de l'Odéon and the Théâtre de l'Odéon, second in size only to the Comédie-Française. With its lofty columns, the theater reminded Sylvia a little of the colonial houses of Princeton. Around its arcades were little bookstalls. Nightly and on Thursday and Sunday afternoons, crowds passed up the street to see classical performances of plays and music. Across from the theater on the right was the Café Voltaire, whose great era had been the last quarter of the nineteenth century, when patrons included Gauguin, Verlaine, Rimbaud, Whistler, Mallarmé, Rodin, and contributors to the *Mercure de France*, which had offices nearby. In 1957, after a long decline, the Voltaire gave way to the Benjamin Franklin Library, an American cultural center—a fitting transformation of the premises, considering the friendship of Voltaire and Franklin.

By 27 July 1921 Sylvia's new shop had opened for business. It was more spacious, the address was easier for customers to find, and the rental included two small rooms above the shop. And more important than all these advantages was the reality that she was now across the street from Adrienne. Although Sylvia and Joyce frankly missed the old place, Quinn was pleased with Shakespeare and Company's new appearance and announced that he was glad *Ulysses* "wasn't going to come out in that shanty."

At the same time, Sylvia moved all her personal things to her room in

Adrienne's apartment at No. 18. According to Richard McDougall, this move "was as symbolic as it was practical," for it "consolidated the physical region of that country of the spirit." Sylvia and Adrienne now divided the rue de l'Odéon between them, presiding over the best of American, French, and English literature. When Archibald MacLeish arrived in Paris, in the summer of 1923, he experienced the same awe that the Odéonia (the name is Adrienne's invention) inspired in other young writers:

Turning up from St. Germain to go home past the bottom of the gardens to the Boulevard St. Michel one kept Shakespeare and Company to starboard and Adrienne Monnier's Amis des Livres to port, and felt, as one rose with the tide toward the theatre, that one had passed the gates of dream. . . . It was enough for a confused young lawyer in a grand and vivid time to look from one side to the other and say to himself, as the cold came up from the river, Gide was here on Thursday and on Monday Joyce was there.

CHAPTER 5

Stratford-on-Odéon

1921–1922

. . . this little renaissance in a French street . . .

— Richard Ellmann

. . . to Stratford-on-Odéon.

— James Joyce

There is more real Shakespeare in Paris right now than there has been in Stratford-on-Avon in one hundred years.

— Sylvia Beach

THE FRENCH were the first and last customers of Shakespeare and Company. They were there before Joyce and the Americans arrived, and they were there when Joyce left and the Americans fled Hitler with their depression-deflated purses. The French writers were the ones who turned the bookshop into what Jackson Mathews called "a fiery center." It was logical and natural, then, to look in 1921 to the French to help her further Joyce's literary reputation. Naturally, she turned first to those who were closest to her. Although Adrienne did not read English, she accepted Sylvia's judgment of and enthusiasm for Joyce. Together they planned to enlist the help of their mutual friend Valery Larbaud, whose knowledge of English literature and command of the language were unsurpassed among French critics. He became the pivotal figure in their French campaign for Joyce, which began on Christmas Eve 1920, when the two writers met at Shakespeare and Company, and culminated in the sensational Larbaud lecture and the reading from *Ulysses* that took place on 7 December 1921.

Sylvia arranged the meeting after Larbaud had responded with interest to *A Portrait of the Artist as a Young Man,* which she had given him to read. In the words of Larbaud,

I met James Joyce towards the end of 1919 [read 1920] in the studio [Shakespeare and Company] of a friend in the Rue Dupuytren. Miss Sylvia Beach introduced us. Joyce is a man who does not speak; he is a man—*tout à fait en bois.* When I went away, Miss Sylvia Beach gave me the numbers of *The Little Review* in which fragments of *Ulysses* had appeared. On my arrival at home, I began to read them, thinking it would be an excellent preparation for sleep, I had a happy surprise, when I finished the last number, it was early morning. . . . My admiration for Joyce is such that I am sure he is, of all contemporaries, the only one who will pass into posterity.

Sylvia remembers accurately, however, that it was several weeks after this first December meeting that Larbaud first read *Ulysses*. In typed comments following the publication of the first volume of Joyce's letters (1957), she records that she gave the *Little Review* numbers to Larbaud in February of 1921. In her memoirs she says, "Larbaud had yet to make the acquaintance of *Ulysses*. Hearing that he was laid up with the grippe, I thought this was the right moment for Mr. Bloom to introduce himself. I bundled up all the numbers of the *Little Review* containing parts of *Ulysses,* and sent them to the invalid with some flowers." He sent her a *pneumatique* in English on the fifteenth to thank her for the flowers and the *Little Review* and to say that he was "reading *Ulysses*. Indeed I cannot read anything else, cannot even think of anything else. Just the thing for me. I like it even better than 'A Portrait.' " He mentioned also that Mlle Linossier had given him Sylvia's copy of *Exiles,* Joyce's only play. Again, on the twenty-second he wrote that he was "raving mad over *Ulysses,*" and that since he had read Whitman, when he was eighteen, he had "not been so enthusiastic about any book." He wants to keep the issues of the *Little Review* a little longer and to translate eight or ten pages if Joyce will "allow" him. He requests, "Will you ask Joyce about it?" In a postscript he exclaims, "It is wonderful! As great as Rabelais: Mr. Bloom is an immortal like Falstaff." Because the *pneumatique* and postcard are dated 15 and 22 February and addressed to Sylvia, they appear to substantiate her memory. She showed the letters to Joyce, who was visibly moved by the praise. He wrote Larbaud the following day, thanking him for all his compliments and requesting that the *Little Review* numbers be returned. Within the week, Joyce confided to Frank Budgen that he (not mentioning Sylvia) had a letter from Larbaud saying that "he has read Ulysses and is raving mad over it, that Bloom is as immortal as Falstaff (except that he has some few more years to live—Editor) and that the book is as great as Rabelais." Joyce cared very much about his reception by the French writers and critics. For information about and contact with the French, he depended upon Adrienne and Sylvia. The French critic and philologist Jean Paulhan, a patron of the bookshops and soon a friend of Joyce, remembers that Joyce "listened to all they told him and never said a word."

Larbaud followed his written praise with talk of promoting the novel. He told Adrienne and Sylvia that the work must be introduced to the French readers and that he himself would write an article on Joyce for the *Nouvelle Revue Française*. Apparently, during the spring there was talk of his giving a lecture in her book-shop, and she suggested that he translate portions of the novel. In the months that followed, Larbaud read *Ulysses,* as Joyce concluded each section, and planned his lecture-article. But there seemed to be no more definite lecture plans until the fall, when Joyce was nearly finished with the novel. In the meantime, Larbaud, who was going to the country, offered his apartment rent free to Joyce, thinking that he would be more comfortable there than in a hotel. On 3 June the Joyces moved to 71 rue du Cardinal-Lemoine, behind the Panthéon and in back of an English-looking square with shady trees. He lay on the bed and recuperated from an eye attack amid Larbaud's polished floors, antique books, and toy soldiers. Joyce was pleased with the rent-free premises, the silence, and the parklike atmosphere that existed only ten minutes from the Odéon, while Sylvia thought it a measure of Larbaud's admiration that he would let the Joyce family live in his bachelor apartment.

The writers of the generation of Larbaud and Sylvia—including Fargue, Romains, and others born in the 1880s or soon before—were the most supportive of Joyce's work. Those of the earlier generation—Paul Valéry, Paul Claudel, Marcel Proust, André Gide (all born around 1870)—were either indifferent to or hostile toward his work. Valéry and Proust were indifferent. Valéry, who did accept invitations from the rue de l'Odéon to attend Joycean events, never subscribed to *Ulysses*. Joyce had only one brief meeting with Proust, who died within months after the publication of *Ulysses*. Claudel was openly hostile to the fiction of Joyce.

Paul Claudel was one of the first poets to whom Adrienne introduced Sylvia. Adrienne lavished on his poetry her greatest love and admiration. Claudel had undergone a mystical experience in 1888 when he read Rimbaud's *Illuminations*, and later that year became a Christian during a revelation at Christmas mass in the Cathedral of Notre Dame. "In a moment my heart was touched and I believed. God exists, He is here. . . . He is just as personal a being as I." Although she was not a believer, Adrienne shared his mystical bent, was strongly attracted to Catholicism, and was greatly influenced by his poetry. Adrienne presented a Claudel program in 1919; published (in Les Cahiers des Amis des Livres in 1920) the lecture Claudel gave preceding the program; and held a second Claudel meeting—with Adrienne, Fargue, and Romains reading portions of his plays—at her library on 28 May 1921. Sylvia thought that Adrienne and Claudel even looked alike—they could have been brother and sister, though there was a twenty-four-year difference in their ages.

With Guillaume Apollinaire (who died in 1918), Claudel was the most important French poet of the early part of the century. He was very kind to Sylvia during his visits to Paris between periods of ambassadorial service abroad. But when Sylvia and Adrienne became involved in publishing Joyce, whom Claudel considered "an enemy of God," he was dismayed. He had read and hated *Portrait*. He never read *Ulysses* for, he believed, Joyce's works were saturated with the "hatred of the renegade." One day Sylvia looked up to see Claudel stop at her shop window, glance at the *Ulysses* display, cross himself, and hurry on past the Odéon theater, intersecting what today is called the Place Paul-Claudel, into the Luxembourg Garden.

An English-speaking visitor walked into Shakespeare and Company, searching the room with her eyes, noting the rows of books, puzzled by the photographs. With a dissatisfied look, she approached the distinguished-looking

Frenchman with the black eyebrows, Chaplin mustache, and dangling monocle who sat at Sylvia's desk.

"Do you carry pencils and paper?" she enquired.

"I am sorry," he responded politely in his quiet voice. "We do not have these in stock." As she turned to leave, a smile crossed Paul Valéry's lips and he called after her, enjoying the moment of playing shopkeeper, "Perhaps we will get pencils and paper for the shop later!" When Sylvia returned and heard about the incident from Valéry, she laughed and added that having stationery "in the immediate proximity of books only puts ideas into people's heads."

Valéry, the greatest French poet of the twentieth century, loved jokes and laughed easily. He began coming in regularly after she had moved to the rue de l'Odéon and he had quit working for the Havas News Agency, and he sat beside her and told humorous stories. He had been a patron of Adrienne's library since 1917, and she had just published his *Album de Vers Anciens* in her Cahiers. Sylvia was still in Serbia when he gave his first reading at Adrienne's library, in 1919; she did hear him give a lecture there on Poe's "Eureka." Though she struggled to read his *La Jeune Parque* (*The Young Fate*, 1917) before she ever met him, she found the man himself easy to know: "I loved Valéry, but then everybody who knew him loved him."

Valéry dropped in to Shakespeare and Company chiefly to hear Sylvia talk. According to a mutual friend, he "loved the completely American way she had of speaking the surest idiomatic French. . . . Any remark she made was likely to have the turn and force of epigram or folklore." Sylvia thoroughly enjoyed his visits. He was natural, kind, "completely unaffected," she avows, and always happy. On one visit to the shop, he found Cyprian sitting in a rather short skirt, legs crossed and knee exposed. Her stockings came only to the knees. Seizing a pencil, he drew a woman's head on her bare knee. Cyprian regretted that she had no way of preserving this sketch signed "P.V." Valéry was a charming man who enjoyed the company of women. Sylvia knew his mistresses as well as his wife and family. In his "valérian English," he would tease her about her "patron." Once he took a volume of Shakespeare from the shelf and, opening it to "The Phoenix and the Turtle," asked, "Now, Sylvia, do you know what it's all about?" "No indeed," she replied with mock wonder. But it was nothing, he said, compared with Musset's obscure lines that he had just been listening to at a poetry reading at the Théâtre du Vieux-Colombier.

"Les plus désespérés sont les chants les plus beaux" ("The most despairing are those most beautiful songs"), he recited. "These lines are completely obscure. And they reproach me for my obscurity!"

Valéry's poetry is obscure, not because it tries to express the inexpressible (as did his mentor Stéphane Mallarmé), but because it is quintessential. The abstract thought is combined with emotion, imagery, and fantasy and condensed into classical form. For example, *La Jeune Parque* is a long musical and metaphysical poem that is a monologue either of Fate torn between serenity and responsibility or of the mind struggling to free itself from the body. Adrienne says that the poem "whets the mind without ever sating it." Although he distrusted emotions, he was a Wagnerian. Joyce would not admit he was one, claims Sylvia. Valéry never read Joyce's work, but to support his two friends, he willingly took part in their various Joycean events. His favorite social and literary spot was Adrienne's library, where he and Romains, both heavy smokers, filled the room with clouds of smoke. When Fargue arrived, late as usual, he would exclaim, "Adrienne has set her shop on fire to suggest that somewhere within these walls is a divine spark!" Then he joined the smoking and heated the room further with his language and stories.

On the eve of Joyce's introduction to the French intellectuals, in 1921, the first generation of writers were about fifty years old. Fort was forty-nine, Valéry fifty, and Gide fifty-two. Claudel and Spire, at whose party Sylvia had met Joyce, were both fifty-three. Although Gide had been the first French subscriber to *Ulysses,* his action was only a gesture of support for her effort. Soon, he expressed privately to Jean Paulhan that the book was a "sham masterpiece." In a lecture on Dostoevski, given several months after *Ulysses* was published, Gide asserted that the interior monologue was not Joyce's invention but the development of Poe, Browning, and Dostoevski. Joyce publicly spoke with respect of Gide's writing and was probably not aware of Gide's real views. Privately he rejected Paulhan's suggestion that the *Nouvelle Revue Française* publish the French translation of *Ulysses.* Sylvia and Adrienne were aware of his reservations.

"Gide is here," Sylvia called from the balcony of their little hotel in Hyères, on the Mediterranean coast. They had come two days before to escape everyone they knew, as well as all the subscription mail, the typing, and the proofreading (Myrsine Moschos was keeping the shop open). Soon they discovered that Jules Romains, who had a summer home nearby, had recommended the hotel to all of them. They agreed to stay and enjoy each other's company. Sylvia and Adrienne were particularly pleased to see Gide, because they had just been rereading and discussing his *Caves du Vatican.*

The Mediterranean was warm and blue in early September, and the three of them went swimming every day. Adrienne "simply floated upright close to the shore" in her cork jacket and lifebelt. Gide and Sylvia, who were both lean and wiry, rowed out to swim deeper, and Gide suggested that she dive from the boat. Though she had "never tried diving" and would have "preferred not to begin in his presence," she took the daring leap into the Mediterranean, only to belly flop. *"Pas fameux!"* ("Nothing wonderful!"), he shrugged.

Adrienne records in detail the literary and social discussions of the three friends in the course of the lunches, teas, and dinners that they shared during those five days: they discussed Fargue and Larbaud, the possibility of Copeau's staging Gide's *Saül,* and, among many other matters, cannibalism. If they discussed Joyce—and it is inevitable that they did, since all Shakespeare and Company was geared to his publication—Adrienne does not say so. They were joined for visits and meals by Jules and Gabrielle Romains (Romains had just published *Lucienne,* one of the most erotic novels written in France) and the English critic

Roger Fry. When it rained, Gide entertained them in the hotel salon by playing an old piano warped by the sea air: he "plays from Schumann, Chopin, Albéniz— with virtuosity, but without soul," observes Adrienne. She notes that on the second day, after Gide and Sylvia had gone swimming, he asked Sylvia to speak to him in English:

> In the afternoon he asks her again to let him read English to her and to correct him; he reads some pages from [Fielding's] *Tom Jones,* which Sylvia brought to reread here, and it was precisely a passage from [Gide's] preface to *Armance* that had made her think [to bring it].

Gide left to join Copeau, who did stage *Saul,* with himself in the title role, in June of the following year at the Théâtre du Vieux-Colombier. Sylvia and Adrienne remained in Hyères for nearly two weeks longer; they went home via Marseilles, where Sylvia expressed keen curiosity in the red-light district. She returned to Paris "sunbaked," but ready to face a busy fall, to tackle those last and most critical months before the publication of *Ulysses*.

Comradeship and mutual admiration marked Sylvia's relationship with the French writers, even with Gide and Valéry, who were nearly twenty years older than she and did not share her enthusiasm for Joyce. She socialized more with those of her own age group, such as Romains, Duhamel, and Durtain—the *copains,* or cronies. Other friends and patrons in this younger group included Larbaud, Reverdy, Perse, Paulhan, Maurois, Giraudoux, and Copeau.

The immediate family of the Odéon consisted of Adrienne and Sylvia; Adrienne's sister, Marie, whom they called Rinette from the word Marienette; her husband, Paul-Émile Bécat; Léon-Paul Fargue; and Valery Larbaud. A picture of this group, occasionally reproduced in books about the period, shows them posing behind the picture of a cardboard boat at the Foire d'Orsay in June of 1924. Marie, who was two years younger than Adrienne, was admired for her beautiful embroidered canvases or tapestries, about which both Fargue and Valéry wrote essays. Temperamentally and physically different, the sisters were nonetheless close friends. Both considered Sylvia their sister.

Marie was married to Paul-Émile Bécat, who had studied at the École des Beaux-Arts. His realistic portraits of the Odéon writers have been reproduced many times. He drew Joyce and McAlmon together in 1921, at the latter's request, and did oil paintings of Adrienne in 1921, of Larbaud and Romains in 1922, of Sylvia in 1923, and of Adrienne and Marie together in 1924. He made his living, however, illustrating erotic literature. His illustrations of *The Adventures of Fanny Hill,* for example, are detailed and explicit poses of a man and woman, often in the act of clitoral stimulation. Bécat picked up his models in cafés, and he often kept them with him after they posed. Free in turn, Marie was for many years the lover of Fargue. They formed an amicable ménage à trois and often traveled together.

One day Sylvia took the trolley with Marie and Fargue to the factory where he lived with his mother and "a long-suffering family servant." His engineer father had invented certain formulas in glassmaking and at his death had left the glass factory to Fargue, who was trying to operate it. The factory was located within hearing distance of the whistling trains of the Gare de l'Est. Fargue loved the sound of the trains and evoked them in his poetry of the streets. According to Sylvia, "He revered his father and was loath to part with the factory, which Fargue père had built up and which, under the proprietorship of a poet, was fast running down." The foreman remained to fill the orders that trickled in. Fargue showed Sylvia his father's handiwork around Paris, including the window at Maxim's. The Fargue stained-glass windows and vases, made in the days of art nouveau, decorated the homes of French millionaires.

While Fargue invented new schemes to save the factory, Marie and Sylvia tried to help. Marie made new designs for his glass. That day Sylvia watched as the workmen were making impractical ceiling lights that looked like "inverted soup plates decorated with weird figures from the Zodiac" and hardly let out any light. Fargue later made the rounds of the department stores, and his wit rather than the design sold the product. To help Fargue, whom Sylvia thought the most interesting character of the French literary world, she asked a photographer from the *New York Times,* who was doing a feature story on the bookshop, to go to the factory; there he took some photos of the glassmaking, with Fargue, Sylvia, and the foreman in the pictures. But Fargue, the resplendent poet, the fabulous noctambulist, the indefatigable teller of bawdy jokes and stories, lacked the business acumen to rescue his father's factory.

Sylvia's closest adult friends were French, but she remained American. Gertrude Stein's declaration that "America is my country but Paris is my home" more accurately described Sylvia Beach than Stein. Unlike Gertrude, Sylvia knew the language well and made her closest friendships among the French. Both wisdom and maturity—she was twenty-nine when she moved finally to Paris—kept her from making the common mistakes of exiles. On the one hand, she never attempted to deny her American heritage by embracing a national identity that was not hers by birth. She did not embrace all things French with uncritical enthusiasm. Nor did she, at the other extreme, choose to live within an American community in Paris, avoiding the French people and customs. She absorbed French culture, preferring many of the French to the American ways. Remarkably, she was, as Adrienne testifies, "so American and so French at the same time." She combined certain unique characteristics of both countries: she was energetic and friendly, yet unselfconscious, discreet, and a bit eccentric.

For Adrienne, Larbaud, Joyce, and many others, Sylvia represented America. They saw in her the best of what they read in the American literature to which she introduced them. Adrienne declared that by her very nature Sylvia was American—"young, friendly, fresh, heroic . . . electric (I borrow the adjectives from Whitman speaking of his fellow citizens)." She remained always young, in looks and spirit. Even when the wrinkles came, she had more energy than had persons half her age. Both Henri Hoppenot and Saint-John Perse (Alexis Leger) allege later that Sylvia reminded them of the daughter of a Wild West sheriff who has just hitched her horse outside the door, enters the room with a decided walk, and takes in all present with a rapid, circular glance. Alice B. Toklas, years later, suggests both Sylvia's strength and patriotism in calling her "flagstaff." She is the American flag in France, claims Toklas, and as strong as a staff—"a less valiant soul" would have been crushed by her work. Myrsine Moschos testifies that the French admired Sylvia for her Americanness and appreciated her understanding of French ways. Like Henry James's *Madame de Mauves,* Sylvia was able to "be very American and yet arrange it with [her] conscience to live in Europe."

Adrienne also stresses Sylvia's democratic spirit—her equal acceptance of young and old, talented and simple (she disliked only snobs). According to Adrienne, Americans "have democracy in their blood; it is their tradition, their reason for being, the voice that speaks to them stronger than any other." But she best sums up Sylvia's character and personality in this excellent recollective description of her friend as she appeared at the time of their beginnings:

This young American displayed an original and most attaching personality. She spoke French fluently with an accent that was more English than American; to tell the truth, it was not so much an accent as an energetic and incisive way of pronouncing words; listening to her you thought less of a country than of a race, of the character of a race. In her conversation there were neither hesitations nor pauses; words never failed her; on occasion she deliberately invented them, she proceeded then by an adaptation of English, by a mixture or extension of French vocables, all that with an exquisite sense of our language. Her finds were generally so happy, so charmingly funny, that they at once came into usage—our usage—as if they had always existed; one could not keep from repeating them, and one tried to imitate them. To sum it up, this young American had a great deal of humor, let us say more: she was humor itself.

The charm and humor may have been characteristically American; but her "exquisite sense" of the French language was unusual. She occasionally used words from the English and French to express her ideas. "She spoke marvelous idiomatic French," one of her friends asserts, "but she had too much character to lose her accent." Although she grew to maturity in an English-speaking country, she lived more of her years (forty-six) speaking French. She coined new French words and eventually forgot some of her English. "I have had enough of your histories [scenes]," she reprimanded a young assistant.

How was she French? Adrienne says she was "French through her passionate attachment to our country, through her desire to embrace its slightest nuances." But she also had some of the French temperament. She was skeptical and perceptive, with a wit that displayed itself both in her love of puns and wordplay and in her mischievous pranks. She saw humor in most situations, could halt or stimulate a conversation with the turn of a phrase. While Joyce saved his wit for the written page and conversed often in monosyllables, Sylvia poured all her wit and wordplay into her conversation.

Her discretion was French. Friendly and free though she was, she evinced a restraint born of the parsonage and nurtured by her years in France. Her younger sister, Cyprian, after years of film acting and living in southern California, mistook the discretion for repression. Yet Sylvia was not conscious of her discretion. Like the French, she had a remarkable degree of unselfconsciousness—a quality that allows them to act out their lives openly, presenting hourly dramas on the streets of the city. Americans might call the behavior eccentric. In Sylvia the behavior was charming. "She did not stop to see if her hat were on straight," says Janet Flanner. "She knew by feeling."

In writing about French "discretion," upon which "both taste and measure depend," Adrienne claims that the French (she uses Saint Bernard and Stendhal's Julien Sorel as sacred and secular examples) are concerned "not to distend their souls, not to abuse the Word, not to dry up the source of their being." If Adrienne is correct about this restraint—and she admits some falling away from measure and taste since the turn of the century—the French have a need to preserve the human spirit, a quality of discernment, of keeping secrets. Sylvia shared this sense of measure, control, and conservation with the French, devoting her life to the preservation of the Word—in the bound volumes of the expression of the human spirit that filled her shelves.

Sylvia was committed to introducing the Americans, the English, and the French to each other. But the example she set of close association with the French was followed by all too few of her compatriots, because of either the language barrier, national pride, or insecurity. Many Americans were in Paris too briefly to learn much about France. For example, the short visits of Edna St. Vincent Millay and Edmund Wilson in the summer of 1921 did not give them opportunity for, as Wilson expresses it, "Walking the picture galleries of other men's minds." Nor was it much different for some long-term visitors. After years in France, George Antheil and Robert McAlmon would make little progress in learning to speak French. As with Gertrude Stein, it was the rule rather than the exception that Americans living in Paris did not associate with the French. They "stick to each other, and seldom read French or speak it badly," lamented an editorial in the Paris *Tribune*. Sylvia seemed to agree: "Some of my friends, for instance Justin O'Brien, Archibald MacLeish [and] George Dillon, shared my fondness for the French, but most of the others seemed to be unaware of living next door to Larbaud's Barnabooth, and of the existence of [Valéry's] La Jeune Parque just across the River. I think they missed a lot." And Matthew Josephson notes that "few of the American habitués of Montparnasse absorbed any French literary influence, for the reason that French writers of note seldom came to those places." To say that most or all of the Americans knew nothing of the French, however, is an error.

There certainly were exceptions during these early years of the twenties. Natalie Clifford Barney, a longtime French resident, and Kay Boyle, who came later for shorter periods, made an effort to learn about the French and to speak their language. Samuel Putnam, William Carlos Williams, Matthew Josephson, John Dos Passos, Malcolm Cowley, Glenway Wescott, Waverley Root, and many others spoke French fluently. John Dos Passos, a brief but frequent early visitor to Paris, was interested in French literature. His writings show the influence of Jules Romains, whose unanimism and urban scenes are echoed in *Manhattan Transfer* (1925) and in the trilogy *U.S.A.* The montage techniques of the Cubist painters and the films of Sergei Eisenstein influenced his own montage technique in the trilogy. Matthew Josephson, who arrived in Paris (via Brooklyn, Greenwich Village, and Columbia University) in the winter of 1921, attended lectures at the Sorbonne. Although he found many of his old Greenwich Village friends (such as Slater Brown, Cummings, Loeb, Djuna Barnes, and Berenice Abbott) in Paris, he spent most of his time with young French writers (Aragon, Breton, Soupault, Paul Eluard, Max Ernst). His memories of the twenties he entitled *Life among the Surrealists*. Josephson was active in many of the little-magazine ventures, such as *Broom* (1921–1924) and *Secession* (1922). For *Broom* he translated the works of his French Surrealist friends Aragon and Éluard, to whom he introduced E. E. Cummings and Malcolm Cowley. The first essay that he sent home to the *Double Dealer* was an article on Jules Romains. Malcolm Cowley studied classical French literature on an American Field Service Association Fellowship at the University of Montpellier and the Sorbonne in 1921–1922, and became the friend of Aragon, Tzara, André Salmon, and other French writers, and later translated works by Paul Valéry, André Gide, and others.

When Sylvia returned from her vacation with her French friends on the Mediterranean, the Joyces were planning their move from the Larbaud apartment. Joyce was finishing the last chapter of *Ulysses*. Harriet Weaver was busy consolidating all English copyrights of James Joyce's works. This was a crucial year in Miss Weaver's relations with Joyce, for while she was working with him and sending him money for advances, she was entertaining doubts about him. As early as May she, who abhorred alcohol and lived simply, had heard rumors of his drinking and his easy, expensive style of life. Joyce, on learning that she was upset, dispatched a long and ingratiating letter to her, and by August she had decided that his style of life should not prejudice her fostering of his talent. She was loyal to any commitment she made. At that point, following an August letter in which Joyce suggested that "it would be well if *Ulysses* makes my name to unify my publishers," she decided to be his sole English publisher. From Elkin Mathews she purchased for £15 the rights for *Chamber Music,* poetry published fourteen years before. From Grant Richards she received the copyright of *Dubliners* and *Exiles* for £150. By mid-October she had all the English copyrights and the resignation of J. B. Pinker as Joyce's agent.

Joyce took care not to offend Miss Weaver, to whom he owed so much. He kept careful record of his financial dealings with everyone. Although his endowments from Miss Weaver were a gift, he took care to call these latest payments "advances" on the sale of the English edition that she expected to publish later. He expressed his gratitude, along with his dramatized suffering: "Many thanks again for your aid which illuminates the dismal labyrinth I seem to walk in." The help that he was receiving he believed to be, as has been noted before, an acknowledgment of his election. But he was capable of scorning others in the same situation. In a discussion with Mme Yasushi Tanaka, the wife of a Japanese painter in Paris, he responded to her praise of Yeats with a dismissal of him as Lady Gregory's lover, stating besides that she financed him.

Sylvia returned to face family visitors and a financial crisis. Her mother arrived for her annual stay, and while she was there her brother Dr. Thomas J. Orbison and their nephew Douglas, son of John Henry (Hal) Orbison (a missionary in India), visited. Sylvia informed Holly that their uncle Tom was "quite breathless to find that his nieces were doing such a lot of stunts." In this same letter to Holly, Sylvia explains her financial situation: from the bookshop income, Myrsine had been able to pay herself a wage; but when Sylvia paid the regular bills, she recognized that there was not enough for the extra expense of the move to the rue de l'Odéon, which amounted to 2,000 francs, plus 120 francs for the printing of a thousand new prospectuses advertising the bookshop in rue de l'Odéon. Business was good; she averaged a daily income of about 100 francs ($12), but the exchange rate for pounds cut her profit, which amounted to only about $100 in 1921. Also, while assured of increasing business, she faced a bill of 1,000 francs from Darantière on December first: "He requires it and naturally the cheques from subscribers will not arrive in time for that first payment." On 22 September she pleaded for a loan from Holly, the sister who always seemed to have a well-paying job and a well-organized financial statement:

. . . I'm asking you to lend me a thousand francs!!! My carpentry bill will be handed in any day now and mother who was going to lend me all the money for my moving expenses had to stop off in the midst, having had a great deal of expense getting Cyprian equipped as a rising star. . . . My business is going well [but I] have to put every single centime aside to pay the printer.

Joyce, though he had to cut back on the number of hours of work he could do each day, was finishing the last section of *Ulysses*. On 3 September he wrote to Robert McAlmon that he would "give Molly another 2000 word spin." He moved out of Larbaud's apartment at the end of September and on 6 October announced that he had finished the Penelope episode, which was at the printers'. At the bottom of the final page of the manuscript, he wrote "Trieste-Zurich-Paris, 1914–1921." "*Penelope* is the clou [nail] of the book," he informed Frank Budgen. "It turns like the huge earthball slowly surely and evenly round and round spinning." The Penelope section, analogous to the return of Homer's Ulysses to his wife, is Molly Bloom's monologue, which she delivers as she lies in bed with a sleeping Leopold. It is clearly the most erotic section of the novel, the section to which the book falls open in libraries around the world:

. . . yes to say yes my mountain flower and first I put my arms around him yes and drew him down to me so he could feel my breasts all perfume yes and his heart was going like mad and yes I said Yes I will yes.

Joyce devoted the month of October to correcting the proofs of the Ithaca section. He complained to McAlmon that the printers are "boggled by all the

w's and k's in our tongue and can do only about 100 pages at a time until they
print off. However I am doing my best to push Bloom on to the stage of the
world by the beginning of November. . . .'' Larbaud continued reading *Ulysses,*
as the page proofs came, and prepared his lecture on Joyce. Although Cyprian
had gone back to work in a film, Mrs. Beach occasionally helped Sylvia and
Myrsine in the bookshop. Her visits were a pleasure and a burden for Sylvia.

On the twelfth, Sylvia received a long-awaited letter from George Bernard
Shaw, whom she had asked, several months before, why he had not subscribed
to *Ulysses.* Joyce was not fond of Shaw, whom he called "a born preacher,"
but he was encouraged by each subscription from a man of letters. It was Sylvia's
belief that Shaw, though he was of her mother's generation, would support a
fellow Irishman who had written a revolutionary book. Because Mrs. Desmond
Fitzgerald, his former secretary, had convinced Sylvia that Shaw was a generous
man when appealed to, Sylvia had announced to Joyce that she was sending him
another subscription blank.

"He'll never subscribe," Joyce asserted.

"Yes, he will," she responded.

"Will you bet on it?" he asked. She accepted, and they wagered a silk
handkerchief for her and a box of Voltigeur cigars for him.

Joyce won. Shaw's letter was addressed to "Dear Madam," whom he calls
a "young barbarian beglamoured by the excitements and enthusiasms that art
stirs up in passionate material." She was amused by the letter, thought it "quite
characteristic" of Shaw, but admitted she was disappointed. She paid her bet.
Shaw, who had read portions of *Ulysses* in the *Egoist,* swore that he found it a
"revolting record of a disgusting phase of civilization, but it is a truthful one."
He compares Joyce's effort to that of making "a cat cleanly by rubbing its nose
in its own filth." He concludes by grumbling that "if you imagine that any
Irishman, much less an elderly one, would pay 150 francs for such a book, you
little know my countrymen." Pound took up the cause, and, in an exchange of
letters, Shaw sent a post card of Christ's entombment with the Marys in tears
about him: "J.J. being put into his tomb by his editresses after the refusal of
G.B.S. to subscribe to *Ulysses.*" He asks Pound whether he has to like everything that Pound likes: "As for me, I take care of the pence and let the Pounds
take care of themselves." Later Pound snaps in his "Paris Letter" in the *Dial*
that Joyce "has presented Ireland under British domination, a picture so veridic
that a ninth rate coward like Shaw (Geo.B) dare not even look it in the face." In
a letter to H. L. Mencken, Pound complains that Shaw is writing "twice a week
complaining about the high cost of *Ulysses.*" Joyce was amused by the exchange
and declared that Shaw probably would be buying the book from a bookshop
somewhere. Shaw's letter was her only subscription refusal, and it did not deter
the work of *notre intrépide Sylvia,* as André Spire calls her. Soon Pound created
quite a stir when he brought in a subscription from William Butler Yeats and laid
it on Sylvia's desk.

In the Shaw matter, Sylvia seems to have had the last say. In a letter written
years later, to thank Shaw for a raw-vegetable cure for migraines, she adds,

And if I came to Joyce's help and published it [*Ulysses*] when it was suppressed, that was entirely the fault of my upbringing—by YOU, dear Mr. Shaw, for I and all my generation were brought up and not "badly braot up" like poor Drinkwotter, by Bernard Shaw.

Although its price was not the issue with Shaw, the book did cost a great deal. *Ulysses* retailed in Paris for 150 francs minimum. And it was neither well bound nor painstakingly printed. It had many typographical errors because of the hastiness of the job and the numerous changes and additions made on the proofs. Yet in 1977, No. 96 of the first 100 copies would sell at auction for $10,000.

The book ledger for England, Ireland, and Scotland was slowly filling with familiar names: Bennett, two Huxleys, three Sitwells, Woolf, Churchill, Wells, Walpole, and Yeats (who would receive the Nobel Prize in literature in 1923). Havelock Ellis, who thought 150 francs too high, bought *Ulysses* when Sylvia agreed to buy his *Studies in the Psychology of Sex* for her lending library. The largest bookstore order was for eleven copies from the Irish Book Shop, which reordered in two years. That was hardly enough for every Dublin "male person . . . between the ages of 15 and 20" who Shaw had suggested be rounded up and forced "to read all that foul mouthed, foul minded derision and obscenity." In spite of Shaw's refusal, some "elderly Irishmen" did pay 150 francs, some even 350, for *Ulysses*. The Paris bookshops did not subscribe and would come begging too late for the first edition. Brentano's ordered only one copy of the first edition, but ledger books show dozens of orders from that store for copies of later editions. Sylvia began a ledger book for other countries of the world, including South America, South Africa, and China; La Librairie Française of Peking ordered ten copies.

During October, Joyce was "snowed up" in proofs, as he expressed it to Harriet Weaver. He had recast the Aeolus section, amplified the Lotus-Eaters section, and added to the others. He worked long on the Ithaca section. The correcting of proofs had gone on—sporadically and sometimes feverishly (as during this month)—for eight months. The first page proofs had arrived on 16 June. Joyce always wrote by hand, using blunt black pencils that he bought at Smith's in Paris. On proofs, according to Sylvia, he used red, blue, and green pencils

to distinguish the parts he was working on. Fountain pens he didn't understand at all. They bewildered him. Once I found him struggling to fill one, covering himself with ink as he did so. Years later, he did think of using a typewriter, and asked me to get him a Remington Noiseless. He soon swapped it for Adrienne's noisy one, and, so far as I know, never used either of them.

The reading and correction of proofs was a creative act, notes his biographer Ellmann. He did not merely correct or change words and phrases, he added to the copy, always complicating the material with interrelated details. He told Jacques Benoist-Méchin, "I've put in so many enigmas and puzzles that it will keep the professors busy for centuries arguing over what I meant, and that's the only way of insuring one's immortality." His statement has proved to be more than jest. Joyce has become the favorite of exegetes the world over.

Joyce sent proofs and copies to Frank Budgen, Robert McAlmon, Harriet Weaver (often through Ezra Pound), Claud Sykes, and Eliot (who with Aldington was writing a review). Pound, according to Victor Llona, a critic and translator friendly to both, spent many days in the bookshop battling with galleys. Joyce often asked for suggestions and associations to keep his text growing. No book has ever been written in this way. His encyclopedic expansion sometimes took him through six or eight galleys. His appetite for proofs was insatiable, Sylvia thought. "Every proof was covered with additional text . . . adorned with Joycean rockets and myriads of stars guiding the printers to words and phrases and lists of names all around the margins." According to A. Walton Litz, Joyce "elaborated like a mosaic worker upon a predetermined pattern." Some parts of Ithaca, on which he worked during October, increased as much as five times! Earlier sections that had been published in the *Egoist* and the *Little Review* were also expanded, usuallly by 20 percent. In total, Joyce wrote probably a third of *Ulysses* on page proofs. No other editor or printer woulld have considered such an allowance. Both were tried to the limits of their endurance. At first Darantière cautioned Sylvia: "M. Darantière warned me that I was going to have a lot of extra expense with these proofs. He suggested that I call Joyce's attention to the danger of going beyond my depth; perhaps his appetite for proofs might be curbed. But no, I wouldn't hear of such a thing. *Ulysses* was to be as Joyce wished, in every aspect." If "real" publishers followed her example, she says later, "it would be the death of publishing. My case was different." Then Darantière threw up his hands each time he saw another galley proof filled with additions. They sent galley after galley, reset the type again and again. Darantière was swamped with *Ulysses*. Sylvia remembers that he no longer had time to look at his collection of books or old pottery or linger over his fine wines. His vine-covered printing house worked overtime. In an early draft of her memoirs, written after *Ulysses* had achieved its place in world fame, she does not reveal her occasional exasperation at Joyce, the pressure that an amazed printer placed on her, and her own fear of bankruptcy:

I let him have as many proofs as he wanted and [he] crowded them with as many additions as he could get onto the page. The final proofs contained more handwriting than print. . . . After the *"bon à tirer"* had been returned with Joyce's and my signature, and the printing had begun on our beautiful handmade paper, the printers would receive a telegram with several extra lines to insert—but they were so obliging. . . . as for me I was mad over Ulysses and would never have dreamed of controlling its great author—so "gave him his head." It seemed natural to me that the efforts and sacrifices on my part would be proportionate to the greatness of the work I was publishing.

After Sylvia's death, the Paris correspondent of the *Guardian* declared, "That *Ulysses* became the sort of book it is is largely due to her, for it was she . . . who decided to allow Joyce an indefinite right to correct his proofs. It was in the exercise of this right that the peculiarities of Joyce's prose style reached their novel flowering." Though Joyce could have perhaps continued revising indefinitely, he confessed years later that *Ulysses* was the most "finished" of all his incomplete works.

There were light moments of friendship and mutual excitement associated with the birth of *Ulysses*. Joyce would read aloud from *Ulysses* for her, often the Cyclops section. They would burst into peals of laughter at Joyce's rendering of the dog and joke about the growth of the novel. Joyce would tell her that *Ulysses* was no longer than many other novels, such as *The Forsyte Saga,* only instead of running into many volumes, his was packed into one "hold all," as she calls it. Joyce's affairs, she acknowledges, were at least seven times as much trouble as an ordinary author's. Joyce, Larbaud, and Sylvia would play the game of spotting Molly or Leopold Bloom on the street or in a restaurant. Finally, he told Sylvia to write for the picture of Mr. Holbrook Jackson, editor of the English review *To-Day,* who looked like Joyce's conception of Mr. Bloom. Everything Joyce saw or heard was a good or bad omen for his book. He drew those around him into his obsession with his Ulyssean world.

Although October had been the original publishing date, they were early aware that it would have to be postponed. By the beginning of November, the Ithaca episode, with its many versions and additions, had been finished. Joyce announced in letters to his friends that the writing of the novel was finished and that he expected about three weeks of proof work left, with publication at the end of November. Yet he kept making additions on proofs and complaining about the printer's mistakes. In the back of his mind, the date of 2 February looked both talismanic and reasonable. He wrote provocatively to Harriet Weaver in November:

A coincidence is that of birthdays in connection with my books. *A Portrait of the Artist* which first appeared serially in your paper on 2 February [his birthday] finished on 1 September [her birthday]. *Ulysses* began on 1 March (birthday of a friend of mine, a Cornish painter [Frank Budgen]) and was finished on Mr Pound's birthday [30 October], he tells me. I wonder on whose it will be published.

McAlmon claims the superstitious Joyce was even concerned about the way the silverware was placed on the table and the way McAlmon poured the wine.

Subscribers became restless—the October date of the announced publication came and went. Because they had not paid any money yet, Sylvia nervously joked, the subscribers could not sue her for swindling them. T. E. Lawrence (of Arabia), who had ordered two of the expensive editions, demanded his copies. Sylvia did not have time to answer him from her own battlefield. She had a handful of inquiries, some irritated, each day. Paris publicity concerning the publication of *Ulysses,* which the press treated like a sporting event of worldwide importance, kept the Paris subscribers notified of the delays.

By November there were 400 subscribers, but the money had not been collected, because the book was not ready. Funds were low; Joyce had been borrowing advances from both Sylvia and Harriet Weaver. While helping him pay his personal expenses, she worried about collecting the full amount for the first payment to the printer, which was due on 1 December. In mid-October, at Joyce's request, she had written to John Quinn in New York, expressing a "desperate need" for money which, if not met, meant "he will not be able to finish *Ulysses:*

I give him everything I can spare but as you may imagine my shop has not been in existence long enough to support a family of four people as well as myself. . . . It is up to all of us who want the most important book of today to appear to come to the help of its author.

Even the Thomas Paine ring in the last line did not move her fellow American. Quinn had given Joyce 2,000 francs (almost $250) in the summer and was paying him regularly for his fair copy of the *Ulysses* manuscripts; he had paid Joyce a total of $1,200 for the manuscript and was angry when he received the letter from Sylvia asking for more money for Joyce. He asked Pound whether Joyce was really starving and added, "if you think I ought to send him 1,000 francs, I will do it, but I'll be damned if I'll do it because Miss Beach asks for it." Quinn had no understanding of the financial dealings of Sylvia, thought she was sharing equally, and was not about to believe "another woman." Pound replied that he did not think the situation was that difficult. Quinn sent nothing. By this time Pound had developed a disapproving attitude toward Joyce's expensive living habits. Pound, who made his own furniture and gave money to beginning artists who needed help, had noticed that Joyce was both receiving and spending freely.

Joyce had borrowed on his royalties from Harriet Weaver and from the bookshop till, where he left little notes when Sylvia was not there. The only recourse was friends. The list of friends who lent or donated money to the Joyce family through the years would fill several ledger books. His borrowings from his brother Stanislaus often went unreturned. Joyce was as deft with the hat in the one hand as he was with the pen in the other. When the letter he had asked Sylvia to write to Quinn brought nothing, he suggested she write to McAlmon. McAlmon had been lending Joyce $150 monthly to tide him over; although McAlmon did not care, some of this money was never repaid. After she sent McAlmon a letter of special appeal for funds, signing her name at Joyce's request, Joyce wrote to him, "I do hope Miss Beach has not been writing to you about me. With the best intentions in the world but saying nothing to me about it she has been writing to several addresses in both worlds. O dear me! I hear a groan going up from the entire globular earth—in which I have to join. Well, it will soon be over." Sylvia was only half aware that Joyce was pulling the strings but remaining invisible in order to deny the tugs. Except with his closest friends, he adopted an air of indifference, of being above all the daily details of money and publicity, paring his fingernails at a distance. For example, in writing to Italo Svevo just months before launching careful plans for a publicity campaign for *Ulysses,* he commented, "I don't know what the outcome will be and I care very little." In fact, he was planning the finest details from the back room of Shakespeare and Company.

When matters became indeed critical, Joyce finally wrote to Harriet Weaver with reluctance ("I have no recourse"). "You will think me mercenary," he admits, adding a request for £75 to pay the printer. For most of the year, she had worried about his physical and financial excesses, particularly his long hours of eyestrain. His behavior did not seem wise. Less than half a year after having received £200 ($1,000) in "advance of royalties," he was out of money again. "It was all very surprising and difficult" for her, conclude her biographers. "And one of the difficulties, though Harriet could not recognize it, was that she was judging another by herself. She was a rational person. He was not. Yet, once her loyalty had been given, to whatever cause or person, she was incapable of withdrawing it."

Preparation for the reading and lecture at Adrienne's library began in earnest in October. They decided to charge admission to benefit Joyce, whose "funds were low." In Adrienne's essay entitled "The Translation of *Ulysses*" and in the varying drafts of *Shakespeare and Company* are found contradictory statements concerning the beginning of the translations. Sylvia states in her memoirs that Larbaud began the translation of portions of *Ulysses* and that, fearing his lecture would not be ready, he asked for help with the translation. But an early draft of the memoirs, as well as Adrienne's essay, states that Larbaud, who had only a month to write the lecture, did not offer to translate the earliest portions of *Ulysses*. Joyce chose fragments from the Sirens and Penelope sections to be translated, and Adrienne made arrangements with Jacques Benoist-Méchin, the nineteen-year-old music student and patron of the two libraries, to do the job. He was young but serious and intelligent, and he could converse with the older writers. Most important, he could read and appreciate the most difficult works in both languages, for he had spoken English during the first fourteen years of his life.

Earlier—probably on 30 April, when he bought *Exiles* from her—Sylvia had given Benoist-Méchin the portions of *Ulysses* published in the *Little Review*. He was "carried away" by Joyce's genius, he told Adrienne. He agreed to the translating if Joyce would help him when necessary. As agreed, whenever difficulties arose, Joyce spent time with Benoist-Méchin in the back room of Adrienne's shop. A second condition was that nothing be said to his father about the work; his efforts must remain anonymous. His aristocratic father would never have approved of his association with *Ulysses*.

One consultation with Joyce concerned Benoist-Méchin's translation of the final words of *Ulysses:* "and his heart was going like mad and yes I said Yes I will." The young man wanted the novel to conclude with a final "yes" following the "I will." Earlier Joyce had considered using "yes" (which appears 354 times in the novel) as his final word, but had written "I will" in the draft that Benoist-Méchin was translating. There followed a day of discussion in which they dragged in all the world's great philosophers. Benoist-Méchin, who argued that in French the *"oui"* is stronger and smoother, was more persuasive in the philosophical discussion. "I will" sounds authoritative and Luciferian. "Yes," he argued, is optimistic, an affirmation to the world beyond oneself. Joyce, who may have changed his mind earlier in the discussion, conceded hours later, "yes," the young man was right, the book would end with "the most positive word in the language."

Léon-Paul Fargue often joined the sessions, working with relish on the bawdy language. Adrienne called him their consultant. He was a kindred spirit with Joyce, who remarked that Fargue's "almost fatal" flaw was that he was "a man of one language only." But Fargue was full of possible wordplay, which prolonged and enriched the translation sessions. He had a feeling for the wordplay, the bawdy language, and the sense of a city's atmosphere. His collection of poetry *Sous la Lampe* (*Under the Lamp*), which had just been published, illustrates these same qualities. His poetry contains such images of Paris as the rats rolling silently from tree to tree, crossing the lengthening shadow of the passerby. Fargue agreed to work on several portions but, typically, delayed the work until the very last minute.

Larbaud worked on his lecture and met with Joyce about the translation and biographical facts. In the midst of his efforts on behalf of Joyce, Larbaud's latest volume, *Amants, Heureux Amants*, appeared, with a dedication to James Joyce, who was pleased. In a suppressed portion of her memoirs, Sylvia explains that Larbaud and Joyce were "sometimes rather snappy with each other" but that their friendship was based on mutual respect.

Sylvia and Adrienne asked a young American actor named Jimmy Light to read the extract from the Sirens episode in English. Homer's sirens are Joyce's barmaids: Miss Douce and Miss Kennedy of the Ormond Hotel bar. It is four o'clock Bloomstime and, appropriately, the section is dedicated to the art of sounds. Light, whom Sylvia identifies as one of the *Little Review* crowd then in Montparnasse, was enthusiastic about Joyce, but agreed to read only if Joyce would coach him. When they met during November in the back room of Shakespeare and Company, Sylvia could hear the two voices, the Irish tenor and the Light baritone repeating the words: "Bald Pat was a waiter hard of hearing, to set ajar the door of the bar. The door of the bar. . . ."

"The shop is so crowded," Sylvia boasted to her father, "it reminds me of Wanamakers." Business was always brisk before Christmas, and publicity concerning *Ulysses* increased the crowd. Proofs were coming in and then going to Joyce, to his friends who were reading them, and to Darantière and back again, always through Sylvia, who was also running numerous errands for Joyce and trying to meet his impossible financial demands. Myrsine worked longer hours, and young Hélène Moschos made her daily runs to the Joyces' apartment. Sylvia sent Joyce to Man Ray for publicity photographs. Ray, the American photographer and Surrealist artist, had agreed to take photographs of the artists she wished displayed in Shakespeare and Company. The primary concern, however, was the rehearsing of Jimmy Light and the meetings between Joyce, Benoist-Méchin, and Fargue regarding the translation of the French portions that had to be ready on 7 December. The men were meeting across the street, where it was quieter. They worked on the translations until the last minute. When Larbaud read them, he was dissatisfied with some of the obscure passages and was also worried about

Joyce's sexual explicitness. "Surprisingly in the land of Rabelais," says Sylvia, the language of *Ulysses* was "almost too daring." As the time for the Joyce reading approached, Larbaud had misgivings about reading the objectionable passages. So there appeared on the program a warning: "Certain pages have an uncommon boldness of expression that might quite legitimately be shocking."

The crowd that passed into the rue de l'Odéon that December evening was not headed, as it usually was, for the theater at the end of the street, but for La Maison des Amis des Livres. Two-hundred fifty people jammed into the two rooms, with hardly space for another person. The rooms were dark, and people craned their necks to see the speaker's table. All the Left Bank literati were assembled except Pound who, in Ellmann's words, did not appreciate having his "discovery rediscovered." When Larbaud saw the crowd, Sylvia claims, he was frightened: "Adrienne had to give him a glass of brandy before he could summon his courage to go in and sit down at the little table, a place that wasn't new to him, since he was one of the favorite readers at Adrienne's 'séances' [meetings]." But he had not read to a crowd of this size, and he was nervous about the language. On his way to the table he whispered to Joyce that he was omitting a few lines.

Larbaud began the lecture with a review of Joyce's life and works. He discussed each work, particularly as it contributed to *Ulysses,* and told the audience what all recent readers take for granted: the key to Joyce's *Ulysses* is Homer's *Odyssey*. Using Joyce's scheme, he drew parallels between Ulysses and Leopold Bloom and talked of the elaborate organization of the chapters, each presented in terms of an hour of the day, an organ of the body, a color, a symbol, and an art or genre. To an audience that considered itself literary, he said, "The reader who approaches this book without the *Odyssey* clearly in mind will be thrown into dismay . . . for the uncultivated or half-cultivated reader will throw *Ulysses* aside after the first three pages." Finally, Larbaud explained that details that might be considered obscene are in fact descriptions and representations of what is. Furthermore, Joyce's choice of a Jew as protagonist is not anti-Semitic; rather, it is based on "symbolical, mystical, and ethnological reasons," which he did not explain. Ireland, he announced, has made a triumphal entry into high European literature.

Larbaud then read the French translation of portions of the Sirens and Penelope episodes. Sylvia thought to herself, "He is actually leaving out an extract or two!" Joyce believed that Larbaud was unnecessarily worried about the reactions: "what he read was bad enough in all conscience but there was no sign of any kind of protest and had he read the extra few lines the equilibrium of the solar system would not have been greatly disturbed." When a much relieved Larbaud returned to his seat in the audience, Adrienne introduced Jimmy Light, reminding the audience that some passages might seem "audacious." Jimmy Light read the Sirens portion in English, during which time the lights went out briefly, a mystical and probably coincidental parallel to the Cyclops section as well as to the young man's name.

Loud applause followed each portion of the program. During the final applause, as the crowd looked for the author, Larbaud walked over to the screen that hid Joyce from view in the back room. The applause swelled as Larbaud pulled a reluctant Joyce forward. Much to Joyce's delighted embarrassment, he kissed him in French fashion on both his cheeks. Sisley Huddleston claims that "Joyce blushed and trembled with confusion."

Thus Sylvia, Adrienne, and Larbaud launched Joyce on the turbulent sea of French criticism. He was an international literary figure. It was a triumph for Joyce, who, according to his friend Stuart Gilbert, set "much store on the good opinion of the French critics and public." While publicity intensified, Joyce simultaneously corrected proofs of Circe, Eumaeus, and Penelope—a feat he compared to playing several instruments with different parts of the body. The subscriptions and the anticipation rose swiftly during the next two months.

Adrienne's response to *Ulysses* resembles that of many of her fellow Frenchmen, who did not respond with the overwhelming enthusiasm that Larbaud showed. Curious about the book, she could not fully judge it until it had been translated. She had first heard portions from her back room, where Joyce and Benoist-Méchin read and reread them that December. Then from 1923 to 1929 she would oversee the work of Auguste Morel, Larbaud, and Stuart Gilbert as they made the first complete translation of *Ulysses*. An essay entitled "Joyce's *Ulysses* and the French Public," given as a speech in her bookshop on 26 March 1931, is an excellent summary introduction both to Joyce's work and to her own mystical philosophy. She frankly admits having had the desire to lay the book down during the second and third chapters; but when she left the bookish and self-satisfied Stephen and began the second part of the book with the "sympathetic" and human Bloom, she was captivated. She calls Bloom "the primitive of the twentieth century. The man born to Science. The nursling of great vulgarizations. Someday," she asserts, "one will say 'Bloomism' just as one says, 'Quixotism' and 'Don Juanism.' "

There was much discussion concerning the inclusive, sprawling, encyclopedic qualities of *Ulysses*. "Is this encyclopedic breadth not radically opposed to its artistic value?" Adrienne inquires. Romains saw the expansion of *Ulysses* in all directions as a "vain imitation of the immensity of the universe." Art, on the contrary, should organize life, not attempt to absorb it all. Related to this objection was the frustration of some of the French with Joyce's deliberate obscurity (no chapter titles or preface explain the correspondence to the *Odyssey* of Homer). Even Larbaud's lecture had to use Joyce's private scheme. Adrienne was puzzled. The book, like life, she notes, baffles and mortifies. But should not art, she concludes, give order and solace?

This final question of "solace" was the basis of the major objection of the French idealist. Adrienne charges that there is no exaltation of life in *Ulysses,* as there is in all other great works of art. This particular French response to *Ulysses* is best expressed by a German, Ernst Robert Curtius, professor of French at the University of Bonn:

Properly speaking, we can call genuises only those men whose production reflects something of the divine meaning of the world, whose creation brings about an exaltation of life. A light and a force emanate from the work of genius. It illuminates the spirit and reflection, it purifies and ennobles the passions, it gives birth to images that form our life. Even the highest intensity of the spirit, the highest degree of inventive and descriptive powers do not constitute genius if this work lacks the force that enlightens and fructifies. The work of Joyce issues from the revolt of the spirit and leads to the destruction of the world. *Ulysses* unmasks, exposes, demolishes, and degrades humanity with a sharpness and a thoroughness that have no equivalent in modern thought.

Many years later, Claude Roy asked Adrienne how "a person as rational as yourself could bowl that monster between our legs?" But Adrienne moved away from the negative charge so well expressed by Curtius. Joyce, she admits, submits the spirit to nature, to matter: "Divine principles invest themselves in flesh so as to be manifest, certain, sensible." To the charge of obscenity and the degradation of humanity, she responds that Joyce exposes, does not degrade, humanity. Humanity degrades itself: "If love, religion, and death seem, through his work, ugly and dirty, that is because we have scribbled over them without end. He administers to us an excellent auto-vaccination!" Philippe Soupault declares that it is the humanity of *Ulysses* that is its most important element. Adrienne concludes that *Ulysses,* although it lacks height and sublimity, is nevertheless a masterpiece of virtuosity and genius.

Another great English masterpiece of the century—this one in poetry—was being readied for publication in the same months of 1921 as was *Ulysses.* "Complimenti, you bitch, I am wracked by the seven jealousies," cried Ezra Pound to T. S. Eliot on January 24 after he had reread *The Waste Land,* from which Pound had blue-penciled out a third of the lines.

During December and January, Sylvia was swamped with circulating proofs and regular shop business. Though her mother did help in the shop during Myrsine's frequent illnesses during those two months, Sylvia was especially burdened by her visit. Cyprian could not help, because she was busy making *L'Aiglonne,* the movie they hoped would bring her fame. Sylvia helped Joyce with last-moment problems, such as finding the correct shade of blue for the binding. It must be the blue of the Greek flag, with white lettering to symbolize the white islands in the sea. Finally they sent the slightly faded flag that had been hanging in the shop for months to Myron Nutting, an American painter living in Paris. Nutting copied the color and on 10 January sent it back to Sylvia. Despite Darantière's efforts to match the color, Sylvia and Joyce were not satisfied. "Alas!" recalls Sylvia, "merely to look at that flag gave me a headache." Darantière's search took him to Germany, where he finally discovered the right blue—but on the wrong paper. He solved this problem by getting the color lithographed on white cardboard, which explains why the insides of the blue covers are white. Because the work days were very long, Sylvia turned down all evening invitations but one: on 20 January, the Joyce family entertained her, Adrienne, and Fargue (Larbaud was ill) with a dinner celebration for the coming publication.

On Monday, 30 January 1922, the last page proofs were sent to Dijon. On Tuesday the proofs were received in Dijon, and the printers worked that night.

The next evening, Darantière notified Sylvia and Joyce, who had been sending him letters urging the date of 2 February, ''Three copies of *Ulysses* have been sent tonight by express post to Miss Beach.'' Not trusting the mails, Joyce urged Sylvia to telephone Dijon, as she did. Darantière suggested that he send two copies on the Dijon–Paris express. Thus occurred the scene that opens this history of Shakespeare and Company: Sylvia met the train on Thursday, Joyce's fortieth birthday, at 7 A.M.

CHAPTER 6

Selling and Smuggling *Ulysses*

1922

I, my eye, my needs and my troublesome book are always there. There is no feast or celebration or meeting of shareholders but at the fatal hour I appear at the door in dubious habiliments, with impedimenta of baggage, a mute expectant family, a patch over one eye howling dismally for aid.

— James Joyce

If you are lucky enough to have lived in Paris as a young man, then wherever you go for the rest of your life, it stays with you, for Paris is a moveable feast.

— Ernest Hemingway

A WIND GUSTED in the December streets as the tall young American reporter hurried back to his wife, Hadley. He was warmed by his good news and by the anticipation of sharing it with his bride of four months. They were very much alone in this city. They had come knowing no one, with a handful of written introductions to the right kind of people from an American friend, the only writer they knew, Sherwood Anderson.

"I have found a wonderful place!" declared Ernest. "We're going to have all the books in the world to read and when we go on trips we can take them with us." He placed on the bed two volumes of Turgenev's *Sportsman's Sketches,* which he would borrow again and again, D. H. Lawrence's *Sons and Lovers,* Tolstoy's *War and Peace,* and Dostoevski's *The Gambler and Other Stories.* Hadley asked whether he was speaking of the library of Sylvia Beach about which Sherwood Anderson had told them.

"Yes, and it is full of all the good books and it is warm and cheerful and she is a fine person. She trusted me to take these books and bring the money later."

"But, Tatie, you must go by this afternoon and pay," she said.

"Sure I will. We'll both go."

When they arrived with the money that afternoon, Sylvia wrote his name and the amount paid in her ledger book for 28 December 1921. The book reads:

Wed		
December 28		
	Extras	1.20
	The Nation	2.25

	Extras 2 fines	12.85
1	Tauchnitz	4.
	Dubliners	22.50
	subc Mr. Hemingway 1 mo 2 vols	12.
	" Mrs. Peets 3 mos 2 vols	30
	dep 14	
		84.80

Hemingway introduced "the Feathercat," as he called his redheaded wife, Hadley, whom Sylvia thought "an attractive boyishlooking girl" and a "delightfully jolly person." Hadley considered Sylvia an attractive woman and her shop a warm place on that cold day when she studied the shelves, looking for the fiction of Henry James. After they left, they walked along the quays, watching the river and talking of their happiness in Paris. They stopped for a drink to warm themselves, but, because they had spent for the book subscription the twelve francs that would have bought them both a restaurant dinner, they went home to eat instead.

"We're lucky that you found that place," Hadley said.

"We're always lucky," he answered.

Hemingway remembers that after reading for a while, they went to bed and made love, full of the joy of Paris and their youth.

When they had met that morning, Sylvia and Hemingway had liked each other instantly. He was bashful, but, trusting in his own tactics and not the Anderson letter in his own pocket, he just walked in and looked around. As he rubbed his hands together over the stove, he looked at the framed photographs of the writers on the wall above it. He recognized Sherwood Anderson and a few others, but most of them he did not know. He was not of that group—not yet. He wanted to be a writer, a published writer, and he was awed by this atmosphere. Anderson had told him he had to go to Paris if he was serious. While he was traveling in Europe for news stories for the *Toronto Star,* he would write. And he could come here, he thought. This would be his library, his connection with the world of literature.

When he had introduced himself to Sylvia, they sat together for a long chat. She noticed his deep all-American voice with no "twang," and she drew him out on his life experiences. He talked "rather bitterly," she remembered years later, about his childhood, his education driving ambulances in the war in Italy, the wounds and recovery in the Italian hospital, and his newspaper work in Canada. Soon he was pulling up his pant leg and taking off his shoe to show her his scarred leg and foot. She expressed her regret at the "dreadful" scars. Her eager listening and unquestioning sympathy encouraged Hemingway's tendency to self-pity and dramatization. Yet she thought that "in spite of a certain boyishness, he was exceptionally wise and self-reliant." He was "grown up" and "old for his years." His size, seriousness, and knowledge of life reinforced her impression. One day many months later, McAlmon whispered to Sylvia, "Hem's younger than he lets on." She admired his self-education, for she too had instructed herself through travel and a variety of life experiences. He was big and handsome in a Latin sort of way, she thought. Hemingway, who was just twenty-two and attracted to women older than himself, thought she must be Hadley's age (thirty), although in fact Sylvia, who looked to be in her late twenties, was already thirty-four.

Hemingway noted her "lively, sharply sculptured face" and her alive, gay eyes and pretty legs. She was a "cheerful" person who "loved to make jokes and gossip. No one that I ever knew was nicer to me." He undoubtedly saw in her the qualities he most admired: personal integrity, a devotion to the arts, and a willingness to work hard. Neither had much respect for those who spent long, wasted hours drinking in cafés. Hemingway would become most critical of this waste in Fitzgerald; and Sylvia of this waste in McAlmon.

Sylvia and Ernest remained very good friends for nearly forty years after this. For twenty years he was a prominent player in the history of Shakespeare and Company. They neither quarreled nor betrayed each other. And in her memoirs, Sylvia perpetuates his stories of childhood suffering, hunger, and bravura. He had a fatal capacity to make people want to tell fantastic stories about him. Their memoirs indicate that their relationship was exceptional. In his memoirs, also written in the 1950s, but published posthumously, he reserves his greatest praise for Sylvia, in sharp contrast, for example, to his recollections of Ford, Fitzgerald, and Stein. Sylvia never received the satiric abuse he aimed at other expatriates. She made no claim to being his tutor, as did some of the others, nor was she a fellow writer, in any competitive sense; but their friendship did involve matters of trust that could have soured their cordiality. There is no evidence of any disharmony between them. Though their friends believe they retold the experiences in exaggerated terms, their friendship was a genuine one, unstrained through four decades. Their reunion in 1944, at the liberation of Paris, was a dramatic and emotional occasion of loyalty that ensured their mutual nostalgia for the twenties.

By January, as the publication date for *Ulysses* approached, Hemingway was caught up in the fervor of the bookshop project and was helping Sylvia collect subscriptions. On the ninth, the Hemingways moved into a fourth-floor apartment in 74 rue du Cardinal-Lemoine, near Larbaud's flat at No. 71, behind the Panthéon. It was a cold-water flat with a toilet off the hall, but Hemingway later remembers that "we were very poor and very happy." If he pretended to be the romantic starving artist, Joyce certainly did not. In a letter to Anderson about Joyce, who has just published "a most god-dam wonderful book," Hemingway warns Anderson not to be fooled by the rumors that Joyce is starving. The entire "celtic crew" can be seen every night at Michaud's restaurant, which Hemingway could afford perhaps only once a week. He agrees with Stein, he adds, that the poor, complaining Irish never starve. In his memoirs he recalls that he and Hadley looked hungrily through a restaurant window to see the four Joyces dining lavishly. He confided to his good friends that he found the company and conversation of Joyce boring. These judgments against Joyce reflect the different styles of life of the Hemingways and the Joyces as well as Hemingway's dramatization of his own hungry years. Hadley's patrimony, a $3,000-a-year trust fund, by no means made them rich, but he was able to rent a room in which to work and could pay for a skiing vacation every winter. Whatever negative personal comments Hemingway offered, his praise for *Ulysses,* which "made it possible for us to break away from the restrictions," remained unqualified.

February was cold, dry, sunny—and frustrating. The copies of *Ulysses* were slow in coming from Darantière. Reviews were even slower to appear. Joyce spent every day at the bookshop, wrapping books to mail around the world, signing deluxe editions, and offering numerous schemes for extracting reviews from literary persons. He took an interest in every detail of the sale and promotion of the book. He talked over each new order with Sylvia, and read and reread the subscription lists, inquiring why a particular writer, such as George Moore, had not yet subscribed. He loved using the rubber stamps, and when the press copies arrived weeks later, he stamped each gingerly "press copy." When Harriet Weaver was preparing the second edition, he wrote requesting that she order some of the stamps. When persons employed at the London *Times* and the British Museum ordered copies, he leaped to the conclusion that the English establishment was acknowledging him and advised McAlmon to "go to confession for the last day cannot be far off." The following month, having realized that these were probably private orders, he asked Miss Weaver to check anonymously at the British Museum for a copy. If none was there, he would send one; otherwise it was "useless to waste a copy." He jokingly reported to several of his friends that Ireland's "minister of propaganda" was nominating him for the Nobel Prize in literature and that he had wanted to know when Joyce was returning to Dublin. Flattered and amused, Joyce assured McAlmon, "I have not the faintest chance of being awarded the prize." He was correct; the prize was never given to him. A reason for this neglect is suggested in the stipulation by Alfred Bernard Nobel that the award go to a literary work of an idealistic tendency.

Fearing piracy of *Ulysses* in the United States, Sylvia had written to John Quinn a week and a half before *Ulysses* appeared. At the request of Joyce, she asked for financial assistance and wondered whether two sets of a work sent to the Library of Congress were necessary to protect a copyright. She repeated her question in a second letter, and Quinn replied angrily that he had already told Joyce that in his opinion the *Little Review* publication secured the American copyright. And, considering the size of the novel and what happened to the *Little Review,* he did not think there was much chance of piracy. He also warned her about John Sumner of the Society for the Suppression of Vice and added, "This isn't an easy game that you are up against." Worried about his own fourteen copies ($291.10 worth), he asked her to wrap and hold them until he sent further instructions. His most positive, and ironic, note was sounded when Joyce's telegram announcing the publication of *Ulysses* arrived within hours of the death of William Butler Yeats's father:

And so the mystical symbol appears, for on the day that Mr. Yeats died, aged eighty-three, the old generation passing away, the birth of "Ulysses," the child of the new age, was announced by cable from Joyce. I am sure that the old man would have appreciated the far-wandering Ulysses if he had only lived to read it. How he would have enjoyed it! Chuckled over it! Read out from it and laughed over it!

He concludes with more advice and a characteristic insult, reminding her that it takes more than money to support Joyce: it takes "time and patience and strength," of which he has reached his limit. He asks that Joyce write to him directly after this, and not through her. Her reply reflected the opinion of Pound and her recent knowledge of the serious illness of Quinn: "I know that no matter how testy you like to seem, you are the kindest man alive." Then she notes, "While you were helping an old man [Yeats] to die, I was helping a young man [Joyce] to live."

The fear of piracy was soon crowded aside by the fear of confiscation. Sylvia warned the American and English purchasers to place the book in another dust jacket. Suitable jackets were *Shakespeare's Works, Complete in One Volume* or *Merry Tales for Little Folks.* She enjoyed the irony and the intrigue. In early February and March she made her first contacts with a Chicago newsman, which would lead in the fall to the most daring technique of smuggling *Ulysses* into the United States.

Michael Joseph once asked, "Is publishing an occupation for a gentlemen or is it a real business?" Is it, one should more pertinently ask, an occupation for a lady? Sylvia certainly was a lady who meant business. Determined to get *Ulysses* past the storm of customs, she found her "Saint Bernard." She would introduce him in her memoirs as "a certain Bernard B." But his unpublished letters are signed Barnet (or Barney) Braverman, 311 Chatham Street, Windsor, Ontario, Canada. He worked as copywriter, advertising-research man, and part-time salesman for the Curtis Company, an advertising agency in Windsor, where he had recently moved from Toronto. Sylvia claims that she got his name from Hemingway, who had known him in Chicago, where both were newsmen. On 7 February, five days after receiving her first copies of *Ulysses* and without waiting for any confiscation of books, she wrote to Mr. Braverman in Chicago to ask whether he would help get the book into the country. For nearly two months she would receive no reply to her unladylike solicitation of a smuggler.

Hemingway made an important new friendship three months following his arrival in Paris. She had a strong German-Jewish face, Hemingway observed of Gertrude Stein after they met. The Hemingways' visit to Gertrude and Alice, during which Hadley was routinely distracted by the latter, was followed by a single visit from the two women to the Hemingways' flat, where they sat on the bed and Gertrude examined his manuscripts. Soon afterward, Hemingway met them in the Luxembourg Garden and was invited to come by any day after five. He went often, without Hadley.

Gertrude was undoubtedly attracted by his promise as a writer and by his seriousness as well as by his admiration for her. She read his manuscripts, penciled out some of his words, offered strong literary opinions and critical suggestions, and wrote the first criticism of his work, calling it "intelligent," for the Paris *Tribune.* Hemingway believes that they "treated us as though we were very good, well mannered and promising children and I felt that they forgave us for being in love and being married—time would fix that.'' She talked of baseball, gardens, American soldiers, painting, bull fighting, and other people—she loved to analyze the character of others. She loved to talk, as she admitted later in a lecture entitled ''The Gradual Making of *The Making of Americans''*:

I always as I admit seem to be talking but talking can be a way of listening . . . I cannot remember not talking all the time and all the same feeling that while I was talking while I was seeing that I was not only hearing but seeing while I was talking . . .

Although much has been written of her influence on Hemingway's writing, Glenway Wescott—no admirer of Hemingway—claims that while Hemingway chose his words carefully, she ''scribbled, scribbled'' with facility. She reserved her strongest criticism, Hemingway remembered years later, for his frankness about sex and violence. She did not think he should be as explicit as he was in his writing. He claims that in conversation he never used indiscreet language that might shock her, avoiding discussion of the ugly scenes from his travels.

Hemingway admired Stein's artistic freedom, integrity, and her willingness to tutor and encourage his young ambitions. There has been some talk, despite the discrepancy in their ages, of a sexual attraction between them. W. G. Rogers, for example, claims Hemingway admitted feeling an attraction with the powerful and masculine Stein—a union blocked by the presence of Alice. He was also initially attracted to her work. Although surviving library cards reveal that he borrowed only her *Composition as Explanation* (November 1926) and *Three Lives* (June 1928), she undoubtedly gave him copies of her books and read portions of them to him in the early years of their friendship.

While Hemingway was making his regular visits to the rue de Fleurus, Joyce waited impatiently for the world's response to *Ulysses*. ''It is very irritating waiting for reviews,'' Joyce complains to Harriet Weaver. ''I suppose it is because the book is so long.'' Soon, he was talking of a conspiracy of silence against him and urged Sylvia to alert Eliot and others about a ''boycott.'' Finally, on the first Sunday of March, one of the first and most important reviews, a 1,500-word essay by Sisley Huddleston, appeared in the London *Observer*. ''Mr. Joyce is a man of genius,'' he declares, and the *''monologue intérieur* [Larbaud's expression] is, I imagine . . . the vilest, according to ordinary standards, in all literature. And yet its very obscenity is somehow beautiful and wrings the soul to pity.'' He concludes the article by asking, ''Has he not exaggerated the vulgarity and magnified the madness of mankind and the mysterious materiality of the universe?'' This was just the sort of article that would sell books. Within days there were 136 new orders for *Ulysses;* by 11 March 145 more had arrived; by 20 March the figure had risen to 148. The 750 copies of the regular (150-franc) edition were now sold out.

Joyce was delighted. He immediately asked Harriet Weaver and Sylvia to send copies of the review to other writers and critics from London to Stockholm. He seemed not to care whether the reviews were positive or negative. He looked first to see whether the Shakespeare and Company address was given; second, he noted the length; third, he looked at the signature to judge the influence of the name. Whether the author disliked or misinterpreted *Ulysses* was of least importance.

Sylvia was angry at Darantière for his delay in sending press copies. With the demand for books created by the Huddleston article and the mid-March appearance of Joyce before a press conference of English and Irish newsmen, she believed that a wide distribution of press copies was urgent. At Joyce's urging, she went to Dijon on the seventeenth and returned on the nineteenth with the copies for the press and libraries. Hemingway received one of these press copies, which now resides with his papers in the John F. Kennedy Library. Only the pages of the first half and the last portion (Molly's soliloquy) are cut.

The proposal of Sylvia for smuggling *Ulysses* into the United States finally reached Barnet Braverman late in March. He had sublet his Chicago apartment, and the letter found him in Toronto, where he was packing to move to Detroit. The move was fortunate, he later stresses: "Circumstances or accident conspired to have me leave Toronto." His new job was a short boat ride across Lake Saint Clair (the small body of water between Lakes Erie and Huron) to Windsor, Canada. From Windsor he telegrammed on 21 March: "Shoot books prepaid your responsibility addressing same to me care Dominion Express Company." When he heard nothing, he wrote three weeks later apologizing for the terse but cautionary telegram. His unpublished letters reveal his eagerness to help and his pride at being asked to get the books to their subscribers. The mid-April letter asks where the books are—"So, here I am, Miss Beach, at the service of James Joyce's 'Ulysse.'" Braverman claims he knows "an art critic on a Detroit daily" and the "secretary of a Detroit advertising association" who might be "glad to help me expedite the transfer of the books." He adds that he is eager to put "one over on the Republic and its Methodist smut-hounds."

In the meantime, probably because she had heard nothing in response to her February proposal, Sylvia had made contact with another person who would act as an agent to get *Ulysses* into the country: Mr. Mitchell Kennerly, who was a personal friend of the captain of an Atlantic transportation liner. The plan was to smuggle twenty-five or thirty copies in bulk a month from London. Kennerly, president of the Anderson Auction Company, with offices on Park Avenue, had been successfully defended by John Quinn for selling a novel called *Hagar Revelly,* on the ground that it contained a "highly moral lesson." In a March letter, Quinn advised Sylvia about the scheme, explaining everything several times in his condescending manner. "You are an amateur," he declares. This is business, not poetry, and she must get a contract and an American distributor. In a final insult, he adds that because she is a woman, she will not take his advice seriously, because she did not pay for it. A second letter, in April, asserts that he does not want another trial if Kennerly acts as her agent. His letter speaks of confiscation, which he is certain Sumner plans. He warns Sylvia that orders for the confiscation of *Ulysses* have been issued and that she must go slowly on the mailing. She apparently took his advice seriously, because for nearly four months she did nothing more on the smuggling schemes.

Correspondence concerning reviews and the shipment and receiving of *Ulysses* continued. Sylvia typed each review that she found, and Joyce wrote a thank-you letter to each critic. In her work for Joyce, Sylvia increasingly called on her skills of typing and filing, which she had acquired in 1918 with the Red Cross. She kept each fan letter and was particularly pleased with the human-interest stories, such as the one concerning three starving artists who came to the book-shop, each with a third of the cost of the book. They had stayed in bed several days to avoid the cost of food so that each could take a share in one copy of *Ulysses*. During the next fifteen years, letters would arrive telling of the success or failure of the buyers in smuggling the book. One Englishman boasted that he carried the book openly on the plane to London. Prof. Dudley Fitts lamented that his copy was destroyed at the port of New York and requested that another be sent in disguise. Waldo Frank received his copy by way of an American tourist returning from Paris. George R. Cook, president of the Princeton Bank and Trust Company, recalls his exciting purchase of the book and his later attempt to hide the book from his adolescent daughters. Of the scores of letters that remain in her Papers, few are negative. One of the rare ones is from a woman who declares that she has just read the last chapter of the vile and depraved book: "No wonder the book was banned, they should all be burned before they con-taminate the minds of youth. We want, and need beauty in literature and not garbage."

Though he usually solicited reviews through Sylvia, Joyce himself wrote to McAlmon. First Joyce, who had recently begun dressing like a dandy, asks for a necktie, presumably one of McAlmon's discards (McAlmon, who thought Joyce a Dublin-Jesuit provincial, sent him a ring and several ties). Next, he asks for a review of *Ulysses*, which McAlmon dashed off. Joyce corrected it and returned it, saying he himself could not place it for publication. He suggests Harold Loeb's *Broom*, Florence Gilliam and Arthur Moss's *Gargoyle*, or Wyndham Lewis's *Tyro*, and adds "I suppose your father-in-law [Sir John Ell-erman] could not place it anyhere?" McAlmon did not see his assignment through, and the article never appeared. McAlmon did not hold Joyce, whom he called "the old man," in awe; he was incapable of awe toward another person. Joyce was a drinking companion and a fellow writer. Moreover, as he later con-fesses, he, like Hemingway, had never read *Ulysses* through: "The book *is* dull. It takes a person highly curious about life and letters, one of those supermorons, an intellectual, to read it through." But the immediate cause of his failure to publish the review is suggested in a letter he wrote to Sylvia a year and a half later, after she had asked him again for a review of *Ulysses:*

I detest reviews, have to belly ache through my own career, instincts and impulses too much to devote myself to criticism that I'd think respectable. . . . But here's this that has taken me just twenty minutes to get off, and I send it to you before a tremor makes me hold it over, and dabble with it.

He adds, in this undated, unpublished letter, that he has not looked at *Ulysses* in a year and a half and is busy correcting his books and grammar.

Of the many meetings with French, English, and American writers whom Hemingway came to know through Sylvia, the most significant occurred one day when Hemingway was reading in the library and Pound sauntered in. To Sylvia's introduction, Hemingway replied that he had come to Paris in part to see Pound. They soon became good friends, boxing together and discussing writing. Pound was advocating the cause of *le mot juste,* which the French writers, particularly Flaubert, practiced: the principles of directness, precision, and economy. Hemingway was certainly influenced by Pound's distrust of the adjective. Pound's advice, together with Hemingway's reading of Twain, his early admiration for Anderson, his newspaper work, and the growing influence of Gertrude Stein, helped to mold his famous style during these formative years in Paris. The only disappointment Hemingway experienced in Pound seems to have come from the latter's declaration that he did not read Dostoevski or other "rooshians." Pound had a greater influence as a friend and teacher than as a writer. Still, Hemingway, though he did not borrow any books by Pound at the library, certainly read all of his poetry in the little magazines. He took the title "The Age Demanded" from Pound's "Hugh Selwyn Mauberley" for a piece in *Der Querschnitt* in February of 1925.

While Sylvia focused her charity on Joyce, Pound planned broader schemes. His exemplary gesture of generosity toward another writer was his Bel Esprit scheme to "release as many captives as possible" to devote themselves full-time to writing. With the help of Natalie Barney, he hoped to collect £10 or $50 from each person for a £300 annual income for a worthy writer. His first target was T. S. Eliot: "In order that T. S. Eliot may leave his work at Lloyd's Bank and devote his whole time to literature" (so read the official statement on a brochure printed by John Rodker). In a carbon outline Pound expressed his purpose more pointedly: "Eliot, in bank, makes 500 pounds. Too tired to write, broke down; during convalescence in Switzerland did Waste Land, a masterpiece; one of the most important 19 pages in English." During the winter of 1921–1922, T. S. Eliot had had a nervous collapse in London and been hospitalized in Lausanne, where he wrote *The Waste Land.* Though Pound was himself poor, he was convinced of Eliot's greatness and solicited the money from poor artists and their rich associates, such as John Quinn, who promised to take six or seven shares but expressed regret that Pound had not kept the matter quiet. By July, Pound had gained twenty-two of the thirty needed subscriptions to set Eliot free of the commercial work. He circulated innumerable letters on behalf of Bel Esprit and other literary causes, in addition to maintaining his own literary production. But gathering the money was not as great a problem as Eliot himself would prove to be. Uninformed of the project and not desiring to leave his job, Eliot refused the money. Though he later moved from banking to publishing, he always held employment apart from his writing, and unlike Joyce, he could not abide artistic panhandling.

If the efforts of Pound were unappreciated, those of Sylvia were not. Harriet Weaver sent a placard of the front page of one of England's most sensational newspapers: SCANDAL OF JAMES JOYCE'S ULYSSES scream the large black letters that fill a third of the first-of-April front page of the *Sporting Times,* subtitled *Pink 'Un*—Largest Circulation of Any Sporting Weekly in the World. The author of the sensational article protests that he has "no stomach" for Joyce, who is a "writer of talent" but a "perverted lunatic" who "has ruled out all the elementary decencies of life and dwells appreciatively on things that sniggering louts of schoolboys guffaw about." Below the bold-faced title is printed the list of handicapped horses. Delighted with the publicity for her own sure win, Sylvia mounted the placard on the wall behind her desk. She and Joyce were pleased with the publicity, which was slow in coming, even from worthy sources. They had their picture taken in front of the placard, and Joyce half boasted to Miss Weaver that the *Sporting Times*'s reputation "is worse than my own." They did not respond to adverse criticism of the book or to any faulty conjectures or interpretations of the work. They cared only that the conjectures and controversy sold books. And this sensational headline increased the sporting chance of book sales.

Yet the words of the *Pink 'Un* set the tone for the swell of indignation and censorship that was slowly mounting against the book. The *Dublin Review* calls Joyce a Titan who "revolves and sputters hopelessly under the flood of his own vomit." Alfred Noyes declares, "It is simply the foulest book that has ever found its way into print." Edmund Gosse swears it is "sheer indecency." Virginia Woolf dismisses Joyce as "underbred . . . a queasy undergraduate scratching his pimples." The *Sheffield Daily Telegraph* names Joyce "Rabelais after a nervous breakdown," and George Moore calls him "Zola gone to seed." Even Joyce's brother Stanislaus suggests that after this recent "inspection of the stinkpots," he should now return to poetry. "Everything dirty seems to have the same irresistable attraction for you that cow-dung has for flies."

In the Pavillon Colombe, a dozen miles north of Paris, Edith Wharton, the sixty-year-old American novelist and venerable literary personality, struggled through *Ulysses,* finally casting it aside (as she informed her close friend Bernard Berenson) as "a welter of pornography (the rudest school-boy kind), and unformed and unimportant drivel." Miss Wharton, who had been away from America a decade now, lived extravagantly in a world quite apart from the avant-garde rue de l'Odéon; only an occasional friend, such as Gide or Valéry, associated with both literary circles.

On his way through Paris after having worked with the Near East Relief, John Dos Passos (twenty-four years younger than Miss Wharton) bought his copy of *Ulysses* from Sylvia, who introduced him to Joyce. Dos Passos claims he "shook the limp hand of a pale uninterested man in dark glasses sitting beside the stove in the back room" of the bookshop. He "read the book at one gulp" while "laid up with a bout of the flu" on board a transatlantic liner and found parts "boring" and parts "magnificent," but concluded that its publication "disposed of the current theory that the English novel was dead."

Amid rumors of a critical boycott of the book, rumors that probably originated at Shakespeare and Company, Joyce confronted a personal crisis with Nora, his uneducated and unlettered wife (she was a chambermaid when he met her), who refused to read *Ulysses* or anything else written by her husband. When he would get drunk or they would quarrel, according to friends' reports, she would declare, "I'll be taking the children and going back to Ireland." Finally she acted. She took the children and went to Ireland to visit her mother, using the £1,500 that Harriet Weaver had sent in March for Joyce's rest and vacation. Before the Irish civil war forced her to return, Joyce visibly suffered from the desertion, looking to McAlmon like a "lost spirit wailing in the wilderness of Paris." To the dismay of Sylvia, he fainted once in the bookshop.

On 1 May they successfully mailed several packages of *Ulysses* to the United States. One went to a poet named Williams, whom McAlmon praised and who lived in Rutherford, New Jersey. One went to Yvor Winters; two to the Way Farer's Bookshop in Washington, D.C.; and twenty-five to New York City's Washington Square Bookshop. The long letters from Quinn continued to come with news of impending confiscations. He had assured Liveright, he said, that no American publisher could publish an unexpurgated edition. He had seen the novel in the window of Drake's and declared it beautifully printed. In one of his typical examples of mixed praise, he says of Sylvia: "She has tackled, with the audacity, if not the ignorance, of amateurs, a really tough job. That is the job of beating the United States Federal and State laws."

Sylvia returned from an Easter weekend of complete rest at Chartres to the second of three outstanding and positive reviews of *Ulysses*. The first had been the appearance of Larbaud's essay, based on his December lecture, published in April in the prestigious *Nouvelle Revue Française*. Before the end of the month, Middleton Murry, in a long article on *Ulysses* appearing in the *Nation and Athenaeum,* declares *Ulysses* a "remarkable book" of "inspissated obscurities" and calls Joyce "an intensely serious man" with "the mind of an artist, abnormally sensitive to the secret of individuality of emotions and things" and a "genius of the very highest order, strictly comparable to Goethe or Dostoevsky." *Ulysses* was, he adds, "an immense, a prodigious self-laceration, the tearing away from himself, by a half-demented man of genius, of inhibitions and limitations." Joyce predicted that this article might "break the boycott." But it was the Larbaud article that prompted the next important review: Arnold Bennett wrote a page-and-a-half-long essay acknowledging that the prestige and integrity of the *Nouvelle Revue Française* and Larbaud had led him to re-examine *Ulysses*. Joyce, though his vision of human nature is "mean, hostile, and uncharitable," is a "very astonishing phenomenon in letters. He is sometimes dazzlingly original. If he does not see life whole he sees it piercingly. His ingenuity is marvellous. He has wit. He has a prodigious humor. He is afraid of naught."

Sylvia typed the Bennett and Murry articles for circulation. Harriet Weaver collected extracts from forty-seven critical responses, headed by Larbaud's words, for immediate publication. She sent the first numbered copy, with Joyce's inscription, to Sylvia. In addition to collecting the reviews for Miss Weaver, Sylvia handled all of Joyce's correspondence. Fan mail continued to come in from as far away as Chile and China. A poor store clerk named Zenichiro Hondon of Tokyo requested that on 1 February Sylvia exchange a copy of *Ulysses* for a group of Japanese popular novels. Some letters were never answered. On 24 April, William H. Barr sent a self-addressed envelope and asked Joyce to explain the relation between the title and book: "I cannot trace a likeness in the history of the one or the facts (or fiction) of the other."

Ulysses was not easy to sell. In its favor were, for the intellectual, its reputation as an innovative masterpiece of fiction and, for the common reader, its reputation as a "dirty book." These two factors, plus the zeal of its author and publisher for promoting it, soon made the work famous. Certainly its association with a quaint little Left Bank shop, where it was always available, helped sustain its sale for a decade. Working against its sale were the neglect of established critics, the fear of confiscation or arrest (which cut off the major markets), and the high cost of the book. At a time when most Parisians bought a book for a few francs, *Ulysses* cost 150 francs in its least expensive binding. In the United States the cost was high for 1922: the $13 edition sold for $20; the $23 edition for $30 (at Brentano's for $35). John Quinn reported to Sylvia in March that one copy changed hands for $50. These prices indicate both its value and its inaccessibility to the mass of readers.

Arthur Brentano came for *Ulysses* one day when Sylvia was out. "But why didn't you subscribe?" she later asked. For the later editions, her major buyers would indeed be the English and American bookstores on the Right Bank. By then even the French bookshops were stocking the book. Messengers from several French shops bought a dozen or two, wrapping them in their large green cloths, which were tied at four corners for carrying. They often stayed to talk about book weights and show their respect to the publisher of a best seller.

Ulysses changed the sale of books at Shakespeare and Company. There were the books that always sold, year after year: *Cassell's French-English Dictionary,* Shakespeare, the *Oxford English Dictionary,* Conrad and Kipling, Yeats and Blake, Whitman and Melville, and the little magazines like *Broom, Poetry,* and the *Little Review.* But the sale of Joyce's books increased, often to several copies in a day, indicating that a customer would come in to buy *Ulysses* and purchase all of Joyce's works. By the end of 1922, Joyce had become the best seller. Another gradual change occurred between 1922 and 1923. Whereas James, Whitman, Conrad, and Shakespeare had been the big sellers, by 1922 Eliot (whose *The Waste Land* was published that year), Pound's *Poems,* and McAlmon's *Hasty Bunch* were competing with Whitman and the other perennial sellers. The moderns now dominated Shakespeare and Company.

Gertrude Stein did not wait for her yearly subscription to run out in May before coming with Alice in Gody (Godiva, their World War I Ford) to inform Sylvia that they would be transferring their membership to the American Library on the Right Bank. They did not approve of the direction—the publishing direction—that Shakespeare and Company had taken. Less than a year before, Gertrude had purchased a year's subscription, just one day after the prospectus for

Sylvia's publication of *Ulysses* had been paid for but before it was circulated. For months now Gertrude had watched with displeasure the growing Left Bank absorption with Joyce. During this time, she had found opportunities to complain at the bookshop. One day, according to Sylvia, she had complained indignantly about the lack of amusing books in the library, specifically *The Trail of the Lonesome Pine* and *The Girl of the Limberlost*. Sylvia admitted she did not carry these books but inquired whether Gertrude, who was serious, could name any other library that had two copies of her *Tender Buttons* circulating. During the war Gertrude had recommended *The Trail of the Lonesome Pine* to the wounded soldiers in the hospital; and the song by the same title was one of her favorites. But she sensed Sylvia's dismay. To make up for her strong criticism of the bookshop, she gave Sylvia several of her rare items, including an inscribed first edition of *Three Lives,* which was later stolen. Their differences ran deeper than *The Trail of the Lonesome Pine,* however; they disagreed about the value of French literature and, more important, about Joyce's work. In *The Autobiography of Alice B. Toklas,* a decade later, Stein refers to the "few stray irish poets" who hung around the bookshop. She does not capitalize *Irish.* Joyce, she adds, was one of the "incomprehensibles whom anybody can understand." He was her rival for attention and praise. She looked upon the publication of Joyce as a breach of friendship with Sylvia.

When Sylvia heard the news that Gertrude was changing her allegiance, she admitted, tongue in cheek, that in Odéonia, they kept rather low company. Sylvia had incurred, at least for a few years, the wrath of the Sibyl of Montparnasse. According to legend, Sylvia responded to a particular slight by Stein with a telegram that read, "Yes a thorn is a thorn is a thorn." Sylvia did not fear her disapproval. The young American writers who took refuge in what Van Wyck Brooks calls "the mature Gertrudian bosom," however, feared the tongue and wit of Stein. They believed the myth, articulated by her biographer John Malcolm Brinnin, that in the background of her salon, "over the noise of teacups, one could hear the sound of rolling heads, the rumbles of dead reputations being carted away."

Stein believed that she was the century's first and greatest experimenter with the English language. She pointed out to more than one young American writer that her first great book, *Three Lives,* was published in 1908, long before *Ulysses,* whose influence she called "local." "Twentieth-century literature *is* Gertrude Stein," she announced to Samuel Putnam. The four big American writers are "Poe, Whitman, James, myself. The line of descent is clear." The two writers who seemed the greatest challenge to her leadership of modernism never paid homage to her at the rue de Fleurus, and so she disparaged them both. According to her, Pound, the "village explainer," and Joyce, the incomprehensible whom "anyone can understand," both smelled like a museum. "It is the people who generally smell of museums who are accepted. . . . That is why James Joyce was accepted and I was not. He leaned toward the past, in my work the newness and difference is fundamental." She said the same thing about Hemingway after their split: Hemingway looked like a modern but smelled like a museum.

This disparagement of those who ignored her or quarreled with her is emphasized by Hemingway in *A Moveable Feast:*

In the three or four years that we were good friends I cannot remember Gertrude Stein ever speaking well of any writer who had not written favorably about her work or done something to advance her career except for Ronald Firbank and, later, Scott Fitzgerald. . . . If you brought up Joyce twice, you would not be invited back. It was like mentioning one general favorably to another general.

A more balanced view of her literary rivalries is suggested by her friends. She did not care for Joyce's writing, but she did not force all friends to choose between them. Thornton Wilder, for example, was one of her closest friends and admirers and yet he openly admired Joyce's work.

What were the reactions of Pound and Joyce to this open disparagement? Pound countered by calling her "an old tub of guts" and a mere parasite on the body of literature. In a parody that he sent to Eliot in 1926, Pound has Stein say, "Yes, the Jews have produced only three original geniuses: Christ, Spinoza, and myself." Joyce said nothing. Perhaps he had the greater, and certainly the more secure, ego. He completely ignored her. Though she had her loyal admirers, the most prominent literary arbiters of the Left Bank openly admired Joyce's work. She could not ignore Joyce while she herself was being ignored.

"The publisher is not a soloist of spiritual exertion, but the conductor of the orchestra," said Thomas Mann in a 1940 tribute to his American publisher Alfred Knopf. Sylvia was both the conductor of the orchestra and its road manager and business manager. After conducting the author and his manuscript through levels of typists and printer's proofs, she took on more and more of the private business of the Joyce family—even mailing tips to his favorite waiters at the Trianon restaurant. Unlike Mr. Andrew Millar, the bookseller who conducted the publication of Samuel Johnson's monumental *Dictionary of the English Language,* Sylvia did not say, as Boswell reports Millar saying when the book was completed, "Thank God I have done with him." Her own work only increased after the publication of *Ulysses.* She handled all the press and fans who came to the shop. Unlike any other of Joyce's publishers, who were separated from him by miles of land and sea, Sylvia was completely caught up in the herculean task of publishing Joyce's work and managing his career. He gave her what he called "grocer's lists" of things to do. If you did anything for Joyce, she knew, you did everything. Joyce saw her less as the conductor of the orchestra than as the beast of burden. The book publisher, Janet Flanner notes of their relationship, is "literature's common carrier, like a donkey, with the authors and occasionally their weight of genius loaded on his back." Malcolm Cowley claims, "Joyce accepted favors and demanded services as if he were not a person but a sanctified cause. It was, he seemed to be saying, a privilege to devote one's life to the cause, and those who paid his debts for him were sure to be rewarded in heaven.

Miss Beach agreed with him." Joyce's biographer and friend Stuart Gilbert agrees: "For him Art was a jealous god, like the Jehovah of the Ten Commandments, and as her priest he, like Modigliani, demanded for himself special rights and privileges."

Myrsine kept pace with Sylvia in meeting the demands of the customers and Joyce. They continued to send Hélène, the youngest Moschos, on daily trips to the Joyce apartment. These were never enough, and Joyce came every day after twelve noon. The shop was officially closed from noon to two, but Americans, who were not accustomed to noon closings, often came by anyway. This crowd had usually thinned out by one o'clock, when Joyce arrived. He came in and sat next to Sylvia. Myrsine, when not at lunch, sat at the other table working with the lending-library books. Joyce liked to have the curtain open so that he could look out the back window at the concierge's son, Charles Tisserand, a cobbler, working in the courtyard. The scene looked like a Dutch painting, he asserted. Myrsine was devoted to Joyce and enjoyed the excitement of the bookshop during the years he frequented it. She also admired the stamina and maturity of Sylvia, who she thought was a year younger than she. Myrsine had heard '97 when Sylvia had said '87 and never questioned Sylvia's relative youth. Not until years later did she learn that Sylvia was not one year younger but nine years older than she.

What was Sylvia's financial profit for so great a task? Her poor and hurried bookkeeping frustrates the historian or accountant who would determine bookshop finances. Although the original agreement had been that 66 percent of the profits would go to Joyce, letters and ledgers suggest he received all the profits. When Quinn assumed that she was sharing equally in the profits, she informed him that after the printers were paid "Joyce will have the rest." More than thirty years later, she recorded that "whether anything was left in his account or not, we had to look after the author of *Ulysses*."

People imagined, perhaps, that I was making a lot of money from *Ulysses*. Well, Joyce must have kept a magnet in his pocket that attracted all the cash Joycewards. . . . I understood from the first that, working with or for James Joyce, the pleasure was mine . . . the profits were for him. All that was available from his work . . . was his. But it was all I could do to prevent my bookshop from getting sucked under.

Joyce disclosed to his brother Stanislaus that the "Paris edition brings me 82,000 [francs] net." The gross is not as easy to determine. But the practice was, according to an unpublished portion of her memoirs, that royalties were paid to Joyce long before an edition appeared and after the royalties were exhausted:

I don't know what happened to the income from Miss Weaver which I suppose he received regularly but it didn't seem to solve his problems, and I had to come continually to the rescue with my *Ulysses* Bank and even with the bookshop cash box. Except for the sums always set aside for the printers bills, everything coming in from *Ulysses* went Joyceward: how could so much money be advanced to the author without drawing on the publisher's royalties? Owing to this system, I never had to wonder how to invest all this fortune I was supposed to be making with Ulysses. After all, I had my bookshop: and if I had wanted to make money I wouldn't have chosen to make it out of anything that belonged to Joyce. My multiple services to Joyce were free, and I felt more than repaid by the fun I got out of knowing him and collaborating as you might say with him. Nothing could have been more interesting, nor have amused me more than having James Joyce coming in and out.

Her pay was the increase in business that came to the bookshop and the glamour that accrued from her association with a great author—she warmed herself at the fire she helped to light for him.

In April, Hemingway left for a month in Italy, reporting on the Conferenza Internazionale Economica di Genova for the *Toronto Star,* where he teamed up with his fellow journalists Bill Bird, George Slocombe, Lincoln Steffens, and George Seldes. The latter two taught Hemingway, who had been mailing in his stories, to use "cablese"—a reporter's shorthand to save money ("aswellas" became one word, for example). Rushing up to the tables where the men were drinking their chianti, Hemingway exclaimed, "It's wonderful! It's a new language. No fat, all bones and structure." Practicing his "new language," Hemingway sent no fewer than fifteen articles to the *Star* during the Genoa conference.

On quite a different linguistic frontier, Joyce had ceded all English rights for the publication of *Ulysses* to Miss Weaver, whom he planned to meet for the first time in London. But a sudden attack of iritis changed his plans. One day in May, George and Lucia Joyce rushed into the bookshop to find Sylvia. She must come quickly, they said; Babbo, as they called their father, must see her at once. She hurried with them to their hotel on the rue de l'Université and found Joyce suffering terribly, cold compresses on his eyes. He had had an attack of iritis in a restaurant, where the pain had begun suddenly, rather than by degrees, according to the usual course of the illness. A famous specialist had just insisted that he must be operated on at once, and an ambulance was about to pick him up. "That is why he sent for me in such haste," she recalls. "He was determined to prevent another operation like the one in Zurich, performed at the height of an attack. . . . I was to get ahold of my oculist [Dr. Louis] Borsch and bring him to the hotel before the other doctor whisked him off to the clinic." Because Dr. Borsch, who was an American, refused to go to the bedside of another physician's patient, Sylvia and Nora helped Joyce into the taxi. At the clinic, Dr. Borsch, whom Sylvia describes as being as fat as Santa Claus, confirmed the glaucoma. As Joyce had hoped, he recommended waiting until the attack had abated before operating. From that day on, Joyce had a new doctor, "and his fees amounted to so little that Joyce, showing me one of Dr. Borsch's bills, seemed to feel quite insulted that it was so small."

In the early drafts of her memoirs, Sylvia extensively records the medical problems of Joyce. Two sections of these appear, out of sequence, in her final version. The tone of her writing is sympathetic; she admires his great patience, particularly when leeches were applied to his eyes:

I arrived at the clinic one day at the moment when the leeches prescribed by the doctor were being applied. Once they could be persuaded to stick around the eye—not so easy—

they drew away the blood and relieved the congestion. The regular nurse was out, and a younger one was replacing her. She and Mrs. Joyce were trying to prevent these wriggling creatures from flopping on the floor instead of waiting their turn around the patient's eye. Uncomplaining, Joyce submitted to this unpleasant ordeal. The leeches reminded me of those that used to stick to our legs in the Russells' swimming pool in Princeton.

Whenever he was hospitalized or ill at home, Sylvia would bring his mail and read it to him. He loved to hear the news of activities at the bookshop. He was often bored and depressed by his long hours of rest and darkness. Her memoirs, written more than thirty years later, recall only that he spent these hours patiently, playing memory games.

"Will you please bring *The Lady of the Lake*," Joyce asked Sylvia on a similar occasion two years later. On her next visit she brought Scott's book.

"Open it," he said, "and read me a line."

She began: Harp of the North! that mouldering long hast hung . . .

And he continued:

> On the witch-elm that shades Saint Fillan's spring,
> And down the fitful breeze thy numbers flung,
> Till envious ivy did around thee cling . . .

For two pages, she claims, he recited the work without a mistake. From that moment, she was convinced that he had a library in his head. When he was sufficiently recovered, she brought a taxi to take the Joyces home. As she did for each doctor's visit, she paid for both the taxi and the doctor.

Though Joyce usually dictated letters and telegrams (concerning his health) to her for Harriet Weaver, on this occasion Sylvia herself wrote to Miss Weaver, who shared her concern that his career would be ended by blindness: "He gets very much depressed and bored lying in bed. . . . I think it is good for him to have something to think of that takes him out of himself however. The doctor says that his eyes are better." Each press clipping from Miss Weaver was taken to the patient's bed and read aloud. A diatribe by James Douglas in the *Sunday Express* particularly excited him, Sylvia reports, and proved a great distraction. Douglas, after comparing the bulk of *Ulysses* to the one-volume London telephone directory, labeled the book blasphemous: "the most infamously obscene book" in all of literature. Readers must choose between "the devil's disciples and the disciples of God" because Joyce "is a rebel against the morality of Europe." The most supportive review this June was an essay by Pound in the *Dial*. "All men should 'Unite to give praise to Ulysses'; those who will not, may content themselves with a place in the lower intellectual orders," announces Pound. He then makes reference to the "ninth rate coward" Shaw, who could not look its reality in the face. And "no one but a Presbyterian would contest the utility of the exactitude" in the hospital scene's focal analysis (of the Oxen of the Sun episode).

The two women corresponded often during the early summer. Miss Weaver was getting more and more entangled in Joyce's private problems. At Joyce's urging, and because she thought Miss Weaver was "Joyce's best friend" (in

fact, she was his greatest benefactor), Sylvia sent news of his personal needs—
for space (he required six rooms) and for a quiet home away from his noisy,
crowded hotel yet (at his insistence) near the Odéon quarter. On her own she
adds, confidentially, the need to find a trade for George so that he would no
longer be a burden on his father. She suggests that perhaps London is the place
for the Joyces to live.

Sylvia and Miss Weaver also collaborated on easing Joyce's professional
problems. Sylvia informed her that the French writers now "have the greatest
admiration" for him; that the first edition of 1,000 has sold out; and that Miss
Weaver should reject the persistent offers of Samuel Roth to print *Ulysses* in his
American magazine *Two Worlds*. They would all live to regret correspondence
with Roth, who insisted (much to their amusement) that he was going to print
the novel in a single issue! Now they were preoccupied with working out
arrangements for an English edition. Sylvia gave her suggestions for establishing
an agreement with Darantière. Both women also communicated their fear of
confiscation of the novel, especially after the attack by Douglas. By mid-July,
Sylvia was writing about the recovery of Joyce after two months of pain, including details about what he was eating and reading. Never having had to deal with
Joyce's personal affairs, Harriet Weaver was nonplussed. According to her biographers, this period "marks a turning point of profound significance in her relations with James Joyce." His visit in August would enlighten and disturb her
further.

During the summer, Sylvia was busy entertaining family and friends, finding
the Joyces a new apartment, and disposing of the first edition of *Ulysses*. All the
members of the Beach family were in Paris during part of 1922. Mrs. Beach had
spent the winter with Sylvia and Cyprian. Holly, who would end her work with
the Junior Red Cross in Florence in July and move to Pasadena, Califonia, entertained Mrs. Beach during the spring and summer. In early June, the Reverend
Beach, in his last year as pastor of the First Presbyterian Church of Princeton,
arrived in Paris to see some of his nomadic family.

In late July or early August, Marian Mason Peter, the friend with whom
Sylvia had lived in Florence during 1907 and 1908, visited with two of her three
daughters. Adrienne took their pictures in Sylvia's room. Although Sylvia and
Marian had chosen entirely different ways of life, they kept in touch with each
other for decades. When Carlotta Welles Briggs, another friend from her adolescence, asked Sylvia whether she ever regretted not having a family, she replied,
"Oh, but I have Adrienne." While Marian was in Paris, Sylvia requested that
she mail copies of *Ulysses* to Americans who had ordered them and paid for
them. Soon after Marian returned home, Sylvia sent, under Adrienne's name,
boxes of the novel to Lake Forest, Illinois. Instructions from Sylvia explained
that she feared that postal authorities would recognize the Shakespeare and Company label, and she asked that her friend distribute them by registered mail to
the enclosed list of subscribers. Marian Peter's husband, who was a lawyer,
refused to allow his wife to send the books through the mails. So on legal prin-
ciple, she sent them parcel post.

Between his trip to Italy, from which he returned in June, and an August vacation in the Black Forest, Ernest Hemingway spent a lot of time around the bookshop, which he used as his mailing address. He had had a poem published in the *Double Dealer* in July and was writing fiction. He was also studying the masters, those Shakespeare and Company volumes he took with him on all his trips: Turgenev, Tolstoy, Dostoevski, Conrad, Flaubert, James. His preference was for the Russians, particularly Turgenev; two of Turgenev's titles, *Fathers and Children* and *The Torrents of Spring,* he eventually took for titles of his own works. Russian writers were also very popular with other English and American authors. During the 1922 Dostoevski centenary, Gide gave a series of lectures on the writer who Hemingway said had the power, despite his inattention to style, to "make you feel so deeply." Hemingway borrowed many Dostoevski books, including, on two occasions, *The Gambler.* Though he did not borrow books of poetry—with the exception of Yeats's *Early Poems and Stories* and Sandburg's *Selected Poems*—he read the latest poetry in the little magazines on the bookshop tables. The influence of poetry, Sylvia observed, is evident in his titles:

As a bookseller and librarian, I paid more attention to titles perhaps than others who simply rush past the threshold of a book without ringing the bell. I think Hemingway's titles should be awarded first prize in any contest. Each of them is a poem, and their mysterious power over readers contributes to Hemingway's success. His titles have a life of their own, and they have enriched the American vocabulary.

In fact, Hemingway took some of his titles from poetry: *The Sun Also Rises* from Ecclesiastes, *For Whom the Bell Tolls* from a prose Meditation by John Donne, and *A Farewell to Arms* from George Peele's poem of the same title.

The yearly summer exodus from Paris brought no relief for the book business. Hemingway bought a three-month subscription to the lending library in August, borrowed an armload of books, and left for Germany. There is no evidence that Sylvia was able to get away for a vacation in August; but Myrsine visited London with a message for Harriet Weaver, probably concerning the plan for an English edition of *Ulysses.* During July, Adrienne had taken on the remaining copies of the Paris edition, raised the price, and given the proceeds of her sale to Joyce. In mid-August, while Miss Weaver prepared for a second printing, Joyce took his family to London, where he met his benefactor for the first time. His behavior had a disturbing impact on Miss Weaver, who was surprised and disappointed by his lavish living. Unlike her, he went everywhere by taxi. She watched him spend £200 in thirty-three days. She was caught up in the hourly needs of the family, particularly when Joyce suffered an attack of conjunctivitis and was advised to have another operation. Because she had long ago morally committed herself to this man's talent, and so could not resign her pledge, she hung on to the hat of her astonishment and disapprovingly went along for the ride, paying all expenses.

While Miss Weaver was coping with the Joyce whirlwind and collecting each review of the novel, Sylvia continued her smuggling activities. John Quinn informed her at the end of August that a shipment of art treasures, with fourteen copies of *Ulysses* sandwiched in the sealed cases, had arrived safely in New York. In Paris, John Rodker, working with Iris Barry, was employed by Miss Weaver to get 2,000 copies of the second edition. They worked out of La Librairie Six in the avenue de Lowendal, near the École Militaire. Much to Joyce's dismay, their hurry ruled out the possibility of making corrections in the text. This second printing would include a list of 200 errata. The announcement of the new printing, which declared it would be ready in mid-October, added, "The first edition, published in April [read February], is already exhausted." Sylvia was designated the Paris agent. Yet as the weeks passed, and as booksellers who still had copies of the first *Ulysses* complained about the "new" and cheaper (£2.2) edition soon to come on the market, she began to change her mind. Years later she would claim that the haste attending the second printing surprised her. Yet, when Harriet Weaver had written on 24 June 1922 requesting that plates be made from the type, Sylvia had agreed, knowing that the book belonged to Joyce and that the high profits being made by the scalpers should be going to the author. A fresh supply, she agreed, would put a stop to the speculation on the book.

On 12 October this second edition was delivered to John Rodker and Iris Barry, who claimed that they sold 800 copies to an English bookseller who cut the books, wrapped the sections, and shipped them to America on a merchant line. When the other packing cases arrived in London, Miss Weaver, fearing an official raid, divided the boxes between her office and home. Bookshops sold the book under the counter. Four days later, the edition was fully subscribed and Miss Weaver was running most of English publication. Joyce, who had stopped in Paris on his way from London to Nice for a vacation, talked of a third, fully corrected edition. Meanwhile, Dr. Borsch informed Joyce that his abscessed teeth must be repaired. Thinking that he would get the dental work done in Nice, he took his family for what proved a month of poor weather and ill health, all of which he documented in his letters to Miss Weaver, who sent his first royalty payment of £200. His full royalty payment for the second *Ulysses* was £1,636.

Sylvia, her full attention devoted to her bookshop, sold the second edition but sent all bookstore orders for *Ulysses* to Iris Barry. Because Miss Weaver handled all publishing business for Joyce—and because the Beach family had left Europe for the Los Angeles area, where Mrs. Beach found a shop in Pasadena for Holly and Cyprian—Sylvia was now free to concentrate on the physical improvement of her shop. She had racks built for the little magazines. Over a period of several months, she had the back room and the two storerooms above the shop repaired, painted and papered, and furnished. One of Sylvia's dreams was to open the two small rooms above the shop as a tearoom. Tearooms were not available in Paris, and Sylvia wanted to have a place where people could read magazines, talk, drink tea, and eat cakes and sandwiches. She considered putting in a charming spiral stairway leading from the shop to the rooms above, but the building codes for the premises, a French antiquity, prohibited it. She had to be content with serving tea from a pot heated on the downstairs stove.

After the New Year, when a toilet was installed adjoining the rooms above, she began renting them to some of the Americans—she called them pilgrims—who were coming in increasing numbers to Paris.

One of the first pilgrims was John Peale Bishop, a 1917 graduate of Princeton, who arrived in Paris late in the summer of 1922. In the conclusion of an article entitled "Princeton," published the preceding November in the *Smart Set*, he had declared,

If I had a son who was an ordinarily healthy, not too intelligent, youth I should certainly send him to Princeton. But if ever I find myself the father of an extraordinary youth I shall not send him to college at all. I shall lock him up in a library until he is old enough to go to Paris.

Bishop was an American son who knew what to do. Upon arriving in the city, he immediately visited Shakespeare and Company and Ezra Pound. When he asked Pound about American writers of talent in Paris, the poet's answer was a taxi ride to Hemingway's flat. Though they saw each other regularly until 1930, Hemingway did not take Bishop seriously; Bishop was, according to their mutual friend Allen Tate, too modest and noncompetitive.

Janet Flanner and Solita Solano, two pilgrims who would become permanent residents of Paris, arrived in September of 1922. They were both independent women, suffragettes of 1917, one year and five years younger than Sylvia, respectively. After a year of touring Europe and the Middle East for *National Geographic,* they came to Paris, according to Solano, "to learn all about art and write our first novels." They wrote their novels in the Hotel Napoleon Bonaparte, where they paid one dollar a day for their room. They eventually moved to larger quarters but did not leave Paris for nineteen years, when the war drove them back to America. Flanner's greatest fame would come from her essays for the *New Yorker,* which she began to contribute to the magazine in 1925 and which appeared regularly in it for more than forty years above her pen name, "Genêt."

They joined a growing number of women who lived in Paris, singly or in pairs, pursuing journalism, art, or publishing in the freedom of the City of Light. Although they were buddies of Hemingway, their closest associations were with other strong and talented women, such as Margaret Anderson, Nancy Cunard, and Djuna Barnes. Djuna, whom Sylvia thought charming, gifted, and "as Irish as Joyce," had already established a literary reputation with her recently published *A Book*. With Nancy Cunard, the British shipping heiress and poet, Flanner and Solano became a striking threesome, dressing in tailored and dramatic clothes. Solano, who had dark short hair and intense blue eyes, had been an actress, drama critic, and journalist and had published a number of short stories. Flanner had a prominent nose and a strong mouth and claimed that she was "going to look like Voltaire one day." They appear as the sisters Nip and Tuck in their friend Djuna Barnes's risqué *Ladies Almanack*. The freedom and independence of foreign women in Paris during the twenties is well known. Kathryn Hulme, who was to write *The Nun's Story,* describes her first encounter with Flanner, Solano, and Barnes; she found them "sitting in a row like three Fates" at the Café Flore one day, each wearing black tailored suits, white satin scarves, and white gloves and each having a martini in front of her on the marble-top table.

Hemingway perhaps first met Janet Flanner when he returned with malaria and lice from a month in Constantinople, where he had covered the war between Greece and Turkey. Flanner's beat was always Paris. Journalism allowed Hemingway to travel extensively in Europe. During his next trip, when Hadley was going to meet him and Lincoln Steffens in Lausanne, she lost nearly all of his writing, including the carbons. His apprentice work destroyed, he continued writing, living more and more the life of the artist in Paris. "He was beginning to feel like a veteran expatriate," writes his biographer Carlos Baker.

Also returning to the Left Bank and Shakespeare and Company was a group of peripatetic Americans, including Robert McAlmon, who spent part of this winter in Berlin. While the defeated Germans virtually starved, Americans could buy, if they wished, a generous fix of cocaine for ten cents and enough caviar, game, and wine for ten persons for $1.65. Though they profited by Germany's chaotic fiscal system, they were critical of life in Berlin, which looked to them like an ugly, stone-gray corpse. The city seemed to be peopled with war cripples, male prostitutes, and Nazi street bands. Among the Americans who soon returned from Berlin to the beauty of Paris and its latest fad—seances of psychoanalysis—were McAlmon, Josephson, Loeb, Cowley, Arthur Craven, Marsden Hartley, Isadora Duncan, Djuna Barnes, and Berenice Abbott.

Two important Englishmen came to Paris in 1922, but only the second stayed for any length of time to become involved in the literary life of Paris. The first was George Moore, a distinguished and opinionated seventy-year-old Irish novelist, whom Sylvia first noticed peering into the window at the bookshop. McAlmon was in the shop reading his mail and Sylvia was talking to Joyce when Moore arrived. She moved toward the visitor, protecting Joyce, who had just recovered from his eye operation. Moore introduced himself as a friend of Nancy Cunard and glanced in the direction of Joyce. He withdrew reluctantly (McAlmon claims he "bolted") and later sent a kind letter from London inquiring whether the gentleman in the shop had been Joyce. She was relieved that he did not hold the incident against her. Joyce also expressed regret to Sylvia that she had not introduced them, though in fact he had met Moore before. Because Moore had collaborated in planning the Irish National Theatre (Abbey Theatre), which Joyce had strongly opposed, they had never been friends. Moore privately called him a "nobody . . . from the docks." Until Moore's death, they maintained an exaggerated politeness in their relationship, for, in the opinion of McAlmon, they both were "masters at the art of *blague* and blarney and courteous formality in their old Irish manner."

The second Englishman was Ford Madox Ford, who arrived immediately before the death of Proust, who, a virtual recluse, was bringing to completion his great novel *À la Recherche du Temps Perdu* (*Remembrance of Things Past*).

Ford immediately elected himself the "representative of English letters" to attend the funeral. Ford (born Hueffer, not Ford), a friend and collaborator with Conrad and editor of the *English Review* (1908–1909), was a rotund man who wheezed when he made the slightest exertion. He either had asthma or had been gassed during the war (he preferred the latter version), and had written a number of books, including his best single novel, *The Good Soldier* (1915). Within a year, Ford (Fordie to his friends) would found the *transatlantic review,* one of the most important little magazines of Paris and the champion of the American midwestern writers.

Increasing literary, commercial, and social demands placed a strain on Sylvia. She was so busy that she wrote only two family letters this year. A 13 November letter to her mother gives an indication of the continual literary exchange she kept going, which included taking Larbaud out to dinner with Iris Tree, whom he had wanted to meet since he had translated one of her poems in the *Revue de France,* and meeting Lady Rothermere, Adrienne, Larbaud, and Fargue for lunch at Foyot's. Despite her devotion to Joyce and her respect for Miss Weaver, Sylvia was being pressured by bookshop proprietors who had not sold their copies of *Ulysses* when the new edition appeared. Sylvia responded with firmness to a long list of requests from Joyce, including his wish that she publish a third edition and contact fifteen critics to ask whether they had written anything about *Ulysses.* She was not interested in "hustling to boom the book," she informed him, and she was worried about the charge that the second edition imitated the first. Resentful of criticism, he ridiculed her in a letter to Miss Weaver, pretending that her concern was trivial. He said that he had hurried back to Paris from Nice after receiving an "unpleasant . . . very rude" letter from her, adding that "the Paris pot cannot be left for more than three weeks by me but it begins to boil over." He sent his seventeen-year-old son to three bookshops to check for any displeasure that they might have with Shakespeare and Company. George returned to say that he had found none. Joyce also wrote to Darantière about any lawsuit concerning a bogus first edition. Darantière assured him that Sylvia could not be liable to charges of fraud, because there was a difference in size and weight between the two editions and because Joyce had not repeated the offer of signed copies. Sylvia's warnings, whether from other booksellers, publishers, or Adrienne, were real, as were her fear and concern. He was accountable only to art, she to the marketplace as well. To some extent he was to blame, for he separated his friends and his business associations from each other. He had not kept her well informed. Thus, on his return to Paris, he met with her several times, for, as he assured Miss Weaver, he wished at all costs to avoid a rupture with "those who have befriended me in time of trouble." He wished also to keep his good name: "About a hundred influential people (French, American, and English) visit the two establishments of Miss Monnier and Miss Beach weekly and there is no reason why rumours to my discredit (undeserved) should be circulated even by implication." He concluded the letter with a poignant image of his appearance at each feast, hat in hand. The image must certainly have secured the sympathy of Miss Weaver:

Possibly the fault is partly mine. I, my eye, my needs and my troublesome book are always there. There is no feast or celebration or meeting of shareholders but at the fatal hour I appear at the door in dubious habiliments, with impedimenta of baggage, a mute expectant family, a patch over one eye howling dismally for aid.

Hurt feelings were calmed, but there would be later quarrels between Sylvia and Joyce.

At this same time, Joyce was quarreling with one of his intimate, longtime friends, Frank Budgen, whom he had first known in Zurich. This quarrel had an ugly side. In an attempt to retrieve a letter in which he had written some compromising confidences, Joyce invited Budgen to an evening's entertainment, requesting he bring the letter so that Joyce could see what he had written. Joyce ordered many rounds in what turned into a drinking bout. While depositing a drunken Budgen at his hotel, Joyce lifted his wallet, took the letter, put the bar bills in its place, and had the wallet returned by a messenger the next morning, claiming he had kept it as a safeguard. They were estranged for three years afterward.

During the last weeks of 1922 and early in 1923, there were two major confiscations of *Ulysses*. About 400 copies were intercepted in the United States. That is, they were accumulated and destroyed all together. Harriet Monroe, the editor of *Poetry* in Chicago, vented her frustration to Sylvia: "It is too absurd that *Ulysses* cannot circulate over here. I feel a bitter resentment over my inability to read it." When news of the destruction reached Joyce and Miss Weaver, she decided to reprint 500 copies in a third edition. They would then have to get the copies into the United States through Sylvia's "official smuggler." But on 22 December, before the third edition was ready, against their knowledge, a copy of the second edition of *Ulysses* was seized at Croydon Airport in London, sent through various British offices, and declared obscene, and all the English ports were notified to be on the lookout for the book. Unknowingly, Rodker mailed the 500 copies of the third edition in January. These were seized at Folkstone. Unwilling to face court prosecution, Miss Weaver did not claim the books, which were burned in the "King's Chimney," as the official incinerator was called.

Before the two major destructions of *Ulysses,* by American water and English fire, Sylvia had again contacted Barnet Braverman. He had been waiting for months, living in Detroit and working in Windsor, knowing that he had the perfect arrangement for the smuggling. She finally initiated the venture with a telegram inquiring whether he was still interested. His 22 August telegram reads, "Glad to receive books basis mentioned first cablegram." A letter of 6 September, which talks opaquely of "planning campaigns for diverse commodities," reveals his enjoyment of the clandestine nature of the adventure and his eagerness to circumvent the censorship impulses of what he called the "Methodist smut hounds."

Renting a single room in Windsor for $35 a month, Braverman explained to the landlord that he was in the publishing business. When the forty books arrived, his first anxiety was over the customs duty on them. Canadian customs duty required 25 percent on the selling price of foreign printed matter. Legally, he owed $300 for customs duty. He asked to see the customs inspector, and after considerable argument, filled with fear that there would be some recognition of this book banned in the United States, he persuaded the man that these forty books were cheap novels valued at no more than fifty cents each. He paid the $6.50—about sixteen cents each—and stored the copies in the rented room. With relief and excitement, he had passed the first hurdle, saving nearly $300. The next step involved the greatest risk, arrest. Although she had assured him that she would "pay all expenses involved in having the books brought into the United States," he knew she "wouldn't care to defray the cost of legal defense in case" he was caught smuggling.

One evening after work at the Curtis Company in Windsor, he stopped by the rented room and wrapped a copy of *Ulysses* to take with him on the ferry back to Detroit, where he lived in a studio apartment. It was only a ten-minute ride across the water, but it seemed like an eternity. His heart raced, and he felt the hair on the back of his neck stand up. Face to face with the U.S. customs officials, he passed his greatest test of courage. He unwrapped the package for inspection. No sign of recognition crossed the officer's face, for the distance between Detroit and the New York City censors was great. The man nodded, and Braverman retied the package.

With alternating waves of confidence and terror—mixed with a loathing of the drudgery of tying and untying—he repeated this series of actions thirty-nine more times during the coming weeks and months until the forty books were safely within the U.S. border before Christmas. "Brought last copy over today letter follows—B.B." Their last journey, to their subscribers, went smoothly. Ignoring her suggestion that the books be sent by registered mail, he sent them express in bundles of three or four—"c.o.d. to make sure that the express company would deliver them in order to get its money for shipping them." Registered mail, he believed, risked seizure and destruction. The largest order, for twenty-three, went to the Washington Square Book Shop. Other orders were destined for Sherwood Anderson and the publishers Knopf and Huebsch. With Braverman's service, yet another American helped to bring *Ulysses* to the American reading public.

"The books—all of them—have been in the hands of their subscribers for several weeks," he reported to Sylvia in mid-January 1923. The experience of getting the books into the United States "legally" was "quite hair-raising." He then gave her a list of his expenses:

First cablegram (from Windsor)	$ 5.40
2nd cablegram from Windsor	2.42
3rd cablegram from Detroit	2.52
Customs duty	6.50
Storage (room for one month)	35.00
Hauling books from customs	1.50
	$53.34

He suggested that she deduct the price of one copy of *Ulysses,* which "you say Mr. Joyce wants me to have," and asked for the name of "the Chicagoan who referred you to me." Because her letters to Braverman are not available to us, it is not known whether she ever gave him Hemingway's name.

Although the cost had been rather small—$1.33 per volume—the risk and personal difficulties for Braverman had been great. He waited patiently for two months for his expense check before writing a "reminder" of the bill and a postscript: "I *wonder* if you have comprehended the difficulties that were involved in the affair." She mailed the $53.34 check on 9 April with the pamphlet of press notices published by Harriet Weaver and with her gratitude. He responded,

You mustn't thank me. My small performance, dangerous as it was, simply enabled me to be of service to a fellow artist and his daring publisher. . . . And you, Miss Beach, merit a good measure of congratulation for your courage in publishing the book. However, I have been told by feminist friends that the woman could always be relied upon when her courage had to be put to any endurance tests.

He came to Paris in early December, on his way to Vienna to study stage direction, in order to get his copy of *Ulysses* signed by Joyce.

CHAPTER 7

"Plurabilities":
On New Compositions
1923

. . . for over twenty years, they never gave me time to meditate.
— Sylvia Beach

THE FAME OF Shakespeare and Company spread with the news of *Ulysses* and with the growing migration of Americans to Paris. "Paris No Place for a Minister's Daughter?" inquired the *Ogden Standard Examiner*—echoing the title of a popular song—in the Sunday edition of 7 January 1923. Its subtitle answered, "Nonsense! Just see what great things the pretty Beach sisters have accomplished there since they left their parson papa for the boulevards." There were accompanying pictures of Sylvia and Cyprian and superlatives concerning the beauty of the women, the "brilliance" of their careers, and the expense of *Ulysses*. The same article and layout appeared in other American newspapers, including the 11 March edition of the *Philadelphia Inquirer*. Cyprian's acting career was praised in these American newspapers that were read by ladies who still meant something else when they referred to a woman as an "actress." A more ironic note was struck by the article's reference to their "riding in luxury on the crest of a wave of fame and fortune." On the contrary, Cyprian's career had reached a dead end and Sylvia was having trouble with her bills. When Germany stopped paying reparations, France invaded the Ruhr valley, causing a sudden devaluation of the franc. Sylvia, "well nigh crushed" by quarterly publishers' bills from London, had to sell her books for less than she had paid for them. She hurried to exchange all her francs for pounds, but "the transfer cost dear." She complained in a letter to her father that if she had paid attention to the political situation that Hemingway was covering in Germany, she might have anticipated this crisis.

The year 1923, which was to bring Joyce the beginning of a new novel and Sylvia exciting new involvements in the music and publishing worlds, had begun with a gloom that matched this cold and damp Paris winter. Joyce sorted through twelve kilos of notes left from *Ulysses,* looking for material that might be adopted for a new work and dreading the beginning of a series of eye operations at the

American Hospital, where Dr. Borsch arranged his admittance as a "bogus American." Lincoln Steffens, who had tea with him, confided to a close friend that he was "an empty man" who talked "only of his ills." After seeing Joyce "mope silently at his restaurants" and Hemingway "forever playing [that] he was what he was writing," Steffens concluded that art is not a matter of morals or intellectual gifts but merely a matter of genius.

Joyce's American publisher had problems of her own. She and her sister Cyprian had quarreled. Perhaps their differences were aggravated by the failure of Cyprian's plans for a comeback in French films as well as by the growing reputation of Sylvia, the older sister. On 16 January 1923, Cyprian wrote to Sylvia and told her that she did not wish to see her again. She expressed her love, but added that when they were together she was "miserable." She left Paris this year, never to return. Thereafter, Sylvia would see her again only on the occasion of a six-week visit to Pasadena in 1936. Sylvia brooded over the quarrel during the late evenings, when she worked overtime in the bookshop— as she did habitually, for business was brisk, new members joined each week, and she had no assistance from Myrsine Moschos, who had been ill for several weeks.

In January, Sylvia attended a dinner at the Joyces' for the Odéon inner cir- cle—Beach, Monnier, Larbaud, and Fargue. Facing his ominous eye operations, he wished (he claimed) to "see" his friends for a last supper before surgery. Afterward, however, he postponed the operation. Though he was almost blind in one eye, his health improved. He enjoyed his daily visits to Shakespeare and Company, where he read portions of *Ulysses* to Sylvia. Dr. Borsch agreed to postponements but treated Joyce's eyes; this improved his vision. The operations were not performed until April.

The first-anniversary party for *Ulysses,* on Joyce's forty-first birthday, was hardly the Rabelaisian revel that the reputation of his book then suggested. His celebrity as the author of a dirty book and all the stories of Parisian revelry and debauchery notwithstanding, Joyce was a middle-class family man. The Joyce parties were very respectable, even dull. Although reminiscences of his singing Irish ballads at the piano or reading from *Ulysses* add glamour to the memory, the double-birthday parties held annually for Joyce and *Ulysses* were usually quiet and often formal affairs. Family members, Irish acquaintances, and literary friends gathered in a local restaurant or at the Joyce flat. According to a pattern that was followed for ten years, Sylvia received a bouquet of flowers on the morning of 2 February 1923. The bookshop window during that week displayed numerous copies of *Ulysses*. It fell on a cold, damp, and bleak February day, but this first anniversary was warmed by a generous supply of food, wine, and music. "Himself sang us a lot of Irish songs accompanied on the piano by him- self," she informs her father. "We drank to the health of Joyce (some nice champagne) and they drank to mine."

Although troubles with the seizures of the second and third printings of *Ulys- ses* had delayed distribution, the critical verdicts continued to arrive at the rue de l'Odéon. Most were strongly expressed. The *Sporting Times* fired a second volley and announced that the latest printing could be bought for ten shillings. "Several readers of the admirable paper," announced Joyce to Harriet Weaver ironically, "sent [Sylvia] treasury notes." Joyce sent his thanks to Stephen Gwynn for a favorable review in the *Manchester Guardian* and encouraged, actually badgered, Sylvia to arrange reviews in other English and French periodicals. "When I have got one review into *La Revue de France* I shall cease—to the relief of my Paris admirers." Sylvia was also expected to thank reviewers, in Joyce's name, as she had thanked Edmund Wilson for his essay in the *New Republic* (5 July 22). A delighted Wilson informed John Peale Bishop that the message from Joyce made Gilbert Seldes (editor of the *Dial*) "green with envy." Only Joyce exceeded Sylvia as his best literary agent and promoter.

"Yesterday I wrote two pages," announced Joyce to Harriet Weaver on 11 March, "the first I have written since the final *Yes* of *Ulysses*. Having found a pen, with some difficulty I copied them out in a large handwriting on a double sheet of foolscap so that I could read them. *Il lupo perde il pelo ma non il vizio,* the Italians say. The wolf may lose his skin but not his vice or the leopard cannot change his spots." He would continue to work on this "history of the world," as he called it, for the next sixteen years, struggling continually against his growing blindness. Later that year, when the first fragment of this new project was published, Ford Madox Ford gave it the title "Work in Progress." Sixteen years later it would be published as *Finnegans Wake,* a title he kept a closely guarded secret for years. He conceived of the situation of the book as a dream, the dream of his protagonist who was dying near the river Liffey, which flows through Dublin carrying the flotsam of life in its currents. The dying man watches the history of Ireland, indeed of the world, flow past. During 1923, Joyce talked often to his friends of dreams and their meaning.

For Joyce, April was a cruel month of dental operations for ten extractions, seven abscesses, and a cyst. Dr. Borsch hoped that the removal of the decay would relieve his eye disease as well as his arthritic symptoms. He underwent three operations on his eyes. To release tension in the muscle surrounding the left eyelid, Dr. Borsch cut the sphincter muscle. Miss Weaver continued to send him royalty checks as well as extra money. It was this series of operations that prompted her to initiate plans to settle a yearly income on Joyce. The pain and boredom of recovery lasted two months and was relieved only when Sylvia brought to his bedside flowers and T. S. Eliot's review of *Ulysses* in the London *Times Literary Supplement.* A year earlier, in response to Joyce's charges that literary critics were conspiring against him, Eliot had declared himself "distressed and indignant" and determined to do what he could to assist him. The poet's praise in the *Times,* though mixed with reservations, pleased Joyce. The flowers were from a group of American admirers. According to Sylvia, "Gilbert Seldes of the *Dial* joined with some other admirers of Joyce and brought me in a sum of money to be extended in a floral offering to be sent to him at the hospital. I ordered a truly magnificent basket of roses and tulips, just like those given to a debutante for her coming-out ball and it seems to have been a great success.''

April ended with Joyce's release from the hospital and the arrival of a few days of hot sun. ''The sun was out so badly this morning,'' Sylvia announces to her father, ''that I had to roll down the awning of my shop.'' This resumption of her correspondence with her father, after a busy year with little family communication, was precipitated by the announcement of his retirement from the First Presbyterian Church of Princeton. As he would be seventy-one on 24 June, his wife and daughters were relieved that he would be done with the preaching of two sermons a week and tending to the demands of a large congregation. ''Father dear, I was reading the description of the Parson in Chaucer's *Canterbury Tales,* the Prologue, and I thought it fitted you exactly. Do you remember it?''

> Wid was his parissh, and houses fer asonder
> But he ne lafte nought for rain ne thonder,
> In sikness nor in meschief, to visite
> The ferreste in his parissh, muche and lite,
> Upon his feet, and in his hand a staf.

Soon after her husband's retirement, Eleanor Beach, always preferring to live abroad, sailed for Naples with her friend Lucy Henry. She was able to finance this trip because Sylvia had begun sending her the monthly check of $50 from Cousin Mary Morris, believing that ''poor little mother'' needed it more than she did. During her mother's sojourn in Italy, Sylvia operated the shop without help while Myrsine spent several months in Spain recovering her health and strength. Then she hired a young, inexperienced Irish woman named Miss Footner. ''The manager from Brentano's told me they were not taking in much there in spite of the crowds of tourists that are pouring in to Paris,'' Sylvia informs her father. ''I made more this month than last however and my business maintains itself at least.''

Hemingway and McAlmon fled cold and rainy Paris for the bullfights in Spain, while Joyce, after a long period of recovery, made plans to take Nora and Lucia to England for the summer. Two days before they left, the Joyces—he wearing a black eye patch—dined with Adrienne and Sylvia at the home of the English journalist Sisley Huddleston. Both Joyce and Sylvia noted the timing of the Joyce family departure: ''Bloomsday,'' as Sylvia had coined it, the 16 June date on which the events of *Ulysses* take place. They went first to London and stayed at the Belgrave Hotel. Then after a visit with Harriet Weaver, whose funds supported the vacation, they and Kathleen Barnacle, Nora's sister, went on to Bognor, on the south coast of England. Sylvia, who notes that ''the places where Joyce and his family spent their summers . . . were related to the work he was engaged on,'' supposed that he had gone off to Bognor to interview the legendary giant (Harriet Weaver had told him about a ''Giant's Grave'' in Cornwall), giants being a theme of his work. Two years later he involved Sylvia in the pursuit of another theme:

During the summer of 1925 he was plunging into rivers. I got a postcard from Bordeaux: "Garonne, Garonne!" But heaven knows how many rivers Joyce was acquainted with personally. He was in love with the Seine, his "Anna Sequana," I know. I remember that Adrienne and I took him in our Citroën to a spot he wanted to visit up the Seine, where some waterworks was situated. . . . He sat on the bank, once he had inspected the waterworks, and gazed intently at the river and all the different objects floating in it.

George, who had remained in Paris, had promised that he and Sylvia would find a suitable flat for the family. Within a month he had paid Sylvia's landlady 100 francs to hold an apartment in her own building. The Joyces, however, soon rejected the apartment, deciding that it was not large enough for their needs, and thanked Sylvia and Adrienne for their fruitless trouble. The transaction had been awkward and embarrassing for Sylvia. She had done her best, but it had not been good enough.

During a very cold June, the little Irish assistant, Miss Footner, daily stoked the fire in the bookshop's heater. Despite the tedious weather, new and old friends enlivened the shop and gladdened its proprietress. One new friend was the American musician George Antheil, who arrived in Paris just days before Joyce's departure. Within months, his musical creations and personal antics would change the bookshop atmosphere and sweep Sylvia and Pound, and to a lesser extent Joyce, into the vortex of the Paris musical world. Old friends included Marian Cleveland, who visited on her way to spend a summer in Saint-Gervais-les-Bains. Marian, a friend from Sylvia's Princeton days and the twenty-eight-year-old daughter of the former president, and her husband, Stanley Dell, were "very anxious to meet Jules Romains." Sylvia and Adrienne therefore invited them to Sunday dinner with the French writer and his wife and two other Americans: Gertrude Schirmer Fay, a friend of Marian, and Regis Michaud, an American scholar and admirer of Romains who had been giving lectures and writing reviews about the Frenchman's work.

In this same month of June, Sylvia was warmed by a tribute from Adrienne in the form of a poem in honor of their friendship. The poem appeared in *La Figure,* a collection consisting of similar poems that Adrienne had written for her sister, Marie, and other friends as well as for Sylvia—among them Joyce, Romains, Fargue, Valéry, Gide, Larbaud, Benoist-Méchin, and Claudel. All but Sylvia and Joyce were French. She calls Sylvia "my sister born beyond the sea!" and celebrates the destiny of their meeting: "Behold my star has found your own."

During the time that Hemingway spent in Paris, between assignments for the *Toronto Star* and skiing and bullfight vacations, he included Shakespeare and Company on his daily rounds. Mornings he wrote and afternoons he often prowled the city, walking along the quays and watching the men fishing from the embankments with long poles. Some late mornings he would hang around the table of reviews, glancing through *Broom, Gargoyle, Manikin,* and the *Dial.* He was particularly interested in McAlmon's *Contact* and Eliot's *Criterion* and in the spring, "Exiles" number of the *Little Review,* which carried six short sketches

of his own. The best little exile reviews, the reviews that would print the stories
he was writing, did not yet exist. But two important publishing companies were
making plans to print new works, and he was a good friend of their owners, Bob
McAlmon of the Contact Publishing Company and William Bird of the Three
Mountains Press. McAlmon would soon publish Hemingway's *Three Stories and
Ten Poems,* and the following year Bird would publish *In Our Time* (without
capitalization in the title). The three men not only met at the bookshop—No. 12
would be McAlmon's Contact address—but also traveled and caroused together,
with McAlmon paying most of the bills. They ran with the bulls at Pamplona
and in Paris drank together at the Dingo. Hemingway's favorite drinking place,
at the time a private one, was the Closerie des Lilas. "In those days the Closerie
des Lilas was only a café and in the mornings very few people went there,"
remembers Morrill ("Wild Bill") Cody. "The management did not mind that
Hemingway stayed over one café-crème all morning and wrote in a copy book.
He always sat in a big window at the far end of the main room. It had a fine
north light and it looked out on the lovely Avenue de l'Observatoire and the
Luxembourg Garden in the distance. I saw him there many times but never
interrupted him as he says Ford [Madox Ford] did on occasion." The Closerie,
which is located at the corner of the boulevard du Montparnasse and the boulevard Saint-Michel—his clean, well-lighted café—had been a gathering place of
writers and artists: Baudelaire, Manet, Cézanne, Degas, Rodin, Strindberg,
Gauguin, and Whistler. Leaving this spiritual company, Hemingway would walk
across the garden to the rue de l'Odéon, where he was always welcomed by
Sylvia and where he met those who were beginning to accept him into the contemporary literary circles. Thirty years later, in *A Moveable Feast,* where he
romanticizes his poverty, he records what he remembers as a typical conversation with Sylvia:

> "You're too thin, Hemingway," Sylvia would say. "Are you eating enough?"
> "Sure."
> "What did you eat for lunch?"
> My stomach would turn over and I would say, "I'm going home for lunch now."
> "At three o'clock?"
> "I didn't know it was that late."
> "Adrienne said the other night she wanted to have you and Hadley for dinner. We'd
> ask Fargue. You like Fargue, don't you? Or Larbaud. You like him. I know you like him.
> Or anyone you really like. Will you speak to Hadley?"
> "I know she'd love to come."
> "I'll send her a *pneu.* Don't you work so hard now that you don't eat properly."

Hadley, however, remembers that they dined with Adrienne and Sylvia only
once, at a large dinner party in their apartment. Though neither of the Hemingways spoke more than passable French, they got along amiably.

    On one of these days nearly a year later, after admitting his hunger to Sylvia,
who encouraged him to get a good meal, Hemingway walked to the Brasserie
Lipp and ordered potato salad, sausage, and beer. He remembers then heading
back via the rue de Rennes, cutting through the rue d'Assas and the rue Notre-

Dame-des-Champs to the Closerie des Lilas, where, sitting in a corner with the afternoon light over his shoulder, and a half-drunk café-crème beside him, he began writing "The Big Two-Hearted River," a short story set in Michigan. "When I stopped writing I did not want to leave the river where I could see the trout in the pool, its surface pushing and swelling smooth against the resistance of the log-driven piles of the bridge. The story was about coming back from the war but there was no mention of the war in it."

Joyce, who had little in common with this young, athletic American journalist, continued writing his new work during his vacation in southern England. He kept in careful contact with Harriet Weaver, who informed him, during the second week of July, that she was giving him more of her inheritance money. A jubilant Joyce, burdened with heavy medical expenses, a family, and a taste for the comfortable life—Sylvia called it living "on the Joycean scale"—informed Sylvia, "You will be glad to hear that Miss Weaver made me a couple of days ago the very great gift of another £12,000. . . ." That was 936,000 francs ($4,376), he added. Nearly thirty years later, in response to a remark of Sylvia's that she had given her fortune to James Joyce, Harriet Weaver replied,

I gave in 1923 a bequest from an aunt of mine which I did not need. I told Mr Joyce the amount of the income that might be expected and it seems (I did not know this till years later) that he immediately sat down with a pencil in hand and attempted a mathematical calculation as to the amount of capital that would be represented—magnifying this enormously—and publishing the result to friends.

If Miss Weaver's generosity had been tempered by the decision to award the money in yearly installments, an extravagant Joyce would have had long-term benefits. Sylvia, though worried about the effects of this sudden financial windfall, was greatly relieved.

For a while Sylvia and Adrienne spent much time with the Hemingways. Ernest wanted to teach his vigorous American friend the joys of boxing, cycling, and bullfighting. He was very active, though Sylvia noted that he never gave the impression of being hurried, and "most people seemed very vague beside him." He gave his full attention to the moment. He attended every new exhibit of painting; skied in the winter and attended bullfights in the summer; watched horse races at Auteuil, Longchamp, Chantilly, and Bagatelle; and boxed with anyone who would put on gloves. When no one else was available, he put the gloves on Hadley. He rode a bike around Paris and studied for a taxi-license exam, which he failed. Sylvia kept the picture of him in the taxi cap, looking like a chauffeur.

Hadley was heavily pregnant when she and Ernest called at the rue de l'Odéon. The four of them headed by metro for the Pelleport Club to witness boxing. Hadley, ever the good sport, breathlessly climbed the subway stairs and the hill to Ménilmontant, a tough working-class quarter. She did not want the baby to miss a good fight, joked Hadley, who knew the rules of the game. During the early matches, Hemingway explained boxing to Adrienne and Sylvia and identified the characters strolling in and out as managers. Sylvia was later to compare

Adrienne and herself to those "bleary persons hanging around Pelleport Ring on the lookout for talent." Ernest was soon distracted from his teaching by the heavy slugging of a Belgian and a Frenchman. When the women commented on the bloody battle, he explained that it was "only their noses." The last fight was clean but miscalled, according to the crowd, who whistled loudly (the French equivalent of booing). They hustled Hadley out before they were "hemmed in," as Sylvia phrases it. "That was a real Western!" she declared when they were safe.

There was less excitement for the women when he took them later to the six-day cycling at the Vél d'Hiver. Sylvia later describes "the little monkey-men, hunched over on their bikes, slowly circling the ring," which she calls a "merry-go-round." In her memoirs she calls these cycling and boxing lessons "engrossing," but she was secretly bored and confided to a friend that she never learned much. Yet she loved Hemingway's enthusiasm, and she believed he had so much talent that she willingly endured the sports lessons. He had "the true writer's temperament," observed Adrienne, his first French admirer. Bryher recalls Adrienne quietly predicting that "Hemingway will be the best known of you all. He cares for his craft." That summer, when Hemingway was preparing his three stories for McAlmon's Contact Publishing Company, he invited Sylvia and Adrienne to hear him read. "Maybe we didn't know much about boxing, but when it came to writing—that was another thing. Imagine our joy over this first bout of Ernest Hemingway's! . . . We were impressed by his originality, his very personal style, his skillful workmanship, his tidiness, his storyteller's gift and sense of the dramatic, his power to create. . . ."

Another young American had been taken into the rue de l'Odéon circle. "I have found a new lodger for my third room above the shop," Sylvia announces to her father. "A young composer [and pianist] from Trenton. How lucky I am to have these rooms to help me balance the budget!" Following a successful piano concert tour in Germany, George Antheil had arrived in Paris on 13 June 1923 with Boski (Elizabeth Markus, niece of the Austrian playwright Arthur Schnitzler), his Hungarian companion and later his wife. The twenty-three-year-old musician was leaving his career as a piano performer, he asserted, to devote himself to composing. Having rejected Strauss, Debussy, and Ravel, Antheil had come under the influence of the unsentimental brilliance of Igor Stravinsky, the revolutionizer of modern music, who had befriended him in Berlin and urged him to go to Paris. Antheil found the French city to be a "green tender morning" compared with the "black night" of the German capital. Here, he was to pioneer his nonmusical sounds.

Paris had emerged as the center for musical innovation by the time Stravinsky's compositions were given their premieres there. His *Sacre du Printemps* (1913) shocked its first audiences with its strange and primitive sounds. Brought to the city by Sergei Diaghilev, of the Ballet Russe, Stravinsky became the company's principal composer. For his spectacular productions, Diaghilev brought together many artists, with results that were often wild and dramatic. He occasionally combined dancing with music, painting, and writing—once Picasso designed the costumes, Stravinsky and Erik Satie composed the music, and Apollinaire wrote the program. Apollinaire coined the word *sur-realism* in his program notes for the revolutionary *Parade* in 1917—a ballet that combined the talents of Picasso, Satie, and Cocteau, and used sirens, typewriter, and airplane propellers to imitate the sounds of modern life. The friendships made in both the bookshops stimulated this cooperation of the arts.

Most of the regular customers of the bookshop were writers, but among them were four composers: Satie, Antheil, Virgil Thomson, and Aaron Copland. Satie, although unable to read Sylvia's books, because he did not know English, was a regular visitor; Antheil and Thomson were both readers. Sylvia claims wryly that "George was well read: that is, he had read all the Horatio Alger books which I was ashamed to admit I had never heard of: but after Horatio Alger he thought nothing came up to *Ulysses.*" Copland, who had joined the lending library in April, had time to read her books in spite of being worked "terribly hard" by Nadia Boulanger, the great French teacher of musical composition to more than a generation of American composers. Sylvia was fond of Copland, his friend Harold Clurman, and Stephen Tuttle. Several year later Tuttle composed a song for her birthday, and he and her assistant sang it. Although other musicians, such as George Gershwin, visited the shop and briefly had subscriptions, they were not regulars among the serious artistic crowd there, nor did they stay in Paris long. Antheil, Thomson, and Satie, on the other hand, collaborated with writers in a creative mix of art forms.

Sylvia first met Erik Satie at a musical program at Adrienne's bookshop. Satie was one of the close group around Adrienne, and a particular friend of Léon-Paul Fargue, some of whose poetry he set to music. Adrienne claims Satie "was to Fargue, if you please, what the Panchen Lama is to the Dalai Lama." Sylvia in her memoirs describes the tragicomic rift in their friendship after an announcer failed to mention that the texts of songs being performed at a concert by Satie had been written by Fargue. Satie was the father figure for The Six: Louis Durey, Darius Milhaud, Georges Auric, Francis Poulenc, Germaine Tailleferre, and Arthur Honegger. Sylvia was particularly fond of the composer's wife, Madeleine Milhaud, a regular patron. Poulenc and Satie were friends of Raymonde Linossier and other patrons of the two bookshops. Satie, whom Debussy had called "a fine medieval musician who had wandered into this century," was becoming a major influence on modern music. In 1940 Virgil Thomson declared that his "musical aesthetic is the only aesthetic in the Western World"—placing him above Stravinsky. Though he had a reputation as a woman hater, he was apparently cordial to Sylvia and Adrienne. "Satie," according to Sylvia, "perhaps because of English blood on one side of his family, seemed to like Shakespeare and Company. He called me 'Mees,' the only English word he knew, I imagine, and turned up regularly, always carrying an umbrella, rain or shine; no one had ever seen him without one."

Because of Stravinsky, Ravel, Schönberg, Strauss, Satie, and the music school of Nadia Boulanger, young American composers went to Europe, particularly Paris, to complete their professional education. In America, musical training was predominantly Germanic and old-fashioned, but in Paris, according to Copland, Boulanger knew "pre-Bach to post-Stravinsky . . . cold."

If Stravinsky had drawn George Antheil to Paris, the bookshop enabled him to stay. He was immediately adopted and cared for by Sylvia and McAlmon, whose Contact Publishing Company books were now being sold at the bookshop. McAlmon got money from Bryher (£100) and her mother, Lady Ellerman (£50), banked it, and asked Sylvia to distribute it to Antheil. Some of his hungrier friends regretted that "not everyone can fall into a bookshop." But Antheil was a slight and boyish-looking young man who had great personal charm and elicited sympathy. In a letter written thirty-five years later, Sylvia describes him as a "fellow with bangs, a squashed nose and a big mouth with a grin in it. A regular American high school boy but Polish looking too." She felt a special bond with Antheil because he was also from New Jersey. Her family, she discovered, had shopped at the Friendly Shoestore, in Trenton, owned by Antheil's father. Antheil lived with Boski in one of the mezzanine rooms above the bookshop. Though the room looked "impossibly small" and though Sylvia doubted that she could allow a piano, he "thought quickly," he remembers, and "decided that I could compose without a piano. To have Sylvia Beach, American ex-ambulance driver [sic] and publisher of James Joyce's Ulysses, as a landlady seemed so enormously attractive that I immediately stated I was willing to forego the other." The room, he claims, in his 1945 autobiography, "has been more 'home' to me than any other place I have ever lived in."

Whenever he forgot his key, George used the Shakespeare sign to hoist himself to his balcony window, much to the amusement of the neighbors. If someone came into the shop inquiring for him (Bravig Imbs says he had a steady stream of callers), Sylvia would step out of the front door of the shop and call his name. In this room, for which he paid Sylvia 300 francs ($17) a month, he composed his Quintet, his two violin sonatas for Olga Rudge, his Ballet Mécanique, his First String Quartet, his Second Symphony, and a number of smaller pieces. Occasionally, until the concierge finally allowed him to have a piano in his own place, he made use of the piano in Adrienne's apartment. Sylvia claims that the neighbors were made aware that the piano is a percussion instrument when George "pounded" it.

Sylvia introduced Antheil to Joyce, Pound, and Hemingway. Joyce had just returned from his summer in England and had moved into the Victoria Palace Hotel. The money from Harriet Weaver allowed such fine lodging and the time to hunt for a suitable apartment. Within a year Joyce and Antheil would be talking of collaborating on an opera. Pound, who was advising Hemingway on the simple sentence and occasionally boxing with him, was taken with Antheil's spirit and music. Antheil would soon become Pound's newest cause. Hemingway and Antheil met in the bookshop not long before Hemingway (who borrowed $100 from Sylvia) returned with Hadley to Toronto for the birth of their baby and a full-time job with the Star. By October, Hemingway had returned the money to Sylvia and was writing letters full of nostalgia for Paris.

Antheil's presence attracted two other young American composers to the bookshop for frequent visits: Bravig Imbs and Virgil Thomson. Of Norwegian stock, Imbs was a Dartmouth student who had plans to become an artist of some kind. He had not yet decided whether he would be a musician, actor, sculptor, or writer when he shyly entered the bookshop, which he refers to in his *Confessions of Another Young Man* as the "holy of Holies." Seeing two women at a desk—one woman young and beautifully dressed, the other with "brown bobbed hair, beginning to grey, nervous brown eyes and a modest retiring manner"— he addressed the wrong woman with his request for a thousand sheets of yellow paper, to launch his writing career. Told curtly by the younger woman that the shop did not sell stationery, he was impressed with the friendliness of "the assistant" who listened sympathetically as he explained his plans to be a writer. Imbs's description of the experience reveals the way in which many young people invested Paris and the activities of the bookshop with a romantic aura:

What a sympathetic listener this nice assistant was, I thought to myself, when a young man in a bright yellow shirt and flannel slacks popped in at the door and shouted, "Good morning, Sylvia!" It was then I realized the mistake I had made and that the person who had been so obliging was none other than the famous Sylvia Beach herself.

"Good afternoon, George," she said laughing, extending her tiny delicate hand. "Have you been sleeping again?"

"No, composing," he answered gaily. "Don't tell me it's three o'clock!" he exclaimed, glancing at the clock, "I haven't had lunch yet."

When Sylvia scolds him for missing his meals, he pleads, "Don't be cross, I'll dedicate my new piece to you." The young Imbs was delighted by this exchange, believing that "it was what I expected was happening in Paris all the time—if only one were within the magic circle." Sylvia turned and introduced Antheil to Imbs, who soon became his disciple, abandoning writing for a music career. While working as a copy editor on the Paris edition of the *Chicago Tribune,* he assisted Antheil by playing at his concerts. In fact, he eventually did pursue a writing career, publishing poetry in *transition* magazine, a novel called *The Professor's Wife,* and a biography of Chatterton. In the United States, he lectured on Gertrude Stein.

Virgil Thomson—who had first come to Paris in 1921 with the Harvard Glee Club and had stayed on for a year after the engagement ended—was one of the first American composers to study with Nadia Boulanger. When he returned to Paris in 1925, after having finished a degree at Harvard and having taught in New York, he became a very good friend of Antheil, visiting him in the apartment above the bookshop. Sylvia and Adrienne made quite an impression on the younger Thomson, from Kansas City—who claims to have become Parisian "instantaneously." Later, he described Sylvia as an "angular . . . Alice in Wonderland at forty," and Adrienne as "a French milkmaid from the eighteenth century." It was at the bookshop that Thomson met Joyce and other writers. Because he was too poor to buy a subscription, Sylvia waived her fee, to enable him to borrow the books he wanted. He hardly supported himself with his music criticism, although by 1935 he was much in demand in the United States for collaborating on productions that combined writing, music, and painting.

One day when Thomson, who had a brilliant, if not brittle wit, came by to find Antheil, he stopped in the bookshop and inquired for him. Finding only Myrsine there, he left a message. With her Greek accent, Myrsine reported to Sylvia that "Virgin" Thomson had come for George. Sylvia laughed heartily and continued the slip-of-the-tongue title for many years afterward. Thomson would have enjoyed the joke.

On a slip of paper in her Papers, Sylvia lists her musical customers: Antheil, Gershwin, Copland, Varèse, Satie, Poulenc, and Milhaud (she forgot Thomson). She does not include Jacques Benoist-Méchin, because he, like Imbs, abandoned music. But in 1923, Benoist-Méchin was still at the Schola Cantorum, which he had been attending when he served briefly as Joyce's translator of *Ulysses* in 1921. Thus Sylvia introduced the music student to Antheil, and they became good friends. For Antheil's famous performance of the *Ballet Mécanique* several years later, Benoist-Méchin made the introduction of Antheil and operated the central player piano.

When Myrsine returned to work at the bookshop at the beginning of September, Sylvia was able to get away for a short vacation in Les Déserts, in Savoy. She returned in October to an exciting flurry of fall musical and literary activities and to the arrival of new friends. On 11 October, Archibald MacLeish, a young American with a law degree and promise as a poet, joined the library and was checking out the fourth volume of Chaucer and *Mont-Saint-Michel and Chartres*, by Henry Adams, when a cable from Hemingway arrived for Sylvia, announcing the birth of a baby boy. In a letter that followed several weeks later, Hemingway said that "if the baby had been a girl we would have named her Sylvia. Being a boy we could not call him Shakespeare." They settled on John Hadley Nicanor, the final name from Nicanor Villalta, the bullfighter.

John Quinn, the New York lawyer and collector of art and literary manuscripts, also returned to Paris in October. He spent three weeks in a flurry of meetings taking depositions for a legal case and conferring with his literary and art-collecting acquaintances. For the second and last time, he visited Sylvia as well as Pound. He also had a strained meeting with Joyce. Terminally ill with cancer (he would die during the coming July), he informed Joyce of his intention to sell the *Ulysses* manuscript, which he thought would go for about $2,000 (it sold, in fact, for only $25 less). Joyce was unhappy at the price. Quinn's meeting with Ford Madox Ford was happier.

Ford was fast becoming one of the most colorful figures of the Left Bank. He was fifty years old and a prolific writer, just finishing his work on *Some Do Not*, the first novel of the Tietjens tetralogy. He was stimulated by the Paris scene and talked of editing a review in the manner of his successful *English Review*, in which he had published work by his friends Hardy, James, Galsworthy, Wells, and Lawrence—the last for the first time.

Much like Pound and Beach, Ford was a magnetic figure around whom people gathered, and like them he was devoted to the cause of literature and the well-being of those who practiced it. One immediately took notice of Ford because of his unusual appearance. His friends often described him as looking like a walrus. He was bulky and bulbous, with a bushy flaxen-colored mustache, a flushed complexion, and multiple chins. Huddleston says that his eyes were the color of forget-me-nots and that his mouth hung half open like a fly trap. He talked endlessly in a rasping voice, sitting on the very edge of a chair at the Deux Magots or the Dôme, gasping and emptying one tall glass after another.

Ford and his wife enjoyed giving parties, and one of their first was for the rue de l'Odéon crowd. They consumed wine and cheese and danced to accordion music. "Ford invited me to dance with him," recalls Sylvia, "first making me take off my shoes—he was already in his bare feet. With Ford, it was more bouncing and prancing than dancing. I saw Joyce watching us from the sidelines with great amusement." Huddleston vividly describes the contrast between the enthusiastic but awkward dancing of Ford and the nimble, smooth dancing of Pound, who during the Charleston closed his eyes and let his feet fly.

Ford explains in his autobiographical *It Was the Nightingale* that he had long kept up with the literary activities of Paris by means of his correspondence with Pound. He was thus ready to move into the various activities with his usual enthusiasm and assertiveness. He had already judged the merits of the French verse of Fort, Spire, Claudel, and Valéry and was curiously amused by the quarrels about the Dada movement, which were still going strong. He soon met Philippe Soupault and Dada's founder, Tristan Tzara, who was a patron of the bookshop. Pound and Sylvia introduced Ford to many artists. "I had my view of foreign literary life in Paris through Miss Sylvia Beach," he testifies. "That untiring lady battered me without ceasing. She demanded that I should write innumerable articles about *Ulysses* and, with lance . . . slaughter all his English detractors." Sylvia, however, may have failed inadvertently to assist Ford in one of his own endeavors. She recalls that during the course of an evening in his apartment he read aloud to her a long poem of his own composition, which, full of the dinner he had prepared for her, and tired out by her early rising, she was too sleepy to appreciate. In fact she dozed several times during the reading, while Ford paced up and down the room. Later she was afraid "he may have been reading me his new poem with the hope that Shakespeare and Company would publish it, though he never went so far as to suggest it to me." The publishing venture he was most interested in, however, was a new magazine that Pound had planned, which they would call the *transatlantic review*.

The two men met at Pound's flat on 12 October to discuss policy; they were joined by Joyce and Quinn, both of whom were interested in the project. Ford and Quinn were putting up $2,000 each for the review. The photograph of this historic occasion has been reproduced in all their biographies. Pound is sitting in his usual slouched position; Ford holds a small sculpture by Pound; Joyce looks, as always, away from the camera light. Only Quinn is standing and only he is looking at the photographer, hand behind his back in judicial fashion. By this time it had been decided that a portion of Joyce's work would be published in the review (though Quinn had initially resisted the inclusion of any work by Joyce). Ford wished to devote the review to the younger artists now in Paris.

In a suppressed portion of her memoirs, Sylvia reveals the perplexing relationship between Joyce and Ford. Joyce usually narrated to Sylvia his experiences with Ford, and she thought he took Ford's horseplay "very uncomplainingly":

He was always goodhumored over anything of a teasing nature and turned it into a limerick like the one about Ford [which follows]. Or he sent me a cartoon or something. The one in *Punch* represents a big taxi with its burly driver looking back angrily at a small car that has bumped into him: he is saying: "Wot you want is a one-car street." The taxi driver looks like Ford and the small car driver looks like Joyce, strange to say, and Joyce marked it with the initials: "F.M.H." and "J.J."

Following a particularly liquid dinner party that Ford had called together in Joyce's honor, Ford, having emptied all his pockets to meet the large bill, found himself short of funds. All emptied their pockets and pooled the money in the middle of the table. According to Sylvia, "there had been so many drinks they couldn't make up the amount of the bill. Confused mutterings from under the table where Bob McAlmon was sprawling, and with effort he got a chequebook out of his pocket and wrote out a cheque." Joyce, who was amused by these antics and by Ford's reputation for female conquests, wrote a poem (which Sylvia calls a limerick) about Ford and gave it to her:

> O Father O'Ford, you've a masterful way with you,
> Maid, wife and widow are wild to make hay with you,
> Blonde and brunette turn-about run away with you,
> You've such a way with you, Father O'Ford.
>
> That instant they see the sun shine from your eye
> Their hearts flitter flutter, they think and they sigh:
> We kiss ground before thee, we madly adore thee,
> And crave and implore thee to take us, O Lord.

Ford's later disenchantment with Joyce, which Sylvia blamed on the latter's growing fame, was expressed in small affronts, which Sylvia called "horseplay intended to put Joyce and his publishers in their place": giving a gift of a moldy package of cigarettes, refusing to pay for a taxi, requesting immediate payment of *transatlantic review* proceeds, and giving Joyce the wrong name of a restaurant for a party.

The first two little publishing companies to emerge in Paris were McAlmon's Contact Publishing Company and William Bird's Three Mountains Press, both in the fall of 1923. McAlmon was inspired by the example of Sylvia's publication of *Ulysses* and Harriet Weaver's Egoist Press, which had in 1921 published McAlmon's *Explorations,* a volume of poems. In the winter of 1921–1922, he had discovered that he could arrange to have his own copy of short stories, *A Hasty Bunch,* printed by Darantière. So in 1923 McAlmon established the Contact Publishing Company, taking the name from the short-lived *Contact* review, which he and William Carlos Williams had begun in 1920 in New York. He would "create a new literature," not "supply public demand," he announced. In the tradition of small publishers, he would issue a limited number of each book, usually 300 copies. The publishing-company address was 12 rue de l'Odéon, and Sylvia forwarded all his correspondence to the nomadic McAlmon—

to Amsterdam, Madrid, Rome, and all points on the compass. Sylvia, comparing his roving to the movements of his itinerant Presbyterian-minister father, took his flights in stride, at least initially. She mailed him manuscripts, proofs, and personal correspondence, accepted shipment of books from the printer, stored the books, and sold and mailed them. The manuscripts—from Bryher, Mina Loy, Hemingway, Williams, Marsden Hartley—never stayed with McAlmon long. He did little proofreading, and very little rewriting, of his own work. Manuscripts were sent on directly to Darantière for printing. The first two volumes, undated, were his own: *A Companion Piece* (to *A Hasty Bunch*) and *Post-Adolescence,* Sylvia's favorite. He published *Three Stories and Ten Poems* by Hemingway, whom he had met that spring in Rapallo with Pound. These Hemingway pieces were the only works left after Hadley's suitcase, which contained his other manuscripts, had been lost the year before. Bird had to wait for new Hemingway material for his Three Mountains Press.

William Bird, a thirty-four-year old native of Buffalo, New York, had come to Paris in May of 1921 to be the European manager of Consolidated Press, which he and David Lawrence had founded. Bird, a slim and reserved man, was a graduate of Trinity College in Hartford, Connecticut. He had met Hemingway when they both covered the Genoa Economic Conference in April of 1922. When Bird talked of his plans for a new printing press, Hemingway suggested that he look up Ezra Pound, whose poems, he asserted, would be publishable. Bird and Hemingway became fishing companions, and later that summer they, with McAlmon, went to the bullfights in Spain. By October, Bird had bought a seventeenth-century press and opened a print shop at 29 quai d'Anjou on the Ile Saint-Louis. By then Pound had agreed to more than the printing of his own work. He had convinced Bird that he must publish only contemporary writing and had planned to edit by himself a series of prose books that would be "an inquest into the state of contemporary English prose." Pound's gestures were always expressed in the most dramatic terms. Henry Strater, who was painting the first portrait of his friend Hemingway, was to create the design. The Three Mountains Press, which would sell its books from its own office as well as from Shakespeare and Company, was named for Mont Sainte-Geneviève, Montparnasse, and Montmartre. Bird, while working full-time as a leading international journalist, devoted all his free time to his press. His books were beautifully printed on large pages of fine paper. In contrast to the casual and careless McAlmon, Bird poured attention to detail, time, and cash into his editions. From August of 1923 through October of 1926, Shakespeare and Company sold Three Mountains Press books. By December, Pound had edited six books, which included his own *Indiscretions,* Ford's *Women and Men,* William Carlos Williams's *Great American Novel,* and Hemingway's *In Our Time.* The Three Mountains book that sold the most at Shakespeare and Company was printed in 1924: *French Wines,* by William Bird, who was a connoisseur. After the initial impulse, Pound, in his typical manner, withdrew for other ventures, and McAlmon became editor. The merger of Three Mountains with Contact was, in fact, only for distribution.

When Ford could find no operating space for the *transatlantic review,* he moved into the cramped Three Mountains Press office, occasionally lending a hand with the heavy press. One day when Sylvia went to talk to Bird, she had to visit with him on the street, for there was no room in his "office" for another person. Ford was holding one of his Thursday-afternoon teas in their office.

For several years Sylvia had been negotiating for the performance of Joyce's play *Exiles.* Before there was any question of her publishing *Ulysses,* she had agreed to assist Joyce with Lugné-Poe, director of the Théâtre de l'Oeuvre and an acquaintance of hers. She arranged the contact, but nothing more was heard. When another inquiry came, she hurried to find Lugné-Poe, who explained that he could not produce Joyce's play, because theatergoers wanted comedy and he had financial pressure to consider. Lugné-Poe instead produced Fernand Crommelynck's *Magnificent Cuckold,* a comedy that ran for months. With each new set of negotiations, Sylvia corresponded and visited personally with the translator, the director, or the producer. Each plan failed to materialize until the play was first produced at the Neighborhood Playhouse in New York City in 1925. It was not seen in Paris until 1954, when it was performed at the Théâtre Framont in a translation by Mrs. Jenny Bradley, who had been one of the first to assist Joyce when he came to Paris in 1920. Sylvia always took a proprietary interest in this orphan play, abandoned on so many theatrical doorsteps.

In the meantime, Ezra Pound, the "world's foremost discoverer of geniuses"—as George Antheil called him and as Pound liked to bill himself—had taken up the young composer's cause. The poet—who was, not incidentally, tone-deaf—was promoting rhythm as the important element in music, studying the troubadours, and composing his own opera based on the poetry of François Villon. Wishing to collaborate with Antheil, Pound praised him extravagantly in the little reviews and claimed that it was their mutual intention to revolutionize music. Perhaps his excessive praise caused Antheil some harm, but Pound did introduce him to Jean Cocteau, who helped launch the composer in the Paris musical salons. Pound borrowed a fragmentary manuscript of Antheil's, which Antheil later said contained his adolescent ideas about music, and prepared it for publication. Antheil found out about Pound's project from Sylvia, who he claims, "always got to know about everything first." In 1924 Pound's *Antheil and the Treatise on Harmony* was published by Three Mountains Press. It was more Pound theory than Antheil.

Antheil's Paris debut, which took place on 4 October 1923, was part of the filming of Marcel L'Herbier's *L'Inhumaine* (1923). In the Théâtre des Champs-Élysées, the city's largest, he performed for an audience that included Sylvia, Joyce, Pound, Satie, Darius Milhaud (who composed the score for the film), Picasso, Man Ray, and a number of Surrealists. While members of the audience were being entertained in a bonus event to their season tickets, they were also—they learned in the course of the program—serving as extras in the movie about a prima donna concert singer named Claire Lescot, played by Georgette Le Blanc. (Le Blanc, the former wife of Maurice Maeterlinck, knew through her friend Margaret Anderson that Antheil's music would provoke a riotous response.) Her fictional audience, outraged at the character she was portraying, erupts in a riot—the actual riot deliberately produced by Antheil's music. Cameras captured the jeering and bellowing audience (but not Antheil) for posterity. Antheil, who claims he did not know he was being filmed, describes his sensational introduction to a Paris audience:

Rioting broke out almost immediately. I remember Man Ray punching somebody in the nose in the front row. Marcel Duchamp was arguing loudly with somebody else in the second row. In a box nearby Erik Satie was shouting, "What precision! What precision!" and applauding. The spotlight was turned on the audience by some wag upstairs. It struck James Joyce full in the face, hurting his sensitive eyes. A big burly poet got up in one of the boxes and yelled, "You are all pigs!" In the gallery the police came in and arrested the surrealists who, liking the music, were punching everybody who objected.

To his delight, Satie and Milhaud of The Six were immediately enthusiastic about his music. "Paris hadn't had such a good time," he boasts, "since the premiere of Stravinsky's 'Sacre du Printemps.' As Jack Benny would have said: 'Boy, they loved me in Paris!' " Antheil kept the publicity going during the coming year with his preparations for and previews of a new work he called the *Ballet Mécanique*.

Sylvia attended all of Antheil's concerts as well as the opening of new plays in Paris. She was particularly pleased, because it was an American play, to see Eugene O'Neill's *Emperor Jones* in French translation at the Odéon in October. In December she and Adrienne attended the opening-night performance of Jules Romains's *Knock,* with Louis Jouvet in the title role, at the Théâtre des Champs-Élysées. However, evening parties, plays, dinners, and concerts were becoming increasingly difficult for her; if the room grew too warm and the voice too monotonous, she nodded, for unlike many of the others, she had arisen early to start her long busy day. When she did not go out, she worked late in the bookshop to deal with her enormous correspondence. Her correspondents this fall included Hemingway, who wrote several times announcing his imminent return and asking her to find them an apartment. Most mail, however, involved *Ulysses,* Miss Weaver, and the solicitation of reviews for *Ulysses*.

A particularly favorable review appeared in November. Eliot's "Ulysses, Order, and Myth" in the *Dial* pleased Joyce, who in February had complained, "It is curious that no critic has followed up on Mr Larbaud's clue on the parallelism of the two books. They think it is too good to be true." For years Joyce referred to the reviews by Larbaud and Eliot as being the best reviews of *Ulysses* because they emphasized the Odyssean parallels. He had earlier offered, then had forgotten, to elucidate for Miss Weaver the parallels to Homer's *Odyssey*. Writing to thank Eliot, he suggested to him that he invent a short phrase that would win critical popularity—as Larbaud had done before with "interior monologue." Absorbed though he was in his new work, he was always thinking of ways to promote *Ulysses;* Sylvia was expected to carry them through. While he had not directly discussed the subject, he wanted her to publish another edition of the novel. To Harriet Weaver he notes, "Miss Beach tells me of crowds asking to see him [Ulysses-Bloom]. I wait for the conversation to go farther. It never does. And so. And all. Ah, poor Leo!''

Sylvia, however, was busy this year with visitors to her library, especially during the fall, when Myrsine, to protect her health, worked only half days. Regular patrons this fall included MacLeish, Janet Flanner with Solita Solano, and Sherwood Anderson. Each visit, for which business was put aside, would turn into a social and literary occasion. T. S. Eliot came from London for an occasional weekend in Paris. Lady Rothermere, with whom he stayed on one such visit in the late fall of 1923, accompanied him to the bookshop. "He is such a charming fellow and so interesting," Sylvia confided in her mother, "the old fashioned sort of American and very good looking. I only wish he lived in Paris. He is our only modern writer I like after Joyce. . . . Everyone that he was exhibited to was carried away with Eliot." At his request, Sylvia gave him the addresses of Larbaud and Joyce, whom Eliot wished to visit that weekend.

The activities of George and Boski Antheil also enlivened the bookshop hours at least twice a day. George would descend from his apartment upstairs to "check in," borrow books, and get his mail. Boski came more frequently. She met often with Joella, the teenage daughter of the English poet and artist Mina Loy, whose *Lunar Baedecker* had just been published (and misspelled) by McAlmon. They all attended several parties that Sylvia and Adrienne gave (Joella was permitted to attend Sylvia's parties but not the afternoons at Barney's or Stein's).

The fame of the bookshop and James Joyce drew solicitations for more literary welfare work. Would she find a translator? A job? Would she publish another work? She was soon besieged with requests to publish erotic books, such as Frank Harris's *My Life and Loves,* Aleister Crowley's *Memoirs,* and, later, D. H. Lawrence's *Lady Chatterley's Lover* and Henry Miller's *Tropic of Cancer.* When she told Hemingway about Harris's request that she publish his sexual autobiography, Hemingway quipped that she should go right ahead: it would be "the finest fiction ever written." Even as late as 1944, Anthony de Losdari (with Canadian headquarters) asked her to read and publish the account of his life with Tallulah Bankhead in the twenties. (She seemed to regret only that she had turned down Lawrence, whom she found personally charming.) One day Sisley Huddleston entered Shakespeare and Company to find an aroused Sylvia:

"What do people take me for?" [she asked.] "The other day——came into my shop and proposed that I should publish his filthy stuff."

"How silly! And what did you say?"

"I told him to go out of the shop. There are plenty of pornographic publishers, and it is an insult to confound me with them." Then she laughed gaily—her good humor returned. "To think of comparing his lewd lucubrations with *Ulysses!* It was really funny, though for the moment I was annoyed."

Although Huddleston's narrative dramatized her anger, she did regret that *Ulysses* was listed in catalogs of erotica. After purchasing *Ulysses,* an Irish priest asked, "Any other spicy books?" In her memoirs she declares wittily that Joyce "was no specialist, but a general practitioner—all the parts of the body come into *Ulysses.* As he himself said plaintively, 'There is less than ten per cent of *that* in my book.' "

Although she would not publish Frank Harris, she had lunch with him in September of 1923 and handled the Paris distribution of his *My Life and Loves*. Their lengthy correspondence between Paris and Nice in the twenties reveals his generous terms for her, the profitable results that each confiscation of his books brought Harris, the numerous times he raised the price of his books, and his need for her assistance ("I ache for your opinion of the 2nd vol. [*My Life and Loves*]," he begs on 25 July 1925). Amid all the affectionate, pestering letters, the one that reveals the most about Sylvia's business relations with authors is the following:

Dear Miss Sylvia; business and you are poles apart: thank God! You've sent me accounts with no years marked, and you discover 50 of my books in a "cobber's remise" and you've only lost 3 and you mean to pay for them! forget it—please . . .

His good-humored response to her business lapse is explained several months later: "I am more content to be in your hands and I hate ordinary business people."

Publicity also brought many offers of assistance. Young people wrote that they would like to move to Paris in order to work in her bookshop and library. In an unpublished portion of her memoirs, she tells an interesting anecdote. One noon she returned from shopping to find the concierges of the vicinity barricaded against an "undesirable visitor" who they declared was *saoul comme une bour-rique* (drunk as a she-ass). With broom resting on her shoulder for defense, the concierge at No. 18 (where Sylvia and Adrienne lived) pointed to a young man sitting on the doorstep of No. 12; he had insisted, Sylvia was told, on mounting the stairs of her house and had urinated on the stairway. The concierge said she had forced him out the door, which was now bolted, as were all the doors on the block where he had tried to enter looking for Miss Beach and Mr. Joyce.

Although the women warned her not to approach him, as if he were a wild beast, Sylvia walked up to where the young boy sat weeping, his head in his folded arms. Sitting down beside the harmless-looking intruder, she calmed him enough to hear the story of his adoration for Joyce. Excited by the prospect of perhaps meeting the writer, he had drunk a great deal in order to calm himself, and so had arrived in the neighborhood out of control. He was here in Paris to offer his services to Mr. Joyce, he announced, adding that he had been kicked out of his high school in the Midwest when a copy of *Ulysses* had been discovered in his desk. Feeling that the school, as well as his whole town, wanted to get rid of him for his fanatical devotion to Joyce, he had joined another young man, also an admirer, for the journey to Paris. Recognizing that the young man was "simply drunk over being in the same town as Joyce," she sent him back to his hotel with assurances that he and his friend would meet their idol the following day, as they eventually did. Soon the older, steadier boy (who had not arrived drunk) was running errands for Joyce.

When William Bird came to Joyce one day with the proposal that his Three Mountains Press publish a cheap Paris edition of *Ulysses,* Joyce sent him to Shakespeare and Company. Immediately Sylvia herself decided to publish another edition—a decision Joyce had been awaiting. While he had feared she was unwilling, she had wondered why he had not brought it up in conversation. Thus, after a year she resumed her role as publisher of *Ulysses*, a role she would continue for nearly ten years. Miss Weaver replied with the request that the edition be called the fourth, "to give a high curiosity value to the single copy of the small edition of 500 printed in December 1922," the edition presumably burned by English customs. According to Miss Weaver's biographers, this return of *Ulysses* to its first publisher was an "intimation that the good days of The Egoist Press were over."

Correspondence and negotiations with Miss Weaver and Darantière kept Sylvia busy the last weeks of the year. She planned for a January publishing date at her own expense and mailed printed postcards announcing the price in five languages. She would include a new list of corrections, a list kept by Miss Weaver, with Joyce's additions. As a gesture of gratitude toward Miss Weaver, Sylvia bought ten copies of the Egoist *Ulysses*.

Sylvia sent one of these copies to her mother in Florence. For her mother's fifty-ninth birthday, on 5 December, Sylvia asked Joyce to sign the book.

I got out Joyce's pen—the "ladies pen" which is his favorite brand—and the Chinese ink, and Joyce sat down with great alacrity to sign. Mrs. Joyce and I suddenly heard a sharp exclamation and on rushing to see what had happened we found Joyce looking in despair at an enormous blot he had made on the page! I told him not to take on, but nothing would calm him. Finally he scraped it all off very nicely with a penknife and I think it doesn't show at all, don't you? He was very much pleased at the idea of you having this copy of Ulysses. You must re-read the Scylla and Charybdis episode, the conversation in the Library about Shakespeare; it is so interesting and exciting—but everything in the book is wonderful!

Since she felt as she did about *Ulysses*, one can understand her willingness to continue as its publisher. She put off a Christmas trip to visit her mother in Florence so that she could get the edition through the printing process. She saw very little of her family any more. The letters seem cordial, but they are infrequent and sweetly strained.

The year 1923 ended with a flurry of publications. Soon after Hemingway announced to Sylvia (in a homesick letter from Toronto), "I'll get on your shelves yet," William Bird issued his *In Our Time* (Bird chose to style the title all lower case). The book began selling immediately at the bookshop. McAlmon, whose Contact books were also selling briskly, wrote that he would soon be meeting in Paris his friend William Carlos Williams, with whom he had coedited the *Contact* review in 1920. The first number of the *transatlantic review* appeared in December, announcing that it was intended for writers in all languages. Finally, Sylvia was waiting for her own publication, the fourth printing of *Ulysses*. Though Joyce was somewhat bored—at least as a topic of conversation—with *Ulysses* (he jokingly referred to it as the "Greco-Bavarian telephone directory"), Sylvia believed it would please Joyce to have a copy of the book ready for Christmas. Joyce and Sylvia liked to refer to this printing, which was made from the original plates, as an edition. It was to sell for sixty francs or $3.60 (December exchange) in a size smaller than that of the first three and with a white paper cover and blue printing—a reversal of the colors or, as Joyce described it, "the Greek flag upside down this time." The 736 pages would include "Ulysses: Additional Corrections," bound inside the book for the first time.

Joyce had a habit of observing the significant coincidences of events in his life. As his biographer Ellmann observes:

He was interested also in variation and sameness in space, in the cubist method of estab-lishing differing relations among aspects of a single thing. . . . That the picture of Cork [Ireland] in his Paris flat should have, as he emphasized to Frank O'Connor, a cork frame, was a deliberate, if half-humorous, indication of this notion of the world, where unex-pected simultaneities are the rule. The characters pass through sequences of situations and thoughts bound by coincidence with the situations and thoughts of other living and dead men and of fictional, mythical men.

This explanation of the universal process or series of coincidences was a con-vincing intellectualization of his superstitious upbringing. But often the artist-god did not let coincidence take its willful way. All efforts had been made, for example, to get the first *Ulysses* delivered on his birthday, 2 February 1922. And the first four copies of this new edition were delivered to Sylvia on Christmas Eve. She took a taxi to Joyce's flat and handed him two. This new coincidence of time implied more than a Christmas gift from his publisher.

Christmas was a festive season at the shop, which was often crowded with gift buyers intent on enjoying its quiet warmth. A lighted tree stood on the table, adding to the cheerfulness. While the Moschos sisters and Sylvia were sampling Christmas sweets and wine there one day, a representative from the ministry of finance entered. His youthful inexperience as well as his formal attire made him ill at ease in this relaxed and merry environment.

"Do you sell books?" he inquired.

"How do you think we live?" Sylvia replied with polite impertinence.

"But I wish to see your records of sales," he responded with some embar-rassment, walking about the room, his eyes examining everything.

"My assistants are too busy to help you at this time," Sylvia maintained, as she set the cake plate on top of a stack of books. But he insisted on seeing her records. Sylvia, exaggerating her somewhat British accent, as she did under necessary circumstances, turned on him: "I am surprised you would badger a woman who works so hard to make a living and pay her taxes." Her "financial assistant"—she nodded toward Myrsine, who was shuffling books on the far table—was too busy. She would bring the books to the minister of finance at the beginning of the following week. Confounded and defeated, the tax man left.

The following day Myrsine carried a set of finance books to the ministry of finance near Saint-Sulpice. To compensate for the books that were given to poor students, for books taken away by regular customers, and for her own imperfect record keeping, Sylvia kept duplicate accounts—cutting profits slightly in one. Like Joyce, she did not allow coincidence or government to take its willful way.

CHAPTER 8

Americans in Paris
1924

> . . . it was not a generation of expatriates who found themselves in Paris in those years but a generation whose *patria,* wherever it may once have been, was now no longer waiting for them anywhere.
>
> — Archibald MacLeish

> You know, dear, all good Americans go to Paris when they die, and we are dead, as far as they over there are concerned. . . .
>
> — William Carlos Williams

D R. DEVON EVANS, the autobiographical hero of William Carlos Williams's novel *A Voyage to Pagany,* arrives in Paris with the same awe and excitement that many young American artists felt during the middle years of the twenties. The train that Evans rides crashes toward Paris: *"À Paris, à Paris, à Paris.* . . . You must not be afraid. —But Evans was uncertain—and American—and this and that and careless. . . . He wanted to write—that was all, and not to have written, but to be writing."

Paris had traditionally called to the American heart—from Benjamin Franklin to Henry James. If art is truly international, as James and T. S. Eliot believed, then its cultural capital in the twenties was Paris. Stein had arrived in 1903 and Beach in 1916; both remained. Pound came in 1920 and stayed four years; Hemingway came at the end of 1922 and stayed nearly five years. But most American pilgrims stayed only a few weeks or months. By 1924 the migration had gained momentum. Paris was having a notable impact on this second great period of American literature. In the first great period—the "renaissance" of Poe, Emerson, Thoreau, Whitman, Melville, and Hawthorne, before 1860—the American literary consciousness grappled with its own space, both geographical and metaphysical. During the twenties that literary consciousness, according to Irving Howe, "collided with the weight of Europe." The First World War had brought many writers to Europe and to an encounter with history and the failure of their religious and political beliefs. Hemingway's young soldier Frederick Henry says in *A Farewell to Arms* that he is "always embarrassed by the words sacred, glorious, and sacrifice and the expression in vain. . . . Abstract words such as glory, honor, courage, or hallow were obscene beside the concrete names of villages, the numbers of roads, the names of rivers, the numbers of regiments and the dates.'' For meaning, Hemingway and his generation turned to art, that is, to its order and beauty, to the preservation of the word. Style was to be a barrier against chaos and loss of faith.

"Writing in Paris is one of the oldest American customs," asserts Van Wyck Brooks in a book on Washington Irving. "It all but antedates, with Franklin, the founding of the republic.'' For two hundred years—from Benjamin Franklin to James Baldwin—writers have sought Paris, walked the same streets, stayed often in the same hotels. Paris—crossroads of the West—is the place away from home where Americans talk and write best, witness Franklin's *Autobiography,* Jefferson's *Notes on Virginia,* Cooper's *Prairie,* Irving's *Tales of a Traveler,* Benet's *John Brown's Body,* Hemingway's *The Sun Also Rises,* and Fitzgerald's *Tender Is the Night.* The aesthetic distance that some writers had gained by going to nature—like Thoreau in the preceding century—these writers found in temporary expatriation in France. For some writers this was a pattern of alienation and reintegration necessary to their understanding of America and to their artistic development. In spite of the loud denunciations of the United States by a few, most never shook off—or wished to shake off—their American cultural values. On the contrary, in Paris many "found" America.

During these two hundred years—from Franklin to Baldwin—most artists went to Paris for their education in the center of art and culture. Paris had always tolerated—even loved—the artists, who in the twenties, even Williams agreed, were little valued in the United States. By 1924, however, there were more immediate reasons to go there. First, the war had eroded American isolationism by bringing many young Americans to France for humanitarian reasons. Second, in 1924 the steamship companies belonging to the North Atlantic Conference created an inexpensive mode of travel called Tourist Third, which brought would-be artists and students by the thousands. Third, there was a favorable rate of exchange (although Italy and Austria had even better rates). The title of one of Hemingway's *Toronto Star Weekly* articles explains this: "A Canadian with One Thousand a Year Can Live Very Comfortably and Enjoyably in Paris." Americans could afford both to go to Paris and to remain there. Besides, to paraphrase Pound, attics were cheap.

In *Paris on Parade,* written in 1924, Robert Forrest Wilson identifies an "interlocking directorate of the Continental advance movement in English letters: Ford, Beach, Joyce, McAlmon, Bird, Hemingway, Antheil, and Pound." As Henry James had gone to Paris to meet Flaubert, Sand, Maupassant, Zola, and Turgenev, so a young writer of the twenties went to Paris to meet Valéry, Picasso, Stravinsky, and Joyce. One of the most important reasons that writers, including Williams, came to Paris was that their readers lived here. The literary community was in Paris: publishers of the new literature, little reviews that carried the latest poetry and reviews of that poetry, a bookshop and library where all the latest work was available. They could read the latest works in little, inexpensive reviews that they could buy or borrow at Shakespeare and Company. In

America, lamented Carl Sandburg, "It's hell when poets can't afford to buy each other's books." In this single metropolis—the Left Bank was still like a small town—communication and support functioned in their favor. Of course they suffered from the competition and the in-group feuding that have been documented as well as distorted in the memoirs. But here they were challenged, stimulated, reviewed, and—above all—read by the community of literati.

Certainly the sociological factors were to some extent influential in driving them into their exile. The United States tried to regulate reading as well as drinking habits (Prohibition had gone into effect on 16 January 1920). Some artists fled the business ethic signaled by the Coolidge landslide in November, the Red Scare, the Spoon Rivers (the majority of American artists in Paris were midwesterners), and narrow puritanism—the latter being the object of Williams's particular hatred. In his study of the nineteenth-century American artist, Matthew Josephson maintains that creative, individualistic people feel vulnerable and alienated in the society that becomes increasingly mechanical and collective. The artist, he asserts, either takes an antagonistic stand toward society (as did Herman Melville), conceals his work (as did Emily Dickinson), or flees (as did Henry James). Those who fled in the early decades of this century went to Paris to exchange business and moral prejudices for their own aesthetic prejudices. Pound deplored both the American intellectual's contentment in sitting "under the great British bum, carefully collecting and cataloging the droppings" as well as America's rejection of her artists. They were "not a generation of expatriates," explains MacLeish, "but a generation whose *patria*, wherever it may once have been, was now no longer waiting for them anywhere."

Though Williams was critical of his country's puritanism and its treatment of the artist, he debated the value of exile. His writings express this tension, as well as his own ambivalence about coming to Paris. For example, in his prologue to *Kora in Hell: Improvisations* (1917), he had called Pound "the best enemy United States verse has." He continued to attack the international school of Eliot and Pound and European modernist influences, which, he implied, led poetry toward imitation and vagueness, away from the welding of word and thing and the hard statement in the American idiom. Pound barked back at Williams that he (Pound) had "sweated like a nigger to break up the clutch" of the old maids "so as to make a place for the real thing," had "imported U.S. stuff here, to the prejudice of my own comfort (remember I have only what I get by my pen)," and had "the whole stinking sweat of providing the mechanical means for letting through the new moment." Pound concludes that it is Williams's first-generation-American blood that allows him to "keep the environment outside him" and remain "decently objective." Williams can afford to love America. He and Eliot, on the other hand, have "blood poison," the "thin milk of New York and New England from the pap."

"I think you are suffering from [lack of] nerve," Pound taunts his friend Williams in March of 1922. So Williams took a year off from his medical practice, spent six months researching and writing *In the American Grain* in New York, and on 9 January 1924 sailed for Europe with his wife, Flossie. He would see Pound and McAlmon again and he would meet Sylvia Beach, with whom he had corresponded, and perhaps Joyce. The excitement of his approach to Paris is captured in his *Voyage to Pagany,* where Evans's opening responses to Paris are full of exhilaration. Using images of penetration, Williams sends Evans's train flying into Paris, a city described as a woman waiting for her lover. The lover "must come of machines, he must break through." Evans (as Williams) is that lover in the heart of the machine. (Three years later, in May of 1927, Lindbergh was to arrive in a flying machine and capture the heart of Paris.) Paris is "the beloved of men," charming, serious; it "kept secrets and it offered its understanding." Yet he hates the "frivolity" created by the Americans. Williams loved an earlier Paris, the Paris his mother called her lost "Eden."

Williams spent six weeks of his first literary voyage—part of January and May 1924—in Paris. His reunion with McAlmon was amiable, for he found that Bob had retained his western manner but had matured and was at home in Paris. McAlmon introduced him to William Bird, who had recently published Williams's *Great American Novel.* McAlmon took them on a fast-paced tour of Paris life. They went to Shakespeare and Company, dined at Brancusi's apartment, went to the Dingo bar, visited a crowded party at the Fords' (Williams admired Ford's mind but not his hectic life), and met many of the Crowd who were in Paris at the time. With McAlmon they spent a month in the south of France, visited Nancy Cunard in Monte Carlo, Djuna Barnes and William Bird in Villefranche. These experiences were heady.

Williams was no stranger to Sylvia, a fellow New Jerseyite. She had written him as early as 1920, when she had gotten his name from the Egoist Press as a possible subscriber to her first edition of *Ulysses.* He had purchased No. 441 of the first printing of Joyce's work in May of 1922. When Williams first approached the bookshop that January, he looked in the window for his books, and he was not disappointed. In 1922, at McAlmon's suggestion, he had sent Sylvia several copies of *Sour Grapes, Kora in Hell,* and *Al Que Quiere!* According to bookshop records at Princeton, his books always sold and circulated well. Sylvia, who had just returned from a short visit with her mother in Italy, introduced Williams to Antheil, about whom he had already heard from Pound's enthusiastic letters. Myrsine hurried across the street to get Adrienne; when Sylvia introduced her to the distinguished-looking poet-doctor, they liked each other immediately.

Adrienne and Sylvia were soon invited to a dinner party that McAlmon planned for Williams—a party that Williams recalls in both his novel and his autobiography. The dinner party was at the Trianons (Restaurant des Trianons, 5 Place de Rennes), Joyce's favorite, an intimate and elegant restaurant at the corner of the boulevard du Montparnasse and the rue de Rennes. With all the literary crowd there—a few not formally invited—they nearly filled the left side of the restaurant. According to the various accounts, the following persons attended: Bill and Flossie Williams, James and Nora Joyce, Sylvia and Adrienne, Ford and his wife, Stella Bowen, Boski and George Antheil, Louis Aragon, Bill and Sally Bird, Kitty Cannell, Marcel Duchamp, Harold Loeb, Mina Loy, Man Ray, Laurence and Clotilde Vail. Williams was uneasy with the French. Perhaps, as

McAlmon suggests, he wanted profound discussion and was disappointed in Joyce, who drank too much and sang Irish ballads—to match McAlmon's Negro spirituals and cowboy songs and Clotilde's blues songs. When McAlmon asked him to give a response to his welcoming speech, Williams made what he later called a "stupid speech," which humiliated him. He was filled with "contempt for [his] drunkenness," but he also adds, "I saw a France that day which had wholly escaped me theretofore." The humiliation of the dinner and his sense of feeling out of place wth the younger crowd only intensified his growing hostility toward expatriation to Europe.

In sharp contrast to Williams's growing doubts about this Paris world, is the example of Hemingway who, within a few days of the Trianons party, returned to Paris with Hadley and their baby. Hemingway's letters of this time indicate that he was fleeing America to gain a perspective on himself and his country. Paris would give this descendant of Mark Twain both perspective and training (via the techniques of Flaubert and Cézanne) to compose his American idylls of upper Michigan. This year, his first after resigning from the *Star,* would be his most productive yet, for he would write nine stories (including "The Big Two-Hearted River") in the next seven months and meet Ford and begin his work on the *transatlantic review* . Sylvia had not had time to find them an apartment, but they soon settled at 113 rue Notre-Dame-des-Champs, where their second-floor apartment looked out on a sawmill and lumberyard. One morning Sylvia dropped in and was urged to watch Ernest give a bath to Bumby, as they had begun calling the cuddly baby. "He took to fatherhood and . . . did everything but breastfeed his baby,"claims Sylvia."Hemingway *père* was justly proud, and asked me if I didn't think he had a future as a nursemaid." Although he never had to hire himself out in this fashion, he did weed a garden to earn extra money for the trip to Spain in July. They were trying to live on Hadley's small inheritance, which was dwindling as a result of poor investment. And Ford paid nothing for service as manuscript scout for the review. But the Hemingways were not exactly poor.

Within a month of Williams's arrival and the return of Hemingway, Ford published in the Paris *Herald* a review of the former's *Great American Novel* and the latter's *In Our Time,* two of the first six volumes of the Three Mountains Press. Ford calls attention to Hemingway's "minute but hugely suggestive pictures" in the "hardest and tightest tradition of the French." He concludes, however, that Williams's "pre-digested pabulum of life" is "more European" than is Hemingway's "raw material." The somewhat exaggerated conclusions concerning Williams were meant to be ironic, for Williams denied the European influence and strove for a distinctive American idiom. On the other hand, Ford's observations on Hemingway's work directly challenged Williams's predictions of a vague and imitative direction for American literature written in Europe.

As the second anniversary of *Ulysses* approached, Williams was preparing to leave Paris for a tour of the Continent. The bookshop windows were full of copies of the fourth edition. Flowers arrived from Joyce that morning, and the *Ulysses* family celebrated that evening. A small cloud hung over the festivities, a cloud of doubt about the acceptability of Joyce's new work. Joyce was worried about the lack of faith of certain friends, such as Harriet Weaver, who had been reading the manuscript. Such worries lay in a private realm apart from the enchantment that *Ulysses* and the Paris bookshop held for the public. Newspaper articles portrayed a life of glamour, wealth, and intellectual sophistication in Paris. One young Princeton woman, a recent college graduate and a friend of the Beach family, describes the excitement the rue de l'Odéon held for her this winter. She walked by the bookshop often, she claims: "I can see [Sylvia] now, striding along the streets of Paris, wearing a huge cowboy sort of hat and a collegiate sheepskin lined coat." Although the independent stride expressed a western spirit, the headgear was in fact the Spanish hat that Sylvia had worn the day she had met Adrienne. The young Princeton woman had no trouble recognizing *Ulysses* when she saw Sylvia arranging the second-anniversary display window, which was crammed with copies of the book in its distinctive white cover. Though she no longer sent copies to the United States or England, Sylvia offered a large discount to booksellers on the Continent. She was excited by the enthusiasm for the novel:

Two large publishing houses here have been trying their best to get permission to publish ULYSSES in French. But we turned them both down as arrangements have already been made with a publisher. Prof. Cazamian of the Sorbonne is now going to write up Joyce in La Revue Franco-Anglaise. Just think of the Sorbonne going in for him. He is becoming more and more famous. The new edition of Ulysses is going off like a streak!

Other than at the Trianons party, Williams had caught only a few glimpses of Joyce. Indeed, Joyce rarely came into the bookshop during the weeks before early March, when he concluded the Anna Livia Plurabelle portion of his new novel. It was to become the center of the novel, which begins and ends with the river. All his characters are multidimensional. Anna Livia Plurabelle, who represents woman and nature, is a river. Her husband, Humphrey Chimpden Earwicker, is a giant, a god, a mountain as well as Everyman (Here Comes Everybody), the keeper of a public house. Their children are twin boys, Shem and Shaun, and a daughter, Isabel, is a cloud. "Time and the river and the mountains are the real heroes in my book," Joyce stressed. But the radical innovation that raised so much doubt for Harriet Weaver and other friends was in the book's language. He told one friend he was at "the end of English" and another that he had "put the language to sleep" to invent another, multilingual speech.

When Joyce finally received the *transatlantic review* proofs of his Mamalujo (a word composed of the opening letters of the names of the four Evangelists, Matthew, Mark, Luke, and John) portion, the proofs were so bad that he asked for a time extension. McAlmon and Sylvia were both giving him money—loans and advances on sales. He wrote McAlmon that he was waiting for the Weaver legacy to be settled, enduring weather that was "like a Methodist minister's dream of purgatory," and waiting for a much needed vacation after having worked like a "galley slave." Joyce's financial woes were eased by a $350 check from McAlmon. At the same time that Joyce received his gift from this American,

France's weak franc was redeemed by a $100 million credit to the Bank of France by J. P. Morgan.

Joyce's realistic language, much acclaimed by Williams, worried Ford. After a special reading with Ford, Joyce, and Sylvia, Sisley Huddleston assured them that they risked no prosecution for blasphemy. Originally scheduled for January publication, Mamalujo appeared in the April issue (No. 4) of the *transatlantic review*. The appearance of Mamalujo and of Herbert Gorman's *James Joyce: The First Forty Years* (Huebsch), which Sylvia promoted and sold alongside *Ulysses,* increased publicity about Joyce. Each news or critical article brought Joyce detractors, against whom Sylvia was expected to orchestrate a counterattack. When Ernest Boyd's review ("Order Established in the Literary Chaos of James Joyce: A Guide to *Ulysses* and Its Author") of the Gorman book appeared in the *New York Times Book Review* on 2 March, Joyce and Sylvia conferred on the defense. Because Boyd was particularly critical of Larbaud's sweeping generalizations on Joyce, Sylvia sent Larbaud a copy of the review. Joyce informed Larbaud that he thought it "ought to be answered." Larbaud replied in English (Paris *Tribune* in June) and French (*Nouvelle Revue Française* in January).

On 19 April, Joyce wrote a note to Sylvia and had Lucia bring it to her: ". . . I would be very glad if you could manage to advance me another 500 francs. I sincerely hope, if things finally straighten out, that this is the last time I shall ever bother you. If you have it please put it in an envelope and give it to Lucia. . . ." The "things" that had not yet "straightened out" were the closing of Harriet Weaver's aunt Emily's estate; the royalty check for the New York performance of *Exiles* (Sylvia had asked for $250 in advance); and the proceeds from Miss Weaver's sale of the English copyright of his first four books to Jonathan Cape. Though Sylvia had trouble collecting from the Neighborhood Playhouse, where *Exiles* ran for forty-one performances from February through March, she believed it was significant that her own country premiered the Joyce play. She remarked that in terms of the performance, publishing, and financing of Joyce and his works, the Americans played early and crucial roles.

The *transatlantic review,* which published the first fragments of Joyce's new work (Mamalujo), championed American writers, including Hemingway and Williams (Ford published four of Williams's pieces this year). The review was published from January to December of 1924 as a major effort of Ford and the rue de l'Odéon crowd. It was a popular feature of the bookshop, for little reviews are the tangible effort—the flag—of new art. They rally the young artists. And the *transatlantic review* flew proudly at Shakespeare and Company. Although edited by a fifty-one-year-old Englishman, it was dedicated to "the attempt to help youth" and was boldly American in its emphasis. The first issues included Conrad and Ford, members of the older generation, but it also published work by Cummings, Hemingway, Antheil, Pound, McAlmon, and (at Hemingway's insistence) Stein, who although she was no longer young, belonged by right in the company of the innovators, her compatriots. Ford hailed the vitality of American literature, especially of that of the Midwest, the region Ford hailed as the birthplace of the best young writers. He would say, in a 1927 essay explaining and defending the Americans abroad, that they have "no conspiracy against the United States, or even against hundred per cent Americanism. They are hundred per centers all right. They make me tired with it most times." He even turned the review over to Hemingway's direction in July, when, on Quinn's death, Ford had to seek new funding in England and the United States. In his absence, Hemingway published an editorial tribute to Conrad, on the occasion of his death, announcing that he would gladly grind up T. S. Eliot and sprinkle him over Conrad's grave if it would get Conrad back and writing. Williams concurred on Eliot, whose *Waste Land* was a "great catastrophe to our letters" because it "gave the poem back to the academics." Ford, who disagreed, lamented, "I really exist as a sort of half-way house between non-publishable youth and real money, a sort of green baize swing door that everyone kicks both on entering and leaving."

Williams was fascinated with the American and English women, who, considering their numbers and talents, were given little voice in the *transatlantic review*. The women, including Sylvia, had come to Paris for the same reasons the men had. But there was also the added pressure of being a female among the last generation of the Victorian era—"the last group to grow up under the formidable discipline of the Nineteenth Century," as Bryher complains. Because their society assumed that one chose marriage or a career, life in a foreign country took the stigma from the "lesser" choice—even gave a singularity to that life. A certain number of these women were lesbian, a choice or inclination reinforced by the idea that marriage and children precluded a life of literature. Friendships between two women, including Sylvia and Adrienne, seem to have strengthened rather than repressed each member of the pair, even in the case of the domestic service of Alice B. Toklas, who had no career apart from Stein. Paris, like any metropolitan, occidental city, offered freedom of behavior to those who came to it as foreigners. In addition, the tolerance of the French, which is probably based to some extent on self-assurance and indifference to other cultures, ignored the behavior of the outsiders. The women did not necessarily find greater feminist awareness there—as their observations of the attitudes of Joyce, Pound, Hemingway, and Gide testify—but they found fewer restrictions and social pressures.

The women artists in Paris between the war years were a diverse group, as fascinating, and at least as vivid—so recent biographers are revealing—as the men. In fact, William Carlos Williams found the women of literary Paris more interesting than the men—and he named Sylvia, Adrienne, Clotilde Vail, Kitty Cannell, H.D., and Bryher as examples. Though he considered Iris Tree and Nancy Cunard self-destructive, he admired most of them, especially Adrienne:

Adrienne Monnier . . . was, to be sure, French, gross, heavy-legged. The English to the north might think themselves more spiritual, but she smacked her lips and enjoyed where they hardly ate at all; hardly, at least, tasted. The French would never commit self-destruction until they had first drunk up the wine in the cellar. This woman loved food, the senses were her meat. She achieved equality with Nancy and Iris on another plane. It was the women, all of them, . . . who in Paris fascinated me.

Harold Loeb agreed with Williams that the "men were less colorful (with the possible exception of Ezra Pound and Laurence Vail)." And Morrill Cody claims the women were the leaders of the Left Bank: "it is perhaps remarkable that the leaders and organizers of Montparnasse were largely women, from the famed Kiki to the inspiring Sylvia Beach, who, as far as I know, never entered a bar in her life." Cody and McAlmon also admired the American Flossie Martin and the English painter Nina Hamnett, a leader of the Paris bohemian world. And they both remark on the elegant wit of Mina Loy, Mary Reynolds, and Djuna Barnes. Mary Butts, a contributing editor of the *transatlantic review,* managed a successful career as a novelist, motherhood (by her former husband, John Rodker), and an active social life of pub crawling and opium smoking. Mina Loy and Kay Boyle were also productive artists as well as the mothers of several daughters. From the shy and brilliant Djuna Barnes to the outspoken feminist Emma Goldman ("Women need not keep their mouth shut and their wombs open!"), these women enriched the life of Paris. The only traits that Margaret Anderson, Isadora Duncan, Sylvia Beach, Berenice Abbott, Iris Tree, Janet Flanner, and Gertrude Stein shared were their individuality, independence, and strong ego—the latter a necessary trait for survival alone in a foreign capital among so many other strong egos. With strong ego and nurturing spirit—a combination evident also in men like Pound and Ford—they founded little reviews and publishing companies, directed salons, wrote and translated poetry, painted, and studied photography and dance.

Although Cody was incorrect in assuming that Sylvia had never entered a bar, he was accurate in identifying her as a leader of Montparnasse. Shakespeare and Company was, according to one Canadian visitor, "the one grand display for international talent . . . if [you] were at all interested in the way the intellectual cloth of the time was being cut you had to be there, even if you couldn't do more than press your nose against the window." It was called "Sylvia's" now. The reporters on the Paris *Tribune* had a standing joke: "Grab your towel and let's go down to Sylvia Beach." Archibald MacLeish says it was "a place to go to . . . a human being." For Bryher, "It was not just the crowded shelves . . . the many informal photographs . . . it was Sylvia herself. . . ."

In a three-page article in the *Publishers' Weekly* of April 1924, Morrill Cody confirmed the growing influence of Sylvia and her library. He describes her patrons of this year as visiting Americans, artists, and the humble classes. According to Williams, she and Adrienne "conspired to make that region of Paris back of the old theatre a sanctuary for all sorts of writers: . . . the younger Americans found it a veritable home."

Joyce was amused by the American writers who came in increasing numbers to the bookshop, where he had met McAlmon, Hemingway, Bird, Antheil, and would soon meet many others, including MacLeish and Fitzgerald. He had long been interested in the American idiom. "He obviously enjoyed the company of my compatriots," writes Sylvia. "He confided to me that he liked us and our language; certainly he made plenty of use of the American vernacular in his books.'' For example, after amusing his guests with a record of Aimee Semple McPherson's sermons, he included her cadences in the latter paragraphs of the Oxen of the Sun chapter of *Ulysses*—a chapter whose style moves from the Anglo-Saxon to the contemporary American evangelistic idiom.

He was also delighted with American generosity and warmth. Bob McAlmon gave him money. Sylvia managed his professional life. Young Americans he had never met had typed his manuscripts and sold subscriptions. He told Sylvia he thought that Hemingway was a sensitive chap. In her memoirs, she says,

> . . . I am going to say this whether Hemingway shoots me or not—I have always felt that he was a deeply religious man. Hemingway was a great pal of Joyce's and Joyce remarked to me one day that he thought it was a mistake, Hemingway's thinking himself such a tough fellow and McAlmon trying to pass himself off as the sensitive type. It was the other way around, he thought. So Joyce found you out, Hemingway!

They were hardly pals, though Hemingway did carry a drunken Joyce home one night.

Although he was a recipient of American generosity and friendliness, Joyce could not warm to American informality, particularly, according to Sylvia, in the manner of address:

> It is a custom in the French literary world to address writers by their last names. . . . You would never think of calling their authors ''Monsieur Valéry'' or ''Monsieur Proust.'' . . . Valéry always called Adrienne ''Monnier'' and myself ''Sylvia'' as all our other French friends did. I know this custom shocked Joyce. In vain did he set a good example by his ''Miss Monnier'' and ''Miss Beach.'' But let no one dare to call him anything but ''Mr. Joyce''!

One noon Hemingway was minding the store when Joyce, whom he was reported to have once called ''Jim,'' came in search of Sylvia.

''Sylvia is not here,'' Hemingway informed him.

''Oh . . . you mean Miss Beach.''

''And Myrsine is not here either,'' responded Hemingway, anticipating Joyce's next question and ignoring the polite correction. ''She will be right back.''

''Oh . . . you mean Miss Moschos.''

Picking up the rhythm and irony, Hemingway continued: ''Hélène is not here either.''

''Oh . . . you mean little Miss Moschos,'' and Joyce retreated. Hemingway repeated the conversation with great glee when the Misses Beach and Moschos returned. Although amused by Hemingway's story, Myrsine also occasionally thought the Americans too friendly. When she was busy working at the desk, one American whom she had met only the day before slapped her on the back, startling her with a ''Hello, Myrsine.'' The new Americans did not use the same familiarity with the proprietor of the store, she noted. When a few of the customers asked her to lunch to talk about the famous people who came to the bookshop, she drew a dignified line at that familiarity and never accepted an invitation. ''They all came to 'express themselves,' '' remembers Myrsine, ''which they could have done at home. They exclaimed about France and the French, but they cared little. When I asked them if they had read a particular French writer, they seemed little interested.'' She was also interested in the way Americans "expressed themselves" in their individual life-style. They dressed individually—Hemingway like a lumberjack, T. S. Eliot like a bank official, and Pound like no one else. When McAlmon adopted a cummerbund used by the peasants, Mme Tisserand, the concierge, who had come from a distinguished French family recently fallen on hard times, objected to these American patrons who dressed like the workers.

The Americans in Paris in the midtwenties ranged from the boatloads of tourist-class students and would-be artists to the permanent residents such as Gertrude and Alice, Natalie Barney, Sylvia, and William Bradley. Some of the early visitors—what Malcolm Cowley calls the "World War I generation"—had returned to America. Even before Matthew Josephson, Harold Loeb, and Alfred Kreymborg published their January 1924, all-American number of *Broom* (which they soon moved to New York), Josephson had returned home to become a Wall Street broker.

Though he would become our official participant-interpreter of the exile twenties, Cowley himself had left Paris by 1924, before the movement had reached its popular peak. He had been in France during the war as an assistant driver of munitions trucks for the French army. After attending Harvard and living in Greenwich Village, he had returned with an American Field Service Fellowship to study and live (1921–1923) in Giverny, fifty miles down the Seine from Paris where Monet still lived, surrounded by his flowers. Cowley did not join Shakespeare and Company until 15 January 1923, but he has since documented and evaluated its famous patrons in numerous articles and books, especially in *Exile's Return*. He returned to the United States to find that "by that time it seemed that everyone in Greenwich Village had heard the good news and was planning to live abroad."

The Greenwich Village (or *Little Review*) crowd, like most of the visitors, swung open the doors of Shakespeare and Company upon entering and leaving Paris. They had been gathering on the Left Bank since 1922—among them Jimmy Light, Djuna Barnes, Berenice Abbott, Max Eastman, and Mina Loy. Sylvia was delighted, saying that they saved her "a great deal of postage by coming over to Paris and subscribing in person to *Ulysses*." By 1924 Jane Heap and Margaret Anderson were giving speeches about their trial in 1921 for publishing excerpts of *Ulysses*. There may have been some resentment on their part that the world looked to Sylvia Beach as the pioneer publisher of *Ulysses*. They gave interviews for the French papers about the trial, and Jane Heap began writing an account of their activities with *Ulysses*. Although Joyce had not yet met them when they published the excerpts of his novel and seemed to share John Quinn's dislike for them, Sylvia expressed sympathy for their sense of exclusion. In a July letter to her mother she says, "I don't blame them. It would be trying for them if their part was forgotten and they were not given the credit for the effort they made." By November her sympathy had thinned. "Jane Heap," she confided to her mother, "is threatening to start a vast publishing business over here with the Three Mountains Press and Contact and Little Review amalgamated and I don't know what all. But I guess the plans are more or less vague. Some people hate me because of my shop and *Ulysses,* but if they had an 'old trouble' like mine they wouldn't think they'd got something for nothing." Nothing came of the proposed merger.

Marsden Hartley, whom Sylvia thought charming but melancholy, and Mary Butts, who "bounced in and out" of the bookshop, were part of the Contact group, which intermingled with the Greenwich Village group. Contact published Hartley's *Twenty-five Poems* and Butts's *Ashe of Rings.* Mary Butts's "red cheeks and red hair" and interesting face are captured in Cocteau's drawing of her. But the most interesting woman in this Contact group was the remarkable Mina Loy. A friend of McAlmon and Williams from their time in the Village in 1920, she would return to Paris in 1926 and with Peggy Guggenheim's assistance open a small art shop off the avenue des Champs-Élysées, selling her paintings and decorated lampshades to support her children. Williams describes her as "very English, very skittish, an evasive, long-limbed woman too smart to involve herself, after a first disastrous marriage, with any of us—though she was friendly." Mina Loy was known for her productivity and talent—*Lunar Baedecker* is her best poetry—her wit and her beauty. Sylvia thought Mina and her daughters were "ravishing beauties."

Another group of Americans gravitated, for their financial support, to the English-language newspapers in Paris. In the Aeolus episode of *Ulysses,* Joyce describes the newspaper office of the *Freeman's Journal* as big, rambling, dilapidated, and crowded with men coming and going in haste. The confusion of this center of city communications—set at noon of Bloomsday—was based on Joyce's visits to the *Evening Telegraph* in Dublin. Aeolus, god of the winds, was the equivalent of the city editor who presided over the streaming movements and the winds of words. This windy scene in Dublin was closer to the newsroom of Ben Hecht's *Front Page* than to the Paris offices of the *New York Tribune* or the *Chicago Tribune* (later merged as the Paris *Tribune*). American news in Paris was a small operation carried on by men who had other interests like writing, composing, translating, and publishing. They were patrons of the bookshop and reported on as well as participated in the life of the Left Bank. Hugh Ford characterizes the scene:

In some ways Jim Thurber was right when he quipped: "The Paris edition of the *Chicago Tribune* was a country newspaper published in a great city." Certainly it paid small-town wages, as staffers never tired of saying, and it was "clubby," and those who worked for it got used to doing jobs they had not been hired for, and although it purported to be America's voice in Europe from 1917 to 1934, and did faithfully print news from "back home," its real beat turned out to be Paris itself, and chiefly that legendary place called the Left Bank.

William Bird, Eugene Jolas, Arthur Moss, Elliot Paul, William Shirer, and Robert Sage are the representatives. Bird ran the Three Mountains Press while working full-time as European manager of the Consolidated Press Association. Al

Laney claims that Sylvia called on several of her newspaper friends to type Joyce manuscripts. Eugene Jolas, who wrote a literary column for the *Tribune,* later emerged as an important figure in the life of James Joyce. Elliot Paul, the only published novelist among them, was one of the editors and contributors, with Ford and Jolas, to the Sunday literary supplement of the Paris *Tribune.* And the twenty-one-year-old Waverley Root, from Providence, Rhode Island, would after thirty years of living and traveling in France write a mouth-watering book, *The Food of France,* revealing his knowledge of the food, wines, geography, and history of the country.

The visitors tended to cluster around Shakespeare and Company, the newspaper office, a publishing company, a review, or a salon. Before the twenties, salon life had eddied around three major personalities—Natalie Barney, Gertrude Stein, and Edith Wharton—and only a few individuals like Bernard Berenson moved among the groups. During the twenties, other groups, less durable or influential, met in the afternoons or evenings, or at dances. Only Shakespeare and Company, however, was open every day and evening—and all factions were welcome. Because of the hours of the bookshop, Sylvia did not have time to attend many salons. She was apt to laugh at the custom, although she herself did occasionally visit the salon of Natalie Barney. One day when Paul Valéry came for his regular visit, she teased him.

"You're all dressed up. You've been in a *salon.*"

Laughing, he took off his hat and placed a finger through a hole in the crown.

"Princess [Bassiano]. You know her, Sylvia?"

"No," she responded impishly. "I know so few princesses."

"But surely you know her, she is an American!"

"Now what would I do in a salon?" she asked. And they both burst into laughter at their exchange.

Shakespeare and Company was open when Dos Passos, who traveled with gusto through Europe, Russia, and the Middle East, returned to Paris and the bookshop in 1924. He was working on *Manhattan Transfer,* the first of his mature works and the first of what he would call his contemporary chronicles of American life. "I met him between *Three Soldiers* and *Manhattan Transfer,*" says Sylvia, "but caught only glimpses of him as he raced by." He slipped his photograph under her door one day, and she added it to her portrait gallery of writers. It was there on 5 September 1924 that he bought his copy of *Ulysses,* which would influence his montage technique in the trilogy *U.S.A.* Perhaps it was through Sylvia that he met the Russian cinematographer Sergei Eisenstein, who spent many hours in the bookshop during a later trip to Paris. Eisenstein influenced Dos Passos's cutback, collage, and speed technique in his novels.

Archibald MacLeish, a "peculiarly unacclimatized young American lawyer," as he later described himself, had arrived in Paris the preceding autumn and discovered "a bookshop of unfamiliar names—a whole generation of new writers no one in New Haven or Cambridge had even heard of." He found Sylvia sympathetic toward would-be writers and began borrowing books from her library. She introduced him to Joyce and Hemingway. He began spending many evenings of 1924 with the Hemingways, the William Birds, and occasionally Sylvia and Adrienne. Joyce was particularly taken with Ada MacLeish, whose lovely soprano voice was soon heard in concerts with Nadia Boulanger's students, Copland, Thomson, Sessions, and The Six. When she gave a concert of Irish songs, Joyce worked on her repertoire, which always included "The Brown and the Yellow Ale." Archie's education and talent soon gained him friends and associates among both American and French writers. Within the next few years Valery Larbaud translated his poetry. He gives Sylvia credit for having introduced him to the French: he feels a "deep debt of gratitude to Sylvia Beach . . . for the quiet *and* excitement of her bookshop and for the friends, mostly French, and including Adrienne Monnier—to whom she introduced me." Soon after his first visit to Paris, he wrote that he felt "awful homesick for you and Adrienne. . . . There are so few *adults* in the world."

A visit from Mrs. Beach, who had been shopping in Europe that spring for purses, pottery, and art objects for her Pasadena store, brought financial relief for both Sylvia and Joyce. With money from her mother, Sylvia was able to build additional shelves in the shop—renovations reported by Florence Gilliam in the Paris edition of the *Chicago Tribune*. And when Sylvia found a flat for the Joyce family, Eleanor Beach, according to Joyce, "kindly offered to lend me the money, which had to be paid immediately." Unfortunately for Eleanor's money and Sylvia's patience, Nora declared the flat inadequate for their books and pictures and Joyce's work, and by the end of the month the family had moved to a higher room in their hotel.

Sylvia Beach's personal relations with those closest to her—those who placed the greatest strain on her—were always cordial, especially those with her mother. Mrs. Beach, much to Sylvia's relief, left Paris soon after her husband arrived there on what Sylvia called a "grand tour . . . in behalf of the churches." Returning from the south of France were Bill and Flossie Williams, for whom Sylvia and Adrienne arranged a dinner with Larbaud, McAlmon, Bryher, and H.D. During the meal a shout from the street announced Pound's arrival from Rapallo. When he refused to come up, Williams went down to embrace his old friend and former classmate. The meal had been specifically arranged so that Williams could spend an evening with Larbaud. Years later Williams would write with fond memories of Adrienne's chicken dinner, the white wine, and the thrill of meeting the French writer. He and Larbaud shared an interest in the history of the Americas. He was startled to learn that Larbaud had read Cotton Mather's *Magnalia,* which he himself had only glanced through, and had written about Bolívar. These discussions with Larbaud were his best moments in France.

Williams spent many pleasant hours with Hemingway. They played tennis, attended prizefights, and had dinner at the apartment above the sawmill, at which time Williams prescribed a diet to supplement mother's milk for Bumby. With Joyce, whose *Ulysses* he admired for its humanity and the banality of its subject, he would remain only casually acquainted. On 12 June he and his wife left France feeling the euphoria that came from having made new friendships and undergone new experiences; but they also had a sense of being out of place and needing to return home. He had written to Kenneth Burke from Austria, "I have heavy bones, I am afraid—there's little here for me . . . only America remains where at least I was born."

In spite of the great influx of visitors this spring and summer, Sylvia remained involved with Joyce and the French. Amid summer heat and hard work, Joyce's vision and powers of attention diminished alarmingly. Warned by Dr. Borsch that he must curtail his writing, he finished the Shaun portion of *Work in Progress,* boxed up his manuscript and notebooks, and telephoned Sylvia to come get them "hastily," thus ensuring rest for his eyes. In June he had his fifth operation, an iridectomy, the second performed on the left eye. Six days later, on Bloomsday, he received flowers from Sylvia, who was now involved with a new French review, *Commerce,* funded by Princess Bassiano. Marguerite Gibert Chapin, a Connecticut woman, had, like a Jamesian heroine, married an Italian prince (Roffredo Caetani). She cultivated and supported French literati, and *Commerce* was to become one of her most important achievements. The title was taken from *Anabase*—"this pure commerce of my soul"—by Saint-John Perse, a contributor to the review. The review was planned by the rue de l'Odéon group: Adrienne would be its first publisher, and its directors (editors) were Valéry, Fargue, and Larbaud. The first issue was to contain translations of *Ulysses.*

To celebrate the new review and its publication of the first French translations of *Ulysses,* Marguerite Caetani hosted a Sunday luncheon. Sylvia had to persuade Joyce to make an exception to his rule of refusing all midday engagements (it was uncomfortable for him to keep his vow not to drink until evening). A car called for Adrienne and Sylvia, then picked up Joyce at his apartment, and finally called for Fargue, at his glass factory near the Gare de l'Est. Predictably, Fargue was not ready. He was still in bed, writing a cat poem. They waited nearly an hour for him. "By the time he had gone through the usual 'visonins' as Adrienne's sister called his inability to decide which hat, coat, tie, shoes etc to wear," claims Sylvia, "he came down, but went right upstairs again to change to another pair of shoes. It took us quite a time to also find a barber as it was Sunday and the barbers shops were all closed: but Fargue must have a haircut." After repeatedly consulting Joyce's watch—he wore four, each telling a different time of day—they arrived in Versailles over an hour and a half late, but received no reproaches: Caetani knew Fargue; they all did. But Joyce was by then full of gloom, could not converse freely, and had cold feet from the long wait for Fargue. The final insult was the arrival of a huge shaggy dog. The dog bounded in and, ironically, went straight for the petrified Joyce, placing his big paws on his shoulders. The dog was hurried out when the Princess became aware of Joyce's terror. She reassured him of the dog's harmless disposition but added a comment about having once had to buy a plumber a new pair of trousers. Joyce leaned over and whispered into Sylvia's ear, "She's going to have to do the same thing for me."

The planners of the review, whose tensions in the following month would eventually place a strain on old friendships, also planned a French *Ulysses*. Joyce and Sylvia had agreed that Adrienne should have the contract for publishing the French translation of *Ulysses*. A year before, Larbaud, whom Joyce wished to be his translator, agreed to translate portions and summarize others. As Larbaud had to give up his plans under the pressure of other projects, Auguste Morel, a young Breton poet whose work Adrienne had published, agreed to do the job, and took the manuscript with him to the seaside, to translate there. Occasionally he came to Paris to consult with Sylvia, Adrienne, Larbaud, and Fargue to prepare for the publication of the first portions in *Commerce*. On 8 June they worked together on the first two-thirds of Telemachus and portions of the Ithaca and Penelope sections. Larbaud included parts of three portions to show the diversity and range of the book. Larbaud's recollection of this session testifies to the contribution that Sylvia made to the French translation:

> It was enjoyable, yes, that translation session on Sunday. . . . Sylvia found the expressions that were most French, and I, dazed by a bad night and the fear of being late at the Gare de Lyon where Ray was waiting for me, I made lamentable efforts to recall some popular expressions that I nevertheless collect in my heart in every country. My Paris housekeeper says, speaking of her concierge, "She's a horror of a woman." Do you see a place where that might go? But Molly Bloom is not as plebeian as Fargue has made her. I believe that the tone discovered by Sylvia is much more exact.

Sylvia was interrupted in these translating sessions by visits from several British friends, including two charming old men whom she adored: Arthur Symons and Havelock Ellis. They were "paying a little visit to Paris together, staying at the Hotel Regina," she informed her mother excitedly. "They come often to my shop and seem to like it very much. Symons talks a lot, reminisces of Verlaine, Swinburne, and everybody and their love affairs and his and the gypsies; he talks very thickly and one gets about a half of his conversation (fortunately)." She was just as enamored with the sixty-five-year-old psychologist: "I love Havelock Ellis. I took him to have a drawing made by Paul-Emile Bécat on Thursday and it turned out marvellously. I am going to have it in my shop."

Sylvia could not avoid the Antheil whirlwind, whipped now into a frenzy by his enterprising promoter, Pound. At a concert in the home of Mrs. Christian Gauss, Pound "sat at the drums which he beat with a will." In the *Criterion* Pound had just published an article praising Antheil as "the first artist to use machines without bathos" and to have "purged the piano." He compared Antheil's music to the "ice blocks" of Picasso. During the first week of July, Pound hosted "Musique américaine: Declaration of Independence," a private concert of his own and Antheil's compositions played by Olga Rudge and Antheil. The guests included Sylvia, Joyce, Margaret Anderson, Jane Heap, and Djuna Barnes. In fact, claims Sylvia, "the whole Rue de l'Odéon family used to attend the concerts of George Antheil, the most memorable of which was the one where Ezra Pound's music was also on the program. Olga Rudge was the violinist. . . . I loved the quintet performed at Miss Barney's. . . . I would even frequent salons if it were to hear Antheil's music." Sylvia, Antheil, and Joyce were excited about George's plan (in which he eventually lost interest) to compose an opera for the Cyclops portion of *Ulysses,* an opera using thirteen electric pianos, each connected to a controlling piano, drums, and steel xylophones.

If Sylvia and Joyce were drawn into the musical world of George, he in turn was involved in the literary life of Shakespeare and Company. In addition to collaborating with Joyce and Pound in musical-literary endeavors, he became friendly with the little-magazine editors who distributed their publications at the bookshop. The next year he acted as a Paris scout for the German magazine *Der Querschnitt* and published musical scores and critical articles in the *Transatlantic Review* and the *Little Review*. An "Antheil Musical Supplement" was published by *This Quarter*. In a *transatlantic review* article entitled "This Quarter: Early Spring" (1924), Hemingway claims, with tongue in cheek, that Antheil is doing drawings of Stravinsky, Sylvia Beach, and others.

When Hemingway commented in the *transatlantic review* that he preferred his Stravinsky "straight" (he later apologized), George was crushed. He came downstairs for comfort, but as the shop was busy, he sat at Sylvia's desk and typed her a note: "You are one of the only friends I have in Paris, and I don't want to lose you." To cheer him, she took him to Barney's salon and to the Moulin Rouge, where he loved the atmosphere. Adrienne enjoyed dancing, and she and George made an amusing pair; she plump, he slight, they danced to the amusement of the women of the Moulin Rouge. When the two American women in the second room above the shop returned to America, Sylvia gave it to Boski and George. To allow him time away from concert tours to compose his music, she solicited the aid of McAlmon, who this summer arranged with his mother-in-law, Lady Ellerman, for two years' financing. Sylvia distributed the money as a sort of allowance to him. On the debit side of her ledger book, she kept nearly daily records—"g.a. 100 fr."—during late 1924 and 1925. The Antheils seem to have asked for their daily bread. More responsibility rested with Sylvia now that Pound was withdrawing from his Paris and Antheil involvements.

Pound, "the complete expatriate," as Huddleston called him, moved to Italy, settling by December in Rapallo. He had spent about four years in Paris, where his tall, lanky figure crowned with wild red hair was a presence central to its literary life. These years had brought his most concentrated effort at sculpting and composing. He left Paris—as he did various schemes and reviews—out of whim or stubbornness or as the result of a certain malaise that came over him, as it had in London in 1920. The malaise was both physical (he had, among other ailments, appendicitis) and spiritual. And Dorothy Pound preferred Italy, which Pound claimed had "civilized Europe twice" and would again. So the medieval knight left the arena for Rapallo. He had succeeded in getting Williams to Paris, and had launched Antheil via book and concerts. He was thirty-eight years old and wanted to concentrate on his own poetry. "It was time for him to stop doing so much for other men and for literature in general, stop trying to educate the public and simply write," claims Cowley. He had begun publishing his *Cantos,* an epic poem that would occupy him for almost the remainder of his life. Bird's Three Mountains Press displayed a specimen of Canto Four at Shakespeare and Company to promote the publication of Pound's *Draft of VII Cantos for the Beginning of a Poem of Some Length*. Henceforth his name would be tied to Rapallo, his growing collections of poems, and his increased interest in economics.

By midsummer Sylvia was eagerly awaiting a vacation at Les Déserts, "the only place I can afford." The Joyces were in Saint-Malo, and planning to winter in Nice. Hemingway, Bird, Dos Passos, and McAlmon were in Spain—it was Hemingway's third trip to Pamplona and the bull run. Even Myrsine was on a month's paid vacation in Les Plombières as a companion to the maharanee of Baroda. "You know her friends from the Far East and how she swarms with them," wrote Sylvia to her mother. Little Hélène, who knew no English, ran errands and Boski occasionally sat in the shop when needed. When Marian Mason Peter came with her two daughters (Sylvia was now six, Phyllis four), Sylvia and Adrienne gave them a tea party. But Sylvia herself had to put off her vacation until her father—who continued to write from Prague or Bucharest that he was delaying his return—appeared. "Naturally he expects me to be here when he gets back," she complained to her mother, "but what about my vacation." Joyce business—each letter contained a list of requests—and his financial demands, also kept her in Paris: "If the New York draft arrives could you forge my name payable to yourself," he wrote, "and remit me the rest? Or if not send it to me and I will return it. Am I right in thinking that I am now 2000 francs in your debt?" In a letter informing her mother of the deaths of Conrad and John Quinn, Sylvia half complains of her "insatiable" vacationing library members ("All day long I am sending off books"), the numerous accounts of the little publishing companies, "la revue de la Princesse" (*Commerce*), and correspondence with Larbaud and Joyce. "Joyce and I keep the international postal service busy with the innumerable communications that pass between us," she adds. "I never worked so hard in my life as this summer but I am never sick."

The only blow to her momentum occurred when she heard that Ford Madox Ford, with Pound's encouragement, was planning to open a bookshop at Bill Bird's office. She was angry but not defeated. The crisis began when Ford placed a notice in his *translantic review,* saying that he would supply readers with books at prices better than the "notorious" ones they had been paying. Although this remark was not directed at her by implication, Sylvia took it personally. The attack, as she took it to be, was twofold: his offer would compete with her business, and his charge implied, to her mind, that she had been fleecing her customers. She did not see the notice until it had appeared several times and McAlmon had casually mentioned that Bird was opening a sort of bookshop on the quai d'Anjou. She called the move "killing the goose that laid the golden egg for I've worked for all that crowd and the only bookseller in Paris who had their books and boomed them at that and made them known to the public and what would they have done without me if I do say it." Although she considered "that old Ford creature only got this thing up to make himself important and a ridiculous old person he always is," she saw an immediate threat and acted at once. In her ironical way she describes the Left Bank showdown:

Well I showed my displeasure immejetly [*sic*]. . . . Their photos disappeared from the walls of Shakespeare and Company, their books from the windows and tables and shelves, and as for the Transatlantic it got buried somewhere so deep that the sales dropped from 50 a month to 0. Great consternation. People dropped in and were convinced that the atmosphere had changed. . . . They wrote to me and visited me to ask what had displeased me which they knew very well already of course. I told them.

Bird, who immediately disassociated himself from any such plan, took Hemingway and McAlmon to pressure Ford, who swore at them and refused to be "coerced." After an exchange of letters with Sylvia, Ford gave in, changed the wording on the notice, and sent all orders for books to Sylvia.

McAlmon and Hemingway and all the others assured me and reassured me and I put back their faces and books in the shop and Adrienne and I invited the Birds and Hemingways to dinner and the incident closed. It taught them all a good lesson and me too.

With her guns still smoking, she turned to her plans for the fifth printing of *Ulysses*, for which she had contracted to pay by monthly 5,000-franc checks. When all the details were arranged, she left for a brief vacation on the Mediterranean with an overworked Adrienne, for whom the "vacation came too late." She fainted one evening at a restaurant in Montpellier. They returned to Paris after ten days, and Adrienne remained in bed. Sylvia arrived to news that her mother wanted her to buy stock for the California shop (a request she did not have time to honor), that her sister Cyprian was ill (Mrs. Beach suspected tuberculosis), and that their cousin Mary was dead. Myrsine was also ill, and Sylvia found temporary help from a Mlle Schroefer, one of Adrienne's customers, and a Miss Kelly, an American librarian on leave, who catalogued her library holdings. All the tensions this fall—after little rest (she wrote Holly that she had had only one dip in the ocean)—caused several attacks of her "old trouble," eczema, which she referred to as "only a tiresome affliction of the outside variety."

One fall visitor she welcomed was Harriet Weaver, brought to Paris in October for a month's visit by H.D., Bryher, and McAlmon on their way to Switzerland. Sylvia and Harriet Weaver liked each other immediately. They had in common their religious rearing, the service to literature, their relationship with Joyce. Although neither woman would talk much of her difficulties with Joyce, there was a sense of mutual admiration and sympathy. Unlike Miss Weaver, Sylvia had been living in daily contact with Joyce, subject to face-to-face exchange and daily problems. Miss Weaver had been spared this ordeal until now, but on this trip she saw Joyce drunk for the first time. Adamantly opposed to the consumption of alcohol, she was upset and disappointed, but refused to renege on her commitment to him. Miss Weaver and Sylvia went to the Joyce flat to hear him read the first watch of Shaun, who falls asleep in "nonland," and the second watch, where jaunty Shaun loosens his "bruisedbrogues." Both she and Miss Weaver could have used help with the passages, Sylvia wrote her mother after her new English friend left: "Miss Weaver stayed a month and we got along like a house afire together."

Sylvia arranged with Victor Records to have made at her own expense a gramophone record of Joyce reading part of the Aeolus portion of *Ulysses,* the only "declamatory" passage that Joyce claimed could be lifted out for recording and the only reading he would make from the novel. Later Sylvia concluded that "it was not for declamatory reasons alone that he chose this passage from Aeolus. I believe that it expressed something he wanted said and preserved in his own voice. As it rings out—'he lifted his voice above it boldly'—it is more, one feels, than mere oratory." For the test and recording, Sylvia "piloted" him to and from the meetings with Piero Coppola, who informed them there was no market for voice reading. Thirty copies were made—chiefly for friends. The record was cut by the end of November, when Joyce underwent his sixth eye operation, at Dr. Borsch's little clinic in the rue du Cherche-Midi, to remove a secondary cataract.

In regard to Joyce, Sylvia Beach always gave half of her attention to posterity, which she believed the recording served, and half to sales. She had begun keeping separate track of the sales of *Ulysses* at the bottom of her ledger book, below the daily sales of Shakespeare, Conrad, Eliot, Whitman, Yeats, Blake, Ibsen, and others. She named or otherwise identified the person who purchased *Ulysses:* two went to Stuart Gilbert; one each to Nancy Cunard, Ernest Walsh, Joseph Beach, a Frenchman, three tourists, a redheaded American, and an English lady. She also recorded such details as "gave press copy to Emma Goldman" and "put aside for Hemingway 60. franc." This listing not only dates writers' appearances in Paris but also reveals the growth of sales of *Ulysses.* For example, she sold large numbers when a new edition or printing appeared. The preceding January she had sold 227 copies of the newly arrived fourth edition. This September she sold her last 46 copies. Sales of the fifth edition also leaped that fall and persisted through 1925.

Sylvia was caught up in quarrels that erupted in October among the friends who were publishing *Commerce.* In the spring after her own full days of work, Adrienne had transcribed poems for *Commerce* that Fargue dictated to her. This unusual method seemed the only way to get Fargue to compose, for, as Sylvia states in an early draft of her memoir, "Fargue had great riches pouring from his tongue but a somewhat constipated pen." Despite all her efforts, he had kept these poems until the end of June, although the review had been planned to appear that month. Sylvia records that Adrienne's patience remained intact even as late as July. Fargue had no conception of her labors or of his own share of responsibility for her collapse later that summer. Tensions mounted. Valéry's copy was also late. Joyce wanted to suppress all punctuation and accent marks in Molly's soliloquy. When Adrienne disagreed, Larbaud, who at the time was staying in Italy, telegraphed his approval of Joyce's decision. Adrienne relented, and when the issue appeared in August, she agreed that it "fulfilled Joyce's intention" of representing "the uninterrupted progression of the earth and its formlessness." A final quarrel, the origins of which are undeterminable, pitted Larbaud against Adrienne, Fargue, Sylvia, and Princess Bassiano. Its resolution, as unexplainable as its origins, had come by the end of November, and the old friends were speaking to each other again.

The year ended with numerous gifts of friendship. A generous and useful gift came fom Bryher, who had asked Harriet Weaver to order files for the accumulating paperwork of the bookshop. Amid the demands and rewards of work, Sylvia always found time for laughter:

Adrienne and I went on a frolic Christmas Eve with the Jules Romains and Jouvet, the actor of the Champs Elysees Theatre. He, poor thing, was low spirited on account of the play he is doing now—a complete fizzle. But we had a good time. After dinner we visited some bal-musettes in the Bastille quarter and danced with low company. We got home at 5. I went to bed for a while, then got up to go over to Joyce's apartment to see him about [an advance copy of] his phonograph record which I had fetched from the "plant" the day before. It is very fine.

The gift of Williams's *In the American Grain,* arriving several months later, contained the essay "Père Sebastian Rasles," which opens with a tribute to all the personalities of Paris, from Picasso to Adrienne, and to Paris itself. Williams, one of many visitors in 1924, was perhaps the most challenging one, because of the deep-seated ambivalence that he felt toward the city and its intellectual and artistic life. He had come to Europe, his essay claims, with his "antennae fully extended," only to find an "old-world culture where everyone was tearing his own meat, warily conscious of a newcomer, but wholly without inquisitiveness—No wish to know; they were served." He returned to America to call Europe "Our Enemy" and to sound a warning that Van Wyck Brooks had made in 1909: travel abroad splits one from the materials and consciousness of one's own country. Although Pound and Eliot were Williams's best exhibits, Hemingway probably disproved his theory. Sylvia, who kept two homes in her heart, knew what Ralph Touchett articulates in the expatriate Henry James's *Portrait of a Lady:* "Ah, one doesn't give up one's country any more than one gives up one's grandfather. They're both antecedent to choice—elements of one's composition that are not to be eliminated." Bryher testifies that Sylvia, who welcomed each visiting American, never gave up her country:

She loved France, she made us feel that it was a privilege to be in Paris, but the common modern mistake never occurred to her, she never tried to identify herself too closely with a foreign land whose childhood myths she had not shared. Great and humble, she mixed us all together instead, the bond between us being that we were artists and discoverers. We changed, the city altered, but after an absence we always found Sylvia waiting for us, her arms full of new books, and often a writer whom we wanted to meet, standing beside her in the corner.

CHAPTER 9

Summer of "a Thousand Parties"

1925

Nor for all our wild dances in all their wild din . . .

— Ulysses

I N HIS *Ledger* F. Scott Fitzgerald calls 1925 the summer of a "1,000 parties and no work." He was right about the parties—and, for himself at any rate, the abstention from work. He partied in Antibes and Paris, where for the first time this summer he met Hemingway. The most famous 1925 party was the trip to Pamplona in July by the Hemingway group—a trip to be immortalized the following year in *The Sun Also Rises*. The French artists partied as well. While the franc fluctuated and students struck (and occasionally rioted) against the government's economic policies, public artistic and cultural life flourished. Often the Americans were the ones to entertain Paris. Antheil's concerts filled the halls and theaters where they were given, many people coming just to treat themselves to a brawl. He even "disappeared" into Africa in order to delight the press. The beautiful black American dancer Josephine Baker was another sensation of Paris this year.

But 1925 was also a year of literary productivity. A new periodical (*This Quarter*) was launched by the expatriates, and a new French periodical (*Le Navire d'Argent*) was founded by Adrienne. Sylvia was involved in some of the parties and a great deal of the literary productivity. She published two more editions of *Ulysses,* arranged for several foreign translations of *Ulysses,* and negotiated with a number of periodicals for the publication of portions of Joyce's *Work in Progress.* In August she managed to escape to Les Déserts, Adrienne's mother's native region, in Savoy, where she would spend part of nearly every summer for the remainder of her life.

Her Joyce work this year was both economic and professional. She continued to have financial worries about him and the bookshop. On 14 February he left a note reading: "Dear Miss Beach: Please excuse this as I can't see well what I am writing. This is the 15 and I have to pay rent. . . ." Withdrawals for Joyce and his family increased, even after the ledger book read "last of royalties." On a larger financial scale, the newspapers gave frequent coverage to the United

States' demands that France pay its war debts. To forestall her own debt and to satisfy continued requests, Sylvia published this year the sixth and seventh editions, or, more exactly, printings, of *Ulysses*. Increasingly, she handled sales by herself because Myrsine spent hours doing research for Joyce in the libraries of Paris. For ten of the seventeen years during which he worked on his last novel, Sylvia was involved with research, arranging for serial publications, and promotion of the novel. Among her papers are notes for Joyce, such as one that lists American cities named Dublin. On many days during 1925 Sylvia sent Myrsine to libraries to search for word derivations and associations for the pun play of Joyce's novel. He called Myrsine his *glaneuse*, that is, gleaner. She sought derivations of words and collected foreign words, work that necessitated spending hours in dusty places. After serious discussion between Joyce and Sylvia concerning Myrsine's health—he thought she looked frail and tubercular—she was sent to the Maison Neuve, a dusty orientalist library, one of the oldest research libraries in Paris. Sylvia gave her a list of key words, including ''love,'' ''like,'' and ''family.'' She pored through European, African, and Asian books—some pages disintegrating in her hands—searching for words. But she remembers the long hours as enjoyable. Proudly she returned with her notes to Joyce each night. She was his eyes. At night he worked late, using a bold pen or crayons of various colors on large cards. Reaching to the chair beside him and picking up a color, he would write, according to Myrsine, holding the paper close to his eyes. ''What are you doing with all those cards?'' asked Nora, who still claimed never to have read a word of her husband's writings. His reply: ''I am trying to write a masterpiece.'' Nora was not the only skeptic. Many friends found the work baffling. Although it was some time before she revealed her true feelings to Joyce, Harriet Weaver confided to Sylvia that she thought he was wasting his time on this new work. She read it chapter by chapter, which he copied out in ink and mailed to her in partial payment for her kindness and financial support.

From Sylvia he asked a different kind of support, for she had unreserved faith in his genius. Apparently she never criticized portions of the work, though she listened bemused to his readings and explanations, for which she was ''never ashamed to ask.'' She also enjoyed the search for words and books. In a letter to Harriet Weaver, Joyce praises her assistance and complains of neglect by other friends in Paris: whenever he recalled a few lines from another's writing or thought of a clever association to be pursued, he asked those friends with him to ''remember it and help me by finding things for me. They all seem to forget about it as quickly as possible except Miss Beach who knows how to whistle books out of the air.''

Ulysses' third birthday party—and Joyce's forty-third—was marred by continuing eye trouble. Conjunctivitis had postponed the operation that was to take place in January. This was again delayed when, two weeks after his birthday, Joyce was rushed to Dr. Borsch's clinic with painful episcleritis. ''I was as near unreason as my worst critics think me,'' he confesses to Miss Weaver. Dr. Borsch applied leeches to draw blood from his eyes and relieve the pressure. All that spring and summer Joyce waited, reluctantly, for his ninth eye operation. Borsch waited for the conjunctivitis to clear and for the dentist to conclude his operations on Joyce's teeth. All his health problems were detailed in the letters he sent to Miss Weaver in London. The working out of his personal matters fell to those in Paris. He dictated some of his letters to Lucia. Even Auguste Morel, busy translating *Ulysses*, helped with correspondence. Joyce did write his own signature on the labels for his recording of the Aeolus episode of *Ulysses*, which was ready in March. Years later she would regret not having known enough to demand the "master" record from the company. "The record *Ulysses* was not at all a commercial venture," she emphasizes. "I handed over most of the thirty copies to Joyce for distribution among his family and friends, and sold none until, years later, when I was hard up, I did set and get a stiff price for one or two I had left." In the last week of March, she played the record in the shop for family and friends to hear. The record, Joyce liked to tell friends, is "on show or rather on hearing in her shop, all this week."

Exiles, Joyce's only play, concluded forty-one performances at the Neighborhood Playhouse in New York, where the sculptor Jo Davidson had helped to get it produced. Although it was not much of a success, the publisher Ben W. Huebsch wrote a letter to the producer Helen Arthur—and sent Sylvia a copy—praising the production. Later in the year a London company presented it; but Paris audiences would not see it for nearly thirty years.

During the first seven months of 1925, Sylvia presided at the crossroads of intense work and some excessive play. After three months' vacation, Hemingway returned in March from the ski trails of Schruns, in Austria, to the streets of Montparnasse. It had not been a time of productive writing; he rationalized to one friend that he probably needed the stimulation of the city life. However, news of two important breaks had come to him on the trip. In January the American Ernest Walsh and the Scottish woman Ethel Moorhead (a prewar suffragette), who were beginning *This Quarter* magazine, gave him 1,000 francs for his short story "Big Two-Hearted River." And in February he learned that Horace Liveright of New York would publish his first collection of short stories, *In Our Time*. When Hemingway came to tell Sylvia his good news, she handed him a pile of mail that included a letter of inquiry from Max Perkins, an editor at Scribners. The letter came too late: just five days earlier, he had signed a three-book option with Boni and Liveright.

This Quarter, to which Hemingway would devote many hours in the early spring, before having a falling out with Walsh, was a short-lived but significant new periodical of the Odéon quarter. McAlmon informed Sylvia that he and Bryher would be published in this "school magazine" with all the other "Paris degenerates." Some of the degenerates were Stein, Hemingway, Williams, Yvor Winters, McAlmon, Bryher, H.D., and Kay Boyle, a young American on the editorial staff. The first issue of what Walsh subtitled an "international quarterly of the arts" was dedicated to Ezra Pound (photographed by Man Ray) with "the gratitude of this generation." Hemingway penned a tribute, more to Pound the man than to his works, commemorating the multifaceted genius for spending four-fifths of his time on advancing and encouraging writers.

A German periodical became important to Odéonia this year. Sylvia was a sort of unofficial adviser for *Der Querschnitt* (*The Cross-Section*), whose Paris representative was Count Alfred von Wedderkop. She began calling him "Mr. Awfully Nice," in acknowledgment of the only two English words he knew. Hemingway played other word games with the name of the periodical. Antheil had been mistakenly solicited for literary manuscripts and sought Sylvia's advice. Soon Joyce's *Chamber Music* poetry, Hemingway's poems (boyish bawdy doggerel), and Hemingway's short story "The Undefeated" ("Stierkampf") were published in *Der Querschnitt.*

Eliot's *Criterion* of London, meanwhile, planned to publish two portions of Joyce's *Work in Progress.* This appearance in *Criterion*, Sylvia excitedly informs her mother, would be "the first time in ten years that anything" from Joyce's pen would be published in England. "And we are a bit nervous." On 14 April, Sylvia mailed the manuscript to Eliot. She would have bad luck with another English periodical, *Calendar of Modern Letters,* when in the summer the printers would flatly refuse to set the type for the Anna Livia Plurabelle portion, beginning "two boys in their breeches" and ending with "blushing and looking askance at her." Next year, for Marianne Moore at the *Dial,* Joyce would also refuse to change a single word of this passage. Each rejection of Anna Livia involved mailings and letters, regrets, and apologies.

With Eliot's *Criterion* and an anthology edited by McAlmon, however, there came some smooth sailing for Joyce's new work. The preceding fall and winter, when McAlmon had conceived of his anthology, he had written first to Joyce. By April of 1925 Joyce was correcting proofs of the four pages from the first version of the Earwicker episode. For this anthology, called the *Contact Collection of Contemporary Writers* and dedicated to Miss Weaver, McAlmon also solicited work from Bryher's London circle: Havelock Ellis, Norman Douglas, Edith Sitwell, Dorothy Richardson, and May Sinclair. The Paris group included Mina Loy, Mary Butts, Djuna Barnes, Stein, and Hemingway. H.D., Bryher, and Williams, of course, were included. The anthology, ready for distribution in July, helped make this a banner year for McAlmon and the Contact Publishing Company. In addition to the anthology, Contact issued five titles, including McAlmon's own best work, *Distinguished Air,* and Stein's *Making of Americans.* When *Distinguished Air* was ready for distribution at Shakespeare and Company, McAlmon dispatched an urgent plea from London not to sell it to anyone who might bring the book to England. He certainly knew that three of the stories (containing scenes of debauchery in Germany) would embarrass the conservative Ellerman family. To her mother, Sylvia explains McAlmon's problem as follows:

[*Distinguished Air*] was seized in England, or the MS was. When the case came up "in Bow Street" the prosecuting attorney accused the book of having the same publishers as *Ulysses.* You see McAlmon's address in Paris being the Rue de l'Odéon, and his printer being Darantière, makes them suspicious. He has detectives on his track over there now; his correspondence has been tampered with and the porter at his apartment bribed.

Norman Douglas, wanting to share Joyce's good fortune with *Ulysses,* proposed, through Bryher and much to Sylvia's anger, a scheme to publish his own book *Experiments,* to include "printed for Shakespeare and Company" on the title page, and to sell all the copies to Sylvia, who would sell them at the bookshop. Sylvia dismissed the scheme as "absurd" and complained to Holly that "Ever since *Ulysses* he has been one of those who longed to have me bring out a little book for him and bring him in a little fortune. They imagine that the success of *Ulysses* was due to me instead of to the book." Sylvia had more than enough work with her own commitments to publishing Joyce, attending Antheil's concerts (now billed as premieres of his *Ballet Mécanique*), assisting Adrienne in her plans for her new periodical, and entertaining a visit from Miss Weaver.

Five days after the French government, fearing riots, had canceled all May Day parades, Harriet Weaver, the gentle future Communist, came to Paris for a brief vacation. Because Sylvia was kind to her, Miss Weaver felt at ease in Odéonia and stayed there three weeks. The formal Englishwoman, exclaim her biographers, "after only eight months' acquaintance" was addressing Miss Beach as Sylvia, and gave Sylvia "the right to use her own pseudonym Josephine." Sylvia, who cared for and respected Harriet Weaver, had the ability to be as comfortable with this prim Englishwoman as she was with Romains and his cronies and Hemingway, all of whom had their boisterous, bohemian side. She often smoothed the relations between her diverse friends, as her correspondence at this time with Harriet Weaver and McAlmon illustrates. When Miss Weaver found out that McAlmon drank, he confided to Sylvia that he did not want to "frighten" Miss Weaver, and Sylvia explained and justified each to the other.

During Miss Weaver's visit, the Joyces moved to 2 Square Robiac, a cul-de-sac off the rue de Grenelle, where they were to live for six years, until 30 April 1931. Sylvia pronounced the apartment "a great success, nice and sunny" with "good room to work." Miss Weaver saw for herself the complicated and demanding business that surrounded any Joyce family activity. She observed that Sylvia was indispensable to Joyce.

With the first edition of *Le Navire d'Argent* (*The Silver Ship*) scheduled to appear on 1 June, both Sylvia and Adrienne were kept busy during April and May with preparations and translations. The periodical—subtitled *Revue Mensuelle de Littérature et de Culture Générale*—was truly international. Sylvia and Adrienne translated Eliot's "The Love Song of J. Alfred Prufrock"—"*La Chanson d'Amour de J. Alfred Prufrock*"—for this issue:

> *Allons alors, vous et moi*
> *Quand le soir est étendu contre le ciel*
> *Comme un patient anesthésié sur une table . . .*

The translation—they thought *The Waste Land* too difficult to tackle—was a work of love, declares Sylvia, "and we never heard any reproaches from our victim." On the contrary, Eliot was proud, he testified later, to owe to them the "introduction of my verse to French readers." When Prufrock sang his love song in the *Navire,* the first complete translation of an Eliot poem was given to the French. Larbaud composed the opening essay of the inaugural issue, a tribute to Paris—a city that, after four years of war, has lived up to its motto: *fluctuat nec mergitur* ("it rocks but it does not sink"). Paris is the "capital of the Occident," he continues, quoting Whitman's "I am a real Parisian." Larbaud appears to address Sylvia when he welcomes "the Parisians born outside of France, that is to say, the foreigners who have been and are able to contribute to the material activity of Paris and to its spiritual power, like Walt Whitman."

Adrienne's partner in *Navire* was the twenty-four-year-old Jean Prévost, a devoted new friend of both bookshops. Prévost, with André Chamson and Marcelle Auclair (whom Prévost later married), had since 1924 been part of a new group of French patrons and friends—all in their midtwenties. Their contemporaries in France were the Surrealists Breton, Aragon, and Tzara, as well as Saint-Exupéry, while their Anglo-Saxon contemporaries were Hemingway, Fitzgerald, Wilder, and Crane. Chamson and Prévost, Sylvia observes, were "utterly unlike each other." Prévost "was rather erratic, temperamental, moody. He was a grammarian and of a philosophic turn of mind." Chamson, on the other side, was "steady, studious, versatile, levelheaded . . . an art connoisseur, a historian, and political-minded." Both temperaments contributed to *Navire;* Prévost served as its assistant editor for a while before turning his full attention to writing essays and novels. Chamson was busy with the publishing details of *Roux le Bandit,* his first novel, which dealt with the hardships of his Protestant past in the Cévennes. Myrsine was particularly fond of Prévost, who was about her own age. He was friendly and strong and would carry for her the heavy boxes of discount books to the sidewalk windows.

Prévost's eyes, however, were on Marcelle Auclair, a young woman recently arrived from Chile, where she had been reared by her French parents. Auclair tells an interesting story of how "a little provincial girl from Santiago, Chile, became acquainted with the great world of French letters." In her early twenties she had published a very successful novel in Spanish. In 1923, fearing that she was being spoiled by all the early fame, she determined to return to her homeland, where she believed competition would be stiffer. Her family and influential friends gave her letters of introduction, which she placed in her briefcase. Before leaving, she showed some of her poetry to the French writer and diplomat Henri Hoppenot, a family friend at the French embassy. He pronounced her poetry poor, except for one verse. For that one good verse he promised her the address of a special person in Paris, a friend of his named A. Monnier. As Auclair was leaving, a messenger arrived with Monnier's address, which she pushed into her cosmetics bag and promptly forgot. Early in her journey to Paris, deciding that France would be a completely new beginning, she opened her briefcase, pulled out the letters—links between Santiago and Paris—and tore them all in half and discarded them.

Later in Paris she discovered the overlooked letter of introduction to A. Monnier behind her mirror in the cosmetics bag. When she realized that she had seen the shop, which stocked the books in which she was interested, she took the letter to its owner. Thus began a long friendship. Although she was only twenty-two, Auclair had already published her successful novel in Chile and was writing articles about literature for a Santiago newspaper. Adrienne introduced her to Larbaud, Fargue, Sylvia, and Prévost. She would marry Prévost in 1926, with André Maurois and Saint-John Perse standing up with them. Because housing was scarce, they would stay for a while in a small room over Adrienne's shop.

Auclair also liked Sylvia, whom she thought "peppy and friendly, with a sense of humor. She spoke excellent French, but used American words to coin new words that looked like French, but were her own coinage." Auclair's description of Adrienne's dinner parties reveals interesting aspects of the personalities of Sylvia and Adrienne as well as of the social role each played with French writers. The dinner parties were frequent during these middle years of the twenties, with eight or ten persons (never more) at table: the Bécats, Auclair, and Prévost were regulars. Fargue was always there—or at least his plate was. Adrienne, who loved the simple peasant dishes of meat and potatoes, often prepared her roast chicken, preceded by quiche Lorraine. She served her meals in their pink dining room. Pink, she informed Auclair, was "good for the appetite." According to Auclair, Adrienne usually led the conversation, often talking of literature. Her large size enhanced her presence. If Sylvia spoke less, as Auclair noticed, she was always involved in the conversation. Her wit served her attentiveness, and at the unexpected moment she spoke a word or two and the group always broke into laughter. Sylvia was small, but her presence was surely felt in the laughter, wit, and liveliness of her personality. The food and fellowship were memorable. "We still had time for friendship and friends in the group around Sylvia and Adrienne," recalls Chamson thirty years later.

The rich aroma of Adrienne's cooking taught Sylvia to appreciate peasant dishes. She would never share Adrienne's passion for food, yet they both had a sweet tooth. One was a light, the other a heavy, eater. "I loved fats," Adrienne would admit in 1942. "I was not afraid of becoming fat; I saw in them the effects of the goodness of the world; in the fashion of the Hindus, I would mentally anoint my gods with them every morning." She often talked of foods and cooking in the same terms she used to distinguish the flavors of books. Novels are the vegetation of society—the "leaves of grass." Poetry is the meat and potatoes (or is it the sweets and nuts?). She savored the artistry of food and words. "I honored flavors as much as genius," she declares.

Sylvia soon learned that Prévost, who this year wrote *Plaisirs des Sports: Essais sur le Corps Humain* (*The Pleasures of Sports: Essays on the Human Body*), was athletic and enjoyed boxing. He was a stocky Norman who prided himself on his hardheadedness, which he proved, according to Sylvia, by banging his head against an iron pipe in the bookshop. "It made the pipe and me shudder." Immediately she introduced him to Hemingway and organized a boxing match between them, the only "violent French / American encounter" that she mediated. Prévost, she remembers,

was ready to take on Hemingway, and we were looking forward to quite a literary sporting event with everybody present. Unfortunately the fighters preferred to have no spectators when the time came, and in great disappointment we had to see them depart to the empty lot (probably the gym) where the affair was to take place but were forbidden to go along and hear the blows thundering on Prevost's head. They came back and nobody had been knocked out and it was a draw, and Hemingway said he had broken his thumb on Prevost's head. . . .

The two young boxers continued to meet during the summer. Four years later Hemingway confessed to Fitzgerald that at this or a later match with Prévost he had asked the timekeeper, Bill Smith, to cut the rounds short if he was in trouble. Some two-minute rounds lasted only forty seconds.

The following year Adrienne and Sylvia were the first to introduce Hemingway's work to French readers. Prévost later wrote favorable criticism of it, quickening Hemingway's literary reputation in France. Years later, in a preface to the French translation of *The Sun Also Rises,* Prévost sounded a prophetic note of warning about Hemingway, whom "nothing would be able to strike down but himself." Although Prévost recognized Hemingway as his own worst enemy (a man with "an obscure need for his own destruction"), he admired his talent—a talent combining the best in American literature with the zeal and discipline of the French.

That spring and early summer, Hemingway continued to box with Prévost and play tennis and box with Loeb, who was forty pounds lighter than he. According to McAlmon, Hemingway often shadowboxed and pranced about, dodging an imaginary opponent's punches. After his first trip to the bullfights, he would indulge in imaginary cape work. Since his return from Schruns in March, he had made many new acquaintances, who would change his personal and professional life. Harold Loeb and Kitty Cannell had introduced him to two slight and stylish sisters from Arkansas, Virginia and Pauline Pfeiffer. Within a year Pauline would capture Hemingway's affections. Loeb also introduced Hemingway to Lady Twysden, a British inhabitant of Montparnasse, with whom Loeb was in love. Hemingway, in turn, introduced Loeb and all his circle to Bill Smith, a childhood friend who had recently arrived in Paris. These were the people who, along with Pat Guthrie, Duff Twysden's Scot companion—a man none of the others seemed to like—were the friends who went to Pamplona with Hemingway and later found themselves in his first novel.

Sometime in late April of 1925 in the Dingo bar, rue Delambre, Fitzgerald met Hemingway. Fitzgerald was at his professional peak; after *This Side of Paradise* and *The Beautiful and Damned,* he had just published *The Great Gatsby.* Hemingway had not yet written a novel, and not until October would he have his first collection of short stories published in America. Six months before he met Hemingway, Fitzgerald (who was only three years older than he) had recommended his work to the Scribners editor Maxwell Perkins. After this meeting at the Dingo, Fitzgerald generously, with no apparent sense of competition, continued to promote Hemingway's work. As further evidence of his assistance, Fitzgerald the following summer read the manuscript of *The Sun Also Rises* and wisely suggested cuts in the early portion.

Hemingway would not be as kind. Although his letters before 1936 reveal his affection for Fitzgerald's work, Hemingway (the apprentice) would intimidate and mock Fitzgerald (the established writer). In 1936, when Hemingway was the established writer, he openly ridiculed Fitzgerald in "The Snows of Kilimanjaro." In his memoirs Hemingway left the distorted portrayal of a one-sided friendship—a portrayal that has become part of myth. After Hemingway had become the world-famous writer, he no longer needed Fitzgerald.

The strain in their friendship was not a professional one. By the time they met, in 1925, their literary subject matter and styles and themes had been established. Any reader of their novels knows they did not influence each other. Yet their very differences, Matthew Bruccoli points out, put a strain on their friendship: "One played the ruined genius, the other played the titan." Failure is the major theme in Fitzgerald's fiction, and he became identified with his own material. Hemingway's mythology, on the other hand, was that of the he-man life of courage and endurance. Later the world-acclaimed he-man would (could) not admire the weak man, the man too influenced (the he-man thought) by his supposedly predatory wife, Zelda. But when they first met this spring in Paris, Bruccoli asserts, the two midwesterners "had great friendship needs. They both sought admiration and companionship. Hemingway needed an audience. Fitzgerald needed heroes." Fitzgerald, a frustrated athlete, admired Hemingway's reputation as an athlete and war hero. He, in turn, introduced Hemingway to Dean Christian Gauss of Princeton and set up weekly lunches for the three to discuss literary topics.

During Fitzgerald's longest stay in Paris, from May to December of 1925, he met no French writers. Nor would he meet Joyce until three years later: not before 1928 would Sylvia introduce him to Joyce and his hero Chamson. He did go, inebriated, to meet Edith Wharton, who thought him "awful" as a person. Fitzgerald was busy partying in what in a letter to Perkins he would call "the hysteria of last May and June in Paris." He sometimes stayed drunk for a week at a time. This dissipated and wealthy (since 1920 his income had averaged $20,500 a year) writer was not highly respected in the Odéon quarter, where he was seldom seen this year.

While Fitzgerald's literary productivity waned in France, Antheil's musical productivity flourished. Publicity for his *Ballet Mécanique* had been building for months. The 21 January edition of the Paris *Tribune* had announced: *"Ballet Mécanique* to Wipe Out Big Orchestras, and Audiences Too." To spread the word and to build the suspense, Antheil had been giving semiprivate previews, at several of which Benoist-Méchin played. Sylvia and Adrienne faithfully attended all his performances. In imagery influenced by the boxing matches she and Sylvia attended with Hemingway, Adrienne describes Antheil's piano playing:

When he plays his music he is terrible, he boxes with the piano; he riddles it with blows and perseveres furiously until the instrument, the public, and he himself are knocked out.

When he is finished he is red, he sponges his forehead; he comes down from the ring with his forehead lowered, his shoulders rocking, his brows knitted, his fists still clenched tight. After a quarter of an hour he is in his right mind again; he laughs, he has forgotten everything.

To add greater punch and orchestration to his concert, Antheil had planned to use fourteen to eighteen (the number varied) player pianos. When informed that there were not that many in all of Paris, he reluctantly settled for a few and ordered three piano rolls to be perforated. When they were finally ready, Antheil took Boski, Sylvia, and Adrienne to the Pleyel plant. There, in a large warehouse room where Chopin had practiced, he test played the rolls, which were eventually inscribed and given to Sylvia.

Although Sylvia advised against the title, *Ballet Mécanique,* Antheil kept it, for he was fascinated by the mechanical. He even referred to *Ulysses* as if it "were a mechanical invention," notes a dismayed Sylvia: he informed her that he liked *Ulysses* because it "works." Sylvia disapproved either of this obsession with the mechanical or of his combination of the beautiful (ballet) with the banal (mechanical). But she did point out to Antheil, who knew little French, that the title contained a clever Dada combination, for it also referred to the French carpet sweeper, the *balai mécanique* (literally, "mechanical broom").

Not certain that everyone in Paris had heard of his coming concert, Antheil planned a sensational publicity stunt. "I have started my enormous publicity campaign," he confides to Sylvia, "so that I can demand and get at least $5,000 [his next paragraph mentions $10,000] for my *Ballet Mécanique.*" He rented a music room at Pleyel's; announced a semiprivate preview of his great composition; and, with funds from Sylvia, went to Africa, presumably in search of "new rhythms." Through Sylvia and Bravig Imbs—who, conveniently, worked at the *Tribune*—the word was spread. Letters from Antheil, portions of which were to be given to the press, describe his travels to places where music is "nothing but sticks." Then he "disappeared." The ensuing publicity was just what he had planned. The preview would have to go on without him. Just as prearranged, Imbs sent *pneumatiques* to Joyce, to Sylvia and Adrienne, to Benoist-Méchin, to representatives of the *New York Herald* and *Paris Times,* and to Elliot Paul, whose writing Imbs greatly admired. When Sylvia and Imbs picked up Joyce in a taxi to go with him to the performance, the day was cool and Imbs wore his checkered black-and-green mackinaw from Dartmouth. The coat made an absurd match for the wild chords and thumping piano music. Imbs played the piano in Antheil's place. In his *Confessions of Another Young Man,* he describes Sylvia as "enthralled" and Joyce as "gripped in spite of himself" by the wild, deafening, and "overwhelming" music on the piano rolls. There was a "gasp of audible relief" when a roll finished. Joyce—who liked Italian opera more than modern music but had great affection for Antheil—asked to hear a portion of the second roll again. When Elliot Paul exclaimed that he was swept off his feet and when the reporter for the *New York Herald* was shocked to hear there might be seventeen pianolas, Imbs assured Antheil that the *Ballet Mécanique* would be a "huge success."

Every day Sylvia answered questions by the press, feeding the sensational story. The *Chicago Tribune* announced him "Lost in African Desert." The *New York Herald* quoted his last interview, in which he claimed new mechanical locks would be needed to keep the audience in the theater once his concert had started. The telegram to Sylvia from Henry Antheil in Trenton reads: "Have you any news of George please cable." Her reply: "George alright only publicity story keep absolutely secret." She herself never revealed the secret publicly—even in her 1959 memoirs, when the deception had long been uncovered. Imbs told all in his 1936 memoirs; but Antheil's memoirs in 1945 admit only that the charges that the disappearance was a hoax "may possibly be true." In her memoirs, Sylvia continues the ruse, claiming that he had become interested in African rhythms while reading *African Swamps,* a book in her library, and "I was beginning to feel very anxious when, happily, Antheil turned up." Yet their unpublished letters establish that she was part of the plot from the beginning. He sends her details of his hiding out in Tunis and asks her to explain everything to Boski: "Sylvia keep an eye upon Boski. I think she is secretly in love with the concierge's son. Write me, is she very good; and be sure to write me if she isn't." For him it was a time of intrigue everywhere. His worries concerning Boski were a projection of his own guilt. He was traveling with a young dance student named Olga. Later he would claim that they had had no carnal relations and that, on the contrary, she persuaded him to marry Boski. He wired his proposal to her; they met in Marseilles and went to her family in Budapest to marry. While they were on the way to their marriage ceremony, a telegram arrived from Sylvia:

FOR GOODNESS SAKE GEORGE COME BACK TO PARIS IMMEDIATELY AND DENY
THIS IDIOTIC NEWSPAPER STORY LIONS ATE YOU IN AFRICA OR ELSE YOUR
NAME WILL BE MUD FOREVER STOP TIME IS OF ESSENCE STOP SYLVIA BEACH

With Boski staying behind to collect the legal documents from Hungarian authorities, George flew to Paris for his "reappearance."

His *Ballet*—his pièce de résistance—needed some sauce. His disappearance brought enough publicity to carry his name across two continents. The preview concert and its missing conductor received widespread notice, including the essay by Adrienne the following January in *Navire.* Interest and anticipation mounted until June of 1926, when the full performance was given in the Théâtre des Champs-Élysées, one of the sensational events of the twenties.

Another friend of Sylvia's left Europe for Africa this summer—André Gide. After finishing *Les Faux-Monnayeurs (The Counterfeiters),* he and Marc Allégret, his young companion, went to the Congo. Unlike Antheil's disappearance, Gide's trip appeared to be a genuine search for the rhythms of Africa. But he took with him on this primitive search the baggage of the literature of Europe—such as Conrad's *Heart of Darkness*—for his journal, dedicated to Conrad, is full of literary quotations. Sylvia's private view of the trip, undoubtedly influenced by Gide's failure to support Joyce, is expressed in a letter to her mother:

Gide and Marc Allegret have just been in to say gooby [*sic*]. They leave tomorrow for Africa where they are going to stay a year. Mark is to send me a picture of Gide. What a funny creature he is. He can't think of anything else to do so he is going to Africa. His last books are no good and *Corydon* only made him ridiculous. He is jealous of Joyce and has tried to influence people here against him, but unsuccessfully I fear.

A major purpose of the trip was to gather material for a movie. Gide wrote the scenario, Allégret (who would later become a director) operated the camera, and Sylvia and Adrienne were in the admiring audience when the amateur movie was shown later at the Théâtre du Vieux-Colombier. "Marc Allégret was a great friend of mine," claims Sylvia in her memoirs; "he used to come often to the bookshop. Once he brought me a little turtle which he said was a present from Gide." Apparently she kept her private feelings about Gide in the family.

Although Pound, Cowley, and a few others had left Paris permanently, many more writers arrived this year. Increasing numbers of patrons multiplied the problem of unreturned library books. For the first time, Sylvia printed a card reminding members of their overdue borrowings. If receiving a reminder created any embarrassment, it was certainly dissolved by the humor of the drawing on the card: Shakespeare pulling out his hair. On Sylvia's ledger, along with the familiar names of those who were renewing their membership in the library, several new ones appear: Booth Tarkington, William Shirer, Elmer Rice, and Glenway Wescott. The name of William Faulkner does not appear, though he was in Paris several times during the latter half of 1925.

Wescott met Sylvia, whom he describes as "a sweet little sparrow," on a Paris street. "She did not like me," he admits, blaming Hemingway, who had revealed his antagonism toward Wescott to their mutual friends. "Paris was a small town, full of crosscurrents of gossip, misunderstanding and bad feeling." Though Stein would say much later that Wescott "has a certain syrup but it doesn't pour," he championed her ("she did not ruin syntax") and took a dislike to Joyce, whom he described on one occasion as a drunken Irishman.

While he was living in New York, Wescott, who was twenty-four years old in 1925, had written an essay satirizing the hypocrisy and vulgarity of American life. By the time the article appeared, in the August issue of the *Transatlantic Review*, Wescott was in Paris—away from "His Censorship Mr. Sumner," Prohibition, and the cultural wasteland that he criticized. "The young people dream only of getting away," he wrote years later in *Good-bye Wisconsin*. Thus began an eight-year sojourn in the middle of an enormously productive period in his life. With his companion Monroe Wheeler, he became a member of the lending library in February; then they moved to southern France, where he wrote poems, novels, and essays about Wisconsin and his familial and regional origins.

Typical of the very young Americans who came to find jobs in Paris was William Shirer, a recent graduate of a small Iowa college. Shirer found an editorial job with the Paris *Tribune*, where he worked with Eugene Jolas, Elliot Paul, James Thurber, and other newsmen with larger ambitions to succeed as writers apart from newspaper journalism. He found the Odéon quarter immediately. Because he wanted to read more French literature, he frequented Adrienne's

PLEASE RETURN :

American Doctor's
Odyssey —

TO :

SHAKESPEARE AND COMPANY

12, RUE DE L'ODÉON - PARIS - VIe

shop, "though I loved to browse among the shelves and tables of Shakespeare and Company, or be invited to tea in the back room, when in winter a fireplace blazed and there was much good talk."

Elmer Rice, now recognized as a prominent American dramatist of the twenties—although his fellow expatriates were unaware of his significance—came to the bookshop in July. He had already written *The Adding Machine* (1923) and *The Subway* (not staged until 1929), and though he would win the Pulitzer Prize in 1929 for *Street Scene,* he had in 1925 experienced a series of failures in the New York theater. He came to Paris to rekindle his creativity. Using European expressionistic techniques, his plays debunk materialism and the mechanization and sterilization of American society. Paris, with its little shops and ancient buildings, gave the appearance—for Rice and other Americans—of individuality and lack of standardization. In a play he wrote several years later, Rice sounds a note for many young Americans living on the Left Bank:

"Good God! Don't you understand that physical sustenance isn't enough—that one must have spiritual sustenance, too? A man can't create in a spiritual vacuum, in an atmosphere that's aesthetically sterile. And that is precisely what America is: a spiritual vacuum, a cultural desert."

Rice occasionally visited the bookshop to borrow books while he and his family lived briefly in a flat on the Left Bank.

Several times during the summer Sylvia also enjoyed the company of her father, who, interrupting his church work in eastern Europe, made brief visits to Paris. At the end of June, she also saw her sister Holly, who was on a buying trip to Europe and Morocco for the shop that their mother, with money borrowed from Princeton friends, had opened for her and Cyprian in Pasadena, California. Although Holly took only a passing interest in the shop, which sold Italian and French art, bric-a-brac, and small pieces of furniture, she enjoyed traveling on its behalf. In a letter to her mother, who had stayed in Pasadena, Sylvia sent a copy of the first issue of the *Navire d'Argent.* The issue, she explains, had provoked a small scene in the bookshop: Lady Rothermere "came roaring around this afternoon," Sylvia confides to her mother. She complained about the little bibliography about Eliot in the *Navire,* which stated that he had founded *Criterion.* Lady Rothermere, who claimed that right, was eventually calmed after a visit to Adrienne's shop.

Among all the patrons of Shakespeare and Company, the children were the least demanding. For them, Sylvia had a shelf of toys and children's books in the back room and a "long-suffering little armchair at a round red table." Often they asked to be helped up to see Larbaud's West Pointers. One five-year-old named Harriet Waterfield, whom Sylvia took to the zoo, called Sylvia her "best friend." Another, Violaine Hoppenot, a precocious young French child who spoke excellent English, read Sylvia's Kate Greenaway books. She was named after the heroine in the play *La Jeune Fille Violaine,* by Claudel, her godfather.(Her father, Henri Hoppenot, was a poet and French ambassador.) Her youngest visitor was John Hadley Nicanor Hemingway, who by now was trained to show off for his father by putting up his fists and assuming a ferocious expression. According to Sylvia,

Bumby was frequenting Shakespeare and Company before he could walk. Holding his son carefully, though sometimes upside down, Hemingway went on reading the latest periodicals. . . . As for Bumby, anything was all right as long as he was with his adored Papa. [Later] his first steps were to what he called "Sylver Beach's." I can see them, father and son, coming along hand in hand up the street. Bumby, hoisted on a high stool, observed his old man gravely, never showing any impatience, waiting to be lifted from his high perch at last; it must have seemed a long wait sometimes. Then I would watch the two of them as they set off, not for home, since they had to keep out of Hadley's way till the housekeeping was done, but to the bistro around the corner; there, seated at a table, their drinks before them—Bumby's was a grenadine—they went over all the questions of the day.

Hemingway describes those mornings with his son in Chapter 5 of his posthumous novel *Islands in the Stream*. Thomas Hudson and his oldest son recall the flat over the sawmill, walking through the Luxembourg Garden, greeting Joyce (Bumby was "one of Mr. Joyce's friends"), and sitting at the café.

Although the summer of 1925 has become known for the partying in Montparnasse, Pamplona, and Antibes, it was a summer of hard work in the Odéon quarter. Sylvia and Adrienne would be the last to go on vacation. To handle her Joyce work when Myrsine could not work, she hired a Mlle Schreiber. In June, at a small party celebrating Bloomsday in Joyce's new, comfortable apartment, Sylvia took a series of pictures of him, with his hands on his hips, wearing the white jacket that he worked in—a jacket that looked like that of a barber or a pharmacist. Harriet Weaver, delighted with the clarity of the pictures, expressed admiration that Sylvia had kept Joyce in a "fixed position for so long." Bloomsday brought a flurry of sales of *Ulysses* V, the supply of which was running low. Plans were under way for another printing. At the end of July, Joyce asked Sylvia, "Does *Ulysses* VI (it's like the name of a pope) come out on Saturday? I suppose you will hand over the fact to your press agents." She did. The 31 July "Latin Quarter Notes" of the Paris *Tribune* read:

And still they are begging for copies of *Ulysses*. Sylvia Beach of Shakespeare and Co. tells us the sixth edition of the Joyce opus is due off the presses tomorrow. Meanwhile, his health being somewhat improved, the author is occasionally seen on the Left Bank. . . . Sylvia herself believes she is entitled to a well-earned rest and is leaving for the Savoie, not to write a book, she says.

Although No. VI did not appear on 1 August, as they had wished, they anticipated an improved edition. The quality of the paper of No. VI would be better, Sylvia was certain, since she had shown a recent article in the *Bookman* to Darantière, in which its author, Robert Forrest Wilson, charged that Joyce's "monument of obscurity" and obscenity was "a muddy slovenly" printing job on "poor quality paper." Though she discounted the article (Wilson was "merely a journalist''), it was "the best piece of publicity in the world"; she showed it to Darantière, she said, precisely in order to "put him on his mettle." Joyce worshipers, whom Wilson describes as sitting "at the feet of Joyce," waited nearly six more weeks for the new printing. When it arrived, it sold briskly, despite (or because of) an occasional hostile review. Criticism of *Ulysses,* such as the early comments of George Bernard Shaw (who received the Nobel Prize for literature in this year), did not prevent Joyce or Sylvia from feeling enthusiasm for his new, and soon to be more controversial, work.

To simplify the duplication and mailing out of various photos of Joyce and early portions of *Work in Progress* to five separate publications, they adopted a sign for each:

Δ Anna Livia Plurabelle
[Shem
Λ First Watch of Shaun

Farming out extracts from it was one of her jobs because she, Joyce had already determined (to no avail, as it turned out), would eventually publish the entire book.

Joycean activities at Shakespeare and Company did not cease when the four Joyces vacationed—usually to places connected with the new book. Sylvia discloses that "everything in his life was relevant to his work. [Even] his regular floral offerings on anniversaries and other gifts to his family and friends always had reference to what he was working on at the time, or some event in his life— never to what concerned them [family and friends] personally." The readers of *Finnegans Wake* will link the vacations to the "giant" in Bognor (1923); to rows of old Menhirs at Carnac (1924); to rivers, such as the Garonne at Bordeaux (1925); to the Battle of Waterloo (1926). On the July "grocer's list" for Sylvia (Joyce once admitted having "a grocer's assistant's mind") were prescriptions to be filled and sent to him; piano bills to be paid; persons to be seen or written; books and papers to be procured; copies of his works to be sent (immediately) to persons in Ireland, Holland, England, America, or Italy. One errand for Joyce took her to the Hemingways' on the evening of 24 June, the day before the Hemingways left to fish in Burguete on their way to Pamplona, the Fiesta of San Fermín, and a summer of partying and drinking. Those who could not afford the kind of first-class tour the Joyces took, or the more moderate Spanish vacation of a Hemingway, stayed in Paris.

Alcohol consumption had doubled, announced the French Academy of Sciences that summer. The only explanation given, according to the *New York Times* (23 July 1925), was the increased spending power among French workers. No one thought to count the bottles in Montparnasse. Nor could anyone have counted, had he tried, the number of poor students, would-be artists, and third-class tourists that summer at the corner of the boulevard du Montparnasse and the boulevard Raspail. They filled the sidewalk cafés, growing beards, laughing gaily, or staring lovingly at their own reflections in the drinks they consumed. Some were drowned. Some were destructive, many sophomoric, clinging together without interest in France or the French culture. There were a dozen hangers-on for every serious writer, drinking and playing in Montparnasse, which Ford calls "the latest of all Cloud-Cuckoo Lands." Hemingway calls these hangers-on "bums" with remarkable kidneys. Westbrook Pegler, writing in America, would call them "a queer bunch of undisciplined and self-indulgent brats who were determined not to pull their weight in the boat and wanted the world to drop everything and sit down and bawl with them. A kick in the pants and a clout over the scalp were more like their needing. . . . ." The sentiment, in the instance of the wasters, was no doubt just; but Pegler and a vast segment of the public had little or no sympathy for those who were trying their best to be serious workers.

In a chapter that presents the gastronomy of Adrienne's savory chicken, one must speak, in contrast, of the Montparnasse heartburn. For these artists and hangers-on it was oysters and champagne if they were flush—a bummed glass of wine if broke. The quarter was full of hungry people from all over the world. An observer could not always distinguish between the serious writer, who dropped into a café after work, and the hangers-on. Indeed, some of the writers who habitually drank—such as Stearns, Fitzgerald, Crane, and Crosby—were more raucous and less responsible and productive during these Paris years than during other periods of their lives. A few American and French artists successfully navigated through what the *Bookman* article had called the two centers of American culture in France: Shakespeare and Company and the Café du Dôme.

The Dôme—perhaps more than the Rotonde, the Closerie des Lilas, the Coupole, Lipp's, and the Flore (on Saint-Germain), or the Dingo—was the central stopping place this summer. The café, at the corners of the boulevards Raspail and Montparnasse and the rue Delambre, is mentioned in more than fifty books in fifteen different languages. In the second number of his *Exile,* Pound would describe the carrefour Vavin by the Dôme as having "an air of Eighth Avenue, New York, on a Saturday night in or about 1910, except for the gaiety of the paper lantern, in place of that of the metal street lamps." At the beginning of the expatriate flood, two or three years later, it had "the air of a suburban strawberry festival in the America of my youth."

Among the schoolteachers, artists, students, businessmen, and tourists from many countries of the world, certain Montparnasse regulars stood out: Kiki, the model who lived with Man Ray; Jimmy, the barman at the Dingo; Harold Stearns; Duff Twysden and Pat Guthrie, who lived high at the Ritz when the check came from England, then moved back to the quarter and poverty when funds ran out; the robed and Byronic Laurence Vail, married to Peggy Guggenheim; the boisterous French Surrealists. In the mid twenties some equally flamboyant visitors also added to the flavor, including Isadora Duncan, now middle-aged and plump, on her return from Moscow.

The crowded memories of this period include Antheil's riotous concerts; Ford's dances at a *bal musette;* a horse-drawn cab in the Bois de Boulogne; Peggy and Laurence Vail's weekends; the Harold Lloyd and Buster Keaton movies to assuage homesickness; all-night drinking and early-morning onion soup;

the bizarre antics of the Fitzgeralds, occasionally followed by a letter of apology to a friend; the Pamplona bullfights in July; the movable parties that transferred people and locations as the night progressed (or deteriorated). Discussions usually concerned art or one's subconscious, for Freud was very much in vogue. But these American games—retold into American mythology—were matched by a boisterous group of French artists.

Louis Aragon, Picabia, Tzara, and the other French Surrealists were highly visible in Montparnasse cafés and cinemas. Their exploits and demonstrations were notorious. Like storm troopers, they would stage a raid or riot against any play, concert, film, publication, or café they did not like. If they occupied a table at the Dôme, claims one American observer, "it was invariably the noisiest of all and they were the center of attraction." They were rebel sons of the bourgeoisie, "wild beasts in a cage," as they described themselves. They tried, perhaps unsuccessfully, not to take anything—even their own disillusionment—too seriously. One evening the year before, when Loeb, Dos Passos, and Cummings were at Malcolm Cowley's country home in Giverny, they had exclaimed loudly about the accumulation of unwanted books. Soon Cowley began to tear up and burn several bad review books and French university texts. As the books and periodicals went up in smoke, Cummings—in a Dada gesture—urinated on the fire. More than one American observed the contrast between the "noise and feuds" of the Surrealists and the "superior stature" of writers like Gide, Valéry, and Joyce, "who in the quiet of their studies went on working out their individual and clearly marked destinies." The contrast is a matter of degree (and age). Joyce got drunk quietly.

French literary social life could range from the quiet—Adrienne's dinner parties and the salon life, such as Natalie Barney's—to the rowdy. This was the year of touring American jazz groups and the nude dancing of the American Josephine Baker. The French were wild about American jazz; the year before, Stravinsky had returned from an American tour excited about this musical form. In the fall of 1925 Sylvia would hold a reception to introduce her French friends to Paul Robeson and Negro spirituals. Her social life was almost exclusively French, unless the American party was literary or included the French, whose parties were often as gay and frivolous as the American expatriate parties. At one such party—attended by Sylvia, Joyce, Adrienne, Gide, Fargue, and others—the guests sat on pillows on the floor and Fargue enlivened the group. He elaborately introduced a magician called Ghilighili, whom he claimed to have discovered looking for a match in Montmartre. When the man touched his finger to his cigarette and it flamed, they all oohed and aahed like children. Before the evening was over, Joyce and Adrienne danced the snake.

The playfulness and daring of Adrienne and Sylvia is illustrated by an incident that McAlmon claims occurred the year before. They had urged him to attend the Quatz Arts Ball, the most notorious yearly dance in Paris: any kind of dress or undress, any form of behavior, was acceptable. "For the first and only time," he testifies, he consented to accompany them. After dinner at Sylvia's, where he drank red and white wine as well as a large portion of brandy, they dressed him in a cheesecloth toga (he does not report what they wore) and made up his face. Because they were not art students, they had to sneak into the party, where they found swirling bodies, some naked except for body paint, and couples openly having sex. Although he does not report the reaction of Adrienne and Sylvia, McAlmon claims (much later, recollecting his emotion in tranquillity) to have found it all "neither upsetting, beautiful, nor exciting." Pushing aside a protesting art student, he helped himself to bottles of champagne. Soon he was trying, at first futilely, to lift the plump Adrienne. After much laughter and with slipping toga, he succeeded. By the time the two women had carted him off to his hotel room, he had lost his toga completely.

McAlmon took Sylvia and Adrienne to the gay bars of Montmartre. They dropped in first at Loyalty, where the transvestites, dressed in hats and furs, sang and danced on the stage. Sylvia remembers that "the shutters were closed and heavy curtains drawn across the windows so that neither the police nor a breath of air would get in." Farther up the hill was a "more authentic" place called La Petite Chaumière, where beautiful "girls" in pearls and diamonds accompanied elderly men. What interested Sylvia most was the swooning and "little false shrieks and the cooing sounds" of the "ladies."

One week-long party of this year became immortalized in Hemingway's *The Sun Also Rises*. The Hemingways, Don Stewart, Bill Smith, and the Duff Twysden / Harold Loeb / Pat Guthrie threesome attended the Festival of San Fermín. Both the fishing at Burguete and the partying at Pamplona were soured—the first by the lack of fish, the second by the bad mix of people. But it was the sourness that fermented Hemingway's creative juices. From 21 July (his twenty-sixth birthday) to 21 September, he wrote the rough draft of the novel he first called *Fiesta*, a novel about the "lost generation." In February of this year, he had expressed the same "lost generation" nihilism in "The Age Demanded," a poem (whose title was borrowed from Pound) in *Der Querschnitt*. The poem ends:

> The Age demanded that we dance
> And jammed us into iron pants.
>
> And in the end the age was handed
> The sort of shit that it demanded.

Harold Loeb, hurt by Hemingway's use of his character and background for the weak Robert Cohn in *Sun*, tells his own version in his memoirs. These conclude with his return to the United States following the Pamplona episode: "Some of us were 'lost' for a time," he admits, "separated from our traditional moorings and attached to nothing whatsoever." However, he adds, "One by one we went on to recognized achievements or succumbed to the attrition of our dreams." Hemingway was disdainful of the "expatriates" who, unlike himself, could not pass physical tests, hold their liquor, or write well.

No talk of the expatriate "good life" would be complete without an introduction to the Murphys, members of the American upper class and occasional hosts to Hemingway. Wealthy by inheritance, they had moved to France in 1921. They owned the Villa America at Cap d'Antibes, on the Riviera, where they delighted in serving hot dogs and playing the latest jazz records, which they received from a friend in Jimmy Durante's band. They were friends of Cole Porter as well as of Picasso—and certainly of Zelda and Scott, who dedicated *Tender Is the Night* to them. Monthly or seasonally they came to their Paris flat for the latest exhibit or costume ball. Hemingway would spend many hours in the following summer with the Murphys, the Fitzgeralds, the MacLeishes, the Dos Passoses. "There was no one at Antibes this summer," Fitzgerald mockingly laments to a friend, "except me, Zelda, the Valentinos, the Murphys, Mistinguett, Rex Ingram, Dos Passos, Alice Terry, the MacLeishes, Charlie Brackett, Maude Kahn, Esther Murphy, Marguerite Namara, E. Phillips Oppenheim, Mannes the violinist, Floyd Dell, Max and Crystal Eastman, ex-Premier Orlando, Etienne de Beaumont—just a real place to rough it, an escape from all the world."

For hardworking bookshop owners, the place to "rough it and escape from all the world" was a mountain in eastern France in the province of Savoy. Leaving Prévost in charge of the *Navire* (the September issue was devoted to Blake and included Sylvia's drawings by him) and Myrsine in charge at Shakespeare and Company, Adrienne and Sylvia left on Sunday, 2 August. They arrived at Chambéry in a train that was ironically called *Le Train de Plaisir*, for they had to sit up all night on hard, wooden seats. They then took the autocar to Plainpalais and walked up the long, steep mountain to a plateau of scattered thatch-roofed chalets. A haywagon carried their trunks. On this 4,250-foot-high plateau (later called La Féclaz), they had no postal facility, transportation, or modern conveniences. Their commune and the group of tiered hamlets down the mountain from them were called Les Déserts, an odd name for a place with cows rather than camels. Les Déserts, claims Sylvia, was as isolated as it was peaceful:

. . . it's peaceful here after the hard life in Paris. We had so much work to do before leaving; up to the last minute I was correcting typescript for "Mr J J" as Adrienne calls him, and declaring my *chiffre d'affaires* [turnover] for the *bureau de contributions* [taxes] and writing sheets of instructions for Myrsine. . . . No sooner did we reach this mountain top than the burdens of all the book and writer business rolled down its sides into the valley.

The smell of clean air and wood fires soon made the fatigue of Paris work and an uncomfortable train ride seem remote. By day they roamed the hills and pine forests. As the night fell behind the high peaks, they warded off the cold with hot water in beer bottles. They were serenaded by dogs barking at night and awakened at dawn by the cry of the cock and the clang of the cowbells.

Sylvia was an athletic bookworm. In her Bridgeton youth she had spent hours curled up with a book instead of attending school. Yet she loved the outdoors, horseback riding, and skating. Walking through the woods, she always expected to come across an Indian from Cooper's *Leatherstocking Tales*. Her pleasure in Savoy was chopping wood. Until two weeks before she died, at seventy-five years of age, Sylvia chopped wood nearly every summer in Les Déserts, where her health improved. Because dairy products are a staple on the plateau, she learned to drink milk, which she had always disliked, and believed that the dairy diet lessened her headaches.

During the summer of 1925, they stayed with Fine (Josephine), Adrienne's cousin, and her husband, Gay, a very generous man who was mysteriously nick-named L'Économe. L'Économe was one of the sons of "La Grosse Jeanne"— all these Savoyards had nicknames. The two women from Paris slept in a corner of the hayloft, partitioned off for two beds. Sylvia wrote her mother, "Strings [were] stretched across the air to hang our clothes on." The hayloft was their dressing room; a chicken crate (containing two hens being fattened for Sunday dinner) was their toilet table (the following year Gay made them a few pieces of furniture). They reached these spartan quarters by an outside ladder. "The privy was on the side of the chalet next to the road, so that you could hold conversations with people passing by," says Sylvia. All the villagers lived this simple life, sleeping in small rooms behind the stable. The room of Sylvia and Adrienne was on the "second floor" right over the stable, so that they "never missed any important event"—"a cow having a calf at three in the morning by lantern light, with everyone present"; and a squealing pig, stepped on by a cow and sewn up by Fine. They were a world away from the dramas of Paris. "At daybreak the stable doors were opened and out poured the cattle like a crowd leaving the theatre," remembers Sylvia.

While the American colony at Antibes played their party games, Sylvia spent her evenings sitting by a lantern listening to the mountain news of her neighbors. A hay wagon had upset coming down the mountain. A cow had fallen down a precipice, and it had taken all the men on the plateau to haul her up with ropes from the ledge. Some young cow would not have anything to do with Ferdinand's bull. An eagle had carried off a rabbit. If personal calamities occurred or the butter would not come in the churn, there was talk that one of the old women had been hexing her neighbor. Remedies included boiling a lot of rusty nails in a pot or checking under the plank in the floor to see whether a toad was underneath. In addition to a few superstitions, Sylvia learned many lessons from the Savoyards: how to slow the pace of life to the bare essentials; to appreciate the smell of hay, wood fires, and warm milk; to recognize an authentic shepherd dog by his one blue and one gray eye. She also learned to admire what she called this "heroic race . . . from the high mountains who could wield axes in the forests, build houses, harvest their crops on the side of precipices, and drink it down when the day was done."

Although they felt "impregnable," mail did break through the solitude of Les Déserts. In August a Hemingway letter from Valencia announced that he was hard at work on a novel (*Fiesta*), having already written 15,000 words and seen seventeen bullfights. She always heard from Joyce, who thought they were in a desert and could not understand their lack of luxurious accommodations, postal service, and taxis. The lack of these three, so vital to Joyce's life, was precisely why they loved Les Déserts. The only disagreeable aspect of Les Déserts was the thunderstorms, which occasionally set fire to the thatched roofs. This summer Joyce wrote from rainy Rouen, worrying about Sylvia's handling of the correspondence with the publishers of the reviews: "How will you manage to send [Anna Livia Plurabelle] from the desert?" Later he confesses, "I had to rob 3000 francs from you but I wrote to Walsh to send my cheque in name of Miss Moschos and to Eliot to send the other payable to you. . . . I hope they send you those cheques to cover my advance."

Neither Joyce's financial problems nor her empty till could mar her nearly three weeks in Les Déserts. "Not a single 'Penman' anywhere near," she marvels; "no one possessed a book." Adrienne calls Les Déserts "one of our homelands, one of the faces of our soul." "I preferred [the rustic home of] *Bal l'Économe,*" claims Sylvia, "to any Ritz." The air was so heady, one needed "no glass of anything to be high."

The Beach sisters: Hollingsworth Morris, Eleanor Elliott (Cyprian), and Nancy Woodbridge (Sylvia) in the Bridgeton, New Jersey parsonage around 1894.

Below left, Nancy Dunlop Harris Orbison, the maternal grandmother of Sylvia Beach.

Below right, Sylvia Beach in 1916 or 1917 during her Palais Royal days with Cyprian.

Sylvia as a volunteer farm worker in Touraine in August 1917, the year she met Adrienne Monnier.

Below, Adrienne Monnier in backroom of her bookshop at No. 7 Rue de l'Odéon, where she lived from 1915 to 1918, taken around the time she met Sylvia Beach. *Princeton University Library*

On the opposite page, Stephen Vincent Benét and Sylvia Beach with unknown woman in front of Shakespeare and Company at its first, location, No. 8 Rue du Dupuytren in 1921. *Princeton University Library*

Alice B. Toklas and Gertrude Stein and Godiva, the car in which they took Sylvia for rides. *Bettmann Archive*

Ezra Pound at the window of Shakespeare and Company around 1920, taken by Sylvia Beach. *Princeton University Library*

Sylvia Beach and James Joyce with early reviews of *Ulysses* in 1922. *Princeton University Library*

Sylvia Beach with her parents, Sylvester and Eleanor, at Cherbourg on 24 July 1922.

Above left, Robert McAlmon in Shakespeare and Company in 1923, taken by Sylvia Beach. *Princeton University Library*

Right, Ernest Hemingway in Shakespeare and Company about 1922, taken by Sylvia Beach. *Princeton University Library*

Below left, Paul Valéry in Shakespeare and Company, taken by Sylvia Beach.

Right, Harriet Shaw Weaver in Shakespeare and Company, taken by Sylvia Beach. *Princeton University Library*

Bryher (Winifred Ellerman). *Man Ray Collection, Princeton University Library*

Ezra Pound, John Quinn (standing), Ford Madox Ford, and James Joyce, *transatlantic review* conference, in Pound's studio, 1923. *Princeton University Library*

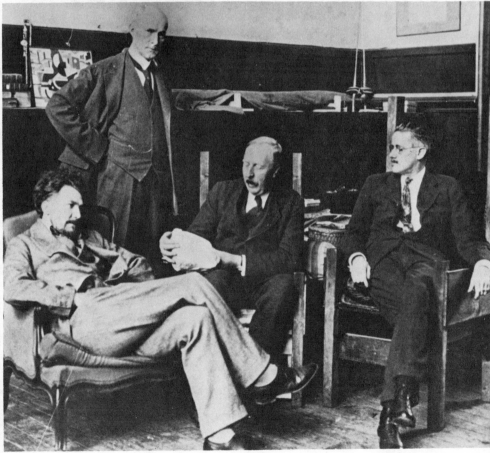

George Antheil climbing to his apartment at No. 12 Rue de l'Odéon.

Nora, James, and George Joyce at a restaurant in the early twenties. *Princeton University Library*

Eleanor (Nellie) Orbison Beach on 14 June 1924. *Princeton University Library*

Some of the Potassons at the Foire d'Orsay during June 1924: Valery Larbaud, Léon-Paul Fargue, Marie Monnier, Sylvia Beach, and Adrienne Monnier.

Left, Sylvia Beach and Clovis Monnier with Mousse, his dog, in Rocfoin around 1925.

Right, James Joyce on Bloomsday 16 June 1925, taken by Sylvia Beach. *Princeton University Library*

A gathering of writers connected with *La Nouvelle Revue Française:* Jean Schlumberger, seated left; standing next to him are Lytton Strachey and Madame Van Rysselberghe; André Gide, center, reading; André Maurois, looking over his left shoulder; standing far right, Jean Prévost; fourth from right, Roger Martin du Gard; seated on the step left, Pierre Drieu de la Rochelle. *Princeton University Library*

Myrsine and Hélène Moschos, Sylvia Beach, and Ernest Hemingway, who came with bandaged head to Sylvia's birthday party during March 1928. *Princeton University Library*

F. Scott Fitzgerald and Adrienne Monnier sitting on the threshold of La Maison des Amis des Livres in 1928, taken by Sylvia Beach. *Princeton University Library*

James Joyce and Clovis Monnier, seated, with Adrienne Monnier, Philiberte Monnier, and Sylvia Beach, standing, at Rocfoin, about 1927 or 1928. *Princeton University Library*

Dejeuner Ulysse, 27 June 1929, Hotel Leopold. Seated: Philippe Soupault, Nora Joyce, Edouard Dujardin, Paul Valéry, James Joyce, Léon-Paul Fargue. Standing behind Joyce: Sylvia Beach and Adrienne Monnier. *Princeton University Library*

A meeting of the staff of the review *Mesures:* seated, Sylvia Beach, Adrienne Monnier, Germaine Paulhan, Henry Church, Barbara Church, and Jean Paulhan; standing,
Henri Michaux, Michel Leiris, and Vladimir Nabokov. *Princeton University Library*

T.S. Eliot reading for the Friends of Shakespeare and Company on 6 June 1936.
François Valéry and Mrs. Paul Valéry are in the front row.

Sylvia and her father in Pasadena, California, August 1936 for his eighty-fourth birthday.

Below, James Joyce, Sylvia Beach, and Adrienne Monnier in Shakespeare and Company for publicity pictures for *Finnegans Wake* in May 1938. *Gisèle Freund*

On the opposite page, Sylvia Beach with a portion of the photographs of the Company. *Gisèle Freund*

Sylvia Beach at her vacation chalet in Les Déserts, in Savoy. *Princeton University Library*

Walt Whitman in Paris:
American Rhythms
1925–1926

My spirit has pass'd in compassion and determination around the whole earth,
I have look'd for equals and lovers and found them ready for me in all lands . . .
— Whitman, *Salut au Monde!*

T HE SUN had not yet blinked over the surrounding peaks and the morning fog clung in cold patches to the earth when Sylvia and Adrienne left their beloved plateau in the mountains. Their 6 A.M. departure, with their trunk in the creaking hay wagon, allowed them to take the Plainpalais autocar at seven and to reach Chambéry by noon, to catch the train to Paris. "Oh dear, it's a short vacation," Sylvia lamented, "but nineteen days here is worth three months of anywhere else and we have only had two rainy days. . . . I feel all made over now after all the sun and air that I've applied to myself. And lots of sleep." The quiet of Les Déserts, punctuated only by crowing roosters and the bark of sheep dogs, was too quickly replaced by the clatter of their twelve-hour train ride to Paris.

They returned to a new theater and symphony season in Paris, which would be highlighted by American rhythms: the rhythms of American jazz, the folk-singing of Paul Robeson, the Chaplin shuffle in his acclaimed film *The Gold Rush,* the erotic movements of Josephine Baker, and the cacophony of Antheil's *Ballet Mécanique.* Years before, when Henry James recorded in his *Parisian Sketches* that "the first symptoms of the winter are to be looked for at the theatres," he could not have envisioned the impact of American art and music on the Paris theaters in 1925–1926. Antheil's infamous concert was the loudest, if not the culminating, event, in this festival of American sounds. Along with the music, American literature made its presence felt in Paris, at least among those who were susceptible to it, such as the readers of the *Navire,* whose March issue was devoted entirely to American writers. Then, in April, came the opening of Shakespeare and Company's Walt Whitman Exhibition.

On a preliminary prosaic note this fall of 1925, Sylvia threaded her way through a maze of negotiations and correspondences for Joyce. He had returned during the first week of September, determined to conclude writing the Shaun portion of *Work in Progress.* Putting off until December his needed eye operations, he left business to Sylvia. She took him to the photographer Martinie; handled photographs and contracts for German and Spanish translations of *Portrait;* unsuccessfully tried to arrange a first meeting between Joyce and his biographer Herbert Gorman; arranged with the *Nouvelle Revue Française* for publication of Morel's French translation (the first installment) of the Hades portion of *Ulysses;* tried to collect monies due Joyce from the *Criterion,* Huebsch, and Cape; and informed a Milanese firm that the Italian rights to *Ulysses* could not be obtained until *Portrait* had been translated. However, it was arranging for the publication of portions of Joyce's new work, which he would take fourteen more years to complete, that gave her the most trouble. For example, both she and Joyce were frustrated by their arrangements with *This Quarter.* Ernest Walsh planned to publish a portion of the Shaun episode in the second number of his review. Walsh, who was dying of tuberculosis, traveled from city to city in Italy while Sylvia tried to follow him by way of his indecipherable letters. When she showed Joyce his explosive letters—full of what she called "guesswords"— Joyce expressed concern for his manuscript: "Goodness knows what sort of text of mine he will offer to his readers if ever the second number comes out." Meantime, Sylvia solved her problem of finding a home for Anna Livia Plurabelle when Adrienne took it, unexpurgated, for her October issue of *Navire d'Argent.* Joyce was delighted when his Anna Livia boarded the silver ship. Appropriately, he sent Adrienne a gift of seafood—"a magnificently dressed gigantic cold salmon from Potel & Chabot," an elegant shop, Sylvia exclaims. Anna Livia was the only English-language text in Adrienne's French review. When the *Navire* issue was printed, Sylvia promptly sent copies to Miss Weaver, who thought it "a good stroke of Miss Monnier's to get her in so smartly," and to Edgell Rickword of the *Calendar,* who thanked her and apologized for his own failure "to cope with the crude forces of convention." Lamenting to her mother that she did not have a "minute to read" any more, she turned down an offer by Newcastle BBC to address the north country of England about her publication of *Ulysses.* But she found time to attend the Surrealist exhibition and various theater and movie events. After seeing Charlie Chaplin's *Gold Rush,* she concludes that "Charley and Joyce are the greatest." She always obliged a customer who wanted Hemingway's signature on *In Our Time,* his enlarged collection of short stories just published by Boni and Liveright in America and, at her arranging, by Jonathan Cape in England. Overburdened by this bookshop, library, and Joyce business, she turned to music:

The phonograph is a great relief to me after the buzzing day's work. I play it every single evening and all day Sunday and you can't imagine how much pleasure it's given me. . . . Every single evening the tired working man sits and listens to pieces such as Beethoven's 5th symphony and other disks he buys with every penny of his saved up savings.

She occasionally used the masculine gender for herself to suggest the difficulty of her work and responsibility. Perhaps there is an implied contrast to the more feminine job of operating a boutique in Pasadena.

A dissonant note began sounding in the background in this fall of 1925. During September, much to his later regret, Joyce became involved with Samuel Roth, who published *Two Worlds* magazine in New York City. Years before, in the spring of 1921, Roth had written Joyce a letter of admiration; on the publication of *Ulysses* in 1922, he had sent a request to Harriet Weaver that he be allowed to present *Ulysses* to America in a number of his *Two Worlds*. Joyce, as usual through Sylvia, had asked Harriet Weaver to decline. "It would be curious to see how they expect to bring out *Ulysses* in *a* number of their magazine!" Sylvia exclaimed to Miss Weaver. In July of 1927, five years after his first inquiries, Roth would begin publishing *Ulysses* without Joyce's permission. Seeds for this piracy were planted that September of 1925, when, with Joyce's tacit permission, Roth began publishing fragments of *Work in Progress* that were available in Europe. Joyce even planned to revise a portion of Shaun "for Mr. Roth," which he did the following April. He also accepted $200, although he waited in vain for further payments that Roth had promised (Roth later falsely declared that he had paid Joyce $1,000). These facts seem to contradict what both Joyce and Sylvia subsequently claimed, or rather allowed to be inferred— namely, that portions of *Work in Progress* were published without their permission and that the $200 was paid after they had protested the publication. Roth published the fifth and last fragment of Shaun in September of 1926. But serious questions had by then arisen about Mr. Roth of New York. He was advertising, without their permission, that Ford, Pound, and Symons were his editors. Hemingway told Sylvia that Roth claimed to be drawing 10,000 subscribers with Joyce's name. Their worst fears were exceeded when Roth pirated *Ulysses* the following year. The ensuing legal battle involved lawyers in New York and Paris, embroiled Roth, Beach, Pound, and Joyce in charges and countercharges, and irreparably strained the relations between Sylvia and Joyce.

Sylvia was worried about her own expenses and Antheil's. Increased sales after the publication of *Ulysses* VI in August brought no relief, because the Joyce family called at least once a week for advance royalties or loans. Soon she arranged with Darantière for *Ulysses* VII to be available in December at seventy-five francs a copy. Shopkeepers and French citizens worried about the increase in taxes as a result of France's twenty-year plan to repay its war debt to the United States. New French governments were in and out of office this fall, as reports of the war in Morocco and Syria and France's political and economic unrest filled the newspapers.

Her resident composer's financial worries were due to personal, not economic or political, predicaments. He depended heavily on charitable donations, particularly Ellerman money. McAlmon, who had been unable to meet Sylvia's request for more funds for Antheil in August, asked Sylvia to have him contact Lady Ellerman, who had been worried about his "disappearance." McAlmon regretted the suggestion when, at the first of the year, Antheil wrote the Ellermans for £200. Upset by the demand, the Ellermans informed McAlmon about it, and he in turn told Sylvia about her friend's indiscretion. Sylvia, who pacified

Mrs. Ellerman, had bigger worries by then, for her own financial situation was perilous. When the exchange rate fell, she considered raising her library subscription charges and dropped the English review *Criterion* (then reorganizing as the *New Criterion*) because they—Lady Rothermere and "the titular people," Sylvia calls them—lost correspondence and had delayed in paying Joyce.

Although the hard work and financial concerns of the fall did not abate when winter came, the cold air brought many creative plans and lively entertainments. Somewhat sadly, Sylvia confesses that because her job obliged her to be a "daylifer," it was only at their "soberer movements" that she saw her friends. "At the end of the day, the prospect of sitting up and talking with people all night in a café didn't tempt me. I usually resisted efforts to get me to 'come along' to some place, unless it was the movies which I always like to see, or a leg show for tired businessmen such as the Folies-Bergère because you didn't have intellectual conversation intruding on your pleasure." One night she and Adrienne managed to get Joyce and Larbaud to a music hall—a form of entertainment the two women (and Fargue) adored. But Joyce, who preferred an Irish tenor, criticized the comedian for perspiring, and Larbaud was bored. "So that was the last time we took those two to a dance hall," swore Sylvia.

The American Janet Flanner, a friend of Sylvia's for the three years she had already lived in Paris, launched a career this fall as a writer for the *New Yorker*. In October, above the signature "Genêt," her first "Letter from Paris" appeared—the title reminiscent of Eliot's "London Letter" and Pound's "Paris Letter" for the *Dial* earlier in the decade. Harold Ross, who had just started the magazine, told her she should write what the French thought was going on in their capital. Thus, she took on the challenge of dramatizing—every two weeks for nearly five decades, as it turned out—some of the historical moments and events of Paris life. Occasionally she reported on Shakespeare and Company and Sylvia, whom she admired for her kindness and eccentricity, her energy and unselfconscious assertiveness. Taking Sylvia's example—and believing that women should "furnish their own plates"—Flanner became an assertive and talented career woman, perhaps America's finest journalist in Europe. Her admiration for her fellow women in Paris grew in her later decades. Her best tribute to Sylvia was not published until 1959: "The Infinite Pleasure," an essay on Sylvia that Stephen Spender considers her finest personal writing.

One of the first events that Flanner reported for the *New Yorker* was the appearance of La Revue Nègre in the Théâtre des Champs-Élysées. Sylvia and Adrienne, who relished the theater, music, and spectacles of each fall and winter season, had seen nothing of this kind of entertainment—nor had anyone else in Paris. Josephine Baker, a nineteen-year-old girl from Saint Louis, had been brought to Paris by the agent Caroline Dudley (Sylvia was a friend of the three talented Dudley sisters). In a new personal-essay section ("gazette") of her *Navire d'Argent* for December, Adrienne praised the comic and sensuous "mocking enticements" of this "Queen of Sheba" and her black male dancer, Louis Douglas, who "lavishes choreographic wonders as much as she herself does."

Adrienne's phrases were as euphemistically restrained as were those of Janet Flanner's first report. Admitting that her first report in the *New Yorker* was timid, Flanner later described Baker that opening night:

She made her entry entirely nude except for a pink flamingo feather between her limbs; she was being carried upside down and doing the split on the shoulder of a black giant. Midstage he paused, and with his long fingers holding her basket-wise around the waist, swung her in a slow cartwheel to the stage floor, where she stood, like his magnificent discarded burden, in an instant of complete silence. She was an unforgettable female ebony statue. A scream of salutation spread through the theater.

Drunk on adulation and champagne during this first week of performances, the cast nearly staggered through its numbers, giving a different performance each night. Paris loved its new American star and La Revue Nègre, which had brought the Charleston to Paris. With the arrival of the Charleston, American jazz finally swept all the clubs and dance halls. The American Negro was in vogue.

When Sylvia invited Paul Robeson to meet her French friends, she was as much curious about him as a black actor as she was interested in helping a fellow former resident of Princeton, New Jersey. Robeson had been starring as Emperor Jones in Eugene O'Neill's play in New York and London. Miss Gwendolyn Bennett, a Negro member of Shakespeare and Company, introduced Robeson to Sylvia. At the tea that she and Adrienne gave, he sang Negro spirituals that, he told a reporter, he planned to sing later on an American tour before returning to the stage. In addition to the reporters from the *Tribune,* who were invited to give Robeson some publicity, Sylvia asked the Joyces, who she thought would appreciate Robeson's fine bass voice. Her thirty-two other guests included the Hemingways, Arthur Moss, and Lewis Galantière, the head of the International Chamber of Commerce. Adrienne devoted a paragraph of the December issue of her gazette to Robeson's arrival in Paris.

In addition to the Robeson tea, Hemingway was a part of all the Shakespeare and Company activities these months. He was in and out of the shop often, as his library cards reveal. Unlike many authors, Sylvia observes, he continued to borrow and buy other writers' books even after he had begun publishing his own. This fall's library card, the earliest Hemingway card to survive, reveals both his preference for Turgenev and his inclination to borrow books related to his own writings. On 23 November, Hemingway borrowed *A Parody Outline of History,* written by Donald Ogden Stewart, whom he had met in 1923 (Hemingway himself was writing *Torrents of Spring,* a brash and reckless parody of the affectations in Anderson's *Dark Laughter*). While polishing the clean, unadorned lines of *The Sun Also Rises,* he would in January borrow a book on bullfighting. On a number of occasions in the years to come, his borrowings from Shakespeare and Company reflect his writing.

In early December, Adrienne and Sylvia began translating a political speech written by Walt Whitman. Sylvia had long been a champion of Whitman's poetry, encouraging her patrons to read *Leaves of Grass* and proudly displaying her

Whitman manuscripts. Jean Catel, a professor at the University of Montpellier, had recently given her Whitman's "The Eighteenth Presidency," an unpublished 1856 speech. Whitman himself had set up the speech in type as small, Adrienne notes, "as the smallest on the charts of an optometrist." They resorted to a magnifying glass to read the emotional words that urged all young Americans to exercise their democratic power against corrupt politicians. Their translation, which took them two months to complete, appeared in the March issue of the *Navire,* which Adrienne devoted to French renderings of work by American writers. The Whitman political idiom, calculated to touch his listeners but difficult to translate, decries slavery, Buchanan, and Fillmore ("two dead corpses . . . two galvanized old men"). After translating lines such as "the President eats dirt and excrement for his daily meals, likes it, and tries to force it on the States," Sylvia would exclaim, "He had his own people there." Adrienne was so stirred by his democratic spirit, she admits, that when at a dinner of the PEN Club she was asked whether she would participate in a movement for the women's vote (although she had "never occupied" herself "with feminism"), she answered yes, "with enthusiasm."

When December chilled the Paris air, the terraces of the cafés filled their large braziers with coal to warm their patrons. Both the temperature and the franc fell. And the waters of the Seine rose, flooding the basements near the quays. The dampness of what Imbs called the "liquid cold of Paris rain" penetrated to the bone. After the rain came snow. Without central heating, businesses and apartments were kept at a temperature of sixty degrees. Sylvia, wrapped in woolen sweaters, moved with her Whitman manuscript closer to her floor heater. After mailing his manuscript of *Torrents* to Boni and Liveright, Hemingway made plans for a second winter of skiing at Schruns, taking five library books with him (including works by Mann and Turgenev). Antheil, who seemed to be perpetually ill this winter, played his cold and glistening dissonances in a rented room around the corner and talked about a full concert of his *Ballet Mécanique* in the spring. And Joyce submitted to Dr. Borsch's knife for his ninth and tenth operations at the Clinique Ophtalmique in the boulevard Raspail. He spent a week at the clinic and suffered an attack of delirium following the operation. For weeks afterward he was too blind to write anything except in the largest letters and would not dictate. He was trying to finish the Shaun section, which consisted of four chapters or watches, on which he had been working through 1925. In the last days of January 1926, Sylvia mailed more than half of the Shaun section to Miss Weaver and Larbaud. She tried not to bother him with the details of the Joycean business except when necessary or when he showed an interest. She was distracted from her worry about Joyce's health by the demands of a busy holiday season and yet another fall in the value of the franc.

Her work in the bookshop, her activities on Joyce's behalf, and her translation of Whitman were interrupted in January of 1926 by flying visits from family and friends. Her father came through Paris on his work for the Alliance of Reformed Churches of Europe. Her mother stopped on her way to Italy on a three-month vacation and buying trip for her daughters' Pasadena shop. Inevitably the visit involved banking, shopping, and mailing chores, for Sylvia kept her mother's Lloyd's account in Paris. While the rains continued and the Seine threatened to flood, Hemingway visited the bookshop after returning from his winter skiing trip. He had written affectionately from Schruns with news of his reading and skiing, his new beard ("They want me to play The Man Moses in the Oberammergau players," he jokes), and their homesickness for Paris ("We miss you all three. . . . What is the dirt in the literary world?"). He was on his way to New York to negotiate with Boni and Liveright, who refused to publish *Torrents of Spring,* his satire of Anderson (one of their best sellers). He would seize this opportunity to move to Scribners. Both before and after this trip, which lasted three weeks, Hemingway spent several days in Paris with Pauline Pfeiffer, who had spent Christmas with the Hemingways in Schruns. Sylvia and his other friends knew—as Hadley did not—of his affair with Pauline, who on 19 January became a member, like Hemingway, of the lending library. Sylvia's final visitor was Miss Weaver, who came to see the ailing Joyce and complete some research at the Bibliothèque Nationale for her friend and publishing associate Dora Marsden. She brought with her Wyndham Lewis's portrait sketch of her, which she gave Joyce for his birthday. She protested blushingly when he playfully suggested hanging it in Shakespeare and Company.

At the end of January, Sylvia was hit with a big increase in income taxes just as an embarrassed Joyce penned a formal request for her financial help: ". . . do you know how I could get at once 6000 or 7000 francs[?]" He admits that he does not want Miss Weaver to hear about his need while in Paris, and explains that "to get the money from the solicitors would involve telling her." About twenty days later, after exhausting other means, Sylvia appealed to her mother in Italy for the money in her Lloyds account: "I would be saved alive mother dearest! . . . You know how the situation is hard for me at times with our Mr. J.J.'s needs. If by any chance you can't spare the money . . . I'll scramble through quite nicely somehow." Her mother, thinking she had the full amount in her Lloyd's account, agreed to rescue her daughter and Joyce. Sylvia, however, would withdraw only 3,000 francs from the account, leaving a cushion of about a 1,000 francs. Sylvia somehow scraped together the remaining funds for Joyce. Later, when a California family, acquaintances of her mother's, visited the bookshop, she "couldn't help noticing (on account of my soul shrivelling up) that they didn't buy a thing."

In the meantime Sylvia and Adrienne (with Prévost's occasional assistance) began another translation for the March issue of *Navire:* McAlmon's short story "The Publicity Agent." Here they faced problems different from their current ones with Whitman's nineteenth-century political idiom and his fine print. It contained "truths," Adrienne explains, "that the French have the habit of expressing by insinuations, not when they speak, but when they write." These two friends of the frank-speaking Fargue were certainly familiar with language "concerning the noble subject of Sex." But they feared shocking some of their friends and readers. But Sylvia, after a serious examination of her conscience, cried, "What! I, the publisher of *Ulysses*, should be afraid of one man when a whole regiment doesn't frighten me?" They took courage from Whitman's ideas on slang and the popular idiom—ideas Sylvia had found in one of the Whitman essays she was reading. Their translation continued, and, in their enthusiasm, they even included footnotes with American and French expressions that dictionaries did not list. "American men who come to Paris can have themselves initiated" into French amorous idiom by "the little women," Adrienne humorously boasts.

Sylvia had been working on the Whitman translation several weeks when she received a visit from Jean Catel that extended her involvement with Walt Whitman. In the United States, Emory Holloway, who had just won the Pulitzer Prize for his biography of Whitman, had recently initiated a plan for a permanent tribute to Whitman in Battery Park in Manhattan. To gain international support, he contacted Catel, who in turn recruited Sylvia, and together they founded the Paris branch of Holloway's Walt Whitman Committee, which in addition to themselves comprised Francis Vielé-Griffin (president), Léon Bazalgette (editor of *Europe*), Jean Schlumberger, Valery Larbaud, Pierre de Lanux, Louis Fabulet, and Henry D. Davray. The committee was a veritable who's who of French Whitman scholars. Their headquarters was naturally Shakespeare and Company, for it was the only American lending library and bookshop in Paris. Sylvia had, from the start, prominently displayed Whitman's work and picture in the shop. Frenchmen who had written about and translated Whitman's work—Romains, Gide, Larbaud, and other members of the committee besides the last—were her friends and patrons.

As a means of soliciting funds for the statue of Whitman, which was being designed in Paris by her American friend Jo Davidson, Sylvia suggested an exhibition at her bookshop. The February issue of *Navire* announced the formation of the Walt Whitman Committee of Paris and the coming exhibition of Whitman manuscripts, early editions, and photographs. Admissions would be donated to help build the statue. Immediately Sylvia talked to her friends who had early editions of the poet. Bazalgette, whose works deified Whitman and interpreted his poems as scripture, lent his *Poème-Evangile de Walt Whitman* (1908), the first French biography of Whitman, and his translation, published in 1919, of *Leaves of Grass*. He also helped Catel and Sylvia collect other contributions. Jo Davidson, who had been cajoling her to arrange a sitting for him with Joyce, suggested that in return she use his model of Whitman in her exhibit.

By the first days of February, she and Adrienne had concluded their translations of McAlmon and Whitman. The Whitman work had put too much of a strain on Sylvia's eyes and she suffered from an obstruction of the lacrimal ducts. At the party for *Ulysses'* fourth birthday, (the forty-fourth for Joyce), at which both author and publisher wore eye patches, they talked of Sylvia's plans for the Whitman exhibit, and Joyce quoted some lines from Whitman's poetry. Later he wrote the following passage in his *Work in Progress:*

old Whiteman self [says] . . . I foredreamed for dreamed for thee
and more than full-maked: I prevened for thee in the
haunts that joybelled frail light-a-leaves for sturdy traeman . . .

In his literary method, Whitman had "foredreamed" Joyce's new novel.

Sylvia did not have the time or money to attend the opening of Joyce's play, *Exiles,* in London. Joyce himself, too ill to attend, waited eagerly for detailed reports from those of his friends who did. Ettore Schmitz (Italo Svevo) and his wife, Livia, Claud Sykes (his former partner in the English Players in Trieste), and Harriet Weaver sent good news about the production and its reception. Joyce and Sylvia exulted together when they heard that Shaw had attended and later, in a debate on *Exiles,* defended the play. Sylvia believed that Shaw had mellowed during the four years since his lengthy refusal to pay three guineas for *Ulysses.*

In the third week of February, Sylvia gathered with a few friends to hear Joyce read the fourth portion (a description of Isabel / Isolde) of the book of Shaun from his *Work in Progress.* The small audience was puzzled by Joyce's language and meaning. Joyce wrote to Miss Weaver, who would soon confide to Sylvia her own confusion about the work, that his reading "produced stupification, I think."

After a brief foretaste of spring, March roared in like a lion, blowing out the furnace of Joyce's flat. When Joyce became ill with swollen glands—or "glanders," as Holly called Sylvia's own frequent similar malady in Belgrade—Sylvia sought a remedy from her neighborhood chemist. The excitement of preparing for the *Navire* and the Whitman exhibit seemed to keep Sylvia herself warm. She closed off the back room, placed her Whitman manuscripts in two show frames, which she had designed (to allow front and back viewing) and which a carpenter had made. Whitman manuscripts were slowly coming in, but no one seemed to be in much of a hurry to set a date for the exhibit. It would be April before she opened the show—largely, it seems, because of Joyce's *Work in Progress,* which, she laments "is at present taking all my time." She decided to ask Joyce, she confides to her mother, whether he would "consider employing a secretary. One of the young Irishmen that come to Paris to study and who would be honored to get the job." On this, as on later occasions, he rejected her idea, wanting all his business under one roof, that of Shakespeare and Company.

Adrienne's major gesture to enhance American literature in France appeared in March: the *Navire d'Argent*'s all-American issue. It featured a drawing of Walt Whitman on page one, followed by their Whitman translation, *La Dix-Huitième Présidence,* and the works of four young American writers—McAlmon, Hemingway, Williams, and Cummings. Sylvia and Adrienne, as mentioned, had translated McAlmon's story, whose French title was *Agence de Publicité.* Auguste Morel, who was laboring on *Ulysses,* had translated extracts from William Carlos Williams's *The Great American Novel.* Georges Duplaix had translated "The Undefeated," (*Invincible*) a short story by Hemingway, and "Sipliss," from *The Enormous Room,* by Cummings, who had just received the Dial Prize.

Adrienne added "Une Lettre à Larbaud," who was in Lisbon. To Larbaud, the man she considered the best proponent and translator of foreign literature in France, Adrienne spoke of their work in translating Whitman and McAlmon. Finally, the March issue contained a portion of Adrienne's *Bibliographie Américaine*, her listing of all American literature translated into French. On the back of the issue was a full-page advertisement for Shakespeare and Company. This issue of *Navire* did much to quicken French writers' interest in American literature. Catel wrote from Montpellier that their Whitman translation "is something great."

Dr. Borsch sent Joyce a bill for 16,000 francs for services (including numerous operations) since 1922. Joyce (who was short on his rent) mailed the bill to Miss Weaver, declaring that "it is really rather moderate for a man of his standing." He adds, in a comment that leaves him innocent of any manipulation, that "Miss Beach wanted to call on him and ask him to reduce it but I would not allow her. She thinks he ought to charge nothing or perhaps make me a present of a telescope!" If this idea did in fact originate with Sylvia, it probably resulted from Joyce's consternation at having to pay the sum or from her own fear that she would have to come up with the money.

With her supply of copies of *Ulysses* running low, and the Joyce family finances depleted, Sylvia made plans for an eighth edition for May. This issue would be "entirely reset" by Darantière, the changes to be based on the list of errors that had been collected, particularly by Miss Weaver. Nora withdrew 14,000 francs (about $400) this month before the book appeared. "Living on the Joycean scale," Sylvia later observes, "while it matched his fame and talents was by no means adapted to his earnings." Stanislaus Joyce, who visited his brother in April, observed with disapproval this Joycean scale of living, his brother's drinking, and the "sycophants" who surrounded him. When requests for translation came this month from Hungary, Poland, Czechoslovakia, and Japan, Sylvia drove "as hard a bargain as possible . . . without holding back any percentage." The money received was never enough.

Hemingway often carried Sylvia away from her Joycean burden. Recently returned from Schruns (where the Dos Passoses and Murphys had joined him in March), he swept her into his sporting world again. He announced one day in the bookshop that she and Adrienne were to attend with him the Vél d'Hiver bicycle races, and showed her the tickets he had bought for the last night, 9 April, of the six-day race. She had recently read about the races in Paul Morand's *Ouvert la Nuit* (1922; *Open All Night,* 1923) and had heard of Hemingway's plans to describe the sport in a short story. Not until thirty years later (in his memoirs) would Hemingway capture the "Vélodrome d'Hiver with the smoky light of the afternoon and the high-banked wooden track and the whirring sound the tires made on the wood as the riders passed," climbing and plunging, "each one a part of his machine." They had an exciting time cheering and swinging their heads back and forth like a pendulum as the cyclists circled about the hippodrome.

As usual, Sylvia and Adrienne spent the Easter weekend with the Monnier family at Rocfoin, a small town near Maintenon, southwest of Paris. The weekend began early, with Joyce expressing his usual anxiety.

If it hadn't been for Adrienne pulling on my side, I could never have got loose. Joyce, as Saturday approached, always thought up so many extra chores for me that it usually looked as if he were going to win. But Adrienne and my own doggedness to hold on to my Sabbath in the country armed me for resistence.

The first time they brought Sylvia's dog, Teddy, the guard at the gate to the train declared that the dog must be muzzled. With aplomb, Adrienne tied her handkerchief around Teddy's jaws, and they walked swiftly past the astonished official. The train took them to the Eure-et-Loire in the direction of Chartres. From the station, they walked three miles through the wheat-growing country to the Monnier family home, Rocfoin. Clovis and Philiberte Monnier welcomed Sylvia as one of their own daughters. They had no telephone, no car, and no indoor toilet. Their only water came from a pump. But they offered a thatch-roofed retreat far from Paris, country cooking, and a view of the cathedral of Chartres across a treeless stretch of land. Here, with Mousse, the Monnier's big, shaggy dog, they all spent each Sunday under a tall elm in the garden, where Sylvia on occasion took everyone's picture. She also took pictures of the Beach family and the Joyce family when they visited. One picture of Sylvia, taken in 1925 by Adrienne, captures her boyish look in the latest style of shirt, vest, tie, and knickers. The photograph shows the bearded Clovis Monnier, Mousse, and Sylvia sitting on the lawn, she in such a way as to reveal shapely legs in long stockings. Her hair is short and full, and she looks ten years younger than her thirty-eight years.

The Walt Whitman exhibit opened to a private audience on the night of 20 April 1926. ''I am going to Stratford-on-Odéon,'' Joyce announced to his friends before attending the reception. The leather-bound guest book reveals that the French outnumbered the Americans that night. The first to pay homage to the American poet was Valéry, France's most distinguished poet. Signing next to Valéry was Adrienne, who glanced proudly at the copy of *Navire* that contained Whitman's ''The Eighteenth Presidency.'' Also recording his name on the first page was Romains, whose unanimist spirit was inspired by Whitman's theory of universal brotherhood. Below Adrienne's name was that of a fellow *copain,* Durtain. Romains and Durtain studied the collection spread out on two long tables made for the occasion—a collection contributed largely by Bazalgette, who had lent twenty books and manuscripts and nine photographs. Before Pierre de Lanux signed the guest book, Sylvia took him to see the three books he had lent, one of them a copy of the original, 1855 edition of *Leaves of Grass.* Other members of the Whitman Committee, including Schlumberger and Catel (who had lent ten items), signed the guest book. Larbaud, who lent three books, had discovered Whitman's poetry when he was eighteen years old, had drawn heavily on Whitman for *Les Poésies de A. O. Barnabooth,* had translated several poems by Whitman, and had written an introduction to selections from Whitman's poetry in French translation, which appeared in 1918.

French experts on Whitman (who had been a major force in French literature since 1910) were most interested in the first edition of *Leaves of Grass* and the handwritten papers that Sylvia had mounted on the wall in movable glass frames. They examined her seven items of scribbled notes and verse on the back of envelopes. These were Sylvia's prized possessions, she explained: they had been given to her by her aunt Agnes Orbison, who had retrieved them from Whitman's wastebasket, with his permission, in the 1880s. Other French literati that night included Benoist-Méchin, Darantière, Prévost and Auclair, Linossier, Michaud, Morel, the Bécats, and Adrienne. "I am a real Parisian," Whitman had once announced. And the French embraced him.

Avoiding the crowded back room, Joyce preferred to spend most of his time in the front of the shop. He arrived with Nora and George, signed on the front page of the guest book, and talked to his good friend Morel, who reported on the progress of his *Ulysses* translation. Morel had called Joyce "the Whitman of prose—a Whitman who speaks all the languages of Whitman and then some." Whitman, Morel could have added, may very well have shown Joyce an example of how the soul of one man can represent all men, or, to use Joyce's words in *Finnegans Wake,* "the soul of everyelsebody rolled into olesoleself."

No American present at the reception would have made Morel's comparison between Whitman and Joyce. Not acknowledging Whitman's modernism, they knew less about Whitman's poetry than did the French with whom they mingled that night. In fact, American universities were just beginning to consider American literature a subject worthy of university study.* During the months of preparation for the exhibit, Sylvia had become very aware that the young American writers in Paris (Hart Crane had not yet arrived) did not share her enthusiasm for their great predecessor, that they regarded him only as the cheerleader of American democracy, technology, and nineteenth-century progress. They felt alienated from the culture they saw him championing. Although Sylvia thought that Whitman was the "father" of this rebellious American generation, she knew that they did not share her insight:

Whitman was anything but the style. "The Crowd" couldn't put up with him, especially after T. S. Eliot aired *his* views about Walt. Only Joyce and the French and I were still old-fashioned enough to get along with Whitman. I could see with half an eye Whitman's influence on Joyce's work—hadn't he recited some lines to me one day?

The chief detractor, as she named him, was Eliot, who, in a tribute to his friendship with Sylvia, came from London for the opening night, despite his antipathy

---

*Matthew Josephson laments that in 1916 many of his own professors knew nothing yet of Melville or Dickinson and that they disparaged Henry James. They completely dismissed modern writers: when his friend Cummings read a paper on Stein in his senior year (1915) at Harvard, the audience was silent with embarrassment. Barrett Wendell, who taught the subject at Harvard until 1921, is said to have told his classes, "Gentlemen, this is a course in American letters; there is no American literature."

to the poet. His signature appears on the first page of the guest book, immediately below Larbaud's and above the signatures of Sylvia's parents. The French receptivity to Whitman, the egalitarian, would not impress the Anglican and monarchist Eliot.

Other expatriates were less reluctant to enjoy themselves: Antheil talked music to Virgil Thomson; Hemingway examined the Davidson model of Whitman, which shows him walking in order to symbolize the open road; Harry and Caresse Crosby, the latter a native New Yorker, discussed plans to place the statue at the tip of Manhattan Island. They all studied the map of Camden and the picture postcards mounted on a large cardboard. Transparent folders guarded the Whitman photographs that Davidson had used for his model. The item that most impressed the American visitors during the next eight weeks was the enormous American flag draped as a screen over the bookshelves in the back room. Sylvia had bought it at the Grand Magasin du Louvre; it had probably been intended for a large building and might have been used to celebrate the armistice in 1918. "I am very patriotic about Walt Whitman and thought he should have a very big flag," she writes.

Among the longtime American residents of Paris at the opening-night reception were Natalie Barney, whose signature heads the second page of the guest book, Galantière, Arthur Moss, and Walter Berry, who at six feet three inches stood above the others in the crowd. The former head of the American Chamber of Commerce in Paris and the friend and counselor of Edith Wharton, Berry was in the last year of his life. The leading English expatriate, Sisley Huddleston, was also present. Stein was not. Knowing that she would not enter Joycean territory, Sylvia had not invited her.

The last name to be written in the leather-bound guest book—its position symbolic of its possessor's reluctant though necessary acknowledgment of Whitman—was that of Ezra Pound, who was visiting from Rapallo. When he had received his invitation, he had sent a news clipping of Whitman's home for the exhibit. Although Pound rejected what he regarded as Whitman's egalitarian love of the "rabble," he knew his kinship with his predecessor. As early as 1909 he had confessed, "Mentally I am a Walt Whitman who has learned to wear a collar and dress shirt although at times inimical to both." Pound had made an uneasy peace with his literary father—a peace or truce best expressed in his poem "The Pact": "I make a pact with you, Walt Whitman," he reluctantly admits. He is "old enough now to make friends" with the poet who "broke the new wood," he declares, adding, "Now is the time for carving. / We have one sap and one root—Let there be commerce between us." Whitman, with his revolutionary style, certainly had broken new wood. What Pound (almost alone of the modernists before Hart Crane) acknowledges in this truce with Whitman is his modernism. Indeed, Whitman was probably the first to use the word "modern" in the sense that this word acquired in the twentieth century. In the following poetic passage from "Thou Mother with Thy Equal Brood," he expresses the modernist credo of its first decades:

To formulate the Modern . . .
Out of thyself, comprising science, to recast poems,
                    churches, art
(Recast, may-be discard them, end them—maybe their work
            is done, who knows?)

This discarding and recasting is what Joyce was doing with prose. It is what
Antheil was doing with his *Ballet Mécanique.* The American writers, at least
until 1950, were the last to acknowledge Whitman's greatness. Larbaud was
correct when he complained in 1914 that Whitman was as "unappreciated in the
United States as Stendhal in Grenoble or Cézanne in Aix."

The exhibit was open to the public for two months every afternoon from two
to six. Tourists, their nostalgia and patriotism aroused by the large flag, proudly
inscribed their names and hometowns. Even when Sylvia raised admission from
three francs to eight, most people failed to pay the fee, because they considered
the entire shop to be a sort of permanent exhibition of writers and writing. She
collected only 561 francs, which paid for the printing but not for the entire cost
of the frames and tables. Fortunately, she sighed, the American committee was
not counting on her to pay for the statue. In fact, plans for placing the statue in
Manhattan were eventually abandoned because New York's art commission
refused to allocate a site. While Holloway struggled to keep Whitman's reputation afloat in America (in 1930 he was barely elected to the New York University
Hall of Fame), Sylvia rode the crest of French enthusiasm, which was never
higher.

The Whitman exhibit, like all her ventures, was not meant to be commercial.
Its success was reflected in the enthusiasm of the French, not in receipts or in
bookshop sales. Sylvia sold only ten copies of *Leaves of Grass* in 1926, the same
number she had sold in 1925. Still, Whitman's poetry ranked first in total American sales, with the exception of works by Eliot and Hemingway, available in
small, inexpensive editions. How many more times his poetry was borrowed—
and Shakespeare and Company was chiefly a lending library—cannot easily be
assessed.

Sylvia was aware that this was a great year in France for American art—
whether it was jazz bands, Negro dance, Antheil concerts, Nadia Boulanger's
concert for American composers, or literary exhibits and publishing. She attended
Boulanger's concert, which the Paris *Tribune* found distressingly modern, with
no "ethnic quality" to give it a "claim to the title American." Ada MacLeish
sang, Aaron Copland played the piano, and other performers presented Thomson's Sonata d'Église and Antheil's String Quartet. Thomson, who had returned
to Paris in the fall of 1925, helped to get Antheil a few concert engagements,
played once on the same program with him, and "loafed at Sylvia Beach's shop."

Two new American publishing companies began this year. Through 1932
Edward Titus's Black Manikin Press (operating out of his Black Manikin rare-
book library) would print twenty-five volumes—the best-known of which was
Lawrence's *Lady Chatterley's Lover,* which Sylvia refused to publish. Harry and

Caresse Crosby, publishing through 1936, issued nearly three times as many as Titus did under the imprint of their Black Sun Press (first called Editions Narcisse). Except for Shakespeare and Company, which published Joyce for a decade, these two presses enjoyed the greatest longevity of all the little expatriate publishing ventures in Paris. The health of the two of them depended both on the talent and dedication of Titus and the Crosbys and on their financial backing. Titus was financed by his wife, Helena Rubinstein, the cosmetics tycoon. Harry Crosby, a nephew of J. P. Morgan, had family wealth.

The Crosbys, who began by publishing each other's poetry in January of 1925, frequently visited Shakespeare and Company, where, according to Caresse, they had their "first encounters with Hemingway, Dos Passos, and Eugene Jolas." Sylvia accepted them as "two of the most charming people" she had ever met. Harry "used to dart in and out of my bookshop," she claims, "dive into the bookshelves like a hummingbird extracting honey from a blossom, or hover a minute around my table" to talk. Crosby, who had been an ambulance driver during the war and a banker after attending Harvard, professed to be a sun worshiper in love with death. Because they did not associate with the French, the Crosbys published only American and English titles. Sylvia, who did not share their enthusiasm for Lawrence, told them about James Joyce, whose *Tales of Shem and Shaun* from *Work in Progress* they would publish in 1929. Upon the death of Walter Berry, who was a cousin, Harry inherited his library and correspondence, including letters from Henry James, which the Black Sun published.

Noteworthy among the expatriates from the United States was Samuel Putnam, who, unlike the Crosbys, did become involved in the artistic life of France. He arrived in 1926 for what would be seven years of active involvement in French life and in magazines sponsored by Americans in France. He would later write one of the best accounts of the expatriate experience in *Paris Was Our Mistress* (1947): "Paris . . . was our spiritual mistress, a wise and beautiful one, at a time when our own America, or so it seemed, had turned a strumpet." Hungry for the sounds of foreign languages, and experienced in translating Italian and French, Putnam intended to support his wife and eight-month-old child by translating for Pascal Covici, a Chicago publisher. His parting salvo to Chicago, where he had served as art and literary critic for the *Chicago Evening Post,* was published in the August *Mercury:* "Chicago: An Obituary." In Paris, Putnam was productively happy. He joined Shakespeare and Company, where, he writes, he stepped into the "sacrosanct stillness" of "another world . . . that shrine of literary pilgrims."

Many other Americans appeared and reappeared in Montparnasse in the spring and summer of 1926. Unlike Putnam, who eventually settled into the French rhythm of life, most of them came for brief visits to the American hangouts. The anarchist Emma Goldman, looking more frumpy than fiery, the *Tribune* snidely notes, had arrived in February. Sherwood Anderson, who had just published a fictionalized autobiography (*Tar*), reappeared in the rue de Fleurus and the rue de l'Odéon. He dined with Joyce, hating the oysters Joyce had suggested he order and taking an increasing dislike for Joyce; feasted on one of Adrienne's chicken dinners; and visited in the Bécat flat, where he announced he would write an essay on Marie's embroidery for *Vanity Fair* (an unfulfilled promise). In addition to Anderson, who was now a friend of the family, increasing numbers of students and tourists turned up at Shakespeare and Company. "Lots of dear old Princetonians visit my shop," Sylvia informs her mother. "How they do travel! I expect you see them all the time in Pasadena too. . . . They . . . have a great awe for me . . . the Princeton people do as a rule. I think it's on account of the article in the *Bookman*. They stand near the door and look at me as if I wuz anthropapagous [*sic*]. (see allynyms [*sic*] and Synonyms)." Articles about the bookshop also appeared in the *Saturday Review of Literature,* in *McNaught's Monthly,* and in *Town and Country.* The two bookshops had become so popular that the literary reporter in the Paris *Herald,* in a piece about Pound, commented that the news was received by "one of the booksellers of the Left Bank (either one will do)." *McNaught's Monthly* ran a two-page feature on Sylvia, who, it indicates,

breezed in, wearing a leather storm coat with a soft hat of the same brown shade. She glowed like her open fire. Her arms were filled with poinsettias and lilacs. Flop went the flowers on the desk—off came the little hat—a shake restored the shaggy bob to its original coil, and she was offering her hand. And between arranging the flowers in several vases, carrying on an animated French conversation over the telephone, selecting some books for an Italian who desired the right kind for a tiresome journey, she managed to answer my question. . . . Eventually she curled up in a big chair and as she drew her feet up under her, in a feminine fashion, I saw that after ten years she still wears sensible American shoes and has not adopted the toppling heels of the Parisian.

Such essays, filled with romantic descriptions of the cozy little shop with its "amber lights and the glow from the grate fire," drew Americans. But often the essays contained inaccuracies or half-truths. The *McNaught's* essay claims that Antheil's *Ballet Mécanique* "depicts in quite a revolutionary way the subjugation of the negro by the factory regime of Industrial America." The large, slick New York *Town and Country* alleges, in an article of 1 May, that Hemingway was a matador in Spain. And a musical version by Antheil of Joyce's "Cyclops," only in the planning stages, is confused with his *Ballet Mécanique.* These articles offer illustrations of the perpetuation of errors, some of which eventually solidified into myth. Fortunately, the reality of Paris was more than enough to satisfy the most romantic and adventurous.

While waves of Americans discovered the sights and sounds of Paris, Joyce continued to construct his rhythms in Shaun, a chapter organized by roads, as the Anna Livia Plurabelle section was organized by rivers, and written in layers and word associations. A transformation of a line in the early version of Anna Livia Plurabelle published in the *Navire d'Argent* shows how Joyce, by reworking his material, added to its meaning: the line that reads "wait till the rising of the moon" becomes, in the final version, "wait till the honeying of the lune, love." This new layer opens the line to suggestive puns on "lunar" and "honeymoon.'' Sylvia took delight both in these layers of puns and in the rhythm of his lines. She observed the rhythm of Joyce's speech as he read completed portions of his *Work in Progress*. All the word combinations, she thought, were "often for the sake of the sounds that rushed through his later work and that he listened to as his sight failed him. His characters are presented in sounds not colors. Even in his earliest works this is already noticeable.'' Sylvia's perceptive observation of the importance of sound for Joyce is echoed by Huddleston, who was also often invited to hear Joyce read. Joyce spoke with "musical intonation,'' Huddleston remembered. His memory of one of Joyce's closing commentaries illustrates both Joyce's layered writing and the importance of sound:

I remember he would take a phrase such as: "Phoenix culpa,'' and would then explain. "Now here you have a suggestion of felix culpa—the blessed sin of the early Church fathers—that is to say the downfall of Adam and Eve which brought Christ into the world; and you have the suggestion, not only of the Garden of Eden, but of Phoenix Park in Dublin, and of Irish history with its wrongs and crimes, and you have the eternal way of a man with a maid, and you have . . .

Sylvia listened to and puzzled over the brilliant echoes of Joyce's new work.

The sound of Joyce's clear, smooth Irish voice reading his work—Sylvia preferred the chattering dialogue of Anna Livia Plurabelle—was only one of the sounds of the Odéon quarter. Meanwhile, Antheil composed his Second Symphony in the apartment above. He occasionally drowned out the voices in the shop—Eliot's quiet Bostonian English (Edith Sitwell called it "High Anglican Asbestos''); Joyce's rich, smooth Irish accent; Ford's hr-r-rmphs and wheezing; Adrienne's high, melodious French; or Pound's nasal slang—a dialect Antheil compared to the intonations of Lum and Abner. Sylvia also had a sense of interior sounds; she claims she treasured the early mornings when she could hear the silence of persons, heads bowed over their reading, listening to an author's words.

Echoing a Protestant hymn, Sylvia describes Antheil's efforts to get funding for a full performance of his *Ballet Mécanique* and his Second Symphony: "After many dangers toils and snares, as Father used to say, correspondence back and forth between Mrs. Bok and George, his prayers were heard and he began to set the table for a performance of the *Ballet Mécanique*.'' Mrs. Mary Louise Bok, his benefactor, sent him a check for the expenses of the performance (Imbs says a quarter of a million francs). Antheil, now occupying with Boski two small rooms above the shop, threw all his energies into the most important concert of his life. Thinking grandly, he rented the Théâtre des Champs-Élysées, which seats 2,500, for Saturday, 19 June 1926. He brazenly approached the young composer Vladimir Golschmann, who agreed to conduct his Second Symphony but told him that one pianola could not be synchronized to eight or even two others. They decided to use real pianists with eight grand pianos and one pianola. Benoist-Méchin would play one of the pianos and Allen Tanner another. Nervous because he had never appeared before a Paris audience, Tanner practiced the "blind blundering chords and breakneck runs for hours a day,'' claims Bravig Imbs. Antheil, of course, was the most frantic, fearing that nobody would attend. Hope, fear, and despair alternated with the rise and fall of the propaganda. How could they have doubted they would have an audience when, by Sylvia's own admission, "for days beforehand we worked without a break on advertising George's concert"?

The concert was a family affair from beginning to end. As a half-jealous Thomson observed, Pound, Joyce, Sylvia, and Adrienne took care of Antheil, "the literary mind's idea of a musical genius—bold, bumptious, and self-confident." On the day of the concert, Sylvia called a taxi to transport them to the theater. While she and Adrienne waited beside the taxi, Antheil, dressed only in his underwear, yanked open the window of his room upstairs and shouted down to them not to wait, as he was not ready. Sylvia repressed a thought that this unreadiness might be one of his pranks ("what if nobody turned up—not even George!"). They were almost late. The old concierge, Mme Tisserand, had departed half an hour earlier—in the first taxi she had taken in thirty years, she declared. She was dressed in her black silk gown, her "nose sprinkled with lots of white powder in the can marked *farine* [flour]" that she had shown Sylvia in confidence.

When Sylvia and Adrienne arrived at the theater, they found they had to push through an unruly throng. In the crowd was Lincoln Steffens, gaping at all the crazies with their wild hair and odd hats. Once inside, they saw a full house— so full that Sylvia imagined for a moment that she would have to arrange the people in double rows like the books on her library shelves. Advance publicity, including the preview performances, which had been amply reported by the Paris *Tribune,* had brought many people there to create, prevent, or witness a riot.

The performance began late. But most people were too absorbed in looking at the celebrities to notice the time. Pound, arrived from Italy, wagged his red beard at everyone he knew. Eliot had come from London to attend in formal dress and top hat, with Princess Bassiano. When the Joyce family entered their box, Sylvia wished that the orchestra would play the Irish national anthem. Kiki, her eyes painted in large triangles to match her triangular earrings, sat among her fellow Dômites in the balcony. Preferring his "Stravinsky straight," Hemingway was out of town. Myrsine, who had heard the music for months through walls, ceiling, and windows, stayed with the shop. But most luminaries of the Left Bank attended: Diaghilev, Koussevitzky, Brancusi, Joyce, William and Louise Bullitt,* and an elegant *grande dame* whom no one recognized but who seemed to be royalty. She bowed graciously. "It's your concierge!" Adrienne exclaimed to Sylvia.

The performance began late because Antheil, who was to play the only mechanical piano at the concert, had to wait until his friend Allen Tanner had

---

*Sergei Diaghilev, the founding director of the Ballet Russe; Serge Koussevitzky, the Russian-American conductor, who took over the Boston Symphony in this year (1924–1949); Constantin Brancusi, the sculptor; William Bullitt, the first American ambassador to Soviet Russia (1933–1936) Louise Bryant, the widow of John Reed, now Mrs. Bullitt.

darned the moth hole in the front of his trousers. After a brief visit to Sylvia's box in order to seat Boski, Antheil went backstage. The concert opened with a Handel concerto grosso, conducted by Golschmann. Antheil's Second Symphony followed, giving the most conservative listeners a false sense of security. There was polite applause. Anticipation seized the audience as they watched the movers bring in the pianos, loudspeakers, and much strange hardware. The tension was electric when the music began. The *Ballet Mécanique* consisted of startling sounds, whistles, hammers, automobile horns, pianos, xylophones, electric bells, loudspeakers—everything but the carpet sweeper (*balai mécanique*) suggested by the title. But the sounds of the music were soon drowned out by the audience. The shouting, whistling (a Frenchman's supreme expression of contempt), and fighting began. Sylvia glanced over to see Pound in motion in the top gallery, among the Montparnassians, where he had positioned himself to see that Antheil, in Sylvia's words, "got a fair deal." He was leading the cheering section, answering the whistles with applause, the shouts of "thief" with "bravo" and "get out if you don't like it." Some left, to calls of "idiot! imbecile! Philistine!" from Pound. Many looked around in amazement. Boski was "frightened stiff." Sylvia, glancing at the stage, could only assume from the gestures of the players that the performance was continuing. A furious Golschmann continued to conduct imperturbably, as though he were at the dead center of a whirlwind. Jacques Benoist-Méchin, who had already performed this score on the player piano to a small audience at the Paris Conservatoire in the preceding November, was not prepared for the noise made by 2,500 people expressing themselves simultaneously. On both occasions, he claims, his fear was mixed with bewilderment: "I said to myself, 'Why do they continue to scream and shout when they cannot hear anything anyway.' It was awful . . . and I was like a bicycle rider in the Tour de France . . . running away from the people at my heels." Suddenly a louder roar distracted the audience at the present concert. The fans (the score called for airplane propellers) began whirring in front of the loudspeakers. They stirred up a breeze that blew the wig off the head of a man sitting in one of the front rows. After only a few moments' pause, the audience began to participate. Men turned up their coat collars; women drew their wraps around them. Then a man rose and opened his umbrella and positioned himself against the imaginary gale. Soon others opened their umbrellas and made the same gesture. When the concert ended, after twenty-eight minutes of pandemonium, cheers drowned out the opposition. If Anthiel had not "had a hearing," he had at least, according to Sylvia, had a *chahut* (riot), and from a Dada point of view, one could not have anything better. Hugh Ford declares, "It was a dadaist's dream: iconoclastic, seemingly formless, dissonant, guaranteed to spread hysteria among the bourgeoisie." In terms of scale and volume, the concert was one of the greatest events of the twenties in Paris.

Antheil was now the toast of receptions, concerts, and teas. Pound, who thought that "nothing was so harmful to a man as obscurity," says Sylvia, suggested he go broaden his fame by taking a walking tour of Italy with his cat,

Crazy, on his back. Antheil rejected the idea because, as Sylvia put it, he "didn't like walking, particularly with Crazy on his back." Instead he stayed in Paris and let himself be lionized. With increasing fatigue and unhappiness, he played in the drawing rooms of wealthy Frenchmen and Americans who, though shocked and baffled with the loud and atonal music, participated in the trendy enthusiasm. He gave several weekly concerts at the palatial flat of Mrs. Christian Gauss on the Champ-de-Mars. In another concert, the Ketterly Quartet played Beethoven and Antheil at the home of William and Louise Bullitt. Imbs remembers that during performances of the *Ballet Mécanique,* many in the audience were always nervous or uncomfortable. But when the piece was over, they burst into loud applause. Imbs, Benoist-Méchin, Sylvia, Adrienne, and Joyce were faithful in their support of each concert. Pound fueled the fires with laudatory reviews, claiming that the *Ballet Mécanique* "takes us out of the concert hall" and organizes the "sounds of the factory" in a "bigger break with the habits of acceptance than any made by Bach or by Beethoven."

America was never more loudly heard in Paris than when Antheil played his music. American rhythms fascinated the French: from Negro jazz to the mechanical Antheil concerts; from the rolling rhythms of Whitman's *Leaves of Grass* to the newly translated midwestern idiom of Hemingway and McAlmon. But the French love affair with America would explode into hysteria in the following May when the whirring propeller of Lindbergh's *Spirit of Saint Louis* were heard above Le Bourget airfield, outside of Paris. A cheering crowd of 20,000 people, who a week before had never heard of Lindbergh, surged past the floodlights set up around the field. In the Paris nightclubs, Americans drank free champagne. For days streetcars flew the Stars and Stripes, and Franglais (*le boy, le shake-hand*) emerged in speech and press. In the rue de l'Odéon, the American members of the Company were proud. Sylvia, long a representative of America in France, was besieged with congratulations.

CHAPTER 11

Transitions
1926–1927

Death is here:
Not in another place, not among strangers.
Death is under the moon here and the rain.

I promise you old signs and a recognition
Of sun in the seething grass and the wind's rising.

Do you ask more?
Do you ask to travel forever?

— Archibald MacLeish,
"Tourist Death: For Sylvia Beach"

LIGHTNING STRUCK a neighboring cottage in Les Déserts one stormy August night in 1926. The thatched roof blazed, lighting the faces of Adrienne, Sylvia, and their neighbors as they helplessly watched it burn. That same week a second bolt, this one in the form of shattering news, struck Sylvia. Samuel Roth had pirated *Ulysses*. In July, in his *Two Worlds Monthly*, he had published in expurgated form the first three books (Telemachiad). When she heard this news in a letter from John M. Price of the *New York Herald Tribune*, the next chapters were in press. There was nothing she could do from her mountain retreat. Even in Paris she would be limited in her defense, because *Ulysses*, except for the portions that had appeared years before in the *Little Review*, was not copyrighted in the United States. However, she immediately wrote to Joyce, who was in Belgium at the time, and they determined not to stand idly by and witness the theft and emasculation of *Ulysses*. When they returned to Paris, they would extinguish the Roth fire with legal and social pressures.

The summer vacation had begun with the promise of calm after the Antheil storm. On 21 July, Sylvia mailed the Shaun portion of *Work in Progress* to Marianne Moore at the *Dial* and, before leaving for Les Déserts with Adrienne, spent a warm July week in Boulogne. While she was there, Joyce (with the reluctant assistance of Myrsine and Adrienne) nearly emptied Shakespeare and Company's cash drawer, bank account, and secret cache and then took his family to the Belgian port of Ostend, on the North Sea. He studied Flemish (incorporating words into his manuscript) and visited Antwerp, Ghent, Brussels, and Waterloo (for descriptive battlefield details). From the back of the bus to Waterloo, the American novelist Thomas Wolfe observed him quietly, hesitant to introduce himself. While Joyce walked the beaches and toured the countryside, haranguing the bus driver with questions, Sylvia and Adrienne relaxed in their mountain retreat, hoping not to have to combine business with pleasure.

Without the knowledge of Sylvia or Joyce, Roth had announced in full-page ads in several English and American publications (including his own review) that he was about to publish a "new unnamed work" by Joyce. This work was not new, of course; rather, it was a piracy of Sylvia's eighth (reset) edition of *Ulysses*, printed by "Maurice Daran Frère [*sic*]" and preceded by an essay on the author by Arthur Symons. The work was altered, however; Sylvia later counted 131 variations from the text in the first eight installments. In the first news of Roth's action, Price asked Sylvia whether the publisher was authorized to issue *Ulysses*, declaring that if he was not, he (Price) was willing to intervene on her behalf. He knew Roth to be a "literary swindler," he explains, because he had "been instrumental in protecting" Pound and Ford against him. Sylvia sent Joyce in Belgium a copy of the letter, along with a cable from the *Dial* requesting deletions in the Shaun section before it could be published. "We do not know what to do" about Roth, Joyce complains to Harriet Weaver in London. "The number is dedicated to me with profound admiration or something like that! O dear!" Why, he wonders aloud, do Sylvia and Adrienne go to Les Desérts? "I wish they were back and the tiresome badtempered summer over." Yet six days later, in a letter to Sylvia accompanying the return of the letter and cable, Joyce writes, "Do not do anything till you return to Paris. . . ." He appears in no hurry to return from his own vacation and fight Roth. He is absorbed in his new work.

Because Joyce did not return to the city until several weeks after Sylvia did, she had time to concentrate on catching up with bookshop business. She met with representatives of English publishing houses in order to place new orders, hired a carpenter to build more shelves, granted interviews with *McNaught's* and the *New York Herald*, brought her business correspondence up to date, and advised the fall tourists who invariably wanted her help in finding apartments. As social and cultural life quickened, Sylvia re-entered the stream of the lives of her friends: she attended a lunch with Jules Romains, celebrated the birthday of the *Tribune* correspondent William L. Shirer (who had just been promoted to the rank of foreign correspondent for the home edition of the *Chicago Tribune*), and dined in the new apartment of Jean Prévost and Marcelle Auclair. George and Boski Antheil had welcomed her return with a new cat, which had "flies," as Boski exclaimed in her Hungarian accent. George caught pneumonia. Fearing it was tuberculosis, Sylvia wrote to their friends for money to send him for a cure.

There would be no cure, she soon learned, for discords that had appeared in the marriages of Hemingway and McAlmon. Letters from Bryher and McAlmon confided news of their final separation. It had always been a marriage for appearances, but by 1926 McAlmon had ceased to keep up appearances. Believing he had Sylvia's loyalty, he wrote to thank her for her translation of his story for the

Navire, hinting that they could undertake other translations. He asked for Sylvia's calming advice, suggested that he might rent Antheil's apartment if it became available, and proposed that someday they "do a magazine, after the others have quit fluttering."

Hemingway, who was beginning to call himself Papa, had returned in August from the Cap d'Antibes, where his neighbors had been the Murphys, Mac-Leishes, and Fitzgeralds. Pauline Pfeiffer had moved in with the Hemingway family, and the marriage finally splintered. Hadley and Ernest returned to separate apartments in Paris. Agreeing to a 100-day separation, Pauline returned to her home in Piggott, Arkansas. Hemingway bought a year's subscription (on 4 October) to the lending library and moped lonesomely about the shop and cafés, heroically contemplating suicide.

The summer of 1926 was marked by a series of transitions in the lives of Sylvia and Company. Disappointments in the lives of McAlmon, Hemingway, and Antheil this year would eventually take these men away from the rue de l'Odéon. The combination of the Roth piracy of *Ulysses* and a death in the Beach family opened a fissure in the Beach-Joyce partnership that in five years would widen irreparably. A gradual shift in Joyce's personal life began in this fall when he met several persons—including Eugene Jolas, Elliot Paul, and Stuart Gilbert—who would form a new set of confidants. Even the café life of Montparnasse was in transition. In the *Herald,* Alex Small lamented the passing of the "villagey venom" and "happy family" atmosphere of the quarter. When angry French workers attacked the Americans in the cafés in August of 1927 after the Sacco-Vanzetti executions, an era began to pass. For Sylvia, the catalyst for change lay in her own family crisis.

On one slow day in September, Sylvia, having the time, wrote to her mother, who was staying in Florence. At the quiet of her desk, she filled a letter with chatty details describing her fall social activities and wardrobe, mining the vein of her mother's interests. Eleanor had urged Sylvia to "dress with distinction" and, on her last visit, had found a new tailor for her. Sylvia assured Mrs. Beach that she would look distinguished in the new suit she had ordered. Before another year had passed, Sylvia would act in a more significant way to save appearances for her mother.

Meanwhile, Joyce returned to Paris to deal with problems regarding *Ulysses* and *Work in Progress.* He was annoyed both with the long hours he had spent in August and September with the German translator of *Ulysses* and with his German publisher's urgency. He vowed to his brother Stanislaus that if the Germans' rush to print caused numerous errors or large gaps, he would "ask Miss Beach to circularize the German press with a disclaimer." He asked Claud Sykes and another friend to read the German translation and postponed its publication. When he refused to alter the Shaun section for the *Dial,* its editors refused to publish it. While censorship and the lack of support by friends for his new work weighed on his conscious thoughts, the Roth matter demanded immediate action. He and Sylvia, who called the piracy a "rape," wrote numerous letters to expose Roth.

Quinn's law partner refused to initiate a suit against the pirate, because there had been no violation of American law. In order to be copyrighted in the United States, a book had to be published there, and *Ulysses,* banned in any case, had been published in Paris. The Bern copyright agreement should have protected the book against piracy nevertheless, but the United States had not signed it.

Roth's piracy was not the first one suffered by Joyce. In 1918 a Boston publisher had printed *Chamber Music* without his permission, and, eventually, pirates in many countries published *Ulysses* and pocketed all the profits. Once a Japanese publisher in Tokyo sent four volumes of his version of the book with his greetings. When Sylvia protested, he thought she was grasping and greedy. The following March, when Sylvia learned that Edward Titus was selling some of her hand-corrected proofs from Darantière (who claimed he had not sold them), she went to the Titus bookshop and demanded to see them. By the time she returned on the next day, they had "disappeared," according to Titus, whom she vowed not to trust again.

In mid-October Sylvia attended a concert by Antheil at the Salle Gaveau. He had recovered from his pneumonia just in time to attend it. She was delighted at the number of bows he took at the conclusion of his Symphony in F. Elliot Paul wrote a long review of the performance for the *Tribune,* complimenting Golschmann's conducting and listing the names and positions of all the distinguished persons present: prominent French musicians, such as Honegger and Milhaud of The Six; the Odéon family, with Joyce in a "pose of absorption and detachment"; the Russian director Diaghilev; and, in front of the "musicians, writers, critics and artists from all quarters of the world," a row of the couturier Paul Poiret's beautiful mannequins. The Antheil whirlwind of concerts, publicity, and plots—which had come to a climax in June at the Théâtre des Champs-Élysées—began dissipating in the winter of 1926. By the end of November, Antheil and Boski had left town on doctor's orders for a change of air in Chamonix. Sylvia protected him from harassment, as she did Joyce, by giving misleading information to inquiries. Because she thought he had "a raft of parasites" swarming around, she told everyone he had gone to Bagnères. Antheil spent longer and longer periods of time away from Paris. Virgil Thomson, alienated by what he considered Antheil's secretive handling of "material benefits," increasingly turned his attention to Stein, with whom he began a long collaboration on two operas and translations. Pound also lost interest in George, claims Boski, when he refused to write another *Ballet Mécanique.* Sylvia, who replenished the Lloyd's account when Antheil needed it, remained loyal to him.

A shift in library membership was evident each fall. Lincoln Steffens, the *Tribune* newsman James Thurber, and the artist Grant Wood left Paris to return to the United States. Longtime patrons remained loyal even after they had left Paris. In November, Sylvia heard from one of her first American members, Thornton Wilder, who had just finished his master's degree in modern languages at Princeton. To her he inscribed his newly published novel, *The Cabala,* which he had begun in Rome and Paris in 1920–1921. In 1927, much to her delight, he became an international celebrity (and won the Pulitzer Prize) for *The Bridge of San Luis Rey*. His fame, which she had correctly anticipated, and steady university employment gave him the financial means to return to Paris for many visits. Among those who came back later this year was Matthew Josephson. New members of the library this fall included Theodore Dreiser, who had just published *An American Tragedy*. He had last visited Paris in 1912. His appearances at the shop were fleeting, for, as Huddleston remembers, the fifty-five-year-old novelist was "dark and gloomy . . . and shrank from the usual round of drawing-room entertainments imposed on American visitors."

At about this time Sylvia became acquainted with two visitors from Russia: Sergei Eisenstein and Ivy Low Litvinov, the English-born wife of Maxim M. Litvinov, the Soviet foreign commissioner. Having purchased *Ulysses* in Shakespeare and Company, she wrote Sylvia from Moscow that she could think about nothing else and was writing an essay on *Ulysses* for a Russian monthly. Wishing to introduce Joyce to Russian readers, she requested Sylvia to send her more books by Joyce and biographical information and later to read her rough draft. "My literary career has come to an end since reading *Ulysses*," she declares. "Don't know whether I'll ever revive and don't even seem to care much." On the contrary, her literary career flourished. Reportedly she tutored Stalin in English, and later, while her husband was Stalin's foreign minister in Washington, she published detective stories, novels, and a number of short stories in the *New Yorker*. When Sylvia sent her copies of *transition* in 1928, she wrote with disappointment that she could not understand Joyce's new work.

Many of the new patrons were obscure, young, and in need of help. In November a young American named Larson, who had been visiting the shop, sought her aid in a case of international misunderstanding. While basking in the warmth of his acceptance at a little tearoom in the Place de l'Odéon (he had been leaving large tips), Larson was suddenly caught short of money. Unable to understand his English, the restaurant owner had him arrested. He had been in jail for eleven days (and had eaten only three pieces of bread and drunk only water), when he got in touch with Sylvia, who bailed him out. That afternoon in the shop, Sylvia and Myrsine gave him tea and listened to the details of his tale of the few missing centimes for the ten-franc lunch. Myrsine recalls many such mishaps suffered by Americans and aggravated by the language barrier, involving restaurants, the metro, concierges, or the police. Travelers always got a sympathetic hearing at Shakespeare and Company.

"I'm busy with all this pirating affair," Sylvia complains in a letter to Holly. "I don't see how publishers of more than one book manage. The work seems to give the maximum of labour any single publisher can furnish." She corresponded with everyone she thought would help, and she urged Joyce to call as much attention to the piracy as possible. She had her father inquire in New York City about legal and social pressures. He called on Frances Steloff at the Gotham Book Mart to talk about hiring a lawyer; at her suggestion, he advised Sylvia against legal action because Roth was "not worth the cannon ball that would put him out of business."

These efforts by the Reverend Beach were a testimony to the elderly clergyman's open-mindedness about art, and his loyalty to his daughter. When an American reporter asked Sylvia what her father thought of *Ulysses,* she replied: "My father thinks that nothing is unworthy of mention if it exists. I should certainly not have published the book without his counsel." Though she did not seek his counsel, she knew the readers of the article might think favorably of *Ulysses* if she had sought it. She told the reporter that she was displeased with the censorship in America and England and added, "You can not successfully legislate against human nature." Apparently her father agreed with her. At least he had learned to take the controversial nature of his daughters' activities in stride. "The cinema for my sister and my *Ulysses* publication must have made life difficult for my father," she mused later. "But he always encouraged us. His only comment on hearing of *Ulysses* was, 'You should have printed a bigger edition, Sylvia.' "

Joyce sought help in other quarters. He wrote to ask Pound whether he knew a lawyer. Pound replied that he did not but explained that when his own name had appeared on the cover of Roth's *Two Worlds* the winter before, he had cabled his father to start legal proceedings against Roth. His father refused because of the expense, but Pound's name was removed from the cover. "You are in worse shape than I was," Pound points out to Joyce, "as you have taken money from him . . . and have known for some time that he was a crook. All I can suggest is that you write to as many papers as possible, denouncing Roth, and stating that the text is garbled and unauthorized." And "SIGN your name," he urges. In the preceding weeks Sylvia had sent sixty letters over her own signature to such American newspapers as the *Evening News* and the *Post* in New York. Stung, perhaps, by Pound's reminder that he had already allowed Roth to publish portions of *Work in Progress*—or prodded by Pound's suggestion that he "organize a gang of gunmen to scare Roth out of his pants"—Joyce decided to do more. His "gunmen" would be scores of international writers; Sylvia would publish a protest with their signatures. By December, the American novelist Ludwig Lewisohn was writing a first draft of the protest. MacLeish revised it with an eye to its legality. The protest reads in part,

It is a matter of common knowledge that the *Ulysses* of Mr. James Joyce is being republished in the United States, in a magazine edited by Samuel Roth, and that this republication is being made without authorization by Mr. Joyce; without payment to Mr. Joyce and with alterations which seriously corrupt the text . . . The question in issue is whether the public (including the editors and publishers to whom his advertisements are offered) will encourage Mr. Samuel Roth to take advantage of the resultant legal difficulty of the author to deprive him of his property and to mutilate the creation of his art. . . .

Sylvia later had copies made and mailed, with a personal letter from her, all over the world. She spent hours telephoning, poring over addresses in *Who's Who,* and writing personal letters. Joyce dictated a letter to Shaw for Sylvia's signature. He found Italian and Finnish addresses; Sylvia suggested many names, particularly those of the French academicians. During December and January she collected signatures and sent several cables a day. For fear of libel, newspapers usually only reported on, and did not quote, her letters and cables. Yet many, such as the *Saturday Review,* continued to print Roth's large advertisements for his issues of *Two Worlds Monthly* that were featuring *Ulysses.* Sylvia and Joyce heard exaggerated rumors that Roth was making one million francs a month from this venture. Finally, Mr. Benjamin Howe Conner (an American lawyer in Paris) agreed to take the piracy case against Roth; at least he thought he could bring backstairs pressure against him. Also, much to Joyce's delight, signatures on the protest began arriving from many writers. Sylvia corralled Hemingway and other well-known customers to sign. Valéry signed, adding his French Academy title. Everyone seemed to be coming to the defense of *Ulysses.*

But few seemed enthusiastic about *Work in Progress.* In May of 1926 Wyndham Lewis had met Joyce with a special request for a piece of his new work for the *Enemy,* a forthcoming review of criticism and philosophy that he would publish. Joyce's work was to be the only fiction represented. Sylvia had the manuscript typed and mailed to Lewis. Months passed without acknowledgment of its receipt or news of its publication. In Brussels, Joyce became impatient, scrawled a letter to Lewis with his biggest black pencil, and dispatched it to Sylvia, asking her to copy it and to send it to Lewis as a letter from herself. "I had no reply to 'my' letter," she reports. The "reply" arrived in March 1927 in the form of the first issue of the *Enemy,* which appeared until 1929. In place of the Joyce text appeared a violent attack on Joyce's *Work in Progress.* In the following September he leveled an even stronger and more personal attack on Joyce himself. With the first volume of the *Enemy,* Lewis sent a letter to Sylvia expressing fear that it would not receive a "warm reception." Yet because she has "a monopoly of the English bookselling trade in Paris," it is to her, he says, that he must send it first.

Portions of Joyce's *Work in Progress,* which he had begun in March 1923, had appeared in 1924 in the *transatlantic review* and in 1925 in *The Contact Collection of Contemporary Writers,* in *Le Navire d'Argent,* and in *This Quarter.* But nothing of it was published in 1926. The *Dial* had refused to publish a portion without deletions, and Lewis had rejected without comment the portion that had been submitted to him. Joyce gave the Anna Livia Plurabelle section to Galantière, who was returning to the United States to work for *Vanity Fair,* but he could not get it published in any periodical. What worried Joyce more than the hesitancy of magazine publishers was the negative reaction of his earliest friends and supporters—such as Miss Weaver, Pound, and Larbaud. They seemed puzzled by, even resentful of, this baffling new work built on a network of puns, esoteric references, and multiple languages. Joyce's growing anxiety can be read in his letters to Miss Weaver, whose support he felt he must have. In June of 1926 he had asked her opinion, suggested collateral reading, and offered to explain any words that puzzled her. In July he asked her to help him by jotting down any ideas that came to her as she read the work. He sent more explanations. In September he sought her complicity in the writing itself by suggesting that she "order" some portion to be included in the manuscript. She sent a piece of local legend about a prehistoric giant's grave near Penrith in Cumberland, England. But with her "order" came the clear indication of her doubt: "Such is my 'order' for this book. But what I would really like is to place an order well in advance when another book is under completion!" Joyce made no open acknowledgment of her hint. Nor had he responded to the first attack by an intimate when his brother Stanislaus had called his new work "the witless wanderings of literature before its final extinction." When Joyce asked for Stanislaus's order, he received no reply. He placed Miss Weaver's legend, he informs her, "in the place of honour, namely the first pages of the book. . . . The book really has no beginning or end. (Trade secret, registered at Stationers Hall.) It ends in the middle of a sentence and begins in the middle of the same sentence":

> brings us back to Howth Castle & Environs. Sir Tristram, violer d'amores, had passencore rearrived on the scraggy isthmus from North Amorica to wiederfight his penisolate war; nor had stream rocks by the Oconee exaggerated themselse to Laurens County, Ga, doublin all the time; . . .

A later game he initiated with Miss Weaver was to keep her guessing the title, which he refused to reveal to anyone. However, no diversion invented by him could make her change her mind. She did not like his deliberate obscurity: "But, dear sir, (I always seem to have a 'but') the worst of it is that without comprehensive key and glossary, such as you very kindly made out for me, the poor hapless reader loses a very great deal of your intention; flounders helplessly, is in imminent danger, in fact, of being . . . totally lost. . . . ."

Sylvia was also taking part in the creation and in reading the decoded lists of words and phrases. She "followed it with him step by step." When he "took up battles" in 1926, she explains, "I ordered Edward S. Creasy's *Fifteen Decisive Battles of the World: 12 Plans,*" and "he read these exciting stories, and went off to have a look at Waterloo. In one of the most amusing passages in *Finnegans Wake* you can see the jumble Joyce made of battlefield, generals, their horses, books and cocked hats." As she testifies in her memoirs, "He explained everything in signs and drawings and alphabets as we went along, and I found all of his ideas so interesting, amusing, and convincing that by the time the whole book appeared I was at home in it and inured . . . to the overflowing Joycean vocabulary." She understood that he was "deliberately misleading" and "blurred" because he explained to her one day that history (and perhaps his work) was "like that parlor game where someone whispers something to the person next to him, who repeats it not very distinctly to the next person, and so on until, by the time the last person hears it, it comes out completely transformed. And he laughed at the poor reader's plight." With this understanding, Sylvia was willing to pick up the meanings and humor where she found them in the work. Miss Weaver, on the other hand, was a critical and careful reader who wanted, as she explained to Sylvia, "to see behind every word and phrase, as far as possible, and to why it is written." She could not find sufficient time to do this with Joyce's new work. Her biographers believe she was caught between a desire to protect Joyce's "peace of mind" and an unwillingness to make "a sacrifice of her integrity." When she asked Joyce whether, when the present book was finished, he would "lend ear to several of your older friends (E.P. to be included)," her implication was clear. He responded, "Do you not like anything I am writing. . . . I am rather discouraged about this as in such a vast and difficult enterprise I need encouragement. It is possible Pound is right, but I cannot go back." She apologized but did not recant. Praising some parts, she confessed honestly that she did not care for his "Wholesale Safety Pun Factory nor the darknesses and unintelligibilities of your deliberately-entangled language system. It seems to me you are wasting your genius. But I daresay I am wrong. . . ." According to her biographers, her mounting perplexity, which in the end forced her to speak, was hard to bear alone. In a confidential letter to Sylvia the following year, she confesses her frustration:

When writing to Mr. Joyce I try now to say all I can in praise of the pieces and nothing against them but I find it difficult as I have the feeling all the time that his genius and his immense labours are being to some extent wasted in producing what appears to me to be—to put it boldly—a curiosity of literature. I daresay I am wrong (*you* certainly believe so) but I cannot help it—and I have neither the art nor the ability to lie adroitly in order to please him. But it distresses me to hurt him and I wish he would not always so insistently ask me how I like the pieces. I *do* like immensely the ending of *Anna Livia* and have told him so.

Sylvia apparently believed that Miss Weaver was wrong. One had, she observes, to "burrow down deep" in the obscurity, for it was "history after all, sometimes private." She believed Joyce was the only writer "brave" and "crazy enough to cut loose from the wornout ideas of writing." She was willing to live with the fact that she herself did not understand all the language. The work was Joyce's choice; she supported him.

In November of 1926 she mailed the Shaun section to Pound, who was talking about publishing a new review. Pound answered Joyce by saying that he did not have the patience to "wade through" this piece and that "nothing short of divine vision or a new cure for the clapp can possibly be worth all the circumambient peripherization." With further prodding by Joyce, Pound still insisted, "Nothing would be worth plowing through like this, except the Divine Vision— and I gather it's not that sort of thing."

McAlmon, who did not sign the protest against Roth, gave only halfhearted support. When Joyce asked for his assurance in the face of Pound's attack, McAlmon told Joyce that he was not mad—just touched by genius. Elsewhere McAlmon confesses that Joyce's new work "was quite beyond [his] capacity" and that "the interest did not carry." McAlmon—like Pound, the Bradleys, Frank Budgen, and other friends of the early twenties—had withdrawn from Joyce's side chiefly because they were annoyed with his egocentrism.

Since Pound and Miss Weaver declined their support and since Larbaud (who had initially thought the work "excellent" but incomprehensible) kept silent,

Joyce, in what proved to be the first step in changing his circle, looked for encouragement among new friends. He invited them to hear him read on 12 December (and again on 26 January at Adrienne's request) the rewritten opening passages of the *Work in Progress*. In addition to Sylvia and Adrienne, the small group at both readings consisted of Elliot Paul, Maria and Eugene Jolas, and Myron and Helen Nutting. "What do you think of it?" he eagerly asked. "Did you like it?" Although they apparently said little, the next day the Nuttings sent flowers and praise. The apparent enthusiasm of this new group (soon to include Stuart Gilbert and Paul Léon) was what Joyce needed. "At the end of 1926," announces his biographer Richard Ellmann, "the *dramatis personae* began to gather for the last period in Joyce's life."

Because Jolas was interested in words and their liberation from conventional language, he had wanted to get better acquainted with Joyce, whom he had met briefly at Adrienne's bookshop in 1924. He had turned to Sylvia, whom he and Paul knew well in their jobs as writers for the Paris edition of the *Chicago Tribune,* and she had agreed to approach Joyce in order to arrange a meeting. It was at her suggestion, perhaps, that the December reading took place. Jolas and Paul had confided to Sylvia that they were thinking of leaving the *Tribune* to establish a new magazine whose program would be to revolutionize language. She respected their credentials and judgment. Jolas, who spoke three languages fluently, had been born in New Jersey of a French father and German mother and educated in the department of Lorraine, near the German border. When she learned about Jolas's publishing philosophy, Sylvia, who was discouraged by the *Dial*'s recent withdrawal of the Shaun portion and by news of the death of Ernest Walsh (editor of the only extant expatriate review), felt new hope for the publication of *Work in Progress*. "Jolas asked me if I knew anything special he might use as a contribution to his review," she explains. "It occurred to me that Joyce, instead of continuing to contribute bits of 'Work in Progress' to reviews here and there, should publish it in monthly instalments. . . ." Soon after the mid-December reading, Jolas asked to be permitted to read the manuscript, and Joyce requested Sylvia to lend him the first 120 pages of it. Finding the work congenial to his own interests, Jolas decided that he would like to publish it. According to Sylvia, "when Joyce called me up to ask what I thought of the plan, I advised him to accept without hesitation. I knew Jolas would be a friend he could depend on; and the name of James Joyce would be a great help in launching a new review."

On the morning after she and Adrienne attended the opening-night performance of Romains's play *Jean le Maufranc,* Sylvia typed and dated the first list of signatures protesting Roth's piracy. This alphabetical list of 6 December ranged from Sherwood Anderson (at his request she had gone to his sickbed to collect his signature) to Virginia Woolf. On that same day she sent a *pneumatique* to Hemingway, whose divorce would be final in a couple weeks, inviting him to dinner the following Saturday with Larbaud, Paulhan, the Joyces, and the MacLeishes. The dinner celebrated Hemingway's new book, *The Sun Also Rises,* which had just been reviewed in the *Tribune,* and the opening at Adrienne's shop (in a new rear gallery) of a six-week exhibit of Paul-Émile Bécat's portrait drawings of writers. The collection ranged from a portrait of Romains, done in 1919, to the portraits of Joyce and Sylvia, done in 1926.

Sylvia was probably too busy to be aware that her family was facing any danger. Although her father had returned to the United States, her mother remained in Italy on another of her extended European stays. Presumably she was buying pottery and antiques for the Pasadena boutique (now run reluctantly by Holly, since illness had made it necessary for Cyprian to move to Palm Springs). Sylvia had a growing sense that she should go to visit her mother, but lack of time and money—she was making monthly payments of 5,500 francs to Darantière and was embroiled in the Roth affair—made it impossible for her to leave Paris.

The familiar hand of the Treasury Department seized Holly's copy of *Ulysses*. In a letter of 27 November, Sylvia had warned Holly (who had requested the book for her friend Mrs. Bullis): "I don't like sending 'em, because we're bringing suit against Roth and don't want it said that we send copies to the U.S. in spite of its being forbidden. So tell Mrs. Bullis to keep her mouth shut about where and how she got *Ulysses if* she gets it. . . ." She did not, as it happened, get it. Instead Holly received the following letter, familiar by now to many Americans:

Miss Hollingsworth Beach
630 E. Colorado Street
Pasadena, California
Madam: December 16, 1926
    One package addressed to you, containing one obscene book "Ulysses," has been seized from the mail for violation of section 305 tariff act, which prohibits the importation of all obscene or immoral literature. (Seizure No. 5217)
    If you will sign and return the inclosed Assent to Forfeiture no further action will be taken by this office.   Respectfully,
                                                          L.H. Schwaebe
                                                          Collector of Customs
                                                          U.S. Treasury Department

At about this same time other potential readers were more successful than Holly's Mrs. Bullis: an Illinois lawyer, Robert Earley, got his copy via Mexico; one W. E. O. Burch boldly carried his copy under his arm as he boarded a plane to England. Students who could not afford to travel were not so fortunate—even if their school library did own a copy of *Ulysses*. Having unsuccessfully attempted to borrow the book from his university library in Columbus, Ohio, a young English major named Sam Steward, who described himself as "an unheard of student," wrote to Joyce asking him to intercede on his behalf with the librarian. Joyce did not respond. Such stories help illustrate the frustration that Roth exploited.

Just months after his wife had given birth to a boy, whom they named Omar Shakespear, Pound informed Sylvia that he was giving life to a new review, "to

advertise the virtues of the elect." It would be called *Exile,* a term that has been
frequently used since to describe the expatriate experience, particularly Pound's
own exile of more than forty years. "Do you want your address on the cover in
SHORT list of places where the reviews may be found?" he inquires. In her
response, which was positive, she inquired whether authors were to be paid for
their work. Pound defensively asserts in a return letter, "It *ain't* that kind of
review. . . . As to sponging on authors, I have had a good deal to do with authors
during the past 15 years, and there have never been but one of 'em who complained about my rates or methods of payments." He declares he is offering
writers "25% on sale, or return stuff." Pound had sent the Shaun section back
to Joyce in the preceding November, and, evidently, he was no longer among
the poet's "elect." However, Sylvia did agree to sell *Exile,* which appeared in
four issues from the spring of 1927 to the autumn of 1928 and which was in its
final phase edited in Chicago by Pascal Covici. Although Joyce would not appear
in this magazine, Jolas and Paul were preparing a home for his *Work in Progress*
in their own review.

In January of the new year, Sylvia wrote what would prove to be her last two
letters to her mother in Florence. "They say it's really repressive down there
now," she writes in one of them. "I hope they don't open this letter and start
having you watched as a dangerous person." Teasing her mother, Sylvia did not
know that it would soon be the police of Paris not Florence who would be watching her. This month Sylvia seemed to be aware only of her own trouble with
Roth. Because there is "no one but me to get the thing done," she complains,
"I have been writing letters up to half past eight every night and on New Year's
Eve stayed in the shop writing till 10:30 and then had to take the letters to the
Central Post." But, she concedes, the efforts are worth it, the list of signatures
is impressive, and the publishing of them "will be really historic." She typed
the list on the evening of the twenty-seventh, closed the shop, and fell into bed.
On the following day, she cabled the protest to hundreds of papers, hoping for a
2 February 1927 publication. She mailed the list to her mother proudly: "Here
is the list as it stands and I'm the one that got all the names." It has been "big
work," she admits.

On 2 February, *Ulysses'* fifth birthday, Sylvia continued to receive signatures
and add them to her growing list. On that night the Joyces, Sylvia, Adrienne,
the Huddlestons, and the MacLeishes celebrated with dinner at Langer's Restaurant; Joyce played host, as usual. A part of the table talk concerned the distinguished list of signatures, of which Joyce was immensely proud. He was
overwhelmed by the support of Albert Einstein and of the two Italian philosophers and senators Benedetto Croce and Giovanni Gentile. "The list of signatures is amazing in its literary dignity and length," declared Janet Flanner (Genêt)
in the *New Yorker.* "One day this protest, with annexed signatures, will be a
bibliophile's item. Today it is a grand gesture to Joyce and Miss Beach and to
the writing craft's spirited solidarity." The list, which had grown to 167 names,
appeared beneath a strongly worded statement that ends with the following words:

The undersigned protest against Mr. Roth's conduct in republishing *Ulysses* and appeal to the American public in the name of that security of works of the intellect and the imagination without which art cannot live, to oppose to Mr. Roth's enterprise the full power of honorable and fair opinion.

Among the distinguished English signers were Bennett, Maugham, and Galsworthy; among the Germans was Thomas Mann; and among the Spanish were Unamuno and Azorín, president of the Spanish Academy. Lady Gregory, Yeats, O'Casey, and James Stephens supported their fellow countryman. The presence of American, French, and Japanese signatures made it a truly international protest. A few writers refused to sign—Shaw and Pound were notable exceptions. The latter thought it a "miss-fire" because Joyce was calling more attention to himself than to the "infamous state of the American law." Pound rather wanted to take on all American injustice: "The minor peccadillo of Mr. Roth is dwarfed by the major infamy of the law." Pound did cooperate in the lawsuit, however. When Roth claimed that Jane Heap had through Pound given him permission to carry on the publication of *Ulysses,* Pound gave a deposition at the American consulate in Genoa, stating that he had not authorized Roth to publish the novel. Shaw did not sign, he explained in a long letter of 18 December 1926 to Sylvia, because the "protest is poppycock." In a tone slightly more sympathetic than that of his 1921 refusal to buy *Ulysses,* he advised Sylvia to have Joyce inform the press of the absurdity of censorship, which in fact often causes a work to be pirated and hence more widely circulated than it would be otherwise.

Ignoring the advice of Pound and Shaw, Sylvia peppered the Western press with the angry protest against Roth, believing that her list of distinguished names could hardly be dismissed by the newspapers. The pressure on Roth and the publicity given to *Ulysses* promised to be great. In a letter to Miss Weaver, after listing the signatures, Joyce concludes, "There are the reserved seats and now let us sit down in peace and wait till the band begins."

The overture was weaker than expected. Fearing libel, many newspapers did not print the full protest. Some French, German, English, and American papers gave it special coverage, emphasizing the prestigious signatures. For example, the London *Times* carried the story and listed the prominent English writers who had signed. The *Publishers' Weekly* (whose editor sent a personal response) and the *New York Times* covered each event in the struggle. Short articles appeared in at least two dozen American newspapers. Ethel Moorhead wrote from Italy asking Sylvia whether she wished her to run the full protest with signatures in the next issue of *This Quarter,* which she was continuing after Walsh's death. The *Humanist,* an English monthly edited by Herbert Devine, printed a full page with Joyce's picture, the protest statement, and facsimiles of some fifty signatures, which Sylvia had had her publishers photograph. When the Associated Press came to do a feature on the shop and the protest, the photographer's flash-bulb sent her cat into hiding for the day. When he read the protest, Roth also may have jumped. But instead of going into hiding as the cat had done, he hired a lawyer and continued to publish *Ulysses* each month through October.

The wrath of Roth, as Sylvia labeled the second movement, was unpleasant. Pound had warned Joyce that they had "a skunk to deal with and the perfume will possibly fly." It did. Roth offered Joyce $1,000 for *Ulysses* and requested a statement from him that the money had been offered before the July 1926 publication. Joyce refused to reply. In letters to individuals and the press, Roth claimed (1) that he was continuing a publication that the *Little Review* had begun with Joyce's permission; (2) that the alteration of the first installment involved only a dozen words and that this was the fault of the subeditor; (3) that he had offered Joyce $1,000 but had received no reply; (4) that he had deposited $1,000 with Joyce's "American attorney Mr. Arthur Garfield Hays"; (5) that he had offered Joyce $2,000 a year in salary for all his rights; and (6) that Miss Beach, not he, was profiting by getting "high prices" from unsuspecting travelers "who think they are buying a dirty book." He, on the contrary, was losing readers who were bored by Joyce's book. The "dirty book" sneer was ironical, a *New Statesman* editor noted, coming from a man who published a pornographic magazine entitled *Casanova Jr's Tales* and who meant to profit from the scandal that had followed in the wake of *Ulysses*. Later Roth accused Sylvia, "that vicious virago, Joyce's secretary," of including dead writers among her signers. In fact two had died since signing. Regarding this charge, Sylvia declared that that's something Roth "might have done himself."

In counterpoint to Roth's claims came pressure from legal and literary camps. Through Chadbourne, Stanchfield, and Levy (Conner's firm in New York), Joyce and Sylvia hoped to force a test case for the reform of the U.S. law. They filed a suit in March to stop publication. The literary pressure probably stung Roth more than did the threat of an injunction. Sherwood Anderson, who had returned to America from Paris in mid-March, charged Roth with piracy and exploitation. Roth replied with a detailed defense of his action. On the back of Roth's letter, Anderson scrawled, "What right have you to publish the work of any living author without his permission?" Roth retorted, "Your note in its brevity was your first composition which I could read through to a finish." Anderson placed these letters in an envelope and mailed them to Sylvia. Later this year Eliot, too, became embroiled in the argument with Roth, who had also pirated Eliot's poetry. In July, Eliot sent a letter to the *New York Evening Post,* the *Nation,* and the *Dial* protesting Roth's piracy of *Ulysses* and his own verses (in an issue dedicated to Eliot). "Mr. Roth chooses to interpret any gift to the world as a gift to himself," Eliot announced. Roth's reply to the three publications and to Eliot charged that the poet was "both a prig and a blackguard" and that his poetry had no commercial value. He sent Eliot a check for $25 to cover what he considered to be its worth. Roth again repeated the false charge that Joyce's agent, Pound, had given him permission to publish *Ulysses*. The international protest, Roth repeated, was all a conspiracy by Sylvia Beach. Elsewhere he described Joyce as a "renegade Jew" with a vast organization behind him. Sylvia was amused that the Jewish publisher would so disparage the "renegade" Catholic and that her efforts were interpreted as being those of a "vast organization."

But Eliot was embarrassed when Roth brought up the Bel Esprit fund raising of 1922. Roth falsely "exposed" Eliot's "beggarly past," claiming that he (Roth) had once contributed to a fund "instigated" by Eliot. It was, of course, Pound's fund, and Eliot was unaware of the fund until it was offered to him. Calling Roth's $25 check "bribery or hushmoney," Eliot sent the check back to the *Post* to return to Roth. The swords on the bloodied deck of literary piracy were sharp and penetrating indeed.

In March of 1927 Joyce asked Sylvia to assist him in publishing a second collection of poems written since he had left Ireland (since *Chamber Music*). In February he had sent the poems, fifteen in all, to Pound, hoping they might soften Pound's criticism of *Work in Progress*. Pound had returned them without comment and, when further pressed for an opinion, had suggested that "they belong in the Bible or in a family album with the portraits." When Joyce inquired whether "they are worth printing any time," Pound answered no. Three weeks later Joyce handed the poems to MacLeish, who was not as blunt or negative as Pound. Graciously, he wrote Joyce to compliment him on the poems and to invite him and Nora to dinner on 14 March. When the dinner plans had to be canceled, he sent Joyce a second letter, saying that the poems "have the strangest quality of 'existence.' " Although Ellmann describes MacLeish's letters as "so enthusiastic as to renew Joyce's self-esteem," the truth is that they contained sincere but qualified praise. Still, cheered by the encouragement, Joyce decided to publish the poetry. In the meantime Sylvia and Adrienne were arranging for MacLeish's poetry (translated by Larbaud) to appear in *Commerce*. Sylvia also arranged, by means of a suggestion to an organizer of the international writers' organization PEN, to have Joyce invited as the guest of honor to a meeting of the London PEN Club. Joyce, delighted to accept, went to London in the company of Morel, and they, together with Miss Weaver, attended.

March brought Sylvia's fortieth birthday, which was accompanied by praise and thanksgiving from her father. Under the bold letterhead of Sylvester W. Beach, D.D., secretary to the Board of Directors of the Theological Seminary of the Presbyterian Church, Princeton, New Jersey, came the following personal message:

Dearest Little Sylvia:—

So your birthday falls this year on the fourteenth of the windy month. This little cheque is perfectly good, and you are to use it in any possible way to help celebrate the greatest event, after that of the illustrious Father of his country. I hope your biographers will be less vituperative than the recent one of G.W. [Washington] once known more favorably. We never know what perspective may do. Anyhow, your illustrious name and fame are so far unsullied, and you stand forth on this side of the Atlantic as the most brilliant American representative in Europe. I would not trust myself to be your biographer, for the book would be so eulogistic that it might be so fulsome as to win but not deserve the condemnation of modern analysis.

Many happiest returns, you dear precious Sylvia. We are all so proud of you that we would like to claim you as a forebear rather than a contemporary.

Love in loads to you and Adrienne.

Your proud and doting father.

Beginning her forty-first year, Sylvia was confident and accomplished. In letters to her sister Holly this month, she mentions three times that their mother is "upset" or "put out" with her for not joining her for a trip. Her defense is to mention the heavy workload, which included writing a personal letter or card to each signer of the protest. "My, it's a Life!" she boasts proudly to her sister, and praises the faithfulness of her library members during the economic recession. In two months her confidence would be put to its severest test by her mother.

Antheil left for the United States to begin a major transition in his career. Never ceasing his plotting and intriguing, he hoped for another chance at success, this time in America. He arranged for a concert at Carnegie Hall, to consist of his *Ballet Mécanique*, First String Quartet, and Jazz Symphonietta. His chief New York backer (the publisher Donald Friede of Boni and Liveright), knowing Antheil's reputation, cabled Sylvia that his "future in America" will be "completely gone if he does not appear this time." She made certain that he was on the boat. "Sylvia, you are the only dearest and darling Sylvia in the world. This is all," cabled Antheil upon arrival. Sylvia warned Holly about the coming concert:

The Ballet Mecanique is to be played with all the pianos and all the drums and all the xylophones and all the aeroplane propellors and all the pieces of tin and all the amplifiers so that it will be amplified 100% and if you hear something out there in Pasadena early in April you won't get scared will you Holly? It'll be a long distance off.

What Holly would hear was dissonance from the critics. The evening of 10 April was a disaster for Antheil. He later fictionalized "the way I was tricked in New York in 1927" in a murder mystery he called *Death in the Dark*. Sensational publicity and garish staging (which Antheil later disclaimed) backfired. According to William Carlos Williams, who was there, the audience reaction received all the attention of the critics. "Every major music critic of New York reacted unintelligently," laments Williams. Antheil writes, "I went back to Paris that 1927 heartsick and broke."

Three years after his first visit, William Carlos Williams returned to Paris and, of course, to Shakespeare and Company, which he claimed (in a letter to Sylvia) "must always be a calling place for right Americans when they are in Paris." This letter, written six months before he sailed for Europe, informed her that he was writing "a kind of novel . . . a straight account of a man of forty [Williams's age at the time of his first Paris visit in 1924] seeing something of America in Europe. It is about America you see." Although begun before this second trip in 1927, *A Voyage to Pagany* depicts experiences he underwent during both visits, and reveals his growing antagonism toward Americans living in Europe.

On this trip the Williamses brought their sons, who were to have a year's study abroad, and the family dined with Sylvia and Adrienne on several occasions. Believing that Sylvia was taking Bryher's side in the divorce charges, Williams sided with his old friend McAlmon, who had written to Sylvia in order to defend himself against the charges by Bryher that he was a "dope fiend." He remembered that Sylvia had taken his side before, in a quarrel with Stein; had translated his work; and had handled numerous details of his Contact Publishing Company while he wandered about Europe. But now she was caught in a quarrel between two friends (at Bryher's request, she found a Paris lawyer), and it appeared to him that she had chosen Bryher's side. During the next four years there would be fewer letters from McAlmon to the rue de l'Odéon.

Williams's second trip to Paris coincided with the first year of *transition* (his first had taken place in the year of Ford's *transatlantic review*). Eventually, two poems of his, two chapters from *A Voyage to Pagany*, and his essay in defense of Joyce's *Work in Progress* would appear in the pages of the new magazine. The essay (November 1927) defends Joyce's work against attacks ranging from Louis Gillet's hostile remarks in the *Revue des Deux Mondes* (1 August 1925) to Pound's private dismissal of it as "backwash" and a "diarrhea of consciousness."

With its plan to publish seriatim his *Work in Progress* (at least the first and third parts of his four-part work), *transition* (1927–1938) promised to be Joyce's staunchest supporter. Jolas and Paul, declaring that literature was too photographic and external, gave their allegiance to the irrational—the evocation of dreams, hallucinations, and the phantoms of half-sleep. Their neoromanticism was strongly influenced by Freud, French Surrealism, and German Expressionism. *Work in Progress,* with its timeless panorama, offered (they hastily concluded) the best example of the exploration of the "night-world." Ironically— or predictably—these newsmen of the Paris *Tribune* fulminated against the cult of intelligibility and damned the common reader. The first issue, dated April 1927, contained poetry by Crane, Imbs, Gide, and Soupault and the first pages of *Work in Progress*. Janet Flanner, in a typical response, was provoked by the "extreme jabberwocky" of Joyce's "Opening Pages of a Work in Progress" and lamented, "Alas, that Ulysses were not still among the Phaeacians!"

Transition represents less the twenties than the transition between the twenties and the thirties. When it first appeared, in 1927, many of the representative figures of the twenties, like McAlmon and Pound, had left Paris, while others, like Antheil and Hemingway, were soon to leave the city. Although it prominently displayed Joyce and Stein, *transition* devoted many of its pages to representative writers of the thirties: Henry Miller, Katherine Anne Porter, Allen Tate, Kay Boyle—writers whom the editors met at Shakespeare and Company, claims Jolas. Years later, in an anthology of writings from *transition,* Jolas praises "our chief agent," Sylvia Beach, who first spoke to Joyce on his behalf and in whose shop he "met many of the writers who later became contributors."

Joyce had earlier rejected a proposal by Sylvia that they find a secretary to help him expedite the new work; but by midspring, exhausted by legal battles, thoroughly discouraged by the lack of moral support from Miss Weaver, and overwhelmed by the enormous task that the completion of his *Work in Progress* entailed, Joyce proposed that Sylvia find a writer-collaborator to finish this work, according to his design. He suggested that she sound out James Stephens, a gentle Dublin poet who Joyce ominously noted has his real first name (James) and the fictional one (Stephen) that he had taken in *Portrait*. He also later learned that Stephens was presumably born at the same hour (6 A.M.), on the same day (2 February), and in the same place (Dublin) as he—a presumed fact (it was really the fabrication of Stephens, an orphan) that convinced Joyce that their collaboration was predestined. But as was her usual practice, Sylvia arranged a dinner meeting for the two men without informing Stephens of Joyce's plan. She left that to Joyce, who did not approach the subject for seven more months. During this summer, Joyce and Stephens became regular companions—part of the Irish mafia, which included the Colums, Arthur Power (the Abbey Theatre dramatist), and (by 1928) Samuel Beckett.

Another important figure who came into Joyce's life was Stuart Gilbert, an Englishman and Oxford graduate who had been a judge in Burma. He moved to Paris with his French wife, Moune, early in 1927 and found Shakespeare and Company, which he called "Stratford-on-Seine." Learning that he had a rich literary background, Sylvia gave him a fragment of Morel's translation of *Ulysses* that had been published in the autumn 1926 issue of *900: Cahiers d'Italie et d'Europe*. Gilbert returned on the next day to express his enthusiasm, to point out several errors in the translation, and to offer his assistance. She then took him to visit her friend in the bookshop across the street, for, she says, "It was up to Adrienne Monnier, who was bringing out *Ulysses*, to consider Gilbert's proposal. . . . Of course she jumped at the chance." Sylvia also immediately notified Joyce about Gilbert's findings and her favorable opinion of him. Joyce wisely appropriated him, to the discomfort of Morel.

Sylvia gave Gilbert a second significant introduction when she offered him the first issue of *transition*, which included Joyce's "famous thunderclap in a dozen languages." Gilbert later honored Sylvia for that "memorable afternoon" when she "handed me a small, green, red-lettered magazine, heartily commending it." Soon Gilbert was a member of Odéonia.

In the spring Joyce was borrowing regularly from the bookshop till, suggesting ominously that the bailiff would soon be walking off with "the furniture and animals in the ark." He traveled in April to London and in May to the Netherlands. Even the May publication of *Ulysses* IX did not relieve the financial pressures on him. Having acquired a Vermeer print of Delft, he had it shipped COD to Sylvia at Shakespeare and Company (he "could not spare the money") with a detailed description of the frame he wished her to purchase for it. By the end of June he would have to turn for financial help to Miss Weaver, as he did not dare approach Sylvia again. Reluctantly he wrote Miss Weaver asking the lawyer for £100 of his capital to settle bills. With increasing frequency after this time, he chipped away at the capital of the Weaver estate.

He also borrowed some of Shakespeare and Company's new acquisitions, such as Anita Loos's *Gentlemen Prefer Blondes* and David Garnett's *Lady into Fox*. Probably in this same month he wrote to his brother for the *Dubliners* manuscript and *Stephen Hero*, which he gave to Sylvia in gratitude.

Sylvia and Adrienne attended the May wedding of Hemingway and Pauline Pfeiffer and a small luncheon given by the Archibald MacLeishes afterward. They probably shared Ada MacLeish's disgust with Hemingway's attempt to nullify his marriage to Hadley in order to give a Catholic sanctity to his new marriage. He did assign to Hadley all the royalties for *The Sun Also Rises,* and he gave Sylvia the corrected proofs of "Fifty Grand," which appeared this same month in the *Nouvelle Revue Française.* The year 1927 was also a year of passage for Hemingway, who was rapidly moving from the lean existence of his early Paris years to the comfortable life of an established author, thanks to the Pfeiffer money and the growing sales of *The Sun Also Rises.* The *Sun* cult had begun in Montparnasse. Although he had spoken pejoratively of the "expatriates," the young Americans imitated his characters—from Barnes's drinking to Brett's short hairstyle.

Three days after Lindbergh had arrived to a cheering throng in Paris, Sylvia made a speech on French radio expressing gratitude to the French for their hospitality and summarizing the events of her bookshop, including her publication of *Ulysses.* Joyce wrote from The Hague that the "wireless is almost unknown here, it seems, so I could not listen in. I am sorry I could not hear you." With this letter he returned the "pomes" with their dates for *Pomes Penyeach* and thanked her for collecting a list of Russian words from Boski Antheil (who knew the language) for his manuscript. Sylvia was busy preparing the manuscript of *Pomes Penyeach* for the printer, to whom she gave the *bon à tirer* on 10 June. Both she and Joyce assumed that she would also eventually publish his *Work in Progress,* when it was completed. Huebsch (perhaps through his junior partner Donald Friede) of Boni and Liveright had just offered Joyce $2,000 down and 15 percent royalties for the new work. He referred all business proposals to Sylvia, as he had done the preceding year when Huebsch wished to issue a special edition of *Portrait.* The amount of work demanded by Joyce—on top of the regular bookshop and lending-library tasks—was almost more than Sylvia could handle. If Joyce needed a collaborator for *Work in Progress,* she needed a relief crew. "I have been very busy this spring," she complained to Holly, "nearly crazed with the stuff!"

The piracies of the years 1926–1928 put a strain on the relations between Sylvia and Joyce. Unfortunately, Joyce tried to induce her to move Shakespeare and Company to New York to fight Roth, presumably by arranging for an American edition and contesting the ban in the courts. As early as March of 1926, he had told Miss Weaver that he needed "an agent over there." Sylvia herself knew that the piracy "could only be ended if an established publisher" in the United States would get the ban lifted and publish the book (as Random House finally did, seven years later). However, as she told Joyce in a letter asking him to release her from the pressure of his demands, she was not the one to act as his emissary in the United States. Her first love was Shakespeare and Company, and she refused to abandon her unique creation: "Shakespeare and Company was my invention, and though it is on a very different level from a Ulysses . . . all the same it was something I could really claim as mine. Don't forget that my book-shop and Company was already in full swing when Joyce came along." In a statement that she did not include in her memoirs, she reveals the strain of this time: Joyce "saw Shakespeare and Company as something God had created for him, but to me it had other sides than the Joycean. Happily for Joyce himself as that was one of the reasons why my little enterprize was so useful to him." She made "every effort" for him short of turning the shop "into a Joyce plant." He threatened "to totally en-Joyce" her when he suggested she "abandon" or "transplant" the shop. "I couldn't do that with something like Shakespeare and Company that had grown up on French soil," she protests. "Besides, the French wouldn't have liked my getting up and leaving after years of their hospitality."

Late in June, a tragic event placeu a greater strain on their relations by delay-ing the publication of *Pomes Penyeach,* canceling the Stephens dinner, and caus-ing Sylvia to withdraw from the Roth fight. Although the tragedy was a testing of her mettle—proof of her strength, courage, and quick-wittedness—it drew her further from Joyce. The events of this June were preceded by two visits from her family. Her uncle Hal (J. H. Orbison), his wife, Lilli, and their daughter Bertha came through Paris on a missionary furlough from Punjab, India. In a letter to Sylvia of the preceding November, Hal had talked about his wandering sister Nellie (Sylvia's mother, Eleanor): "The Orbisons have something of a wild and wandering streak in them! We don't stay *put*—we don't like to lead a very stable existence." His wandering Nellie had completed the last stage of her restless journey.

Eleanor Beach had arrived in Paris from Italy in May in order to visit her middle daughter, who had been too busy to visit her. The daughters had always worried about this delicate and unhappy woman who, after they were grown, had spent as little time as possible in Princeton. She had wandered from the homes of family and friends to Italian pensions, a Pasadena cottage, and Paris hotels—always carrying digitalis for her heart condition. But Sylvia's last report about "Poor Little Mother" is optimistic: "I never saw her looking so fat and hearty. She says she hasn't felt so fine for nine years. And she is well dressed too and living on a comfortable pension. I see her every day and she comes to dinner at our house very often." Twenty days later she was dead.

Because the circumstances of her death profoundly affected Sylvia and her relationship to Joyce, it is necessary to deal briefly with this tragedy. As closely as the facts can be determined, Mrs. Beach was in June of 1927 arrested on a 1924 charge of shoplifting, for which she had mistakenly or naively ignored a summons. Although the merchandise, which had been taken from the Galeries Lafayette, consisted of trinkets worth only a few dollars, the police arrested her. Anxious to protect her mother from public humiliation, Sylvia called Conner, her lawyer in the Roth fight, and asked him for his advice. He recommended a lawyer named Le Paulle, who proceeded to handle Mrs. Beach's release and to arrange for secrecy. It was his suggestion that they solicit two character endorse-ments, one of them from the pastor of the American Church, and a report from a doctor, who testified to the mental strain that Mrs. Beach had undergone and to the bad effects produced by self-medication.

Despite the efforts that had been made to preserve her privacy, Eleanor Beach, whose spirit had been weakened by years of unhappiness that she had been forced to keep to herself, believed that her reputation had suffered a deathblow. The shock was too much for her. Eleven years earlier, in a letter to Sylvia, she had echoed a similar anguish at what she called a "breakdown." In that 1918 letter she cried out that she was "nearly crazy" with the pain of hurting her daughters (whom she had urged to return from Europe) and with living "my terrible marriage." She speaks of the fury of her husband's "rages" over the children's spending of money and declares twice that her "brain will give way" under his pressure, which was like "a spiked band into my head." Her ability to endure these early years is explained in her closing remark to Sylvia: "There is something indestructible in us all that springs up after the worst blows of fortune, and that carries us through . . . and we refuse to be destroyed utterly."

The "something indestructible" in her spirit had weakened with the years, and the arrest was too strong a blow; Eleanor Beach was destroyed. She spent an afternoon in the apartment of Adrienne and Sylvia, talking part of the time to Myrsine. Then she recorded an eight-page denial of her guilt and took a massive dose of her medication. She was rushed to the American Hospital on 22 June and died at 5 P.M., leaving, along with the handwritten statement of innocence, a will dividing her few possessions among her three daughters. Shocked and sickened by her mother's actions, Sylvia arranged to avoid an inquest and telegraphed her father, Holly, and Cyprian about Eleanor's death at the American Hospital—correctly assuming that they would believe that her heart had failed. Sylvia carried the heavy secret with her to her death, sparing them the humiliation. She alone would live with recrimination. Her actions gave her mother a privacy that protected her freedom to choose suicide and preserved her dignity in death—a right Sylvia would claim for Adrienne in 1955 and Hemingway in 1961. Pride, parsonage discretion, and a belief that suicide is a private decision forced Sylvia to keep her own counsel. She paid the bills and had her mother's body cremated and buried at Père-Lachaise. The nomadic Eleanor Orbison, born of missionary parents in Rawalpindi, India, bore three children in a land in which she never wanted to live, loved the beauties of Europe, and in the sixty-fourth year of her life was buried in what she had regarded as the friendly soil of Paris.

CHAPTER 12

Of Translation Treaties and Travels
1927–1928

The American invasion was seemingly at its flood tide when we arrived in Paris again
in the spring of 1927; our ship alone had brought 531 American tourists in cabin class.

— Matthew Josephson

ON BOARD THE SHIP with Josephson, who was returning to France
with a publisher's contract to write a biography of Emile Zola, were the singer
Helen Morgan and a large jazz band from Chicago. They entertained the dancing
tourists who were on their way to visit the Paris bars made famous by Hemingway's *The Sun Also Rises*. These tourists also flooded the rue de l'Odéon in tour
buses, frustrating an overworked Sylvia, who complained that she had to lock
herself in the back room in order to complete business without being disturbed
by swarms of the curious. She preferred to see the visitors arrive singly or in
pairs. The American Legion convention, which was held in September this year,
was a special inducement to many to come to the city. The French response to
Americans turned from euphoric enthusiasm following Lindbergh's landing to
hostile riots at the execution of Sacco and Vanzetti.

On the Fourth of July following her mother's death, Sylvia wrote Benjamin
Conner asking him to withdraw her from the Roth suit: "After such a terrible
[tragedy,] . . . I feel that it would be impossible for me to do anything more
concerning the prosecution of Mr. Roth so will you please communicate directly
with Mr. Joyce in the future." Her resignation reflected her personal fatigue and
mourning as well as a reassessment of her priorities. She felt that the time she
had spent on the Roth piracy and the preparation of *Pomes Penyeach* for the
printer had, perhaps, kept her from meeting her mother's needs. Conner promptly
and coldly replied, sending M. Moreau's bill for "securing release of" Mrs.
Beach and M. Le Paulle's fees, which came to 1,000 francs. Angered at his
insensitivity in sending a bill so soon after her mother's death, Sylvia asked
Joyce to change lawyers. He sympathized with her but did nothing. He justified
his continued association with Conner on the grounds that it was hard to find
another lawyer who would act against literary piracy and that Conner was an
"influential" lawyer who, as he confessed to Miss Weaver, frightened him: "his

letter [to Sylvia] was so callous in any case that I thought it better not to anta-
gonise him." Fearing problems for himself, he refused to join her in her grievance. Besides, she had withdrawn from his side in his battle with Roth.

On the day of her mother's death, Sylvia had given the publishing order for
Pomes Penyeach to Herbert Clarke, an English printer in Paris. By 7 July, when
Clarke had the first 300 copies of the tiny volume of poetry ready for her, Sylvia
had paid Joyce 12,000 francs, in accordance with their agreement. Thirteen large,
numbered copies were printed on Dutch paper for his family and friends. He
gave the first copy to Sylvia, the second to Miss Weaver, and the seventh to
Adrienne. He took the thirteenth. In gratitude for his help on the protest and his
encouragement of the poetry, Joyce inscribed a copy to MacLeish. His new
circle of friends and supporters, including Jolas, Paul, and Helen Nutting (who
had first suggested its publication), received numbered and initialed copies.

Pomes Penyeach contained thirteen poems—a dozen plus a "tilly," the title
of the first poem and a word meaning the thirteenth in a baker's dozen or the
extra half-cup from the Dublin milkman. Faithful to its title (and of necessity
cheaply printed), the volumes cost a shilling, or twelve francs. As they had done
for the Greek blue of *Ulysses*, they chose a special color—the shade of the Irish
Calville apple. Colors were symbolic for Joyce, who was very particular about
this shade of green, which unfortunately, remembers Myrsine Moschos, "faded
fast." So did sales. *Pomes Penyeach* sold slowly at Shakespeare and Company
in Paris, the Gotham Book Mart in New York City, and (despite ads in the
Times) the Poetry Bookshop in London. Reviews were not encouraging, certainly not for Joyce, who hoped the poetry would moderate criticism of his new
work.

Sylvia sold one copy to the English novelist and biographer Rebecca West,
who claims that the business took place in a manner "different from the ordinary
commercial transaction . . . as if it had been a saint's medal on the porch of
Westminster Cathedral." Walking slowly from the rue de l'Odéon to the boulevard Saint-Germain, Miss West read one "mediocre" poem after another. Using
this visit to Shakespeare and Company to frame her long essay "The Strange
Necessity," published in the next year, she calls Joyce a prose writer of "majes-
tic genius," yet a sentimental man "without taste" for preserving this "bad"
poetry. "I do not particularly like *Ulysses* or James Joyce," she admits. When
she criticized *Work in Progress*, William Carlos Williams sprang to the defense
in an essay in the September issue of the *Bookman*.

Leaving Myrsine to fill the remaining orders for *Pomes Penyeach* and *transition* and leaving Joyce to complete a piece of his new work to be inserted
between the Shaun and Shem sections, Sylvia departed for Savoy. Adrienne,
who knew the extent of Sylvia's physical and mental strain following her Roth
work and the loss of her mother, insisted that they go to Les Déserts as soon as
possible. This time Joyce, who had described the Odéon atmosphere as "greatly
strained and tragic," did not play his tug-of-war with Adrienne.

Joyce was very discouraged this summer and fall while he revised Shem. His new work was ridiculed and attacked in every press clipping that came to the shop. In his book *Time and Western Man,* Wyndham Lewis leveled a second volley against Joyce, Pound, Hemingway, and the decay of left-wing romantic literature. He began his brilliant and prejudiced assault by accusing the two "Left Bank bookshops" of being agents of Joyce and the "Super-realists." Specifically, Lewis marked Joyce as "the poet of the shabby-genteel, impoverished intellectualism of Dublin" and Pound as a "revolutionary simpleton." As a result of direct and occasionally accurate hits, Joyce and Pound cooled their relations with Lewis. Elliot Paul's answer to all charges against a so-called cult of "unintelligibility" appeared in the third number of *transition* as KORAA ("Kiss Our Royal American Ass"—after the KMRIA heading in *Ulysses*). Lewis's personal attack hurt Joyce. The "grievance collector," as Leon Edel labels Joyce, noted the affront and quietly wrote his revenge. A careful reader of the February and March issue of *transition* sees Joyce's reply to Lewis's "knowall profoundly impressive role" in a section of *Work in Progress* in which Butt describes to Taff his experiences in war—a metaphor for the battle between *transition* and Lewis. Like Dante in *The Divine Comedy,* Joyce repaid old grudges and settled scores by scattering his enemies throughout his work. *"Finnegans Wake* is both a work of art and an act of revenge," claims Edel in an essay entitled "The Genius and the Injustice Collector," published in 1980.

Complaining that Picasso gets "20,000 to 30,000 francs for a few hours' work" while he has labored 10,000 hours each writing Parts 1 and 3 and is "not worth a penny a line," Joyce spent each day in the shop poring over the reviews and the order forms. Five years before, when hostile reviews of *Ulysses* had arrived from the press service, Joyce had only counted the lines and checked to see whether they included the Shakespeare and Company address. This time his reaction was different. He did not have a base of support from Miss Weaver and Pound or a sufficient mixture of high praise amid the negative reviews. His task was too large, and month after month was taken up by the job of revision or physical illness. He did, however, find assurance in Sylvia's promise to remain his publisher. In an unpublished letter to Miss Weaver, he claims, "I have obtained Miss Beach's promise" that when Parts 2 and 4 of *Work in Progress* are completed, "she will publish the hotchpotch resulting therefrom." Later this fall, Joyce again stated his assumption that Sylvia would put out his new work. In a letter to Pound, who had suggested the American Pascal Covici as the publisher for *Work in Progress,* Joyce declares, "Miss Beach, of course, has first claim on the right to publish but if my American copyright is secured I shall bear in mind your suggestion."

Since the appearance of the first number of *transition,* in April of 1927, Joyce had used it to promote his new work. He had given Sylvia a list containing the names of about forty persons to whom she was to send free copies of the magazine each month. Because the cost was prohibitive, amounting to 400 francs a month, they had abandoned this method of promotion by late fall. Joyce returned then to requesting his friends and admirers to write friendly critical essays about the book for *transition,* in order to win a sympathetic and enlightened readership. Elliot Paul's "Mr. Joyce's Treatment of Plot" (*transition* 9) clarified the circular plot in which events are presented associationally, not chronologically. The major motif, Paul goes on to explain, is the Fall of Man, and the two major characters are H. C. Earwicker (Adam) and A. Livia (Eve). Joyce needed, furthermore, to justify his innovative techniques: Jolas's "The Revolution of Language and James Joyce" (*transition* 11) does this. Joyce also wished to reply to certain attacks: in a defense of *Work in Progress* as a part of literary tradition, Frank Budgen wrote "James Joyce and Old Norse Poetry" (*transition* 13). Joyce planned and discussed each essay with its author.

Sylvia and Adrienne left Les Déserts reluctantly, after too brief a stay. Sylvia had to prepare for the arrival in August of Sylvester Beach and his oldest daughter, Holly. Cyprian, ill for some time and devastated by her mother's death, did not accompany them, but she wrote to Sylvia, in ignorance of the truth, that she was pleased that their mother had "had such a tidy short and artistic death." Sylvester stayed long enough to have his portrait sketched by Bécat and his picture taken by Sylvia one Sunday at Rocfoin. He and Holly had brought Sylvia a new Remington typewriter, moccasins (Adrienne also got a pair), and American phonograph records, which delighted Joyce.

Holly stayed for a month, but her vacation was severely restricted by the rioting that broke out when the state of Massachusetts—after having imprisoned Sacco and Vanzetti for six years—executed the shoemaker and fish peddler. The Paris police placed long wooden barricades across the street to check papers and arrest agitators. By mid-September the police were checking foreign identity cards and fortifying themselves for the finale of the American Legion decennial convention—a parade down the Champs-Élysées. After days and nights of drunken reveling, lavish spending, backslapping, and breaking furniture in gay Paree, the legionnaires staged their huge parade. On the same day, the dancer Isadora Duncan, killed when her scarf caught in the wheels of a speeding car on the French Riviera, was buried at Père-Lachaise. Isadora, who had with American pride welcomed Lindbergh at Le Bourget airport, had recently scrawled across a newsphoto of the Massachusetts governor Fuller on her mantel "Down with Philistines!" On that drizzly day in mid-September, as a silent procession of her friends accompanied her body to its grave, the Philistines marched thousands strong behind blaring bands down the Champs-Élysées.

The return voyage of Holly was unfortunately timed to coincide with the departure of the remaining legionnaires. Williams, who was leaving his wife and sons in Europe to return to his medical practice, was also scheduled to sail on the S.S. *Pennland.* He ended his second trip to Paris with mixed feelings. Part of his ambivalence was expressed in his nearly completed novel, *A Voyage to Pagany,* which he showed to Sylvia. A portion of the novel appeared the next month in *transition* (next to a short story by his new friend Philippe Soupault). Sylvia, just recovering from a long bout with migraine headaches and needing to get out of Paris, accompanied Williams and Holly on the train to Cherbourg.

With them on the train were five Siamese cats that Holly was taking to Cyprian, who planned to breed and sell them in Palm Springs, where she was recuperating from surgery. While Williams formed the opinion during their voyage together that Holly was tolerant (she put up with the raucous legionnaires), intelligent, and a "most interesting talker and an able little slat of a person," Cyprian thought that she was too much her father's daughter—overly ambitious and overly concerned with respectability. Unsuccessful in her attempt to breed cats, Cyprian (her mother's daughter) returned reluctantly to Pasadena.

Sylvia seemed more involved with the lives of her friends in Europe than with the affairs of her family. Bryher, whom she and Williams had discussed at length on the journey to Cherbourg, ended her marriage of six years to McAlmon and wedded a Scotsman named Kenneth Macpherson. She firmly believed she must have a husband—though in name only. Macpherson, who had briefly been H.D.'s lover, would have his longest affair with Jimmy Daniels, the favorite black singer of Paris and later of the New York crowd. A talented if lazy man, Macpherson became part of the circle that Sylvia would frequently visit in Switzerland when her work for Joyce abated. An authority on films, he began, in partnership with Bryher, the first English-language magazine entirely devoted to the "art of screen" and probably the finest magazine devoted to the art of silent film. Called *Close-Up*, it was distributed at Shakespeare and Company. Together, Macpherson and Bryher also built Kenwin, a large home and studio in Montreux, Switzerland, and legally adopted Perdita, the daughter of H.D. and, it was then presumed, Richard Aldington. With Bryher (who had very strong views on child rearing), her mother H.D. (whom she calls "a beautiful spirit who lived on Mt. Olympus"), McAlmon (who called her "the Lump" and "it"), Aldington, Macpherson, and their various friends, Perdita grew up in a confusing environment without playmates. One of the few adults who treated her "as an important person," she remembers, was Sylvia, whom she visited in 1928.

The English poet Richard Aldington (H.D.'s former husband) made many visits to Paris after 1927. Because *Ulysses* was banned in England, he explains in his autobiography, one of his first stops was the rue de l'Odéon: "It was obligatory as soon as one arrived in Paris to buy a copy of *Ulysses* from the publisher. . . . It is surprising that the Paris municipality, with its passion for honouring the artists by giving their names to streets, didn't change the rue de l'Odéon to rue James Joyce." At Shakespeare and Company, Sylvia introduced him to Hemingway and to Jean Paulhan of the *Nouvelle Revue Française*. Aldington, who had not been in Paris since 1913, was surprised at the changes that had occurred, particularly the expansion of the Montparnasse cafés to handle the crowds of visiting Americans.

During this fall Sylvia tried to put her life in better order. She had withdrawn from the Roth case; her family had gone home; and she had bought a plaque for her mother's crypt. Now she had her teeth repaired, took a test for her driver's license, and made plans to buy a car with Adrienne. She also tried to relax more by taking short trips on weekends and playing records on her phonograph in the evening. She kept active socially with friends like Romains, whom she consulted about the American rights for his play *Dr. Knock,* a satire on doctors that is in the true spirit of Molière. The young American producer Roscoe Ashworth, to whom she had raved about the play, wrote from California of plans to produce it there, requesting her to secure permission from Romains. Sylvia also met with Hadley Hemingway, back from an American visit, looking healthy and appearing recovered from the troubles attendant upon her divorce; dined with the Colums, friends of both Cyprian and Joyce; and tried to encourage George and Boski Antheil. In a letter to Holly, Sylvia writes: "If you hear of any large sum of money for poor little George, just let me know. He is pretty low now."

Sylvia took Adrienne in their new Citroën, bought on the installment plan, for its first drive. In negotiating a crowded Paris intersection, she collided with an autobus. Shaken but determined, she learned to master the machine and was soon driving the eighty-two kilometers to Rocfoin each Sunday. She and Adrienne also drove to Normandy for a weekend with the novelist Jean Schlumberger, who had been one of the founders of the *Nouvelle Revue Française.* The three of them enjoyed talking in front of the bright fireplace in a cottage (where he preferred to live) adjoining Braffye, his ancestral home. Schlumberger ordered his dachshund to perform tricks for them. Standing on her hindlegs, she showed them, according to Sylvia, "the buttons on her waistcoat." The next morning Sylvia appraised his large English library in the main house, finding, as he had feared, that it "reflected the tastes of English governesses who had taught successive generations of young girls at Braffye."

Their second trip was to Versailles, where Sylvia took the remaining members of the Williams family. The two boys fell in love with Sylvia and her dog, Teddy, with whom they played in the backseat of her car. They thought she was a "demon driver," Williams later reported to her in a letter.

Joyce had more fear than the Williams boys had. He thought all cars should be forbidden except for those of government officials—and except for taxis, which he used regularly. Cars were too dangerous, declared the partly blind Joyce. Yet he entrusted himself to Sylvia for a Sunday trip to Rocfoin, where she took his picture with Adrienne's parents, and a trip to inspect the waterworks above the Seine. Sylvia remembers that he "sat on the bank, once he had inspected the waterworks, and gazed intently at the river and all the different objects floating in it." At the end of October he excitedly finished rewriting the Anna Livia Plurabelle section, into which he had woven the names of 350 rivers. "The stream is now rising to flood point," he announced, "but I find she can carry almost anything."

In the early fall, Hemingway had returned from a summer in Spain with Pauline, who, at thirty-two, was now pregnant. His short story "Hills like White Elephants" had just appeared in the fifth number of *transition.* On his library card, Sylvia had earlier this summer written, "ask Hemingway about 'Grandmother,' " a reference to Glenway Wescott's recently published *The Grandmothers.* Soon after borrowing the book she had suggested, Hemingway was approached in the shop by the reporter Alex Small, who, according to his sub-sequent article in the *Herald,* engaged the novelist in conversation concerning "recent books and the denizens of Montparnasse, some of whom he advertised, you may remember, in a celebrated novel." Picking up Wescott's novel, Hem-ingway observed sharply, "There are only two troubles with that book. One is that every word of it was written for immortality." The second, Mr. Small left the reader to conclude, was that they were not.

Hemingway was preoccupied with his new family and growing fame. His literary reputation was confirmed when the PEN club invited him to be honored by them at a banquet on 17 November 1927. The invitation was sent to Sylvia, who forwarded it to Hemingway with her congratulations.

At 3:30 on the first Wednesday of November, she listened to Joyce read Anna Livia Plurabelle, which was to appear in the November issue of *transition.* When Joyce slipped him a whisky before reading, McAlmon assumed that the reading would be "a severe test." But it was the pretentious seriousness of the audience, particularly Mary Colum's knowing smiles at the puns, that tested McAlmon's patience. The twenty-five guests included MacLeish, who wrote Joyce the next day that he was "moved and excited" by the "pure creation that goes almost beyond the power of the words." Much as Joyce was delighted with the enthu-siastic response of his listeners, there was one who remained outside the fold. Privately he complained to Sylvia that Miss Weaver, to whom he mailed each section, was "wallowing" in the "verbiage" of his new work and denying him her approval. At his suggestion, Sylvia told Miss Weaver that Joyce had taken to his bed and was "very unhappy because the new work doesn't please you for whom it is being written. He wouldn't mind anybody else not liking it. He often says to me bitterly, 'Miss Weaver doesn't care for it' and yet he feels that some parts of his new book are the best work that he has done and that he can do." Sylvia certainly knew the pressure she was placing on her sensitive and gentle friend. A conscience-stricken Miss Weaver immediately responded that she was grieved at her inability to be enthusiastic and that she had "neither the art nor the ability to lie adroitly in order to please him." As her biographers accurately conclude, Joyce was punishing her for the negative comments she had made—only after he had begged for her opinion. Both fearing and courting persecution, Joyce "defended himself . . . by appealing to Harriet's conscience and reducing her self-esteem." She decided to go to Paris on the first of the year to assure Joyce of her support.

The year ended with only a 3,600-franc profit for the bookshop, with the death of her beloved cat, Lucky, and with the beginnings of two misunderstand-ings. The first was the appearance of the ninth number of *transition* without a selection from *Work in Progress.* Joyce, on doctor's orders not to work this month (he had colitis), had notified Jolas that he needed a rest. This December issue carried three interesting items: a half-page box explaining that Joyce was exhausted from the "painstaking perfection and expansion" of his text; an essay, "The Case against Mr. Roth," which called him an "ignorant blunderer" and a "liar and sneak thief"; and a small announcement inside the back cover that Titus's bookstore, to the relief of the editors, would no longer sell *transition* (probably in part because Titus had dealt with Sylvia's stolen *Ulysses* proofs). The appearance of the magazine without an installment from Joyce led the Paris *Times* to suggest that "one of the high priests of modernism" had "recanted his new style." Because he refused all requests for interviews, Sylvia had to explain his illness to the patrons and the press.

A second misunderstanding, which later erupted into open hostility, involved the translators of Adrienne's French version of *Ulysses*. Adrienne, with Sylvia's occasional involvement, was trying to work with Morel (the translator), Gilbert (who was now checking the translation), and Larbaud (who was overseeing their work). Each man had his private understanding with Joyce, who wished all the help possible as long as his helpers remained harmonious. But Larbaud was now disturbed that he was not clearly recognized as the one with final responsibility.

These misunderstandings—like all Joyce business, including the continuing Roth case—involved Sylvia. This winter she also tried to secure a U.S. copyright for fragments of *Work in Progress* that were to appear in *transition*. Joyce's plan was to send the proofs, before publication, to the lawyers in New York, who would then send them to the U.S. copyright office to be registered. The plan was probably not legally sound, and it eventually led to several litigious and personal quarrels. Sylvia was tiring of the numerous cables to the lawyers and the fine points of the law. Despite the planned retreats from her work and the loving concern of Adrienne, she suffered from bouts of ill health and migraines this year.

Following a Sunday drive to Chantilly in the third week of January, Adrienne and Sylvia welcomed Miss Weaver to Paris. She arrived for a fortnight visit to see Joyce, who, unable to live on the interest on her gift to him, had just sold another £300 of stock. Miss Weaver listened for many hours to his explanation of the book and assured him he had her support for a work he must certainly continue. The spirits of both were raised by the visit.

The sixth birthday of *Ulysses* (Joyce's forty-sixth) was celebrated at the Joyce flat. Sylvia and Adrienne and Boski and George Antheil picked up Miss Weaver on their way. The Irish writer Arthur Power was there, along with the Nuttings, McAlmon, and Kitty Cannell. The evening began rather stiffly, as the Joyces stayed in the background. All Joyce's parties, Soupault understates, were "slightly monotonous." It was Adrienne, "whiter, more blue-eyed and golden than ever, immense and shapeless . . . bright and talkative," Helen Nutting recalls, who tried "to keep the conversation going." She succeeded with her stories of table-tapping and messages from the world of spirits. Soon there was singing and dancing, particularly by McAlmon and Joyce. McAlmon sang Negro blues and jumped with jazz dances; Antheil played anything requested; and Joyce sang Irish ballads and dipped his head and snapped his fingers to Greek dances. In the midst of this somewhat boisterous crowd, only Miss Weaver kept her serenity.

On 15 February, Sylvia attended a lecture on Joyce and Eliot sponsored by the Society for the Propagation of the English Language in France. The lecture was given by the young Irishman Thomas McGreevy, who was a graduate of both University and Trinity colleges, Dublin, and who since 1926 had been *lecteur* or assistant teacher of English at the École Normale Supérieure. McGreevy was one of Joyce's compatriots in Paris who were devoted to him. He had agreed to do some Joycean secretarial work (chiefly copying) for Sylvia; later he would, at Joyce's suggestion, write an essay defending *Work in Progress*. Sylvia was pleased to have his help, for she was just getting over a severe cold, which Adrienne and Myrsine had caught from her. Joyce was eager for them all to recover, so that there would be "a general brisking up of the artillery."

Sylvia was sufficiently recovered to get embroiled in a heated argument with Jolas. Her attempt to serve Joyce's best interests by getting *Work in Progress* copyrighted in the United States (before each European publication) necessitated bothersome maneuverings. First, Jolas had published and sent the eleventh number of *transition* to the United States before Sylvia had had time to send a copy of the proofs to Joyce's lawyers, who were registering each section of Joyce's work with the patent office. Second, at Elliot Paul's suggestion, Donald Friede in New York—in another effort to ensure U.S. copyright—had printed a fragment of *Work in Progress* there in January. Much to Joyce's alarm, Friede had taken out the copyright in his own name. Thinking he was now in the power of Friede, Joyce (always quick to litigate) asked Sylvia to intervene and consulted his lawyer and *transition*'s lawyers. (Friede soon ceded the copyright to Joyce, as he had always intended to do.) Following a pattern she and Joyce had agreed to, Sylvia went to do battle with Jolas and others, while Joyce remained aloof. She could be brisk, especially when she believed that he was being put upon. Her willingness to march into the fray, knowing that he would avoid conflict at all cost, occasionally aggravated more problems than it solved. Furthermore, it made her appear arbitrary and Joyce conciliatory. Occasionally the playing of their agreed-upon roles left her deserted in a contest that he had orchestrated.

To the surprise of both of them, Joyce walked into the shop as Sylvia was arguing with Jolas about the early publication and distribution of *transition*. Immediately Joyce heard what he described to Miss Weaver as the "snappy thunder in the air." Fearful of alienating Jolas, he attempted to calm both friends. "Jolas has just written a very good article," he explains to Miss Weaver, "and while I want an explanation I don't want a quarrel. . . ." Aware of the value of a good editor, Joyce avoided taking part in any accusations against Jolas.

The advantages of Joyce's partnership with Jolas were manifold. Primarily, Jolas had an understanding of and enthusiasm for Joyce and his work that included no questioning or censoring of the text. He arranged for Joyce to have proofs set in large print—and as many proofs as Joyce wished (he once used five). Jolas had sound financial backing, a large magazine that circulated in America, and he printed more copies if any were confiscated. It was also important to Joyce that Jolas was apolitical in a time of growing dogmatism. He shared Joyce's knowledge of languages, his Catholic childhood, and his devotion to art as a secular religion. He was energetic, a good listener, a lover of spirits, and open to assisting an eclectic group of experimental writers. Maria and Eugene Jolas were a valuable addition to the Joyce corporation.

Joyce and Sylvia were, at the same time, a great advantage to Jolas. The regular appearance in its issues of portions of *Work in Progress* elevated *transition,* which would otherwise have been one of a number of excellent periodicals, to its prominence as the best expatriate review published between the wars. Sylvia introduced Jolas and his magazine to her French colleagues. According to their friend Victor Llona, she and Adrienne were "successful in casting a limelight on James Joyce" and consequently on *transition,* particularly among "the French writers who centered around *La Nouvelle Revue Française.*"

In the early spring, while she was caught in the midst of an "overflow of work," as Sylvia calls it, the doctors discovered that Antheil was tubercular and prescribed a rest in the mountains. With McAlmon's assistance, Sylvia raised 10,000 francs from their friends to pay the composer's expenses. William Bird wished his donation to be anonymous and gave twenty-five copies of Pound's Antheil book to be autographed and sold for the fund. Declaring that McAlmon could not afford it, Sylvia refused to accept his own offer to pay 500 francs a month to the fund. She was tired of caring for the Antheils. "Oh dear," she sighs to Holly. "How glad I would be if I could get him over to America and into the arms of some of his other friends and just let them look after George and Boski for a while (indefinitely). It is too great a responsibility for me with my shop and other cares." Joyce also was tired of Antheil's problems, particularly of his failure to complete the opera *Hero and the Cyclops,* based on the Cyclops episode of *Ulysses.* George talked seriously of going to the Cologne Opera to stage it if Joyce appeared for a reception. Joyce, though he did not think George had "written 20 bars of the piece," knew he was in poor health and agreed to go. Although six months later Antheil was still declaring that the Cologne deal was a "sure thing," he never completed the opera.

On the weekend before Sylvia's birthday, on 14 March, Adrienne prepared a birthday dinner for her, to which she invited the Hemingways. While they devoured the chicken and vegetables, Hemingway—his wounded head wrapped in a wide cloth bandage—painted a vivid picture of his recent accident. His tendency to exaggerate and Sylvia's tendency to believe his stories are revealed in her description of the event:

Ernest has a great gash on the top of his forehead. The skylight in the toilet (at his apartment) fell down on his head and two arteries were severed and a large piece was sliced right out of him. With great presence of mind he plastered the wound with toilet paper which is the only thing that will stop an artery from flowing it seems. He lost over a quart of blood they told him at the American Hospital where they were sewing him up for an hour and 20 minutes.

The photograph of Sylvia and the bandaged Hemingway standing in front of the shop has since become a classic. Hemingway was in the shop a dozen times in February and early March; then he and Pauline left Paris and moved to Key West. In the following September he wrote from Sheridan, Wyoming, to tell her of his son Patrick's birth, the wonderful fishing, and his completion of *A Farewell to Arms*.

Further controversy arose at this time concerning the job of putting *Ulysses* into French. Thinking that Sylvia and Adrienne were accepting the Morel-Gilbert text without acknowledging his authority, Larbaud had complained to Joyce. The two women, on the other hand, believed that the publisher (Adrienne) should have a direct say in the translation. Joyce called them all together and played the referee or, as he liked to fancy himself, the diplomat. He invited them to the Trianons, his favorite restaurant, which was on the boulevard du Montparnasse. Here, his extravagant tipping had earned him royal treatment. With his guests assembled, Joyce established that Larbaud was to be the final authority for the French translation. When disagreements continued to arise, Joyce proclaimed the "Trianons Treaty."

That these different and strong personalities could agree as much as they did is a testimony to their dedication to a common goal. They expended great effort and endured personal affronts not in response to warm friendship from Joyce but in reverence for the written word and the genius of Joyce. Morel had been doing the translating since early 1924, on the Île de Bourbon. His imagination tended to emphasize the coarseness or violence of the text, causing Joyce occasionally to remark to Adrienne, "A little too much Madagascar here." Gilbert had the advantage of daily contact with Joyce in Paris. According to Sylvia, he became "an expert on deciphering the Joycean hieroglyphics." His tact and precision made his suggestions invaluable. Joyce declared that, even with these two excellent translators, Larbaud's "final revision" was "absolutely necessary" because "he is very accurate, slow, fastidious, and rather timid." Larbaud was, according to Richard Ellmann, "brilliantly sensitive to style."

Either at her own initiative or at his request, Sylvia gave Gilbert a copy of the key to *Ulysses* (made by Joyce in 1921), a briefly sketched outline comparing the novel with Homer's *Odyssey*. Gilbert informed her that he had read the key with "much interest" but that he thought it only "skims the surface." He concludes, prophetically, "This 'key' may serve to open the gardengate. . . . I can forge, I think, an ampler key!" Assisted by the author, he began the key or commentary that summer while he and his wife and the Joyces shared part of their vacation together. In 1930 he published the standard key, *James Joyce's "Ulysses,"* read by every navigator through *Ulysses*.

Joyce resumed his travels at the end of March with a few days vacation in Dieppe and Rouen, where Sylvia sent him mail, including a prospectus for a new Lewis book (*The Childermass*) that compares that work to *Ulysses* in size and importance. Joyce returned to Paris, where he stood as godfather (Jenny Bradley was godmother) at the Catholic baptism of Ford's baby daughter, Julia. In late April and May he took Ford's small house in Toulon, returning on 24 May to correct proofs of Anna Livia Plurabelle (to be published by Crosby Gaige in October) and the watches of Shaun (for *transition*) and to give sworn testimony concerning Roth.

In mid-May Sylvia had driven Adrienne and the Joyces in the Citroën to Chartres. They had planned the trip for April, to include Fargue, but heavy rains had made it necessary for them to postpone it. Adrienne wanted Joyce to see where she planned to have *Ulysses* printed in that town, which was conveniently near her family home. When she suggested that they light a candle for him in the cathedral, he complied uneasily and declared in a letter to Miss Weaver that Adrienne "becomes more and more superstitious, thinks that V.L. is bewitched by L.P.F. and I wish she could find out who is bewizarding me, for I have at the present moment, and all for my own self, episcleritis, conjunctivitis, blepharitis, and a large boil on my right shoulder. So much for candles."

Many travelers besides the Beaches, Williamses, and Josephsons returned to Paris and the rue de l'Odéon this year. Among those who returned were Frank Budgen, who immediately found Joyce through Sylvia. Among visitors new to Paris was George Gershwin, whom Sylvia thought "a very attractive, lovable fellow." She attended a large, crowded party and heard him play and sing to enthusiastic applause. Gershwin told a *Herald* reporter in April that he was writing a new musical called *Americans in Paris* (*An American in Paris*)—"to be handled lightly, in the spirit in which many Americans come here, to play, carefree and happy." Two arriving Americans who did not come just to play were Allen Tate and Kay Boyle.

Tate was a twenty-nine-year-old visitor from Nashville and Vanderbilt College via Greenwich Village. Although a friend of Josephson and other New York writers in Paris, Tate had been particularly critical of Americans who went to stay there. On receiving a Guggenheim Fellowship, however, he left the United States immediately with his wife, Caroline Gordon, to spend a year in the city. He became very friendly with Ford (Putnam remembers that Tate and Ford held sonnet-writing contests on Saturday nights) and with Sylvia, dropping into the bookshop frequently. "Sylvia was kind to me from the beginning," recalls Tate. "I never knew why, except that true kindness needs no reason."

Kay Boyle was a shy twenty-five-year-old American who, having married a French exchange student, had lived in France since June of 1923. In Paris briefly in the fall of that year, she had her heart set on glimpsing Joyce and other writers at Shakespeare and Company. But when she saw the shop sign, she confesses, her courage failed: "I stayed on the other side of the street, my back half turned, glancing at the bookshop from the corners of my eyes." In 1927 she wrote Sylvia asking for a job as "secretary or saleslady" in the bookshop because, she explains later in her memoirs, she "wanted to give my daily allegiance to the words that others were able to set down." In the following year, 1928, having left her husband and borne a child fathered by Ernest Walsh, who had died five months before its birth, she came to Paris. But even then she was "far too shy to go to Sylvia's bookshop." Early one morning after a night of wandering and sleeping in the Bois de Boulogne, she courageously approached the door of the bookshop intending to ask Sylvia to give her McAlmon's address so that she might contact him and ask him for a job. Seeing that it was not open, she walked on—then saw a clock that indicated seven. The shy-mannered Boyle, who gave the appearance of a brazen femme fatale, with her red lips and dangling earrings, became a more active participant in expatriate literary life in later years.

Transition, which had begun publishing Boyle's poetry and short stories in 1927, turned consciously and analytically American in its focus in 1928. The thirteenth number of *transition* (summer), the first issue expanded now to appear quarterly (with a cover by Picasso and more *Work in Progress*), was an American number that featured "Inquiry among European Writers into the Spirit of America." The fall issue featured a compendium of answers to the question "Why do Americans live in Europe?" "That the world is become overweeningly interested in America flatters us," announces Josephson; "it flatters us more that we have not clamored for the spotlight."

Boatloads of Americans continued to disembark at Cherbourg. On board the *Paris* were Fitzgerald, returning for a four-month visit so that Zelda could study dance, and King Vidor, the Hollywood film director who was to see France for the first time (although he had already directed three films presumably set principally in France). These two men would add an interesting chapter to the lives of Sylvia and Chamson. "It was through Scott," asserts Sylvia, "that I met King Vidor, of Hollywood, and through me that Scott met the young French writer André Chamson." Because Fitzgerald worshiped Joyce too much to approach him on his own, Sylvia and Adrienne invited the Fitzgeralds, Joyce, and Lucie and André Chamson to dinner on Wednesday, 27 June, in their apart-

Paris, July 1928

18 Rue D'Odéon

Festival of St. James

ment. Fitzgerald called the evening the "Festival of St. James" in a drawing he made of the guests at table inside her copy of *The Great Gatsby*. He drew himself kneeling in worship beside a haloed Joyce. Sylvia, her hand or fork raised on high, and Adrienne, presiding at either end of the table, look like mermaids. They are portrayed as sirens, Chamson declares. (Either he or Fitzgerald confused the two bewitching mythological species.) In this same year Sylvia caught an image of Fitzgerald in a snapshot she took of him sitting beside Adrienne on the threshold of La Maison des Amis des Livres. Although Sylvia calls Fitzgerald a "great pal" in her memoirs, she adds that "he streaked across the rue de l'Odéon, dazzling us for a moment." That moment was this summer of 1928. It was Fitzgerald, however, who was really bedazzled—by Joyce and Chamson. It is said that he offered to show his esteem for the Irish writer (whom he addressed as "Sir") by jumping out of the window. An amazed Joyce is supposed to have prohibited the display and exclaimed, "That young man must be mad—I'm afraid he'll do himself some injury." Fitzgerald did in any case request and receive an autograph from Joyce in his copy of *Ulysses*. Fitzgerald found Chamson, who was closer to his age, more congenial. Chamson himself later expressed amazement at the immediate "brotherhood of the heart" which existed between men so dissimilar. They often met during this summer, and on one occasion Fitzgerald, drunk and depressed by his failing marriage, was dissuaded by Chamson from jumping from a balcony in his apartment to the street, six floors below.

Fitzgerald introduced Vidor, at the height of his reputation as a director, to Sylvia and the bookshop. On one of his visits he brought a large, rather romantic-looking picture of himself, which he inscribed, "To Sylvia Beach, encouraging! 22 June 1928." When he announced that he wanted to film a book by a French author, she suggested he use Chamson's novel *The Road* (*Les Hommes de la Route,* 1927), which dealt with the building of the road on Mont-Aigoual (in the Cévennes), Chamson's favorite mountain. Sylvia and Adrienne had visited the mountain with Chamson, who promised, in turn, to visit their "holy mountain, Les Déserts." When Sylvia explained the plot of Chamson's novel to Vidor, he seemed delighted. A mutual meeting, at which the scenarist Eleanor Boardman and Sylvia translated, led to a month's work and much talk about future fame and wealth for Chamson. But to the embarrassment of Sylvia and Fitzgerald, Vidor suddenly left for the United States without a word about continuing the film. "I lost face in this affair, and, what is worse, so did my country," admits Sylvia. "As for Scott Fitzgerald, he was horrified." Chamson soon forgave them, and years later he and Sylvia could laugh over the dream of sudden glory and riches of the Hollywood variety. Chamson, a secretary to the minister of state, kept his job and later found greater (and more dignified) fame as a member of the Académie Française and as the director of the Archives Nationales.

Despite the aborted Vidor scheme, Chamson praises Sylvia for weaving *la guirlande des étrangers sur cette guirlande française:*

Sylvia carried pollen like a bee. She cross-fertilized those writers. She did more to link England, the United States, Ireland and France than four great ambassadors combined. It was not merely for the pleasure of friendship that Joyce, Eliot, Hemingway, Scott Fitzgerald, Bryher and so many others so often took the path to Shakespeare and Company, in the heart of Paris, to meet there all these French writers. But nothing is more mysterious than such fertilizations through dialogue, reading or simple human contact. . . . I know, for my part, what I owe to Scott Fitzgerald. . . . But what so many other writers owe to each other, is Sylvia's secret.

Sylvia added an eminent Swiss woman to her garland of friends. During this spring in Shakespeare and Company, she introduced Joyce to Carola Giedion-Welcker, a Zurich art critic who had just published an article on *Ulysses*. Joyce invited her to tea in his apartment. Two years later Sylvia sought Giedion-Welcker's assistance when Joyce went to Zurich for an eye operation. After a decade of loyal friendship she would help him and his family find refuge in Switzerland following the outbreak of World War II.

Sylvia brought an important young English writer into her Franco-American circle—Cyril Connolly. Only twenty-five years old at the time, Connolly would play a larger role in the life of the bookshop in the thirties. In an unfinished novel, he captures his own naive excitement of 1928. Its protagonist Kenneth finds a "modern bookshop" (Shakespeare and Company) as his "spiritual home," where he "prepared for his private revolution, by which he was to put an end to the divided reign of art and experience, of literature and life. Somewhere on those walls was the sword he would pull out to make an end of such tyrants and proclaim the reign of a happily integrated modern soul." When Kenneth narrates the plot for his great novel to Miss Greville (Sylvia Beach), she responds, "it sounds very neat," whereupon he resolves "immediately to tear it up." Her judgment was unhesitating. And her character, as suggested in the following passage from Connolly's unpublished novel, is dynamic:

O if you could have known that woman, her gay fierce generous character, her American courage, her extreme wit! She made it seem possible, after all, to Kenneth that he could become a real person and so write like one, her library held the essence of that new wisdom, the technique of which Americans seemed to possess the secret and which he helped to apply, writing at last non-intellectually about intellectual things.

In the bookshop, Kenneth (Connolly) caught a glimpse of the "published silhouette of Joyce, the swarthy face and broad shoulders of Hemingway, the beard of Fargue, Gide in his cape, Sherwood Anderson—it was a place where people who normally existed, lived, and people who lived, enjoyed themselves."

In reality, the lives of these writers were far from being as exciting and fulfilling as Connolly imagined. Joyce's own existence was plagued by money and health problems. He took with him 75,971 francs in royalties and overdraft when he went on an extended vacation in July; he was not gone a week when he asked Sylvia for an additional 10,000 francs. Wherever they went, the Joyces stayed in the best hotel while the Gilberts, who joined them for the first of several summer trips, stayed nearby at a cheaper place. Once, when they traveled together by train, Joyce dictated to Gilbert a letter with itemized instructions and questions for Sylvia. This summer the Joyces and Gilberts traveled to Zurich, Innsbruck, Frankfurt, Munich, and, finally, Le Havre. In September, when he returned to Paris, his eyes were severely painful and he collapsed, unable to see and unable to prepare a portion of his work for the fall issue of *transition*.

Eager for their vacations, Sylvia and Adrienne—after a busy spring social calendar of weddings (Elliot Paul), baptisms (daughter of Ford), and theater going (at Cocteau's invitation)—left Paris in mid-July to travel for the first time in their Citroën to Savoy. They journeyed first to Touraine to visit Romains and his vineyard and garden. Romains, always the playful tour guide to his *copains*, mapped out a route for them to take from Touraine to Savoy through villages out of his *Cromedeyre-le-Vieil*. In an unpublished portion of her memoirs, Sylvia describes their trip. First they visited "Romains's mountain," Mezenc, a volcanic and "curiously shaped" formation. The high point of their trip through Romains country was the village of Saint-Front (holy forehead), near a lake. They spent the night in a pension because the quaint inn was "reserved for traveling salesmen." The next morning, they heard the rumble of the two-wheeled carts pulled by stout horses that were taking the farmers to Sunday mass. Sylvia and Adrienne hurried through the courtyard past rows of unharnessed carts, their shafts in the air, to join the farmers at mass. Sylvia fidgeted a little when the sermon ran too long; she envied the children the buns that they munched to keep themselves occupied. On the next day, having crossed the Plateau of a Thousand Cows (where only sheep were grazing), they approached Savoy and their own sacred mountain. Holding firmly on to the wheel of the Citroën, Sylvia bounced all the way up the poor road to Les Déserts in low gear.

Occasional day trips in the car brought on fatigue that was with them when they returned to Paris, on 13 August. They found Marie Bécat excitedly at work on an embroidery of Dublin for Joyce. They also found the latest issue of the *Nouvelle Revue Française,* which contained Joyce's *Protée*—the Proteus section of *Ulysses* as translated by Morel and Gilbert and reviewed by Larbaud. Also, with great amusement they read Huddleston's book about them all, *Paris Salons, Cafés, Studios*. Sylvia had allowed him to choose some of his illustrations from her gallery and asked in return that he write a review of Joyce's *Anna Livia Plurabelle,* which he politely declined to do. At about this time Huddleston moved to a country mill on the Seine, which took him, after nearly a decade, out of the daily life of the Odéon quarter. The Jolases also moved to a country house (later bought by Charles de Gaulle) in Colombey-les-Deux-Églises. But old friends, such as Emma Goldman, who published an article about Sylvia in this year, continually returned. Loeb and Wilder came in September for brief visits. Wilder, basking in the fame of his Pulitzer Prize, for *The Bridge of San Luis Rey,* was accompanied by the boxer Gene Tunney, who drew a crowd at Lipp's when they dropped in for a beer. On his way to Rome from Paris, Wilder stopped in Villefranche (near Nice) in order to visit Wescott and other writers at the colony there. In Rome he stood as best man for Tunney's marriage to the heiress Mary Lauder.

Late this fall, through McGreevy, Sylvia met another Irishman, a twenty-two-year-old recent graduate of Trinity College named Samuel Beckett, a tall, thin young man with light-blue eyes magnified by small round glasses. Beckett, who took over McGreevy's room at the École Normale, began in October a two-year appointment in a position similar to his as *lecteur* at that prestigious institution. McGreevy introduced him to Joyce and Sylvia at about the same time, in October or November. Joyce, whose *Ulysses* he had read and admired, fascinated Beckett, who went with McGreevy to see him as often as he could. During the two years he was in Paris, Beckett remained only a peripheral member of the writer's circle, yet became increasingly useful to him. As he had done with Budgen, Joyce gradually took over Beckett's life. Increasingly he asked Beckett to read for him, write a critical article about his work, run errands, do research, and give him total, unqualified allegiance. Beckett has since captured the megalomania of his adopted father figure in his portraits of Pozzo (*Waiting for Godot*) and Hamm (*Endgame*).

Beckett stopped in occasionally at the bookshop, not to borrow books (which he had in abundance at the École Normale), but to be in Joyce headquarters. During these two years he caught glimpses of Hemingway and McAlmon in the shop but never met them. Sylvia observed the shy and quiet Irishman bent in a corner with his head in a book. He, in turn, saw her as a woman of courage, determination, and friendliness. Unaware of her fatigue or the extent of Joyce's demands on her, he believed that she was "passionately devoted" to Joyce. Yet by this time, while burdensome commitment remained, the passion was gone. After her mother's death, she tried to withdraw, to reclaim some of her time. But Joyce enveloped the lives of his friends, demanding full-time devotion. She gave all she could, then became angry, either at Joyce or herself. She had persistent migraine headaches and two major colds this year and soon became afflicted with facial neuralgia.

Joyce undoubtedly perceived her fatigue, although this was one of the lowest years for him as well. He depended increasingly on a group of young men who idolized him. He asked Jolas, McGreevy, Gilbert, Beckett, and others to read to him, transcribe for him, or take him for walks. On many days, Beckett would return from the university to hear from his concierge that "Mr. Joyce called." Immediately Beckett reached for her phone and gave the operator the number: Ségur 95-20. *Ségur quatre-vingt-quinze-vingt,* he spoke the words with a poetic rhythm that he would remember vividly for more than five decades. Joyce wanted a companion for his evening walk, and Beckett hurried to meet him, honored by the demand, which it was a privilege to fulfill.

Sylvia's chores multiplied with the Joyce family's return from vacation, the serious illnesses of James and Nora, and the preparation of *Ulysses* X for November. Adrienne was ill with a bad cold. So was Joyce, who, after attacks of colitis and eye disease, suffered what Sylvia described privately as a "nervous breakdown." He could no longer see print, except for capital letters, and thus could not read or write. Short of money, as he chronically was, he could not pay his bills. Sylvia sent Hélène Moschos to him with a 7,000-franc check for his rent, then a 2,000-franc check to pay Dr. Borsch. He was many thousands of francs overdrawn on his royalties. (He had been overdrawn nearly 18,000 francs by July.) His eyes had improved slightly when, on 8 November, Nora was suddenly hospitalized for exploratory surgery for suspected uterine cancer. "She had not been well for sometime," Sylvia confides to Holly. "She would never see a doctor, saying that it was enough for her husband to be in their hands." Sylvia kept Miss Weaver informed about the illness, swearing her to secrecy concerning its seriousness, which they kept from Joyce. Joyce remained in the room next to hers off and on for a month while she was receiving radiation treatment, which eventually proved ineffective. Sylvia drove them home in her Citroën, ran their errands, arranged to have the Shaun section returned in large print (so that Joyce could add another layer from the notebooks of details that he had collected at the hospital), urged him to find an eye specialist in Munich or a younger doctor in Paris, and tried to keep him informed and amused.

Critical articles on *Work in Progress,* such as those by John Rodker, Robert Sage, and McGreevy—solicited and encouraged by Joyce—continued to appear in *transition.* Joyce asked Sylvia to send copies to many interested and influential persons. When he asked Sylvia to send all issues of *transition* that contained *Work in Progress* to H. G. Wells, whom he had just met, Wells politely refused to support Joyce's work. In late October the small but well-printed ($15 for the deluxe copies) book of *Anna Livia Plurabelle* (published by Crosby Gaige of New York, and with a preface by Padraic Colum) was ready for distribution at Shakespeare and Company.

A second and even more expensive book that sold at the shop this fall was Pound's *Draft of the Cantos 17–27,* published in September in London by John Rodker. It sold for from £5 to £50. The most disappointing book this fall, with respect to sales, was Dora Marsden's *Definition of the Godhead,* the first volume of a lifework of philosophic and scientific research financed and assisted by Harriet Weaver. Miss Weaver, who had for years been supporting Marsden as well as Joyce, revived the Egoist Press just to publish Marsden's initial volume. When Miss Weaver asked for sales figures and comments on the book, Sylvia reluctantly reported that only a handful had been sold.

Two controversial books by women did sell and circulate well this year. Radclyffe Hall's *Well of Loneliness,* a novel about a lesbian, was banned in England and New York before its Paris printing. Copies sold at high prices from vendor's carts and Sylvia had a waiting list of borrowers, particularly after the stage version in Paris nearly provoked an opening-night riot. She herself was fascinated with the book; her curiosity superseded her skepticism about its literary merit or psychological accuracy. Natalie Barney, thought to be the model for Valerie Seymour in the novel, invited a large crowd for tea, cucumber sandwiches, and a meeting with Miss Hall. Before the party, she sent to Shakespeare and Company for the book, but Sylvia had to inform her that she would have to wait several days, as all the copies had been sold "as soon as they got in." Sylvia adds, "Yes, you are the heroine in all the outstanding books this season." Certainly Sylvia was referring also to Djuna Barnes's *Ladies Almanac.*

Ladies Almanac, printed by Darantière, and written "By a Lady of Fashion," was a clever little chapbook full of drawings and disguised portraits of the women (including Barney) in the American colony of Paris. As the thirty-three-word subtitle suggests, the book shows their "signs and tides," their "diurnal and nocturnal Distempers." The Left Bank crowd had great fun identifying the figures in the book, particularly Evangeline Musset, who, like Natalie Barney, went "riding all smack-of-astride." Djuna Barnes had written the book, and she and two helpers had hand-colored her illustrations in twenty-five copies. Sylvia (who was not caricatured in the book) helped by selling twenty copies during October and November.

As the publisher of *Ulysses* and as the distributor of both privately printed and controversial books, Sylvia had a shady reputation in some quarters. It was not unusual for her to receive a letter, such as the one she opened this year from a "bibliophile," asking for the "complete list of your pornographic publications." She was offended by the assumption that she dealt in contraband books, but not for reasons of prudery. If she turned down D. H. Lawrence's request to have her publish *Lady Chatterley's Lover,* it was because she did not like it. Aldous Huxley—who "was making a sacrifice . . . condescending to come to the headquarters of James Joyce, to whose *Ulysses* he was not friendly"—begged her assistance for Lawrence, who was his friend, because the book had been pirated and was circulating in Paris with no profit to its author. Sylvia sympathized with Lawrence's plight and informed Huxley that she would sell copies of the unexpurgated Florence edition in her shop. Lawrence himself wrote to assure her that, although *Lady Chatterley's Lover* had been seized by U.S. customs, no legal action there or in England had ensued and that she must not fear selling it. He also asked her again to publish the book: "I suppose you are too busy to take charge of the French edition for me, if I pay the costs of production? You know all the ropes and everything, and I should feel more sure. But of course you may have too much on hand." She was too busy, he was correct about that, she agreed; but she did not tell him that the work left her indifferent. Privately, she called it a "kind of sermon-on-the-mount—of Venus." Finally, he made several visits to the shop, bringing first their mutual friend Millicent Beveridge (whose photograph of himself he autographed for Sylvia), and on later visits his wife, Frieda. But no amount of persuasion worked. Sylvia felt some guilt and regret in refusing his request, as she explains years later:

It was sad refusing Lawrence's *Lady,* particularly because he was so ill the last time I saw him that he had got out of bed to come to the bookshop and had a flushed, feverish look. It was distressing trying to explain my reasons for not undertaking other publications than *Ulysses* [lack of capital, space, personnel, and time]. . . . It was difficult to tell him that I didn't want to get a name as a publisher of erotica, and impossible to say that I wanted to be a one-book publisher—what could anybody offer after *Ulysses*?

She suggested Titus, who published *Lady* the next year. It became one of Shakespeare and Company's best sellers.

The "Trianons Treaty," which held together the translators of *Ulysses,* unraveled for good in October. Adrienne and Morel quarreled, Joyce reported to Miss Weaver, in a simplified version of the truth. Even though Joyce announced that he would "approach him and bring him back into the fold under one shepherd life without end amen,'' the differences were never resolved. Larbaud, critical of Morel's phrasing, had sent a list of suggestions and rewritings to Joyce, who approved them. Adrienne, following Joyce's wishes, accepted them. She was caught in the middle, a position that Sylvia recognized. Sylvia reveals that "in the *mic-macs* Adrienne was the principal sufferer.'' Years had passed since the translation had begun, and weeks since Adrienne had circulated her prospectus. Before November all copies of the deluxe edition of the work and 500 to 600 copies of the regular edition had been subscribed for. The treaty had come undone at the most critical moment. Sylvia remembers that at the end of the quarrel, Morel, perhaps justifiably offended, left the project:

He had a temper and said things, I believe, to Larbaud. Then he got annoyed at Gilbert, who, he thought, was too exacting, and went away in a huff. Meanwhile, Larbaud, whose health was never good, fell ill and retired to his home near Vichy. The survivors, Gilbert and Adrienne, spent many an afternoon . . . completing the work in the back room of her bookshop.

The case against Roth was finally resolved at the end of the year. A year before, when the arm of the law, twisted by Conner, had begun to encircle Roth, he had ceased publishing *Ulysses*. His issue of October 1927 had contained the fourteenth and last episode of the pirated book. Yet in that same year Roth had published a full pirated book edition of *Ulysses* IX. Before the suit was tried in the fall, Conner's firm in New York cabled requesting Joyce's permission to change the suit to an injunction against the use of Joyce's name. Although there had really been no legal case against Roth, the law firm had stayed with Joyce because of his stature as a writer. Wisely, Joyce had had Sylvia send through the law firm all requests (such as one in May from John Rodker) for the publication of *Work in Progress*. The firm had been kept aware of his value as an author. The injunction against Roth's "publishing, printing, stating or advertising" the name of Joyce was filed and swiftly issued in December of 1928.

The year ended with the mailing of Christmas books and with the receipt of letters from former patrons. Notable among the letters was one from MacLeish, who enclosed money for Sylvia to buy three or four bottles of white wine for Joyce for Christmas. "Do you like my Hamlet [*The Hamlet of A. MacLeish*]?'' he asked Sylvia. "The critics hate it. Ernest, whom I have never pleased before, says perhaps I'm a great poet. Which is a nice way of saying he likes it. He is almost alone. He and Galantière. Please join up.'' The letter ends with "our best to les Bécats and the merchants as pappy puts it.''

In a note to Hemingway, Sylvia celebrates the turn of the year by reciting a litany of crises: Nora is in the hospital; Joyce has broken down from the strain; recovering from facial neuralgia herself, she must run the shop alone because Myrsine is ill; and Adrienne is busy correcting proofs and keeping three translators from "springing at each other's throats.'' She could also have added that she was looking everywhere for a "runner" because Hélène Moschos, tired from going on errands, had quit. But these relatively minor problems would soon pass, and the year 1929, with the arrival of Morley Callaghan, Hart Crane, and the American financial crash, would bring a grand finale to the twenties.

CHAPTER 13

"Exagminations"

1929–1930

A hundred cares, a tithe of troubles. . . .
— *Finnegans Wake*

SYLVIA WAS WRESTLING WITH the tedious details of her bookkeeping for taxes and inventory when she received a call from the doctors attending Nora Joyce. The results of Nora's exploratory operation and radium treatments were unsatisfactory, and the doctors believed that she needed a radical hysterectomy. Revealing to Sylvia the extent of Nora's cancer, they asked her whether she would bring Joyce and his son, George, to the clinic to be told of the necessity for an operation. As Sylvia and the doctors had expected, Joyce was reluctant to consent to it. He finally approved, however, and the hysterectomy was performed at the Neuilly clinic three days after the Joyce-*Ulysses* birthday party. Harriet Weaver had arrived on 20 January to spend two months ministering to the stricken family. While she saw to the personal needs of Nora and the others, Sylvia continued to manage Joyce's literary and financial business. Though all remaining royalties were turned over to George Joyce on 9 February, Sylvia went on paying doctor bills from her own funds.

"Well, I have had a certain amount of luck in my life, don't you think so. And one piece of it I consider is NOT being married," Sylvia discloses in one of the few references to her sister Holly's marriage. Joyce's "Holly Hazeleyes" (Sylvia called her "Miss Terious") married Frederic James Dennis on 21 January 1929 in San Diego, California. Cyprian stood as witness for her sister, and their father performed the wedding. Holly, who was forty-five years old but who had decided many years earlier to be five (then ten) years younger, married a forty-year-old Columbia Law School graduate. Dennis was the editor of the Pasadena *Spectator* and the *Pasadena Realtor* and a contributor to several magazines, such as *California Arts and Architecture*. Sylvester Beach held his son-in-law in high regard; Cyprian thought he was "staid and stuffy." And when Cyprian informed her that Fred hated France, he was not endeared to Sylvia either.

If Holly had married a bore, Carlotta Welles, Sylvia's childhood friend, had found her happiness with the convivial James Briggs—a banker and a man who loved to exchange suggestive jokes and double entendres with Sylvia and bathe nude at the beach in Bourée. In 1929, two years after their marriage, the couple moved permanently to Paris. Sylvia would spend many family vacations (especially Thanksgiving) in their city apartment or at Carlotta's family home in Bourée, where as teenagers the two girls had spent a delightful year away from school. Her association with the Briggses during the next two decades reinforced Sylvia's American identity.

While her oldest sister and her childhood friend settled into domestic life, Sylvia made plans for her own progeny, her third Joyce publication. In the preceding summer she and Joyce had conceived of a collection of critical essays on *Work in Progress*. Joyce had since generated and overseen the writing of most of the essays, which had been appearing in *transition*. During the first months of 1929, Beckett wrote the essay ("Dante . . . Bruno. Vico . . . Joyce") that was to head the 194-page collection. The essay by William Carlos Williams ("A Point for American Criticism"), the only unsolicited critical response, appeared last. Joyce had decided to limit the essays to twelve by "latter-day apostles"— a reflection of his numerological interest (there were twelve customers at Earwicker's pub) as well as his mocking messianic megalomania. Joyce had already begun calling Eugene Jolas and Elliot Paul Saint Peter and Saint Paul (he himself was by implication the Master) since Wyndham Lewis had referred to Paul's essay "New Nihilism" (*transition* 2) as "the new Paul's creed." Among the numerous references to the apostles in *Work in Progress* is "you was bad no end . . . so whelp you Sinner Pitre and Sinner Poule."

Anticipating objections to twelve positive, and thus presumably biased reviews, Joyce penned a negative response himself ("Dear Mister Germ's Choice"), signing it Vladimir Dixon:

Dear Mister Germ's Choice, in gutter dispear I am taking my pen toilet you know that . . . I am so disturd by my inhumility to onthorstand most of the impslocations constrained in your work that . . . I am writing you, mysterre Shame's Voice, to let you no how bed I feeloxerab out it all.

Though the style was undeniably Joycean, Sylvia always alleged that it appeared on her desk anonymously, addressed to Brentano's, the distinguished Right Bank bookshop. There was also a second letter of protest, which she claimed to have solicited from a female journalist and customer ("G. V. L. Slingsby"), who she knew disliked Joyce's new work. She herself may have written the piece. The collection of the twelve disciples and two dissenters would be published in the spring under the title *Our Exagmination round His Factification for Incamination of Work in Progress*. In his letters, Joyce referred to it as *O*. Sylvia called it *Our Exag*.

Adrienne was occupied by her own publication. *Ulysse* (without the *s* in French) was finally ready in February, for Joyce's birthday. The event historically linked the two rue de l'Odéon bookshops. Sylvia took pride in her own early contribution to the translation and distributed it when her English and

American friends wrote for copies. Adrienne, after years of translators' quarrels, concluded her Joycean work with pleasure. More than three months elapsed before she mustered the enthusiasm to celebrate the appearance of the book.

During the first weeks of 1929, despite a bout of facial neuralgia, Sylvia ran the shop alone. She began treatments for her headaches with a friend of both bookshops, the thirty-three-year-old Dr. Thérèse Bertrand-Fontaine, who had been Sylvia's first customer. (With Sylvia's recommendation, she also treated Joyce, Hemingway, and Mary Colum.) Greater than the physical discomfort of headaches and neuralgia was Sylvia's disappointment in Myrsine, who she discovered was feigning illness in order to be absent from work for weeks at a time. She bragged to another person about her deception, and the word got back to Sylvia, whose disappointment was a further aggravation. Some relief came in the form of a new and more dependable errand girl who worked from 9 A.M. to 7 P.M. each day (Hélène Moschos had worked only afternoons). Also, Wilhelmine Moschos filled in at the desk until Myrsine returned from her "illness" and a vacation in Biarritz. "Now she has come back," Sylvia confesses, "but my confidence in her is gone for good."

Late on the last night of 1928, at the mill (Le Moulin) north of Paris rented by Caresse and Harry Crosby, amid drunken revelry, McAlmon had looked at Kay Boyle with searching eyes and cried, "It's too damned depressing, so depressing that I can't even get drunk. They're wraiths, all of them. They aren't people. God knows what they've done with their realities." Then he added prophetically, "The good days are finished." McAlmon took a taxi to Paris and some months later left for America. By the end of the year, Crosby had also examined his life in France and concluded that for him it was "The End of Europe." The following December he was dead in New York City, a gunshot wound in his temple.

The end of the twenties brought both quest and inquest. The successful quests were numerous: Hemingway published *A Farewell to Arms* and was now, in his own mind, a successful author. Fitzgerald continued work on *Tender Is the Night*. Hart Crane wrote the "Cape Hatteras" portion of his great epic *The Bridge*. Sylvia published the collection of critical articles on Joyce's *Work in Progress*. McAlmon contributed two excellent short stories to *transition*. The Crosbys published Joyce's *Tales Told of Shem and Shaun*. Adrienne held her celebration luncheon for the publication of *Ulysse*, in June. In *That Summer in Paris*, his portrait of this gay and exciting period, which marks the end of an era, Morley Callaghan has given a popular, but incomplete, impression of 1929. It was, to a certain extent, a year of celebrations and important publications. Yet, for Joyce it began a two-year period in which he did little writing. He and Nora were ill, and by the end of the year, his only enthusiasm was for the tenor voice of the Irish singer John Sullivan. He would throw his creative energies into the promotion of another man's career. Others threw their creative energies to the winds. The opium and alcohol central to the Crosby weekend parties only hastened death. McAlmon felt increasingly isolated, frustrated, and desperate. For him

1928 and 1929—not 1921—marked the beginning of the so-called lost generation. He would blame Paris, using, as seems traditional, female terms: "I knew all too well that Paris is a bitch; and that one shouldn't become fascinated with bitches; particularly when they have wit, imagination, experience and tradition." Earlier Hemingway had also blamed the seduction of Paris nightlife for the dissipation of some of the Americans and Englishmen. In *The Sun Also Rises,* Jake Barnes exclaims, "You're an expatriate. You've lost touch with the soil. You get precious. Fake European standards have ruined you. You drink yourself to death. You spend all your time talking, not working. You are an expatriate, see? You hang around cafés." Though the testimony of McAlmon and Hemingway seems to ring true—especially in 1929 and in the lives of men like Crosby and Crane—one must also account for their productivity during this year.

The meeting of Crane and Crosby in January was, one might assume, preordained by their mutual self-destructiveness. "He is of the sea as I am of the Sun," Crosby exclaims prophetically in his diary. Four days after Jolas had introduced them, Crosby agreed to publish *The Bridge,* Crane's as yet unfinished epic poem. Although he did not share Crosby's fondness for opium, Crane was dazzled by his wealth and the comfort of Le Moulin life. Crane, for his part, loved sailors and Cutty Sark, and both were his undoing. He had left his Ohio home (his daddy concocted the candy Life Saver) at the age of seventeen; had been befriended by Tate, Cowley, and Josephson in New York; and had lived on fellowships, grants, and the charity of friends. An inheritance from his grandmother brought him, in 1929, to Paris, where Crosby became his major benefactor.

The lives of Crosby and Crane embody one of the paradoxes of the twenties most evident in 1929—a paradox that Leon Edel describes as a "strange stream of creativity and pseudo-art meandering in and out of libidinous bars." Crosby was a mediocre poet whose Black Sun Press books were beautifully printed contributions to literature. Yet he was a petulant little boy—in a more destructive fashion than was Hemingway with his big-boy posturings. While decrying the noise and vulgarity of America, he dropped water balloons from hotel balconies, swallowed opium, and kept his neighbors awake with his drunken revelry. Crosby's dissipations—like his suicide—were calculated; Crane's were not. Crane had lost control. His frantic search for sailors often left him beaten and ill. He wrote infrequently, in concentrations of productivity (to the strains of his favorite music, Ravel's *Bolero*). He was not a part of the literary circles of Paris, although he met Stein, Soupault, and Sylvia (but not, presumably, Joyce).

During this last, wild year for Harry, the Crosbys frequently visited Shakespeare and Company. On 6 February, Harry recorded in his diary that he and Caresse had gone to the bookshop to see Sylvia "to ask her if Joyce would be willing to let us edit a fragment of his *Work in Progress.*" They wanted, as Caresse phrases it in her memoirs, "a piece of the Irish cake then baking on the Paris fire." Sylvia listened to their plans, then talked to Joyce, who arranged for the Crosbys to visit his flat in the first week of March. In the meantime, Caresse brought copies, which Sylvia was to sell, of their collection of Kay Boyle's short stories. On the twentieth, Harry confided enthusiastically to his diary, "When I got home a letter from Sylvia Beach to say we can have Joyce." They conferred with Joyce on 27 March, signed on 6 April, and then worked out the contract and printing details with Sylvia.

The Crosbys planned to print three tales that had already appeared in *transition:* "The Maddest Thick That Ever Heard Dump," "The Mookse and the Gripes," and "The Ondt and the Gracehoper." By May they were calling the book *Tales Told of Shem and Shaun*. His contract with the Crosbys gave Joyce $2,000 for 600 copies, 100 of them signed: excellent pay for Joyce, thanks to the generosity of the wealthy Crosbys and the persistence of Sylvia. "I was very grasping in matters concerning Joyce," she admits, "and was reputed to be hardheaded in business." Although she had his power of attorney, her "services were free" in the sales of portions of Joyce's work.

Publication by Crosby offered Joyce an opportunity, in "The Mookse and the Gripes," to retaliate against Wyndham Percy Lewis, whose recently published *Childermass* (like his later *Doom of Youth*) imitates the "master Joys of Potluck . . . whom the gods call just Joys or Shimmy." Using the language of *Work in Progress,* Lewis cleverly mocks Joyce's self-publicity at Shakespeare and Company:

Sweet Will as shop-sign is the best high-brow stop-sign—to say *We have* that Swan of Avon *right here inside* with us forkeeps, beard brogue pomes and all (in a hundred in-edited poses from youth up to be seen on all hands tastefully snapshotted) ponderating "meggs-in-progress" and "wirk-on-the-way" in our back office (with Vico the mechanical for guide in the musty labrinths of the latter-days to train him to circle true and make true orbit upon himself) so STOP!—but there is more in confidence, for twixt me you the shop sign and crooked counter Sweet Will is all very well but for tourists only, and there are others, non-tripping, that are surely stopping and wanting and quite otherwise wanting. So our sign's reversible—get me? there is a fourth dimension of introverted Swans of Avon unseen by the profane, we have *that* in the shop *too* ant many narfter thorts as well as swan-songs, so walk right in we'd be glad to be met by you.

In "The Mookse and the Gripes," Joyce fought back with his own puns on the "enemy the Percy" who is "weltall Ondt in his windhome" and "sair sair sullem and chairman-looking when he was not making spaces in his psyche." Sylvia calls the satire a "harmless, almost affectionate" retaliation. She enjoyed a little revenge herself.

Joyce was eager to have a portrait frontispiece for the book drawn by Picasso, but the latter refused to accept Caresse's commission. He was, after all, in the Stein camp. Brancusi agreed to do it. Sylvia and Joyce liked his drawing, but the Crosbys thought it less than modern. Brancusi, who later gave this first drawing to Sylvia, then composed another, simpler, abstract design for the volume: a curlicue and three lines, showing Joyce "reduced to the essentials," as Sylvia remarks with disdain. When Julian Huxley (Joyce wanted a scientist) refused the request to write an introduction, C. K. Ogden (the creator of Basic English) accepted. Immediately Joyce began reworking his tales for Crosby, who confided to his diary that he and his wife were leading a "most stimulating" life.

After having concluded contractual details with the Crosbys, Sylvia turned her final efforts to the collection of criticism of *Work in Progress*. Joyce composed the title and double-checked all the references in the essays. Sylvia, aided by an astronomy book in her library, created the cover design: a wheel ("an orbit upon himself" says Lewis) around whose ring appears the title *Our Exagmination round His Factification for Incamination of Work in Progress*. The names of the twelve authors form the spokes of the wheel: Beckett, Marcel Brion, Budgen, Gilbert, Jolas, Victor Llona, McAlmon, McGreevy, Paul, Rodker, Robert Sage, and Williams.

In *Work in Progress,* Joyce refers disparagingly to these apostles: "Imagine the twelve deaferended dumbbawls of the whole above-beugled to be the contonuation through regeneration of the urutteration of the word in pregross." Later in the same work, he writes, "His producers are they not his consumers? Your exagmination round his factification for incamination of a warping process." Playfully, Joyce deflected criticism of his work by leading the criticism against his "deaferended" and "dumbbawls" defenders.

The end of May, when *Our Exag* appeared, Joyce was dismayed to find that, despite his last-minute checking, there were errors; but he approved of the book as a whole. In a letter to Larbaud he proudly claims credit for the title, cover design, and conception of each article. Williams, writing to Sylvia, praises the efforts of the various contributors to defend Joyce's new work:

I am tremendously stimulated by this new book about Joyce. I see it as another stroke against the bulwark of literary intolerance and veritable stupidity which is holding back an unsuspected ocean. God how I do see it and how powerless and prone I feel myself. But not always. I'd rather be engaged in this momentous undertaking (it hasn't a name) than to have all there is else in the world.

McAlmon did not share Williams's enthusiasm. He had written his essay ("Mr. Joyce Directs an Irish Word Ballet") at the insistence of Sylvia. Yet he included enough such phrases as "he hopes he has done this or that" and "I cannot say" to catch the knowing eye of Joyce. But Jolas, who declared the McAlmon essay "sensitive, very sensitive," did not feel the slight tug at his own leg.

Joyce was very active in promoting *Our Exag*. He arranged for reviews and asked friends to translate several of the essays for publication in Italian, German, Danish, and Swedish periodicals. He defended his "intriguing" by claiming he had "little or no support . . . to defend a difficult cause." Though sales of this book barely covered costs, he and Sylvia talked about putting together and publishing a second defense of *Work in Progress,* but the project never got beyond the planning stages.

Spring brought Cyril Connolly and Hemingway back and a new friend, Justin O'Brien, into the Franco-American circle. Sylvia encouraged young Connolly (who borrowed nearly one thousand francs from the bookshop till) to write an

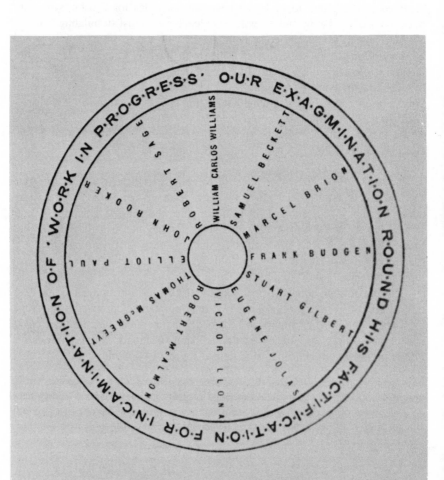

SHAKESPEARE AND COMPANY

12, RUE DE L'ODÉON, PARIS

M CM XX IX

article on Joyce; after its appearance in *Life and Letters* (April 1929), she thanked him for his work. O'Brien, a French instructor at Harvard who was beginning his scholarly work on French literature, successfully sought Sylvia's aid in securing permission from Larbaud to translate *Amants, Heureux Amants* and in placing his "Notes for a Study of Jean Cocteau" in *transition*. Hemingway returned from America in April for a spring and fall in Paris, a summer in Spain. He came with Pauline, their baby (Patrick), and Bumby, whom they were returning to Hadley after a long Christmas visit. In May, Hemingway's *Farewell to Arms* began appearing serially in *Scribner's Magazine*.

Hemingway boxed with the Canadian writer Morley Callaghan, whom he had known in Toronto. Callaghan and his wife, Loretto, had come to Paris for the spring and summer. His short stories had appeared in *This Quarter* and *transition*, and Scribners had published his novel *Strange Fugitive*. He and Hemingway had the same Scribners editor, Max Perkins, and they also shared a love of boxing. On different occasions the painter Joan Miró and Fitzgerald (who had returned that spring to try and finish *Tender Is the Night*) served as timekeepers when they sparred together.

Callaghan, who had run a little lending library in Toronto while studying for a law degree (and working summers at the *Star*), was naturally drawn to Shakespeare and Company. But he did not particularly like Sylvia. When he first arrived in Paris, he came to the shop, introduced himself, and asked her for Hemingway's address. Always protective of her friends, she replied that she was not certain Hemingway was in town but that she would take his name in case Hemingway contacted her. Unconvinced that she was telling the truth, Callaghan was examining the bookshelves when, he says, "suddenly Miss Beach left her desk and approached us. Had I seen 'the piece about my work in the Harvard *Hound and Horn*' she asked, handing it to me, then leaving us. 'See,' I whispered to my wife, 'she knows who I am and she knows Hemingway's address and won't give it to me. To the devil with Miss Beach.' " They then left. Two days later they returned with a note for Hemingway, which Sylvia immediately delivered, and the friends were reunited. Callaghan was pleased to have McAlmon inform him later that "Miss Beach in her role of den mother sometimes made ridiculous mistakes." McAlmon told him about her failure to introduce George Moore and Joyce. In *That Summer in Paris,* written more than thirty years later, Callaghan calls Sylvia "fair and handsome" and admits that he was "too young and arrogant to have respect for her consideration for her friends." Yet the dominant impression he leaves is one of dislike for the "severe and mannish" Sylvia and her "protective screen." What Callaghan could not have known is that Hemingway had given her specific instructions to keep his whereabouts secret, especially from Fitzgerald, whose behavior had gotten him evicted from an apartment. He wanted no one, not even friends, to drop in on him.

Callaghan hung about the "very small, backbiting, gossipy little neighborhood" of Montparnasse with McAlmon and his two very young friends from Montreal who had come to Paris in 1928: John ("Buffy") Glassco and Graeme

Taylor. Callaghan saw examples of this small-town bickering in the feuds between McAlmon and Hemingway (each one belittled the other's manhood), between Fitzgerald and McAlmon, between Hemingway and Ford, and between Fitzgerald and Hemingway. According to Callaghan, one needed a fight card to keep track of the snubs and squabbles. The reminiscences of Glassco (*Memoirs of Montparnasse*), who was nineteen at the time, and those of Callaghan (*That Summer in Paris*), who was twenty-six, have helped to create the myth that expatriate life in Paris was all drinking, boxing, and having trivial spats. Neither gives more than a glimpse of life in the rue de l'Odéon.

Tales Told of Shem and Shaun was ready on 17 June 1929. An amusing incident occurred at the last minute when the printer, discovering that the final page contained only two lines, begged Caresse Crosby for more copy. She refused with disdain, exclaiming that she could never approach Joyce with such a request. The printer returned on the next day with eight more lines that he himself had requested from Joyce, who, he told Caresse, "had been wanting to add more, but was too frightened of you, Madame, to do so." Proud of his Black Sun Press edition, Crosby took one of the first copies to Sylvia, then went to the mill for four days to lie naked in the sun ("I penetrate into the Sun I am the sun"). Within weeks he was in the shop telling Sylvia about his new passion, flying, which would take him closer to the sun. Lindbergh was his hero. She thought him far too nervous to earn a pilot's license. He would, she claims, "dart in and out of my bookshop, dive into the bookshelves like a humming-bird extracting honey from a blossom, or hover a minute around my table. . . ." But on the day he earned his wings "he stopped in at the bookshop to give me a snapshot of himself in front of his plane. He said he had learned to fly as it would be a pleasant death."

According to Joyce's wishes, Sylvia, not the Crosbys, handled all the press copies for *Tales*. She and Joyce were experienced in promotion and arranged for each review. The Crosbys were already busy publishing other books. Soon after they published a book by Jolas, Crosby's name replaced Elliot Paul's on the *transition* masthead as a contributing editor. Of the fifteen Black Sun Press books that he and Caresse published in 1929, they seemed most proud of the Joyce work.

By the spring of 1929, Joyce had slowed his work pace and was devoting more time to worrying about his family: to his eighty-year-old father, whose pleas to visit him in Ireland he ignored, and to the potential careers of his two children. April ended with family and friends cheering the debut of George, who sang two Handel songs in concert. In the following month, they attended the last dance performance by Lucia, whose behavior became increasingly bizarre during the next two years.

Sylvia was concerned about Lucia. Moved about from country to country, language to language, by her father, she had developed few friends outside his circle. She was eager to be creative and began studying dance—ironically at about the same time that Zelda Fitzgerald became obsessed with that art. Both women, who devoted long, grueling hours to practicing, would have their first mental breakdowns within a year of each other. Sylvia attended each dance recital in which Lucia performed, the last on 28 May. After this, Lucia decided she was too weak to continue her career and became concerned with finding a husband, particularly when George announced his intention to marry. She fixed her attention first on the sculptor Alexander ("Sandy") Calder, then on Samuel Beckett. Beckett, who was one of the rivals for her father's time and attention, was often with the Joyce family. His presence threw her into a flutter. He was either unaware of the effect ("his emotional development was somewhat arrested," asserts his biographer Bair), was afraid to jeopardize his standing with Joyce by openly rejecting her, or was feigning ignorance of the infatuation. He was instead fixated on Joyce: "First he affected Joyce's manners, then he aped his dress. He had become so close to George Joyce that many persons remarked how much they were 'like brothers.' Now, in what was for Joyce the ultimate adulatory gesture, Beckett consciously began to pattern his writing after his." If Lucia had been well, they might indeed have married. In a childlike autobiography that she wrote in 1961 at the request of Sylvia, Lucia, having described each one of her "boyfriends," remarks, "Then I knew Samuel Beckett who was half jewish [read half Protestant] he became my boy friend and he was very much in love with me but I could not marry him as he was too tall for me. He was a writer and pianist."

In June, their Joycean publications behind them, Sylvia and Adrienne took a short holiday and then returned to host one of their most elaborate festivals for Joyce. *Déjeuner Ulysse*—a luncheon honoring the publication of the French translation of *Ulysses*—was held on 27 June, eleven days after Bloomsday. Adrienne and Sylvia carefully planned the event, which was held at the Léopold restaurant (obviously chosen with Leopold Bloom in mind). Because the Léopold was in Les Vaux-de-Cernay, a tiny village past Versailles, in the Chevreuse Valley, they rented a bus to transport their party from the rue de l'Odéon. The majority of the nearly thirty guests were friends of Sylvia and Adrienne, such as Fargue, Romains, and Valéry (of the three, only Fargue cared particularly for Joyce or his work). Other leading French writers at this very French occasion were Paulhan, Soupault, Chamson, Pierre de Lanux, and Édouard Dujardin, whom Joyce had called the father of the stream-of-consciousness technique. To the regret of Joyce, the translators Morel, Gilbert, and Larbaud were conspicuously absent. With the Joyce family came Helen Kastor Fleischman (the American whom George planned to marry) and the two young Irishmen Beckett and McGreevy, whom Pound (who had just met them at a luncheon with Joyce) considered sycophants.

A printed menu listed six courses, beginning with paté Léopold and ending with a selection of liqueurs. After a few speeches, the presentation of copies of *Ulysse,* comic turn-of-the-century songs sung by Fargue, and the signing of menus, the party loosened up. The youngest members—McGreevy, Beckett, Soupault, and Nino Frank—"romped around engaging in all sort of antics."

Frank, a young journalist whose birthday fell close to the day of Bloom's odyssey (a fact that in part accounts for the invitation from his casual friend Joyce), remembers that Joyce joined their foolish antics. The Irishmen were particularly drunk; the French were apparently annoyed. Adrienne had trouble gathering them all together for a group photo of the historic event. She and Sylvia stood immediately behind Joyce on either side, and twenty others (Beckett was apparently too drunk or too shy to pose) grouped themselves around these three. She then herded everyone back into the bus, where the jokes and singing continued. When Beckett asked the bus driver to stop, so that he could go to the toilet, four or five of the most inebriated (including Joyce) immediately headed for a bar. Several more times the bus stopped, the driver now joined the drinking, and the local inhabitants along the route silently watched the noisy celebrators. The others, including an indifferent Nora Joyce (accustomed to her husband's behavior), waited on the bus. Paulhan was disgusted and scolded Frank; Valéry was full of Gallic disdain; Adrienne was angry and dismayed; Sylvia finally, at one stop, persuaded Joyce to stay on the bus.

Ulysse was well received by the French. Joyce spent several months assiduously culling reviews both of *Ulysse* and of *Work in Progress*. Although the response to the former was considerably more positive, Adrienne's efforts at promotion produced one negative response. Ambassador Claudel, in Washington, D.C., returned the *Ulysse* that she had mailed him. In an accompanying

MENU

LE PATÉ LÉOPOLD
LES QUENELLES DE VEAU TOULOUSE
LE POULET DE BRESSE RÔTI
LES POMMES NOUVELLES AU BEURRE
LA SALADE DE LAITUE MIMOSA
LES FROMAGES VARIÉS
LA TARTE AUX FRAISES DU JARDIN

VIN BLANC, VIN ROSÉ, VIN ROUGE
PASSE-TOUT-GRAIN DE NUITS
MOULIN A VENT
CAFÉ FILTRE
LIQUEURS

letter, he declared, "I once wasted a few hours reading *Portrait of the Artist as a Young Man* by the same author, and that was enough for me." Both books, Claudel concluded decisively, are "full of the filthiest blasphemies, in which one feels all the hatred of a renegade—afflicted, moreover, by a really diabolical absence of talent." The youngest French writers evaluated *Ulysse* differently, testifies Simone de Beauvoir:

After the monumental *Ulysses* appeared in French, a door was opened for us to a new world of foreign writers—D. H. Lawrence, Virginia Woolf, the great American Hemingway, Dos Passos; Faulkner, who totally transformed our concept of what a novel should be; and Kafka, who transformed our vision of the world in which we lived.

While Callaghan spent his "summer in Paris," Sylvia and Adrienne went to Les Déserts, and the Joyce family (with the Gilberts) went to Torquay, in the west country of England. In July, Hemingway was in Pamplona; McAlmon, after eight books and nine years of bouncing about Europe, was headed toward the United States; Josephson was in New York with many returned Americans, celebrating in what he describes as a hard-drinking and fighting summer before the crash; and Fitzgerald was again in Cannes, but very unpopular because of his drunken behavior. For those who remained in Montparnasse—whose nightmarish quality Fitzgerald would capture in *Tender Is the Night* and "Babylon Revisited"—the big event was Crane's imprisonment in July for resisting arrest. After having smashed furniture at the Café Select, he was clubbed into insensibility by police and dragged off to jail feet first. Maria Jolas found him a lawyer. The Crosbys, Kay Boyle, Bill Bird, and others attended his trial. Within days of Crane's release, Crosby had bought him a ticket and put him on board a ship headed for the United States.

During the nearly two months that Joyce spent in England, he was busy arranging publicity in English reviews; meeting with English men of letters; listening as Gilbert read to him aloud each chapter of his *James Joyce's "Ulysses,"* portions of which Joyce helped him place in various magazines; recording, at Sylvia's suggestion, the last pages of the Anna Livia Plurabelle section for Ogden, at the Orthological Institute. To Joyce's delight, James Stephens had agreed he would carry on Joyce's work if "sight or the opposition demanded it."

At Les Déserts the hay "smelled sweet" and the cock they were fattening awakened Sylvia and Adrienne each morning. Gay had built a "sort of garage" for their car. But they spent only ten days at the mountain retreat, because Sylvia suffered from an infected thumb, which required a stay near the clinic in Chambéry, where the doctor opened the thumb three times in the process of treating it.

While on vacation, Sylvia learned that her younger sister, Cyprian, had recently gone into business with Helen Gerome ("Jerry") Eddy. They opened The Frog Footman (named after a character in *Alice in Wonderland*), a restaurant that served "cosmopolitan cuisine" (with Cyprian as chef) at 495 South Lake Avenue in Pasadena. With unfortunate timing, the opening took place only weeks before the stock-market crash, and the restaurant survived less than a year. Helen, who had met Cyprian in the Beach boutique, had been acting with the Pasadena Community Players and was beginning an active career in Hollywood films. She found a few parts for Cyprian, who eventually withdrew from public life to be Helen's faithful companion for twenty-four years, until Cyprian's death, in 1951.

Sylvia and Adrienne, before returning to Paris, spent several therapeutic days swimming and sunning in the Mediterranean near Marseilles. When Joyce learned that she was rested, he wrote from London, "I am glad to see you are better. Go on like that for I am coming back early next week, exhausted, penniless. . . ." Hemingway arrived in Paris before Joyce—just days before the appearance of his *Farewell to Arms*. It would be a best seller by November. One afternoon near the end of September, Hemingway was leaving the bookshop when Sylvia called him back to meet a new arrival, Allen Tate, who would make frequent visits during this year from his Hôtel de l'Odéon residence. With delight, Sylvia introduced Hemingway to this young poet, who had written several laudatory reviews of his work. Hemingway's only response was to scold him for saying that Defoe and Captain Marryat had influenced his work. In the shop and later at the Café Voltaire, Hemingway offered opinions on the alleged impotence of Ford Madox Ford, recently separated from Stella Bowen, and on a man's need to limit his ejaculations, while young, so as to have a supply of them in his old age. Sylvia, who knew all about Hemingway's opinions, spoke privately with disapproval about his views on women and sex. His literary work was another matter.

A twenty-two-year-old American graduate student, destined to be one of his country's best critics and biographers, was now a frequent visitor at both libraries. Leon Edel glanced around the shop during each visit, hoping to see his culture hero Joyce. Much later, Edel rendered some of the most perceptive judgments of the man Joyce. But his view of him this year was from a distance, and was colored by awe. Sylvia was the one he knew at close range: she "had a soft, musical voice and was one of the pleasantest women I have ever known." She was "patient, discreet," and "tactful," he adds, a woman who "wanted to have her modest little bookshop, her literary foyer modeled on Adrienne's, but fame, in the figure of the tall, slouching Irishman with his cane and his arrogance, thrust itself through her doorway." Years later, after Edel had become aware of her difficult association with Joyce, he marveled that he "never heard her say anything that did not enlarge the legend she had helped to create." Edel believed the "fairy tale" legend of the true genius. Not until Jolas enlightened him when they were together in occupied Germany after the war (and after Joyce's death) did Edel learn the truth about Joyce's alcoholic evenings, his habit of drinking until he was anesthetized, until cigarettes burned and blistered his unfeeling fingers. "Great God, Edel," Jolas explained to his friend. "Great God! A man can't be a hero when you've seen him cold stiff, night after night."

Late 1929 was not the best time to be living abroad (as was Edel) or to be beginning a new business in America (as was Cyprian). The U.S. stock market plummeted in October. When the news was carried in French newspapers, Sylvia worried about her family in the United States, particularly about the boutique and the restaurant businesses; about her small bank account in Princeton; and about how the crash would affect European businesses, especially her own. The effects of the "Wall Street killapse," the "fall of the Wall" (as Sylvia called it), were slow in reaching Paris; but by early December she was reporting that all businesses involved in the tourist trade were feeling the depression. The drop in tourism was evident first in Montparnasse, where the expatriate community, according to Putnam, "began dying" in 1929.

Montparnasse—considered a center for visiting students and artists—was bankrupt, both spiritually and economically. Its decline had been foreshadowed by the French workers' invasion of the café terraces in August 1927, to protest the execution of Sacco and Vanzetti. The exit of its foreign denizens was hastened by the U.S. stock-market crash in October of 1929. In the spring of 1931 the country went off the gold standard, and the old way of life came to a definite end. There remained this year 25,000 permanent American residents in France, half of them in Paris. But in the coming winters fewer tourists sat close to the large coal braziers in the café terraces. And fewer came to Shakespeare and Company to buy copies of *Ulysses* or other books. Still, despite the erosion of her business, Sylvia continued to fulfill her commitments to Joyce and to bear the burden of his financial demands.

In October she was caught up in a thousand details for Joyce, who was finishing the last Watch of Shaun for the November issue of *transition* and trying to mollify his wife, who disliked returning from England to the café life in Paris, and their daughter, who had wept for a month over her failed dance studies. Perhaps in part to cheer Nora, Joyce planned an 8 October celebration of their silver anniversary together. Sylvia sent the invitations to the Hemingways, Fargue, Soupault, Adrienne, the Gilberts, the Crosbys (who would soon afterward leave for America), and many others. The party was crowded and jovial. Joyce wore a tuxedo with a white carnation; Crosby wore, as was his custom, a black flower. After Irish whisky and champagne were served, Joyce sang Irish ballads that he was hoping soon to record. Gilbert, now that Antheil was gone, played the piano. Fargue arrived late and immediately began to eat the pink angel food cake, asserting that it "reminded him of young girls cut into pieces."

Joyce's final work (until February 1933) for *transition*—he had now written Parts 1 and 3 of the novel—coincided with the temporary suspension (for financial reasons) of the magazine. The June and November 1929 issues had reached new limits of mystical jargon. The double issue No. 16/17 contained the "Revolution of the Word"; the first section of No. 18 was entitled "The Synthetist Universe: Dreams and the Chthonian Mind" and was overwritten in a combination of social-science jargon and mystical generalizations. In McAlmon's judgment, the editors were chasing "the hallucinatory word over the sleepwalking realms of a mythos," making "any balanced writer" think he was "having delirium tremens." *Transition* was, he concluded, "a constant example of how not to write." However esoteric and windy its literary philosophy, *transition* had provided an invaluable service to Joyce. In fact, Edmund Wilson, one of the best early critics of *Work in Progress,* claims that it is "rather doubtful whether without the work done by *transition* it would be possible to get the hang of the book at all."

Sometime before *transition* suspended its publication until 1931, the Jolases invited their contributors and friends to a large party. The rooms were crowded with guests sipping champagne. Suddenly talk hushed and they moved back to clear a passage for Maria Jolas, who led two persons toward two large armchairs, "from which the occupants, as if touched by an unseen finger, quickly arose." The unmistakable figure of Gertrude Stein, followed by that of Alice B. Toklas, moved regally to the chairs. Soon a group of young men who knew or wanted to know Miss Stein had squatted in a half-circle before her chair. Across the room sat Nora and James Joyce, seeming not to notice the commotion. The Jolases, by inviting both Joyce and Stein to the same party, had done a daring thing. Kay Boyle has described this party, at which she first met Joyce, in great detail:

Nora and James Joyce had given no sign that they had seen the ceremonial cortege pass, but Sylvia Beach, who had been chatting with Soupault and Elliot Paul and Adrienne Monnier near one of the wide windows that opened on the mild spring night, turned and crossed the room, making her way through the guests who had now begun to talk and drink and laugh again, and drew up a footstool, and sat down in her gray, mannish suit before the Joyces. "Isn't she the true picture of an Irish colleen, with her dark hair and her misty blue eyes?" Nora said to Sylvia as she introduced us, and nothing else but this introduction might have been taking place anywhere in the room.

Boyle claims she never talked to Stein that evening, for it would "have seemed almost a disloyalty to have crossed the room and genuflected before [her]." Neither did Joyce make the trip. Stein had made clear her opinions of Joyce, both to Sylvia (when she withdrew her library membership) and to Jolas. "Poor Eugene Jolas stopped in at my bookshop one day," declares Sylvia. "Pale and shaken, [he] told me what a dressing down he had just had from Gertrude Stein because his review was paying too much attention to the 'dirty Irish politician James Joyce.' "

His appearances in *transition* seemingly ended, Joyce turned to private presses for publication of reworked portions that had appeared in that magazine. He was so busy with promotion, with securing a favorable audience, that he did not continue work on his unfinished novel. In the back of his mind was the idea that James Stephens would finish or ghostwrite the remainder of it for him. Joyce would take years to write Part 2 (the first portion of which would not be undertaken until 1932) and Part 4. Both relieved and let down by the conclusion of his *transition* contract, he threw his enthusiasm and promotional skills into boosting the career of another man, the Irish tenor John Sullivan.

Joyce first heard of Sullivan, who had lived in France since his twelfth year, from his brother Stanislaus, who had met him in Trieste and had learned that he was reading *Portrait.* The Irish writer and the Irish singer must meet, vowed

Stanislaus, and they soon did, after Joyce heard *Tannhäuser* sung by Sullivan. "Joyce was carried away by Sullivan's voice," Sylvia declares. "He said to me that it was cleansing and reminded him of the men that came for the garbage in the early morning." In her opinion, Sullivan lacked the warmth, theatrical presence, acting ability, and charm of John McCormack, the Irish tenor whom Joyce had first admired. But she admits that offstage—particularly at after-concert suppers at the Café de la Paix—Sullivan was very attractive. The personal charm of Sullivan and his interest in Joyce's work made the difference for Joyce, who boasted to Miss Weaver that Sullivan was not only the "most powerful dramatic tenor at present alive" but also "a great admirer of mine." The friendship seems to have been stronger on Joyce's part. Soon they were drinking together and sharing stories of persecution. Sylvia believed that they both imagined themselves persecuted—a fancy, she adds, that proved a fortunate thing. With great sympathy and with a sense of identification, Joyce decided to take on the supposed conspiratorial forces that kept Sullivan from singing at Covent Garden and at the Metropolitan Opera; eventually he wrote "From a Banned Writer to a Banned Singer" on Sullivan's behalf.

The fanatical cheerleading for Sullivan seems curious behavior for the egocentric Joyce unless one looks closely at his personality and predilections. First of all, Joyce loved the opera. From grand opera to the crudest vaudeville, Joyce relished the spectacle of drama—the atmosphere, lights, spectators, the hush before the curtain rose. Opera filled him with childlike fascination and worship. He sacramentally abstained from food before a performance, eating supper afterward. Second, Joyce had finished nearly a decade of difficult writing, had essentially stopped writing on his novel, and was ready for a change (as his activities of 1930 would illustrate). Sullivan came into his life at the right moment. Perhaps Joyce initially thought that Sullivan could help George's career. But more important than these circumstances were the psychological factors. Joyce began to identify himself with Sullivan to the point, some observed, that Sullivan became more an idea in Joyce's mind than a real person. "Joyce saw Sullivan as an alter ego," concludes Ellmann, "who had pursued the career he himself had rejected, and had then encountered the same opposition in music which Joyce had encountered in literature. Roused by the challenge of making another career, now vicariously in another art, Joyce extended to Sullivan an almost motherly solicitude." The applause for Sullivan became applause for Joyce. In order to love and care deeply for another person, Joyce had to see that person as an extension of himself (as was his family) or as an alter ego (as were for a time James Stephens and John Sullivan).

Sylvia could not understand the fanatical devotion that Joyce gave Sullivan. Nor had she understood the "infatuation" that Joyce had earlier had with the operatic tenor John McCormack, with whom he had once sung on the same program in Dublin. Joyce had on that occasion noted every curl on McCormack's head, as well as the way he walked and bowed; he pleaded with Sylvia to note the striking resemblance between his own voice and McCormack's. Eventually she purchased all of his records and wildly applauded with Joyce at each concert. His infatuation with McCormack, who was indifferent to Joyce's work, she found "amazing and touching." Perhaps it prepared her for what she called "the Joyce-Sullivan affair, one of the most extraordinary in the Joyce history." Joyce attended each concert, got to his feet to cheer, shouted curses at the competition; wrote to every connection he had in order to promote Sullivan's career; arranged at least fifteen notices in American and English newspapers (several mentioning the so-called conspiracies against Sullivan); and tenaciously badgered Nancy Cunard to use her mother's connections to hire Sullivan for the London opera (going so far as to suggest that she could have a piece of his work for her Hours Press). He even broke his silence with reporters—but only to talk of Sullivan.

The director of the Paris Opéra, harassed by Joyce's excessive promotion and badgering, gradually dropped Sullivan, whom he did not consider a major talent, from the programs. Joyce worked even harder on Sullivan's behalf, appealing for support to all of his friends and admirers. According to Sylvia, they "would call up the box office and book seats for *Guillaume Tell*, maybe a whole box. But we made it clear that it was John Sullivan we wished to hear as Tell. And if we were told it was not to be Sullivan, we canceled the booking. This happened so often that the box office got riled and stopped answering the telephone." Sullivan was eventually dropped completely.

Sylvia and Adrienne watched the Sullivan affair with amusement, wondering whether Joyce had gone "soft in the head." Adrienne, who shared the disdain of French intellectuals for the Paris Opéra, inquired bluntly one day, "Why do you do so much for a little known tenor?" Joyce replied that since coming to Paris, he had been introduced by them to many "geniuses," all of whom he considered "perhapses." About Sullivan's voice, there was "no perhaps." They remained unconvinced.

Only because she cared for Joyce and saw the operatic nature of his *Work in Progress* did Sylvia assist in his Sullivan campaign. She asked her brother-in-law Fred Dennis whether he could generate some publicity in California magazines. She collared every patron to fill the house for Sullivan's performances. One of these patrons was Leon Edel, who agreed to Sylvia's request. He did not care for the opera and had little money; but he would, he reasoned, catch a glimpse of the "legendary" and "invisible" Joyce, subject of his youthful idolatry. He splurged on a one-dollar, second-tier front seat and eagerly watched Joyce appear and walk down the left aisle "like blind Homer." When Sullivan appeared, before he sang a note, Joyce applauded wildly and shouted bravos, as he did after the tenor finished each of his arias. He and his camp followers stopped the show. Edel confesses that he was probably applauding Joyce himself, just as "Joyce's applause was as much for the banned writer as for the allegedly banned singer. For Joyce had linked himself wholly to his countryman's voice and read his own dilemma into the life of Sullivan. . . . Having crowned him king of the tenors, Joyce, super performer of the writers, was satisfied."

Joyce's enthusiasm for Sullivan carried through to the following March, when the tenor went on tour. Not in an artistically productive period for his own work, Joyce confessed to Miss Weaver that there were times when he was "incapable of thinking, writing, reading or speaking." Sylvia also confided to Miss Weaver that she was depressed. The only one who seemed to be riding high was Hemingway, who left in his new Ford to ski in the Alps (with the Murphys and the newly married Dos Passoses), trailing good reviews and escalating book sales in his wake.

Antheil, who had been wandering about Europe since his disastrous Carnegie Hall concert, arrived in Paris in December. Joyce immediately tried to enlist his support for Sullivan by asking Antheil to contact all of his musical connections to bombard the Metropolitan Opera. But Antheil was wrapped up in his own plans for a new opera to be performed the coming April in Frankfurt. If the opera was a success, he boasted to Sylvia, he would be a success forever! The bravado was an attempt to cover the awkwardness of months of absence from Paris and his embarrassment at the rumors of his opportunism. His letters to Sylvia during the preceding months had contained a note of defensiveness about his not having written the Cyclops opera for Joyce and about gossip that Sylvia was supporting him financially. He begged her to help counter this spreading rumor, which he blamed on his friends Walter and Lillian Lowenfels. While he had wandered through Germany, Italy, and southern France all year, Sylvia had kept his room unrented and forwarded him small checks from Mrs. Bok and the money she had solicited from friends. The years of "favors and services you have always rendered me," Antheil whines, "coupled with the fact that I owe you still very nearly a half-year's rent, do not make my conscience easy in this journeying around the southern countries in search of health, particularly so that health makes it imperative that I have first class accommodations. I still also remember that I owe the doctor and the tailor in Paris." She publicly continued to give her support to young Antheil but privately confessed that "he is a regular little cad as time has shown. An ungrateful *arriviste* [climber]."

Antheil left Boski in Paris and sailed for New York in time to be able to spend Christmas with his family in Trenton. Two weeks later, Allen Tate left Paris after thirteen months of study, and Hemingway, while declaring his enthusiasm for Paris "in temporary decline," joined the migration to the United States. Of these three, only Antheil soon returned, to discover that his room had been rented to Crown Prince Norodeth of Cambodia.

"If you really wish, it is quite possible for you to see your apartment again," Sylvia informed Antheil. "The young crown prince is an enthusiast of your music. He plays the piano very well and has been attempting to play your 'Airplane Sonata.' I often hear him, above, playing the rolls of 'Ballet Mécanique,' which, incidentally, shakes the whole building!"

"I'd like to meet him," exclaimed George, greatly impressed to be admired by a prince who would some day be king.

"The French Government is scared to death about the young prince," Sylvia disclosed as she called his attention to a French detective who paced the sidewalk outside. George asked why the prince was staying in his humble quarters.

"The prince is very democratic," Sylvia explained. "He refused to come to Paris to study unless his uncle, the regent, permitted him to bring along some thirty other Cambodian lads; he's paying the expenses of all of them, and so he's living here in the same sort of Latin quarters as are they."

The prince had undoubtedly found the apartment through Dr. Moschos, who trained many Cambodian medical students, or through Myrsine, who told him about his humble flat but prestigious Left Bank address. When Antheil saw his old room, he was impressed by the oriental rugs, the Cézanne paintings, and the Pleyel grand piano, at which he sat, in gratitude to the prince, to play several of his own compositions. Sylvia and Adrienne, confident that their street was being well guarded by French police, spent the Christmas weekend with Jeanne and Sisley Huddleston in the Normandy mill house in Saint-Pierre-d'Autils, on the Seine.

The colorful and artistically productive twenties ended in a season of deaths. Almost prophetically, MacLeish had earlier this year published in *transition* a poem entitled "Tourist Death: For Sylvia Beach," dedicated to the woman who had particular insight into the nature of those whom the poem condemned. Some of the Shakespeare and Company patrons and friends who died this year were among the ones MacLeish describes as living their lives as tourists, asking "to travel forever" in search of a new Rive Gauche. They had what Cowley, in *Exile's Return,* calls the "spectatorial attitude." In August, Diaghilev died in Venice. In November, the French Surrealists Jacques Rigaut and Jacques Vaché took their lives. And on 10 December in New York City, Harry Crosby, only thirty-one years old, pulled the trigger to end his life. Two months later, D. H. Lawrence died of consumption.

The rue de l'Odéon lost two close friends this year—friends who did not approach life as tourists. The year opened with the death of Dr. Borsch. It closed with the death of Raymonde Linossier—lawyer, author, patron of both shops, and one of the first of Joyce's typists. Sylvia, Adrienne, and Joyce mourned the loss of both. For those who remained, the greatest test would be not the loss of friends but the economic collapse. Sylvia knew that no decade is, in the words of MacLeish's poem, "a prize box or a terminus." The twenties had given her both the prizes and what MacLeish calls the "sweat bitter." This new decade, with its economic restraints and its prevailing sense of the need for change, would bring a final crisis in the relationship between Sylvia and Joyce.

CHAPTER 14

The Flowers of Friendship Fade
1930–1931

Hirp! Hirp! for their Missed Understandings!
chirps the Ballat of Perce-Oreille.
— *Finnegans Wake*

All me life I have lived among them but now they are becoming lothed to me. And I
am lothing their little warm tricks. And lothing their mean cosy turns. And all the
greedy gushes out through their small souls.
— *Finnegans Wake*

R AIN FELL CONSTANTLY throughout the spring of 1930 and continued
to do so until the end of July, when Sylvia was laid low with pneumonia. The
cold rain was an appropriate accompaniment to the chill of the economic depression and the cooling of several friendships.

Decisions by Joyce during 1930 and 1931 estranged him from his most faithful supporters, including Harriet Weaver, Sylvia Beach, and Samuel Beckett,
and moved him into the final phase of his life—a more lucrative, but relatively
joyless, decade. In a March letter to Harriet Weaver, he complains that he is
temporarily alienated from Sylvia and Adrienne and is suffering "miniature
fainting fits." The causes of his unhappiness, he explains, are threefold.

The first cause, and one that underlay all of the others, was financial. "I am
continually placed in difficult situations which I am not quickwitted enough to
know how to handle by the sudden exaltations and depressions of the Odéon
Bourse," he explains. He is feeling the pinch of Shakespeare and Company's
shrinking purse—even though Sylvia had been paying him between 7,000 and
10,000 francs monthly on *Ulysses* royalties and had negotiated large advances
for portions of *Work in Progress,* for the second German and the second French
editions of *Ulysses,* for Polish and Czech translations of *Ulysses,* and for productions of *Exiles* in Berlin and Milan. He does not ⎯ke the fluctuations of the
purse personally, he hastens to add, for "where I am concerned, they have never
wavered in their loyalty to me." He was building up larger and larger overdrafts
at Shakespeare and Company. At the end of February his overdraft or "advances"
amounted to nearly 13,000 francs. Despite the economic depression, he spent
lavishly on food, clothing, and entertainment. To regain her advances and

replenish her supply of copies, Sylvia planned the eleventh printing of *Ulysses* for May. It was her largest order to date: 4,000 copies.

Joyce's second annoyance had to do with the publishing of his new book, which he and Sylvia had always assumed she would handle. However, the financial stakes had become higher by now and he wanted the book published in the United States, believing that "American wealth, law and power" dictated this step. He complains to Miss Weaver that "Miss Beach naturally feels that the book that she has been waiting for and has helped me so much with, is not being energetically enough given to her by me." Yet Sylvia was not resentful or anxious, as a letter written that same week to Holly indicates: "He says he will have to have it come out in America, otherwise there is no possibility of securing a copyright, and that is true."

The third source of tension in Joyce's life was that he had stopped writing. His creative energies were given instead to promoting Sullivan and selling his own earlier work. "Apart from [their] sales," he confesses, the editions and publications of *Ulysses* do not interest him any more. He was inclined even to allow Stephens to "write the rest" of his new work. The "state of tension" between himself and the rue de l'Odéon (created less by money than by his Sullivanizing) was so acute that he avoided the bookshop for a week. Soon he asked the London executors to cash £200 of the principal of Miss Weaver's gift. His tension and ennui are so unnerving, he says at the end of his litany of complaints to Miss Weaver, that he is "light in the head."

The changes he considered this spring, though drastic, were slow in coming. He decided to leave Paris for London or at least to move out of the expensive Square Robiac apartment: "I do not think that if I cease working there is much point in my continuing to live in Paris. It involves sacrifice of capital for one thing." To avoid having to transport his books, which he could no longer read, he disposed of most of his library. Upon Dr. Borsch's death, he decided (on the advice of several people) to seek treatment from Dr. Alfred Vogt of Zurich. A third decision, he confided to Miss Weaver, was to marry Nora, his common-law wife of twenty-six years, in order to secure inheritance rights for his family in England. Joyce was primarily concerned about his future security and his health.

How many of these plans Sylvia anticipated is not known. She was fully informed about his concerns for securing copyright for *Work in Progress*, because she herself handled all this business. Always informed about his eyesight, she had been one of the first to urge him to find a specialist in Switzerland. She still knew nothing of the marriage plans. Joyce now had several people who would run his personal errands, and his stops at the bookshop were less frequent. More often he dialed Littré 33-76 and talked on the phone to Sylvia, who saw to a growing stream of requests for pieces for anthologies, translations, and photographs.

The Reverend Beach arrived in mid-April to visit Sylvia and Adrienne. They were soon settled into a comfortable domestic routine, which had him eating every meal with them. Though a day maid relieved the two professional women of the household chores, Adrienne planned, shopped for, and prepared each meal. Other family scenes were less tranquil. This month Zelda Fitzgerald had the first of her serious mental breakdowns; by June, Scott had placed her in a clinic in Geneva. Lucia Joyce was periodically irrational. She moved from placidity to distracted staring into space to blunt and flighty behavior—the last in the presence of Beckett. Her aggressive pursuit of Beckett, now in his second year of employment at the École Normale, had finally forced him to speak. When he informed her in May that he did not have a romantic interest in her, she became seriously distraught. The Joyces were furious at him for having (they believed) led her on.

A break with Joyce followed, to the distress of Beckett. He clung to weak consolation from friends, who assured him that the Joyces would eventually have to face the truth about Lucia. Since December (at the request of Joyce) Beckett had been working, with his friend Alfred Péron, on a translation of the Anna Livia Plurabelle section. Although his daily attendance on Joyce seemed over, Beckett continued the translation, wrote poetry (his *Whoroscope* won the poetry award of the Hours Press), and spent a summer alone in Paris writing a long essay on Proust. His visits to Shakespeare and Company brought him as close as he could now get to his idol and father figure.

While Sylvia was on a short trip to Le Bourget with her father, Adrienne received from Lucia a letter full of chores that Joyce wanted Adrienne to perform in Sylvia's absence. Adrienne was to mail *Our Exag* books to four persons, with notes enclosed in two; to call George to ask him to make a doctor's appointment and give a certain notebook to Paul Léon; and to call Léon, who was to change several words in Joyce's manuscript. This letter, similar to ones that Joyce had sent Sylvia for more than a decade, upset Adrienne, who had never made a commitment to the daily business of Joyce. Judging by her behavior in the coming months, she was rapidly convinced that Sylvia had also had enough of this business.

A new recruit had joined the Joyce industry. The aforementioned Paul Léon, who had met Joyce several months before, was helping him transcribe his work. Léon and his wife, Lucie—(she later wrote for the *New York Herald Tribune* under the name Lucie Noël)—were Russian Jews, emigrants who had lived in London three years before moving to Paris in 1921. Joyce liked Léon because he had a lighthearted manner, was a friend of George and Helen Joyce, was trained in law and literature, and carried a name (Paul Léopoldovich) that seemed to foreordain his association with the creator of Leopold Paula Bloom. Léon's legal training appealed to the lover of litigation. The lawyer, in turn, was devoted to Joyce, whom he believed (by reputation) to be the greatest living writer. In response to an April letter from the writer, thanking him for his assistance, Léon replied that he owed the gratitude to Joyce, who had "allowed [him] to observe the formation of [Joyce's] thoughts." Although he had not read Joyce's work, he was by June giving a great deal of clerical help. To assist Joyce, he soon learned, was to have one's life taken over by him.

One day Jack Kahane, whom Sylvia called a "friend and colleague in the publishing business,'' strode in with his usual inquiry, ''How's God?'' Sylvia informed him that Joyce was in Zurich submitting to a cataract operation by Dr. Vogt. Kahane admired Sylvia ''no end'' for her discovery of such an ''obscene'' book, as he characterized *Ulysses*. He published only the ''spicy kind of books,'' and he had long urged Sylvia to allow him to take over the publication of *Ulysses*. After much badgering, she had finally agreed to take Kahane to the Joyce apartment, where the honor of shaking the hand of ''the greatest expatriate'' almost caused him to swoon. When Joyce agreed to give him a segment of *Work in Progress,* Kahane promptly paid him an advance of 50,000 francs ($2,000). By June *Haveth Childers Everywhere* was available in 600 beautifully printed, outsize copies, costing the publishers nearly 100,000 francs. Only by selling the American rights were Kahane and his partner saved from bankruptcy. Disappointed in the fragment, he complained to Sylvia that it lacked sexual interest. She laughed, admiring Kahane ''for his good humor and scorn of pretenses.''

In this year, early in the depression, four other established little presses sold their publications at Shakespeare and Company: Nancy Cunard's Hours Press, which printed sixteen books from 1930 to 1932, when it closed; Edward Titus's Black Manikin Press, which stayed in business until 1932; and Caresse Crosby's Black Sun Press, which functioned until 1936. In 1930 Crosby published nine books, including Crane's *The Bridge.*

Several new Paris presses, begun during 1930 and 1931, supplied Sylvia with books. Henry Babou and Jack Kahane jointly owned the Vendôme Press and Obelisk Press (1930–1939). She sold their edition of *Haveth Childers Everywhere* and (later) a re-edition of twenty-five copies of *Pomes Penyeach* with lettering by Lucia, a reissue of Radclyffe Hall's *Well of Loneliness,* and books by Henry Miller and Anaïs Nin. Sylvia also sold the Gertrude Stein books of the Plain Edition, a press founded by Stein and Toklas when the agent William Bradley could not place Stein's books with any publisher. Using profits from her writings and the sale of a Picasso painting to finance the venture, they released *Lucy Church Amiably,* their first book, in January 1931. Their second, *How to Write,* was followed by the poem ''Before the Flowers of Friendship Faded Friendship Faded.''

There was considerable vitality among the small presses in these years. Michael Fraenkel and Walter Lowenfels founded Carrefour in 1930 and issued their own works anonymously; Bob Brown brought out his own books under the imprint Roving Eye (1930–1931); Samuel Putnam published seven books during 1931–1932 under the name New Review Press; and in October 1930 the Harrison Press, directed by Monroe Wheeler (financed by Barbara Harrison and advised by Glenway Wescott) issued the first of its beautifully printed books.

Although the little presses flourished during the early thirties, there were few Paris-based little magazines in English. The only one that appeared regularly was *This Quarter,* now edited by Titus with the assistance of Samuel Putnam. The latter soon quarreled with Titus, who did not want to print James Farrell, and left to begin the *New Review.* Harold J. Salemson, who had published *Tam-*

bour off and on during 1929 and 1930, joined Putnam. Only *transition* persisted through the decade. One issue appeared in 1930 (there was none in 1931); nearly 400 pages long, it contained sections bearing such titles as "Dreams and Mythos," "Evolution of the Sense," and "Reality and Beyond." In addition to Jung's "Psychology of Poetry," the editors (Jolas, Gilbert, and Sage) printed a memorial to Harry Crosby and a Shakespeare and Company advertisement, but nothing from *Work in Progress*.

Faber and Faber had *Anna Livia Plurabelle* ready in June, with a verse on the dust jacket that Joyce had given to Eliot:

> Buy a book in brown paper
> From Faber and Faber
> To see Annie Liffey trip, tumble and caper . . .

Sylvia had been selling the booklets *Haveth Childers Everywhere* and *Anna Livia Plurabelle*—Joyce's only 1930–1931 publications—for several days when Joyce returned from Zurich with improved sight in one eye. He asked her to keep the news secret. One day in June he stood in a Sullivan concert of *Guillaume Tell*, raised his dark glasses, and announced dramatically, "Thanks be to God for this miracle. After twenty years I see the light once more!" The newspapers carried this latest and greatest publicity stunt. Sylvia and Adrienne were astounded.

At about this time Sylvia met a woman who was an important friend in the coming decades. Marian Willard, a young New York and Long Island socialite was studying bookbinding in Paris. They met socially through a mutual friend, Martha (Toni) Hughes, and talked about art and psychiatry. Marian was in Paris on her way back to the United States from Zurich, where she had visited Carola Giedion-Welcker and had attended a series of lectures by Carl Jung. She soon discovered that the Joyce circle did not like Jung, who had just written an unfavorable introduction for the third German edition of *Ulysses* (the publisher did not use the essay). Jung, whom Joyce had once called the Swiss Tweedledum to the Viennese Tweedledee (Freud), would adopt a more favorable view of Joyce before Miss Willard returned from the United States for her second visit to Paris.

Sylvia's vacation this year began unusually early and unexpectedly. Long before the Joyce family left for an extended English vacation, where Joyce persisted in his Sullivanizing, Sylvia fell ill with exhaustion and a cold. Dr. Thérèse Bertrand-Fontaine X-rayed her chest, diagnosed pneumonia, and demanded that she rest. Adrienne immediately took her to Rocfoin and the Monnier family bosom, where Sylvia was fed and cared for with love. Adrienne spent long weekends there and prepared Sylvia's favorite dishes. With the instruction of Mrs. Welles (Carlotta's mother), Mrs. Monnier planted six stalks of imported American sweet corn, a vegetable fed only to the pigs in Europe. But there was little sun this summer—one of the rainiest in half a century—and the corn ripened with large bald spots. Nevertheless the family gathered around to watch their American daughter eat the vegetable. Next year, they all exclaimed, they would plant more. During dry spells, Sylvia walked around the soggy garden and among the fruit trees in her wooden shoes, breathing the fresh air and allowing her body to heal. "The life is so restful after the strainfulness of Paris," she assures Holly. On this same day, Joyce sent a postcard in his own hand from Switzerland. "Very glad to hear the good news about you. Have a good rest." Then, pleased with the results of his latest operation, he adds, "I wrote this all MYSELF."

By mid-July she was well enough to travel with Adrienne. They were forbidden to go to Les Déserts because of its high altitude, which might endanger Sylvia's health. Abandoning plans to visit the Vosges, located in the rainy area near the Rhine, they headed south in their car, spent a few days with the Romains near Tours, and then drove through the Cévennes mountain region and the gorges of the Tarn. Their last week, they spent amid gales and winds on Mont Aigoual, eating fish from the mountain rivers each night. Sylvia returned to Paris at the end of August, healed and refreshed, to face the mail that had piled up in her absence.

She had never been away from Shakespeare and Company so long—three months. Summer trade had been sufficient to pay business bills and to keep up with Joyce's requests. She had had no personal expenses, because neither the doctor nor the Monniers had allowed her to pay for anything. Her absence had forced Joyce to rely more on Paul Léon and others, another important step toward her slow withdrawal from the Joyce industry.

Joyce returned to Paris in time for the opera season. He made a stop in the rue de l'Odéon to hear the French literary news and seemed most interested when Adrienne told him that the *Nouvelle Revue Française* had taken up the cause of Lawrence's *Lady Chatterley's Lover,* a novel Joyce thought "lush" and "sloppy." (Lawrence, in turn, thought *Ulysses* a "filthy" novel.) He resumed his obsession with Sullivan by trying to persuade Antheil to write the music and libretto of Byron's *Cain,* so that the singer might star in it. By the end of the year, Antheil had to beg Sylvia to help him get out from under Joyce's pressure. *Cain* was hopeless for the stage, he confided to Sylvia. Perhaps because he had failed Joyce before, he tentatively agreed to compose the music if Joyce would write the libretto. Joyce, who was willing to be a "scissors and paste man," refused to rewrite Byron's text and promptly replied that if Antheil had only heard the magnificent Sullivan voice, his ear would have "at once" found "the way out of the difficulty." If he cannot write the opera "at once, with enthusiasm," then Joyce will "offer poor Byron and poorer Sullivan elsewhere." Antheil was undoubtedly pleased with the polite ultimatum and, with the urging of Pound, abandoned the opera.

Joyce also cultivated wealthy English and American patrons of the arts in an attempt to get Sullivan into Covent Garden and the Metropolitan Opera. He even put off another needed operation in Zurich in order to hear Sullivan sing his last *Guillaume Tell* of the season in Paris. When the singer went on tour that winter, the writer at last started to write again. Using a new typewriter, he began the first chapter of Part 2 of *Work in Progress,* matching the games of children ("Angels and Devils" or "Colours," which he played as a child) to the combat of Shem and Shaun.

While Sylvia handled negotiations for a new project—the setting to music of *Pomes Penyeach* by Antheil, Darius Milhaud, and other composers (it was published as *The Joyce Book*)—Léon was involved in a new French translation of Anna Livia Plurabelle. Péron had turned over to Joyce in late summer the Anna Livia translation on which he and Beckett had spent half a year. Because of his estrangement from Joyce, Beckett had not dared to accompany Péron with the fruit of their labors to the Joyce apartment. Joyce sent it to the printer, then took it back to show to friends. At first they suggested only a few changes, but then they began a new translation that was completed in May of 1931 (the original was eventually lost). Joyce met weekly with the new translators—Jolas, Léon, and Ivan Goll. He was also meeting during these months with Herbert Gorman, who had agreed to write his full biography with the tacit understanding (Gorman soon realized) that he be treated "as a saint with an unusually protracted martyrdom."

By the end of the year, the depression was being felt beyond the tourist areas. "A whole street full of diamond merchants is scheduled to go into bankruptcy next week. I don't know why they are putting it off until then!" asserts Sylvia, who was herself feeling the effects of the crisis. Social life and the arts, however, did not seem to be affected by it. In this "very social" month of December, Sylvia visited Carlotta Briggs, gave dinner parties, planned a reading by Edith Sitwell for the following month in the bookshop, and attended films and plays. She was proud that Romains had four plays running in Paris. "The only drawback," she announces to Cyprian, "is that we are always going to First Nights." Her social life remained French; her professional life centered on the English and Americans.

The American writers who dropped in during the last weeks of 1930—they included Ludwig Lewisohn, Emma Goldman, and Elmer Rice—were full of talk about Sinclair Lewis's winning the first Nobel Prize in literature awarded to an American writer. In his Nobel address Lewis saluted (after having on earlier occasions disparaged) the young writers, "most of whom now live in Paris," who refused to be "genteel and traditional and dull." Despite his salute and the European assumption that *Babbitt* was typically American, many of the American writers in Paris felt that Lewis lacked the innovative greatness of some others, who had been passed over. He had been put above the Americans Dreiser, Pound, O'Neill, Wharton, Eliot, and Frost, and above the Europeans Galsworthy, Hardy, Gide, and Joyce. (Lewis himself thought Willa Cather should have won the prize.) When Lewis visited Montparnasse, many young American writers snubbed him, leaving him to sit in the cafés alone.

Suddenly, when his son was about to marry and he himself was contemplating marriage to ensure an inheritance for his family, Joyce insisted that he and Sylvia sign a contract for *Ulysses*. Years before, when she had casually suggested drafting one, he had wanted to have nothing to do with it (though in 1927 they had signed a contract for *Pomes Penyeach*). Because he knew the legal costs of his suit against Roth were growing and because he had already claimed in the deposition against Roth that *Ulysses* was her property, he wished to confirm the

MEMORANDUM OF AGREEMENT made this nineth day
of December, 1930 BETWEEN James Joyce, Esquire,
c/o Shakespeare & Co., 12 Rue de l'Odéon, Paris
(Hereinafter called the Author) of the one part
and Miss Sylvia Beach, Shakespeare and Company,
12 Rue de l'Odéon, Paris (Hereinafter called the
Publisher) of the other part, whereby it is
agreed by and between the parties as follows:
THE AUTHOR HEREBY AGREES:

1.   To assign to the Publisher the
exclusive right of printing and selling throughou
the world, the work entitled ULYSSES.

THE PUBLISHER HEREBY AGREES:

1.   To print and publish at her own risk
and expense the said Work

2.   To pay the Author on all copies sold
a royalty on the published price of twenty-five
per cent.

3.   To abandon the right to said Work if,
after due consideration such a step should be
deemed advisable by the Author and the Publisher
in the interests of the AUTHOR, in which case,
the right to publish said Work shall be purchased
from the Publisher at the price set by herself,
to be paid by the publishers acquiring the right
to publish said Work.   *les et epprouves*

James Joyce
Sylvia Beach

ownership or responsibility. He purchased stamped official paper and drew up an agreement according to his specifications on 9 December 1930. She was given "world rights" (she later noted sardonically that "the world was his own") to the publication of *Ulysses* in exchange for 25 percent of the published price. This "strange Jesuitical document," as Janet Flanner calls it, contains an important last section that allows Sylvia's rights to be purchased "at the price set by herself" if both Sylvia and Joyce should deem the circumstances of a sale "in the interests of the author." Ironically, the need for tangible evidence of their agreement, their bond, was a cruel portent of the coming breach of trust. The contract that Joyce initiated, he himself would breach.

Joyce's relations with Sylvia and Miss Weaver (as well as with other, less involved women friends) during these months reveal his growing dislike of women. His long dependence on them, burgeoning financial pressures, and the personal problems that resulted from his years of poor health, led him into frequent tirades against them. After one of his diatribes, Frank Budgen reminded him that he had once found women physically desirable. *"Macchè!* Perhaps I did. But now I don't care a damn about their bodies. I am only interested in their clothes." He swore argumentatively to Mary Colum that "what they call love is merely a temptation of nature in one's youth." He told Helen Nutting there was no such thing as a beautiful woman, informed Arthur Power that Italian women were "cold like all women," and confessed to Jolas that the word *love* made him "feel like puking."

He had lost interest in women as personified by Molly Bloom, that is, as sexual beings and also seemed to be losing interest in them as intellectual companions. He owed a good part of his professional success and income to a number of intelligent women (Margaret Anderson, Jane Heap, Harriet Weaver, Sylvia Beach, Adrienne Monnier, and, later, Maria Jolas—to name only the most important). Yet when the outspoken Mary Colum expressed her view that he would do better to credit the influence of Freud and Jung than that of Édouard Dujardin in his work, Joyce declared with annoyance, "I hate women who know anything." Although Mary Colum did not believe this, a few days after the outburst, he penned a verse about "poor Joyce Saint James" and seven "extravagant dames" with bees in their bonnets and bats in their belfries. He may never have liked Mary Colum; but he did at one time like Harriet Weaver and Sylvia Beach. His letters to Miss Weaver before this time reveal his great respect for her intelligence and perception. In the early years of 1921 and 1922, he had spent hours in the bookshop nearly every day working with Sylvia, reading portions of *Ulysses* and sharing jokes and puns, each amused by the other's accent and idioms. A decade of personal and financial demands and scores of courteously perfunctory letters dissipated this camaraderie. He had no close personal friends apart from his family. His demeanor in Sylvia's presence was elaborately polite and old-fashioned. But as women have long known, chivalry often masks dismissal, if not contempt. Although he owed much to a type of independent, creative, courageous, and intelligent woman, he did not create such a woman, with the possible exception of Beatrice in *Exiles,* in his art.

Nor was Joyce interested in women as maternal or nurturing persons. He told both Mary Colum and Carola Giedion-Welcker that women had been his most active supporters, yet consciously or unconsciously he resented their aid because of the obligation it put on him. This dependence only strengthened his misogyny. Without Miss Weaver's money and encouragement he could not have sustained himself or his family. He took freely, spent lavishly, and asked for more. He badgered her for her opinions, yet took offense when she honestly found she could not give him her full support for *Work in Progress*. His attitude toward her was always cool afterward. Her roles as financier, worrier over his health, and judge of his work were really too motherly for his liking, though he depended on her playing them. As with his actual mother, he at once needed and scorned her encouragement. His relationship with Miss Weaver, according to her biographers, suffered an irreversible strain or coolness during these months: "He had fled from his mother, from Mother Ireland and from Mother Church; but the inescapable mother appeared again in the person of his benefactress. Her 'alms' supported him; her frown disturbed or irritated him."

He was only half jesting when he said that his only interest in women had to do with their clothes. He watched approvingly as Helen Kastor Fleischman, who married George in December, taught Nora about dress and fashion. Joyce enjoyed being a dandy, eating in the finer restaurants, and having the women of his family well appareled. Helen, financially secure and ten years older than George, dressed beautifully. Ellmann asserts that "as he grew older, women more and more seemed to him dolls, unfortunately not mindless."

To what extent did the creator of Molly Bloom understand—even before he lost interest in her body—the mind, body, or psyche of woman? In two years Jung would write to Joyce praising his provocative and profound understanding of human psychology. After reading Molly Bloom's forty-page soliloquy, Jung confided, man to man, "I suppose the devil's grandmother knows so much about the real psychology of a woman, I didn't." He rewrote the unfavorable preface of 1930 on Joyce and published it separately in 1932. Nora, however, passed what is probably the final judgment on Joyce, Jung, or other men, when she said of her husband: "He knows nothing at all about women."

The financial crisis that began for Joyce during the final weeks of 1930 was not caused entirely by the cost of women's clothes. Joyce was spending more recklessly than ever. By the standards of 1930, he had an excellent income. From the interest on the Weaver principal, Joyce earned approximately $350 (9,000 francs, or £70) a month. His *Ulysses* royalties came to between $300 and $470 a month. Translations, reprints, and records increased these figures. Despite the growing income, he now borrowed $400 from Sylvia and confessed to Miss Weaver, "My royalty reserve dropped with a bang just when the wedding, Xmas and New Year announced themselves so that I have to realise another £100 [$500 from the principal] immediately. . . . The solicitors in charge of the fund strongly suggested to Joyce that he live within his income. Dramatically, he canceled plans for the celebration of his forty-ninth birthday and later informed Miss

Weaver, in the tones of a persecuted man, that he had disposed of four-fifths of his books, could not afford to get his broken plate repaired by the dentist, and had had "the worst birthday in history" because there was "no money" to hold a "reunion of all my friends." In order to move from the Square Robiac apartment, he accepted £160 from Miss Weaver, who, living frugally herself on a small income, had to sell some of her own stock to be able to give it. According to one friend, the Joyces "were extravagant on things like clothes, hotels, restaurants and vacations: they simply thought the money would last forever."

For the small cost of renting chairs and printing invitations, Sylvia held her first poetry reading at Shakespeare and Company on 7 January 1931. It is testimony to the breadth and generosity of her spirit that the poet was Edith Sitwell, who was more closely associated with the rue de Fleurus than with the rue de l'Odéon. Sylvia paid allegiance to no single coterie. "I managed somehow to have them all get along with each other, rather difficult when you mix writers," she confesses. She invited her French friends, Joyce, and the Stein group. Once she had sent the invitations, she feared no one would come. When almost everyone accepted, she was even more afraid. Joyce, who had to be persuaded to put in an appearance, squeezed into a chair on the back row in the front room. Even Fargue came. It was fortunate that he had a backseat in the back room, because not knowing a word of the language, he fell fast asleep when Sitwell read from the Elizabethan and modern English poets. When she concluded, he awakened, applauding louder than anyone else.

According to a list made by Sylvia, the Stein party (including Elizabeth Bowen, Pavel Tchelitchev, and Allen Tanner) had front-row seats. Stein expected to hear her own poetry read, but Sitwell, in a gesture of loyalty to Tchelitchev (with whom Stein had quarreled), did not read a single Stein poem. Sylvia, apparently unaware of Sitwell's poetic revenge, had met the Englishwoman several times before the reading. Though she was the same age as Sylvia, Sitwell—who became Dame Edith in 1954—presented a physical contrast to her. Unfortunately, no one took a photograph of the diminutive Sylvia standing with the angular, eccentrically dressed, six-foot-tall British poet. A picture of herself, which she gave Sylvia for the bookshop gallery, shows her lying on her back with her eyes closed and her hands on her chest—like the sculptures of Angevin kings on their tombs, she confided. She autographed her *Collected Poems* and her study of Alexander Pope and examined with interest Sylvia's Whitman manuscripts (for she and her brothers had, more than any modern poets, enhanced Whitman's reputation in Great Britain).

Stein did not greet Joyce this evening. They would meet only once presumably, several years later at a party at the studio of Jo Davidson when Sylvia, after receiving their permission, presented them to each other. They shook hands peacefully, Sylvia reports. Toklas, twenty-five years later, recalls the meeting:

Sylvia asked her if she would come across the room and speak to him—his eyes were very bad—which of course she did. (By that time he wasn't an Irish fairy to her any more—he was just an Irish legend.) She told me that she said to him—After all these years. He said—Yes and our names always linked together. She said—We live in the same arrondissement. And he said nothing so she went back to talk to a Californian.

In April, Stein told an interviewer from the Paris *Tribune,* "Joyce is good . . . [but] his influence is local."

A more fruitful introduction occurred immediately after the Sitwell reading, when Sylvia brought to Joyce's seat the tall, bearded Louis Gillet, a member of the French Academy. This meeting, according to Gillet (who had once attacked Joyce), was the culmination of a long campaign on Sylvia's part:

I used to see Sylvia Beach every so often, the Rue de l'Odéon being not too far from my home in the Rue Bonaparte. There was however a greater distance between the chronicler of the *Revue des Deux Mondes* and the young literary school. This sprightly woman enjoyed bringing them closer. When I browsed in her book shop, she amused herself by trying to convert me. [She gave him *Our Exag* and *transition.*] A lady is always an amiable servant of Parnassus: she is clever, tactful—in one word—a woman. Moreover Miss Beach knew how to talk; soon we became good friends. I already regretted my first move and was willing to learn. On thinking it over I began discerning the greatness of the phenomenon *Ulysses.* I did not know Joyce, I wished to meet him but was afraid I had offended him. Miss Beach recognized my inclinations and arranged an interview.

Sylvia's conversion of Gillet proved both personally and professionally valuable to Joyce. That night the academician apologized to the writer for his hostile review of *Ulysses* in the *Revue des Deux Mondes* (1 August 1925) and he volunteered to write another article on *Ulysses* and one on Joyce's new work ("M. James Joyce et son Nouveau Roman" appeared in his *Revue* in August). They agreed to meet for dinner.

When Joyce and Gillet had gone their separate ways, the Sitwell guests slowly walked to No. 18 for refreshments prepared by Adrienne and Marie. According to Sylvia's description of the reception, the guests filled every room in the flat, including the toilet. Sylvia continued her literary charity work by trying to enlist Natalie Barney, who had just received a postcard from Antheil, for the realization of Joyce's plans for *Cain.* The effort was futile because by mid-February, Joyce, by his own admission, had "almost given up Sullivan's case as hopeless though I hate being beaten."

"Extraordinaire! Extraordinaire!" exclaimed Adrienne the next day when she learned of Gillet's conversion to the Joyce cause. She and Sylvia found money for Joyce's dinner with Gillet on 19 February. Joyce was immensely impressed with Gillet's reputation in Paris. He would soon, in Joyce's mind, replace Larbaud as the leading French critic of his work. "People in Paris gasp at the hold I seem to have got there," Joyce confided in Frank Budgen. Gillet, now an admirer of Joyce's creative genius, has given us one of our most vivid descriptions of Joyce:

I can still see his long, delicate and aristocratic silhouette, surmounted by a strange cylindrical head, whose bony face with its enormous forehead in the shape of a tower seemed to have been cut out in the zinc of stovepipes, like certain surrealistic sculptures: I had never seen in anybody else more haughtiness, a demeanor more courteous and at the same time more aloof.

Gillet describes Joyce's "wending his way down the street tapping the iron point of his cane on the pavement, with a gesture groping and self-assertive." He was "not of this world," but "a stranger, a phantom whose shadow only was among us and who wandered with sureness in the universe of his thoughts and memories."

While Soupault and Adrienne made final suggestions on the French translation of Anna Livia Plurabelle, which Joyce pronounced "one of the masterpieces of translation," Sylvia concluded an inventory of her stock, both in the shop and upstairs in the storage room. She counted 4,600 books, 75 of which were checked out. During 1931 and 1932 (no record for 1930 remains) her best sellers were *Pomes Penyeach*, *Lady Chatterley's Lover*, *Ulysses* (and Gilbert's Key to that Work), Stein's *Lucy Church Amiably*, and the literary magazines. Among these magazines was Putnam's *New Review*, which editorialized against the excesses (specifically the "Joycean-Stein stutter") of *transition*. Sylvia sold it anyway.

As Sylvia's birthday and Patrick's Day (Joyce usually dropped the "Saint") approached, she planned to give a dinner party (Léon calls it "Miss Beach's Dinner") at the Trianons restaurant to celebrate the Irish holiday. She knew that Joyce enjoyed festive celebrations, and he had let her know that he had sulked alone through his birthday the month before. She and Adrienne invited all the associates of Joyce who were in Paris, including Mary and Padraic Colum, Herbert Gorman, Stuart and Moune Gilbert, Maria and Eugene Jolas, Bill Bird, and Paul Léon. Bob McAlmon, who had recently returned to Paris, came late, a few drinks ahead of the others. He disliked associating with the translators, imitators, and worshipers who had accumulated in the decade since he and Sylvia had met Joyce. But he was soon, according to his own memory, the lively center of the party. He gave a short speech about this being the day that Saint Patrick drove a lot of snakes out of Ireland but left "many things" that "he might better have driven out." No one, including McAlmon himself, knew what he meant. Joyce and Bird sang; then McAlmon (at Joyce's request) wailed his "Chinese Opera," a "performance that has had me thrown out of several bars and most respectable households and the police of various stations know it well." Although McAlmon remembers only the drinking, the hostess had provided a grand meal with champagne. Each guest contributed to the expense and most, including Joyce, ordered beforehand. According to Mary Colum, the waiter appeared with just a dish of lentils for Joyce. The most charitable of the group thought he intended some symbolic "correspondence" to which he gave intellectual and psychic allegiance. Mary Colum claims that Sylvia and Adrienne were shocked at Joyce's gesture of "pure cussedness." Sylvia, in a letter to Holly nearly twenty years later, denied that they had been shocked. But Colum believed he was sulking, perhaps over his financial problems and his missed birthday party.

Possibly with a little less enthusiasm, Adrienne concluded preparations for a reading of the French version of Anna Livia Plurabelle on 26 March at her book-shop. She had been the first to publish the English version of Anna Livia, in 1925 in her *Navire d'Argent*. Since that time, Joyce had worked on the episode, greatly enriching and expanding it. Now that it was to be given a hearing in French translation, he hoped to "break the back of the resistance" to his *Work in Progress*. If it did not do so, the reading might close his Paris career, as the Larbaud reading in December of 1921 had opened it. Though Larbaud was increasingly ill during the thirties and no longer present at the rue de l'Odéon festivities, Adrienne called on many other influential French writers. Sylvia invited the Joyce associates; Miss Weaver came from England and Beckett from Ireland. In addition, she invited a few of her new enthusiasts, including the young Leon Edel, for whom she had already played the record of Joyce reading Anna Livia. At this first meeting, Edel was tongue-tied when the distant and aloof Joyce, with his deep "shut-in" gloom and poker face, slouched into a small wooden chair beside him.

The long and elegant program had four parts. Adrienne introduced the read-ing; she spoke of her first meeting with Joyce at the Spire party in 1920, of his growing reputation in France, and of her criticism of *Ulysses*. Her elaborate analysis, which included quotations from numerous French critics, was one of the best (though subsequently neglected) early French responses to *Ulysses*. Then Soupault addressed the company, explaining the process of translation and mak-ing only passing reference to Beckett and Péron, who had begun it. Beckett, still estranged from Joyce, felt slighted. Soupault explained every detail, including the size of the table around which the translating committee had held its twice-a-week sessions. Adrienne then played the record (on Sylvia's gramophone) of Joyce reading Anna Livia in English. Finally, Adrienne read (Beckett claims Soupault read) from the French translation. She read too quickly and unemotion-ally for McAlmon's taste. She read in the familiar singsong French manner, noted Edel, who watched her lips become a circle as she spoke the word *ondes* repeatedly. "I think Miss Monnier," exclaimed Joyce, who must have liked the reading, "should record" it and "sell the discs."

McAlmon, a somewhat reluctant guest and unaccustomed to the solemnity of French homages, was cynical about the badly dressed and "dumbly worship-ful" guests packed into both rooms. During the reading, he lifted his hands in a gesture of mock prayer. After the ceremony, Édouard Dujardin, who was unknown to McAlmon, walked over to and slapped the face of McAlmon, who was stunned by the old man's gesture. Harriet Weaver responded to the slap with tight-lipped, shocked disapproval. Sylvia, who hurried to her side to coax her back to gentleness, thought that he must have arrived drunk and been smacked for making a stir. At the reception afterward in the apartment of Adrienne and Sylvia, when McAlmon explained the intent of his gesture, Joyce whispered to Sylvia that the next time McAlmon and Dujardin gave a performance, they should hire the Cirque d'Hiver. The official explanation of the slap surfaced several days later: Dujardin, sensitive about his wife's thick ankles, had thought McAlmon had glanced at them and expressed mock horror.

Adrienne fled to Rocfoin in order to recover from their "triumphant" soirée. On the Easter weekend, Sylvia drove Marie and Paul-Émile Bécat to join the Monniers. The unavoidable topic of discussion was the economic crisis, *le krach américain,* or what Sylvia called "crashing noises all around us." Sylvia had just heard that Holly had had to sell her Pasadena store and take a job as a buyer for two shops. She wrote Holly, in turn, that she and Adrienne, after three and a half years, were for financial reasons forced to sell their car.

In order to secure an inheritance for his family under English law, Joyce moved out of the Square Robiac apartment, stored his furniture, and went to London, leaving Shakespeare and Company as his permanent address. He had planned this move, as previously mentioned, in a letter to Miss Weaver the year before. He wished to establish residency for his marriage to Nora—though he led Sylvia, who opposed the move, to believe that his intention was to save money. Joyce complained to Miss Weaver, "It is useless to discuss my present condition with Miss Beach. As she does not know what my motive is . . . she naturally regards my acts in a wrong light and has no idea of what I have to face in the way of expenses over there." For a different reason, Miss Weaver also opposed his move: she thought he should first go to Zurich for an eye operation.

Joyce lived in England for five months, establishing English domicile for the sake of marriage and inheritance. During that time, he kept Sylvia occupied with requests for royalties, with urgings that she sell her limited editions of *Work in Progress* publications, and with literary business. Miss Weaver carried the burden of providing for the Joyce family. Although he indulged in one more burst of Sullivanizing, attempting unsuccessfully to get the tenor an engagement at Covent Garden, Joyce was generally in a passive mood—tense, brooding, and nervous. Nora disliked their apartment, which was dreary; Lucia behaved strangely; and Joyce drank heavily and spent wildly—he once gave, in the presence of Miss Weaver, a £5 tip to a waiter in Kettner's restaurant. He seemed to court her rejection. Yet he drew up a will leaving her all of his manuscripts and naming her his literary executrix.

At this time, Joyce's work was almost pirated once again. In a letter dated 15 April 1931 from East Cleveland, Ohio, Alexander Buchanan announced to Sylvia that when he had discovered that *Pomes Penyeach* was not copyrighted, he had decided to print 100 copies. Would Mr. Joyce sign one of the copies, he naively asked. Sylvia immediately asked her father to have Princeton University Press publish the small volume of thirteen poems. Two days after receiving the poems from the Reverend Beach, the Princeton press informed her that 50 copies (for a total cost of $27.06) had been printed and two sent to Washington for copyright. She then informed Buchanan that *Pomes Penyeach* was indeed a copyrighted book. If only she could have secured protection for *Ulysses* so easily and rapidly.

The spring of 1931 brought new and old friends to Paris and the bookshop. Ford had returned with a new wife, Janice Biala—Joyce facetiously said he could not remember whether it was his eighth or his eighteenth. McAlmon enjoyed the drinking company of Gorman, before heading for southern France and Germany, where he watched Hitler speak in Munich. Cummings was busy studying Russian and waiting for visa confirmation for a trip to that country. Pound came from Rapallo in June and talked to Sylvia about his plans to have his cantos published. And Hemingway, on his way to Spain for another summer, stopped to give her details about the car accident he had had the preceding fall in Montana. She had been keeping him abreast of Paris gossip and the *crise des affaires* suffered by the writers. Louise Norledge, one of the few English visitors who did not flee when the pound was devalued, joined the library this year and became one of its faithful friends. Making his first short visit to Shakespeare and Company was the twenty-seven-year-old Chicago writer James Farrell, escorted by Putnam. Sylvia was not certain that she liked Farrell, even after the appearance of his first novel, *The Young Manhood of Studs Lonigan,* with its Joycean honesty and stream of consciousness.

She immediately liked the frail and dark, "Japanese looking" woman who joined the library on 20 May. Anaïs Nin, a twenty-eight-year-old French-born American, borrowed Cummings's *Enormous Room.* Her literary inspiration had come not from Cummings but from Lawrence, whose *Lady Chatterley's Lover* had awakened her from a protected life. She had just written a tribute to Lawrence, which she offered to the Black Manikin Press. Though she did not impress Titus—who eventually published it, however, as *D. H. Lawrence: An Unprofessional Study* (1932)—the manuscript won the admiration of a young down-and-out American writer named Henry Miller, who became her lifelong friend.

Fruit from the Joycean tree—in the form of offers to publish *Ulysses* in America—began to fall about Sylvia. Joyce had given the tree a firm shake when he had visited his agent James Pinker in London. He obviously needed money and wanted to take advantage of the potentially large American sales. The first letters came in May with Huebsch's Viking offer—sent to both Sylvia and Joyce— to publish an American edition of *Ulysses.* Voluminous correspondence also began with Lawrence E. Pollinger and Claude Kendall of the Curtis Brown Company, who wished to publish *Ulysses* "as a test case." By July offers to publish *Ulysses* and *Work in Progress* (some from publishers of erotica) had become so numerous that Sylvia frantically had to juggle publishers' inquiries along with regular bookshop business and repeated requests from Joyce to mail his work and royalty payments. She cut short her vacation in Rocfoin in order to pound out dozens of letters on her typewriter.

On 19 May, Adrienne protested in a letter to Joyce that she and Sylvia had been put out long enough. Although Gide may have supposed that Joyce was so dedicated to his work that he never thought of fame and money, she avowed, their experiences had been otherwise: "you are . . . very concerned with success and money." He had importuned them to sell the limited editions of sections of *Work in Progress* and had repeatedly inquired about royalties from *Ulysses.* Angry because she believed that Sylvia's health had been destroyed and both their physical and financial resources strained ("we're travelling now third class"), Adrienne stressed that they could do no more for him than they were already doing. This letter was one she had probably thought of sending already many times before. She had long urged Sylvia to resist his encroachment on her time and energy. Maria Jolas, perhaps not fully aware of the history of occasional tensions between Sylvia and Joyce, blames the jealous "Sapphic heart" of Adrienne, who wished to "rid Sylvia of an importunate suitor." Although Joyce ignored the letter, it undoubtedly excited his sense of persecution. Mary Colum declares that a "deeply wounded" Joyce showed the letter to her. "Joyce was a more sorrowful man after this estrangement." The breach between them widened, but business (most immediately, the publishing offers) loosely maintained their alliance.

Sylvia shared her frustration and concern with few friends, least of all with her family. But she sent a note to Hemingway requesting that he come by for a discussion: "I am anxious to ask your advice about a matter concerning Joyce." Hemingway noted, as had Adrienne, that in all the cables and letters of offers, she was known as Joyce's "representative" in Paris, and that there were no offers for her rights as publisher. Later she claimed that it had not occurred to her that she might be recompensed—"until I realized that it hadn't occurred to anyone else. Then I began to be exasperated at being ignored." So in a letter to Lawrence Pollinger of Curtis Brown, she speaks as Joyce's publisher—the one who has negotiated all his *Ulysses* and *Work in Progress* contracts—and as the one who by contract has "exclusive right of printing and selling" *Ulysses:*

In reply to your letter of the 3rd, if Mr. Joyce is in favour of Ulysses being published in America and he receives an advantageous offer I will not oppose the proposition. . . . If an arrangement were made to publish Ulysses there I would not continue the Paris edition. Of course I am unable to send copies to England and America and the sale is necessarily slow, but it is steady. I pay a 25% royalty to Mr. Joyce on every copy, the price per copy is Frs. 125 or about $5.00, and he makes $5,000 a year from Ulysses. The conditions for securing the American rights would be roughly:

  1. The sum of $25,000. to be paid to Shakespeare and Company upon signing the contract:

  2. At least a 20% royalty to Mr. Joyce:

  3. $5,000. in advance royalties to be paid to Mr. Joyce upon signing the contract.

The request for $25,000, which she thought showed the worth of *Ulysses,* was from Pollinger's perspective an extravagant amount. His response on 25 June— "I understand you control the English language rights in this book"—suggests he had not been informed of the contract by Joyce or his agent James Pinker. Pollinger offered a $1,000 advance, 10 percent on signing, and 15 percent if Joyce would write a preface. On 9 July the offer was raised to a $5,000 advance (her original request), but it made no mention of payment to her.

On 4 July—the birthday of Joyce's father—Nora Barnacle and James Joyce legalized their marriage at Kensington Registry Office in London, an event caught by reporters for the front pages of several newspapers. Joyce, Sylvia believed, "thoroughly enjoyed the scandal" created by the press. She repeated his fabricated story that he had already married in Trieste, but that in order to legalize his will he had had to get married under English law. Just as Joyce had insisted on a contract for *Ulysses* with Sylvia when their personal bond and trust was dissolving, so Joyce was now legalizing a marriage when its physical ties were weakening.

On the day of the Joyce marriage, Sylvia left for what was to be an aborted vacation at Rocfoin (they could not afford the trip to Les Déserts). Before leaving—she took her typewriter with her, because she was working on a translation of Valéry's ''Littérature''—she dispatched a letter to Pinker in London: the Pollinger offer is too small for Joyce, she asserts, adding, ''Will you kindly take note of the fact that I have a contract with Mr. Joyce for *Ulysses*.'' Because she believed that an American edition would stop her own publication, she expected any offer to include the $25,000 that she had mentioned earlier. ''Considering that much time, expense and influence have been used in developing the sales during all these years, this is a modest estimate of the value that *Ulysses* represents to me.'' To her sister Holly she confides, ''It must be because of my sex that they think I wouldn't charge them anything.'' By the end of the month, Curtis Brown had decided to withdraw the offer because of the ''absurd'' demand by Miss Beach: ''She is apparently treating our offer, not seriously, but angrily, as if we were trying to take the book *away* from her.'' She was preparing, in fact, to say good-bye to *Ulysses*.

A further complication for Curtis Brown—and for Sylvia—was the appearance of a pirated *Ulysses* in New York, another example of diabolical timing by their old nemesis Samuel Roth. In mid-June, Sylvia received the unhappy news from Boski Antheil, who had been to the Gotham Book Mart and had there learned that ''10,000 bogus copies'' were circulating. Because Frances Steloff wanted to stay out of the controversy, Sylvia asked Holly to check at the Gotham for a copy of the pirated book. But it was the Reverend Beach who purchased the book for $6.50 and mailed it to Sylvia. ''It is rather a peculiar position for you, a clergyman, isn't it?'' Sylvia chuckled.

While continuing her correspondence from Rocfoin, Sylvia dreamed of a longer rest. ''I would like to live in the country entirely, and raise rabbits and chickens, and ride a bicycle to the nearest village whenever [I] need a few provisions,'' she fantasizes to Holly. ''And I am beginning to get the hang of mowing and don't hold the scythe quite so badly as I did at first, and would like to work in the fields very much.'' Before she exchanged her scythe for her Remington, she and Adrienne spent a week at the seaside with Carlotta, Jim, and the two-year-old Jimmy Briggs. The sea baths with the Briggs and the fresh vegetables at Rocfoin were an antidote for Sylvia's headaches. She soon converted Harriet Weaver to a nutritious diet of raw vegetables, which Joyce declared ''were created by the Lord (only) to be thrown at Covent Garden tenors.''

Adrienne's letter had done nothing to slow the stream of the Joyce business. His letters concerning the U.S. publication of *Ulysses* and Roth's piracy and his requests for royalties only increased in frequency. While Adrienne pressured Sylvia to resist, the Joyce family claimed that they were not getting their due from Sylvia. Certainly, they thought, she was making a great deal of money from *Ulysses*. By July they were inundated with offers for the publication of *Work in Progress,* which Joyce had decided to sell at a time when he was least inclined to finish it (he wrote virtually nothing on it in 1931). "About a dozen publishers have been cabling and writing" for the unfinished novel, Sylvia confides to Holly. "It shows that he occupies the biggest place now among living writers." T. S. Eliot for Faber and Faber, Heubsch for Viking, and Harper made offers. Despite her option to publish the book—and because "it would be to his advantage to have a big publishing house handle" it—she cabled him: "advise you accept best offer." He signed with Viking, adding a clause providing that if Huebsch left for another firm, he had the option of taking the contract with him. For the English rights, he received a £150 advance from Faber and Faber.

Another legal problem pestered Sylvia when Joyce became excited by the thought of another bout of litigation and sounded the battle cry for her (and nearly a dozen others). A German newspaper, the *Frankfurter Zeitung,* had published a crime story by Michael Joyce, but mistakenly attributed it to James Joyce. Even after the author, the translator (who was responsible for the mistake), the editor, and a published editorial had explained the error, Joyce pressed for an elaborate apology and damages. He reluctantly gave up the pursuit when German and English lawyers warned him that public opinion would be outraged by such a trivial matter. By this time Joyce had paid a large legal fee and Sylvia had spent hours, on top of her regular bookshop business, typing letters and recruiting support for the cause (Joyce himself sent thirty-six letters and eleven telegrams). With Myrsine gone, Sylvia's August days ran from 8 A.M. to 7 P.M., and still, she complains, she "cannot get through with the work there is to do." When Thornton Wilder came through Paris this month, they invited him to dinner to discuss the *Zeitung* controversy as well as his six plays soon to open in the United States. Although they enjoyed entertaining the August visitors, Sylvia and Adrienne could completely forget their cares for a few hours only at the movies. Although Adrienne had trouble understanding American talkies, which were very popular in France, they enjoyed Eddie Cantor in *Whoopee* and Greta Garbo in *Anna Christie.*

Sylvia cut all unnecessary expenses, sold their car, and canceled their Les Déserts vacation, and yet she had financial difficulties. The exit of American and English customers (the pound fell by one-fifth) slowed the lending library noticeably. She lowered the library rental rates. Only the sale of a few books, particularly *Ulysses,* gave her the margin to pay utilities, her modest rent, and the Joyce royalties (and advances). Her personal expenses, as always, were meager. Most of the fruit, vegetables, and fowl that they ate was raised at Rocfoin.

Early in September 1931 Sylvia dismissed Myrsine "for economic and for other reasons." After a decade of daily work and friendship, Sylvia could not afford to pay the full-time salary. She would pay the unemployed husband of the concierge across the street to run a few errands. But she feared that when Joyce returned from his vacation she would have to hire a full-time errand runner.

Sylvia had for some time been unhappy with Myrsine's deceit about her absences, concerned that the subscribers' cards and books were not kept in order, and annoyed with the "endless visits" from Myrsine's friends. Despite her relief at being rid of these small annoyances, Sylvia felt the loss for herself and for the bookshop when Myrsine left.

On his way from Spain back to the United States, where Pauline would give birth to their second son, Hemingway stopped for two weeks in Paris. He had been working on his bullfight book, *Death in the Afternoon,* and seemed to have no worries. Unlike Sylvia and the other literary friends in Paris, he had no money problems. He talked to Sylvia at length about the piracy of *Ulysses,* promising (though nothing came of the promise) to help the woman who had once helped him. His lawyer, he assured her, was an expert in literary matters and accustomed to not charging writers. With a promise and a kiss, he sailed to America with his family. "I felt sorry to see them go off again," confided Sylvia to her father.

On 29 September at Shakespeare and Company, Sylvia and Joyce held a "council of war" concerning Roth. Joyce had just returned from London, where he had sublet his apartment (expecting to return, though he did not, in the spring of 1932) and had received a stern parting lecture from Miss Weaver on the need for temperance. His immediate concern—Sylvia describes him as "terribly upset"—was the pirated edition of *Ulysses.* If Roth had indeed printed 10,000 copies, publication in the United States would be jeopardized. The copy of the pirated edition, which soon arrived from Sylvester Beach, bore no Roth markings. The title and copyright pages were exact reproductions of Sylvia's *Ulysses* IX (May 1927). The cover was imitated, but the pages were yellower and thicker. Joyce told his London agent that Sylvia did not wish to inform American publishers who were interested in buying *Ulysses* about the pirated edition, because publishers would then "conclude they had the knife at her throat."

The only way to stop further piracy, Sylvia and Joyce agreed during a long discussion in the shop this fall, was to sell *Ulysses* to an American publisher with worldwide distribution. Both Huebsch and Soupault, the latter recently returned from a lecture tour in the United States, assured them that the climate in America was ready for the legal acceptance of *Ulysses.* Though they did not agree on Sylvia's fee, Joyce himself neither encouraged nor discouraged her with the publishers. He was hoping, he confided to Harriet Weaver, that Pinker would come to Paris to convince Sylvia to revise her contract and accept £1,500 instead of £5,000 for the American rights. He also wrote to Pinker asking him to find a publisher who would pay Sylvia what she wanted for *Ulysses.*

Relinquishing *Work in Progress* had been a sensible and relatively easy task for Sylvia. She could not give him an advance. He had worldwide fame now— a fame she had helped him gain—and only a large publishing house could distribute a sufficient number of copies to all the countries that would want the book. But it was "not the same case for Ulysses," she asserted. She was already the publisher of *Ulysses.* And she stood to lose what she believed to be the only source of profit for her bookshop. Also, she had (at the instigation of Joyce) a contract stating that "the right to publish said work shall be purchased from the Publisher at the price set by herself." Finally, and perhaps most convincing to her in her pursuit of her rights, she had the encouragement of Adrienne and other friends. Her family, who had now been taken into her confidence, agreed that it would be "unjust" if she were not paid. Harriet Weaver also assured her that she deserved to have "men publishers recognise your rights and position as first (and most courageous and enterprising and hardworking) publisher. . . . And I hope they will see this and make a really substantial offer so that a working arrangement can be come to as soon as possible." Later Sylvia admits, in an unpublished draft of her memoirs, that "it was perhaps more the advice of my friends who urged me to assert those claims, than my own convictions on the subject of *Ulysses* proprietorship that influenced my behavior."

Huebsch suggested that Sylvia might be willing to take a portion of the royalty on copies sold. "I waited for Joyce to speak up," she later recalls, "but he never did." In another suppressed version of her memoirs, she says that Joyce would not consent to a reduction in his royalties. He felt no financial obligation to Sylvia. "No doubt he was right," she states with humble resentment. Sylvia and Adrienne (who refused to see Joyce) busied themselves by participating in the lives of their French friends. Joyce, who believed they were both avoiding him, sent his son to a French lawyer to have the contract interpreted. George reported that Joyce could demand 25 percent of what she received in any form.

Sylvia relieved the tension that had developed between them when she told Joyce in the bookshop on 19 October that she had considered reducing the amount of her request. Joyce immediately informed Pinker that she had accepted the inevitable and had asked him "to write to you to know what is the best counter offer an American house will give, the offer to be in French money." While she awaited the result, the relations between Joyce and the rue de l'Odéon remained cordial and businesslike. Léon-Paul Fargue arrived one day as Sylvia was giving Joyce a large box of cigars. She had just lost a bet that Sullivan had run off to South America with his mistress. Adrienne arranged a dinner party for a dozen people at the end of November, so that they and Joyce could listen to a special BBC broadcast on Joyce by Harold Nicolson. They gathered around the Bécat radio, only to hear Sir Harold announce that he had been forbidden to give his lecture. After surprised exclamations, then laughter, they went to the table and had what Sylvia calls a "merry meal." The talk was finally given three weeks later, when the ban was lifted, and they all sent Sir Harold a congratulatory telegram. "Everything seems now to be well disposed" around the Odéon, Joyce confided to Miss Weaver. "It is strange that my presence has this effect and my absence produces a violent reaction." Certainly Joyce's cultivated politeness and what Marianne Moore calls Sylvia's "unfailing delicacy" allowed business to proceed without an open breach this fall.

Huebsch informed Joyce that anyone was legally free to publish *Ulysses* (that is to say, his injunction against Roth was worth nothing); that Joyce should purchase the rights from Sylvia; and that Viking would pay £200 in advance of 10 percent royalties. Pinker advised Joyce and Sylvia to accept the offer and counsel of Huebsch. Sylvia, at the request of Joyce (who believed the offer was far too low), informed Pinker that he should break off the Huebsch-Viking negotiations.

A week later she met in the bookshop in order to plan further anti-Roth strategy with Adrienne, Léon, Soupault, and Joyce. Soupault, who was returning to the United States, was to enlist the French consul general's support in order to fight against Roth's counterfeiting of a French printer's product. Sylvia even persuaded Darantière to write to the U.S. ambassador to France. Despite these efforts, Joyce was becoming increasingly frustrated by the "firstrate . . . bungling" by Pinker, his agent; by a letter he had received from Conner, his lawyer, who called him a swindler; and by Huebsch's offer, which Eliot agreed was "ludicrous." The trouble with Conner began when the lawyer asked for the $2,000 balance due him on Joyce's case against Roth. When Conner asked Joyce for the money, Joyce claimed that he did not believe he was the owner of *Ulysses* when it was published. He implied that Sylvia should pay the lawyer's fee. But when she insisted that he had known he was the owner until their contract, and when another lawyer agreed with her, Joyce accepted his responsibility for the Conner bill.

Soon he concluded that the major obstacle to a speedy settlement of the business surrounding *Ulysses,* particularly to the sale of *Ulysses* to a U.S. publisher, was Sylvia's unwillingness to give up all claims to her publishing rights. In an unpublished letter to Harriet Weaver, Joyce refers disparagingly and accusingly to the increasing influence of Sylvia's "more intelligent partner," their lesbian relationship, Eleanor Beach's suicide, Cyprian's poor mental health, and Sylvia's migraines.

Sylvia had not seen Joyce in a few weeks, and there seemed to be no more correspondence about an American *Ulysses.* But she was visited nearly every day by Padraic Colum, who pursued the problem in his conversation. What she did not know was that Joyce was carrying on the negotiations without her knowledge. "I never saw such a man for secret maneuverings," she notes in a suppressed portion of her memoirs. "It seemed only a harmless little amusement when I was aware of his manipulations of others, but when I began to get some of it myself, I didn't find it so funny." Joyce had begun serious negotiations with an American publisher and had recruited Colum for a special assignment. Each day Colum came from the Joyce apartment to Shakespeare and Company to talk of the need for an American edition. In a suppressed section of her memoirs, she recalls in detail their last conversation, in which he, in his Irish brogue, urged her to relinquish her selfish claims.

"What right do ya have to *Ulysses?*" he insisted.

"But what about my contract? Is that imaginary?" she asked in exasperation.

"There's no real contract. It doesn't exist, your contract," Padraic replied.

Angry at his interference as well as at Joyce, who she thought was "hiding behind a friend," she showed him her contract. Then he blurted out the true message:

"You are standing in Joyce's way!"

She was flabbergasted. When she had recovered and Colum had left, she called Joyce in anger and released all claims to *Ulysses*.

CHAPTER 15

In the Wake
1932–1933

Bring out number, weight and measure in a year of dearth . . .
— William Blake

O what the grief of my mund be . . .
—*Finnegans Wake*

TEN YEARS, almost to the day, after Sylvia had handed Joyce his first printed copy of *Ulysses,* she resigned as his publisher, giving him full custody of the book. Both the copy and her resignation were birthday gifts—the first for his fortieth, the second for his fiftieth. Another significant gift in this year came from another American: Helen Kastor, his daughter-in-law, gave birth to his first and only grandchild, Stephen James Joyce.

These events were almost overshadowed by his grief and guilt over the death of his eighty-two-year-old father, on 29 December 1931, and the mental collapse of Lucia four weeks later. His father's death left him with no heart for writing. "I am thinking of abandoning work altogether," he divulged to Miss Weaver. He was maudlin and full of "self-accusation and prostration of mind." He rationalized to Pound, Eliot, Weaver, and other friends that he had not been able to return to Ireland at the request of the old man, for fear that physical harm would come from his enemies. But the birth of his grandson on 15 February gave him some solace and the sense of a replacement for the life lost. He was torn between "joy and grief," he confesses in a poem sent to Eliot for publication: "A child is sleeping; / An old man gone."

A greater and more prolonged grief, one that Sylvia and a few other friends had anticipated, was the mental breakdown of Lucia. This grief would preoccupy him until his death. On the morning of his birthday, Lucia lifted a chair in the air and flung it at her mother, whom she accused of breaking off her relationship with Beckett. Missing Nora, the chair shattered—and with it all family peace.

The years 1932 and 1933 were among the darkest for Joyce as well as for Sylvia. They marked the lowest point thus far in Joyce's life: he suffered a number of physical collapses; used sleeping pills immoderately; squandered hundreds of pounds of his Weaver capital while awaiting the U.S. court settlement on *Ulysses;* wrote only one section of *Work in Progress;* and fought the doctors' opinions concerning Lucia's insanity by keeping her with him—a decision that brought pain and harassment into his daily existence. Though shorter in duration, the lowest point in Sylvia's life (apart from the year of her mother's death) came during the winter of 1931, when, betrayed by Joyce, as she felt, she feared losing her shop along with *Ulysses.* She lived continually with migraine headaches until the winter of 1932, when the current of her life, unlike Joyce's, seemed to change toward a slower pace and warmer relationships with family and friends.

During these two years, Joyce was estranged from both Harriet Weaver and Sylvia. His relations with Sylvia were characterized alternately by strain and cordiality. She amicably called him on the telephone before his birthday (probably before the Colum incident), eager to plan what he called his "jubilee," and offered to cancel a brief vacation trip if he responded positively (he was, he explained, "too dejected to make a reply"). He was, however, in quiet contact with Random House concerning the American publication of *Ulysses.* Even after she learned, weeks later, of the negotiations, she welcomed him cordially, collected his reviews, and sent all correspondence to him. He in turn was very courteous and expansive. On the tenth anniversary of *Ulysses,* he sent her ten white lilac branches with a large blue bow for the *Ulysses* colors and a magnificent pair of forged-iron deer.

However, the underlying resentment that Sylvia and Joyce felt toward each other had a way of emerging at moments in the form of irritating trifles. During one of his visits to the bookshop, she accidentally knocked to the floor some reviews of his work. When she did not pick them up, he imagined she was challenging him to do so. He proudly ignored them and reported the incident to Miss Weaver. On more than one occasion, according to a shop assistant who was unaware of the cooling of their friendship, he placed his wet umbrella across the books on her table.

At the same time, Joyce challenged Harriet Weaver with displays of extravagant spending. When she conveyed another reprimand from the solicitors that his divestment of the principal "could not go on," he sent her a list of his essential expenditures and, with annoyance, informed her that she had spoiled his "jubilee" birthday. Typically contrite and apologetic—and blaming herself for their strained relations—she responded by annulling his indebtedness on all his outstanding loans as a birthday gift. His feelings of guilt for not having returned to his dying father and for the breakdown of Lucia, together with some sense of responsibility for the estrangement from his two long-suffering and faithful angels, made 1932 and 1933 miserable years for Joyce.

The early months of 1932 mark the beginning of the ascendancy of Paul Léon in Joyce's affairs. The first sign of his official role as secretary and agent (Joyce called him "my lawyer in Paris") was an 8 February letter to Sylvia, in which he acknowledges the receipt of the "annulment on your part of the contract existing between you and Mr. Joyce and the recognition by you of his ownership of the rights of *Ulysses.*'' His second was to ask Sylvia whether she would publish a new edition (the twelfth) of *Ulysses,* which she agreed to do, on condition that the costs of 60,000 francs be prepaid. His morning errands occasionally brought him to the bookstore on the business that was gradually making him (in the words of his wife) ''Joyce's alter ego and guardian in practical details of life.'' What she does not reveal is that within a year this relationship also became strained and weakened by distrust.

Alliances had now shifted. Among the early friends, Pound was unenthusiastic about and Lewis openly critical of Joyce's new work. Larbaud, too ill to assist him, also lacked enthusiasm for it. Joyce had courted Harriet Weaver's disapproval and forced Sylvia's resignation. According to a pattern evident throughout his life, these first Paris friendships were darkened by friction, poor judgment, and misunderstandings. Of his new friends, Stuart Gilbert, Louis Gillet, and Eugene Jolas certainly understood and applauded his innovation. Léon, who still had not read his work, served him out of admiration for his mind and reputation as well as out of compassionate recognition that Joyce needed help after Sylvia resigned.

Sylvia's emotional response to the break with Joyce was contradictory, as was her treatment of him, which was by turns affectionate and reproachful. Joyce was like a lover in whom she had invested nearly twelve of her best years. She never wavered in her support of his work, tried occasionally to recapture their comradeship, and never betrayed him publicly. There is no recrimination in her memoirs, written long after his death. The flowers of friendship fade, she admits, ''but enmity fades faster I have noticed.'' Privately, she occasionally expressed anger and a sense of betrayal. What had happened to her was—in a Joycean phrase from *Work in Progress*—''truly deplurable.'' In letters to her family, she vacillated between blaming the Roth piracy for her loss and resenting Joyce for letting her ''drop'' or throwing her ''overboard.'' In early drafts of her memoirs, suppressed before publication, she calls it an ''injustice'' that a work she ''had been nursing at least as many years as Joyce had spent in writing it,'' should be taken from her without compensation—a complaint that ironically echoes Joyce's repeated cries of thievery against Roth and other pirates. About Joyce personally, she adds, ''I saw him in another light after this, not only as a very great writer but also as a great business man, hard as nails.'' And in other drafts she calls him ''the great lovable but merciless man'' whose ''one-sided business methods are the least admirable side of the Joycean character . . . cold and determined.'' To Holly, who had pressed her for an opinion, she confides, ''It's all bumps when you're working with him. I prefer peace and being with people who have some human sense of the existence of others.'' She adds, in her harshest judgment of Joyce, ''He thinks, like Napoleon, that his fellow beings are only made to serve his ends. He'd grind their bones to make his bread.'' But she suppressed all these statements—as if in the mere writing of them she had satisfied her sense of justice. Instead she told the world, in a note reminiscent of Harriet Weaver's self-recrimination, ''As for my personal feelings, well, one is not at all proud of them, and they should be promptly dumped when they no longer serve a purpose.

. . . And, after all, the books were Joyce's. A baby belongs to its mother, not to the midwife, doesn't it?'' In a penciled-in addition to an unpublished draft of her memoirs, she confesses, ''it was the right thing to do but it did cost me pain.''

The response of Joyce was less mixed: *Ulysses* was his creation, and it had brought her increased business for a decade; he was in debt and had a right to all the money he could get. To his collection of injustices recorded in *Work in Progress,* Joyce added: ''The black and blue marks athwart the weald, which now barely is so stripped, indicate the presence of Sylvious beltings.'' Mary Colum blamed their friends: ''There were always a few people who tried to make a breach between them.'' Léon believed Adrienne was behind the contract demands. The Joyce family suggested that the fault was Sylvia's. Unaware of the expense of paying for the printer, postage, publicity, and overhead for handling copies, they were certain that Sylvia had made a great deal of profit, which the Joyce household should have received. When Joyce repeatedly asked the Colums whether he was right or wrong, they claimed later, they could never bring themselves to say he was right, for ''separation'' from his ''greatest helper'' was a ''tragic one.'' Though his question suggests self-doubt, he appeared never to waver from his single-minded determination to present his work to the world and to force the world to read it. He had what Eliot eleven years before had termed ''the true fanatic's conviction that every one ought to forward the interests of his work.'' Joyce's aggressiveness, Eliot adds, is ''not the artfulness or pertinacity of ordinary push'' but the ''conviction of the fanatic.'' He was what Gorman called ''that high type of literary artist who is thoroughly selfish and inwardly gazing at all times.''

Malcolm Cowley, in discussing the relation between ethics and literary life, has recently denied Faulkner's claims that amorality is justified in the case of artists (''If a writer has to rob his mother, he will not hesitate; the *Ode on a Grecian Urn* is worth any number of old ladies''). Cowley counters that ''no complete son-of-a-bitch ever wrote a good sentence.'' Supposing that Cowley's belief is true, that such a close relation between character and art exists, many geniuses with moral failings, such as Hemingway and Frost, have been pardoned by posterity because, for all the failings, the best parts of their natures found expression in their works.

The harshest judgment of Joyce has in recent years come from Leon Edel, who criticizes

Joyce's way—I suppose by the combination of helplessness and mockery—of commanding always a circle of friends hypnotized by his virtuosity and prepared to immolate themselves on his altar. They received scant thanks for their pains, and are immortalized in the puns of *Finnegan.* Joyce wrote not for literature but for personal revenge. His motivations are confused, but there is something heroic in his ideal and in his sense of myth. He belongs to the witchcraft of words. He was Faust, but he thought of himself as Jesus—and Judas was everywhere.

Though Edel's judgment is accurate, it must to a small extent be qualified, for both Sylvia and Harriet Weaver received more than ''scant thanks.'' Joyce gave all his manuscripts to these two women. In an unpublished letter written in March of this year, Joyce confesses to Miss Weaver that he feels "personally unworthy" of her "munificence" and of his wife's "constant devotion." He adds, with less honesty or insight, that he does feel worthy of the friendship of Sylvia and Adrienne because he never, so far as he knows, "betrayed their friendship." Several years later, in defending Sylvia against a friend of his who was belittling her, he reveals more awareness: "All she ever did was to make me a present of the best ten years of her life."

Harriet Weaver came to Paris in the beginning of March to smooth her ruffled relations with Joyce and to discuss a regular English edition of *Ulysses*. She and Sylvia, who had long shared a concern for the Joyce family, discussed Lucia, whose condition had taken a turn for the better, and her recent engagement to Alex Ponisovsky—a sort of European-family settlement conceived, arranged, and nurtured by Joyce and Léon, the brother-in-law of Ponisovsky. The plans had to be called off when Lucia became catatonic following her formal engagement party and was hospitalized and diagnosed as having "hebephrenic psychosis," a form of schizophrenia characterized by bizarre adolescent behavior. On the matter of Sylvia's generous relinquishing of *Ulysses*, there was no agreement between Harriet and Sylvia. Although Miss Weaver had encouraged Sylvia's hopes for a publisher's settlement, she appeared not to sympathize with Sylvia's grievance. Miss Weaver, who lived a simple life but never had to face bankruptcy or starvation, placed first, as always, the best interests of Joyce. She herself had sacrificed for Joyce; Sylvia should do the same.

What no one told Sylvia, who continued to make plans for *Ulysses* XII, was that Random House had in February offered Joyce $2,500 ($1,000 at signing, $1,500 at publication) and a 15 percent royalty, assuming all the risks of a court battle, in order to publish *Ulysses* unexpurgated. Negotiations had begun in December of 1931 between Bennett Cerf and his friend Robert Kastor, the forty-year-old brother of Helen Joyce. Joyce had known that the offer was coming in when he had sent Colum to Sylvia. Joyce signed the contract with Cerf on the last day of March, and the publisher then hired the noted civil-liberties lawyer Morris Ernst to take their case to court—promising a lifetime royalty from the book if he won. Two days later, on 2 April, Léon informed Sylvia of the signing. On that very day Joyce wrote to Cerf the letter that would serve as the author's preface, in which he sums up Sylvia's contribution: "My friend Mr. Ezra Pound and good luck brought me into contact with a very clever and energetic person Miss Sylvia Beach. . . . This brave woman risked what professional publishers did not wish to, she took the manuscript and handed it to the printers." His two verbs—*took* and *handed*—describe with enormous understatement her efforts in the publishing of *Ulysses*.

Joyce soon paid her an official visit and, against the advice of Paul Léon and George Joyce, informed her and Adrienne about the terms of the contract. They both "expressed satisfaction," he confides to Stuart Gilbert in an unpublished letter: "The interview was perfectly friendly but it has cost me an entire winter to preserve that friendship. . . . The whole affair stumps me." The letter establishes that George and Léon were probably Sylvia's chief antagonists and that Joyce believed he had acted diplomatically and within his right.

Sylvia immediately assumed she would drop her plans for *Ulysses* XII when she heard that Random House planned a small $2.50 edition for a court case and a $1.00 Modern Library edition when the case was won; she worried also about the remainder of her *Ulysses* XI (which cost $5.00). She need not have worried. They settled on the importation and seizure of a Shakespeare and Company edition, and the Modern Library edition did not appear for two more years, long after she had sold out her eleventh edition. After she read Joyce's preface letter to Cerf during this April meeting, she wrote to Holly that Joyce "has written a preface to the new edition connecting me up with Ezra Pound [now a self-appointed defender of Fascist Italy] in the first publishing of *Ulysses*. So as you might say, he has not only robbed me but 'taken away my character.' "

With the loss of rights to *Ulysses,* Sylvia's financial boom-and-bust cycle ground to a halt. With each new edition of *Ulysses,* she had been flush, able to pay Darantière, errand girls, and even a small percentage of her own expenses. When the Joyce royalties on each edition had been paid in full, however, the Joyce expenses always continued—postage, paper, legal fees, medical expenses, gift copies, telephone calls, taxis. "Advances" for family expenses usually meant eating up whatever publisher's profit there was. Business expenses usually came from bookshop profits. Then, with each new edition, Sylvia thought she was catching up. When her business on Joyce's behalf ended in 1932, her bookkeeping grew simplified. Out of habit, she continued to watch her cashbox, but her fears that it would become empty were, now that Joyce had gone, groundless.

Sylvia made a concerted effort early in the year to secure new library subscriptions. In December two events gave her excellent publicity with American tourists: kind words by Max Eastman in an article in *Harper's* and Holly's successful submission of her name to *Vanity Fair*'s hall of fame. By March she was able to increase her monthly income. Several of the Joyce circle became library members, including Peter Neagoe, Louis Gillet, and Maria Jolas, who purchased a two-volume Montessori for the private school she planned to open outside Paris. Other short-term visitors included Ludwig Lewisohn, Sinclair Lewis, Dwight Macdonald, and the Antheils, who returned to France because George had a Guggenheim Fellowship to write an opera with John Erskine. This new business in the spring gave Sylvia the confidence necessary to paint the interior of her shop a "nice new cigar brown" and to hire another assistant. Though she suffered emotionally, she appeared in a small way to profit financially by the loss of her Joyce responsibility.

On the recommendation of the longtime library member Marie Bruneton, Sylvia hired a young American woman named Jean Henley to work half-days. Jean, who had attended Vassar and who later practiced medicine in New York City, was studying sculpture in Paris and had lived at the student hostel run by Bruneton and Mary Dixon. She became a salesgirl and general helper for Sylvia, who described her to Holly as "a large, fine looking German girl, very anxious to help me all she can, and not deceitful . . . she is intelligent in the college girl way, though knowing nothing of books, and seems rather too susceptible falling in love. . ." Because of her disappointment in Myrsine and more likely because of her depression over the breach with Joyce, Sylvia kept to herself and did not cultivate the friendship of Jean Henley. Though unaware of the complicated Joyce affair, Henley knew that Sylvia was depressed and subject to many migraines—in short, a woman in pain.

The headaches were persistent during this year. Sylvia's letters to Holly reveal that she tried (unsuccessfully) several specialists; temporarily gave up smoking, coffee, tea, and sweets; took massage treatments, pills, and injections; and went on a milk diet. In May, when a doctor recommended by her friend the composer Darius Milhaud took her off all dairy products, she thought she was better. She could find only temporary relief. The origin of the headaches was undoubtedly physiological—they had begun in her preteen years. Stress—and she was a high-strung personality—triggered the pain. Katherine Anne Porter, whom Sylvia met this year, describes Sylvia as "a thin, twiggy sort of woman, quick-tongued, quick-minded and light on her feet. Her nerves were as tight as a tuned-up fiddle string and she had now and then attacks of migraine that stopped her in her tracks."

When Sylvia was a captive of her pain, she remained upstairs, fully dressed in her workroom. When Jean Henley had a question, she walked up the wide, dark stairway and hall to the eighteenth-century apartment, where she found Sylvia working on her books or correspondence. She had several family problems this year: the death of the father of Fred Dennis, an eye operation for the Reverend Beach (details of which she discussed with Joyce), and her cousin's runaway wife (who soon came to Paris with her lesbian lover). Her family kept her informed of American book interests, the Lindbergh kidnapping, and news of kin. But her French family was the center of her private world: life with Adrienne and Sundays at Rocfoin with the Monniers. For some time Sylvia had been assisting Adrienne—who called 1931 her "year of confinement"—in preparing for publication the latter's *Catalogue Critique de la Bibliothèque de Prêt* (the first part of a critical catalog of her library). In its preface, which is a "statement of faith in her vocation," Adrienne testifies that she would not have been able to publish it without the aid of Sylvia. Adrienne also published in this year *Fableaux (Fables)*, a collection of her prose pieces, most of which, according to her translator, "draw their inspiration from the life of Les Déserts, her mother's native commune in Savoy, and reproduce the direct, robust speech of the country people."

Joyce wanted Sylvia to publish *Ulysses* XII—a cheap Continental edition to keep the novel available and the cash flowing until the Random House edition was printed. Although he had received the $1,000 advance when he had signed the contract, it was soon gone and Joyce feared that the court process might delay U.S. publication for some time. Two London firms, contacted by Joyce and Miss Weaver, had failed to make an offer: Cape would print only an expurgated edition; Faber and Faber was afraid of the legal consequences of publishing an unexpurgated one. Léon hinted in letters to Sylvia of March and April that the Random House edition would be a long time in coming and that, in the meantime, she could exercise her rights to a Continental edition. She went as far as to ask Darantière for the prices, then decided against publication for three reasons: it was too costly and Joyce would not advance the printing costs; she believed that the Random House edition was imminent and would wipe her out; and she wished no more Joyce business, which she discovered she could survive without. In response to Léon's persistent hints, Adrienne informed him on 14 April that *Ulysses* was now in the hands of Random House. Joyce, who waited several weeks to broach the subject again, called her to discuss the issue. He found out that she was truly uninterested; that she planned to turn over to him her files on *Ulysses;* and that if another publisher wanted to buy her plates, she would sell them for what she had paid Darantière for them. Later, when representatives of the Albatross Press dropped in, she suggested they see Joyce about a Continental edition. She wanted the *Ulysses* business to be out of her life—a life now centered only on her bookshop, lending library, and Adrienne.

As a part of their full social life, Sylvia and Adrienne gave a dinner party this May for Jean Schlumberger, who had just received English (Northcliffe) and French (Femina) prizes for his novel *Saint-Saturnin*. Among the guests was Desmond Harmsworth, a customer of Shakespeare and Company in the early years, who was just starting a little publishing company at the same time that most of the others were closing down: Titus's Black Manikin Press, Stein's Plain Editions, Putnam's New Review Press, and Shakespeare and Company's Joyce enterprise. The small magazines did not fare much better. The distinguished *Commerce,* for which Sylvia had been a consultant, expired this winter, after eight years of publication. Even *Poetry* in the United States was threatened for a time with extinction. A Carnegie grant eventually saved it, but until that help came, Sylvia kept a large handwritten sign posted in her shop pleading for fifty-cent donations on behalf of the magazine. *This Quarter* persisted to the end of the year, helping to keep alive a threadbare Beckett (who had become reunited with Joyce this July) by paying him translation fees for a fall Surrealist number. Of the well-known little magazines based in Paris, only *Transition* survived, in a new biannual, capital T version honoring Joyce on his fiftieth birthday and mocking Goethe on his centennial.

When doctors said that Lucia should stay in isolation, away from her parents, and could offer no specific treatment, Joyce planned to take her to Maria Jolas in Feldkirch and go to see Dr. Vogt in nearby Zurich for treatment of his eye. Jane Lidderdale and Mary Nicholson characterize well Joyce's obsession with Lucia: "he saw her as a genius in his own image, distorted and frustrated by a world that conspired against his genius too. He felt very close to her because they were both victims; and then despaired because she was also his victim, sacrificed to his work and to his wanderings." Ellmann adds, "He had always before put his writing beyond all other considerations; now, as an expression of guilt, he put his daughter's health beyond his art, and punished himself for past obtuseness by writing hardly at all and by devoting his thoughts frantically and impotently to his daughter." In 1934 Carl Jung, her twentieth doctor, concluded that she was Joyce's "own Anima" and that "they were like two people going to the bottom of a river, one falling and the other diving."

Before leaving for Austria with Lucia, Joyce came to Shakespeare and Company to discuss his royalties from *Ulysses* XI, recent Japanese piracies of *Ulysses,* and his need for a Continental edition. He confided in Harriet Weaver that he had been intimidated by her "negative" attitude and by the presence of Jean Henley—a "footballing female" he would "not care to encounter on a dark road at night." Sylvia asked whether she might settle payment of his royalties for *Ulysses* XI after her holiday. Though he was feeling the personal and financial loss of her daily services, he agreed to a delay in payment until after the few remaining copies were sold. When he asked whether she would publish a twelfth edition, she again answered no. Yet through July—due perhaps to false rumors—he was still not convinced that she was finished with him, and feared that if he found a publisher for the twelfth edition, she would be angry. But despite his suppositions, she had made up her mind to have nothing more to do with *Ulysses.*

On Bastille Day, 14 July, while revelers were dancing in the streets, Sylvia and Adrienne left Paris for Les Déserts. Because of Sylvia's bout with pneumonia in 1930 and the financial crisis of 1931, they had not been able to visit their mountain for three years. Heavy rains notwithstanding, Sylvia went for long walks in thick trousers, boots, and a rubber cape, while Adrienne prepared the printer's copy for her catalog. With only Adrienne's knowledge, Sylvia made a $40 down payment (1,000 francs) on a small chalet—the only property she ever owned. Unknown to Joyce, she had briefly borrowed from his last royalties to invest in her future happiness.

The concern of most people in the literary world was how to make enough money to survive. Adrienne was banking on her catalog; Sylvia had her own plans. When Holly sent an article on the Olympic Games that she had written for the *Los Angeles Times,* Sylvia replied, "I would like very much to make a little something extra on the side if I could write in my spare minutes." But, she concludes, she lacks Holly's "power of synthesis" and gets lost in details. Sylvia was, in fact, writing a piece about why she loved France for the October issue of *Bravo: Arts, Lettres, Spectacles.* But her strength lay in translating. She completed this fall her English rendition of "Littérature," an essay by Valéry, which begins, "A poem must be a holiday of the mind." The original French version had appeared in *Commerce* and was afterward reprinted in two deluxe editions. The translation was undertaken after an English journal had asked Valéry for a sample of his work for a special number featuring French authors. He had come to the bookshop wanting to know whether Sylvia thought he should give them "Littérature." When she said yes, he asked whether she would work with him on the translation. Though flattered by his consideration, she demurred:

Valéry, however, insisted on "our" doing it. If I got stuck, he said, all I had to do was to run over to the rue de Villejust (now rue Paul Valéry) for a consultation. Unfortunately, whenever I took his suggestion and ran over . . . I found that I couldn't count on him as a collaborator. "Just what did you mean here?" I would ask. Pretending to look carefully at the passage, he would say. "What could I have meant to say?" or "I'm positive I never wrote that at all." Confronted with the text, he still denied any knowledge of it. Finally he would advise me simply to skip it.

Sylvia enjoyed the sessions with Valéry; but, even with the signature of "Sylvia Beach and the Author," she felt she had mutilated his fine work. When she tried to share the publisher's fee, he returned her check with a letter, in which he addressed her as a "female devil" and signed himself "Mephisto": "Honourable men only receive money for distinguished and delightful intimate services." He adds, "Dr. Faustus Lit.D.Ox. is very shocked and The Right Foul Mephistopheles is really aggravated by your kindness."

When Adrienne's catalog proved more financially successful than did Sylvia's translation, Sylvia talked of publishing her own library catalog. Though she never compiled the catalog, she and Adrienne devised another plan. They printed a prospectus offering reduced rates to students and professors. The prospectus brought a flurry of late-fall business.

Jean Henley had her own plan for increasing business. After several customers had asked her for erotic books that the shop did not stock, Henley suggested to Sylvia that they carry titles like *Fanny Hill*. "Sylvia was aghast," Henley remembers. She did not reject the book itself—she had seen Paul-Émile Bécat's explicit illustrations for it—rather, she questioned its right to a place in Shakespeare and Company. Soon she reconsidered, however, and looked the other way while Jean ordered it.

Gertrude Stein was also hard pressed to find a means of making money. In this summer she had written *The Autobiography of Alice B. Toklas* and taken it to the literary agent William Bradley, who had just accepted *Tropic of Cancer* from an unknown writer named Henry Miller. Bradley found an offer for Stein from Harcourt, Brace and an offer for Miller from Jack Kahane. The *Autobiography* appeared in an abridged version in the *Atlantic Monthly*, in which she had long tried, unsuccessfully, to get her work published, and in book form in 1933. She surprised a number of people by saying that she and Anderson had virtually created Hemingway, who was, she charged, "yellow." She also bragged that Sylvia was "very enthusiastic" about her. And, much to the surprise of the Jolases, she claimed to be the inspiration for *transition*. To no one's surprise, the book was a best seller. She had written it largely to make money, an artistic compromise that Hemingway used in order to get his revenge in a review of "The Farm," by Miró: "If you have painted 'The Farm' or if you have written *Ulysses*, and then keep on working very hard afterwards, you do not need an Alice B. Toklas."

Joyce, spending more freely under the stress of Lucia's illness, also had his money problems. He informed Harriet Weaver that he wanted to sell £1,000 of stock in order to be able to join Lucia in Austria and to pay hotel bills at the

Carlton Elite hotel in Zurich. When she remonstrated that he was "throwing his money away like a drunken sailor," he appealed to her sympathy by claiming that he also needed the money for new false teeth and a tombstone for his father. She sent him a quarter of the amount (enough to cover his immediate needs) and never again objected to his requests for money.

Only a few of Sylvia's friends were flush. Antheil was living well on his Guggenheim money in the south of France and encouraging Adrienne and Sylvia to visit his spacious villa. One of his grand parties included all the members of the Berlin Opera Ballet. While Antheil's success was temporary, Hemingway enjoyed a success that was solidly based on popular acceptance of his work. He had driven to Wyoming in the hunting season this year in his new V-8 Ford roadster (past the burdened jalopies of migrant workers) and was now planning an African safari.

Sylvia had recently bidden good-bye to Jean Henley (who would return to work part-time during the first half of 1933) and hired the twenty-two-year-old Jane Van Meter, who ran the American University Union at the Cité Universitaire. Van Meter, who proved to be the most professional assistant to work at Shakespeare and Company, was, inevitably, compared to Myrsine, whom Joyce had recently hired to look after Lucia for half of each day. Joyce's love and indulgence of Lucia (he had given her 4,000 francs for a new coat) was proving no cure for her insanity. When the Joyces relocated to an apartment in the rue Galilée, Myrsine moved in with them for several months.

Exhausted, moneyless, distracted by his concern for Lucia, and feeling increasingly persecuted, Joyce was in the winter of 1932 taking six sleeping pills each night—until he collapsed on a train in January—in an effort to find relief from acute insomnia. Sylvia, by contrast, seemed to perk up in this winter. Her headaches were less frequent and painful, and her letters to her family and friends reveal a playful wit and ease. She was busy renewing herself. She spent more time with Adrienne, wrote more often to her family, went swimming in a local indoor pool, entertained many friends, frequented the movies, and walked (even in freezing, January weather) in the Bois de Boulogne. With high spirits, she also challenged the American Library and other competitors by refurbishing her shop and promoting its activities—painting the walls of the back room, building more bookshelves, and taking out more advertising. Between the beginning of October and the end of November, business doubled.

Sylvia was encouraged. Though the depression was threatening, what she had feared might be a financial catastrophe—the loss of *Ulysses*—had not been that. On the contrary, many of her daily expenses diminished. Because she had been so busy juggling her American, British, and French bank accounts and had cared little for the intricacies of bookkeeping, she had not kept separate accounts for Joyce. Only the sales of *Ulysses* had been listed separately, at the bottom of each page in her daily account books. But the costs of the cables, telephone calls, typing jobs, advertisements, errands, postage, and a score of other professional services on behalf of Joyce and his family had become enmeshed in

Shakespeare and Company business. She had had only a vague idea of her fluctuating profits and losses. Now, after eight months without the Joyce business, she concluded on the basis of her observations, that she had made no direct financial profit from *Ulysses*.

Feeling confident on her own, she had talked first to Kahane and then to the Albatross Press about buying her Continental rights to publish *Ulysses* for 60,000 francs. Before Joyce returned to Paris this fall, she had settled with Albatross. Joyce, who had been bombarded with requests from Albatross, did not know that Sylvia had already given her assent. Unfortunately, instead of consulting Sylvia directly, he sent Léon to her, thus antagonizing her and complicating both communications and negotiations. The second- and third-hand reporting of events only polarized the factions. When Adrienne implied that Joyce had ruined Sylvia's health, he promptly called a Zurich specialist for her. Léon, Myrsine Moschos, and George and Helen Joyce spoke against Sylvia to Joyce, and their words got back to her. When Joyce attempted to arrange a meeting with Sylvia, she avoided him. He duly recorded her behavior in *Work in Progress* ("Sylvias sub silence"), and agreed to the payment to her of 25 percent of both his advance and his royalties of the first five years. When his family and Paul Léon urged him not to share his royalties, he did eventually arrange (without informing Sylvia) for her percentage to come directly from Albatross and not from his royalties. After another confrontation between Sylvia and Léon, in which she insisted that she had made no profit on the copies of *Ulysses* that she had sold during the preceding decade, Joyce and Albatross extended payment of royalties to her—after five years she would get 7.5 percent. Joyce thought the stance of Adrienne and Sylvia had been "idiotic" (because "all the cards are in my hands"); she thought it was "decent of him" to share his royalties, but suspected that "every breath" he drew was "calculated within an inch." During the next year, his interpretation of her motivations is even more deprecating—as numerous unpublished letters written to Harriet Weaver attest. Joyce now had a new Continental publisher. In December, after careful editing by Gilbert, *Ulysses* was published by Albatross under the Odyssey Press colophon. Sylvia was paid for her rights—but not, as she had been led to believe, out of Joyce's royalty.

Soon after signing the Albatross contract, Joyce penned a verse entitled "Portrait of the Artist as an Ancient Mariner." The mariner "dreamed of the goldest sands uprolled / By the silviest Beach of Beaches." The third stanza honors the early promotional work of Sylvia:

> Shakefears & Coy danced poor old joy
> And some of their steps were corkers
> As they shook the last shekels like phantom freckels
> His pearls that had poisoned porkers.

After a knockout in the eleventh edition, Albatross takes over: "With K.O. 11 on his prow . . . an albatross / Abaft his nape was hung." Sylvia ignored what she suspected might be a double meaning in shaking "shekels" and was soon encouraged by a thaw in her relations with Joyce. By January of 1933 Léon could confide to Miss Weaver, "Mr. Joyce's relations with the Odéon quarter are very good."

Because Sylvia and Adrienne loved to entertain, the Christmas season of 1932 was crowded with social life. Adrienne devoted hours to pastry making ("her great amusement and indoor sport," Sylvia calls it) and several weekends at Rocfoin to jam making and preserving. The season began with gatherings of old friends: a leave-taking dinner with Penny O'Leary Ybarra and several meals with Margaret Sloane, the Princeton friend who had giggled when Cyprian opened the Paris-cabaret fan in church. On Allen Tate's return this winter, Sylvia introduced him to Adrienne, who invited him and his wife, Caroline Gordon, to a dinner that proved to be friendly and full of high spirits. When the guests told Sylvia about their "Southern States Renaissance," Adrienne remarked, "Monsieur Tate is so conservative that he's almost radical." He vowed he would profit from her warning. After entertaining Jane Van Meter and two French teachers for a Christmas Eve dinner of goose, Sylvia and Adrienne had Christmas Day dinner with Sylvia's childhood friend Carlotta Briggs, who was expecting a second child. To Adrienne's delight, it turned out to be a traditional holiday feast of turkey, stuffing, cranberries, sweet potatoes, and holiday pudding. Dinner was followed by the singing of carols. Among the "twice a week invitations" after New Year's Day were a dinner with the Desmond Harmsworths and one with the Jacques Lemaîtres and Lucien Romier, the editor of Le Figaro, who had recently returned from a tour of the United States. The French guests were aghast and Sylvia dismayed as Romier told of aggressive young American women bent on seducing all the frightened young men. When he declared that there was no longer any such thing as an innocent American girl, Sylvia accidentally dropped a piece of potato on the rug.

Katherine Anne Porter, in Europe on a Guggenheim Fellowship, became one of the few new American friends of Shakespeare and Company at this time. She had heard about Sylvia from two longtime customers of the bookshop: Sergei Eisenstein, whom she had met in Mexico (where she had spent the preceding four years) and McAlmon, whom she had met in Germany early in 1932. Though Porter's first library card, which reads "no charge," is not dated until 3 January 1933, the two women, according to Porter, had met earlier:

When I first saw [Sylvia], in the early spring of 1932, her hair was still the color of roasted chestnut shells, her light golden brown eyes with greenish glints in them were marvelously benign, acutely attentive, and they sparkled upon one rather than beamed, as gentle eyes are supposed to do. She was not pretty, never had been, never had tried to be: she was attractive, a center of interest, a delightful presence not accountable to any of the familiar attributes of charm. Her power was in the unconscious, natural radiation of her intense energy and concentration upon those beings and arts she loved. She loved her hundreds of friends, and they loved her . . . each one sure of his special cell in the vast honeycomb of her heart. . . . Her genius was for friendship; her besetting virtue, generosity . . . and courage that assured even Hemingway.

From this winter until the fall of 1936, when Porter left Paris, she and Sylvia visited and dined together often. They were to remain friends for nearly thirty years longer. Sylvia and Adrienne attended her marriage to Eugene Pressly, in that March, and signed their marriage certificate. Sylvia had enormous admiration for this lovely forty-two-year-old Texan, who in 1930 had won immediate critical acclaim for her collection of short stories *Flowering Judas* from American writers in Paris, such as McAlmon and Josephson. She was also translating an old *French Song Book* (published by Harrison of Paris in 1933). Porter was grateful for Sylvia's encouragement and delighted to be invited to the Odéon parties, which she informed Sylvia were "full of the sparkle of life in *everybody* present, which you two could always bring out." Sylvia enjoyed visiting Porter and her large, sleepy tomcat, named Skipper, at her apartment in the rue Notre-Dame-des-Champs, where she had visited Pound a decade before.

On 16 February Shakespeare and Company was closed—as were all Paris shops—in protest against a proposed increase in taxes. Sylvia and Adrienne took the day to prepare a feast for Miss Weaver, who came to see her closest friend in Paris, Sylvia, and to determine what she could do for Joyce and his family. He was vexed when he learned that Miss Weaver, in trying to assess the situation, had talked to several friends of his concerning, among other things, his excessive drinking. He was particularly angry when he learned that she had visited Sylvia. He suspected the motives of his friends as well as those of the doctors who treated Lucia; he saw betrayal all about him. Thinking that Miss Weaver, too, had betrayed him, he sat in stony silence when she came to call. Her biographers believe that "like many men with a habit of dependence on women, he had a wild terror of being trapped in their monstrous regiment. Their compassion, eagerly sought, moved a net around him, detested and feared whether or not it was meant for his own good." Yet his sense of persecution had gone beyond the helping women in his life. By April he had also become estranged from Léon. He had always seen himself as the "melancholy Jesus." Now, virtually blind and afflicted by the behavior of his daughter, whom he would not commit to an institution, he felt the pricks of his persecutors: "Wherever I walk," he had complained to Miss Weaver, "I tread on thistles of envy, suspicion, jealousy, hatred and so on." Certain that Sylvia had "maltreated" him, he succeeded in convincing Léon and the Jolases that this fantasy was true. Miss Weaver, who took the time this year to talk about this subject to Sylvia, knew better. Burdened by Lucia, Joyce veered—in the words of Léon—"from states of great irritation and impotent fury to sudden lachrymose fits."

Though Sylvia kept herself informed about Joyce through Léon, the news was infrequent, and she cared chiefly about her bookshop, the renewing of old friendships, and a variety of new interests beyond the shop. She even attended weekly horticulture classes in the Luxembourg Garden—though she claimed she did not "own so much as a clothes tree." She also became interested in the political crisis in Europe, which absorbed Adrienne, who feared that Hitler's rise to power in Germany would lead to a war. Sylvia, too, worried occasionally but thought that the country was becoming panicky when it began selling gas masks and inspecting cellars for "retreat when the Italian planes begin to buzz overhead."

For her forty-sixth birthday, on 14 March 1933, Sylvia received a number of gifts from family and friends, including flowers and fresh eggs from the farm of Louise Norledge, a member of Shakespeare and Company. Joyce, despite his anger of the month before, gave Sylvia a lovely silver basket with thirteen Calville apples, the color they had chosen for the cover of her first edition of *Pomes Penyeach,* and a signed copy of the new English edition—the first copy to reach Paris. Above all else, he wished to avoid hostility between them.

Harriet Weaver, who had meantime returned to London, informed Sylvia that she was coming again to Paris to persuade Joyce to go to Zurich for a long-delayed treatment of his eyes, which was supposed to be given quarterly. Léon, though he was himself estranged from Joyce, had been sending her occasional medical reports of the writer's real and imagined illnesses. He had confided that Joyce was in a state of "listless disgust and apathy," writing nothing, and in need of both a visit to Dr. Vogt and £100 from his stock. Miss Weaver came and stayed for ten days. With the help of the Giedions of Zurich, she succeeded in persuading Joyce to go to Zurich for the summer and to put Lucia in a clinic nearby. Ignoring the potential disapproval of Joyce, she visited several times with Sylvia and Adrienne.

The early summer of 1933 was gloomy: the weather was cold and damp, business was poor, and citizens resented the presence of the many Algerian soldiers in the street. As if to punctuate the gloom, Sylvia learned that the rental on her shop would soon be tripled. Only the visits and news of friends brought warmth: Fred Dennis and Holly visited Paris, Willa Cather paid her first visit to Shakespeare and Company, Carlotta wrote that she had a new son, named Thomas, and Hadley Hemingway announced her marriage to the newspaperman Paul Scott Mowrer.

When her six-month calculations revealed a small deficit of 1,160 francs, Sylvia decided to do without the part-time services of Jean Henley but to keep Jane Van Meter, when she could work. In order to save money Sylvia and Adrienne spent more days than before at Rocfoin; they decided that during the slow business season their savings would be even greater at Les Déserts. They also needed to get away from what Sylvia called the "cave life and garage atmosphere" of Paris. They spent July and part of August there, rising at sunrise to the clang of cowbells; chopping wood for the fire in the cold evenings, when they took beer bottles filled with hot water to bed with them; hiking to visit storage caves for cheese, where they could smell the huge cakes of ripening Gruyère. They had breathed the cold, thin mountain air for more than a month when they were called back because Jane Van Meter had to leave on short notice for America, where her father was ill. Thanks to Holly's insistence and financing, Sylvia spent the last week of August with her sister and brother-in-law who were vacationing in Dinard. She swam in the Channel, visited Saint-Malo and

Mont-Saint-Michel, and relished the sisterly companionship.

The new customers during both the spring and fall seasons of 1933 were only passing through Paris—friends of Cyprian and Helen from Hollywood and the Pasadena Playhouse, academics and friends of Sylvester Beach from Princeton, and a few old friends such as Marian Peter, who brought her daughter, Sylvia's namesake, now fifteen years old. The tide of American travelers was beginning to reverse direction, running back to the United States. One by one they dropped by the bookshop to say good-bye—Leon Edel, many American students, and English and American businessmen. The most significant departures, however, were those that signaled the end of the American expatriate era: the exit of the longtime residents Samuel Putnam, Gerald and Sara Murphy, Glenway Wescott, and Monroe Wheeler.

The last waves of the peripatetic twenties in Montparnasse were barely visible. Wambly Bald had pronounced the collapse of Montparnasse in his final "La Vie" column of the Paris *Tribune,* on 25 July 1933. "Farewell to Montparnasse" he announced in a light tone, "I am tired of jiggling a corpse." Though written two years earlier, two works of literature portray the wake of the American expatriate movement. *The Left Bank,* a play by Elmer Rice (a Paris visitor of 1925), expresses a dominant theme of this final exit, in the argument of Claire, who insists on returning to America:

It's simply that my roots are there. I want to go and live in my own country, among my own people. I'm tired of being an exile; tired of drifting—of this aimless, wandering existence that we live here. . . . I want to go home and dig for turnips in my own garden.

Samuel Putnam, who had arrived in Paris in 1926 and who had spent the last three years in the south of France, where his children had grown up speaking French, left for the same reason: "a change was going on in our native land and we were out of it. We were out of it, and we were not sure that we liked being out of it any too well." He was tired of the "chronic petulance of the long-term expatriates" like Stein and Pound and discovered he could no longer brook any criticism by "little American deracinates and little untraveled Europeans" of his "big-breasted country." The end of expatriation was for Putnam and many others, such as the archetypal expatriate Harold Stearns, the rediscovery of America.

The world of wealthy American expatriates was best represented by Sara and Gerald Murphy, who had lived with their children in France since 1921. In 1933 they left their elegant Paris apartment and their Villa America at the Cap d'Antibes and went home. Fitzgerald, who had belonged to the Murphy circle, was now finishing *Tender Is the Night,* whose hero and heroine, Nicole and Dick Diver, are inspired by the style of life of the Murphys. The novel portrays the spiritual malaise that undermined the lives of some Americans during the twenties; his short story "Babylon Revisited" portrays the aftermath. Charlie Wales, the central character, returns to a "Paris so empty" in the thirties. Feeling guilty about the excess and irresponsibility of those earlier days, Charlie limits himself to one drink at the Ritz, where the bartender sighs that since the depression he has "half the business."

Others left in 1933 because they felt they had stayed abroad too long. Glenway Wescott, who had moved to France in 1925, at the age of twenty-four, had written there his best work about his familial and regional origins in Wisconsin. But in 1932 his collection of essays, *Fear and Trembling*, received sour reviews, and by the next year, when his *Calendar of Saints for Unbelievers* made an effete mockery of his search for self and art, Wescott had reached the nadir of his creative life. He, Monroe Wheeler, and Barbara Harrison (who would marry Wescott's brother) returned to New York and the family estate in New Jersey.

Success had also changed many writers. One of the signs of the new era, Wambly Bald had noted in his farewell to Montparnasse, was Stein's entry into the pages of the *Atlantic Monthly* with *The Autobiography of Alice B. Toklas*. It was not just that they had begun reminiscing about the lives they had once led, but that they were writing for mainstream American publications. Hemingway was receiving $250 for each article published in *Esquire*, a new magazine for men, and *A Farewell to Arms* was being made into a Hollywood movie starring Gary Cooper. Malcolm Cowley was book editor at the *New Republic*, and MacLeish was working for *Fortune*.

Europe, too, was changing. The Communists had just won six million votes in Germany; Hitler and his storm troopers were on the march; and the French feared an Italian invasion and a takeover by French Nazis. The Dôme was now brimming with German refugee artists. In fact, the catalyst for the departure of Putnam had been his glimpse in southern France of a dirigible passing directly over a peasant plowing his field behind his oxen: "Did that peasant realize the distance of the Graf Zeppelin from his oxen—the distance, and the nearness? If he did not, *I* ought to realize it. My semi-medieval retreat, my 'isolation,' was as false as the man-made 'ruins' about me." He and other Americans who had for a time settled in Europe believed, when they left it, that its historical twilight had come. There were others, however, who dared to stay on in the Old World, despite the growing storm warnings. Among them were the few assimilated Americans, the Ameropeans—such as Sylvia—who had been there long before the expatriate invasion. Sylvia never wavered in her allegiance to her adopted culture, even though the political and economic changes—which drove home many settled Americans—threatened the very existence of Shakespeare and Company.

Joyce called Sylvia in September when he returned to Paris from Zurich to thank her for the news clippings and mail that she had forwarded to him. She thought he seemed "very grouchy over everything": his bad nerves brought on a stomach disorder that caused him to collapse with pain (his fourth breakdown this year), he had lost weight in Switzerland, he did not think he was receiving enough of a royalty on the Continental edition of *Ulysses*, and he considered the delay in the court appearance of *Ulysses* interminable. Doctors in Switzerland had reconfirmed the diagnosis of Lucia's schizophrenia, yet he still refused to institutionalize her. Though "distrustful" of Léon, to whom he had not written during his summer in Switzerland, he called on him for any necessary assistance—for example, to pressure the publishers of Albatross for either advances on royalties or monthly payments. Unlike Sylvia, who had paid daily when asked, they refused both to give advances and to increase the frequency of royalty payments.

Sylvia received an amusing letter from a young man in Virginia announcing that during an audience with the pope this summer, he had carried *Ulysses* discreetly under a prayer book, where it had received the benediction of His Holiness. Full of admiration for Joyce that "could not be contained in a letter," Dewitt Eldridge informed Sylvia that "whatever treatment *Ulysses* may have had in America, in Vatican City it was blessed." Adrienne "laughed till she cried" when Sylvia translated the letter, and Joyce, delighted, sent it to Harriet Weaver. All of them—especially Joyce—enjoyed the papal blessing. In two months the United States—by means of a court decision—bestowed a greater blessing on *Ulysses*.

"My business is suffering excruciatingly from the exodus of Americans," Sylvia lamented to Holly. "They say about 13 thousand have left since the dollar fell. But the ones who are still here try their best to encourage me." Carlotta Briggs, for example, encouraged her wealthy friends to patronize the shop and placed a large Christmas order herself. A few Englishmen returned, notably Cyril Connolly, who borrowed a number of books during this fall and winter. But the threefold rent increase, which had begun in October, threatened to bankrupt her business. Adrienne now refused to allow Sylvia to pay her half of their apartment rental. And Clovis Monnier, who lived on a very small pension, offered Sylvia, his "third daughter," 3,000 francs from his savings as a gift. She refused it.

To the delight of Sylvia, Hemingway arrived in Paris the evening of 26 October and came to see her the next morning. "He and I are good old friends," she declared in a letter she sent Holly later that day. "He looks fine and handsome. His new book of short stories, *Winner Take Nothing,* will soon be out and he has finished a new novel and is writing another." He was full of bluster in the wake of attacks, particularly one by his friend Max Eastman, on his *Death in the Afternoon.* First Stein had called him "yellow" in her "autobiography" of Alice, then Eastman had made insinuations about his manhood. Morrill Cody, for whom he had promised to write a preface for *This Must Be the Place: Memoirs of Montparnasse,* describes Hemingway as "living in a hotel under a false name and fearful of being followed by the press . . . and begging me not to divulge his real address." He trusted Sylvia, who had always protected him, and Cody, whom he met in November in the bookshop to discuss the preface deal. Paris, about which Hemingway now talked in the past tense, was "a fine place to be quite young in." While Sylvia and many of their mutual friends were struggling financially, Hemingway and Pauline left for a three-month ($22,000) safari for four in Africa.

When *Ulysses* went to court on 25 and 26 November in the United States, Joyce was impatiently negotiating English rights, first with Faber and Faber and finally with John Lane of the Bodley Head. The possibility of English publication rested to some extent on a successful outcome of the court case in New York. The legal brief that the attorney Morris Ernst had presented to Judge John M. Woolsey of the U.S. District Court in New York quoted a number of artists' opinions of *Ulysses* and argued that it was not obscene by the standards of 1933. On 6 December, Woolsey, who had spent part of his summer reading the novel, delivered an emphatic decision, in which he calls the book a "very powerful commentary on the inner lives of men and women." He ruled that "in spite of its unusual frankness," he did "not detect anywhere the leer of the sensualist. I hold, therefore, that it is not pornographic." He concludes, "whilst in many places the effect of *Ulysses* on the reader undoubtedly is somewhat emetic, nowhere does it tend to be an aphrodisiac. *Ulysses* may, therefore, be admitted into the United States." Morris Ernst links this historic decision with another one rendered this week: "The first week of December 1933 will go down in history for two repeals, that of Prohibition and that of the legal compulsion for squeamishness in literature." Within ten minutes after Cerf heard the news, the typesetters were at work. The Random House *Ulysses,* which began selling at the end of January, had by mid-April sold 35,000 copies—more than all the copies of the Shakespeare and Company editions combined. The ship *Ulysses* had left the Shakespeare and Company tugboat in its wake.

CHAPTER 16

Storm Clouds

1934–1935

It darkels . . . all this our funnanimal world.
— *Finnegans Wake*

Loud, heap miseries upon us yet entwine our arts with laughters low!
— *Mime of Mick, Nick and the Maggies* (1934), Chapter 9 of *Finnegans Wake*

THREE MONTHS LATER, while Sylvia's birthday flowers—a large basket of irises and lilies from Joyce and two dozen tulips from another friend—were still fresh, Hemingway rushed into the shop. Tanned from his African safari, he eagerly showed her photographs of the five lions that he and his party had killed, each defeated animal lying at the feet of its victor. While Sylvia and Pauline chatted, he strolled over to the reviews and browsed among them, noting that the first installment of Fitzgerald's *Tender Is the Night* had appeared in *Scribner's Magazine.* Suddenly in the midst of reading *Life and Letters,* he bellowed and turned purple in the face. Twisting around, he delivered a right uppercut to the tulips, decapitating them and knocking the vase to the floor, where it broke. The water from the vase spilled on the new books on the table, soaking them. Hemingway, embarrassed, repeatedly muttered humble apologies, as Pauline and Sylvia mopped up the water with cleaning rags, struggling to contain their laughter at the absurdity of the incident. Then, as they blotted pages of the wet books, he read to them the passages in the magazine which had caused his cry of outrage. They were from Wyndham Lewis's essay "The Dumb Ox: A Study of Ernest Hemingway." The piece as a whole attacked what Lewis called his imitation of the "Stein stutter" and his anti-intellectual cult of action in which characters are without will and intelligence. Sensitive to criticism, aggressive by nature, just back from the big-game competition in which Charles Thompson had shot a larger lion than he had, and now attacked by a literary opponent and unable to respond on the spot, verbally or otherwise, Hemingway struck the tulips, acting more like a "mad bull" than a "dumb ox," Sylvia confided to Holly. "Poor Ernest, he is really a very good boy but primitive, which doesn't interfere with his writing, on the contrary." When Lewis heard of the incident, he delightfully added, in the retelling, that more than tulips were involved: "large inkwells drifted through windows and tables overturned."

Hemingway wrote a check for 1,500 francs to pay Sylvia for the vase, flowers, and thirty-eight books. He would repay Lewis thirty years later by calling him a nasty-looking man with the face of a frog and the eyes of an "unsuccessful rapist." Walking out with his purchases—he took all the books he had damaged—Hemingway grimaced slightly as he noticed among them four books by Virginia Woolf, another of his unkind critics. Sylvia returned 500 francs as overpayment the next day. When Adrienne heard of the "boom" in Sylvia's business, she envied her luck and suggested that she would get some flowers ready if Sylvia sent Ernest across the street. Lewis had unknowingly precipitated a small redistribution of the literary wealth.

During his relatively short, nine-day visit, Hemingway spent a liquid evening with Joyce, whom he had to carry home like a sack of potatoes, and gave rise to yet another dramatic event in Shakespeare and Company. Early one cold, wet evening, Sylvia and Katherine Anne Porter were chatting together when Hemingway, wearing an old raincoat and a floppy hat pulled over his eyebrows, rushed in. Sylvia hurried to embrace him, then, with what Porter would describe as "that ominous apostolic sweetness in her eyes," she spoke their names in full and, holding each one by the hand, declared, "I want the two best modern American writers to know each other." She had no sooner bestowed this blessing on what she hoped would be a fast friendship than the telephone rang and she withdrew to answer it. Hemingway, standing stock still, looked hard and expressionless at Porter. Though time has proved that her skill as a writer of short stories is the equal of his, he felt challenged yet again, perhaps even offended, to have this unknown writer—a woman, at that—compared to him, the famous Ernest Hemingway. She looked back unblinkingly at him, thinking that she had seen all the bullfights she had wanted to see, in Mexico, and that she preferred Joyce, Yeats, and James as writers. Though they faced each other for a full ten seconds, they did not exchange a word. Then, turning silently, Hemingway bolted from the shop and into the rain.

Though Joyce had remembered Sylvia on her birthday, she had not attended his birthday party in February, because Adrienne had refused to go to it. Harriet Weaver, who was in Paris to try and help Joyce, had not been invited, nor had she even seen Joyce on this visit. At the moment of his success—when *Ulysses* was available to all the world (England would soon follow the United States) and selling by the thousands of copies—the two women who had helped him the most were not at hand to celebrate with him.

There had been little else to celebrate. At the birthday party, Lucia had hit Nora, against whom she had long directed her hostility. Though Joyce continued to treat her as a normal but willful and eccentric girl, Lucia had run away from home and created numerous embarrassing incidents. Following the Woolsey decision, she had twice cut the telephone line when she was annoyed at the congratulatory calls to her father. Finally, after having struck Nora, she was sent to a sanatorium in Nyon. Joyce spent nearly half of 1934 traveling and living near this and other clinics where she was being treated.

"You would not know Paris!" Sylvia exclaimed to Holly after weeks of sporadic demonstrations and a "bloody Tuesday" riot on 6 February 1934–actually an uprising involving all political factions—which brought hundreds of thousands of Parisians into the street to protest against state taxes, corrupt politicians, the escalating cost of living, and state-protected swindlers. She and Adrienne bought supplies of candles and groceries and spent hours reading the papers each day to keep up with scandal investigations, demonstrations, and political reactions. During a lull in the spring street demonstrations, Sylvia talked to the American University Women's Club. Though expecting the members to be "revulsed" by her connection with *Ulysses*, she needed the publicity, because her chief competitor, the American Library, was planning to move to her territory, the Left Bank. Her fears proved to be groundless, because the women were fascinated with her talk and sought her help in preparing for their next lecturer, Gertrude Stein, who consented to answer questions only during her appearance. The women, who had read nothing except the *Autobiography*, came to Sylvia for copies of her books and a list of appropriate questions.

Sylvia saw almost nothing of Joyce in 1934. When he had called for appointments in the preceding fall and winter, she had, with one exception, offered the excuse that she and Adrienne were going out for the evening. According to Léon, however, in a letter to Miss Weaver, it was Joyce who had "cast them out of his life"—though "keeping exteriorly on decent and polite terms." That he still needed them is clear, for in this same letter, Léon suggests to Miss Weaver that if she has "kept good relations with the rue de l'Odéon it would be a great thing should you be able to induce Miss Monnier to bring out a cheap edition of the French *Ulysses*. I am loth to begin with her as her contract is almost entirely in her favor and I know she will not abandon it ever." This letter, which is unpublished, portrays an abandoned Joyce, isolated behind a "barrier of solitude . . . irritable and almost hypochondriac." Joyce's complaints were many: the publicity for *Work in Progress* was poor, Gorman was not finishing his biography, Joyce was the only one who had hope for Lucia, his publishers were not paying him all his royalties, he needed more money (though only £1,500 of stock remained), and betrayal was all around him. When a call to Sylvia revealed that she knew the latest news about Lucia's confinement, Joyce accused all his associates of talking to her about his personal problems. The Odéon, he complained to Léon, was "a chain on his literary work[,] a chain on his life . . . [which now] "cut him off from the litterary [*sic*] circles of France and England." Léon, a relative newcomer to the Joyce circle, believed Joyce's complaints and seemed unaware that Sylvia and Adrienne had introduced and maintained Joyce's chief connection with French literary circles. He begged Miss Weaver to assure Joyce of her continued support.

Miss Weaver, who had returned to London on "Bloody Tuesday," came again to Paris to urge what Léon had suggested: that Joyce take a better apartment in which to complete his work, that he make a trip to Zurich to see Dr. Vogt, and that he have confidence in her unfailing support. After a motor trip with friends to Zurich in April and a successful visit with Dr. Vogt (who gave him a new eyeglass for his vision), Joyce rented a fifth-floor apartment at 7 rue Edmond-Valentin, which was, until April 1939, his last permanent address in Paris. Leaving Léon to furnish the apartment, he went to Nyon to see Lucia, who was not, he asserted, a "raving lunatic"; rather, she was clairvoyant—the victim of "people [who] have warped her kind and gentle nature." He prepared *The Mime of Mick, Nick and the Maggies* (Chapter 9 with initial and tailpiece letters designed by Lucia) for June publication, but did not return to his writing. Despite Miss Weaver's continued attention and support, according to her biographers, Joyce "was increasingly ready to interpret anything she did in the way of friendship as a sign, at best, of her lack of understanding, and, at worst, of treachery." He was finding it difficult this year to live by the prayer that closes *Mime:* "Loud, heap miseries upon us yet entwine our arts with laughter low!"

Though she kept herself informed about the miseries of European political and economic upheavals, Sylvia found her "laughter low" by participating in the social lives of her French friends, and she refused to allow all the conversations to be dominated by worrisome talk about the present crisis. She also resisted the demoralizing effects of her migraines. Because her talk to the women's club had increased business, she joined the women's Rotarians. When Cyprian hooted (Holly would have been a founding member), Sylvia explained, "They asked me to get together with them and I didn't like to seem sniffy . . . [and] it means mutual help in our business." After Sylvia confided to Holly that she could not "go on indefinitely like this," her sister urged her to propose herself for a lecture tour of the United States this spring. Holly secured the addresses of agencies that handled such tours and Sylvia went as far as to compose a letter to them in April. By May she had decided that the ship passage would be too expensive and that she would "be so god-awful at those womens clubs" that she preferred to remain "peacefully" in Paris: "I think I'd rather give up the shop and get a job at Adrienne's than go on an awful lecture tour."

Bob McAlmon came to Paris this spring with a manuscript entitled *Being Geniuses Together,* his memoir of the twenties. He read the work to Joyce, who mistook his honesty for maliciousness and called it an "office boy's revenge." Pound, obsessed with financial theory and Mussolini's proposed solution for Italy's troubles, claimed that Hemingway and McAlmon were "reduced to bulls and memoirs." Sylvia, who recorded no opinion on the book, did agree at this time to write a recommendation for him for a Guggenheim Fellowship. At the end of this year, having failed to receive the grant and having exhausted the pleasures of Europe, he returned to America and virtual literary oblivion.

Philippe Soupault, James Stephens, and Sisley Huddleston worked the American lecture circuit, and Stein was considering a tour herself. Joyce refused to do the same, even though he needed the money that personal appearances would have brought him. Still, he would have been wealthy, had he lived simply. *Ulysses* sold 33,000 copies in ten weeks, and Bennett Cerf in person brought a royalty check for $7,500 to Joyce, who dined nightly with the Jolases and Léons at Fouquet's on the avenue des Champs-Élysées. *Ulysses* also made the lawyer Morris Ernst and the young publishing company of Random House financially happy. Cerf claims that *Ulysses* was its "first really important trade publication." In this same year it published a four-volume edition of Proust's *Rembrance of Things Past* and Stein's libretto (Virgil Thomson wrote the music) of the opera *Four Saints in Three Acts.* While in Paris, Cerf dined with Stein, whom he urged to make a lecture tour, and with George and Helen Joyce, who left in May, much to Nora's displeasure, for a year in the United States to meet her family and advance his singing career.

During this summer, for the first but not the last time, came suggestions from her family and friends that Sylvia return to America. Cyprian thought both she and Adrienne should emigrate to California, and Jean Wright, the former wife of Herbert Gorman, suggested that she come to New York. Sylvia confided to Wright and to Frances Steloff that many businesses, including her own, were in their last days. Because only Adrienne could afford to pay Jane Van Meter, who now worked for her, Sylvia ran Shakespeare and Company alone. "Everyone is very upset and anxious over here," she informed her American friends. She had just received notice that her Princeton bank was adding a surcharge to her checking account because its balance had fallen below $100, when Holly, who had sold Sylvia's violin, sent her a $20 check—"a gift from heaven." With each evening meal, there was also talk of war: the Nazis had just attempted to seize power in Austria by murdering Chancellor Engelbert Dollfuss. She read *The Life of Trotsky* and John Strachey's *Coming Struggle for Power* and shared the view of Miss Weaver, Gide, Chamson, and other friends that the Fascist powers threatened peace in Europe. She was none too happy with Ezra, who openly supported Mussolini.

When some visiting Woodbridge relatives told her that the Woodbridge family motto was *nil desperando* ("There is no reason for despair"), she determined to infuse her life with more laughter. During this hot summer she frequently went to the swimming pool with Juliette, the cousin of Adrienne, entertained friends, and rode a bicycle around the parks of Paris—one Sunday coasting down the Champs-Élysées, the breeze cooling her face. Outdoor physical activities had always had restorative powers for Sylvia, from taking surrey rides as a child to doing farm work in Touraine and chopping wood in Les Déserts.

With the increasing numbers of tourists visiting in the summer and skiers in the winter, Les Déserts was changing. Sylvia regretted the threat to their "wild primitive spot." While Van Meter managed the bookshops, they breathed the cold mountain air of the Savoy August. Two pieces of good news reached their mountain. First, the U.S. Circuit Court of Appeals upheld the Woolsey decision when, on 8 August, Judges August and Learned Hand, overruling Judge Manton, found that *Ulysses* "has not the effect of promoting lust." Second, Sylvia learned that Holly and Fred, who had claimed they were going to London for a writing assignment, had adopted an eleven-month-old English baby boy ("of fine old ancestry," Holly claimed). The addition of Frederic Beach Dennis to the family surprised Sylvia as much as Holly could have wished.

At this time Sylvia had made the acquaintance of Sir Theodore Morrison of the British Institute. In July he had paid a visit to Shakespeare and Company and learned of its contribution to English letters. "When I told him how the American Library had cut into" the business, Sylvia declared mischievously, "I thought he looked a bit uncomfortable." (Sir Theodore had given 12,000 francs to the American Library.) Perhaps as a means of balancing the scales of American library service, he became a member of both Odéon libraries, sent British embassy employees as new customers, asked Sylvia to help him select lectures for the British Institute, and commissioned her to superintend a book exhibit for the embassy. Sylvia fell in love with the "fine old gentleman" and introduced him to Romains, Schlumberger, Paulhan, and the Valéry family. Sylvia informed her young-looking fifty-one-year-old sister Holly, "While you were adopting an English baby the English have been adopting me, you see. Only I can walk without holding onto anything, and have more than five teeth already."

In this fall Sylvia faced her clients with the thought that they might be her last. Though Shakespeare and Company had never been very profitable, it was not—as were many of the French shops—threatened with immediate extinction. She considered selling the few stocks that had been left to her by her Aunt Emma this year, and friends talked of incorporating Shakespeare and Company and selling shares. When the *Tribune*, also facing financial difficulties, was bought by the *Herald*, the last article by its arts editor featured Sylvia. Still, the additional publicity—even the wave of news about *Ulysses* that followed its publication by Random House—brought chiefly lookers. Though her business did do better by nearly 21,000 francs ($2,971) in the second half of 1934, she had, because of inflation and a threefold rent increase, a 3,238.40-franc ($462.63) deficit. Rising costs threatened eventually to engulf her.

When Gertrude Stein, after thirty years in Paris, returned to the United States for a lecture tour, she was not just responding to financial need. *The Autobiography of Alice B. Toklas* had finally made the sixty-year-old writer a celebrity in her own country. She reveled in the attention as the press followed her from lecture to lecture—each one limited, at her insistence, to 500 persons. Her success far exceeded that of Huddleston, Eastman, Soupault, and other literary figures who toured women's clubs and the college campuses during these depression years. Stein would return to Paris the following May, declaring that when she rediscovered America, she felt "like a bachelor who goes along for twenty-five years and then decides to get married."

While Stein lectured to the university students in her homeland, Sylvia kept in touch with American graduate students who gathered for the school year 1934–1935 in Paris. They had Beaux-Arts Fellowships and were taking doctorates at the Sorbonne. They met at Shakespeare and Company and at the Café de Flore in Saint-Germain-des-Prés and considered Sylvia part of their group, as Edwin Popper (on a Harvard graduate fellowship) recalls: "She was about thirty-eight years old at the time, but she appeared to be thirty-two or thirty-three [actually she was forty-eight] . . . and had a fine quiet voice, and the appearance of shyness, but could come to the fore with firm opinions, always liberal, on politics and economics.'' Apart from their discussions of the arts, they talked only politics—the assassination in Marseilles of Alexander of Yugoslavia, on a state visit to France; the increasing power of Hitler, now president as well as chancellor of Germany; the scandals and riots in France. "We were in bad times," Popper remembers, but the conversation was stimulating and the camaraderie warm.

MacLeish, who had also (since his *Poems, 1924–1933*) turned to political concerns, asked Sylvia for assistance this fall. He had not been paid royalties for the Paris performance of *Union Pacific,* a ballet for which he had written the scenario, and he knew that Sylvia was his most dependable friend in Paris. He sent her his power of attorney but begged her to turn it over to a lawyer if it became "too dirty." On the next day, she went to the Society of Authors and Composers, pled his case—successfully, as it turned out—and left the dossier for the society's next meeting. On 3 November she called for the royalty check and sent it to him. "I am amazed that you were able to put it through so quickly," he responded with enthusiasm, enclosing a check for bottles of white wine for Christmas for Sylvia, Adrienne, and Joyce.

Though Sylvia was able to help MacLeish, she could do nothing for Chamson, who had just seen the latest King Vidor movie (probably *Our Daily Bread,* 1934) and swore to her that he recognized the plot. The plot of the Chamson novel—*Les Hommes de la Route,* which Sylvia, Vidor, and Chamson had discussed in 1928—was set by Vidor in America instead of the Cévennes. Though she suggested a lawsuit, he decided that "the grandson of a French peasant" should never take on Metro-Goldwyn-Mayer. Embarrassed, she could do nothing but express her frustration to Holly and a few newspapermen.

What she could do successfully for her French friends was assist in the publication of *Mesures,* a new review planned to appear in January 1935. *Mesures* was managed by Adrienne (with the help of Jane Van Meter), sponsored by Henry Church (a wealthy French-speaking American member of both libraries since 1927), and directed by Paulhan, Henri Michaux, the philosopher Bernard Groethuysen, and the Italian poet Giuseppe Ungaretti. The group—assisted by Sylvia, Michel Leiris, and later Vladimir Nabokov—met often during this fall and the coming year at the Church home in Ville-d'Avray. Sylvia, using the skills that MacLeish had called upon, contacted English authors for manuscripts and arranged to get translators for their works. *Mesures* soon published translations of works by Auden, Isherwood, Forster, Edgar Lee Masters, and Frost (Prévost, who translated "Stopping by Woods on a Snowy Evening," borrowed the book containing this poem from Shakespeare and Company). Early in this winter Sylvia arranged, with the help of his nephew, whom she had met at the shop, for the publication of several letters by Gerard Manley Hopkins. She and Adrienne translated the essay "About Punctuation" by the English novelist Dorothy Richardson for the first issue, in January of 1935.

Sylvia admired Henri Michaux increasingly as they worked together on *Mesures.* Michaux, a thirty-five-year-old Belgian poet and artist, was a friend of the Surrealists but belonged to no single group. Sylvia ranked his poetry, which had appeared in *Commerce,* with that of Valéry, Perse, and T. S. Eliot. Her admiration for him culminated in her most challenging feat: the translation, in 1949, of his first book to appear in English, *Un Barbare en Asie* (1933).

As her work on *Mesures* illustrates, Sylvia often explained English and American literature to the French. An unusual opportunity came during this winter when Sylvia and Adrienne attended a Paramount film version of Lewis Carroll's *Alice in Wonderland,* with W. C. Fields as Humpty-Dumpty, Cary Grant as the Mock Turtle, and Gary Cooper as the White Knight. In a review of the film for the *Nouvelle Revue Française* (January 1935), Adrienne quotes Sylvia at length on the importance of *Alice* to English and American children. Sylvia had long enjoyed the Carroll classic and discussed its linguistic feats and imagery with Joyce, who had once helped her solve a puzzle about the Jabberwock. For French readers, she and Adrienne now discussed Carroll's linguistic fantasies and his kinship to Joyce, Fargue, and the Surrealists. According to Sylvia, "Joyce could say, like Humpty-Dumpty: 'When *I* use a word it means just what I choose it to mean. The question is which is to be the master.' No wait, that's not it, Joyce would say rather: 'When I use words I let them go wherever they want, in all four directions.' " In French and English they recited lines from Jabberwocky. Adrienne ends her essay by noting that the younger customers of Shakespeare and Company were upset that the movie mixed Carroll's two works *Alice* and *Through the Looking Glass.*

The year 1935 was marked by strenuous efforts to raise money to carry Shakespeare and Company through the depression. The first plan was discussed during a New Year's dinner attended by, among others, Fargue, Romains, the Prévosts, and Francis Poulenc: Sylvia would prepare a catalog and offer some of her rare books and Joyce manuscripts for sale this coming spring. Her friends— including Adrienne, who had had to sell many of her manuscripts in 1926— understood the necessity. Keeping Shakespeare and Company open should be her first priority.

When she shared her plans with Janet Flanner, the news appeared on 16 February in her "Letter from Paris" in the *New Yorker.* Sylvia assumed that the feature was the gesture of a friend, and she gave Flanner an early edition of *Ulysses,* two pages of corrected manuscript, and her calling card expressing her "love and gratitude." Flanner responded by scolding Sylvia for not knowing how "to make money out of events." The sale of her manuscripts was legitimate news, part of her job, and, she added, "if it served you whom I admire, all the better."

Unfortunately, the news reached Joyce, who had just returned to Paris in late January, before Sylvia informed him. He conveyed to George and Helen Joyce news of the sale, of which, he said, he was still "officially ignorant." What apparently bothered Joyce more than being "journalistically informed," was the "rumour" that Sylvia "by her generous sacrifice of all her rights in *U[lysses]* to me, resigned herself to abject poverty. Frailty, thy name is woman." Though in all her family letters Sylvia blamed the economic depression for her poverty, Adrienne had undoubtedly confided to a few of their French friends information about Joyce's bad treatment of Sylvia.

Late in January, Stuart Gilbert lectured on Joyce's works at the Sorbonne, under the auspices of the British Institute, and played portions of the records of the Anna Livia and Aeolus episodes. Nora reported the event to Joyce, who, in a letter to George and Helen, listed those who had sent him cables of congratulations. "Neither Miss Beach nor Miss Monnier sent anything," he adds, "though the former was at the lecture well to the fore." What Joyce did not know was that the proprietress of Shakespeare and Company, who was sitting on the front row, was responsible for the lecture, for she had suggested it to her friend Sir Theodore Morrison, the director of the institute.

By the first of April, six weeks in advance, Adrienne asked Joyce whether he had any objections to the sale of the manuscripts in Sylvia's possession. He said he did not, but he expressed regret to Miss Weaver that *Stephen Hero*, his early version of *Portrait*, would be made public: "I dislike the putting up for sale of the first MS of the *Portrait*, about 1000 pages. And what rubbish it is! (I threw these MSS at her because I really did not know what to do between her acts of insane adulation and meaningless rage.)" This note of bitterness came out of the darkest and most irrational period of his life. His remarks about *Stephen Hero* notwithstanding, Joyce valued all his manuscripts, but his mental wretchedness overwhelmed his better judgment. He was now convinced that Cerf was "neglecting *Ulysses*" in favor of Stein, and, while he was deeply troubled by Lucia's madness, he tried to deny its existence, keeping her out of institutions all year, insisting that her mind was "as clear and as unsparing as the lightning." When his sister Eileen and Miss Weaver each tried in vain to care for her, despite her truant and violent behavior, he blamed them for the failure. By this summer, according to Ellmann, Joyce had "reached his life's nadir."

Sylvia's problems this year were only financial. Her headaches were less severe, but she received injections of her own blood and calcium from Dr. Thérèse Bertrand-Fontaine. She kept the shop and library open every day by herself, devoting spare moments to preparing the catalog descriptions for her sale. Family and friends wanted to help: Sylvester Beach sent $50; Gide, who bought a copy of *Moby-Dick*, became a steady member of the library and took out a subscription to *National Geographic;* her aunt Agnes Orbison, on leave from the mission field in India, took out a two-week library subscription; and Clovis Monnier demanded that she accept 2,000 francs ($80) for a skiing vacation in Savoy with his daughters (Sylvia decided that she could not leave the shop). Though friends were solicitous, nature and the economy were hostile. Heavy rains and gales flooded parts of Paris. "The Seine has risen alarmingly," Sylvia announced, "and I must say, no one here seems to care. They are more interested in the rise of the cost of living. Where will it end?"

William Bradley, the literary agent, had a plan for fattening Sylvia's purse.

This spring, he and Alfred Knopf visited Sylvia to inquire whether she would write her memoirs for publication by the latter. Sylvia informed Holly that when Knopf "said he would probably bring them out provided [she] didn't bring in too much about Joyce and the French and Gertrude Stein and talked mostly about [herself]," she replied that she "couldn't guarantee to please him at all and [they] had better just let the matter drop." She added, "If and when I have a *mopus agnus* ready to show them they can take or leave it, huh?" When she finally began the long-delayed process of writing her memoirs, a decade later, she undertook no *magnum opus* but a sketchy, witty recollection that devoted only eight or nine pages to her own life. Ignoring Knopf's advice, she featured Joyce and her French friends.

MacLeish, who had written from New York to offer his help in selling her manuscripts, was himself the object of her goodwill. She asked him for a poem and had it published in *Mesures* this spring. In May he returned the check for 500 francs ($75) that he had received in payment and asked her to use it to cover his mailing costs (for several books by Romains) at Adrienne's shop and the cost of subscriptions at both libraries, and to keep the remainder for herself. "Please don't be angry with me for doing this," he concluded, "because it isn't real money anyway being money for a poem which has already been printed."

One day in March, Thomas Wolfe unfolded his large frame from a taxi in front of Shakespeare and Company. Max Perkins had put him on the boat for Europe to await the reception of his novel *Of Time and the River*. Fortified by four drinks—though Sylvia thought him fairly sober—he talked to her about the influence of Joyce, which he was trying to shake. From Shakespeare and Company he found his way, after days of drinking, to the house of Adelaide Massey, an American expatriate who studied at the British Institute, served numerous charities, and occasionally filled in for Sylvia at the bookshop. "Wolfe was indubitably a young man of genius," judged Sylvia, but "perhaps very unsatisfactory as a social being. My friend—and his—Adelaide Massey, to whom he had a letter, took him in after several days and nights in the bars . . . cleaned him up, dosed him with castor oil, treated his black eye and bruises, and put him in bed for a couple of days." Wolfe's psychotic depression was unnecessary—*Of Time and the River* became the literary sensation of 1935.

A more stable and mature (by twenty-five years) American writer was in the final weeks of her tour of the United States. What the audiences and newspaper cartoonists in America found appealing was not Stein's "maturity" but her eccentricity, illustrated by her dress, manner, and unpredictable and outrageous statements. While she arrived in Pasadena greeted by a front-page story in that city's *Post*, there appeared in Paris the "Testimony against Gertrude Stein," a February supplement to *transition*. Georges Braque, Eugene and Maria Jolas, Henri Matisse, André Salmon, and Tristan Tzara denounced the "sordid anecdotes" and megalomania of her *Autobiography of Alice B. Toklas*. It was appropriate that the charges appeared in *transition*, which she claimed to have inspired. Sylvia endorsed their attack on her version of the events, which Jolas's preface labeled full of "hollow, tinsel bohemianism and egocentric deformations." Stein was never "ideologically intimate" with her epoch, it added. Her brother Leo, who had earlier rejected her, confided to a friend, "God what a liar she is!"

Before the beginning of a very busy May, Sylvia sent her catalog to the printer (at Adrienne's expense), and the Monnier family gathered at Rocfoin for the forty-third birthday of Adrienne, on 26 April. Among other things, they talked about the exhibit of Marie's embroidered tapestries, to be held from 15 May through 15 June at La Maison des Amis des Livres, and about Sylvia's fears that she would have to close Shakespeare and Company.

On the day before the exhibit opened, Valéry, Gide, and Schlumberger met at Adrienne's to discuss a plan intended to save Shakespeare and Company. They drew up a petition for subsidy to be submitted to Pierre Laval, the minister of foreign affairs, and considered whose signatures of support might be secured from among the leading writers, academicians, and diplomats of France. While awaiting news concerning the subsidy, Sylvia was occupied by the sale, which called attention to her need.

On the opening day of the embroidery exhibit, Nora Joyce and Carola Giedion-Welcker, who was visiting from Zurich, joined the well-wishers and chatted amiably with Sylvia. Nora learned that Lucia had sent three pieces of embroidery to Sylvia as a gesture of friendship expressing her desire that her father and his former associate become reconciled to each other. Joyce's only response when he heard of her gift was "But why send vases to Samos?"

The sale of Joyce's own gifts to Sylvia was a failure. "Joyce gave me great treasures, which ought to compensate for the loss of *Ulysses,*" Sylvia admitted to Holly, "but I fear that like most great writers, his price will only begin to soar after we are all dead and gone. Alas, there's more glory than money in them MSSSSSSS." She sold only one page of *Ulysses* manuscript, containing scribblings, to "an optometrist in Duquoin [Duquesne], Illinois." The letters that poured in expressed more interest in saving Shakespeare and Company and buying first editions of Hemingway than in purchasing Joyce, Blake, or Whitman materials. Perhaps if she had been able to sell her documents at auction at Sotheby's in London, as she had originally planned to do, she would have received more money. When Sylvia had insisted, despite Sotheby's assurances, on a statement from the British authorities that her Joyce manuscripts would not be seized and burned, Sotheby's learned unofficially that the realization of her worst fears could, in fact, be precipitated by any private complaint. Rather than risk seizure of the manuscripts, she sold a few items on her own.

Though she sent the catalog to a few wealthy patrons of the arts in America, it was her friends who responded. Bryher, who had just purchased the financially troubled English review *Life and Letters,* "bought" a Blake drawing, insisting that it remain in the bookshop. Barbara Church would buy the second Blake drawing. Carlotta sent 5,000 francs ($700) and two weeks later, on receiving an acknowledgment from Sylvia, a reprimand: "You must never again write me such a grateful letter as you wrote after getting the check." Fitzgerald wrote

from Asheville, North Carolina, to say he had given her sale "immediate attention." Because they both wanted Princeton to have her manuscripts, he got in
touch with three "well-to-do former Princetonians plus Henry Strater." He
enclosed an autographed copy of *Tender Is the Night.*

In June, learning that there could be no government subsidy for Shakespeare
and Company, in as much as Sylvia was not a French citizen, Gide, Valéry, and
Schlumberger discussed the possibility of organizing a group of "Friends" to
pledge financial support. Marian Willard, who was visiting again from New
York, announced she would organize a New York chapter. By the fall the plans
would be set and an announcement concerning the formation of the Friends would
be circulated. In Sylvia's letters to her family—she wrote fewer than in previous
years—she did not speak in detail of her financial troubles or of her political
views, which were considerably to the left of Holly's and her father's.

In the years following the financial collapse and preceding World War II,
politics and economic theory engrossed writers in the United States and in France,
as elsewhere. In June, Sylvia and Adrienne attended a large rally organized by
Gide and André Malraux and called the International Association of Writers for
the Defense of Culture. The meeting, "strongly communistic," Sylvia notes,
was truly international, but it was dominated by men (Virginia Woolf and Rebecca
West, who had been invited, were ill and unable to attend). Though Sylvia
described with amused detachment the "dreamy attitude" and bright orange shirt
of Waldo Frank, who sat on the platform, and the numerous men "roaring away"
with great seriousness (Adrienne declined to speak), she cared very much about
these writers and about the strong antifascist views that most expounded.

This was the summer in which Mussolini invaded Ethiopia. The rise of fascism in Europe and the effects of five years of economic crisis in the United
States had turned American literature to the left. Dos Passos, Farrell, Odets, and
Steinbeck were portraying the struggles of the masses caught in economic chaos.
Because American criticism judged a work by its social concern, Faulkner was
virtually passed over. Michael Gold in the *New Republic* attacked Wilder's
novels for avoiding the "modern streets," "child slaves," and the "passion and
death of the coal miners." In *America: A Re-appraisal,* Harold Stearns, once the
harshest critic of his country, praised American democracy and romance, at the
expense of Europe. These new winds blew through Shakespeare and Company,
which now stocked *New Masses, New Statesman,* and *Red Front* magazines.
Except for *transition,* the little magazines dedicated only to art were now collector's items.

Young French faces that would dominate postwar French literature began
haunting the rue de l'Odéon. Though the thirty-year-old Jean-Paul Sartre rarely
crossed the street from Adrienne's library, Simone de Beauvoir, a twenty-seven-
year-old Sorbonne philosophy graduate student and teacher, was an avid reader
of American literature. She confided to Sylvia that there had been little to do in
her home but "take cold baths and drink tea all day." She joined Shakespeare
and Company on 4 September 1935 and for the next six years borrowed scores

of American titles. Of the group who frequented Adrienne's shop—de Beauvoir describes them as "young rebels intent upon transforming the traditional form of the novel into a weapon of social protest"—she was the most faithful to Sylvia, who admired her "brilliant" mind and her facility with the English ("and even American") language. She eventually shared her interest in Dos Passos and Faulkner with her fellow rebels Sartre and Malraux; together they gave these American writers critical acceptance in Europe before they won it in America.

The two bookshops symbolized for de Beauvoir and other Sorbonne graduates, as for many others before them, the world of modern literature. She recalls the names and faces at Adrienne's library:

I eavesdropped when the owner of this sanctuary—who intimidated me with her nunlike apparel and lofty friends—spoke in the most casual and intimate way of famous people whose very names left me somewhat dazed. She would tell some old client, for instance, that she had seen Valéry just the night before, or perhaps Gide wasn't feeling very well. Léon-Paul Fargue and Jean Prévost were two other writers who could often be seen talking to Adrienne on the most affectionate terms. And sometimes with beating heart I suddenly saw the most remote and inaccessible of them all materialize before me in flesh and blood: James Joyce, whose *Ulysses* I had read in French with utter amazement.

The established writers of French literature were intent on saving Shakespeare and Company for this new generation. During a visit with Sylvia, Gide declared that it was "impossible" for her to close her shop, because she played "a role among us that we could not do without now. . . . Something must be done!" It was then that he, Valéry, and Schlumberger proposed forming the Friends of Shakespeare and Company, a group that would pay annual dues for two years, after which time (Gide and Sylvia assumed) the shop would be financially stable. Jenney de Margerie and Jean Schlumberger suggested offering readings for the Friends. The Committee of Patronage, officially responsible for the venture, consisted of Duhamel, Gillet, Valéry, and Jacques de Lacretelle—all members of the French Academy—as well as Durtain, Gide, Maurois, Morand, Paulhan, Romains, and Schlumberger. Adrienne, who served as secretary-treasurer, wanted (but did not dare to ask) Claudel to join this distinguished list of French men of letters.

Schlumberger drew up the appeal for membership, asking fifty persons each to contribute 300 francs ($45) annually for two years. Shakespeare and Company was, he declared, "a place where letters are loved for their own sake, are honored and served." The announcement mentioned four or five readings a year open free of charge to all Friends and open for a modest charge to outsiders. The membership fee seemed large in these economically difficult years, but the organizing committee was distinguished and the readings were tempting bait for anyone with literary hunger. "It's going to be corking!" Sylvia announced.

A separate appeal was printed for the English. Jenney de Margerie, whose husband, Roland de Margerie, was first secretary to the French embassy in London, suggested that Joyce (a banned writer) and Gide (a Communist) should not be mentioned. "Now think of that!" exclaimed Sylvia, who ignored her friend's suggestion. Adrienne assured her that "the whole fun for these people to attend our performances is the naughty guilty feeling they have about approaching some of our risky 'personages.' "

While the appeal pamphlet was in the mails, Sylvia made two sales from her catalog, including a signed first edition of *Lady Chatterley's Lover* to a Syracuse, New York, woman for $50. If the sale was otherwise slow and disappointing, the appeal for the Friends was immediately successful. Many of the first subscribers gave money before the 1936 beginning date, and gave far more than the $45 yearly membership fee. In her record book of donations for 1935–1955, Sylvia lists the early Friends (as well as catalog sales), beginning with MacLeish's return of the *Mesures* check in May:

20 May 1935	Archibald MacLeish	500 francs	($75)
9 July 1935	Carlotta Briggs	5000 francs	($758)
27 July 1935	Jeromes (or James) Hill	1000 francs	($152)
10 Oct. 1935	Bryher	4000 francs	($606)
? Nov. 1935	Bryher	2500 francs	($379)
18 Nov. 1935	Mrs. [Helen] Baldwin	300 francs	($45)
23 Nov. 1935	Marian Willard	1000 francs	($152)
18 Dec. 1935	Barbara Church	600 francs	($91)
21 Dec. 1935	Mme de Margerie	600 francs	($91)

Thus Sylvia received 15,500 francs ($2,364) above ordinary shop receipts for 1935. According to one set of her figures, compiled in July, this was close to the amount of her 1934 deficit and slightly less than what she had estimated her 1935 deficit would be. The doors of Shakespeare and Company would remain open.

The joy of friendship and French cultural life continued despite all the signs of economic crisis and impending war. Sylvia took Adrienne and Jane Van Meter past police barricades to Thanksgiving dinner at the home of Carlotta Briggs. On another day, they wove their way around the patrolling French police in the student quarter and outside the Chamber of Deputies (which debated devaluing the franc) to attend a concert by Marian Anderson. They skirted a Jeunesses Patriotes demonstration in order to see Wallace Beery in *Barnum;* and to see *David Copperfield,* they made a detour around the student Action Française monarchists, who marched each Sunday in their quarter. It was a "bright new improvement," in December, announced Sylvia, when these leagues, which had stockpiled arms, were outlawed. Paris is "dark and dread," concluded Sylvia. "Paris is like myself," admitted Joyce, "a haughty ruin or if you like a decayed reveller."

The buildup toward war in Europe both strengthened old friendships and engendered new ones. An important new friend this winter was Gisèle Freund, a young Jewish refugee from Berlin, who had been ordered out of France. She had no passport and could not return to Germany. Adrienne assisted this accomplished photographer and graduate student in dealing with her visa complications. Freund spent an increasing amount of time in the apartment of Sylvia and Adrienne. With the help of Adrienne, she remained several more years in France by marrying a Frenchman named Bloom—a name that would secure Joyce's permission for photographs in 1938. This happy new friendship was within a year to effect an enduring change in Sylvia's life.

But December of 1935 was a joyful month, crowded with the visits of friends and the preparations for the Friends of Shakespeare and Company. Bryher, who visited Sylvia this month, was one of the first and certainly the most generous Friend. When her father, Sir John Ellerman, had died, in 1933, he had left one of the largest fortunes (estimated between £183 million and £280 million) ever recorded in Great Britain. Though Bryher lived rather simply, she gave generously to her friends in the arts. On her way from Switzerland to England, Bryher stopped early in December to meet Aragon, who appeared this month in the second volume of her *Life and Letters To-Day,* at a dinner arranged by Sylvia and Adrienne. Bryher's request for "good quiet talk" was guaranteed when Sylvia came down with tonsillitis. Nevertheless, they managed to talk about the coming readings at Shakespeare and Company; about approaching war (Bryher was in the midst of her valiant campaign of smuggling of refugees out of Germany); about the work that Bryher and McPherson were doing in films; and about *Life and Letters To-Day.* With the encouragement of Sylvia and Adrienne, Bryher added a European (chiefly French) flavor to this English review.

The only sad note during the closing days of 1935 was Jane Van Meter's imminent return to America. After her three-year absence, her family declared that she had stayed long enough in the "war area" and must complete her university work at home. Jane spent her last month in Paris at both shops—helping Adrienne with *Mesures* and Sylvia with the Friends. On the fifth she stayed with Shakespeare and Company when Sylvia took the metro to Père-Lachaise cemetery in order to place flowers on the grave of her mother, Eleanor, who would have been seventy-one years old then. On the next day, Sylvia applied for a new passport, listing her occupation as "literary" and her date of birth as 1896, not 1887. It was her energy and courage—not the shaving off of nine official years—that would take her into her seventy-sixth year.

CHAPTER 17

Les Amis de Shakespeare and Company

1936–1937

Joyous your mingled selves . . .

— Paul Valéry, *Fragments du Narcisse*

O̲NE COLD Saturday night in February 1936, guests streamed into Shakespeare and Company for the first reading of the Friends. The rue de l'Odéon was dark at 9 P.M., but lights shone brightly from under a new Shakespeare sign painted by Marie Monnier. A tense excitement was created by the presence of distinguished members of the audience and by the reader of the evening, André Gide. After latecomers had entered the back room via the courtyard, sixty-four Friends and paying customers were present—fewer than the many who had besieged Sylvia for cards of admission. All the furniture had been removed to make room for folding chairs. Joyce, who had been ill for some time, but who admired Gide and had paid his $45 fee in the Friends, was not going to miss this important series of French literary events. He sat, with a black patch over one eye, near Gillet, Chamson, Schlumberger, and the Valéry family. Sylvia, who nearly twenty years before had first heard Gide read (the poetry of Valéry) in Adrienne's shop, thrilled to see him sit at a table before her fireplace—his bald head tilted in characteristic manner, two fingers pressed against his square forehead as if he were propping up his head. From the moment when Gide spoke the clear and precise opening sentence of his unpublished novel *Geneviève,* he held the attention of his audience. "His voice moves through a text with the timbre and an authority that awaken a world," declares Adrienne. His elocution, his very presence, radiated severity and energy. Enthusiastic applause followed his performance, which, according to Sylvia, "went off beautifully!"

It was appropriate that Gide, the guiding spirit of Les Amis de Shakespeare and Company, the champion of the oppressed, and the advocate of service to others, should be the one to initiate dramatically the 1936–1937 readings at the Shakespeare and Company library. The thirties, because of the absence of Hemingway and Antheil and the obscurity of Joyce, had made Shakespeare and Company less glamorous than it had been in the twenties. But this two-year series of readings by the French, Sylvia announced after the Gide performance, "give new life to the place!" They revived both the bookshop and the French literary world, long preoccupied with the economy and divided by political issues. Writers of the left and right joined to save Sylvia's enterprise.

Two young people, not yet launched in their careers, exemplify the vitalizing effects of these readings. The first was François Valéry, long a friend of Sylvia, who would help him prepare his English for a diplomatic career. The second was a shy young American woman, Elizabeth Bishop, who would become one of America's important modern poets. Not as fortunate as François, who came with his father, Elizabeth could not get into the crowded Gide reading.

The bashful Bishop, a recent graduate of Vassar, was traveling in Europe with a college friend, Harriet Tompkins, who had come early to Paris from the south of France and had found Shakespeare and Company. When Bishop arrived to spend the first three months of 1936 in Paris, she borrowed and bought regularly from the bookshop, not knowing that its proprietor was the publisher of the blue-covered *Ulysses,* which a wealthy girlfriend at Vassar had lent her. Even in ignorance of Sylvia's reputation, she was painfully shy, hiding her nose in a book whenever Sylvia looked her way. Keeler Faus, a patron of this period, explains why Sylvia did not introduce herself:

Sylvia had hidden warmth, and she waited to learn about people. One had to wait to win her respect. Also, the environment she created was that of the library, not the store. When a new customer walked into the shop, she did not jump up to serve. With an attitude which verged on the indifferent, she waited until a customer had a question. Only then would she take a personal interest in the customer. Often she asked a question to see the extent of the customer's knowledge and seemed to part reluctantly with each book.

Apparently she decided, after several visits by Bishop, that she would have to wait forever for the young woman to ask the first question. So one day when Bishop was browsing the shelves alone, Sylvia approached her with a copy of *Life and Letters To-Day* in her hand and asked whether she was addressing the young woman whose long poem was published in this current issue. "Yes," replied Bishop, blushing crimson and too embarrassed to continue the exchange. Though she would not publish her first poetry collection (*North and South*) until 1946, Elizabeth Bishop had received early critical praise for her sharp and searching individual vision. A week later, when Sylvia saw her at the opera, she asked Bishop whether she wished to meet other writers at a reception in her apartment. Bishop's heart raced when she heard that Joyce and Gide would be among the guests. "I got all dressed up with fear and anticipation," she remembers, "and my college friend borrowed a car to drive me to the rue de l'Odéon." Though appropriately dressed and chauffeured to the party, she had no sooner placed one foot on the sidewalk then she whispered, "No, I cannot do it . . . I am too scared." As her friend drove her home, she was filled with relief and regret. The regret still lingered forty years later when she called this missed opportunity "one of the saddest stories of my life." Though she saw Sylvia again on this and later visits to Paris, Elizabeth Bishop never met Joyce or Gide.

François Valéry, less bashful than solitary, attended each reading, usually with his entire family. Unlike Bishop, young François had known Sylvia and his father's literary friends all his life. He was not star struck, nor was he much interested in French literature. He was now a tall, blond young man—the only fair-haired member of his family—whom his father called "this great Nordic brute." Sylvia was fond of François, who struggled for a career apart from his father and pursued music studies with Nadia Boulanger. He had always spent all of his pocket money on concerts, but now his interests were turning to literature—not to the French poetry of his father's circle but to the English and American literature of Shakespeare and Company. He bought the two-volume, shorter edition of the *Oxford English Dictionary* on the installment plan. Dozens of titles on his library cards—from the King James Bible and Shelley's prose to the *Letters of Mark Twain* and Frost's poetry—mark his self-education from 1936 to 1941. His studies culminated in a degree in English studies at the Sorbonne. Though Sylvia recalls in her memoirs that Paul Valéry suggested the theme of his son's thesis, Robert Browning's *The Ring and the Book,* implying the father's sympathetic interest, François remembers their relationship differently. He remembers the feeling of youthful rebellion he experienced in telling his surprised father, the greatest poet in France, that he considered English poetry superior to French. Valéry *père* was speechless.

Before François left France for a year of schooling at Exeter (Sylvia asked Eliot to welcome him to England), he spent many cold afternoons sipping hot tea at Shakespeare and Company. Of all his parents' friends, Sylvia seemed to him the youngest and most understanding. His father liked her urbane world view and her sense of humor; his mother and aunt, who lived in a quiet and bourgeois world markedly different from his father's, thought her distinguished and charming. Young François, on the other hand, sought her worldly understanding. To Sylvia he could confide anything, for she was unflappable, broadminded, and utterly natural in her approach, not only to the subject of his father's mistresses, but to things in general. She offered him, then, both personal and professional support.

Sylvia was as interested in building new friendships with Bishop and Valéry and others of their age as in maintaining her old friendships. Two girlhood friends visited in January: Penny O'Leary Ybarra, who attended the Gide reading, and Marian Peter, who promised financial aid to Shakespeare and Company. Longtime patrons as diverse as Tristan Tzara (who came to announce that young French writers were no longer interested in Surrealism) and Jacques Benoist-Méchin (zealous now in spreading the surrealistic propaganda of Hitler) renewed their library membership to help Shakespeare and Company.

Les Amis de Shakespeare and Company were for the most part French. The "official" Friends, chiefly men of the arts, publicly tendered Sylvia loyalty and affection. For many, such as Duhamel and Romains, it was a return to the rue de l'Odéon. Duhamel, whose novels were now best sellers, and Romains, whose plays often ran to 200 performances, had since forsaken their regular vigils at Adrienne's "little chapel." Some devotees of the library believed, probably incorrectly, that the popular success of Duhamel was a sign of his artistic defeat. In any case, his fame and that of the other Friends called attention to Sylvia's plight and helped Shakespeare and Company.

Among the unofficial Friends who privately rallied to the support of Sylvia in 1936 were many women for whom no amount of money, time, or care was too much to lavish. Dorothy Richardson and Bryher recruited members among the English, Marian Willard among the New Yorkers. Marian's major donors this year were Helena Rubinstein, who gave $246, and Anne Morgan, the daughter of the financier, who gave $460. Miss Morgan, her secretary assured Sylvia, "is intensely interested in what women are doing." Others who this year gave more than the $45 membership fee were Adelaide (Polly) Norledge ($91), Carlotta Briggs ($758), Marian Peter ($152), and Bryher ($379). The women of the Odéon also worked together on the readings. Sylvia asked Miss Dorothy Plummer—"little Plummer" she called her new assistant—to clear the books from the tables, which were removed on the day of each reading. Plummer, an Englishwoman who had been teaching in Paris for three years, consistently delighted Sylvia with her accent and shared afternoon tea with her. It was she who mailed printed invitations for each reading, kept track of seat reservations, and helped arrange signs, chairs, and flowers. Adrienne and Marie always prepared the food that Sylvia purchased for the reception that followed each program. "We women must stand together! *Pour la culture!*" Marian saluted Sylvia.

During the four weeks between the Gide and Valéry readings, excitement mounted. Bryher and Carlotta, her most generous supporters, had disappointed Sylvia by their absence from the first reading. For the Valéry night, however, Carlotta stayed in Paris for the weekend and Bryher came from Switzerland. The organizing committee, leading French writers, and diplomats were there, including Schlumberger, Paulhan, Prévost, and the head of the British Institute, Granville-Barker. Although Lucia, now at home again after a stay at Saint Andrews Hospital in England, was a burden to them, Nora and James Joyce attended. Joyce undoubtedly noted the auspicious leap-year day, 29 February.

Leaning over his manuscripts, his gray hair parted in the middle and his black eyebrows showing prominently over his glasses, the sixty-five-year-old Valéry read prose pieces of his *Alphabet* and, at the prior request of Sylvia and Adrienne, *Fragments du Narcisse*. Unlike the commanding Gide, Valéry read weakly, almost slurring his words through closed teeth. Joyce later informed Beckett that the performance was poor. François, who had never before heard his father recite his poetry, thought his voice simply "bad" and the final syllables of each line nearly inaudible. Yet he was moved, unexpectedly, by the wit of his father's poetry. In an article published in the *Nouvelle Revue Française* six months later, Adrienne adds that Valéry, "not as an actor, but as an author, yes, the whole author," moved her: "when we think of it, our hearts beat in our heads." Consequently, when Valéry concluded his reading, several in the audience called for an encore. In the manner of poetry and music concerts in Parisian cafés, one guest called out "Le Cimetière marin!" Accordingly, Valéry read that long poem whose title in English is *The Graveyard by the Sea,* his soliloquy on death set near Sète, his birthplace. No sooner had he finished its final lines, which read in translation,

> Fly away, my sun-bewildered pages!
> Break, waves! Break up with your rejoicing surges
> This quiet roof where sails like doves were pecking

than Joyce called in a clear tenor voice for "Le Serpent." Joyce smiled with pleasure as Valéry began his *Ébauche d'un Serpent.* Despite Valéry's halting delivery, the last verses of the poem struck the audience. In English they are rendered as follows:

> Enough for me if, in the air,
> The giant promise of bitter fruits
> Should madden the children of clay. . . .
> —The very thirst that made you huge
> Can raise to the power of Being the strange
> All-probing force of Nothingness!

Though most shared François's delight in the play of intelligence, Carlotta turned and whispered to the woman next to her, "I am afraid I do not understand most of what he is saying!" With amused sympathy, the woman replied: "Well, I have heard it before. I am Mme Valéry."

Sylvia provided a final link between the Briggs and Valéry families nearly nine years later. When Valéry died, after the liberation, the family did not have appropriate burial clothes for his state funeral. Sylvia hurried to the Briggses' Paris apartment, which they had left in her care when they fled France quite suddenly before the Nazi occupation. On 25 July 1945, Frenchmen stood vigil all night in the Place du Trocadéro, before the Palais de Chaillot, where Valéry lay in state; the national funeral, on the next day, was the largest one since that of Victor Hugo. France paid her last respects to Valéry, dressed in Jim Briggs's striped pants and morning tails.

For her birthday, in March, Sylvia spent five days in London. She had last been in London in 1919, when she and Holly had purchased their poetry books for the library. Now, seventeen years later, she returned on her first plane trip, to negotiate with Faber and Faber to take over stock (boxed since 1929 in her storeroom) and rights for *Our Exag,* and to attend several plays, including *Murder in the Cathedral,* T. S. Eliot's first. She complimented Eliot by calling *Murder* "by far the loveliest play of our time"; but she confided to her Presbyterian minister father that the Anglo-Catholic author "looks as if he were getting papish." To Holly she added, "He has become more and more a Catholic, and at the same time, more and more of a poet." She stayed with Harriet Weaver in Gloucester Place and cheered her with her gaiety. Sylvia and Harriet saw John Gielgud in *Romeo and Juliet* and visited numerous tourist spots. Sylvia dined in the homes of Cyril Connolly and T. S. Eliot; Eliot promised to give, sometime in April or May, so as to coincide with the Paris premiere of *Murder in the Cathedral,* the first English-language reading for the Friends. Though it was a literary visit—paid for by the Faber deal and the sale of three Hemingway first editions at the Anderson Galleries—Sylvia kept up a busy social schedule. Returning home—she admired the view from the plane of the white-capped Channel waves and winding Seine—Sylvia congratulated herself that she had flown to England "before the Germans got there with the gasses."

During the ten days that preceded a reading by the novelist Jean Schlumberger, she consented to newspaper interviews and hired a new part-time student secretary, Margaret Newitt, who could speak fluent French and would work through the following year. However, when she learned that Elizabeth Bishop was in the American Hospital being treated for an eye infection, Sylvia was too busy to visit her in spite of Margaret's assistance. Instead, she sent her armloads of books, which were brought to the hospital by Harriet Tomkins. Bishop, who remembers that Sylvia "looked like my favorite boarding-school teacher," was cheered by her "extreme kindness." Despite the urging of Sylvia, Bishop (who thought Sylvia was "small and shy" like herself) was too ill to attempt another celebrity reading and reception.

On Saturday, 28 March, at 9 P.M., the Friends gathered to hear Jean Schlumberger, a founder of the prestigious *Nouvelle Revue Français,* and the cofounder with Gide of the Friends. He read portions from an unpublished comedy, *La Tentation de Tati (The Temptation of Tati),* that delighted the audience with its humor. If Gide read with force and Valéry without it, Schlumberger read, according to Adrienne, "ravishingly well, in a simple, adept, and gay manner." More than the other two, she adds, Schlumberger "helped us to recover the atmosphere of the salons of the eighteenth century, in which the most enjoyable exchanges of the spirit took place."

Sylvia reported news of politics and of the readings to her father, who was busy planning his own gathering—the reunion of the Princeton class of 1876. She remarked that in April the French elections "all went LEFT in a landslide that has quite scared the old standpatters and canon-merchants. Now they are trying to revenge themselves by sitting on the franc so as to flatten it out." She enclosed an article from the New York *Sun* that William Bird had written about her readings, anticipated the excitement over Eliot's reading scheduled for the end of May, and expressed gratitude for her Friends: "I would never have dreamed that people could be so kind."

On 9 May, Jean Paulhan read from *Les Fleurs de Tarbes (The Flowers of Tarbes,* 1941). The fifty-two-year-old Paulhan—a critic, philologist, and long-time editor of the *Nouvelle Revue Française*—riveted the gaze of his audience as he moved to and from his seat at the table. Adrienne, charmed by Paulhan's performance, envisioned, as he read, a snake charmer: "The line of his voice moved toward the idea like the sound of a flute, and the idea, undulating, reared up like a cobra; it sometimes seemed that the idea was about to throw itself upon its charmer. Paulhan quickly arose, stepped away a bit, fixed the creature with a look (the fangs had not been drawn, I assure you), then his voice went on, insidiously." But if his delivery was riveting, his work, Sylvia judged, was "incomprehensible." At the reception afterward, others confirmed her judgment that the passage from *The Flowers of Tarbes* was difficult to follow. All, indeed, except her errand girl, who claimed that she understood every word!

Because Paulhan had recently begun a translation of *Pomes Penyeach* for *Mesures,* Joyce though besieged by tragic circumstances, attended the reading out of courtesy. Physically, he was vexed again by his eyes, nerves, and an attack of colitis; psychologically, he was vexed because he believed that neither of his children had done anything with their lives. After only three weeks in Paris following her release from an English hospital, Lucia had to be taken in a straitjacket to a sanitarium and then to an asylum. Over half a million francs had now been spent in a futile search to cure her. George, who faced a thyroid operation, had never established a successful singing career. And occasionally, when Joyce drank to excess, Nora packed a suitcase and went to a hotel. To encourage Joyce during this siege of troubles, Harriet Weaver financed half the publication costs of Lucia's lettering of *A Chaucer ABC.* A grateful Joyce sent her the originals and urged her to apply "strong moral and personal pressure" on subscribers, and he showed her how by promising to cut off any friend who would not subscribe. In letters from May to August of this year, Léon confided to Miss Weaver that Joyce was quarreling for trivial reasons with many of his old Paris friends and living in virtual seclusion.

In order to avoid Pentecost, on 30 May, Eliot postponed his appearance until 6 June, when he came to Paris for a busy four-day visit, accompanied by Mr. and Mrs. Christopher Morley. Sylvia was delighted to have her longtime friend and best seller (after Joyce) read at Shakespeare and Company. Adrienne, who had helped Sylvia translate "Prufrock" a decade before, was similarly taken by the forty-eight-year-old Anglicized American. His face, she recalls, was "that of an archangel who has too much work to do, and so does only half of it, leaving the rest to the North Wind." Certainly, Eliot was a busy editor and, since the recent openings in London and Paris of his first play, a dramatist of growing fame. But he claimed not to have new poetry to read; "it would perhaps have been better for your purpose," he remarked regretfully to Sylvia, "if I could have given a reading before my *Collected Poems* appeared." But his adoring listeners hardly cared that he did not have a work in progress; they treated him as a holy visitant.

The reading took place, as did the others, at the hour of nine on Saturday, when the Friends and their general-admission fans had gathered in the library of Shakespeare and Company. Sylvia, fortunately, had ordered extra chairs, which were all taken. The crowd included a photographer from the *New York Times* and a few gate-crashers. The knees of the front-row Valéry family brushed the table where Eliot sat, head down, reading in, according to Adrienne, "a pure voice with reverberating intonation" that passed "his trance on" to the audience. Young Gisèle Freund was impressed with the "cosmopolitan audience" and the "grave, beautifully modulated voice of Eliot." He read his best-known poem, *The Waste Land,* which is about the spiritual sterility of modern times and concludes with thunder—thunder that prophesies rain, hence salvation: "DA . . . Datta . . . Dayadhvam . . . Damyata!" He closed, at Sylvia's request, with early written parts of what would become *The Four Quartets,* the consummate expression of his religious beliefs. Adrienne, in that quasi-religious fashion that often marks her comments on literature, describes the poetry as "full of incommunicable motifs, slight and overwhelming states of grace that the Zen Buddhists call *satoris.*"

Gide stayed in Paris for this last reading of 1936, then left later in June for a celebrated trip to Russia to observe the Communist experiment at work. He was only one of many European and American artists and intellectuals who saw the communism of Russia as a social and political alternative to the rising fascism of Italy and Germany. Ashamed of his privileged economic status, Gide had been converted to communism by a reading of the Gospels. Meanwhile, in England, Harriet Weaver was converted to the same cause by a reading of Marx; according to her biographers, she had during the preceding summer had an "apocalyptic vision of Karl Marx" in which "universal social justice and universal peace were inevitable." In Paris, however, Sylvia, though politically influenced by both Gide and Weaver, was converted by neither.

On 18 July, while she was spending a week with Adelaide Norledge at Long Barn in Trinity, Jersey, Gen. Francisco Franco joined the military uprising that would precipitate the Spanish civil war. On this quiet island, with its lovely lanes and old manor houses, Sylvia ate "tomatoes and grapes under glass" and rested from persistent abdominal cramps, unaware that Franco was "liberating" his country from Marxism. She returned to Paris on the nineteenth to be caught up in the frenzy that had begun to develop concerning the position that France should take in the conflict, especially vis-à-vis Germany and Italy, which had sided with the Fascist forces.

Sylvia, however, who had many months before made plans to visit the United States, did not linger in the city. She went home—it would be her first visit in nearly twenty-two years—on 24 July, her trip having been paid for by her father, whom she went to meet in Princeton upon her arrival. Together they flew to California to celebrate his eighty-fourth birthday. Because he had been ill, his daughters worried about his waning capacity to care for himself. In California, Sylvia stayed with Cyprian and Helen ("Jerry"), whom she met for the first time, and visited Holly, Fred, and their three-year-old son, Freddie. The Antheils (George was writing music for Hollywood films) visited her one afternoon and conjured up the old times in Paris, invoking an atmosphere as heady as strong wine. "Whenever Hollywood stupidity depresses us," Boski wrote her later about that conversation, "we think of it and we feel better right away." The many photographs of this California family reunion, which would be the last, show Sylvia tanned, clad in white shorts, and deceptively healthy looking. In fact, she was suffering at the time from persistent menstrual bleeding.

Leaving California, Sylvia flew to Newark in order to visit Princeton, where she promised the university library a first edition of *Ulysses*. Later, while visiting Marian Willard in Locust Valley, Long Island, she underwent a hysterectomy and six radium treatments. In exchange for her donation to the Friends and the promise of further payment, Sylvia gave Marian her set of corrected proofs of *Ulysses*. She also counseled her to open a gallery that rents art—an idea that Marian incorporated in the East River Gallery, which opened this fall. Nursed back to strength by Marian and her grandmother, Mrs. William D. Guthrie, Sylvia was able, by October, to visit Jane Van Meter, who came up from Washington to New York City. Several times she dropped in to see Frances Steloff at the Gotham Book Mart, admiring the Gotham's courtyard and bookstalls in the back and arranging for Miss Steloff to sell *Mesures*. During the week before she left, in mid-October, she kept up a frantic pace. "New York City is an endurance test," she declared. But she responded to all invitations. Peggy O'Leary, secretary to Dorothy Thompson at the *Herald Tribune,* gave a cocktail party at which reporters interviewed Sylvia. Hoping to sell Joyce material, she called on Dr. A.S.W. Rosenbach, the owner of the Quinn *Ulysses* manuscript. The location seemed providential, Sylvia notes: "His Rosenback [*sic*] Co. is right beside St. Patrick's, and Joyce would think that symbolic—a mystic relationship." Rosenbach himself was not attuned to this suggestion: he wanted no more Joyce, but was fairly sure he knew someone who would be interested in the manuscript of *Stephen Hero,* which Sylvia left with Marian.

During this last week in New York, Sylvia also had appointments to meet Marianne Moore and Archibald MacLeish. The poet Moore, her correspondent of a decade, she met for the first time. In a letter of 17 October to her father, she records her initial impressions:

The most interesting friend I made in America, after Helen Eddy, was Marianne Moore. Her poems and her portrait have always been in my shop, and Bryher told me to be sure to see her. She came all the way from Brooklyn to the picture gallery on 57th street, interrupting a "piece" she is writing for the *Nation* on Gertrude Stein, and leaving her mother alone and ill, and she took me back there to a negro performance of *MacBeth* which she wanted me to be sure and see before I left. And she signed her poems that Bryher had given me. She looks like a little old maid school marm but only at first. When you take a good look at her and hear her talk she is unique and fascinating.

Perhaps because she overextended herself in her long visit with Moore, the doctor asserted she was not well enough to travel to Conway, Massachusetts, to visit the MacLeishes. Regretfully, she canceled. Before Sylvia sailed for France on the SS *Normandie,* Marianne Moore—astounded by Sylvia's persistent showering of small gifts upon her—sent her a photograph inscribed "to courageous generous unselfish *wilful* Sylvia Beach." Several publishers talked to Sylvia about her memoirs—Clifton Fadiman of Simon and Schuster even pursued her on board the ship before she sailed. But she seemed more interested in seeking American publishers for the young French writers than in publishing any book of her own.

While Sylvia was in the United States, Margaret Newitt was operating Shakespeare and Company, which was closed for three weeks in August. Joyce, vacationing in Denmark, read proofs of the first British edition of *Ulysses,* to be published now that the ban in England had been lifted. And Adrienne and Gisèle Freund vacationed in Venice. When Sylvia left the United States, in mid-October, she was full of her rediscovery of her homeland and eager to continue to absorb all she had missed during her nearly twenty-two years away. Still, though she carried in her suitcase phonograph records of western songs she had played at Marian's home, she was "homesick for France." She was weak from her medical treatment, but felt "like a new person."

Returning to what she called her "problematic little business," she found the franc depreciated. The cool autumn air was full of talk about Spain—whose insurgent government was now controlled by Franco. Though the chief worry of almost everyone else in Paris was a possible European war, Sylvia was more upset about a vexing change in her living arrangement with Adrienne. In her absence, Gisèle had moved into the apartment they had shared together for so long.

Within days Sylvia moved out of 18 rue de l'Odéon and into the small rooms above her shop. For the first time in fifteen years, she lived alone. To inquiring friends and family she spoke of the noise and crowded conditions of No. 18, of the wisdom of saving on rent payment (the mezzanine rooms had always been included in her shop rental), and of her displeasure with Gisèle. Her parsonage discretion has left no documentation of this lovers' quarrel. Indeed, in only one, suppressed segment of her memoirs does she speak of her love life:

I think Gide was very much disappointed in me one summer when he joined Adrienne and me at Hyères and nothing funny ever happened. A lady who attended the American Church and used to know my respectable father told someone she would not set foot in my shop where she had heard dreadful things went on. My "loves," as any lists may have perceived, were Adrienne Monnier and James Joyce and Shakespeare and Company. And once I felt so drawn to Robert McAlmon that I wrote and told him so. . . . But by the time he [returned] my thirteen generations of clergymen had regained their ascendancy and to McAlmon's evident relief, we talked only of the weather. Adrienne used to call me *Fleur de Presbytère*—"Flower of the Parsonage." Whether from my puritan ancestry or puritanical upbringing—once when I was in my early teens my mother told me "never to let a man touch me"—I was always physically afraid of men. That is probably why I lived happily so many years with Adrienne.

Though these intimate years with Adrienne ended, Sylvia continued to take her evening meals with Adrienne and Gisèle and to maintain her close professional association with Adrienne. She kept her separate apartment at No. 12, even after the approach of the Germans made it necessary for Gisèle, who had fled her homeland, to leave Paris in turn. The friendship of Adrienne and Sylvia remained fast until 1955, when Adrienne committed suicide after a long illness. The thirty-eight-year devotion of these women is similar in its duration and character to the forty-three-year friendship of Bryher and H.D. and the thirty-nine-year union of

Stein and Toklas. Eros channeled into sorority yielded both personal and literary fruits.

In November, at a dinner of the PEN-club in honor of Spanish writers—to which Sylvia took Carlotta Briggs—its president, Jules Romains, opened the program with a salute to the recent triumph of American democracy: the re-election of Franklin Delano Roosevelt to the presidency. Sylvia shared Romains's delight in the Roosevelt victory, but Joyce was irritated with PEN's shifting focus when six months later, his paper denouncing U.S. censorship and piracy of *Ulysses* was overshadowed by political discussions. Sylvia attended a second dinner of the club, honoring German writers and presided over by Schlumberger. This group of French writers, who were each month honoring writers of countries with repressive governments, feared war. "As for us French," Sylvia confided to Holly, "we're so scared you've no idea how."

Because the radium treatments had temporarily diminished her energy, Sylvia put off for a few months further readings by the Friends. At Adrienne's urging, however, she planned the appeal to the Friends for 1937, and Adrienne drew it up. They talked with the founding committee, and Romains agreed to give the first reading of the new year. Sylvia asked Aldous Huxley to join the lineup. He declined with regret, because he was leaving for the United States.

During November, Sylvia welcomed Harriet Weaver to Paris for a week's visit. She had come to encourage Joyce, whom she had not seen in two years. Léon, who saw him only occasionally, had kept her informed about Joyce, who was working to complete *Work in Progress,* but who "in his practically total estrangement from people" was for long hours listless and silent. Again, Miss Weaver met with him and promised her support until the novel was published. She never saw Joyce again. Her relations with Sylvia were easier and without strain. Sylvia prepared several meals for Harriet; because of the latter's preoccupation with Spain, they spoke much about politics. They tried futilely to attend a Socialist meeting that was to be addressed by Léon Blum, the Socialist prime minister, that was so crowded they could not enter the auditorium.

Because she had Margaret Newitt to tend the shop, Sylvia was able to spend several days over Christmas in the country with the Huddlestons and then to take a two-week skiing vacation in Les Déserts. She hiked around with a pack on her back, looking like, in her own words, "a perfect animal specimen." Rid of all traces of her operation and full of fresh zeal for arranging a new series of readings, she returned to Paris a week before the Romains program was held. Meanwhile, Adrienne had printed and mailed the new bulletins to the Friends, and contributions had begun arriving: $100 from Anne Morgan and $1,000 each from Bryher and Carlotta. "The Friends," she disclosed in a timely metaphor, "have been coughing up so kindly again—those who have not gone away or who can afford to help—and we are hoping the coughing will continue, as it should with the vile weather we are having."

On 30 January 1937, according to Sylvia, Romains "read an hour and a half of beautiful things out of *Les Hommes de Bonne Volonté* [*Men of Good Will*]" and his poem *L'Homme Blanc,* published the following year. The audience glittered with fellow *copains* and with literary figures like Kahane, Soupault, and Valéry. The reception that followed celebrated both the success of the reading and the two honors that had been announced that very day: France had elevated Romains to the rank of commander of the Legion of Honor and made Adrienne a knight of the Legion of Honor. In the festive spirit of the occasion, the two winners congratulated each other: Adrienne saluted Romains with a kiss; Romains promised to play the godfather and pin the ribbon on Adrienne when it arrived. Along with the flowers, telegrams, notes, and calls that arrived following the announcement of Adrienne's elevation, a customer who for a year had owed her 400 francs, came rushing in to pay his bill. When Adrienne narrated the incident to Valéry at the Romains reception, he gave her a wink and quipped, *"Monnier, c'est utile."*

For Sylvia, the awards led only to embarrassment. When Cyprian received the news in California, she misunderstood it. In an interview with the *Pasadena Post* about the readings at Shakespeare and Company library, she informed the reporter that Sylvia had received the Legion of Honor. Recognizing her mistake after the appearance of the *Post,* she telegrammed the eastern papers that had picked up the story, but it was too late to make a rectification. Holly and her father circulated numerous clippings from the *Post* and other papers among their friends. When the news reached Sylvia, she was shocked and distressed—but forgiving. Cyprian, in turn, was dismayed that her only gesture to publicize her sister had backfired. Her letters and telegrams begging Sylvia's forgiveness reveal that she did her best to make amends. In contrast to them, Holly and Sylvester were too embarrassed to tell anyone of the mistake, and, according to Cyprian, they "began to say hell and damn the way [they] do when they get mad."

Fortunately for Sylvia, American events seemed far away during this February. In comparison with the spring floods in France and the war in Spain, a mistake made in American newspapers seemed trivial. The war in Spain, which would be a dress rehearsal for world conflict, brought visits from Stephen Spender and Hemingway. Spender, who was going to Valencia to do some broadcasting for the government there, offered to give a reading of his poetry upon his return. By her own admission, Sylvia had been occupied "quite a lot getting" the work of Spender and W. H. Auden "translated and published here and with more or less success—it's so hard to interest people in poetical writings in a language not their own." Sylvia also asked Hemingway to read. He was in Paris for ten days, on his way to Spain as a sort of antiwar correspondent for the North American Newspaper Alliance. Tentatively committing himself to appear on his return, though he dreaded reading in public, he went on to Spain to issue news releases and to do a documentary film (*The Spanish Earth*) on the plight of the Spanish people. On this visit he borrowed no books and expressed only faint interest in the new *Transition* (No. 26), which contained more of *Work in Progress.* His focus, like that of many artists, was on world events. His muse was married to action, as Wyndham Lewis would observe in 1950, and he was fully enjoying what Carlos Baker calls his role as "America's leading war novelist."

Bryher was another literary friend to visit Sylvia this February. Though Sylvia, Adrienne, and she shared leisurely dinners, Bryher was in Paris chiefly on business for *Life and Letters To-Day*. Sylvia arranged for her to meet French writers and, at the request of Bryher, was planning for the Paris Exposition of that summer a booth or stand that would feature both *Life and Letters To-Day* and Shakespeare and Company. Although the work demanded of Sylvia more time and energy than she had, she resolved not to disappoint her friend. She gained the requisite energy for this work, she confided to Holly, from liver extract: "it makes you bouncing. It makes you paint bookcases and undertake repairs of all kinds."

Though work toward arranging other readings was now well underway, Sylvia needed her reserve of energy. On the last day of April, André Maurois, one of the first members of the Shakespeare and Company library and a member of the organizing committee to save the bookshop, read "a delightful unpublished story." Though no record remains of what story he read, we do know that later in this year he published both a biography of Chateaubriand and a popular history of England. The fifty-two-year-old Maurois, a great French interpreter of the Anglo-Saxon spirit, "was always present," according to Sylvia, "whenever Franco-American relations were to be encouraged."

One of Sylvia's successes on behalf of English letters in France was the publication during this spring, in *Mesures,* of *The Dog beneath the Skin* (1935), by W. H. Auden and Christopher Isherwood. Featuring satiric scenes from European politics, *Dog* is a rather episodic play that Sylvia believed would amuse the French. Paulhan had found a translator to "adapt" a shortened version of the work, and Sylvia handled all the arrangements. Isherwood and Auden informed her that they liked the translation "very much" but asked, too late, that she explain in print that it was an abridgement of the English original. She tactfully apologized, assured Isherwood it would be entitled an "adaptation," and suggested how difficult it was these days to get any translation published. She told him that she had secured Paulhan's assurance that a note of explanation would appear in the *Nouvelle Revue Française.* Finally, she promised Isherwood with characteristic wit: "I will talk to theatrical people about producing your play. Only they would be sure to transform and transpose it beyond recognition."

On 12 May, the readings of the Friends of Shakespeare and Company came to a boisterous conclusion. According to Sylvia's breathless account, the joint reading by Hemingway and Spender, who had met each other in Spain, was hastily arranged when Hemingway decided he could not appear alone:

Hemingway suddenly arrived on his way home [from Spain] and Spender was here too, and [Spender] and W. H. Auden were to give a reading later. And I'd told him to come back with his pal Auden, but Hemingway said what fun it would be to have Spender and him together, and I thought so too. So Spender stayed on and Hemingway promised to read a part of his novel [*To Have and Have Not*], and we wrote out a whole lot of invitations by hand and then twice a day he came in and said he could never read that novel—twasn't any good anyway and as for himself he just wanted to go back to the Spanish front and get killed right off. So Spender and I cheered him up and on and

Hemingway wanted beer and whiskey which I told him could be managed, and I bought two large beer mugs at the Bon Marché and lots of the best beer and a bottle of White Horse.

Hemingway's fear intensified. At Adrienne's apartment prior to the reading, he drank steadily before, during, and after dinner. Gisèle Freund noted that his face grew redder and redder as he drank. Between sips of whisky and drafts of beer, he and Sylvia reminisced about a private reading of his first stories, given thirteen years earlier in Paris for Sylvia, Adrienne, and Hadley.

2 INVITATIONS

" SHAKESPEARE AND COMPANY "

— SYLVIA BEACH —

ERNEST HEMINGWAY 192
and STEPHEN SPENDER
who are in Paris for a few days
will read — Hemingway from
his unpublished novel — Spender
some poems — at the Shakespeare
& Company Bookshop on
Wednesday May 12th at 9 o'clock

12, RUE DE L'ODÉON   Please let us know as soon as
PARIS (6ᵉ)   possible if a seat is to be reserved
for you.

As Hemingway fortified himself for the looming event, Shakespeare and Company began filling with Friends and eager outsiders. Even that somewhat disdainful patron Helena Rubinstein was there, though she slept through most of the reading. The Joyces sat in the shadows of the back room with the Jolases. Others who crowded into the two rooms included Stuart Gilbert, Natalie Barney, and the new U.S. ambassador to France, William Bullitt; Romains, Maurois, Duhamel, Paulhan, Prévost, Chamson, and the Valéry family; and two newspaperwomen, Hemingway's longtime chum Janet Flanner and Martha Gellhorn, with whom Hemingway had recently begun an affair in Madrid.

Dwarfed by her two tall friends, Sylvia slowly threaded her way to the center of the crowd. "I introduce to you Hemingway and Stephen Spender," she announced proudly. The pale, lean English poet and the tanned, robust American novelist sat together behind a single table, on which reposed a bright lamp and two beer mugs, though they nervously drank from the same one, Hemingway's. Extra beer bottles and the White Horse whisky bottle sat on the floor beside the table.

Intimidated, Hemingway, who was to read first, stammered through a few comments on writing and war and the difficulty of writing in a fascist country. Then he gulped down some beer and began reading "Fathers and Sons" from *Winner Take Nothing* (1933). He was whispering, and a woman asked him to speak louder. He then began to read, according to a French news reporter, "with the air of an innocent child and a strong American accent. This shyness could only make him seem more likable." Growing gradually more assured, according to the reporter for the Paris *Herald Tribune,* "he began to put expression in his clean, terse phrases. He was beginning to show grace under pressure." Pausing, he downed more of the foamy beer. It was grace under pressure, fortified by alcohol.

During the applause for Hemingway, Joyce and several others slipped out through the courtyard door. But if Spender was embarrassed by this desertion, he did not show it. He had been critical of Joyce in *The Destructive Element* (1935) and was as fervently committed to his socialist beliefs as Joyce was fervently indifferent to politics of whatever stripe. Caught in his poetry of war and enraptured by the socialist groups stirring in Spain, Spender later during this year would join the English Communist party. He read five (of a projected ten) poems he had recently written, some of the first literature to come out of war experiences in Spain. He forewarned the audience that the poems concerned war in general, not only the Spanish civil war. In a clear tone, contrasting sharply with that of Hemingway, he read,

> The guns spell money's ultimate reason
> In letters of lead on the spring hillside.
> But the boy lying dead under the olive trees
> Was too young and too silly
> To have been notable to their important eye.
> He was a better target for a kiss.

The poetry captured the antiwar romanticism of this Shelley of the thirties. For Spender, Hemingway, and other writers gathered at Shakespeare and Company on that evening, the Spanish civil war was a poet's war—a war in which some fine young writers would die, a war that Spender thought resonated a "poetic purity" and intensity as well as "Spanish passion, idealism and violence of temperament." Here was an open and genuine resistance to fascism; as such, it foreshadowed for Spender and others the combat of the modern individual against machinery, militarism, and bureaucracies.

Amid loud applause, particularly from the politically partisan people in the audience, Spender took a final drink of Hemingway's beer. A roar of chatter followed the joint reading. Everyone, Sylvia observed, considered the event a "great sensation." Hemingway kissed Adrienne on both cheeks and was overheard to mumble that he would never read in public again—not even for Sylvia Beach. Sylvia, deeming Spender "frightfully sensitive," contrived a medical excuse for Joyce, whose leaving she privately thought had been meant as an insult. But he, with commendable credulity, believed her tale and saluted Joyce as a great contemporary writer.

A rainy Whitsuntide vacation at the home of Polly Dennis, the daughter of George Washington Cable, brought Sylvia a needed rest and a slow release from the excitement of her Hemingway-Spender reading. Living alone now, as she had been since her return to France, Sylvia was free to spend more time with a variety of people. Later this spring she spent several weekends with different friends in the country and many hours in Paris with Carlotta, who had recently lost both parents. Together they saw films, a Roland Hayes concert, and Giraudoux's sensational new play, *Electra*.

The Paris Exposition Internationale opened in June amid strikes, a new devaluation of the franc, and demonstrations and relief efforts on behalf of Spain. Perhaps because of these political crises, Paris was particularly enamored of the Palace of Chaillot, the grand pavilion, the garden and fountains of the Trocadéro, and the terraces along the Seine opposite the Eiffel Tower. Sylvia took Marian Willard, who had stopped in Paris on her way to Zurich, to the opening ceremonies, which Sylvia described as "grand and gaudy." She scrutinized the Russian building, topped by a sculpture done by a woman—"gratifying," she confesses, "to feminists."

For many months now, Sylvia had been involved in the Exposition; for, as Bryher's Paris distributor, she was in charge of the *Life and Letters To-Day* booth—located in the Pavillon de la Presse (Valéry managed the writing section) between the venerable *Revue des Deux Mondes* and the children's *Mickey Mouse* magazine. Sylvia's booth, usually run by her assistant, Margaret Newitt, featured the all-French number of *Life and Letters To-Day*. Sylvia confessed that she did not have big plans for profit: "I would rather have a nice peanut stand with a machine steaming, than try to do something [commercial] with littrachur at the Exposition." Her best draw was, she added prankishly, the "sumptuous proportions" of her "beautiful blonde" assistant.

On 2 July 1937, two days after the opening of the Exposition, Sylvia held a formal reception to honor Bryher and her *Life and Letters To-Day*. The reception was, for all practical purposes, the last gathering of the Friends of Shakespeare and Company. The gathering comprised French and English Friends (including the editor Robert Herring from London), who cheerfully consumed an excess of both speeches and refreshments. Adrienne read aloud the account of Bryher's visit, at the age of five, to the Paris Exposition of 1900, *Paris 1900*—an account that Sylvia and Adrienne had translated into French. The audience was delighted with the historical parallel, but the naturally shy Bryher, intimidated by the presence of French writers, did not attend the reception. At the last moment, to everyone's disappointment, she had sent a note of regret to Sylvia. The party went on without her.

For all the receptions, readings, and expositions, Sylvia's meager business earnings could not cover burgeoning bookshop costs. Each year since 1932, rent and taxes had run to more than $2,000. Though Bryher herself gave nearly $1,400, special donations were down in 1937. There were at least eighty paid library subscriptions—Simone de Beauvoir borrowed armloads of books this year—but few people could buy books. Her visitors during the first half of 1937 included Isherwood, Spender, Leon Edel, Irving Babbitt, and Hemingway; but of these, only Hemingway was affluent.

One week in July during this sultry summer, while the International Congress of Writers angrily boiled over in Spain, Sylvia, vacationing in Jersey, was braced by the cool, tranquil marine air of the Channel, which cleared away every headache and fear of the future. She swam in the brine, ate potatoes—Jersey's chief crop and topic of conversation—and visited Polly Norledge, who had recently lost her husband. She then returned to Paris for a brief stay, after which, having thanked Margaret for a year of faithful help and bid farewell to Adrienne and Gisèle, she closed the shop and went back to Jersey, where she spent August and part of September. "Everyone here wants to flee to America away from wars and dictators," she confessed to her father a week before she left the tense city. Though the future had never been more cloudy, she had no intention of returning to the United States. Bryher assured Sylvia that come what may to Shakespeare and Company, she herself would be cared for: in fact, during the next seven, lean years, Sylvia would receive monthly payments from a special fund set up by Bryher for her common expenses. Feeling blessed with loyal friends, Sylvia sat down to begin her memoirs.

CHAPTER 18

Hanging On

1937–1939

> What has gone? How it ends? Begin to forget it. I will remember itself from every
> sides, with all gestures, in each word. Today's truth, tomorrow's trend. Forget,
> remember!
>
> — *Finnegans Wake*

TWO YOUNG AMERICAN WOMEN, who had met on board the *Cité du Havre,* arrived in France during September 1937: one was a nineteen-year-old debutante, the eldest daughter of a prominent Lake Forest family; the other was an attractive and intelligent married woman whose husband would spend the academic year just beginning at the Institute for Advanced Study at Princeton. "Aunt Sylvia," cried the first, as they were approached dockside in Le Havre by a thin little woman in loose-fitting clothes. Wearing no makeup and showing the first signs of arthritis, she certainly offered a strong contrast to her beautifully dressed godchild, Sylvia Peter, who had come to France to finish her education. The child's mother, Marian Mason Peter, had named her after the friend she had made in 1907 in Florence, where the two had spent a year together, living in a pension. Marian, married to a vice-president of the Long Island Railroad, had been a generous donor to the Friends of Shakespeare and Company. On this day her daughter brought an additional 500-franc ($90) gift. Young Sylvia, in the course of attending art classes at the school of André Lhote, was to help a little by "sitting" with the bookshop when her aunt Sylvia had to write letters or run errands. Eventually, however, it was her shipboard friend, whose name was Eleanor Oldenberger, who would become the shop assistant.

The elder Sylvia had just returned from her summer vacation with Polly Norledge in Trinity on the island of Jersey. Because Margaret Newitt had kept the shop open only a few days during her absence, Sylvia was swamped with the work of reopening the shop and preparing for the Sorbonne students: "no time for golf or bridge, even if I knew how to play either of those games," she gently complained to her father. Even when she had caught up with the paperwork after a two-month absence, she remained busy with her lending library and lunch and dinner engagements at Lipp's, the Deux Magots, and the Coupole. She found little time to work on her memoirs. These last years of the thirties were full of political turmoil, as war approached. Yet friendship and literature flourished.

Adrienne began publishing the periodical she called her *Gazette,* and Sylvia watched closely each detail of the preparation of what would be Joyce's last work, his *Work in Progress.* Weaving their way through her life and activities during these years were several young American women who assisted in the bookshop.

Paris was abuzz with the talk of war, particularly the war in Spain: two-thirds of the country was now held by Franco. During this autumn 12 writers in the *Left Review* posed a polemical question "to the writers and poets of England, Scotland, Ireland and Wales": "Are you for, or against, the legal government and the people of Republican Spain?" They declared that "Ivory Tower" ironic detachment "will no longer do . . . for it is impossible any longer to take no side." Only 5 of the 12 signers were friends of Sylvia Beach: Louis Aragon, W. H. Auden, Nancy Cunard, Stephen Spender, and Tristan Tzara. Of the 148 writers responding, 127 supported the Loyalists (as did Sylvia), 16 were neutral, and only five sided with Franco. A more lasting response was Auden's "Spain 1937" and scores of poems, essays, novels, and plays from the politically engaged writers. Many of them, such as Hemingway (whose *To Have and Have Not* had just been published), were in Spain observing, reporting, or fighting.

Hemingway and his fellow journalist Martha Gellhorn came to Paris from Madrid every two or three months during the coming year. Sylvia carefully followed the fighting in Spain, not simply because Hemingway was there but because Spain had been her home for almost two years before she moved to Paris in 1916. In a letter to her father, she declared that with all the trouble in Spain and China, it was probably time for a new Flood. She reported that "Roosevelt's speech about wars has been a sensation here." Adrienne is "quite lyrical" about Roosevelt (whose speeches were always translated and widely disseminated) as the "only hope of everyone." Though well-informed, Sylvia was not as politically involved as her friend Harriet Weaver, whose letters from London tell of her marching in the May Day parade and handing out the *Daily Worker* in Hyde Park. To her father, Sylvia reported, "We have been having great gunpowder plots and Ku Klux and all. But no blood shed, fortunately."

Sylvia was late to the grand opening, on 14 November, of the new home of the French PEN club in the rue Pierre-Charron, partly financed by government funds. While she was hurrying to close the shop, the president of the French Republic, Albert Lebrun, arrived at the ceremony with all due pomp. As the formally dressed writers pushed into line, President Lebrun paused to greet some of them. Adrienne, with her red Legion of Honor ribbon on her chest, drew his formal salutation. The host and president of PEN, Jules Romains, presented Lebrun to Joyce for a long handshake. Standing between Adrienne and Joyce was Nino Frank, who had accompanied Joyce. Frank, who was taken aback when the president also greeted him, assumed "that the chief of state suddenly took pity on the poor devil installed like a hyphen between the glory of Ireland and this high-placed Legion of Honor; in any event he held out his hand." Frank was so "flabbergasted" that his babbled response alerted Joyce, who could "hardly stifle his hilarity." Escaping down the stairway, where Joyce could indulge his mocking spirit, he whispered, "He probably took you for Sylvia Beach!" An embarrassed Frank and a mischievous Joyce abandoned the pompous speeches by the president and several of his ministers. By the time Sylvia arrived, she too had missed the speeches but not the "swell reception" and buffet. She talked both with Romains and with the secretary of the English branch of PEN. They agreed that the British and American governments would never contribute a home and a subsidy for their writers, as the French government had done.

Because business was poor and the only security seemed to be on the personal level, Sylvia took time to enjoy friends and nature. One day, after nodding to God and mammon—she had picked up a copy of *Pilgrim's Progress* for a customer and paid her taxes at Saint-Sulpice—she stopped in the Luxembourg Garden to sit for an hour on a bench, listen to the fountain, and smell the flowers. While her pace slowed, Joyce's quickened. While her circle of friends broadened, his shrank. Isolated in a dark apartment, Joyce labored away on *Work in Progress* for serialization in *Transition* and, he hoped for the following year, full publication by Faber and Faber in London. "A kind of destitution [replaced] the former animation and numerous friendships," claims Nino Frank, who paints the most detailed picture of Joyce's solitude during these final years of his life.

In the course of one of their occasional conversations, Joyce informed Sylvia that he had lost his copy of his early pamphlet "The Day of the Rabblement." Sylvia had Joyce Reeves, the young English girl who came twice a week to help in the shop, make a transcription of her own copy. The two-penny broadside against Irish parochialism denounced the proposed National Theatre as a betrayal of the artist, who should know no national boundaries. Joyce had had to publish it at his own expense in 1901. When he thanked Sylvia for the effort of copying the text, she responded with delight and to his surprise remarked, "Oh, that's all right. Joyce did it for me."

In addition to the occasional assistance from Joyce Reeves, Sylvia counted on the help of Sylvia Peter and Eleanor Oldenberger. On their arrival in Paris, Sylvia had taken them both to tea at an elegant pastry shop and then back to see the bookshop, which seemed very crowded by their American standards. The proprietress spoke very carefully—they thought pedantically—to the two young women, explaining the shop and Paris life. Soon, the two were acting as occasional shop sitters. Though they took her generosity for granted, they certainly were of assistance to her, freeing her to leave the shop when she wished. Young Sylvia, whom Sylvia considered a "baby vamp" but still a "dear little girl," showed up less and less at the bookshop, for she lived some distance away at the Cité Universitaire, studied art, and led a busy social life. Eleanor, who lived around the corner at the Hôtel l'Univers, took on more responsibility. Her difficulty with the French language in lectures that she attended at the Sorbonne and her fascination with the small and lively proprietress increasingly brought her from the university to the Odéon quarter. Soon after Adrienne had examined her handwriting and declared her trustworthy, Eleanor began working full-time at the shop. To enable Sylvia to have full-time help and thus the leisure to write her memoirs, Carlotta Briggs deposited $120 each month in a New York bank for Eleanor's salary, thereby avoiding the need for a work permit in Paris. The young Oldenbergers, who were paying only $20 for Eleanor's rent, considered the $120 a generous amount.

Friends who remained in Paris were loyal. Among the few who returned to stay was Samuel Beckett. By December, after years of "self-imposed isolation" and unhappiness in Dublin, Beckett had made Paris his permanent home. Within weeks, he had visited Sylvia and all his old friends; had had his novel *Murphy* accepted for publication after years of effort and a dozen rejections; and had taken up with Joyce, who again treated him as a servant. Because he loved Joyce, he corrected proofs and accepted the occasional humiliation. Being too poor, and at the same time too proud, to accept, as many others did, a free library card, Beckett came to Shakespeare and Company to browse and to talk to Sylvia, not to borrow or buy books. Eleanor did not particularly like him—he belonged to the decadent group, she believed; but he was on friendly terms with Sylvia. One day, Eleanor remembers, he and Sylvia had a long conversation about their love of mountain climbing. Beckett, though he might not have known the full extent of the personal and professional stress she had suffered, recalls that Sylvia had a "permanent worried look," as if she "had been battered against something."

Among her new members was the young daughter of William Butler Yeats, Anne Yeats, who borrowed only *Ulysses*. Sylvia took the eighteen-year-old girl into her care and escorted her to a meeting in the new quarters of PEN. Romains, who also attended this meeting, which was an affair for the Mexican writers, was delighted by Sylvia's guest. Another young friend of these years was Tania Whitman, daughter of the Crocker bank family of California and soon an *amateur riche* of Joyceana. Because Tania loved literature and wrote poetry, Sylvia forgave her her wealth. Tania often took Sylvia to lunch and occasionally worked in the bookshop when needed.

Despite the continuing literary activity and the support of new and old friends, the business suffered. Sylvia raised library charges, took out an ad in the *Herald Tribune,* and had the "best October" in years; but inflation ate up all profits. Henry Church and Tania Whitman were the only two who made large purchases. She could not have stayed open without her settlement from Bryher, who, anticipating the war, urged her to move to New York City.

Paris was full of refugees. Many French citizens were unemployed, and few could afford to buy the expensive hardback books of the American and British publishers. Sylvia warned James Laughlin of New Directions, who wanted his new anthology of experimental literature sold in the bookshop, to send only a few. Most of the English and American intellectuals are gone, she adds, and "the French rarely go as high as a dollar and then only for a classic." Soon, she would be able to sell only three copies of each issue of *Life and Letters To-Day* for Bryher. But Eleanor, young and American, saw the economic crisis—which dominated many of their conversations—as a challenge rather than a necessity to which they must bow. She handled the daily fluctuation of the franc and did her best to promote business. She took the eight-by-twelve-inch signs advertising "The Famous Bookshop and Lending Library" (printed in 1933) to hotel lobbies. She subsequently introduced Sylvia to Mme Hazenberg, who sat behind the information desk at the American Express office, directing hundreds of Americans to spots in Paris. She took the two women to lunch, then left a stack of bookshop calling cards on the desk for Mme Hazenberg to give to anyone who showed an interest in books. Eleanor increased the amount of the children's literature in the lending library—as Jean Henley had done with erotica, to help business. Finally, she brought a friend of hers, a tax expert named Alexis Roubin from the finance ministry, to help with the books. By the time Eleanor left, at the end of 1938, the bookshop showed a smaller deficit than usual.

During the first Christmas season that Eleanor worked in the bookshop, Pauline Hemingway arrived in a flurry from her home in Florida looking for her husband, who had been vacationing in Catalonia with his fellow war correspondent Martha Gellhorn. Young Eleanor, who was alone in the shop, knew nothing of the troubled marriage of the Hemingways and could do little to comfort Pauline, who plied her with questions. Though he was gloomily reunited with Pauline and returned to the United States, Hemingway was back in Europe with Martha in the following spring and the autumn. Sylvia watched the Hemingway wives come and go, commenting to Eleanor that his "first trouble is he wants to marry everybody." (He would marry Martha in 1940, immediately after his divorce from Pauline, and divorce her in 1945, three months before marrying Mary Welsh.) Sylvia's strongest judgment against this man, whom she considered her good friend, was delivered during a discussion of his literary treatment of women: "Hemingway just thinks that women are something to fuck."

War moved closer in the early months of 1938. Hitler announced "a further understanding" with Austria, as Sylvia, with ironic understatement, describes his invasion of that country. Each evening Lord Halifax explained to Londoners on the BBC the procedures for air raids. The "French are trembling and miserable" and beginning to move their troops to frontier locations, Sylvia informs Holly. She refers to the dictators as "the Bullies"—Hemingway's term—yet approves the government's appeasement measures: "the government has gone more to the right in the hopes of conciliating fascist neighbors, and I hope it works—but wonder." She had been convinced since her Serbian days that war is insanity, and shared the maxim that most other French friends held: "peace at all costs." Everyone's attention was turning toward daily survival. While Sylvia depended on the monthly charity of Bryher and Carlotta, her sister Cyprian, recently recovered from shingles and needing to pay her bills, had applied to the Federal Theatre Project.

The charity that she herself could afford to give she reserved for young people, who adored her. She denied them neither books nor small loans. In only one area was she intransigent—that of overdue books. Yet it was the people with money—not the students—who were most guilty of keeping books too long. One Frenchwoman who returned a book long overdue refused to pay the fine. "Well," responded Sylvia, "if you are so poor as not to be able to pay this small fine, I will give you some money." Insulted, the woman—who could have well afforded to buy the book—claimed that she had never been talked to in such a manner. Those who had the money, Sylvia observed to several of her assistants, often failed to pay their bills. Small wonder that she cared more for the poor students, who, as a group, were more respectful of books and lending privileges.

Ford Madox Ford borrowed his last books from Shakespeare and Company on 2 March 1938—a handful on the metaphysical poets—and withdrew from the world of patriotism, technology, and urbanization. In *Provence* he declares, "I want a civilization of small men each laboring two small plots—his own ground and his own soul." The man who had first published a piece of Joyce's new novel under the title "Work in Progress," who had encouraged the young midwestern writers in his *Transatlantic Review*, who had bounced Sylvia around the dance floors of Montparnasse—this man would, in the last months of his life, cultivate his own vegetable garden.

In 1937 Adrienne resigned her directorship of *Mesures* magazine and sold the rights of her French translation of *Ulysses* to Gallimard publishers, thus freeing herself to renew an interrupted literary adventure. *La Gazette des Amis des Livres,* a small pamphlet or bulletin of about thirty pages, was her own garden. Each pamphlet consisted of one or more essays by her—a continuation of the personal "gazette" section of her *Navire d'Argent* of the twenties—and a section of a bibliography of world literature and history. The bibliography was intended to be a sequel to her catalog of French literature available at her lending library (Catalogue Critique de la Bibliothèque de Prêt, 1932). The *Gazette* printed readers' correspondence and some quotations and announcements. Her first issue (January 1938) is made up chiefly of her essay entitled "Numéro Un." Adrienne speaks directly to the French, who, because they "want to be rich" believe their "poets must be poor." The French book business, she declares, is suffering; only the Italian and Spanish are worse buyers of books. She concludes with a request for a dialogue on books with her readers. This first *Gazette* was well received; 200 people, including Holly and the Reverend Beach, subscribed to it almost immediately. Gide praised her work and declared that "one hears you speak" in the essay.

In the same month in which the first *Gazette* appeared, Adrienne and Sylvia published their translation of Bryher's sixty-two-page booklet *Paris 1900,* from which Adrienne had read in the preceding year, at the *Life and Letters To-Day* reception. Bryher was delighted, and inscribed in Sylvia's copy, "The only writing of mine I have ever read with pleasure thanks to your translation."

In the eyes of the world, Joyce again became associated with Shakespeare and Company. It was, however, only for a day in May, and it was only to pose for publicity pictures for *Work in Progress,* whose final title, *Finnegans Wake,* was known only to him and Nora at the time, when it was being prepared for simultaneous publication in England and the United States. Joyce himself arranged the meeting with Adrienne and Sylvia as part of one of his five sessions of posing for Gisèle Freund. He had definite ideas about how he wanted himself presented to the world, Gisèle remembers. As he was well aware, the world would associate him with the two women who helped him so much on the way to success. The pictures of the three old friends, posed rather formally around the small table below the photograph of William Shakespeare, is one of the most popular pictures from the rue de l'Odéon. They appear suspended in a sea of books and photographs. Sylvia looks severe with her hair pulled back, yet younger than her fifty-one years. She is wearing a dark dress with a white collar and is smoking. Joyce is slouched in his chair and looks tired. He was, in fact, very ill and talked of this book as his last, almost foretelling his death, thought Gisèle later. She remembers the meeting of the estranged friends as happy and full of memories.* This was Joyce's last formal visit to the rue de l'Odéon. He would be dead in less than two years.

While Europe cracked and burst around him, Joyce with studied detachment corrected proofs for the most recent issue of *Transition* and prepared his great novel for publication. He saw to all the details, from the cover, publicity photographs, and early reviews to the appearance of Gorman's biography, which Joyce delayed until the novel appeared. Beckett first agreed to, then abandoned, an essay on demand; but he corrected proofs with the others. The Jolases and the Léons played a guessing game that he made up about the title of his work. When Jolas guessed the title in August, Joyce paid him a 100-franc wager and swore him to secrecy. "It is surprising," Léon confided to Miss Weaver, "what a minute circle of friendship surrounds him."

By contrast, the spring social calendar of Shakespeare and Company was crowded with visits from old friends, students, and wounded veterans of the Spanish war. Sylvia's friendships were catholic in scope. Perdita Macpherson, the natural daughter of H.D. and the adopted daugher of Bryher, visited Paris alone this year. She was nearly nineteen and ready to establish friendships of her own. She liked Sylvia very much, visited the bookshop often, and went to the theater with her. During a visit to Sylvia's apartment, Perdita saw a box of letters from Joyce. Sylvia, who was sorting her papers for her memoirs, talked of Perdita's parents and the twenties. The young woman was impressed less with the past than with Sylvia's nervous energy and interest in the present—the concierge's son, the neighbor's cats, the theater, and her friends.

Though the volume of business was now a trickle, compared with the flow in the twenties, fame brought Sylvia unsolicited manuscripts and fan mail. She

---

* "Early in March [1939, Freund writes], *Time* magazine asked me to persuade Joyce to pose once more, in color this time, because they wanted to use my portrait of him on the cover. After my promise to Joyce that I would never bother him again, I was reluctant to do so. . . . It was Sylvia who suggested the one way I might get Joyce to pose for me in color. . . . . . 'Write him a letter,' she said, 'and sign your married name this time.' " Immediately after receiving the request to pose for Mrs. Bloom, Joyce responded favorably.

kept up a regular correspondence with many of her friends and patrons of the twenties, such as the Antheils, who were now parents of a son; Kay Boyle, who lived in the south of France with her husband, Laurence Vail; and MacLeish, Williams, and many others who lived in the United States. McAlmon, Natalie Barney, Elliot Paul, William Bird, Beckett, and Hemingway dropped in occasionally this year to see her. Holly, whom she would not see again for fourteen years, paid a one-day visit during a London vacation. When Barney ordered books and added 300 francs for a donation, Sylvia expressed her gratitude. Sylvia and Adrienne finally had time during the last years of the thirties to visit Barney's salon.

During a brief visit in March to Shakespeare and Company, Hemingway purchased two plays: Charles Bennet's *Blackmail* and Stephen Spender's *Trial of a Judge* (1938). Though he had always been interested chiefly in fiction, Hemingway had as early as 1927 discussed with his editor, Maxwell Perkins, the possibility of writing a play. And in February of the following year (1928), he had borrowed from Sylvia's library O'Casey's *Plough and the Stars* and O'Neill's *Emperor Jones*. These two were the only plays he borrowed until his 1938 purchases. His renewed interest in drama had begun in the fall of 1937, when he wrote his only play, *The Fifth Column*, a contemporary spy thriller full of autobiographical elements and set in Madrid. He had this manuscript with him in March and left it with Sylvia to mail to Perkins on the twenty-seventh. Uncertain about his success as a playwright, he waited until August to make the decision to include the play in a collection of his short stories.

Friends of the thirties, such as Padraic and Mary Colum, Henri Michaux, Anaïs Nin, and Henry Miller, were faithful this year. Miller and Saroyan, working with Alfred Perles, Nin, and Lawrence Durrell, had started a sort of Dadaist anthology called *The Booster,* later called *Delta* (1937–1938), which Sylvia distributed. Farrell, whom Sylvia had met through Putnam in 1931, visited Paris again this year. She took a stronger dislike to him this time, because he acted like a "pushy upstart" and bragged too loudly about living with a mistress.

Among the new friends—Gisèle Freund calls him a "shy, silent visitor"— was the fifty-nine-year-old English novelist E. M. Forster, whose work Sylvia enthusiastically admired and collected for her library—from the novels *Where Angels Fear to Tread* (1905) and *Passage to India* (1924) to his minor classic of criticism *Aspects of the Novel* (1927).

One must, in observing the literary and personal associations of Sylvia, note her growing contact with several wealthy persons, which is accounted for in part by the financial need of Shakespeare and Company and by their generosity. Yet there remains a paradoxical element in her relations with them, which is not explained entirely by this need. Theoretically, she had contempt for mere wealth. Beginning in this spring and summer, however, she repeatedly visited the homes of Polly Dennis, Mr. and Mrs. Romilly Feddens, Polly Norledge, and Carlotta and Jim Briggs (only Carlotta was a childhood friend). Though Sylvia had fame, her style of life (including an apartment without running water) was dramatically simple, and her political views were far to the left of those of such friends. Still, though she could turn her wit against them, she enjoyed their company. They, in turn, found her undemanding, easy to entertain, and, above all, amusing.

However, Sylvia reserved her greatest respect for the creative artists, and they enjoyed her company for the same reason the wealthy did. She was a clever conversationalist, curious and animated, delighted with everything she saw and did. She did not talk about herself, but absorbed the world around her as if each day were her last on earth. Perhaps it was her parsonage training that gave others the impression that she thought herself unimportant and placed others first. But the trait that may have endeared her most to her literary friends was her loyalty. "I'm a clingstone-beach," she once observed with a pun. One of her strongest loyalties was to Bryher (who combined wealth and creativity) with whom she spent Whitsun weekend in Vevey, Switzerland—though since her abortive school experience there, she had never liked the country. While in Vevey, she sunbathed, swam in the lake, and went for a drive in the mountains with "Uncle Norman" Douglas, the English author of the famous novel *South Wind* (1917) and many volumes of travel literature. Douglas was a close friend of Bryher and her husband Kenneth Macpherson. Later, they faithfully took care of Douglas in his old age. Bryher, who again warned Sylvia about the inevitability of war, had been busy for six years smuggling German Jews through Switzerland to France and beyond. Sylvia was also helping Germans resettle and was raising money for the republican cause in Spain by selling prints of contemporary artists in her shop.

One of the most important gestures of friendship for her artist friends was her determination to protect them. She became upset when a young assistant would rush up to a writer and make that writer aware of his public reputation. The bookshop was to be a haven. During the twenties, she had told inquirers that Joyce was not in the shop when he was in fact standing in the back room. Now she protected Hemingway when he visited. Even in her memoirs, written after many of these persons had died, she protected their privacy. Though it weakened her memoirs, she never traded on her literary friendships.

On a cold and rainy May day, Sylvia and a few other friends from the twenties and thirties joined a large crowd of villagers to attend the wedding of William Bird's daughter in Houx, near Maintenon. Sylvia rode in a chauffeured bus with the musicians, McAlmon, and other guests who had no car. She sat with McAlmon directly behind the bus driver, whom she directed to the wedding, which, because of inclement weather, took place in a big loft. McAlmon had returned early in 1938 for what would become a final, two-year drift through Europe. He gave Sylvia the proofs of his Paris memoirs, *Being Geniuses Together*, finally published in London this summer, after many cuts by the publisher Secker and Warburg. If the publishers considered it too vulgar and the reviewers too vengeful, Sylvia considered it candid but honest. The visits with McAlmon in this year were amiable, though Sylvia, as she had already said years before, was disappointed by what she believed was a waste of his talents. When she returned to the bookshop from the Bird wedding, she discovered that in her absence Hemingway had dropped in with a group of friends and would return the following day.

When Hemingway came, she served him whisky from the bottle that she had bought for his reading at the shop, in the preceding year. During their hour together, while he sipped his drink and told of his experiences in Spain, she listened with her usual enthusiasm and wonder. He returned her hospitality and attentiveness by declaring that he would give another reading the next time he came to Paris (the war and sober reconsideration intervened). He took Sylvia to lunch with Martha, Freddy Keller, and Marty Hourihan; the latter two were wounded friends from the American battalion in Spain. Sylvia paid careful attention to the stories of Spain and battle wounds. But though she always listened closely to Hemingway's stories, she did not share his view of war or his macho approach to crises. She confided this reservation to Holly:

Stephen Spender is shocked at Hemingway's war lust and the way he seems to thrive on the front lines amid shells and bombs. Stephen is definitely horrified at violence, and I feel as he does and with [Aldous] Huxley in his *Ends and Means* [1937 essays]. . . . [But, she adds,] I am very fond of Hemingway and accept him *tel quel* [as he is].

This was her secret of friendship.

Norman Douglas came for a visit during the summer. Sylvia and he both loved the southern lands: she Greece and he Italy. The British novelist was now seventy years old, but his conversation was exuberant and free and, declares his friend Bryher, he was both "erudite and adventurous." Sylvia gave him Hemingway's whisky bottle, and the two friends, bottle in hand, strode up the street to the Luxembourg Garden. They took with them a little sailboat that Sylvia had recently purchased for her young nephew Freddie Dennis:

Norman and I launched it on the Luxembourg lake. He christened it the "Norman Douglas" with some whiskey in a bottle that Hemingway didn't finish when he was here. But Freddie [she tells her sister] will have to come and fetch it if he is ever to get it. Douglas teased me by saying that the boat was really for myself. . . .

This childlike quality of delight in the daily adventure of life—a quality she shared with Douglas—remained with her until the day she died.

On the dark side were the migraine headaches, which had plagued her since childhood and which only long periods of quiet away from Paris could cure. "I never mention the head to Father," she confesses to Holly, "as it would only worry him unnecessarily, but you know that I suffer from continual migraines. Being away from everything and everybody is the best treatment and I have only one month that I can devote to the cause of my health." Both for her health and for the solitude necessary to work on her memoirs (Clifton Fadiman had been urging her to complete them), she went in August to her little mountain chalet at Les Déserts. She rejected kind invitations to visit Carlotta in Bourée and Polly Norledge in Jersey and even to enjoy the company of Adrienne. She had not been in Les Déserts in three years and had never been there alone, as she was now, though Marie Monnier spent the first two weeks with her. It rained so hard that snails clung to the bottom of her damp shoes, forcing her to ask the carpenter to remove them. Nevertheless, she walked the mountain paths, carried water each morning to her little cottage, and chopped wood for her cooking stove. After Marie left, Sylvia typed out on her Remington the memories of her youth and of the opening of her bookshop and library. Because of the war, she believed, there was "no hurry for publication" (indeed, it did not come until twenty years later). As she had excluded Adrienne from this vacation, so she kept her far in the background of her memoirs. She confessed to Jackson Mathews years later, "I didn't really say in my book what I wanted to about Adrienne Monnier. She was such an interesting person that I was afraid she'd take the whole show." Because the writing went well and Eleanor Oldenberger was managing Shakespeare and Company, Sylvia stayed through September. Only rumors of war and the evacuation of the Savoyards drew her home to Paris.

In addition to helping her run Shakespeare and Company economically, which meant just breaking even, Eleanor filled Sylvia's need for a close personal friend during this year. Since she had moved into the bookshop apartment, Sylvia had yearned somewhat for daily companionship, and Eleanor provided this. Sylvia, who loved to walk, took Eleanor with her on long hikes along the banks of Mr. Joyce's Anna Sequana and about the city she loved. She explained the origin of street names and architecture and told stories about the occupants of the buildings they passed. Interlaced with these anecdotes were tales of the twenties and Joyce and the crowd that used to gather at the bookshop. For the younger woman, these walks were intimate lecture tours. Sylvia took upon herself the education of Eleanor, who was bright and eager to learn about literature, and gave her, one at a time, the books of Joyce, beginning with *Exiles* and moving on to *Dubliners, Portrait,* and finally *Ulysses,* each with explanations and reminiscences. It was with the study of *Dubliners* that Eleanor became interested. As she read *Ulysses,* Sylvia gave her a chapter-by-chapter explanation. She revealed to the younger woman that she felt she had been wronged, and yet it was apparent to Eleanor that she revered Joyce's work without qualification. She gave Eleanor a copy of one of her early printings of *Ulysses* with the soft-blue cover and warned her never to cut the pages, because that would decrease the value of the book. She directed her reading to a variety of other books, including Forster's *Passage to India* and Radclyffe Hall's *Well of Loneliness,* and took her to excellent restaurants and to cultural events, including productions of Garcia Lorca's *Bodas de Sangre (Blood Wedding)* and Bach's *Saint Matthew Passion* and a lecture by Auden at the Sorbonne.

Priscilla Curtis began working for Sylvia during Eleanor's last months in the shop and took over before Christmas, when Eleanor left. Priscilla, who had attended Bryn Mawr for two years, was a school chum of Sylvia Peter's sister Phyllis and a member of another prominent Chicago family. After Priscilla attended classes in the mornings, she opened the bookshop at 2 P.M. and stayed until 6. Her mother gave her a little allowance and secretly paid Sylvia 450 francs (about $50) a month. "She is to think I am paying her myself," confesses Sylvia to Holly. "I don't approve of these subtleties," but the mother believes that Priscilla will "take interest if she thinks it's a real job."

Priscilla's most vivid memory of working for Sylvia, whom she thought "quite a character," was the odd nature of the business, which was "hardly business-like." Sylvia did not seem to want to part with anything. When a customer asked for one of her first editions, which filled many shelves, Sylvia would take it down and talk with growing enthusiasm about the book and its author. Finally, according to Priscilla, she would replace the book, declaring that she could not part with it. Like the homeowner who reads his own description of his house in the newspaper, she had sold herself the book.

Except for Eleanor, Sylvia's assistants of this period learned little about her private life, but observed that she spent long hours in the tidy, crowded, musty rooms above the shop, where she answered letters from around the world, kept the books, and occasionally added new portions to her memoirs. For relaxation she read mysteries and contemporary fiction. Now she had time—as in October, when she read Thomas Mann's *Magic Mountain*—to catch up on the reading she had put off in the frantic twenties. Now, when she least needed assistance, she had a number of young American women to sit in a nearly empty shop.

Alexis Léger, a permanent ambassador at the Quai d'Orsay, telephoned Sylvia in early June of 1938 to inform her that she had received the French Legion of Honor (created by Napoleon in 1802). She, Adrienne, and Léger (the great poet, whose nom de plume was Saint-John Perse) celebrated with lunch at the home of Henri Hoppenot, who along with Édouard Herriot had made the nomination. Sylvia's father was the one most pleased by the honor that the French government paid his middle daughter. He confessed, "I am so proud of you that I am maudlin." He and Holly took the honors of the world seriously. His letters, until interrupted by the war, were filled with effusive expressions of his pride in her career. He lavished endearing names on her. Cyprian was greatly pleased, or to be more precise, relieved, to hear the news of the Legion of Honor. Her embarrassing mistake of the year before was forgotten. With relief, she confided to Sylvia, "I should have delayed my heroic exploits as star publicity agent another year." Sylvia, too, was pleased with the honor, but she took it with her usual ironic humor, referring to the "little ribbon gibbon me by the French." She was innocent of pride, claims Hoppenot, and accepted the award as a sign that she was confirmed as French. Only four months earlier, when an English award had been bestowed on Maurois, she had humorously suggested that the British should also honor her for "keeping their old Bard fresh here all these years." When the French honored her, she received, according to her own description, "tons of letters . . . most from French friends." The British and Americans would be much slower to recognize her contribution to literature.

Now that Joyce was gone, Gertrude Stein and Alice Toklas more frequently strolled down the rue de l'Odéon, Gertrude wearing her brown velvet hat, which to the young American assistants looked like a baseball cap. With her close-cropped gray hair, the large Stein was a presence that commanded attention. Alice would come in first to survey the shop. If Sylvia was there, Alice occupied herself with the assistant so that Gertrude had Sylvia to herself. If Sylvia was not there, she engaged the customers so that Gertrude had the full use of the assistant. One day, when Sylvia was out late in the afternoon, Alice stopped by at Adrienne's bookshop, while Gertrude slowly stepped into Shakespeare and Company. The Sibyl of Montparnasse was now sixty-four, but her round face was nearly unlined. She inquired of Sylvia's assistant, "Are you busy?" Eleanor assured her that they had many customers, but few Americans. "What books are being bought?" Stein asked in a voice that Eleanor considered beautiful, and with a look that caught her straight in the eye with its undivided attention. Stein was charming and beautiful, Eleanor thought, but full of distracting questions. Eleanor had to respond negatively when asked whether they had sold any copies of Stein's *Everybody's Autobiography* (1937), the account of her American lecture tour. After an occasional glance out the window for Alice and after a few more questions concerning business, Stein left without making a purchase. When Sylvia returned before dinner she concluded that they had been inspected.

On another day, while Priscilla was working in the bookshop and Hemingway was browsing around the shelves, Stein arrived, led by her black dog, Basket III, and was confronted by the man with whom she had not conversed in years. The barbs that had been traded (Hemingway was to deliver the last and cruelest in his posthumous *A Moveable Feast*) were notorious. But on this occasion, in Shakespeare and Company, good form prevailed: they hugged and exchanged enthusiastic greetings for the wide-eyed assistant. That is, the short and rotund lady grasped the arms of the burly thirty-nine-year-old Hemingway, who leaned down to press his cheek against hers.

Stein considered her borrowings from Shakespeare and Company to be on a personal and not a business basis. Though she drove a new car and Sylvia a bicycle, she assumed that her lending privileges should be free. Increasingly, she invited Sylvia to her new apartment in the rue Christine, into which she and Alice had recently moved with their 130 canvases. Sylvia occasionally took a young assistant with her. On one such visit in the following year, when Sylvia brought Tania Whitman and Priscilla Curtis, Stein took the three on a tour of her gallery and spent fifteen minutes of analysis in front of the painting of a chair by Francis Rose, one of her discoveries. Rose had, she announced, "captured the chairiness of the chair." On these visits, Sylvia and Gertrude spent most of the time exchanging information about their mutual friends.

Aside from Stein, Hemingway, and Beckett (the latter comparatively unknown at that time), Sylvia's most distinguished English-speaking patrons during these last years of the thirties were the Oxford English poets, inheritors of *The Waste Land* and active opponents of fascism in Europe. The following men considered themselves the heirs of her patrons of the twenties: Spender, Auden, Isherwood, C. Day Lewis, and their friend Cyril Connolly. Unlike the others, Connally was a journalist who had done rather little creative work—he had written only one novel. But among the group, he was Sylvia's closest and oldest friend. When his collection of essays, *Enemies of Promise,* was published, in this year, he inscribed two copies, one "To Sylvia the only *friend* of Promise" and the other "To Sylvia without whom this or nothing else would have been written." Auden, who had been dropping by Shakespeare and Company for several years, published this year *Overtures to Death and Other Poems.* Normally pale, with an unhealthy, doughy look, Auden flushed red when he was excited. The bookshop assistants thought he suffered by comparison with the fair-haired Spender, who looked like a tall Lord Byron. Sylvia talked of his recently published verse play *Trial of a Judge,* and the assistants whispered of his love life. The presence of these young English writers, Hemingway's visits from the war, and Sylvia's interest in political events changed the tenor of Shakespeare and Company in the late thirties.

Even Valéry had turned his attention to social issues when he published *La France Veut la Liberté* this year. He now occupied the chair of poetry at the Collège de France, a post created for him in 1937, and stopped by each week following his afternoon at the French Academy. Priscilla remembers the day on which he came to congratulate Sylvia for her Legion of Honor:

Just after dusk and at closing time there was a knock on the window. A masklike face, gray moustache and black rimmed glasses, was pressed up against it. Paul Valéry always peered in to ensure Sylvia's presence before he came in. Tonight he was joyful; as one of Sylvia's enthusiastic admirers, he took a personal pride in her award.

Proud of his accomplishments, Sylvia gave Miss Weaver a copy of Valéry's *La France Veut la Liberté* for Christmas.

Of all the books dealing with war, peace and freedom this year, the most important was George Orwell's *Homage to Catalonia.* The work reveals his compassion for the Spanish people and a knowledge of the political background of the war, in which he himself had fought. Spender borrowed Shakespeare and Company's copy of the book on 7 September; Hemingway borrowed it on 30 September and never returned it. He had also borrowed earlier that month (and never returned) Elliot Paul's *Life and Death of a Spanish Town,* about the Fascist invasion of Santa Eulalia. In March he had begun writing his own novel about the Spanish civil war, to be called *For Whom the Bell Tolls.* The conspicuously engaged older American writer paid careful attention to the literature of the younger English writers, whose essays, novels, and plays focus on European communism's conflict with fascism. Defensive about his playboy image, Hemingway confessed to George Seldes, "I had to go to Spain to prove to you goddamm liberals that I was on your side."

By contrast to these writers, Joyce appeared to be paring his fingernails while Europe ignited. Paul Léon expressed his fear to Harriet Weaver that Joyce would be accused of elitism, of writing capitalist art for elitists. Two friends, by defending Joyce, acknowledged this tension. In "Homage to the Mythmaker," in the final issue of *transition,* Jolas defended Joyce's neutrality and apparent lack of social consciousness. Several years later, Carola Giedion-Welcker claimed that Joyce was not indifferent to war, because of his Saint Patrick's Day party in 1938 he spoke briefly about Hitler's demonic character.

"My old Pal Hemingway is back and working hard on a book," Sylvia announced to Holly. "He is also delivering large quantities of food to the Spanish, risking his life every day to get it through." The quantities were not large, and probably most of the food he smuggled was for himself and Martha, claims George Seldes, who stayed in the same Madrid hotel. Hemingway always held court when he arrived at Shakespeare and Company. He was the center of any group. Sometimes he brought the group of friends with him; at other times he attracted a small crowd. He was a famous writer, a big, bearlike man. Eleanor took an immediate dislike to him. He swaggered and was too busy being the center of everyone's attention, she observed. More important, he walked out with magazines and books without paying. Eleanor was under the impression—a mistaken impression, she later learned, as far as it concerned writers like Hemingway—that she was there to help the bookshop remain solvent. She began keeping a record of the magazines and books he took. Occasionally she would have to invent an excuse to walk across the room to get a look at the title in his hand. The list grew, and she kept it on her desk for the opportune moment.

One day in the fall of 1938, Hemingway came to the shop with Martha Gellhorn. They were very interested in each other and in the latest journals and books. Sylvia was not there. Though he had never paid her attention before, this time he walked to Eleanor's desk with two books and asked her what he owed. She calculated the expense of the two volumes and then suggested:

"Perhaps you would like to settle your account, Mr. Hemingway." He raised his eyebrows in surprised interest. She took the list that she had been saving from her desk and handed it to him.

"These are the books you have taken on previous occasions." With his future wife looking on, he opened his wallet and took out twenty dollars and some change. They left immediately.

When Eleanor returned from lunch, Sylvia met her with an anxious look on her face and took her to the back room for a confidential chat.

"Hemingway was here this morning?"

"Yes, he was," Eleanor replied.

"Well, he telephoned at noon to be certain I was here. Then he came over to express his anger," declared Sylvia. " 'I was here this morning,' raged Hemingway, 'and she cleaned out my pockets. Get rid of that female before you lose all of your pals.' " When Eleanor tried to explain how Hemingway had been taking books from the shop, Sylvia showed no apparent surprise and remained annoyed with her.

"Never do that again, Eleanor. Friends can have anything that they want. If they do not want to pay for what they take, they do not have to pay." Eleanor was bewildered and hurt. She had expected to have a businesslike behavior approved of. Sylvia concluded the discussion by adding, "Brentano's would *pay* Hemingway if he would come to their shop!"

The following month, on his last trip from Madrid, Hemingway walked in as if nothing had happened, greeting the assistant curtly. "My new book [*The Fifth Column and First Forty-Nine Stories*] is coming out soon and I want to order twenty copies for Christmas gifts." Eleanor wrote down the order and excitedly told Sylvia. "You see," Sylvia cheered, believing that Eleanor had finally understood the code of the literary salon and bookshop. "He is a friend of Shakespeare and Company."

In order to ensure delivery before Christmas, they had to order by cable. They were concerned about spending $5 for a cable. When the order arrived, they stacked their large investment of books on the desk and waited for his visit. When he finally dropped in a week or two later, he sat at the desk to autograph his copies. From the top of the stack he took one and signed his name, asking Sylvia to send it to the Spanish ambassador-in-exile. The second he sent to a friend in the French diplomatic service in the Quai d'Orsay. Opening the third, he asked Sylvia for the name of her assistant and then inscribed "To Eleanor Oldenberger with very best wishes from her friend Ernest Hemingway." Surprised and pleased, Eleanor considered it a truce.

When the third book had been signed, he took out his money and paid for just three books, then walked out, leaving them bewildered and dejected. What would they do with the other seventeen copies of his book? During the final weeks of her employment, Eleanor did her best to sell the books to any customer who looked solvent, but there were few English-speaking people in Paris at that time of the year, and the French would probably not have bought the copies even if they could have afforded them. According to Hemingway's library card, Eleanor sold only six of the seventeen copies.

Act 5 of the thirties tragedy began in the fall of 1938, when the Munich Pact in effect surrendered central Europe to Hitler. The English poet Louis MacNeice expressed the mood of England, as well as that of France, in his *Autumn Journal:*

> Conferences, adjournments, ultimatums,
> Flights in the air, castles in the air,
> The autopsy of treaties, dynamite under the bridges
> The end of *laissez faire*.

This poem about the autumn of 1938 expresses the sense of the apocalypse—that "beast / That prowls at every door and barks in every headline." Paris began to look more and more like a refugee camp. Citizens hoarded food staples, especially chocolate and coffee, which Sylvia, Adrienne, and Eleanor agreed were among the best pleasures of the palate. By January, Sylvia would have the required foreign-identity card, with her photograph on it, a right-profile view with her ear showing. The American embassy, where her friend Keeler Faus worked, advised all Americans to leave Europe. She would stay. To relieve financial pressures, she sold her manuscript of *Pomes Penyeach* to Tania Whitman.

With the French economy in shambles and only a few thousand Americans remaining in Paris, Sylvia joined the Briggses for Thanksgiving. The small group of Americans at their house included Arthur J. Knodel, a recent graduate of the University of Southern California. The young American was delighted to meet the famous Sylvia Beach, whom he thought "an extraordinary little lady." He was to pay regular visits to Shakespeare and Company, until June of 1939. Sylvia served him tea and cookies and introduced him to the works of Sartre, Michaux, and Saint-John Perse. Later, as professor of French at the University of Southern California, Knodel devoted much of his professional life to the works of Perse.

In one of the many articles that spread her fame this year, Sylvia is described as having a "gift for listening [and] a spring of sympathy and spiritual vitality; but she is also like a deposit of many rich minds, delicate, small-boned, clear skinned.. . . . Her femininity is of a rare sort that does not need clothes to express individual taste and character. It is all done with the face, the deep-set eyes, the presence." The essay also captures the atmosphere in which Knodel and two generations of young scholars and artists were nourished: the "spell of stillness" in Shakespeare and Company, "its somewhat littered appearance," and rooms "smelling pleasantly of print and paper and old wood."

After having delayed her departure for several months, Eleanor left for the United States to join her professor husband in Chicago. She sailed on a ship crowded with Jewish refugees and anti-Semitic employees, carrying with her the manuscript of *Stephen Hero*, which Marian Willard had in the meanwhile returned to Sylvia. Eleanor offered the manuscript first to the Collector's Bookshop in New York which decided not to buy it. Then Marian, for Sylvia, negotiated with Harvard, which, to raise the money, arranged an exhibit of the Joyceana that Sylvia had left in the safe of Marian's grandmother, Mrs. Guthrie: *Chamber Music, Stephen Hero,* and the protest letter with its signatures. Although Marian thought the initial Harvard offer for *Stephen Hero*—only $450—ridiculously low, Sylvia made no attempt to raise the price until it was too late, after Marian had sold the manuscript for a trifling $500 in January 1939. Sylvia wanted her manuscripts used, not "possessed," but if a library did gain possession, she believed, it should have paid a fair price. Nevertheless, the sale to Harvard helped Shakespeare and Company, which had a 8,000-franc deficit for 1938. Since having said farewell to the manuscript of Joyce's first novel, she had been awaiting the publication of his last. "Finished *Work in Progress* tonight," he wired Miss Weaver on 14 November, then collapsed, having brought the waters of the Liffey River and the Irish Sea together. One thousand pages of proof awaited correction. Friends other than Sylvia would help Joyce correct proofs on this novel.

While Priscilla kept the library members happy, Sylvia posed for Gisèle, who photographed a color portrait of her face. She used a newly discovered process by which she was able to project the pictures onto a large screen. Through Adrienne's assistance, Gisèle had photographed a number of French writers. They planned to show this December the larger-than-life faces on a screen in Adrienne's shop. Sylvia enjoyed seeing all her friends in "gigantic size" but found it "scaring" to see herself. Adrienne published a loving description of Gisèle's talent in her *Gazette*.

Though Sylvia continued to express the hope that there would be no war, Hitler made it inevitable in March 1939 by invading Czechoslovakia and uniting it with the Reich. In the weeks before, as the Spanish civil war had ended, half a million Spaniards had swept across the border and into France. Britain made treaties with Poland, Greece, Romania, and Turkey. With irony, Sylvia informed her father (now undergoing a mental storm of confusion and under the care of Cyprian and Helen) that the "he-men neighbors" are "pacifying" the "little nations that can't help themselves." Auden responded in his "In Memory of W. B. Yeats":

> In the nightmare of the dark
> All the dogs of Europe bark,
> And the living nations wait,
> Each sequestered in its hate . . .

In Paris, Sylvia and her friends, fearing the approaching war, turned to one another for comfort and support. One day, when Valéry had dropped by for a chat with Sylvia, the Elliot Paul family arrived to join the happy conversation. Within half an hour Gertrude and Alice arrived, amazed to encounter so many visitors, particularly their old friend Paul, whom they had not seen in a decade. It seemed for a moment a renewal of the lively years of Shakespeare and Company. When they all scattered—Alice with two new American cookbooks that had been gifts from Cyprian to Sylvia—they pledged to see each other more often.

Realizing that her freedom of movement would soon be limited, Sylvia called at the homes of her friends, dined with the visiting Spender, and took several trips to Les Déserts, where she skied and saw old friends like Fine Gay; to Jersey, where she stayed for two weeks with Polly Norledge; and to Bourée, where she spent Easter with Carlotta and her family. Bryher sent her a ticket to stop in Vevey on the way home from Les Déserts. "In my skiing suit and boots complete with Savoy peasant house smell," claims Sylvia, she traveled to see Bryher and H.D. in their "large glass house by the lake." She felt awkward having the white-jacketed Swiss boy bring her breakfast on a silver tray in bed. But the talk was not of skiing or of luxury but of the war and Bryher's efforts to help Jews escape through Switzerland. Unlike Bryher, who was openly alarmed, Sylvia seemed to assure herself there would be "a somehow peace." When she visited Bourée, outside of Paris, she felt secure in the old house, which was partly underground. The "caves are bombproof," she assures her sister Holly. "The view of the garden and little Cher was soothing after Paris and war cries." The Briggses confirmed that their home would be hers if war came. "If there's a whatyoumaycallem," she confides to Holly, "Carlotta told me I could go down and stay at Bourée." In six months their worst fears were realized.

CHAPTER 19

"How It Ends?"

1939–1941

The deed is everything, not the glory.

— Goethe, *Faust*

Though much is taken, much abides.

— Tennyson, *Ulysses*

THE FINAL CHAPTER in the history of Shakespeare and Company opened with the publication of *Finnegans Wake* in May 1939. It closed in December 1941, when a Nazi officer threatened to confiscate the stock of the bookshop if Sylvia did not sell him her only copy of the novel. Between these two events lay the prelude to war, the gradual paralysis of business, the Nazi occupation of Paris, and the deaths of James Joyce and Sylvester Beach. Despite all her losses, Sylvia managed, in the end, to hide the contents of Shakespeare and Company three floors above the shop she had occupied since 1921, and then to hang on and endure a second world war in France.

When *Work in Progress* was published as *Finnegans Wake,* * on 4 May, it appeared simultaneously in England and the United States, at a time when everyone was preoccupied with Hitler's rhetoric and German tanks rolling into Czechoslovakia and Poland. Though its appearance was delayed until long after Joyce's birthday because Viking Press printed from photocopies of the Faber and Faber edition, Joyce did receive a single paper-covered copy of the British edition on 30 January, in time for his fifty-seventh birthday. When Sylvia received her first copy of the "real" first edition (Faber and Faber), she mailed it to Eleanor Oldenberger, her last and favorite pupil of Joyce's work.

The 9 May issue of *Time* magazine carried a color photograph of Joyce by Gisèle Freund on its cover and a full review of *Finnegans Wake* in the book section. Most international publications featured or at least acknowledged this last novel of his. This worldwide attention for the new work contrasted sharply with the general indifference to *Ulysses* that had followed Sylvia's publication

---

*The title, not known until the binding stage, was based on the ballad about a hod carrier who is revived by the smell of whisky at his own wake. Without a possessive apostrophe, the title puns the waking Finnegans; the first word is plural and the second a verb. In addition to *wake*'s implying

of it seventeen years earlier. Without experience or training, Sylvia had published a novel no one else would print; but *Finnegans Wake* was published after
lively bidding by two of the largest English and American firms. Whereas Joyce
had lengthened *Ulysses* by a third on the numerous proofs, he added to and
rewrote *Finnegans Wake* during more than a decade of serial publication in *Transition* and of bringing out small editions of his individual chapters. Beyond the
differences in these financial and publishing circumstances were the changes in
the times. *Ulysses* appeared, in the same year as Eliot's *Waste Land,* during a
postwar climate favorable to personal expression and artistic innovation. By the
time *Finnegans Wake* appeared, the attention of the world, including the part of
it that cared about literature, had turned to the incipient war, which weakened
the effect of the enormous publicity. Furthermore, the new novel defied assim-
ilation. Although it was widely reviewed, the critics, to his discouragement,
expressed confusion, anger, and hostility toward Joyce's multilanguaged style.
Public interest soon waned. *Ulysses* had, by contrast, entered the world quietly
and slowly; but through the persistence of two excellent promoters (its author
and its publisher) and the publicity that censorship and piracy brought, its reputation ultimately became worldwide. Joyce read both of these works of the inner
self—the first a record of the day, the second the night—to Sylvia. Nighttime
itself would soon encircle him, and the thunder of war would drown out the
voice of even the harshest critic.

In the Briggses' Paris apartment, Sylvia had finished reading *Black Beauty,*
to Carlotta's two young sons, and the women were quietly lunching, when Jim
Briggs returned early from a weekend in Bourée with a copy of *Time* magazine
under his arm. He was enraged that Joyce had written such an "unintelligible"
book. Sylvia, proud of Joyce and assured of his genius, listened patiently. She
was to receive both negative and positive criticism with equanimity, and even
cope with the bizarre responses the book provoked. In 1954, one young man sent
letters and telegrams announcing that he had "solved the riddle" of *Finnegans
Wake:* When would World War III break out? On page 517, he discovered, Joyce
declares, "Tick up on time. Howday you doom? . . . The uneven day of the
unleventh month of the unevented year. At mart in mass." Atomic war, the
young man concluded, was going to start on 11 November (Martinmas). In forty
letters to Sylvia, his family, and his friends, he demanded that they evacuate the
cities. Though he contacted Sylvia later to apologize ("half the jazz musicians
and dope peddlers in Greenwich Village, Harlem, and San Francisco must be
thoroughly disgusted with me today"), he was waiting again in the next year for
Moscow and Mecca to attack Europe.

Sylvia sold *Finnegans Wake* and Miller's *Tropic of Cancer,* which was also
published this May. Her best sellers during this year in which the war began
were not political books: Eliot's collected poems, his first two plays (*Murder in*

both a funeral wake and an awakening, *Finnegan* refers to both end (fin) and recurrence (again)—
thus resurrection—and reflects the circularity of the novel, which begins and ends with the same
sentence.

the Cathedral and *Family Reunion*), Hemingway's *Men without Women,* works by Gertrude Stein, and Melville's *Moby-Dick,* which was popular following a new, full French translation, published this year. Adrienne, on a separate working vacation in this summer with her parents, exclaimed in a letter to Sylvia (who had recommended the novel during their first meeting in 1917) that she had just read the "profound" book: *que c'est profond! C'est vraiment un des grands livres du monde.* In 1940 Sylvia more than doubled her sales of it. During the war, young French students who, according to Adrienne, had already reached "the Sartre point" read it with enthusiasm. It appeared in French—with its tragic sense, irony, and despair—"at a good moment," she adds.

Because business was at a trickle during the first months of the war, Sylvia had more time at her disposal. She was free to read, dine occasionally with Gide, party at the Church home, attend plays, and greet visitors like William Saroyan and Thornton Wilder. Saroyan claims that in July of 1939, when he visited Shakespeare and Company, Sylvia insisted he meet Joyce and dialed his home. When they spoke on the telephone, Joyce told him he was mispronouncing his own name ("a concession to the American limitations of speech," Saroyan explained) and invited him to visit, but Saroyan left for London on the next day, and so they never met. Sylvia and Adrienne kept Wilder, whom they had not seen in more than a decade, to themselves. To celebrate his return and his recent Pulitzer Prize, for *Our Town,* they had him to dinner on 27 June. On the following day he came to the shop to have his photograph taken. After a visit to Stein in Bilignin (where she had her summer home), he returned to America to read *Finnegans Wake.* "The last time we saw him," declares Sylvia, "he was holding hands with Anna Livia Plurabelle." The result, three years later, was *The Skin of Our Teeth,* a Joycean play that won the author another Pulitzer Prize. Sylvia later observed that "Thornton Wilder, contrary to most people, began by being conservative and grew up into a revolutionary."

Though fewer in number, literary friends continued to come to the rue de l'Odéon; but there were "no American tourists," Sylvia informed Eleanor, who was sending her the ten-cent Golden Books for Children, unavailable in France. "Adverse circumstances" led Sylvia to cease advertising in the *Herald Tribune.* With each new speech by Hitler, more foreigners left Paris, taxes rose, and the government talked of preparedness for war. As a foreigner, Sylvia was not entitled to one of the gas masks that the government gave to all citizens; but she felt a certain spiritual protection inside Shakespeare and Company.

Inevitably, Anne Yeats had to leave for England and Priscilla Curtis for the United States. In early summer, Sylvia took her assistant to the railroad station— reluctantly, for, she confided to Holly, "my Priscilla has turned out a perfect success." Tania Whitman stayed on awhile longer, offering to help in the fall. Most of the young English and American girls who helped Sylvia in the thirties were, as their letters reveal, greatly influenced by their experience at Shakespeare and Company. They in turn enriched Sylvia, who took pride in their maturation and education. She would have three more assistants after Priscilla left: one Scot and two French Jews, both of whom would be seized by the Germans.

Sylvia's service to Joyce and the world of literature was acknowledged, in the late summer, in Herbert Gorman's biography of Joyce. This authorized version, delayed by Joyce's demands that elements be changed, presents a faultless Joyce as martyr. For example, he insisted that his marriage to Nora in 1931 be called a second ceremony and that no mention be made of Lucia's illness. He also paid some old debts to Sylvia and others. She is described as an "extremely vital personality with great courage" and with literary tastes "animated by a lively scorn for the standardized fiction of the time." Yet, Gorman echoes Joyce's false belief that she made her living solely on Joyce's work and that *Ulysses* is the "only book that goes on selling" in Shakespeare and Company.

The summer of 1939 in Paris was punctuated with masked balls, dancing until breakfast, a garden party at Versailles for 750 guests, and Elsa Maxwell's party for Mrs. Louise Macy in a rented mansion illuminated by several thousand candles. Ambassador William Bullitt gave a huge ball for the visiting Yale Glee Club. The approaching war seemed to call for a swell time. Sylvia retreated to Les Déserts. Her only complaint—one she shared with the "entire male peasant population," who were as indifferent to religion as she—was about the increasing number of priests and nuns recently quartered in Savoy, particularly in Les Déserts. Though Bryher sent her a train ticket to Vevey and Stein offered to pick her up by car at Chambéry for a visit to Bilignin, Sylvia stayed put. Only the nonaggression pact signed on 23 August by Hitler and Stalin, followed eight days later by Hitler's invasion of Poland, dislodged her. Surprised and angry (Harriet Weaver persisted in trusting Russia), Sylvia hurried to pack and return to Paris. In the villages, she passed posters calling the boys of Savoy to join their regiments. She took the last bus down the mountain before its young driver was mobilized and the bus requisitioned.

World War II began on the first day of September, when German tanks rolled into Poland. Two days later, England and France declared war on Germany. Like many other Americans, the Briggses made plans to leave Paris for home. Stein and Toklas returned to the city for their two most valuable paintings: Picasso's portrait of Gertrude and a portrait by Cézanne of his wife—the latter picture they would sell for food during the war. Joyce arranged to transfer Lucia from Paris to La Baule. Sylvia, however, despite the urging of family and friends that she leave, planned to stay in Paris with Shakespeare and Company. During a fortnight in Bourée, she helped the Briggses pack just traveling clothes for their plane flight to California, where they settled near the Beach family in Altadena. They left the key and $100 for Sylvia, who packed and stored their belongings— leaving their local maid and gardener, a flourishing garden, and enough goods to provide a possible refuge for Sylvia in this house, half-hidden by the rocks. Because they told her to keep or distribute anything she wished, she would give Jim's clothes to aviators who had been shot down during the war. His morning suit would await Valéry.

Sylvia assured her worried family and friends that she could "manage on Bryher's fund. You know I can take care of myself and am a prudent person." For a time in this fall, business in Paris was virtually paralyzed, though Sylvia kept Shakespeare and Company open half of the day and a young Frenchwoman volunteered to work three evenings a week. Occasionally the shop was full of friends who, she informed her father, "preferred books to bandages." Now when she had volunteer help, there was little for either of them to do. She rode her bicycle all over Paris, even in the rain. When the cold weather came, she wore leather boots and a motorcycle hat with flaps. Undaunted, she sailed through the half-deserted streets with a powerful sense of mobility. When the opening and censoring of mail delayed its delivery, she resorted to postcards. When foreign students were no longer accepted at the Sorbonne, she welcomed them at Shakespeare and Company. As long as she could, she would keep it open as a warm refuge.

Although the snow-blanketed city during the holiday season may have looked, in Sylvia's words, "as good as a New England Christmas Card," the picturesqueness was deceptive. Walking through the Luxembourg Garden, she thought that the faces of the Jews she passed reflected their desperation. She missed her usual Thanksgiving and Christmas celebrations with the Briggses, but shared Christmas Eve turkey dinner with Adrienne, Marie and Paul-Émile Bécat, and several Jewish friends. One couple brought caviar. A week later, she renewed her passport for the maximum of six months. "I am staying on and doing fine," she reassured her family; "I will not be a quitter."

In the Jolas home, at Saint-Gérand-le-Puy, Joyce spent a glum Christmas. Helen Joyce had had a nervous breakdown, George had left her, and their son was now enrolled in Maria Jolas's bilingual school. Though ill with an undiagnosed duodenal ulcer—he had earlier ignored a doctor's suggestion for X-rays—Joyce spent heavily, ate little, and drank much. He had recently quarreled again with Paul Léon and Miss Weaver. "What is the use of this war?" he had complained to Beckett, angry that the world was distracted from *Finnegans Wake*.

Bryher made two trips to Paris this winter, the first on 4 December, on her way to London following her mother's death. She and Sylvia had dinner with Adrienne and Walter Benjamin, whom Bryher had helped escape from Germany. Bryher, who apportioned a third of her money to friends, spent the night in Sylvia's apartment and again assured her of her continued support. Benjamin took her to the railroad station by metro the next day. When Bryher returned from her visit to London early in 1940, Sylvia, through Henri Hoppenot (director of European affairs for France), helped her get a three-month extension on her visa so that she could come back to Paris at Easter time. Depressed by her mother's death, the war, and the absence of H.D. (who was in London), Bryher wanted to leave her big house on Lake Geneva and be close to her friends in the rue de l'Odéon.

In addition to Walter Benjamin, who borrowed books from Shakespeare and Company from February through April of 1940, Sylvia had fifty-nine other members, including the students, who got a discount. The approaching war seemed to feed their hunger for books and literary talk, and they lingered in the shop until after seven each evening. The loyal former assistants longed to return. Jane Van Meter wrote from the University of Virginia, concerned about the cold Paris weather and food shortages. Eleanor Oldenberger offered to return and help, but abandoned her plan when Germany invaded Norway and Denmark. Typical of the many letters from her friends abroad was one from MacLeish, who extended "warm handshakes across a very bloody ocean. We all think of you these days. God keep you." Sylvia was surrounded by friends as the Germans drew closer. One of the richest celebrations of literary fraternity in this spring was a dinner feast that Bryher gave at the Tour d'Argent, one of Paris's finest restaurants. Bryher, Sylvia, Adrienne, Chamson, Prévost, and Michaux cheered themselves with pressed duck and friendship.

The Reverend Beach again suggested in vain that Sylvia come back to the United States. There were several reasons why she did not take refuge there: she considered it a dangerous time to travel, had no career there, and feared she would not have the funds to return to Paris. For safety in France, she assured herself and others, she could always flee to Carlotta's house in the rocks. Underlying all these factors was a determination to keep Shakespeare and Company alive and to remain with Adrienne.

In her last letter to Holly, who soon moved with her family from Pasadena to Princeton, Sylvia complained that the war, like the winter, seemed to persist too long. What she did not realize was that the war, after several deceptive months of relative calm, was in fact about to begin in earnest. Germany attacked the Netherlands on 10 May 1940, and three days later its army entered France. Polly Norledge telegrammed from Jersey that day: "Very Welcome here at any moment." Sylvia, still believing with the others in Paris that the French would never surrender, assured her father, now eighty-eight, that despite Hitler's latest "snatches," she was safe. It was her last communication to him.

By mid-May, Sylvia and Adrienne had learned that refugees of German origin were to report to refugee camps. They met frequently with Hoppenot, who intervened for several of their friends. Sylvia and Adrienne, worried about Gisèle and other Jewish associates, provided lodging, clothes, food—even went to the police station to secure good-character certificates. In particular, they aided Walter Benjamin and Arthur Koestler. Koestler, the Hungarian-born English writer, at the time thirty-five years old, had been editing an antifascist, anti-Soviet weekly in Spain until arrested. Following four months of internment, he came to Paris and hid for several days in Adrienne's apartment. While he was reading on Adrienne's couch (Stendhal's *The Red and the Black* held over his head), a four-leaf clover fell on his forehead from the book, touching a spot right between his eyes. She kissed the spot and declared he would escape safely. In 1941, after having fled to England, he published the work he had begun in Paris—his most important novel, *Darkness at Noon*. The German critic and translator Walter Benjamin was not as fortunate. After the occupation of Paris and the capitulation of France, he fled to Marseilles to pick up a visa to the United States, where he planned to take refuge. On his way to Lisbon, where he hoped to embark, he was stopped at the Spanish border and told that he and his group would be turned over to the French police, who would probably pass them on to the Gestapo. That night Benjamin, despairing of his future, took his own life.

At the end of May, Sylvia complained to Bryher that the weeks were "getting more and more weakly." Most literary activities, including the publication of *Mesures,* edited by Paulhan, came to a halt. But Adrienne, with the help of her young assistant Maurice Saillet, was able to publish what proved to be her final issue of the *Gazette.* It contained her essay "Our Friend Bryher" and the excellent "Joyce's *Ulysses* and the French Public," the text of the speech she delivered at the reading of Anna Livia Plurabelle in March 1931. Sylvia placed another order for books, including Graham Greene's *The Power and the Glory,* Richard Wright's *Native Son,* and Pearl Buck's *Other Gods,* all published in this year. This order, though a gesture of optimism about the future, would be her last. Her largest sales in this final, lean year were the following: twelve books by Hemingway (including eight copies of *A Farewell to Arms*); nine copies of Faulkner books; twelve copies of *Moby-Dick.* Most business (though financially negligible) was in the lending library. Business slowed, but social life persisted. Even after the bombing of the Renault factory on the Seine, Virgil Thomson held his Friday-night open house for the Surrealists Breton and Éluard, in uniform, Peggy Guggenheim, and a few American journalists.

When the air raids and bombings of Paris began, in early June, Thomson, Guggenheim, Freund, and scores of the other American and European expatriates fled Paris for the south of France. Gisèle eventually made her way to Argentina. Thomson, Man Ray, and Salvador Dali escaped to the United States via Lisbon. McAlmon, ill with tuberculosis, without adequate food, and a victim of the theft of his books and papers, was briefly interned but managed also to make his way to Lisbon and thence home. In the days before the Germans entered Paris, the rue de l'Odéon was streaming with people headed for the railroad stations, where they would camp and wait for trains. Others left the menaced city on bicycle or on foot, pushing wheelbarrows. Then the streets were empty except for bicycles and speeding government staff cars. Dark trains full of families threaded their way out of Paris, now periodically paralyzed by air raids.

Friends who remained during the last, hollow, waiting June days, before what Adrienne called the "black rain," made almost daily visits to the bookshops, where Sylvia and Adrienne held open house. Among them were Robert Sage, Katherine Dudley, Fargue, Michaux, the Hoppenots, Dr. Bertrand-Fontaine, and Marie and Paul-Émile Bécat. The atmosphere of the city itself, according to Adrienne, became increasingly "anguished" and "people are hugging one another on the metro." Worried friends living elsewhere made inquiries: Victoria Ocampo wired from Buenos Aires, "Say if safe am with you all," to which Adrienne replied, "Victoria be with us. Long live the Argentine Republic." Dismayed and cut off in Switzerland from Perdita and H.D., who were in England, Bryher lamented to Sylvia: "I . . . tried always to do what [I] could for the real artists, and especially for the woman artist." Sylvia responded with love: "Don't worry about us, it's only the time between one holiday and the next, we shall soon be together again."

During the final three days of free Paris, one of Sylvia's young student volunteers, a Canadian named Ruth Camp, fled—only to be shot at, captured, and interned. Keeler Faus, a friend and patron for eight years, and Tyler Thompson, both with the American embassy, came to place red embassy stamps on the doors of Shakespeare and Company and Sylvia's apartment to indicate to the Germans that Sylvia was American. On Wednesday the twelfth, because Adrienne desired to flee to Rocfoin, Sylvia bicycled to the Gare Montparnasse to see whether trains were leaving. But Marie intervened, insisting that they remain in Paris. The three women—Sylvia like a third sister for some twenty years now—went to the boulevard Sébastopol to watch the exodus. Sylvia movingly describes the scene:

A lovely June day in 1940. Sunny with blue skies. Only about 25,000 people were left in Paris. Adrienne [, Marie,] and I went over to the Boulevard Sébastopol and, through our tears, watched the refugees moving through the city. They came in at the East Gate, crossed Paris by way of the Boulevard Saint Michel and the Luxembourg Gardens, then went out through the Orléans and Italie gates: cattle-drawn carts piled with household goods; on top of them children, old people and sick people, pregnant women and women with babies, poultry in coops, and dogs and cats. Sometimes they stopped at the Luxembourg Gardens to let the cows graze there.

On Thursday the thirteenth, it was Sylvia's turn to want to leave. She went to the American embassy, where she discussed the details and implications of flight, then changed her mind. After visiting the embassy, she lunched with Dr. Bertrand-Fontaine, at her hospital. From the windows, says Sylvia, they "watched the last of the refugees pouring in. Close on their heels came the Germans. An endless procession of motorized forces: tanks and armored cars and helmeted men seated with arms folded. The men and the machines were all a cold gray, and they moved to a steady deafening roar." Friday the fourteenth was the first full day of the occupation.

To the surprise of Adrienne and Sylvia, the streets of Paris were peaceful, and they were free to walk around and shop for food that weekend. They opened their bookshops on Monday the seventeenth, from 2:00 to 6:00, and had tea at the Dôme after closing. According to Adrienne's journal, which is liberally sprinkled with details of the food they found and ate, their mood during the first weeks of the occupation ranged from hope that life would be orderly under the Germans to "great depression" and resignation "to defeat and fascism." They spent each afternoon visiting with members of their libraries and shared dinner with each other and Sunday tea with Keeler and Colette Faus and other friends. On her bicycle each morning, Sylvia foraged for sweets and fruit. Adrienne stood in long lines for meat and butter. Food became as time-consuming an obsession as books.

With the signing of the armistice between France and Germany, their Paris customers who had fled returned, finding to their delight that the two libraries were still open. Because Shakespeare and Company remained open, Sylvia felt justified in having stayed. "I never left Paris," she explains to Polly Norledge,"—hadn't the energy to flee, luckily, as nothing happened to us nor to the other monuments." New members included students of Sartre. Françoise Bernheim, Sylvia's volunteer helper, who had been studying Sanskrit at the Sorbonne, was now excluded from classes and forced to wear a yellow Star of David on her chest. When Sylvia was with her, she shared Françoise's ostracism. Since the young woman was forbidden to enter public buildings or sit on public benches, they one day shared a lunch on the ground beside a park bench. According to Sylvia, "we hurriedly ate our hard-boiled eggs and swallowed the tea in our thermos bottles, looking around furtively as we did so. It was not an experience that we cared to repeat."

Until the end of 1940, Joyce was trapped in Saint-Gérand-le-Puy, which German troops occupied for only six days. In the third week of June, following Léon's arrival by donkey, the two men were, in Ellmann's words, "reconciled insofar as reconciliation was possible for Joyce." Léon helped Joyce compile a list of misprints in *Finnegans Wake,* then returned to Paris, where he went to the Joyce apartment and saved the writer's books and papers from confiscation by the Germans. The list of misprints was given to Maria Jolas, who fled to the United States at the end of the summer. With the urging and financial assistance of the Giedion-Welckers, Joyce began the complicated process of trying to get papers so that his family could leave France and flee to Zurich.

Probably as a result of efforts on the part of Faus, Sylvia was able to get word of her safety to her family. In return she heard that her father, shocked by news of the war and already nearly blind and deaf, had lost his memory. Because Cyprian and Helen could no longer deal with his senile behavior, they had placed him in the Rosemead Sanitarium in Pasadena. "The greatest blessing," Cyprian assured Sylvia, "is that he has forgotten there is a war in Europe, and thinks of you only as you were before." The former "President's Pastor" could neither read nor write and spent his days waiting for a visit from "the President, Mr. Roosevelt." In a final bit of ironic good news, Cyprian informed Sylvia that, inexplicably, Sylvia's Princeton bank account had more than $2,000 in it. Now, when she needed money, it was out of reach.

While Germany was bombing Britain, Bryher reached her family in London, and Sylvia kept together the Company that remained in Paris. Because her rent was now a gift of the owner, she could meet expenses with her meager library income. She still had fifty-three library members, including twenty-eight students, who needed their weekly (sometimes daily) supply of books. Simone de Beauvoir renewed her subscription and borrowed titles by Hemingway and Dos Passos. The demand for American and English literature was high, but the supply was diminishing. Sylvia's only source of books was the Germans, who had taken over Hachette, which distributed the inexpensive Tauchnitz and Albatross books she always purchased. Soon the Germans banned the sale of all English books published after 1870.

Within two months, Sylvia lost the two most important men in her life: her father died on 16 November, in the Rosemead Sanitarium, and Joyce died on 13 January, in a Zurich hospital. Her father expired of old age, having lived "happily till the very end," Cyprian assured Sylvia, "and that end couldn't have been more merciful." Her letter was written immediately after his funeral, which Cyprian called "a grand send-off." Joyce died as a result of a neglected ulcer, which perforated his stomach and caused peritonitis, just twenty days short of his fifty-ninth birthday.

Pale, thin, and shabby, the members of the Joyce family had arrived by train in Zurich on 17 December, looking, Carola Giedion-Welcker later told Edel, "like some of the angular figures in a Picasso drawing." Brooding over the poor reception of *Finnegans Wake,* worried about having left Lucia in an occupied area, and short of funds (which Harriet Weaver soon sent), Joyce was in severe pain. He was taken to the hospital on Friday, 10 January, and operated on on Saturday; he died on Monday at 2:15 A.M. At his burial, on Wednesday, Lord Derwent (of the British legation in Bern) spoke on behalf of England, Ireland, and those—such as Larbaud and Sylvia—who were grieving in other cities: "Sylvia Beach, whose devotion to him and his work have [sic] an epic quality and must never be forgotten—must be a very sad woman today."

Two weeks later Paul Léon, who was living as inconspicuously as possible in Paris, came to Shakespeare and Company to talk to Sylvia about the man they had both loved and served. No record remains of that sad conversation. But the ledger shows that he bought Gorman's biography. Soon afterward, Léon was arrested and interned by the Germans. In 1942 he was executed in an extermination camp for Jews.

During the occupation, Sylvia often saw French friends, such as the Valérys and the Bécats, and the few American friends remaining in Paris, such as Katherine Dudley and the Fauses. One day, Katherine Dudley and Françoise Bernheim accompanied Sylvia to one of Valéry's lectures on poetry at the Collège de France. Françoise was allowed in after a kind doorman offered to hide her coat, with the yellow Star of David. Though she found that Valéry pursued his subject in "devious ways," often taking "a certain wicked pleasure in losing his hearers," Sylvia believed the lectures were "among the few things that counted during those days."

In the preceding September, Valéry had read portions of his *Mon Faust* to Sylvia, Adrienne, and Marie. With Adrienne's encouragement, he read it again to a larger group that gathered one day this March at her apartment. Adrienne was particularly intrigued by the character of Lust, which she analyzed after the war, when *Mon Faust* was finally published. On another occasion, some months later, Sylvia toured Valéry's disordered study in his apartment, in the street later named for him. He half boasted to her that he could not find anything in the clutter, then accompanied her to his wife's well-ordered dining room. Just as they sat down to lunch, an air raid sounded and Valéry "jumped up and rushed to the window and hung out to see the planes come over Paris, dropping bombs." According to Sylvia, "if the police had passed at that moment they would have whistled him back. The family seemed accustomed to this behavior: François [his younger son] said, 'Papa adores these raids.' "

The German occupation was a more personal and threatening matter to her friends in the resistance than it was to Valéry. Violaine Hoppenot, a member of Shakespeare and Company since childhood, asked Sylvia to hide her from the Gestapo. She had recently abandoned plans for graduate study in the United States (for which Sylvia had secured MacLeish's assistance) and become active in the resistance. She stayed for the night and borrowed some of Sylvia's clothes to change her appearance. Though she was captured by the Gestapo, the clothes and some false identity papers did protect her from recognition, and she was released. Jean Prévost was less fortunate. On 1 August 1944, he was shot to death by the Germans in the Vercors, a wooded plateau in the Alps that was a center of the resistance. When Françoise Bernheim was taken by the Germans, Sylvia was beside herself. Swallowing her hatred of both the collaborators and the Gestapo, she begged them for the release of Françoise. A man at Gestapo headquarters snarled at Sylvia, "You have a black mark against your name on account of your Jewish friends." Françoise died in Auschwitz.

Sylvia was successful in helping Gordon Craig and his family, whom she had first met in 1920, in Rapallo. She admired the Craigs and had distributed his *Mask* theater magazine (1908–1929) and lent his *Marionettes* magazine. When a German patron expressed interest in copies of these publications, Sylvia succeeded, despite the language barrier, in conveying to him the plight of the Craigs, who had been imprisoned by the Germans. The patron seemed to share Sylvia's sorrow, murmured something she did not understand, and left. A short time later, he returned with a Gestapo officer who spoke perfect English. The officer asked her to gather all the information on the Craigs, establishing that they were not Jewish, and to take it to Gestapo headquarters. Soon after she had done this, the two men returned to the shop to say that the Craigs would be released by Christmas. The man who had first looked through Shakespeare and Company's books on theater history and art was, Sylvia later learned, a "highly placed official."

Sylvia herself would later be helped by a man who had strong ties with the German government: Jacques Benoist-Méchin. One of her earliest customers, the first translator (1921) of portions of *Ulysses,* and an accompanist in Antheil's *Ballet Mécanique,* Benoist-Méchin was now secretary to the notorious Darlan, who contacted Hitler on behalf of the French fascist government in Vichy. Benoist-Méchin claims that when he learned, in 1943, that Sylvia had been interned for several months in Vittel, he gave the order to have his friend released.

Other former patrons of Shakespeare and Company had fled to America: Romains and Breton were in New York; Maurois was at Princeton, where he had a professorship; Isherwood and Huxley had settled in Los Angeles. Among

the former patrons in New York and Washington, D.C., Saint-John Perse organized aid—too late, as it turned out—to bring Sylvia, and possibly Adrienne, to
a refuge in America. Michaux and Stein, like many others, had sought refuge in
safer parts of France. Ford Madox Ford and Havelock Ellis had died. Sylvia was
out of communication with her former American patrons and regular correspondents such as MacLeish, Antheil, and Hemingway. Their letters to her were now
marked "undeliverable" and returned to them.

The faces of the Company had changed considerably. Since Germans patronized the shop, some of her old patrons, such as Gillet, had their books delivered.
Perhaps because Sylvia herself had changed under the stress of the war, she
ceased altering the date of birth on her passport. Just days before her fifty-fourth
birthday, she began to write 1896 again, then corrected it to 1887. The physical
privations of war—for example, the scarcity of food and the restriction that she
could operate her radiator only three hours a day—took their toll. So did her later
internment by the Germans. The pictures taken after the war show a Sylvia who
has considerably aged.

When the Japanese bombed Pearl Harbor, on 7 December 1941, and America
entered the war, her safety was immediately threatened:

. . . my nationality, added to my Jewish affiliations, finished Shakespeare and Company
in Nazi eyes. We Americans had to declare ourselves at the Kommandatur and register
once a week at the Commissary in the section of Paris where we lived. (Jews had to sign
every day.) There were so few Americans that our names were in a sort of scrapbook that
was always getting mislaid. I used to find it for the Commissaire. Opposite my name and
antecedents was the notation: "has no horse." I could never find out why.

If she could not understand this reference to her missing horse or German bureau-
cratic logic, she did sense her own danger. One December day a big gray military
car stopped in front of Shakespeare and Company. A high-ranking German officer stepped out and studied the display window. Could he please buy *Finnegans
Wake,* he requested in perfect English on entering the shop. "It's not for sale,"
Sylvia responded, explaining it was her last, hence a personal, copy. But he was
very interested in Joyce's work, he explained angrily. She stood firm. He turned
on his heel and strode out with a stomping of his boots. "Those boots always
made them seem much more enraged than they were," she later told a friend.
"You know how Henri Michaux talks about the noise pigeons make as they fly
away? Just like boots, he says. Whenever you heard boots at night you let them
alone. Boots were Germans," she concludes. With the echo of boots in her ears,
she hid *Finnegans Wake,* fearing the officer would return.

Just days after she had made her last recorded sale—*Wuthering Heights, The
Forsyte Saga,* and Shelley's poems—Sylvia received a call from Gordon Craig.
Her German visitors had been true to their word. The Craigs, who had been
freed before Christmas, were in a Paris hotel. Craig came to Shakespeare and
Company on that afternoon and told Sylvia that her German interlocutor had
supplied them with coal, warm clothes, and a Christmas tree. Inside the library's

copy of *Gordon Craig and the Theatre: A Record and an Interpretation,* by Enid Rose, he wrote, "to Sylvia from E.G.C. December 17, 1941."

At the end of December, the German officer who had wanted her only copy of *Finnegans Wake* appeared again at the door of Shakespeare and Company. Where was the book, he demanded. It was put away, Sylvia explained. This time her resistance was unavailing. "We're coming to confiscate all your books today," the officer shouted, trembling with rage. As soon as he drove off, she ran to the concierge, who promised to give her free of charge the unoccupied fourth-floor apartment. Sylvia recruited Saillet, who asked whether she could wait until the beginning of the new year to move her stock. She could not. She feared confiscation of Shakespeare and Company more than imprisonment of herself. In record time—Sylvia claims two hours—using boxes and clothes baskets, she, Adrienne, Saillet, and the concierge carried more than 5,000 books, thousands of letters, pictures, tables, chairs, signs, and electric-light fixtures up four flights of stairs for safe hiding. She called a carpenter to remove the shelves and a painter to cover the name of the shop on the building. Compared with the years of dreaming, the months of planning, and the twenty-two years of what she called "steering a little bookshop between two wars," Shakespeare and Company disappeared in a flash. The long weekend between the wars ended as rudely as any Monday-morning reality. What years of economic hardship could not accomplish, the Nazis did. There is no record that the officer returned or that Sylvia was interrogated concerning the disappearance of the contents of her shop. Though other Nazis eventually came to arrest her, they never found the contents of what had been Shakespeare and Company, which remained hidden, a secret kept until the liberation.

CHAPTER 20

The Official Period

1942–1962

I am a citizen of the world!

— Sylvia Beach

ON THE TWENTIETH ANNIVERSARY OF the first publication of *Ulysses*, its author had been buried for a year and the stock of Shakespeare and Company had been in hiding for a month. Six months later the Germans occupying Paris would come for Sylvia. Before they came, Adrienne collected books returned by the Shakespeare and Company customers, while Sylvia lived as inconspicuously as possible among those who were her first friends in Paris, the French artists. In what turned out to be a farewell to Fargue's gang of *potassons* of the early days, she attended a private playing by Francis Poulenc of the score of his ballet *Les Animaux Modèles* (dedicated to Raymonde Linossier and affirming his faith in France). Not long after the ballet opened at the Opéra, Sylvia was arrested by the Germans.

When their truck came to pick her up, at 9 A.M., one day late in August 1942, she had time to pack only a few clothes and the most condensed portable reading: the Bible and the collected works of Shakespeare (the latter would be kept by the censor until shortly before her release). Climbing into the truck, she discovered her friend Katherine Dudley. In their numerous stops around the city to collect other American women, Sylvia and the others cheered loudly when their captors returned from a building empty-handed. After a brief internment at the zoo in the Bois de Boulogne, the women were taken to Vittel, a watering place in eastern France, where they were lodged in a converted hotel. The Americans—joining hundreds of British women who had been assigned to another hotel—included titled ladies, prostitutes, dancers, teachers, artists, chambermaids (who considered internment a vacation), fifty nuns, and "quite a few crazy women whose case was not improved by capture," exclaims Sylvia. With a certificate from Dr. Thérèse Bertrand-Fontaine, she was housed for several months at the hospital, which the British had thoroughly colonized with punctual organization, afternoon tea, a working library, and secret stocks of food. The women had also devised a successful system for escapes. As she had done during her Serbian experience, in 1919, Sylvia expressed preference for the British over the rather helpless American women at times of physical and emotional stress.

With the same unbiased concern that made her bookshop a sanctuary for all races and creeds, she led a delegation to protest anti-Semitic views expressed by the British president of the internment camp, served as postmistress (one of her jobs at Shakespeare and Company), assisted the nuns of the camp in caring for the sick Americans, and cheered the others. "Who can be as entertaining as our dear Sylvia," testifies Sarah Watson of their internment together. Sylvia's adventurousness, flexibility, years of physical labor, and spartan life in Paris enabled her to take the experience in stride.

When, after more than six months, Sylvia was released through the intervention of Jacques Benoist-Méchin at Vichy headquarters, she borrowed money for the train back to Paris and, with her rucksack full of Red Cross goods, was met by Maurice Saillet at the Gare de l'Est. She spent most of the days on the top floor of Sarah Watson's students' hostel in the boulevard Saint-Michel, eating her major meal of the day with Adrienne and Saillet, where she kept abreast of the latest literary news and read the underground *Editions de Minuit*, published at great risk by her friend Yvonne Desvignes. She kept her legal residence in the mezzanine apartment at No. 12 and registered weekly with the police. Rarely did she open the flat on the fourth floor, where the books of Shakespeare and Company slumbered.

Hemingway "liberated" the rue de l'Odéon, on Saturday, 26 August 1944, the day after the German surrender of Paris, arriving in the street with four BBC cars. The story of his visit—somewhat unreliable in its details after so many years—forms the dramatic conclusion of Sylvia's memoirs in 1959. "I flew downstairs," she recalls; "we met with a crash; he picked me up and swung me around and kissed me while people on the street and in the windows cheered." After receiving Sylvia's assurance—his concern was hardly necessary—that Adrienne had not collaborated with the Germans and hence was not in need of his protection, he took his men to the roof to check for snipers.

The following months were punctuated with visits from members of the Company: Leon Edel and Richard Ellmann stopped by in uniform; Keller Faus and the American embassy friends returned to work. Several weeks after Paris had been freed, Sylvia held, at the urging of *Life* magazine, a literary party in the liberated fourth-floor apartment—among all the books, pictures, and furniture of Shakespeare and Company—for Faus, Louis Aragon, Janet Flanner, Hemingway, Henri Michaux, Adrienne, and Paul Valéry (who was to die in a few weeks). Before the party, Sylvia posed in her foodless kitchen for a *Life* photographer. Though Shakespeare and Company had physically ceased to exist on the day the name had been hurriedly painted out in fear of the Nazi officer's return, its influence lived on in the lives of its illustrious friends, now scattered around the world.

Members of the Company from England—notably Cyril Connolly, Stephen Spender, and T. S. Eliot—urged her to reopen Shakespeare and Company. Connolly wrote of his own first visit to Shakespeare and Company that he was "indescribably happy" to be back again and close to the "sacred rue de l'Odéon, where those two bilingual sirens who have so long enchanted us with all that is best in two literatures . . . still decoy." Eliot called immediately before V-E Day, in May of 1945, with soap and Chinese tea, an invitation to the opening night of the French version of *Murder in the Cathedral*, and assurances of the need for Shakespeare and Company in postwar Paris. Without her encouragement, these subjects of England unsuccessfully appealed to the British council for funds. Even if she had received special funding, however, she could not and would not have reopened the bookshop: she was tired, and, after years of frugality and hardship, she was—at fifty-eight years of age—afraid of taking risks. Besides, she assured her friends, one should not attempt anything twice. By this time the premises at No. 12 had been leased to an antiques dealer.

Though life in the forties after the war was free and enriched by literary activities, Sylvia and Adrienne, like other Parisians, were preoccupied with the scarcity of food, fuel cutoffs, and strikes. "We are like the missionaries," confesses Sylvia, "crazy about parcels." Former assistants, family, and friends sent boxes of clothing, chocolate, coffee, and staples. Packages from Bryher and Holly came almost monthly. She gave many of the clothes to French friends and the chocolate to neighborhood children and Valéry's grandchildren. She was happy to be living in her fourth-floor apartment with her book collection and pictures and enjoying the outdoors with Adrienne every summer at Les Déserts.

The war had shifted the priorities of Sylvia, who had once been preoccupied with the survival of Shakespeare and Company. In the forties following the war, before beginning what she called her "official period," she spent her time looking after the needy, serving afternoon tea to visitors, and working at a hospital in Versailles—once guiding two truckloads of GIs ("crutches and all") on a tour of Paris. Her literary charity work included serving on the board of the American Library of Paris (once her rival) and helping Adrienne distribute abundant supplies of clothes, food, and coffee, sent from Argentina by Victoria Ocampo, to French writers and newsmen. By contrast, she kept university people, who were full of personal questions about her friends, at a distance. She lent books only to old friends, such as Michaux, Gide, and Simone de Beauvoir, and to a few new ones, such as the black American novelist Richard Wright.

Wright, who lived in Paris from 1946 until his death, in 1960, became one of her closest literary friends. He was also a friend of de Beauvoir and Sartre, moved easily through the French intellectual community, and served as a sort of elder statesman among expatriate American writers then in Paris. "Of all writers I have known, he is the most unselfish and thoughtful," Sylvia confides to Holly. "In fact, none of the others—the so-called white ones—were interested in anyone but themselves. Fellas like Hemingway appear uncouth beside Dick Wright." As he lived around the corner in the rue Monsieur-le-Prince, it was easy for him to visit and to borrow from Sylvia.

Literary life thrived in the freedom that came with the liberation of Paris. Only the cast of characters was changing: Prévost and Valéry were dead; Sartre drew capacity crowds at his lectures; André Malraux was "crown prince now," Sylvia informed Bryher; Wright and the French poet Yves Bonnefoy became important new friends; and Stein and Toklas brought her visiting American scholars. Old animosities had been dissipated by the war and the passage of time, and the survivors of the American colony in Paris—Stein (who died in 1946), Toklas, Sylvia, and Barney—kept in frequent touch with each other. But Sylvia's closest friends, in a sense her family, were Adrienne and Marie Monnier, Maurice Saillet, and Camilla Steinbrugge, whom she had met in Vittel.

Sylvia attended lectures and the latest movies and plays—from a GI production of Saroyan's *Time of Your Life* to the opening of Schlumberger's *Tentation de Tati*, which he had read in part at Shakespeare and Company. Her personal literary work, aside from the occasional loan and sale of some of her library books, lay in writing and translating. Though she planned to write regularly for the *New York Herald Tribune* (Paris), she published only one article—on the underground press during the occupation. She worked sporadically on her memoirs, encouraged by Richard Wright. After having corresponded with Houghton Mifflin and Harper about the publication of her memoirs, she signed a contract with Harcourt, Brace in July 1950. Sylvia also translated several short works, including Adrienne's essay on *Ulysses* for the *Kenyon Review* and (assisted by Adrienne, who wrote the preface) Bryher's *Beowulf*, a short novel based on the fortunes of an English tea shop and its owner during the war. When the *Mercure de France* published it, in 1948, Bryher came to sign the 100 copies and celebrate with Adrienne, Sylvia, and the Chamsons. Inspired by the translation of her *Beowulf*, Bryher sent Sylvia and Adrienne to England for a glamorous twelve-day visit, during which they saw Harriet Weaver in Oxford. Sylvia also looked up fellow prisoners from the Vittel days who were now living in London, and the two women dined together with Eliot and Connolly on separate occasions. At Sulgrave Manor, the home of George Washington's ancestors, Sylvia signed the guest book, adding "Princeton."

Sylvia's largest translating assignment, for James Laughlin of New Directions, was Henri Michaux's *Barbare en Asie*, impressions of the poet's journey on that continent. She worked on the book—which she called "a labor of love," adding that "translating is the devil"—for more than a year. She had high expectations for this introduction of Michaux to English readers. When the translation appeared, in the summer of 1949, she gave a large party for Michaux and more than fifty of their friends, at which the marionette finger puppets presented Michaux's play *Chaines*. Reviewers observed that her taut, faithful translation was a continuation of her cross-fertilization of literatures. In 1950 the translation received the Denise Clairouin Award.

Literary interest in Joyce, which usually included Sylvia, had greatly increased by the late forties. Some young scholars asked to be allowed to make use of her Joyce collection—a few came every day to work during their Paris visit—prompting Sylvia to talk of "fending off the harpies." Her own work on Joyce's behalf during this decade was concentrated in two meetings with Harriet Weaver.

During a two-week visit from Miss Weaver in June 1947, they dined with Stuart Gilbert and talked of his collection of letters by Joyce. The two women met again when Sylvia spent two weeks in Oxford and London. Though she saw Eliot, who had just won the Nobel Prize, she was there chiefly on Joyce business. She and Miss Weaver struggled with the question of a proposed theatrical production of *Finnegans Wake,* which Miss Weaver eventually rejected.

Two final Joycean events of the forties were the recording of her impressions of the writer for a two-hour BBC broadcast and the staging of an exhibit of Joyceana. During the last two months of the decade, some of Sylvia's Joyce collection and all of the Joyce material rescued by Paul Léon were on exhibit at the Librairie La Hune, a new Left Bank bookshop in the heart of existentialism. Lucie Léon and Maria Jolas arranged the exhibit; Mrs. Joyce, whom the proceeds were to benefit, came from Zurich to attend; Harriet Weaver came from London early and stayed with Sylvia; and they all (except Miss Weaver) talked about Joyce on the radio. These women excited interest in Joyce's work in hopes of selling the collection on exhibit (except for Sylvia's materials and the manuscript of *Finnegans Wake*) to an American university. Eventually, the Lockwood Library of the University of Buffalo bought the items in the La Hune exhibit for $10,000. Harriet Weaver wanted to give the *Finnegans Wake* manuscript to the National Library of Ireland, but Nora refused when Ireland rejected her request for the reburial of Joyce in his homeland.

In 1951, Sylvia lost Cyprian, who, unknown to her, had been ill for months with cancer of the bladder. Cyprian had talked of going to Paris to see her sister, from whom she had always kept news of her illnesses, but slipped into a coma and died on 26 July. Helen Eddy, who had shared Cyprian's life for twenty-four years, had her body cremated, and scattered her ashes among the rosebushes of a Pasadena mausoleum. In the following year she came to Paris for a six-week visit with Sylvia. While walking along the Seine, Helen told Sylvia of the loving and unselfish sister she had never really known since their Palais-Royal days during World War I. Sylvia's decision to remain a Parisian had perhaps robbed her of one of her most devoted friends.

In 1953, for the second time since having settled in Paris in 1916, Sylvia visited her homeland in order to see her last remaining family member. She spent the spring of that year in Greenwich, Connecticut, with Holly, who had been widowed in 1945. Among the Paris friends she visited in New York were Katherine Anne Porter and Saint-John Perse—the latter at a Bollingen Society cocktail party in his honor. Donald Allen of the Grove Press, who alleged that she was "the only American [he had] ever known who possessed a truly French wit," gave her a night tour of New York City attractions. Upon her return and after only a week to catch her breath and open her mail, Sylvia accompanied Adrienne to London. Bryher had invited them over for a week of music and theater during the coronation of Queen Elizabeth II, about which Adrienne wrote a long descriptive article for the *Lettres Nouvelles*. Except for one more vacation at Les Déserts, this would be Adrienne's last trip.

Adrienne had been ill with rheumatism since 1950, when she talked of getting someone to take over her library and flat and of moving in with Sylvia. Despite cortisone treatments and considerable pain, she worked hard on her lectures and articles. But she suffered fainting spells, like the one that had occurred on a trip during a visit with Helen Eddy to Mont-Saint-Michel. While vacationing with Sylvia and Camilla in Les Déserts in September 1954, she was stricken with Ménière's syndrome (aural disturbances of the inner ear). For nearly nine months she suffered from the delusion of maddening noises. On 20 May 1955 Sylvia informed Jean Schlumberger that Adrienne was "very ill," and on 18 June she confided to Bryher that Adrienne "often threatens to beat it off this planet." That very day, after reciting some of Valéry's poetry aloud, Adrienne asked Sylvia and Marie to leave her alone, and took an overdose of sleeping tablets. They found her in a coma on Sunday, the nineteenth. She died at 11 P.M. in the hospital. "She died last night," a brokenhearted Sylvia informed Bryher; "I'm glad she hasn't got to go on suffering anymore." To Harriet Weaver she expressed the wish that Adrienne "had been spared all the suffering." Among Adrienne's papers, which she had secretly and with difficulty arranged the week before her death, they found the following statement:

I am putting an end to my days, no longer able to support the noises that have been martyrizing me for eight months, without counting the fatigue and the suffering that I have endured these recent years.

I am going to death without fear, knowing that I found a mother on being born here and that I shall likewise find a mother in the other life.

Though the details of Adrienne's death were released reluctantly, condolences poured in from old friends, even from Ezra Pound, confined now to Saint Elizabeths Hospital in Washington, D.C., who wrote, "Sorry you have lost your good friend." Only the Bécats, Sylvia, Saillet, Camilla, and Holly (who was concluding a month's visit with Sylvia) accompanied the body of Adrienne to its grave. There was no ceremony. Her public memorial would be a special, 1956 edition of the *Mercure de France,* edited by Saillet. Her private memorial lay in the hearts of those who loved her, particularly Sylvia, who had now lost to suicide the two women to whom she was closest.

In a handwritten response to the loss of Adrienne, Sylvia expresses her grief and confesses that Adrienne had suggested she accompany her in death:

Can see no remedy at all for the swooping down of death on someone you love . . . [especially] the realization that the person is gone for good, without giving you another chance to do things better and not be so inattentive to what's really important—yet you were given plenty of time—years to improve! Maybe—surely she had something more to disclose if you had listened closer. This feeling of incompleteness is one of death's worst cruelties. Sometimes you wish you had left with her as she suggested—she knew what living without her was going to be like. She knew everything—Adrienne.

Personal happiness went with the death of Adrienne, who for thirty-eight years had been a sister, lover, mother, and mentor. The rest of Sylvia's life, as one friend notes, was marked by mere honorary awards.

An honor she considered dubious was that of being sought out by Joyceans.

Though she joined the readings by the close Joyce circle, usually organized by
the devotees Lucie Léon and Maria Jolas, and though she continued helping
Gilbert collect Joyce letters, she wanted nothing to do with university scholars.
The exceptions were her old friend Justin O'Brien, who had many Columbia
University graduate students doing dissertations on French literature, and Jackson Mathews, who came to Paris to translate the work of Valéry and who later
worked for the Bollingen Foundation. Marie Monnier Bécat rented the apartment
of Adrienne to Jackson and Marthiel Mathews, who soon became not only neighbors but devoted friends and protectors of Sylvia. The encouragement of the
Mathewses, pressure for Sylvia to finish her memoirs, several trips to New York,
and increasing interest in the twenties pulled her out of her grief and into a
greater international role.

She was honored by the publication of her memoirs. In 1956 Harcourt, Brace
published the Joycean portions of her memoirs, entitled *Ulysses in Paris,* as a
Christmas gift book. While in New York in that August to deliver the manuscript, she heard that Hemingway was in town and wrote him about her work,
telling him that she was hesitant about publicly mentioning his early domestic
life. Hemingway, who in the next few months would begin writing his own
memoirs of the twenties, called to chat with Sylvia. When her editor sent him a
copy of the portions about Hemingway, he scrawled across the envelope, "Cable
Sylvia—anything she writes OK. Perfectly OK about Hadley—EH."

Three years later the memoirs were ready for final publication. They had
been delayed by the numerous distractions that literary activities created and by
the difficulty of writing. Though she had reservations about her book—she thought
it too condensed and "old-trunk-in-the-attic"—it was generally well received by
critics, who regretted its brevity. Connolly called it "a charming, gay astringent
scrapbook." It contained both accidental and deliberate errors, the largest one
her decision—perhaps made because of her social standards—not to be critical
of anyone, particularly not of Joyce. Her complimentary judgments of Joyce and
her patrons were nonalcoholic, to use her own term; they presented her public
diplomacy of goodwill and not her private, occasionally bristling wit. Her friends
agree that contrary to the star-struck attitude that her memoirs convey, her genius
lay in knowing precisely how to choose and discriminate.

A second honor that focused international attention on Sylvia as the chief
representative of Joyce and the American and British expatriates in the Paris
twenties was the sale of her Joyce collection to the University of Buffalo (now
the State University of New York at Buffalo), which had bought the Joyce exhibit
at La Hune and had received donations from Ben Huebsch (the American publisher of *Dubliners, Portrait of the Artist as a Young Man,* and *Exiles*). Jackson
Mathews handled the arrangements for Sylvia, and Prof. Oscar Silverman, then
chairman of the Department of English, drew up the informal agreement on 6
December 1958 on Shakespeare and Company stationery: her remuneration was
$55,510. The sudden wealth in her seventy-second year appears ironic in light
of the many difficult years of penury.

The third and perhaps most personally rewarding honor for Sylvia was the monumental exhibit in Paris of the memorabilia of the writers of the twenties. At the suggestion of Morrill Cody, the cultural attaché and a former member of Shakespeare and Company, she assisted the cultural center of the United States Embassy in Paris in preparing *Les Années Vingt: Les Écrivains Américains à Paris et Leurs Amis, 1920–1930* (The Twenties: American Writers and Their Friends in Paris). The exhibit consisted chiefly of Shakespeare and Company's photographs, letters, manuscripts, and first editions, arranged by author—from Margaret Anderson to Thomas Wolfe—in specially built display cases. It opened on 11 March 1959 to public and critical acclaim. For ten weeks, Sylvia reigned over *une passionnante rétrospective,* giving radio talks, interviews, lectures, and guided tours of the exhibit—tours she described as "something like driving through the literary traffic in Paris." At the exhibit, she posed with Alice B. Toklas and Thornton Wilder, at a café table in front of a wall-size photo of the Dingo bar, while a pianola beat out music from the *Ballet Mécanique.* André Maurois and André Chamson gave speeches at the exhibit. In a time of anti-American sentiment in France, the exhibit attracted nearly 20,000 visitors (the following year it attracted 15,000 in London). It was not an adjunct to commerce, but an endeavor to inform the public and to increase appreciation for American and British artists in France. Because most of the 600 items belonged to her, the exhibition was a tribute to Sylvia's central role in the world of international letters.

The public rewards continued in June of 1959, when Sylvia flew to Buffalo to receive—"as representative of the best in American and French culture"—an honorary doctorate of letters from the University of Buffalo. From 1959 until her death, in the fall of 1962, she was a different woman. The modesty and reclusiveness that were the habit of the minister's daughter and the Frenchwoman—qualities sharpened by the war—were abandoned. She had survived the rationing of food, the lean life of postwar Paris, the loss of her closest friends. Not only had she influenced the literary history of her period, but also, having outlived most of her contemporaries, she had the advantage of sharing in the glory of its revival. She would have, on the other hand, the disadvantage of being remembered as the little old lady of the revival rather than the young and lively woman of the great days. Her chief concern during her last two years was finding a home for what she called her "Joyce-less Collection," the Shakespeare and Company Papers. Though she never failed to assist the aspiring artist, she remained uncomfortable with the "business scholars." She received requests for photographs and reviews, continued a voluminous correspondence, and gave many radio talks. After the death of Hemingway, she appeared on French television with two bullfighters and the manager of the Ritz Hotel.

Following a trip with the Mathewses to Greece, the Middle East, and Egypt (where they were joined by Yves Bonnefoy), Sylvia culminated her public life by dedicating the Martello Tower at Sandycove, near Dublin—the setting for the opening passage of *Ulysses*—as a center for Joyce studies. Dressed in Irishtweeds by the Anna Livia Boutique, on 16 June 1962 (Bloomsday, a name she had coined), she was carried by an old Dublin horse-cab of the period of 1904, the date on which the action of the novel occurs, to the Martello Tower. There she opened the ceremony by speaking of Joyce and Ireland and raising the Munster flag high above the James Joyce Tower. After standing in the warm afternoon sun while Donagh MacDonagh read the poem he had dedicated to her—"this one courageous woman" without whom "Joyce might have waited long"—she led devoted Joyceans down the winding steps of the tower to a reception lubricated by Guinness stout.

After an active vacation at Les Déserts (she broke her wrist chopping wood!), Sylvia returned to Paris the end of September. On 6 October, Maurice Saillet found her dead in her apartment. Apparently she had suffered a heart attack a day or two earlier. A simple funeral service was held at the Père-Lachaise cemetery. Thereafter her body was cremated. Literary persons and embassy friends—each group mistakenly thinking the other had planned an elaborate ceremony—sat in embarrassed and overdressed silence. Keeler Faus thought he heard above the somber organ music the laughter of Sylvia. Over the objections of her friends, who believed that after forty-six years she belonged to Paris, her ashes were sent to Holly in Greenwich, Connecticut, and buried in the following spring in Princeton. When Archibald MacLeish heard that she had died alone in her apartment, he insisted that "she is not alone, then or ever. She had that Company around her."

ACKNOWLEDGMENTS

To THE NATIONAL ENDOWMENT FOR THE HUMANITIES, I am indebted for a fellowship that enabled me to devote a full year to the writing of this book. In addition, for research and travel grants, I thank the American Philosophical Society, the National Endowment for the Humanities, and Point Loma College. I am indebted to Gailyn Fitch and to the staff of Ryan Library for their research assistance; to Mary Polley, Kathi Ellis, and Sherri Lippiatt for their typing; to Kathee Dayvolt for photography reproduction; and to the relatives of Sylvia Beach who gave me assistance and encouragement.

I wish to thank Richard M. Ludwig and his excellent staff at the Rare Book and Manuscript Collections, Princeton University Library, which houses the Sylvia Beach Papers. I also thank the Department of Manuscripts, British Library; Robert Bertholf and Melissa Banta of the Lockwood Memorial Library, State University of New York at Buffalo; Donald F. Gallup of the Beinecke Library, Yale; Jo August of the Hemingway Papers, John F. Kennedy Library; Alan Cohn of the Morris Library, Southern Illinois University at Carbondale; the John Quinn Memorial Collection, Manuscripts and Archives Division, and the Berg Collection, New York Public Library; Cornell University Library; the Bibliothèque Littéraire Jacques Doucet of Paris; the Humanities Research Center, University of Texas at Austin; the Research Library, University of California at Los Angeles; the Library of Congress; the McFarlin Library, University of Tulsa; Lilly Library, Indiana University; Butler Library, Columbia University; Houghton Library, Harvard.

To the participants who told me this story, I express my gratitude. In England: Martha Gellhorn Hemingway and Arthur Koestler. In Italy: the late Caresse Crosby. In France: Marcelle Auclair Prévost, Helen Baltrusaitis, Samuel Beckett, Jacques Benoist-Méchin, Yves Bonnefoy, Jenny Serruys Bradley, André Chamson, Keeler and Colette Faus, Gisèle Freund, Florence Gilliam, Maurice Saillet, the late Solita Solano, and François Valéry. In the United States: the late Boski Antheil, W. T. Bandy, Joella Bayer, the late Elizabeth Bishop, the late James Briggs, Kay Boyle, Jacqueline Campbell, Morrill Cody, Malcolm Cowley, the late Holly Beach Dennis, David Diamond, Silvia Dobson, Helen Eddy, Leon Edel, the late Mrs. Carl Ernlund, the late Janet Flanner, Joseph Foster, Frank Hanley, Marian Willard Johnson, Arthur J. Knodel, the late Archibald MacLeish, the late Jackson Mathews, Marthiel Mathews, Leigh Mercer, the late Marianne Moore, the late Hadley Hemingway Mowrer, Agnes Morris Orbison, Edwin Popper, the late Katherine Anne Porter, George Seldes, Perdita Schaffner, Douglas Schneider, Eisig Silberschlag, Frances Steloff, the late Irwin Swerdlow, the late Allen Tate, Virgil Thomson, Glenway Wescott, and the late Thornton Wilder. My best resource for unpublished material was the women who worked as assistants in Shakespeare and Company. Several of these women gave me days of their time: Myrsine Moschos, Dr. Jean Henley, Eleanor Oldenberger Herrick, Sylvia Peter Preston, and Priscilla Curtis Veitch.

In addition to the numerous persons who were patrons of Shakespeare and Company, I thank the following: Jane Lidderdale and Freda Luttrell, in London; Joseph Barry, Darthea Speyer, George Whitman, and the late Marcelle Fourier, in France; David Scherman, Avis Drake, Leslie Katz, the late Howard Rice, the late Mary Streets, and Donald Morrison Meisel, in the United States; John Elwood, who first told me about Sylvia Beach; and Lewis E. Buchanan, who supervised my first research. Thanks also to my fellow historians and biographers Carlos Baker, Richard Ellmann, Hugh Ford, Carolyn Burke, Emily Wallace, Deirdre Bair, Ernest Kroll, Oliver Pilat, Willard Potts, Bonnie Scott, Marcia Holly, George Wickes, and Geoffrey Wolff—all of whom shared information and ideas with me.

For permission to quote material here, I am indebted to Harcourt, Brace, publisher of Sylvia Beach's *Shakespeare and Company* (© 1959); Random House for quotations from James Joyce's *Ulysses* (© 1934, 1946), "In the Memory of W. B. Yeats," from *W. H. Auden: Collected Poems*, (© 1976), and Stephen Spender's "Ultima Ratio Regum," from *Selected Poems* (© 1965); Viking Press for quotations from James Joyce's *Finnegans Wake* (© 1968) and from *The Letters of James Joyce*, edited by Stuart Gilbert (vol. 1, © 1957, 1966) and Richard Ellmann (vols. 2 and 3, © 1966); Viking Penguin and Faber and Faber for Jane Lidderdale and Mary Nicholson's *Dear Miss Weaver* (© 1970); Charles Scribner's Sons for quotations from Adrienne Monnier's *The Very Rich Hours of Adrienne Monnier*, translated and edited by Richard McDougall (© 1976), and Ernest Hemingway's *A Moveable Feast* (© 1964); Oxford University Press for quotations from Richard Ellmann's *James Joyce* (© 1982); Faber and Faber for quotations from Louis MacNeice's *Autumn Journal* (© 1939); Princeton University Press for quotations from *The Collected Works of Paul Valéry* (© 1977); Houghton Mifflin for quotations from Archibald MacLeish's "Tourist Death: For Sylvia Beach," in *New and Collected Poems, 1917–1976* (© 1976); Mercure de France for quotations from *Sylvia Beach (1887–1962)* (© 1963); Keeler Faus, Marthiel Mathews, and other individuals for permission to use and quote letters, photographs, and tapes in their possession; the Estate of Sylvia Beach for quotations from her letters and manuscripts; the Estate of Harriet Weaver for quotations from her unpublished letters to Sylvia Beach; the Society of Authors for quotations from the published and unpublished letters of James Joyce.

Though the responsibility for the translations of passages from letters and essays in French is mine, I am grateful for the help of Richard McDougall, whose knowledge of the language and of Odéonia was invaluable to me. Portions of the manuscript that dealt directly with them were also read by Kay Boyle, Malcolm Cowley, Leon Edel, Jean Henley, Arthur Koestler, Archibald Mac-Leish, Eleanor Oldenberger Herrick, and others. I wish also to thank Mina Bryan, who shared her knowledge of the Beach family; James O. Allsup, a valiant advocate of style; A. Walton Litz, who gave me the opening scene; and Albert Sonnenfeld, who shared the journey.

My special indebtedness to certain institutions and individuals is recorded in the notes that follow. Unless otherwise specified, all Beach family letters as well as all letters to Sylvia Beach are in the Sylvia Beach Papers in the Princeton University Library. Letters from James Joyce to Sylvia Beach are in the James Joyce Collection in the Lockwood Memorial Library of the State University of New York at Buffalo. Letters from James Joyce to Harriet Weaver are in the Harriet Weaver Papers in the British Library. All correspondence between Sylvia Beach and Bryher is in the Beinecke Library of Yale.

NOTES

ABBREVIATIONS

INITIALS are used for the principal figures (Sylvia Beach, James Joyce, Adrienne Monnier, Eleanor Beach, Sylvester Woodbridge Beach, Holly Beach Dennis, Harriet Weaver) and for the author (NRF). Other abbreviations in the notes are as follows:

Ellmann — Richard Ellmann, *James Joyce*, rev. ed. (New York: Oxford, 1982.)

Mercure — *Sylvia Beach (1887–1962)*, compiled by Jackson Mathews and Maurice Saillet (Paris: Mercure de France, 1963; reprinted from "Memorial Edition to Sylvia Beach," *Mercure*, 349 (Aug.–Sept., 1963)).

McDougall — Adrienne Monnier, *The Very Rich Hours of Adrienne Monnier*, trans., with an introd. and commentaries by Richard McDougall (New York: Scribners, 1976).

SC — Sylvia Beach, *Shakespeare and Company* (New York: Harcourt, Brace, 1959).

III, 562 — Volume and page numbers are cited for *Letters of James Joyce*, ed. Stuart Gilbert (vol. 1) and Richard Ellmann (vols. 2 and 3) (New York: Viking, 1957, 1966).

NY — New York.

INTRODUCTION

SC, 12–13, 35, and several unpublished drafts and suppressed portions of the memoirs; Tom Stoppard, *Travesties* (London: Faber and Faber, 1975), 23; Archibald MacLeish, "There Was Something about the Twenties," *Saturday Review*, 31 Dec. 1966, 11.

1. A GIFT OF TONGUES
1922

Publication day: SC, 84–86, 40; Sisley Huddleston, *Back to Montparnasse: Glimpses of Broadway in Bohemia* (Philadelphia: Lippincott, 1931), 194; Cyril Connolly, *Enemies of Promise* (London: Routledge, 1938), 75; Interview with Myrsine Moschos, 22 June 1978; Janet Flanner, *Paris Was Yesterday* (NY: Viking, 1972), x; JJ to HW, 8 Feb. 1922, I, 180; Among the Sylvia Beach Papers are numerous handwritten and typed drafts of her memoirs. In several cases, the details of these versions vary considerably from or were excluded from the published memoirs.

Printing problems: "There had been typesetting machines for 30-odd years," explains Hugh Kenner ("An Insane Assault on Chaos," *NY Times Book Review*, 22 June 1980, 7), "but *Ulysses* was surely the biggest book of any importance to be set by hand since William Morris handset the Kelmscott Chaucer in 1893–

96." A facsimile of the *Ulysses* manuscript and the 1922 edition are now available from Octagon Books for $200. Prof. Hans Walter Gabler of Munich is, with the aid of a computer, identifying the estimated 4,000 errors that have accumulated in all of the published versions of *Ulysses,* and he will establish a corrected text.

Contribution of Shakespeare and Company: E. Morrill Cody, "Shakespeare and Company—Paris," *Publishers' Weekly*, 12 Apr. 1924, 1261; Ernest Hemingway, *A Moveable Feast* (NY: Scribners, 1963), 35; SB is "a symbol of the early twentieth century feminist," concludes Lisa McFarlane in her senior thesis "For-Who-Is-Silvier" (Princeton, 1979); Marianne Moore, "How Do Justice . . . ," *Mercure*, 13; Bryher, *The Heart to Artemis: A Writer's Memoir* (NY: Harcourt, Brace & World, 1962), 208.

2. WHO IS SYLVIA?
1887–1919

The major sources for the life of Sylvia Beach prior to the founding of Shakespeare and Company are early, unpublished drafts of her memoirs, portions of which were selected for pp. 3–14 of *SC;* family documents of the Orbison, Beach, and Dennis families; SB letters to Eleanor Beach, Sylvester Woodbridge Beach, Holly Beach, and Cyprian Beach, 1904–1919 (specific dates will not be cited in this chapter); Grace Z. Brown, "Sylvia Beach: American Publisher in Paris," *McNaught's Monthly*, Sept. 1926, 77–78.

Childhood and adolescence: Agnes Morris Orbison to NRF, 29 June 1977; Mary Streets to NRF, 11 Apr. 1969; SB interview, "From Presbyterian Vicarage to Ulysses," BBC (24 Oct. 1959); Ezra Pound "Unanism," *Little Review*, 4 (Apr. 1918), 26, and untitled note, ibid. (May 1918), 62; Joseph Barry, *Infamous Woman: The Life of George Sand* (NY: Doubleday Anchor, 1978), 27; SWB, "The American Student in Paris," *Independent: A Weekly Magazine*, 25 Sept. 1902, 2307–8; SB to Margaret Marshall, 23 Jan. 1958, Harcourt, Brace; Interview with James Briggs, 6 July 1978; SB to Bryher, 4 Apr. 1949; John Peale Bishop, "Princeton," *The Smart Set* (Nov. 1921), reprinted in *Collected Essays* (NY: Scribners, 1948), 391; Interview with Sylvia Peter Preston, 1 June 1978; Hamlin Hill, *Mark Twain: God's Fool* (NY: Harper & Row, 1973), 174.

Final trip to Europe: EB to Mary Morris, 28 May 1915; In William Butler Yeats's speech in a *Poetry* dinner in his honor, 1 Mar. 1913, he declared that he "metrical experiments of French poets" and "French criticism" arc dominating "the best English writing," *Little Review*, 2; Charles Fenton, "Ambulance Drivers in France and Italy: 1914–1918," *American Quarterly*, 3 (1951), 337; Malcolm Cowley, *Exile's Return: A Literary Odyssey of the 1920's* (NY: Viking, 1951), 38; In 1915 in Spain, villagers threw rocks at Sylvia and Cyprian, who were dressed in riding pants (interview with Helen Eddy, 27 May 1978); Mrs. Beach's 11 Dec. 1918 letter to SB is, by her own admission, the message of a nearly "crazy" woman who cares only for her children, yet wishes they had never been born; her "only accompaniment at meals" is "a person I feel like murdering."

Sylvia meets Adrienne: To Holly (31 Jan. 1918), Sylvia expressed enthusiasm for the poetry of Paul Fort, to whom she had sent a box of fruit. He sent her a note (7 July 1918) of gratitude for the offering; AM, "La

Maison des Amis des Livres," *Rue de l'Odéon* (1920), in McDougall, 69; Bryher calls Adrienne a "thoughtful reader" who was "a part of that timeless nucleus that has, as its purpose, the transmission of a wisdom that cannot be written down, even in poetry," *Heart to Artemis*, 208; Sylvia took out a second subscription (15 Mar. 1918) in the A. Monnier library; Molyneux designed Adrienne's dress; Interview with Marcelle Auclair, 9 June 1978; William Carlos Williams, *The Autobiography of WCW* (NY: New Directions, 1967), 193; Malcolm Cowley, "When a Young American," *Mercure*, 57; Sisley Huddleston, *Paris Salons, Cafés, Studios* (London: Lippincott, 1928), 208; Interviews with Myrsine Moschos (22 June 1978), Gisèle Freund (11 Aug. 1969), Jackson Mathews (3 May 1969), Morrill Cody (17 July 1978), and Yves Bonnefoy (23 June 1978); Jackson Mathews, "Conversation with SB and Company," *Kenyon Review*, 22 (winter 1960), 139; Samuel Putnam, *Paris Was Our Mistress: Memoirs of a Lost and Found Generation* (NY: Viking, 1947), 97; According to SB, Adrienne's "little shop was the rendezvous for mental cocktails during those ghastly days when Paris was being bombarded"; Adrienne's poem quoted in McDougall, 12.

Serbia: Henry James to Howard Sturgis, 5 Aug. 1914, *The Letters of HJ*, ed. Percy Lubbock, vol. 2 (NY: Scribners, 1920), 384; According to Oliver Pilat, *Drew Pearson: An Unauthorized Biography* (NY: Pocket Books, 1973), 71, Drew Pearson and SB had an affair during their Red Cross service in Serbia and aborted a child; No verification of this incident, which Pilat acknowledges was mere rumor, remains; Interview with Pilat, 27 Dec. 1981; *SC*, 16, 18–19, 21, and early drafts; Records show that her first business day was 17 (not 19) Nov.; Eugene Jolas, quoted in Hugh Ford, *Published in Paris: American and British Writers, Printers, and Publishers in Paris, 1920–1939* (NY: Macmillan, 1975), 3.

3. . . . AND COMPANY

1919–1920

Opening: Linda Simon, *The Biography of Alice B. Toklas* (NY: Doubleday, 1977), 108; SB to EB, 19 Nov. 1919; Robert Sage, "Shakespeare and Company's Sylvia Beach," (13 Oct. 1962) news clipping; *SC*, 17–21; Sisley Huddleston, *Paris Salons, 209.

French customers: SC, 16, 22, 54–57, 146–62, and early versions of these chapters; SB to EB, 24 Nov. 1919, 15 and 18 Mar. 1920, and 10, 23, and 27 May 1920; SB to HB, 7 and 11 Dec. 1919; Ernest Hemingway to Bernard Berenson, 20–22 Mar. 1953, in *EH: Selected Letters*, ed. Carlos Baker (NY: Scribners, 1981), 809; Huddleston, "The House of the Friends of Books," *Paris Salons*, 196–207; McDougall, 17, 36; AM, "Fargue as Talker" (1960), in McDougall, 207–9; AM, "In the Country of Faces" (1939), in McDougall, 233; Interviews with Marcelle Auclair (9 June 1978) and Myrsine Moschos (22 June 1978); Jackson Mathews, *Kenyon Review*, 140; AM, "On Pre-Columbian Mexico" (1954), in McDougall, 383; Claude Mauriac, *Conversations with André Gide* (NY: Braziller, 1965), ix.

Librarian and bookseller: NRF, "Sylvia Beach's Shakespeare and Company: Port of Call for American Expatriates," *Research Studies*, 33 (Dec. 1965), 198; All the library cards that have survived are in the Sylvia Beach Papers, Princeton; Interview with Eleanor Oldenberger Herrick, 7 Mar. 1978; *SC*, 105; Janet Flanner, "The Great Amateur Publisher," *Mercure*, 48–49; Leslie Katz, "Meditations on Sylvia Beach," *Mercure*, 82; SB to HBD, 3 and 9 Feb. 1920; Huddleston, *Paris Salons*, 251.

Arrival of Stein: William Shirer, *20th Century Jour-*

ney: A Memoir of a Life and Times (NY: Simon and Schuster, 1976), 288; Glenway Wescott, "Memoirs and Opinions," *Prose*, 5 (fall 1972), 192; *SC*, 27; Matisse, in Georges Braque et al., "Testimony against Gertrude Stein," *transition*, 23 Supplement (Feb. 1935); Simon, *Biography of Alice B. Toklas*, 122–25; Alice B. Toklas, "Sylvia and Her Friends," *New Republic*, 19 Oct. 1959, 24; Stein poem, in *Mercure*, 95–97, and vol. 5 of the Yale edition of Stein's works; SB to EB, 10 May 1920; *SC*, 28–29.

Stein and the French: Gertrude Stein to SB, n.d.; Eugene Jolas and André Salmon (in "Testimony against GS") and Matthew Josephson concur that Stein had, in Josephson's words, "rather slight contact with the literary world of Paris," *Life among the Surrealists* (NY: Holt, Rinehart & Winston, 1962), 12; In a 24 July 1952 letter to Donald Gallup, Sylvia implies that Larbaud's mother became ill and that he was unable to get to the Stein dinner. In *The Autobiography of Alice B. Toklas* (NY: Harcourt, Brace, 1960), 196, however, Stein states that the meeting took place; SB to GS, 2 Oct. 1921.

Benét and other visitors: SC, 29, and unpublished drafts; SB to EB, 23 May 1920; SB to Stein, 27 May 1920.

Arrival of Pound: SC, 45, 26–27, and early drafts; JJ to HW, 2 Dec. 1928, I, 277; Pound, "The Island of Paris: A Letter," *Dial*, 69 (Oct. 1920), 406.

Pound and the little magazines: Solita Solano to NRF, 29 Aug. 1969; Frederick J. Hoffman, Charles Allen, and Carolyn R. Ulrich, *The Little Magazine: A History and a Bibliography*, 2nd ed. (Princeton: Princeton University Press, 1947), 2; Charles Allen,

"Advanced Guard," *Sewanee Review*, 2 (July–Sept. 1943), 425; Bryher, *Heart to Artemis*, 205; Pound to SB, n.d.; *SC*, 137.

Arrival of Joyce: SC, 40, 34–37, and early drafts; SB, "*Ulysses* à Paris," *Mercure de France*, 309 (May–Aug. 1950), 12–29, and "*Ulysses* a Parigi," *Inventario*, 3 (1950), 77–87; After SB's first (*Mercure*) telling of her meeting with JJ, Pound insisted that he never had blue eyes and Spire wanted her to change the story, insisting that there were no birds singing that day and that he had not served any cheese or wine, only tea with

food; AM, "Joyce's *Ulysses* and the French Republic" (1940), in McDougall, 112–26; Benda's attack, in *Belphégor*, which takes its name from an Old Palestinian devil who comes to the earth in human form, continued in *The Treason of the Intellectuals* (1927); Padraic Colum, *Our Friend James Joyce* (Garden City, NY: Doubleday, 1958), 119; Prof. Albert Sonnenfeld further suggests the association of Sylvia (sylvan, sylva) with the dark wood or forest image of the opening line of Dante's *Divine Comedy*; André Spire, "La Rencontre avec Joyce," *Mercure*, 41–45.

4. THE BATTLE OF *Ulysses*
1920–1921

Joyce's first visit: Fritz Vanderpyl quoted in Ellmann, 492; *SC*, 37–41; JJ to HW, 11 Mar. 1923, I, 201.

Writing Ulysses: Ellmann, 357; A. Walton Litz has established that 40 percent of the manuscript Quinn bought is "of dubious authority," review of *Ulysses: A Facsimile*, in *James Joyce Quarterly*, 14 (fall 1976), 9; JJ to HW, 25 Feb. 1920, I, 137; Sisley Huddleston, *Back to Montparnasse*, 258; JJ to Carlo Linati, 21 Sept. 1920, I, 146.

Joyce adjusts to Paris: Ellmann, 485–90; *SC*, 41; Interview with Jenny Serruys Bradley, 16 June 1978; Wyndham Lewis, *Blasting and Bombardiering* (Berkeley: University of California Press, 1967), 165–70, 272, 293–94; Hemingway, *A Moveable Feast*, 108.

Harriet Weaver: Leonard Woolf, *Beginning Again* (London: Hogarth, 1964), 246–47; Virginia Woolf, *A Writer's Diary* (London: Hogarth, 1954), 363; Jane Lidderdale and Mary Nicholson, *Dear Miss Weaver: Harriet Shaw Weaver, 1876–1961* (NY: Viking, 1970), 225, 174, 87, 162; JJ to HW, 25 Aug. 1920; Letters between John Quinn and Ben Huebsch, in Herbert Gorman, *James Joyce* (NY: Rinehart, 1948), 277–81.

Natalie Barney: SB to HB, (?) Nov. 1920; SB to EB, 7 Nov. 1920; Valéry's remarks on salons, in unpublished portions of *SC;* Interview with Morrill Cody, 17 July 1978; Putnam, *Paris Was Our Mistress*, 73; Williams, *Autobiography*, 229; *SC*, 114; SB to HB, 16 Oct. 1920.

Love of the theater: McDougall, 237–88; SB to CB, 21 Dec. 1920; SB to HB, 20 Dec. 1920.

Financial adjustments: JJ to Frank Budgen, 10 Dec. 1920, I, 151; SB to EB, 16 Dec. 1920; JJ, *Ulysses* (NY: Random House, 1946), 593.

Joyce meets Larbaud: SC, 57.

Revelry and repentence: SB to HB, 20 Dec. 1920; SB to EB, 17 Feb. 1921.

Little Review trial: John Quinn to JJ, 13 Apr. 1921 in Myron Schwartzman, "Quinnigan's Quake! John Quinn's letters to James Joyce, 1921–1924," *Bulletin of Research in the Humanities*, 83 (Apr. 1980), 35; Margaret Anderson, *My Thirty Years' War: An Autobiography* (NY: Covici, Friede, 1930), 220–21; JJ, *Ulysses*, 354, 359, 360 (*lovely* in the next to the last line was for years ironically misprinted as *lively*); *NY Times*, 22 Feb. 1921, 6; Anderson and Quinn clearly did not like each other—she shows more sympathy for Sumner, whom she found shy, charming, and convinced of his beliefs.

Sylvia agrees to publish Ulysses: SB to EB, 1 Apr. 1921; JJ to HW, 3 Apr. 1921, I, 160; Not until 13 Apr. 1921 did Quinn send Joyce the full details of the trial; Early draft of *SC*, 47; Gorman, *James Joyce*, 286; JJ to HW, 10 Apr. 1921, I, 162; Power quoted in Ellmann, 504; Arthur Power, *Conversations with James Joyce* (NY: Harper & Row, 1974), 29; HW to SB, 12 Apr. 1921; Lidderdale and Nicholson, *Dear Miss Weaver*, 181.

Typing Ulysses: SC, 63–65; Quinn to JJ, 5 June 1921, Schwartzman, *Bulletin*, 38–42.

Darantière: SC, 48–50, and unpublished versions; SB to HB, 23 Apr. 1921. (Marjorie Reed promised Sylvia an article in the *New York Sunday Herald*, and Sisley Huddleston promised one for the London *Observer*.)

Gilliam and Moss: SC, 137; Interview with Florence Gilliam, 16 June 1978.

Thornton Wilder: Richard Goldstone, *Thornton Wilder: An Intimate Portrait* (NY: Dutton, 1975), 39; Wilder to NRF, 22 May 1969; Unpublished drafts of *SC* and p. 111; Stein quoted in Samuel M. Steward, ed., *Dear Sammy: Letters from GS and Alice B. Toklas* (Boston: Houghton Mifflin, 1977), 37; Wilder to NRF, 8 Oct. 1968.

Sherwood Anderson: Huddleston, *Paris Salons*, 78; James Schevill, *Sherwood Anderson: His Life and Work* (Denver: University of Denver Press, 1951), 135–36, 28, 42; Sherwood Anderson, *France and Sherwood Anderson: Paris Notebook, 1921*, ed. Michael Fanning (Baton Rouge: Louisiana State University Press, 1976), 34, 9; *SC*, 30–32, and unpublished drafts; Anderson to SB (?), 1927.

Chicago Tribune article: Hugh Ford, ed., *The Left Bank Revisited: Selections from the Paris "Tribune," 1917–1934* (University Park: Pennsylvania State University Press, 1972), 58–59.

McAlmon and Bryher: McAlmon letter to Williams, quoted in Robert McAlmon and Kay Boyle, *Being Geniuses Together: 1920–1930* (Garden City, NY: Doubleday, 1968; Originally published as McAlmon's *Being Geniuses Together: An Autobiography*, 1938), 50; *SC*, 99–102, unpublished portion, 51; Interview with Perdita Schaffner, 7 July 1978; AM's "Our Friend Bryher" (1940), in McDougall, 204; Bryher, *Heart to Artemis*, 201, 207–8; McAlmon and Boyle, *Being Geniuses Together*, 24, 130–31; Robert E. Knoll, *Robert McAlmon: Expatriate Publisher and Writer* (Lincoln: University of Nebraska Press, 1957), 6.

Subscriptions: The book for England, Ireland, and Scotland contains 364 names, among them Havelock Ellis, T. E. Lawrence, Elkin Mathews, Dora Marsden, John Rodker, W. B. Yeats, T. S. Eliot; the France book contains 183; the U.S. book, 243; Jane Heap to SB, June 1921; Lidderdale and Nicholson, *Dear Miss Weaver*, 188–89.

Joyce writing Ulysses: JJ to Frank Budgen, (?) Feb. 1921, I, 159–60; Holly Beach Dennis statement concerning the Beach women in *Ulysses* (she misses the reference to her father), in SB Papers; JJ, *Ulysses*, 518, 321, 293; A. Walton Litz, *The Art of James Joyce: Method and Design in "Ulysses" and "Finnegans Wake"* (NY: Oxford, 1964), 89.

Bank and post office: T. S. Eliot, "Mr. T. S. Eliot writes:—" *Times* (London), 13 Oct. 1962, 10, reprinted in *Mercure*, 9–10. "If any of the Joyce family needed money," write Mary and Padriac Colum, "they went to Miss Beach for it," *Our Friend James Joyce*, 189; *SC*, 23, and early drafts.

Myrsine Moschos: Interviews with Myrsine Moschos, 22 and 24 June 1978; *SC*, 49–50; JJ to HW, 11 Nov. 1932, I, 327; The Ritarasi decision was not in honor of the novel or Joyce, but was the result of bookshop talk. According to Moschos, he never read the novel. *Quinn visit: SC*, 61–62, and early drafts; B. L. Reid, *The Man from New York: John Quinn and His Friends* (NY: Oxford, 1968), 492; Schwartzman, *Bulletin*, 27–66.

To the rue de l'Odéon: SC, 12, 62; McDougall, 5; Archibald MacLeish, "What One Remembers . . . ," *Mercure*, 35; MacLeish to NRF, 11 Apr. 1969.

5. STRATFORD-ON-ODÉON
1921–1922

Fiery center: Mathews, *Kenyon Review*, 137.

Larbaud and Joyce: JJ mistakenly takes credit for giving *Ulysses* portions to Larbaud; Larbaud quoted by Jolas, "Rambles through Literary Paris," *Paris Tribune* (8 June 1924), in *Left Bank Revisited*, 96–97; *SC*, 57–58, 69–70; Larbaud's letters to Sylvia are reproduced in *Mercure*, 99–100; JJ to Budgen, (?) Feb. 1921, I, 159; Ellmann, 489.

Claudel: McDougall, 22–24; Mathews, *Kenyon Review*, 140–41, 145–46.

Valéry: Interview with Myrsine Moschos, 22 June 1978; unpublished portion of *SC;* Jackson Mathews, "My Sylvia Beach," *Mercure*, 25; *SC*, 13–14, 158–60; Interview with François Valéry, 20 June 1978; AM, "Valéry in the Rue de l'Odéon" (1945), in McDougall, 77; Huddleston, *Paris Salons*, 200.

Gide: Ellmann, 530, 488, 695; *SC*, 156–57; AM, "With Gide at Hyères" (1921), in McDougall, 93–98; SB to HBD, 22 Sept. 1921.

Sylvia Beach and the French: Interview with Keeler and Colette Faus, 25 June 1978; *SC*, 150–51; Interview with Myrsine Moschos, 22 June 1978; Mathews, *Kenyon Review*, 78; AM, "Americans in Paris" (1945), in McDougall, 413; Henri Hoppenot, "Pendant près d'un Quart de Siècle," *Mercure*, 15; Alice B. Toklas (*New Republic*, 24) claims SB is "the most American after Gertrude Stein"—high praise from Toklas; Henry James, *Madame de Mauves* (NY: Scribners, 1908), 247; AM, "Mémorial de la rue de l'Odéon," quoted in McDougall, 40; Interview with Marthiel Mathews, 18 July 1978; Interview with Eleanor Oldenberger Herrick, 8 Mar. 1978; According to Eugene Jolas, JJ was "never an easy conversationalist and had a tendency to monosyllabic utterances," "My Friend James Joyce," *Partisan Review*, 8 (1944), reprinted in Seon Givens, ed., *JJ: Two Decades of Criticism* (NY: Vanguard, 1948); Dwight Macdonald, "James Joyce," *Against the American Grain* (NY: Random House, 1962), 124–26; Interview with Janet Flanner, 29 July 1977; AM, "The Nature of France" (1940), in McDougall, 418–19; Edmund Wilson, *The Twenties: From Notebooks and Diaries of the Period,* ed. Leon Edel (NY: Farrar, Straus and Giroux, 1975), 96.

Other Americans and the French: Unpublished drafts of *SC;* Interview with Myrsine Moschos, 22 June 1978; *Left Bank Revisited;* Josephson, *Life among the Surrealists,* 87; Fenton, *American Quarterly,* 326–43; Between 1920 and 1942, in keeping with the intellectual quality of the ambulance volunteers during the war, 215 scholarships were given to Americans to study at French universities.

Joyce and Miss Weaver: JJ to HW, 24 June, 7 Aug., and 2 May 1921, I, 165, 168, 164; Lidderdale and Nicholson, *Dear Miss Weaver,* 189; Ellmann, 491.

Financial strain: SB to HB, 22 Sept. 1921; Bookshop ledger for 16 July 1921.

Penelope completed: JJ to Robert McAlmon, 3 Sept.

1921, III, 48, and 6 Oct. 1921, I, 172; JJ to Frank Budgen, 16 Aug. 1921, I, 170.

Soliciting Shaw: SC, 50–53, which includes the Shaw letter; Ezra Pound, "Paris Letter," *Dial* (June 1922), in *Literary Essays of Ezra Pound* (London: Faber and Faber, 1961), 407; Pound to Mencken, 22 Mar. 1921, *The Letters of Ezra Pound: 1907–1941,* ed. D. D. Paige (London: Faber and Faber, 1951), 240; André Spire, "La Rencontre avec Joyce," *Mercure*, 43; SB to Shaw, 17 Nov. 1949; Howard Woolmer, "*Ulysses* at Auction with a Preliminary Census," *James Joyce Quarterly,* 17 (winter 1980), 143; Bookshop records.

Ulysses proofs: JJ to HW 7, Oct. 1921, I, 172; *SC,* 65, 58–60, 63, and unpublished drafts; Ellmann, 513, 521; Interview with Jacques Benoist-Méchin, 10 June 1978; Victor Llona, "With Ezra Pound before Rapallo," *Cimarron Review,* 7 (Jan. 1973), 15; Litz, *Art of James Joyce,* 92; the *Guardian* correspondent Darsie Gillie, quoted by Flanner, *Mercure,* 47; Joyce, quoted by Adolph Hoffmeister, "Portrait of Joyce," in *Portraits of the Artist in Exile,* ed. Willard Potts (Seattle: University of Washington Press, 1979), 129.

Light and superstitious moments: Unpublished drafts of *SC,* and pp. 88–89; JJ to HW, 1 Nov. 1921, III, 52; McAlmon and Boyle, *Being Geniuses Together,* 35.

Joyce borrowings: SB to John Quinn, 17 Oct. 1921, NY Public Library; Quinn letters to Pound, in Lilly Library, Indiana University, Bloomington; Stanislaus Joyce to JJ, 26 Feb. 1922, III, 58; SB statement concerning her solicitation of McAlmon, in SB Papers; JJ to McAlmon, 6 Nov. 1921, I, 175–76; JJ to Italo Svevo, 5 Jan. 1921, I, 154; Lidderdale and Nicholson, *Dear Miss Weaver,* 190.

Translations of Ulysses: Unpublished drafts of *SC;* AM, "The Translation of *Ulysses*" (1950), in McDougall, 126–28; Interview with Jacques Benoist-Méchin, 10 June 1978; Feminist critics, who assert that Molly is a male fantasy of female sexuality, would be amused by this lengthy discussion by Joyce and Benoist-Méchin (the Benoist-Méchin translation is lost); JJ to Valery Larbaud, 30 July 1929, I, 284.

Seance at Adrienne's: SC, 58, 73–74; *Ulysses,* 269; SB to SWB, 3 Dec. 1921; Man Ray, *Self-Portrait* (Boston: Little, Brown, 1963), 186; AM, "Joyce's *Ulysses* and the French Public" (1940), in McDougall, 112–13; Ellmann, 520–23; Valery Larbaud's lecture "The *Ulysses* of James Joyce" appeared in English in *Criterion: A Quarterly Review,* 1 (Oct. 1922), 94–103; JJ to HW, 10 Dec. 1921, I, 178; Huddleston, *Paris Salons,* 203; Gilbert, introd. to I, 29.

French response to Ulysses: AM, "Joyce's *Ulysses* and the French Public" (1940), in McDougall, 114–26, which quotes Romains, Curtius, and Soupault; AM, "Occupation Journal" (1940), in McDougall, 391.

End of the Year: Ezra Pound to T. S. Eliot, 24 Dec. 1921, *Letters,* ed. Paige, 234; SB to SWB, 20 and 24 Jan. 1922; *SC,* 63, 84, and unpublished drafts.

6. SELLING AND SMUGGLING *Ulysses*
1922

Hemingway's arrival: Most dialogue is from Hemingway's account of these Paris years in *Moveable Feast,* 35–38, 211; The same letter from Sherwood Anderson was written to SB, Pound, JJ, Stein, and Lewis Galan-

tière, employed by the International Chamber of Commerce and Anderson's translator; Though his subscription rate was for two volumes at a time, EH remembered (thirty years later) borrowing five (his borrower's cards before 1925 are lost); Early drafts of "My Best Customer," *SC,* 77–83; Hadley Hemingway Mowrer to NRF, June 1969; Carlos Baker, *Ernest Hemingway: A Life Story* (NY: Scribners, 1969), 78–87; NRF, "EH & Shakespeare and Company," *Fitzgerald / Hemingway Annual, 1977,* 157–81; Morrill Cody to NRF, 7 July 1978; Interview with Myrsine Moschos, 24 June 1978; EH to Sherwood Anderson, 9 Mar. 1922, *EH Selected: Letters,* 62; EH, *Writers at Work: The* Paris Review *Interviews* (NY: Viking, 1963), 226.

Waiting for first reviews: JJ to HW, 17 Nov. 1922, I, 194; JJ to McAlmon, 11 Feb. 1922, I, 181; JJ to HW, 20 Mar. 1922, III, 62.

Quinn: John Quinn to SB, 4 / 6 Feb. 1922; SB to JQ, 21 Feb. 1922, NY Public Library; Michael Joseph, *The Adventure of Publishing* (London: Wingate, 1949).

Stein and Hemingway: Hemingway, *A Moveable Feast,* 14–15; Glenway Wescott, "Memories and Opinions," *Prose,* 5 (fall 1972), 193; W. G. Rogers, quoted by Goldstone, *Thornton Wilder,* 52.

First review and sales: JJ to HW, 3 Mar. 1922 (British Library), and 11 Mar. 1922, I, 183; Sisley Huddleston, *Observer,* 5 Mar. 1922, 4; Bookshop records; JJ to McAlmon, 17 Mar. 1922, III, 60; JJ to Stanislaus Joyce, 20 Mar. 1922, III, 61; JJ to HW, 16 May 1922, I, 184; Dudley Fitts to SB, n.d.; George R. Cook to SB, 13 Mar. 1959; Kate Crane-Gartz to SB, (?) Feb. 1934.

Joyce solicits McAlmon: McAlmon and Boyle, *Being Geniuses Together,* 29, 128; JJ to McAlmon, 17 May 1922, III, 60.

Pound's Bel Esprit: Reprinted in *Letters of EP, 1907–1941,* 238–42.

Negative reviews: "Aramis," "The Scandal of *Ulysses,*" *Sporting Times,* 1 Apr. 1922, 4; JJ to HW, 10 Apr. 1922, I, 183; "Domini Canis" (Shane Leslie), "Ulysses" (Review), *Dublin Review* (Sept. 1922), 119; Alfred Noyes, "Rottenness in Literature," *Sunday Chronicle,* 29 Oct. 1922, 2; Edmund Gosse to Louis Gillet, 7 June 1924, in Louis Gillet, *Claybook for James Joyce* (NY: Abelard-Schuman, 1958), 31–32; Woolf, *Writer's Diary,* 49, 47; Barrett H. Clark, "George Moore," in *Intimate Portraits* (Port Washington, NY: Kennikat, 1951), 110; Stanislaus Joyce to JJ, 26 Feb. 1922, III, 58; R. W. B. Lewis, *Edith Wharton: A Biography* (NY: Harper & Row, 1977), 442; John Dos Passos, *The Best Times: An Informal Memoir* (NY: New American Library, 1968), 148.

Nora to Ireland: Ellmann, 557; McAlmon and Boyle, *Being Geniuses Together,* 280; JJ to Nora Joyce, (?) Apr. 1922, in Ellmann 534; Unpublished portions of *SC;* JJ informed Stanislaus Joyce (20 Mar. 1922, III, 61) that HW "has made me another gift of £1500 in addition to the £2000 and the previous £5000 making £8500 in all, as well as the reversion of a country house somewhere."

Positive reviews: Quinn to SB, 4 Apr. and 27 Mar. 1922; Middleton Murry, "Mr. Joyce's Ulysses," *Nation and Athenaeum,* 22 Apr. 1922, 124–25; JJ to HW, 30 Apr. 1922, III, 64; Arnold Bennett, "James Joyce's *Ulysses,*" *Outlook* (London), 29 Apr. 1922, 337–39; Ellmann, 531–32; Unsolicited letters concerning *Ulysses,* in SB Papers.

Stein's hostility to Joyce and Pound: SC, 28, 32; Stein, *Autobiography of Alice B. Toklas,* 239, 196, 200, 212; John Malcolm Brinnin, *The Third Rose: GS and Her World* (Boston: Little, Brown, 1957), 269; Putnam, *Paris Was Our Mistress,* 138; Hemingway, *Moveable Feast,* 27, 28; Interview with Joseph Barry, 12 June 1978. Pound's parody quoted in *Exile* (1938), and McAlmon and Boyle, *Being Geniuses Together,* 225.

The Joyce burden: James Boswell, *Life of Samuel Johnson* (NY: Oxford, 1948), 192; Janet Flanner, "The Great Amateur Publisher," and Malcolm Cowley, "When a Young American," in *Mercure,* 45, 58; Stuart

Gilbert, introd. to I, 31; Interview with Myrsine Moschos, 24 June 1978; SB to John Quinn, 21 Feb. 1922, NY Public Library; *SC,* 198, 201, and early drafts.

Hemingway learns cablese: Interview with Gilbert Seldes, 23 July 1981. Baker, *EH: A Life Story,* 89. Baker mistakenly places this incident at a Lausanne conference, claims Seldes.

Joyce's eye troubles: SC, 66–68, 70–72, and unpublished drafts of these passages; JJ told HW he had learned 500 lines of Scott's poem in three days, 27 June 1924, I, 216; Bookshop ledgers.

SB and Miss Weaver on Joyce: SB to HW, 6 June, 9 June, 18 June, 26 June, 7 Sept. 1922; Pound, "Paris Letter" (May 1922), in *A Dial Miscellany,* ed. William Wasserstrom (Syracuse: Syracuse University Press, 1963), 97, 101; Lidderdale and Nicholson, *Dear Miss Weaver,* 199.

Visits from Marian and Carlotta: Interview with James Briggs, 6 July 1978; SB to Marian Peter, 8 Aug. 1922.

Hemingway's reading habits: His library cards are deciphered in NRF, *Fitzgerald / Hemingway Annual, 1977,* 157–81; *SC,* 83.

Joyce to London: SB to HW, 26 June and 9 July 1922; Ellmann, 536; Lidderdale and Nicholson, *Dear Miss Weaver,* 202.

A second printing of Ulysses: SC, 95–97; Lidderdale and Nicholson, *Dear Miss Weaver,* 203–4; Ellmann, 505–6 n.; SB to HW, 9 July 1922; Interview with Myrsine Moschos, 24 June 1978.

John Peale Bishop: Bishop's "Princeton," *Collected Essays,* 400; Bishop, "Homage to Hemingway," *New Republic,* 11 Nov. 1936, expanded in *Collected Essays,* 37–46; Allen Tate, *Memoirs and Opinions, 1926–1974* (Chicago: Swallow, 1975), 61.

Flanner and Hemingway, journalists: John C. Broderick, "Paris between the Wars: An Unpublished Memoir by Solita Solano," *Quarterly Journal of the Library of Congress,* 34 (Oct. 1977), 306–14, 351–53; Solano to NRF, 29 Aug. 1969; Interview with Flanner, 29 July 1977; Kathryn Hulme, *Undiscovered Country: A Spiritual Adventure* (Boston: Little, Brown, 1966), 100; Baker, *EH: A Life Story,* 100.

Berlin: Josephson, *Life among the Surrealists,* 101, 105; McAlmon and Boyle, *Being Geniuses Together,* 107.

George Moore and Ford Madox Ford: SC, 72 –73; McAlmon and Boyle, *Being Geniuses Together,* 249; Ellmann, 618; Clark, *Intimate Portrait,* 110; Malcolm Cowley to NRF, 17 Apr. 1982.

Joyce quarrels with Sylvia and Budgen: SB to EB, 13 Nov. 1932; JJ to HW, 13 Nov. 1922; *SC,* 96–97; Ellmann, 541–42; JJ to HW, 17 Nov. 1922, I, 197.

Smuggling Ulysses: Harriet Monroe to SB, 16 Sept. 1922; Only two copies of this third edition (the second Egoist edition) survive. One, sent by Rodker to HW, was given to SB to be sold for a "fancy price" for JJ. Bought by Rodker himself, the copy is now at Yale. The second copy, given to JJ, is now at SUNY, Buffalo; Lidderdale and Nicholson, *Dear Miss Weaver,* 215–17; K. W. Dandie, president, Curtis Company, Ltd., to NRF, 19 Nov. 1976 — "Two of our retirees remember Braverman as a shy man . . ."; Braverman / Beach correspondence, Princeton; *SC,* 86–88.

7. "PLURABILITIES": ON NEW COMPOSITIONS
1923

Trouble for Sylvia and Joyce: SB to SWB, 3 Feb. 1923; Ellmann, 545; Lincoln Steffens to Laura Suggett, 12 Dec. 1922, *The Autobiography of LS* (NY: Harcourt, Brace, 1933), 610–11, 833, 835; Interview with Helen Eddy, 27 May 1978.

At the Joyces': JJ to Valery Larbaud, 17 Jan. 1923, III, 71; SB to SWB, 20 Jan. and 3 Feb. 1923.

Soliciting and thanking reviewers: JJ to HW, 11 Mar. 1923, I, 201, and 30 Mar. 1923, III, 74; Edmund Wilson to John Peale Bishop, 5 Sept. 1922, *Letters on Literature and Politics, 1912–1972* (NY: Farrar, Straus and Giroux, 1977), 94.

Joyce begins Finnegans Wake: JJ to HW, 11 Mar. 1923, I, 202; According to A. Walton Litz (*Art of James Joyce*, 77), he wrote the King Roderick O'Connor fragment; Ellmann, 546–50.

Dental operations: Nora Joyce to HW, 6 Apr. 1923; Ellmann, 543; SB to EB, (?) 1923.

Sylvia writes her father: SB to SWB, 20 Apr., 3 May, and 1 June 1923.

Joyce travels: Unpublished portions and *SC*, 184; Lidderdale and Nicholson, *Dear Miss Weaver*, 222–23; JJ to SB, 12 July 1923, III, 79; SW to SWB, 29 June 1923.

Arrival of Antheil: Boski Antheil (interview, 28 Jan. 1978) claimed they arrived on 4 July; George Antheil claimed it was 13 June, for the premiere of Stravinsky's ballet *Les Noces*, in *Bad Boy of Music* (Garden City, NY: Doubleday Doran, 1945), 98; SB to SWB, 13 June 1923.

Hemingway's routine: Baker, *EH: A Life Story*, 111; Morrill Cody to NRF, 7 June 1978; EH, *Moveable Feast*, 70; Hadley Hemingway Mowrer to NRF, 5 June 1969; "Big Two-Hearted River" was begun in May of 1924.

Weaver bequest: JJ to SB, 12 July 1923, III, 78; HW to SB, 25 May 1950.

Playing with the Hemingways: Unpublished drafts of *SC*; Hadley Hemingway Mowrer to NRF, 5 June 1969; *SC*, 79–81; Interview with Morrill Cody, 7 June 1978; Bryher, *Heart to Artemis*, 213.

Antheils move in: SB to SWB, 29 June 1923; Antheil, *Bad Boy of Music*, 97, 109–13; McDougall, 39; Roger Shattuck claims that Satie played his dramatic symphony *Socrate* in Shakespeare and Company for Cocteau, Gide, Jammes, Milhaud, Sylvia, and Adrienne (*The Banquet Years: The Arts in France, 1885–1918* (Garden City, NY: Anchor, 1961), 160, but the location was probably Adrienne's bookshop; *SC*, 153–54 and early drafts; George Wickes, *Americans in Paris* (Garden City, NY: Doubleday, 1969), 193–233; SB to Margaret Marshall (her editor), 30 Jan. 1958.

Imbs, Thomson, and Benoist-Méchin: Bravig Imbs, *Confessions of Another Young Man* (NY: Henkle-Yewdale, 1936), 39–40; Virgil Thomson, *Virgil Thomson* (NY: Knopf, 1966), 77; Interview with Virgil Thomson, 26 July 1977; Interview with Myrsine Moschos, 24 June 1978.

Hemingway and Ford: EH to SB, 6 Nov. 1923, *Mercure*, 106; Huddleston, *Paris Salons*, 117, 121; Stella Bowen, *Drawn from Life* (London; Collins, n.d.), 111; Interview with George Seldes, 23 July 1981; *SC*, 137–38; Ford Madox Ford, *It Was the Nightingale* (Philadelphia: Lippincott, 1933), 200.

Ford and Joyce: Chief source for this relationship, as well as for the JJ poem, is unpublished drafts of *SC*; JJ to HW, 10 Oct. 1923, I, 204.

New publishing companies: *SC*, 130–32, and early drafts; Ford, *Published in Paris*, 34–94.

Peddling Exiles: *SC*, 163–68, and early drafts.

Antheil's debut: Antheil, *Bad Boy of Music*, 117–18, 131–33; Richard McDougall to NRF, 8 Jan. 1980; "Marcel L'Herbier's *L'Inhumaine*," Museum of Modern Art film introduction; Hugh Ford, "George Antheil: The Composer Upstairs" (Paper read at Modern Language Association Meeting, San Francisco, 29 Dec. 1979); AM, 'The *Ballet Mécanique*' (1926), in McDougall, 247–48.

Plays and correspondence: SB to EB, 12 Dec. 1923; Hemingway to SB, 6 Nov. 1923, *Mercure*, 105–7.

Reviews and visitors: JJ to HW, 6 Feb. and 23 Oct. 1923, I, 200, 206; JJ to HW, 19 Nov. 1923, III, 83; SB to EB, 3 Dec. and 12 Dec. 1923; Interview with Boski Antheil, 28 June 1978; Interview with Joella Bayer, 5 July 1981.

Requests to publish erotica: EH to Harriet Monroe, 16 Nov. 1922, *EH: Selected Letters*, 72; Anthony de Losdari to SB, 12 Oct. 1944; Huddleston, *Back to Montparnasse*, 194–95; *SC*, 90–95; Frank Harris to SB, 17 July and 12 Nov. 1924.

Sylvia resumes Ulysses publication: JJ to HW, 2 Nov. 1923, III, 82; Lidderdale and Nicholson, *Dear Miss Weaver*, 230; SB to EB, 3 Dec. 1923.

The Hemingways write: Hadley Hemingway lamented to SB (24 Nov. 1923) that returning to Toronto was "the first big mistake we've made"; EH to SB, 6 Nov. 1923, *Mercure*, 106 (recently reprinted in *EH: Selected Letters*, 97–98).

Ulysses IV: JJ to HW, 26 Feb. 1923, III, 72–73; JJ to HW, 5 Feb. 1924, I, 210; Ellmann, 551.

Christmas: Incident with the tax man, from interview with Myrsine Moschos, 22 June 1978.

8. AMERICANS IN PARIS
1924

William Carlos Williams, *A Voyage to Pagany* (NY: New Directions, 1970), 9, 15.

Historical perspective: Irving Howe, "Literature of the Latecomers: A View of the Twenties," *Saturday Review*, 10 Aug. 1974, 32; Hemingway, *A Farewell to Arms* (NY: Scribners, 1957), 185; Van Wyck Brooks, *The World of Washington Irving* (NY: Dutton, 1944), 338; Hemingway, "A Canadian with One Thousand a Year," *Toronto Star Weekly*, 4 Feb. 1922, 16; "For the arts to exist the attic must be cheap," declares Pound in his "Paris Letter," *Dial*, 71 (Oct. 1921), 462; Robert Forrest Wilson, *Paris on Parade* (Indianapolis: Bobbs Merrill, 1924), 224; Carl Sandburg, quoted by Pound, *Literary Essays*, 13; Harold Stearns, ed., *Civilization in the United States: An Inquiry by Thirty Americans* (London: Jonathan Cape, 1922); Archibald MacLeish, *Saturday Review*, 11.

William Carlos Williams's first trip: Ezra Pound to

WCW, 11 Sept. 1920 and 18 Mar. 1922, *Letters of Ezra Pound, 1907–1941*, 221, 223, 239; WCW, *Voyage to Pagany*, 13–14, 235; NRF, "Voyage to Ithaca: WCW in Paris," *Princeton University Library Chronicle*, 40 (spring 1979), 193–214; SB to EB, 22 Jan. 1924; WCW, *Autobiography*, 194; Harold Loeb remarks that Williams called the talk and food "disappointing," *The Way It Was* (NY: Criterion, 1959), 202; McAlmon calls WCW "overimpressionable," *Being Geniuses Together*, 185.

Hemingway returns: EH to SB, 6 Nov. 1923, *Mercure*, 105–7; *SC*, 82, and early drafts; Ford Madox Ford, "A Few Friends" (24 Feb. 1924), in *Left Bank Revisited*, 259.

Second anniversary of Ulysses: Lucy Hodge Ernlund to NRF, 10 Mar. 1969; SB to HB, 7 Apr. 1924; SB to EB, 22 Jan. 1924.

Anna Livia and Mamalujo: JJ, quoted by Eugene

Jolas, "My Friend James Joyce," in *JJ: Two Decades of Criticism*, 11; JJ quoted by August Suter, "Some Reminiscences of JJ," *Portraits of the Artist in Exile*, 64; JJ, quoted by Beckett, in Ellmann, 546; JJ to McAlmon, n.d., I, 209 (JJ confided that he thought the *transatlantic review* "very shabby"); JJ to Valery Larbaud, 24 Mar. 1924, III, 91; SB to EB, 2 Aug. 1924.

transatlantic review: Ford Madox Ford to H.G. Wells, 15 Nov. 1923, *Letters of FMF*, ed. Richard M. Ludwig (Princeton: Princeton University Press, 1965), 157; FMF, "Some American Expatriates," *Vanity Fair*, 28 (Apr. 1927), 98; Malcolm Cowley remembers that the review was "hard-boiled and midwestern," *Exile's Return*, 275; FMF to Gertrude Stein, 18 Sept. 1924, *Letters of FMF*, 165.

Women in Paris: Bryher, *Heart to Artemis*, 203, 207; Williams, *Autobiography*, 222, 193; Loeb, *Way It Was*, 165; James Charters (with Morrill Cody), *This Must Be the Place: Memoirs of Montparnasse* (Lincoln, Neb.: Herbert Joseph, 1934), 48; McAlmon and Boyle, *Being Geniuses Together*, 55–56, 103; Morley Callaghan, *That Summer in Paris* (NY: Dell, 1963), 108–9; Archibald MacLeish, "What One Remembers," *Mercure*, 34; Morrill Cody, "Shakespeare and Company—Paris," *Publishers' Weekly*, 12 Apr. 1924, 1261–63.

Joyce and the Americans: SC, 40–41, 78; Interview with Myrsine Moschos, 22 June 1978.

Cowley and the Greenwich Village crowd: Malcolm Cowley, "The Twenties in Montparnasse," *Saturday Review*, 11 Mar. 1967, 55; SB to EB, 12 July and 4 Nov. 1924; SC, 112–14; Interview with Joella Bayer, daughter of Mina Loy, 5 July 1931; WCW, *Autobiography*, 138.

Newspapermen: Hugh Ford, introd. to *Left Bank Revisited*, 1; Interview with George Seldes, 23 July 1981; Al Laney, *Paris "Herald": The Incredible Newspaper* (NY: Appleton-Century, 1947), 160.

Valéry and salons: Early draft of *SC*, 160.

Dos Passos and Eisenstein: SC, 109–11, and bookshop records.

MacLeish: Archibald MacLeish, "What One Remembers," *Mercure*, 34; MacLeish to NRF, 17 Oct. 1981 and 23 Oct. 1968; MacLeish to SB, 23 June (no year).

Joyce apartment: JJ to HW, 13 May and 22 May 1924.

Williams, Larbaud, and Hemingway: SB to HB, 23 May 1924; WCW, *In the American Grain* (NY: New Directions, 1956), 109–10; Alice Hunt Sokoloff, *Hadley: The Story of the First Mrs. Hemingway* (NY: Dodd, Mead, 1973) 71; WCW to Kenneth Burke, 14 Apr. 1924, *The Selected Letters of WCW*, ed. John C. Thirlwall (NY: McDowell, Obelensky, 1957), 64.

Commerce: JJ to HW, 24 May 1924, I, 214; *SC*, 142–43, and early drafts; McDougall, 49–50; Larbaud quoted by AM, "The Translation of *Ulysses*" (1950), in McDougall, 131.

Symons and Ellis visit: SB to EB, 28 June 1924.

Pound promotes Antheil: Sisley Huddleston, *Paris Salons*, 83; Ezra Pound, "George Antheil," *Criterion*, 2 (Oct. 1924), 324–25, 331; Unpublished portion of *SC;* the concert at the salon of Natalie Barney took place on New Year's Day, 1925; George Antheil to SB, (?) 1924; Interview with Boski Antheil, 11 Feb. 1978.

Pound leaves Paris: K. L. Goodwin, *The Influence of Ezra Pound* (NY: Oxford, 1966), 40; Alan Holder, *Three Voyages in Search of Europe: A Study of Henry James, Ezra Pound, and T. S. Eliot* (Philadelphia: University of Pennsylvania Press, 1966), 315–16, claims Pound could find no venerated circle of contemporary writers in Paris; Noel Stock, *The Life of Ezra Pound* (NY: Discus, 1974), 335, adds that there were no contemporary French writers of the first magnitude in Paris and that because Pound was not a drinker, he did not always fit in; Cowley, *Exile's Return*, 122.

Summer crises: JJ to SB, 17 Aug. 1924, III, 106; SB to EB, 2 Aug. and 4 Nov. 1924; SB to HB, 26 Sept. 1924.

Miss Weaver and Victor Records: Lidderdale and Nicholson, *Dear Miss Weaver*, 248–59; SB to EB, 4 Nov. 1924; *SC*, 171.

Commerce quarrel: SB to EB, 2 Aug. 1924; AM, "The Translation of *Ulysses*" (1950), in McDougall, 132; Valery Larbaud to JJ, 6 Nov. 1924, III, 109; JJ to HW, 28 Nov. 1924.

Christmas gifts: SB to HB, 27 Dec. 1924; WCW, "Père Sebastian Rasles," *In the American Grain*, 105–6; Van Wyck Brooks, *The Wine of the Puritans* (NY: Kennerly, 1909), 121–26, 138; Bryher, *Heart to Artemis*, 208.

9. SUMMER OF "A THOUSAND PARTIES"

1925

"A thousand parties": F. Scott Fitzgerald, "Autobiographical chart," 179, Fitzgerald Papers, Princeton.

"Writing a masterpiece": Interview with Myrsine Moschos, 22 June 1978.

Whistling books: JJ to HW, 17 Apr. 1926, III, 140.

His master's eyes and voice: JJ to HW, 26 Feb. 1925, III, 114; *SC*, 171–73; JJ to HW, 31 Mar. 1925.

New periodicals: *EH: A Life Story*, 140–41; Robert McAlmon letter to SB, undated; SB to EB, 13 July 1925; JJ, "Fragment of an Unpublished Work," *Criterion*, 3 (July 1925), 498–510, is the fifth chapter of *Finnegans Wake* (104–25); Sanford J. Smoller, *Adrift among Geniuses: Robert McAlmon, Writer and Publisher of the Twenties* (University Park: Pennsylvania State University Press, 1975), 165; McAlmon to SB, 1 July 1925; SB to HB, 4 Mar. 1925.

Miss Weaver visits: Lidderdale and Nicholson, *Dear Miss Weaver*, 256; McAlmon to SB, 1 July 1924; SB to EB, 27 June 1925.

Translating "Prufrock": SC, 127; T. S. Eliot, "Miss Sylvia Beach," *Mercure*, 9; McDougall, 51–52.

Prévost, Auclair, and Chamson: SC, 119–21, and unpublished drafts; Interview with Myrsine Moschos, 24 June 1978; Interview with Marcelle Auclair, 9 June

1978; André Chamson, "Le Secret de Sylvia," *Mercure*, 2.

Adrienne's cooking: Interviews with Marcelle Auclair (9 June 1978) and Eleanor Oldenberger Herrick (4 Jan. 1979); The table conversation convinced Auclair that AM and SB were not lesbians. Auclair and Françoise Prévost, *Mémoirs à Deux Voix* (Paris: Éditions du Seuil, 1978), 130; William Carlos Williams testified that she locked the kitchen door while preparing her famous chicken dinner, "Père Sebastian Rasles," *In the American Grain*, 106; AM, "A Letter to Friends in the Free Zone" (1942), in McDougall, 403.

Prévost and Hemingway: SC, 120; Unpublished drafts of *SC;* Hemingway to F. Scott Fitzgerald, 24 Dec. 1929, *EH: Selected Letters*, 313; Roger Asselineau, ed. *The Literary Reputation of Hemingway in Europe* (Paris: Minard, 1965), 46; Prévost, introd. to *Le Soleil se Leve Aussi* (Paris: Gallimard, 1949), viii; Auclair and Prévost, *Memoirs à Deux Voix*, 416; Baker, *EH: A Life Story*, 142; Prévost, *Way It Was*, 245–52.

Hemingway meets Fitzgerald: Baker, *EH: A Life Story*, 145–47; Matthew J. Bruccoli, *Scott and Ernest: The Authority of Failure and the Authority of Success* (NY: Random House, 1978), 1, 5, 155; Lewis, *Edith*

Wharton, 468; FSF to Max Perkins, 28 Aug. 1925, Perkins Papers, Princeton; Arthur Mizener, *The Far Side of Paradise: A Biography of F. Scott Fitzgerald* (Boston: Houghton Mifflin, 1965), 196; Interview with Myrsine Moschos, 24 June 1978.

Preparing for Ballet Mécanique: Jacques Benoist-Méchin (interview 10 June 1978) declares he played a preview performance because Antheil was weak from illness; AM, "The *Ballet Mécanique*" (1926), in McDougall, 247; Antheil, *Bad Boy of Music*, 104, 169; *SC*, 122–23; Antheil to SB, 16 Aug. 1925; Imbs, *Confessions of Another Young Man*, 56; *SC*, 125 (in reality, Antheil had been to Africa before, in 1923); Many of the Antheil letters are undated.

Gide to Africa: SB to EB, 13 July 1925; The Gide picture appears in her memoirs; This is the same year that Élisabeth van Rysselberghe gave birth to Gide's daughter, Catherine; *SC*, 158.

Arrival of Wescott, Shirer, and Rice: Joseph Blotner to NRF, 26 May 1969; Phone conversation with Glenway Wescott, 7 Aug. 1980, and interview, 4 Nov. 1980; William H. Rueckert, *Glenway Wescott* (NY: Twayne, 1965), 33; William Faulkner was in and out of Paris between August and December of 1925, and it is possible that he dropped in to the bookshop, though no evidence exists that he did (Joseph Blotner to NRF, 26 May 1976); William L. Shirer, *20th Century Journey*, 240–41; Putnam, *Paris Was Our Mistress*, 103; Elmer Rice, *The Left Bank* (NY: Samuel French, 1931), 38.

The children: SC, 106, 82; correspondence between Henri Hoppenot and SB, in Jacques Doucet Library, Paris; Loeb, *Way It Was*, 194; Hemingway, *Islands in the Stream* (NY: Scribners, 1970), 57–64.

Ulysses V and VI: In 1962 SB would write an article in the Irish *Times* about her Bloomsday photographs;

HW to SB, 22 Sept. 1925; JJ letter, undated, I, 229; Paul Shinkman article, in *Left Bank Revisited*, 102; Robert Forrest Wilson, "Paris for Young Art," *Bookman*, 61 (June 1925), 403–12; SB to EB, 13 July 1925; JJ to SB, 22 Aug. 1955, III, 126.

"Farming out" Work in Progress: SB, "James Joyce Care of Shakespeare and Company Paris," typed MS; SB has "the first refusal of my next book!" JJ to HW, 12 Apr. 1924, III, 93; JJ to Frank Budgen, 2 May 1934, III, 304).

Summer parties: Ford Madox Ford, *Your Mirror to My Times: The Selected Autobiography and Impressions of FMF*, ed. Michael Killigrew (NY: Holt, Rinehart & Winston, 1971), 105; Westbrook Pegler (at Fitzgerald's death), quoted by Glenway Westcott, *Images of Truth: Remembrances and Criticism* (NY: Harper & Row, 1939), 232; Loeb, *Way It Was*, 270, 168–69; Malcolm Cowley to NRF, 17 Apr. 1982; Putnam, *Paris Was Our Mistress*, 181–82, 189; Cowley, *Exile's Return*, 158–59; McAlmon and Boyle, *Being Geniuses Together*, 185–88; Smoller, *Adrift among Geniuses*, 138; numerous unpublished versions of the McAlmon section of *SC*; in *EH: A Life Story*, 147–55, has sorted fact from fiction; Loeb, in *The Way It Was*, 259–300, has told his version; Calvin Tomkins, *Living Well Is the Best Revenge* (NY: Viking, 1971); F. Scott Fitzgerald to John Peale Bishop, 21 Sept. (1926?), *The Letters of FSF*, ed. Andrew Turnbull (NY: Scribners, 1963), 359.

Les Déserts: Most of the details of Les Déserts are based on typed and holograph versions of *SC*, 191–96, and on family letters; SB to EB, 7 Aug. and 21 Aug. 1925; SB to HB, 12 July 1933 and 7 Aug. 1945; EH to SB, 3 Aug. 1925; JJ to SB, (end of July?) 1925, I, 229; JJ to SB, (22?) Aug. 1925, III, 125; AM, "A Sketch of Les Déserts" (1935), in McDougall, 356.

10. WALT WHITMAN IN PARIS: AMERICAN RHYTHMS
1925–1926

From Les Déserts: SB to EB, 21 Aug. 1925; Henry James, *Parisian Sketches: Letters to the "New York Tribune," 1875–1876* (NY: NYU Press, 1957), 7.

Fall Joyce business: SB to EB, 13 July and 30 Oct. 1925; JJ to HW, 5 Nov. 1925, III, 131; Unpublished portion of *SC;* HW to SB, 17 Oct. 1925; Edgell Rickword to SB, 3 Oct. 1925; SB to HW, (?) Oct. 1925; Jonathan Cape, who first read Hemingway's work, at SB's insistence, met EH at her arrangement, in Shakespeare and Company that May (Jonathan Cape to SB, 17 May 1936).

Initial Roth involvement: Samuel Roth to JJ, 10 May 1922 (Roth offers $100 plus 15 percent and requests a review copy); SB to HW, 6 June 1922; Ellmann, 580; JJ to HW, 5 Mar. and 17 Apr. 1926, III, 139–40; SB letter of protest to the press, dated 18 Nov. 1926.

Lady Rothermere and company: SB to EB, 30 Oct. 1925.

Music halls: Unpublished portion of *SC.*

Janet Flanner: Interview with Janet Flanner, 29 July 1977; JF, "The Great Amateur Publisher," *Mercure*, 46–47; JF, "A Foreword: Three Amateur Publishers," in Ford, *Published in Paris*, xi–xii; Stephen Spender, "European Places, People and Events," *New York Times Book Review*, 18 Nov. 1979, 54, a review of *Janet Flanner's World: Uncollected Writings, 1932–1975* (NY: Harcourt Brace Jovanovich, 1979), which reprinted the 24 Oct. 1959 *New Yorker* essay on SB.

La Revue Nègre: AM, "La Revue Nègre" (1925), in McDougall, 240–41; Adrienne wrote numerous essays about the theater, which she had learned to love from her mother. McDougall has devoted a section to translations of her essays ("Spectacles"): the circus, opera, plays, dance, actors, and musicians–including pieces on

the Folies-Bergère, Gian-Carlo Menotti, and Maurice Chevalier; Flanner, *Paris Was Yesterday*, xx.

Paul Robeson: Paul Shinkman, "Latin Quarter Notes," in *Left Bank Revisited*, 103.

Hemingway's borrowings: See NRF, "EH—% Shakespeare and Company," *Fitzgerald/Hemingway Annual*, 1977, 175–81, for a list of books borrowed by Hemingway. A fifth of all the titles, excluding children's books, were written by Turgenev, whose *Sportsman's Sketches* he borrowed on numerous occasions.

Translating Whitman: AM, "A Letter to Larbaud" (12 Feb. 1926), in McDougall, 108–11; AM and SB attended the International Suffrage Alliance meeting in Paris, 28 May 1926.

Hemingway fun: EH to SB, ca 15 Jan. 1925, *Mercure*, 109–10, reprinted in *Selected Letters*, 146; Baker, *EH: A Life Story*, 139–44.

Another Joyce loan: JJ to SB, 29 Jan. 1926; SB to EB, 19 Feb. and 6 Mar. 1926.

Translating McAlmon: AM, "A Letter to Larbaud" (12 Feb. 1926), in McDougall, 111–12.

Jo Davidson: JJ did sit for Davidson (JJ to HW, 18 Mar. 1926, I, 240); SB mistakenly remembers that the exhibit was planned before she learned of the monument, *SC*, 128.

JJ on Whitman: SC, 128; Richard Chase, *Walt Whitman Reconsidered* (NY: William Sloan, 1955), 89–90.

Joyce friends: Italo Svevo visited the bookshop in the years 1924–1928, and his photograph hung on the wall; JJ to HW, 29 Feb. 1926, III, 139; SB to EB, 6 Mar. and 8 Apr. 1926.

Catel letter: Jean Catel to SB, 25 June 1926.

Borsch bill: JJ to HW, 30 Mar. and 3 Apr. 1926.

The Joycean scale: Unpublished drafts of *SC;* Stanislaus Joyce, quoted in Ellmann, 579.

Bicycle races and Easter vacation: SB to EB, 8 Apr. 1926; EH, *Moveable Feast,* 64; *SC,* 191, and unpublished drafts.

Whitman exhibit: JJ to HW, 17 Apr. 1926 (unpublished portion), III, 140; Gay Wilson Allen, *The New Walt Whitman Handbook* (NY: NYU Press, 1975), 286; Betsy Erkkila, *Walt Whitman among the French* (Princeton: Princeton University Press, 1980), 226; Logan Pearsall Smith, *Unforgotten Years* (Boston: Little, Brown, 1939), 102; *SC,* 20; Morel, quoted by AM, "The Translation of *Ulysses"* (1950), in McDougall, 131; Robert Duncan, Roger Asselineau, and Richard Chase have found specific Whitman influences in *Finnegans Wake;* Josephson, *Life among the Surrealists,* 29–30; Barrett Wendell quoted in Ernest Earnest, *Expatriates and Patriots: American Artists, Scholars, and Writers in Europe* (Durham, N.C.: Duke University Press, 1968), 225; SB and Co., Paris," *Listener,* 2 July 1959, 28; Ezra Pound, "What I Feel about Walt Whitman, 1909," reprinted in Roy Harvey Pearce, ed., *Whitman: A Collection of Critical Essays* (Englewood Cliffs, N.J.: Prentice-Hall, 1962), 9; Larbaud quoted in Gay Wilson Allen, *Walt Whitman Abroad* (Syracuse: Syracuse University Press, 1955), 72; Davidson's model caught the attention of Mr. Averell Harriman, then president of the Union Pacific Railroad, who commissioned the statue to be completed and erected as a memorial to his mother at the beginning of the Appalachian Trail at Beach Point. The Davidson statue was first exhibited at the New York World's Fair in 1939 and then moved to its permanent site. The walking posture of Whitman is especially appropriate for the permanent site, a granite hilltop beside a woodland trail; The ten-best sellers at Shakespeare and Company (1919–1941) were Eliot (231), Hemingway (190), Whitman (114), Stein (89), Poe (65), Pound (63), Cummings (63), James (59), Bird (56), and Melville (48).

American rhythms: Irving Schwerké, "Notes of the Music World," (10 May 1926), in *Left Bank Revisited,*

219; Thomson, *Virgil Thomson,* 76.

Titus, Crosby, and Putnam: Caresse Crosby to NRF, 18 July 1969; CC, *Those Passionate Years* (NY: Dial, 1979), 191; *SC,* 134–35; Putnam, *Paris Was Our Mistress,* 7, 96.

Bookshop visitors: "Goldman Scoffs at U.S. Morals" (27 Feb. 1926), in *Left Bank Revisited,* 157; SB to EB, 30 Oct. 1925; Alex Small, "Latin Quarter Notes" (1 Feb. 1927), in *Left Bank Revisited,* 108; Grace Z. Brown, *McNaught's Monthly,* 77–78.

Joycean rhythms: Early typed draft of *SC;* Huddleston, *Paris Salons,* 215; Nino Frank, who worked with JJ on translating, concluded that he cared more for rhythms and harmony than for meaning, "The Shadow That Had Lost Its Man," in *Portraits of the Artist in Exile,* 97.

Ballet Mécanique: Numerous unpublished drafts of *SC,* 123–25; Bravig Imbs, *Confessions of Another Young Man,* 97–103; Thomson, *Virgil Thomson,* 78; Lincoln Steffens to Ella Winter, 20 June 1926, *The Letters of LS* (NY: Harcourt, Brace, 1938), 749; Steffens declares, "I don't know why the kicks. It's new; it was discord, true, but beautifully, as one uses rough prose to lead into harmony"; Interview with Myrsine Moschos, 22 June 1978; Hugh Ford, "George Antheil: The Composer Upstairs" (Paper delivered at the MLA meeting of 29 Dec. 1979); William L. Shirer (*20th Century Journey,* 243) remembers Pound bounding onto the stage; Interview with Boski Antheil, 28 June 1978; Interview with Jacques Benoist-Méchin, 10 June 1978 (he remembers he was playing the pianola because Antheil was weak from the grippe); Ezra Pound, "Antheil," *New Criterion,* 4 (Oct. 1926), 698.

Lindberg arrival: Falnner, *Paris Was Yesterday,* 22–23.

11. TRANSITIONS
1926–1927

Summer crises: AM to SB, 27 July 1926, *Mercure,* 111–13; Thomas Wolfe to Aline Bernstein, 22 Sept. 1926, in *The Letters of TW,* ed. Elizabeth Nowell (NY: Scribners, 1956), 114–15—"[JJ] had a large powerful straight nose—redder than his face, somewhat pitted with scars and boils," notes Wolfe; SB to editor, *New Statesman,* 23 May 1927; JJ to HW, 18 Aug. 1926, I, 243–44; JJ to SB, 24 Aug. 1926, I, 244–45.

Divorces: Bryher-Beach correspondence, Yale; McAlmon and Boyle, *Being Geniuses Together,* 288; McAlmon to SB, n.d.; Baker, *EH: A Life Story,* 176; Alex Small, "Latin Quarter Notes" (2 July 1926), in *Left Bank Revisited,* 105–6.

Dealing with pirates: JJ to Stanislaus Joyce, 5 Nov. 1926, III, 145; *SC,* 179, 182; SB to Edward Titus, 4 Mar. 1927; In a suppressed portion of her memoirs, SB claims that the rare-book dealer Ronald Davis sold the proofs to Titus.

More Antheil concerts: SB to EB, 21 Oct. and 6 Dec. 1926; Elliot Paul, "Literary and Artistic Paris Cheers Rendition of Antheil's Symphony" (17 Oct. 1926), in *Left Bank Revisited,* 221–22; SB to HB, 23 Nov. 1926; Thomson, *Virgil Thomson* 81, 96; Interview with Boski Antheil, 11 Feb. 1978.

Fall visitors: Matthew Josephson, foreword to *Left Bank Revisited,* xxiv; Sisley Huddleston, *Paris Salons,* 319; Ivy Low Litvinov to SB, 14 Nov. 1926 and 27 Sept. 1928; Interview with Myrsine Moschos, 24 June 1978; SB to EB, 6 Dec. 1926.

Piracy and the Beach family: SB to HB, 27 Nov. 1926; SB to SWB, 28 Dec. 1926; Interview with Frances Steloff, 27 July 1977; Grace Z. Brown, *McNaught's Monthly,* 78; SB, "From Presbyterian Vicarage to *Ulysses,"* BBC interview, 24 Oct. 1959 (transcription courtesy of Willard Potts).

Writing the protest: Ezra Pound to JJ, 19 Nov. 1926, *Pound/Joyce: The Letters . . . with Pound's Essays on Joyce,* ed. Forrest Read (NY: New Directions, 1967), 225; *SC,* 181; SB to EB, 18 Jan. 1927; Both JJ (JJ to HW, 8 Nov. 1926, I, 246; JJ to Stanislaus Joyce, 15 Dec. 1926, III, 148) and SB (SB to EB, 6 Dec. 1926) mistakenly believed Roth was selling more than 40,000 copies a month!

Lewis requests: Wyndham Lewis to SB, 20 Mar. 1927; the *Enemy* attacked *transition,* communism, Surrealism, Joyce, Stein, Lawrence, Negroes, and Indians.

Explaining Work in Progress: JJ to HW, 7 June and 24 Sept. 1926, I, 241–42, 245; HW to JJ, 1 Oct. 1926, quoted in Ellmann, 582; Stanislaus Joyce to JJ, 7 Aug. 1924, III, 103; JJ to HW, 8 Nov. 1926, I, 246; HW to JJ, 20 Nov. 1926, quoted in Ellmann, 584; *SC,* 183, and early draft of 185; HW to JJ, 29 Jan. 1927, quoted in Ellmann, 589; JJ to HW, 1 Feb. 1927, I, 249; Lidderdale and Nicholson, *Dear Miss Weaver,* 259; HW to SB, 20 Nov. 1927; Ezra Pound to JJ, 15 Nov. 1926, in *Pound/Joyce: The Letters,* 228; Pound, quoted by Ellmann, 585; McAlmon and Boyle, *Being Geniuses Together,* 285; Frank Budgen (*Horizon,* Feb. 1941, in

JJ: Two Decades of Criticism, 20) says that "Joyce was a self-centered man" who would yawn through a discussion of Marx's theories but perk up when he heard that Marx's birthday coincided with his own.
    Enter the Jolases: Valery Larbaud to AM, 6 June 23, quoted in Ellmann, 552; JJ to HW, 21 Dec. 1926, III, 149; Ellmann, 587–88; Eugene Jolas, "My Friend JJ," in *JJ: Two Decades of Criticism,* 5; *SC,* 140–41.
    Celebrations and smuggling: Robert Earley to SB, 31 Aug. 1926; W. E. O. Burch to SB, 5 Aug. 1927; Sam Steward to SB, n.d.
    Exile: Ezra Pound to SB, 15 Jan. and 22 Jan. 1927.
    Signatures of protest: SB to EB, 18 Jan. and 28 Jan. 1927; JJ informed HW (1 Feb. 1927, I, 249) that SB sent the protest to 900 people; Flanner, *Paris Was Yesterday,* 17–18; Ezra Pound to JJ, 25 Dec. 1925, in *Pound / Joyce: The Letters,* 226.
    The Roth "band begins": JJ to HW, 1 Feb. 1927, I, 494; Humanist (April 1927), 173; Ezra Pound to JJ, 19 Nov. 1926, *Pound / Joyce: The Letters,* 226; JJ to HW, 23 Feb. 1927, III, 155; Samuel Roth to Sherwood Anderson, n.d., SB Papers; Roth to the editor and the editor's note, *New Statesman,* 19 Mar. 1927, 694–95; *SC,* 182; JJ to HW, 8 Jan. 1927, III, 149; Roth to Anderson, 2 May 1927, SB Papers.
    Pomes Penyeach: JJ to HW, 18 Feb. 1927, III, 155; MacLeish's letters to JJ concerning *PP* are in the Harriet Weaver Papers, British Library; Archibald MacLeish to NRF, 17 Oct. 1981; Ellmann, 591; AM to JJ, n.d., Harriet Weaver Papers, British Library.
    Sylvia's birthday: SWB to SB, 14 Mar. 1927; SB to HB, 2 Mar. 1927.
    Antheil at Carnegie Hall: SB to HB, 2 Mar. 1927; William Carlos Williams, "George Antheil and the Cantilene Critics," *transition,* 13; Donald Friede, *The Mechanical Angel: His Adventures and Enterprises in the Glittering 1920's* (NY: Knopf, 1948), 44; Antheil, *Bad Boy of Music,* 197.
    McAlmon-Bryher divorce: WCW to SB, 18 Aug. 1926; SB to Bryher, 15 Dec. 1926; McAlmon to SB, n.d. and 24 Nov. 1926; WCW reports that McAlmon was furious when SB claimed that his drinking was affecting his writing; WCW to Florence Williams, 24 Sept. 1927, *Selected Letters of WCW,* 72; After Ellerman settled $75,000 on McAlmon, some friends referred to him as Bob McAlimony.
    Williams's return and transition: Eugene Jolas, ed., *transition Workshop* (NY: Vanguard, 1949), 394, 14; Dougald McMillan, *transition: The History of a Literary Era, 1927–1938* (NY: Braziller, 1976), 1; Flanner, *Paris Was Yesterday,* 20–21.
    James Stephens: JJ to HW, 20 May 1927, I, 253;

"I have asked Miss Beach to get into closer relations with James Stephens" to "finish the design"; Ellmann (III, 169, n. 3) claims that Stephens was an illegitimate child whose name, birthdate, and birthplace were invented.
    Stuart Gilbert: Gilbert to SB, 19 Dec. 1927; SB mistakenly identifies 900 as *Commerce,* in *SC,* 144–45; Gilbert, "Transition Days," in *transition Workshop,* 19.
    Joyce borrowings: JJ to HW, 27 Mar. 1927; JJ to HW, 3 July 1927, I, 257.
    Joyce MS: JJ to SB, n.d., cited in *SC,* 89 (Sylvia mistakenly believed that Joyce gave the MSS to her in January 1922); Joyce had sent the 1912, burned Dublin edition ("the abortive Maunsel printing"—Ellmann) of *Dubliners* with MacLeish to offer to the book dealer A. S. W. Rosenbach. Joyce tells Miss Weaver he hopes the sale will pay for his trip to the Dutch coast, JJ to HW, 12 May 1927, I, 252.
    Hemingway remarries: Baker, *EH: A Life Story,* 346; The MacLeishes do not remember attending the wedding or giving a party, MacLeish to NRF, 17 Oct. 1981; According to McAlmon, who admired her wit, dignity, and discretion, Hadley responded to the Hemingway annulment proposal with "All right, then the child is altogether mine," *Being Geniuses Together,* 346.
    SB radio talk: SB's radio speech (Tuesday, 24 May 1927) for the Institute Radiophonique d'extension universitaire de la Sorbonne is printed in *Mercure,* 91–93; JJ to SB, May or June 1927; SB, unpublished "Diary of the Publication of *Pomes Penyeach,*" SB Papers; Ben Huebsch to SB, 22 June 1926; SB to HB, 31 May 1927.
    Piracies cause strain: JJ to HW, 18 Mar. 1926, I, 240; Unpublished drafts of *SC;* SB to JJ, 12 Apr. 1927.
    Death of Eleanor Beach: J. H. Orbison to SB, 24 Dec. 1926; SB to HB, 31 May 1927; The two character witnesses were Mrs. J. March (Helen) Baldwin and the Reverend Mr. Joseph W. Cochran; EB to SB, 11 Dec. 1918; EB to SB, 1918; Interview with Myrsine Moschos, 22 June 1978; Interview with Helen Eddy, 27 May 1978; Joyce, who returned from Holland on the day of the tragedy, guessed the truth after talking to doctors at the hospital, and confided it to Miss Weaver, whom he pledged to secrecy. It was, he regretted, a "very bad case of stupidity, panic, brutality, and incompetence,'' JJ to HW, 23 June, 5 July, and 10 July 1927; In her handwritten will, dated January 1927 in Florence, EB declared she was "very much opposed to graves" and wished cremation; Helen Eddy, for more than twenty years a companion of Cyprian, declares that the family knew nothing of the suicide.

12. OF TRANSLATION TREATIES AND TRAVELS
1927–1928

Tourists: Josephson, *Life among the Surrealists,* 314 (Josephson's first visit was in 1921–1923); 300,000 Americans went to Europe in 1928, Francis P. Miller and H. D. Hill, "Europe as a Playground," *Atlantic Monthly,* Aug. 1930, 226; SB to HB, 4 May 1928.
    Withdrawal from lawsuit: Benjamin Conner and M. Moreau correspondence with SB, in the SB Papers; JJ to HW, 26 July 1927, III, 162.
    Pomes Penyeach: SB, "Diary of the publication of *Pomes Penyeach,*" SB Papers; Interview with Myrsine Moschos, 24 June 1978; In an undated letter to SB, Helen Nutting assumes that Joyce wanted apples pictured on the cover; Rebecca West, *The Strange Necessity: Essays and Reviews* (London: Jonathan Cape, 1928), 13–198; William Carlos Williams, "The Strange Case of JJ," *Bookman,* Sept. 1928, 9–23; JJ to HW, 26 July 1927, III, 162–63; JJ to HW, 3 July 1927, I, 257.
    Lewis versus Joyce: Wyndham Lewis, *Time and*

Western Man (London: Chatto & Windus, 1927), 93; McMillan, *transition,* 204–8; Leon Edel, "The Genius and the Injustice Collector," *American Scholar,* 49 (autumn 1980), 476; JJ to HW, 14 Aug. and 14 Sept. 1927, I, 258–59.
    SB to publish Work in Progress: JJ to HW, 30 Aug. 1927; JJ to Ezra Pound, (8?) Nov. 1928, III, 166.
    JJ promotes Work in Progress: JJ to Stanislaus Joyce, 29 Jan. 1928, III, 169; Williams's essay in *transition* 8 was the only unsolicited piece; "I have tried to keep off the stage as much as possible in the interest of other people's finer feelings," says JJ to HW (20 May 1927, I, 255), "but evidently it is not enough."
    Beaches' visit: Interview with Helen Eddy, 27 May 1978; Cyprian Beach to SB, 11 July 1927; SB to HB, 26 Sept. and 14 Oct. 1927; William L. Shirer (*20th Century Journey,* 312) describes the Duncan funeral.
    Williams and Holly sail together: WCW to SB, 24 June 1928, in *Mercure,* 115; For an analysis of the WCW

trip to Paris, see NRF, *Princeton University Library Chronicle*, 193–214; WCW to Florence Williams, 30 Sept. 1927, in *Selected Letters*, 71–79.

Cyprian and Holly: Interview with Helen Eddy, 27 May 1978; SB to EB, 18 Jan. 1927 (Penney soon married Toni Ybarra and left California).

Bryher remarries: Interviews with Perdita Schaffner (7 July 1978) and Glenway Wescott (4 Nov. 1980); AM, "Our Friend Bryher" (1940), in McDougall, 205.

Aldington: Richard Aldington, *Life for Life's Sake: A Book of Remembrances* (London: Cassell, 1968), 296.

SB's active social life: SB to HB, 14 Oct. 1927; SB to HW, 14 Nov. 1927; *SC*, 148–49; Williams to SB, 28 Oct. 1929.

Joyce inspects the waterworks: SC, 184; JJ to HW, 29 Oct. 1927, I, 260; JJ spent 1,200 hours on the seventeen pages, he informed Larbaud, (18?) Oct. 1927, III, 164; Huddleston, *Paris Salons*, 14.

Wescott and Hemingway: Alex Small, "Notes of Montparnasse" (12 Oct. 1927), in *Left Bank Revisited*, 109; Glenway Wescott's version of this incident varies, *Prose*, 196; Though Wescott always praised Hemingway's writing, he declared he was an exception in their generation, because of his "excessive consciousness of [his] position, pedestal, or niche in literary history" (p. 190); Interview with Wescott, 4 Nov. 1980.

Joyce reads Anna Livia: McAlmon and Boyle, *Being Geniuses Together*, 315; Undated MacLeish letter, quoted by Ellmann, 598.

Pressure on Miss Weaver: SB to HW, 14 Nov. 1927; HW to SB, 20 Nov. 1927; Lidderdale and Nicholson, *Dear Miss Weaver*, 275.

Two misunderstandings: SB to SWB, 17 Jan. 1928; An article in the *St. Paul Dispatch* (8 Dec. 1926) notes Joyce's refusal to talk to the press but his deliberately passing "a quiet order to Miss Beach" to do so; JJ to Valery Larbaud, 18 Oct. 1926 and 19 Jan. 1927, III, 164, 168–69.

Copyright for Work in Progress: SB to SWB, 17 Jan. 1978; JJ to Donald Friede, 20 Mar. 1928, III, 172.

Birthday and lecture: Helen Hutting diary, quoted by Ellmann, 599; HW to SB, 22 Mar. 1928; JJ to HW, 15 Feb. 1928, III, 171.

Eugene Jolas: JJ to HW, 15 Feb. 1928, III, 171; McMillan, *transition*, 182; Ernest Kroll to NRF, 28 June 1977, on the unpublished Llona autobiography.

Collections for Antheil: McAlmon (*Being Geniuses Together*, 220) claims that when William Bullitt demanded a medical examination, the doctors diagnosed Antheil's lungs as being clear; William Bird had sold his Three Mountains Press to Nancy Cunard; SB to HB, 12 Mar. 1928; JJ to HW, 28 Mar. 1928, III, 174; JJ to HW, 20 Sept. 1928, I, 269.

Hemingway injury: SB to Holly Beach, 12 Mar. 1928; Robert O. Stephens, "Hemingway and Stendhal: The Matrix of *A Farewell to Arms*," *PMLA*, 88 (Mar. 1973), 271–80.

"Trianons Treaty": Unpublished drafts of *SC;* JJ to Valery Larbaud, 18 Oct. 27 and 19 Jan. 1928, III, 164, 168–69; JJ to HW, 20 Sept. 1928, *Selected Letters*, 335; Ellmann, 601.

Gilbert's key: Stuart Gilbert to SB, 29 Mar. 1928; JJ to Stanislaus Joyce, 5 Aug. 1928, III, 181.

Joyce travels: JJ to HW, 28 Mar. and 16 Apr. 1928, III, 173, 176. JJ to SB, 22 May 1928, I, 262; JJ to SB, 28 Apr. and 2 May 1928.

Gershwin and Tate: SC, 125; "Gershwin Picks Americans in Paris for Subject of Next Jazz Symphony" (3 Apr. 1928), in *Left Bank Revisited*, 224–25; Putnam, *Paris Was Our Mistress*, 124; Allen Tate to

NRF, 13 Apr. 1969; Allen Tate, "Memoirs of SB," *Mercure*, 38.

Kay Boyle: Boyle, in *Being Geniuses Together*, 93, 114, 117–18; Boyle to SB, 2 Dec. 1927; Boyle to NRF, 12 Feb. 1978 and 12 June 1981.

Fitzgerald, Vidor, and Chamson: King Vidor, *A Tree Is a Tree* (NY: Harcourt, Brace, 1952), 171; Vidor's films with French settings were *The Big Parade, Bardelys the Magnificant*, and *La Bohème; SC*, 116–19, and earlier drafts; Lucie Mazauric with André Chamson, *Ah Dieu! Que la Paix est Jolie* (Paris: Plon, 1972), 111–24; Arthur Mizener, *The Far Side of Paradise*, 230–31 (JJ remark to Gorman, p. 146); "Remarks by André Chamson," *Fitzgerald/Hemingway Annual, 1973*, 69–78; Chamson, *La Petite Odyssée* (Paris: Gallimard, 1965), 45–52; Chamson, "Le Secret de Sylvia" *Mercure*, 23–24.

Giedion-Welcker: Richard M. Kain, ed. "An Interview with Carola G-W and Maria Jolas," *.'J Quarterly*, 2 (winter 1974), 103.

Cyril Connolly: Connolly, "A Rendezvous for Writers," *Mercure*, 160–61.

Vacations for Joyce and Sylvia: Unpublished drafts of *SC;* JJ to SB and AM, 3 Sept. 1928, I, 265; The embroidery represented the Liffey River, the Irish Sea, and the arms of Norway, Ireland, and the Joyce family (SB had sent to England that year for the Joyce, Beach, and Orbison coats of arms), JJ to HW, 20 Sept. 1928, I, 268; SB to Sisley Huddleston, 21 June, 2 Nov., and 6 Nov. 1928, Humanities Research Center, University of Texas, Austin.

Beckett: Deirdre Bair, *Samuel Beckett: A Biography* (NY: Harcourt Brace Jovanovich, 1978), 69; Interview with Beckett, 27 Aug. 1980.

Joyces ill: SB to HW, 5 Oct. and 3 Dec. 1928; HW to SB, 18 Nov. 1928; JJ to HW, 2 Dec. 1928, I, 276.

Robert Sage: Sage, obit of SB, in *New York Herald Tribune*, 13 Oct. 1962, clipping.

H. G. Wells: When Joyce asked Wells to help propagandize his book, Wells politely refused, pointing out how vastly different their lives and works were and adding, "Your last two works have been more amusing and exciting to write than they ever will be to read," 23 Nov. 1928, I, 274–75.

Radclyffe Hall and Natalie Barney: Interview with Eleanor Oldenberger Herrick, 4 Jan. 1979; Flanner, *Paris Was Yesterday*, 48; SB to Natalie Clifford Barney, 4 Nov. 1928, Jacques Doucet Library, Paris.

Requests to publish erotica: I. H. Barkey to SB, 16 Feb. 1928; Although she claims (*SC*, 92) that Aldington also begged her assistance for D. H. Lawrence, he denied any involvement, asserting he came to the shop with Hemingway, not Huxley, whom he did not know, Bryher to SB, 5 Dec. 1959; Lawrence to SB, 24 Dec. 1928; *SC*, 93; Joyce did not speak well of Lawrence's work, in part because it was linked to *Ulysses* as being pornographic, JJ to HW, 27 Sept. 1930, I, 294.

"Trianons Treaty" unravels: SC, 145; JJ to HW, 23 Oct. 1928, I, 271.

Roth quits: When Roth asserted, on 6 Dec. 1950 (at the JJ Society meeting in the Gotham Book Mart), that he had made no money on *Ulysses*, one assumes he was referring to the serialized version in *Two Worlds Monthly*, not to the full pirated edition, which he never acknowledged having published.

Correspondence with MacLeish and Hemingway: Archibald MacLeish to SB, 9 Dec. 1928; SB to Ernest Hemingway, 30 Jan. 1929; In his return letter, EH tells SB of the suicide of his father (EH to SB, (?) Feb. 1929); SB to HB, 3 Dec. 1928.

13. "EXAGMINATIONS"
1929–1930

Nora's operation and Holly's marriage: SB to HBD, 8 Sept. 1928, 30 Mar., 4 June, and 4 Dec. 1929; Inter-

view with Helen Eddy, 27 May 1978; CB to SB, n.d. (1934); Interview with James Briggs, 6 July 1978.

Collecting essays for Our Exag: SB solicited and rejected at least one other essay, by Édouard Roditi, SB to ER, 10 Jan. 1929, UCLA.

Disappointment with Myrsine: SB to HBD, 29 Jan. and 30 Mar. 1929.

End of the twenties for McAlmon: McAlmon and Boyle, Being Geniuses Together, 368; Smoller, Adrift among Geniuses, 190; Hemingway, The Sun Also Rises (NY: Scribners, 1954), 115.

Crosby and Crane: Harry Crosby, Shadows of the Sun: The Diaries of HC, ed. Edward Germain (Santa Barbara: Black Sparrow, 1977), 236; John Unterecker, Voyager: A Life of Hart Crane (New York: Farrar, Straus and Giroux, 1969), 575–99; Malcolm Cowley to NRF, 17 Apr. 1982; Leon Edel, introd. to John Glassco, Memoirs of Montparnasse (NY: Oxford, 1970), ix.

Crosbys to publish Joyce: Harry Crosby, Shadows of the Sun, 238, establishes that they met JJ through SB; Caresse Crosby, Passionate Years, 191; SC, 134–36; Wyndham Percy Lewis, Doom of Youth (London: Chatto & Windus, 1932), 175–76 (Childermass and Doom are part of a larger work, The Human Age); Caresse later regretted having abandoned Brancusi's first drawing, which was "vastly more interesting," 195; Harry Crosby, Shadows of the Sun, 248.

Our Exag: JJ, Finnegans Wake (NY: Viking, 1939), 284, 497; JJ to HW, 27 May 1929, and JJ to Larbaud, 30 July 1929, I, 279, 283; Williams to SB, 8 June 1929; McAlmon and Boyle, Being Geniuses Together, 285–86; SB to HBD, 4 June 1929; JJ to HW, 28 May 1929, I, 281.

Lewis attack: Enemy, 29 Jan. 1929; Joyce had already sent for early Lewis writings; JJ to HW, 12 and 18 Apr. 1929, III, 188.

Crosby proofs: Ellmann, 614; Caresse Crosby, Passionate Years, 196; According to the HC diary, they corrected proofs on 9, 14, and 29 May 1929.

Connolly, O'Brien, and Hemingway: SB to Cyril Connolly, 28 Mar. 1929, McFarlin Library, University of Tulsa; Justin O'Brien, "For a Young American in 1930," in Mercure, 326 (Jan.–Apr. 1956), 75.

Callaghan: Morley Callaghan, That Summer in Paris, 209–14, 125; McAlmon and Boyle, Being Geniuses Together, 181; Mizener, Far Side of Paradise, 234–36; Bruccoli, Scott and Ernest, 92, 73; Both Callaghan (84–86, 134) and Harry Levin, rare critics of SB, found her intimidating.

Tales Told of Shem and Shaun: Caresse Crosby, Passionate Years, 197; Harry Crosby, Shadows of the Sun (21 June 1929), 258; SC 134–35, and early drafts; JJ to Caresse Crosby, 17 July 1929, III, 191; SB to Williams, 15 Oct. 1929, Buffalo.

Joyce family: Ellmann, 610–11; Bair, Beckett, 83; Lucia Joyce's manuscript, written at the request of SB (for Richard Ellmann), is in the SB Papers, Princeton.

Déjeuner Ulysse: Gilbert and Larbaud were out of town, and Morel had another engagement, JJ to Lar-

baud, 30 July 1929, I, 282–83; Chamson remembers that Jean Schlumberger was missing, "Le Secret de Sylvia," Mercure, 23; Hugh Kenner, The Pound Era (Berkeley: University of California Press, 1971), 396; In a letter to Larbaud (20 July 1929, I, 283), JJ claims that Valéry wanted to make speeches but I put a veto on that"; Nino Frank, "The Shadow That H Lost Its Man," in Portraits of the Artist in Exile, 84–86; Frank does not mention that SB, who he thought had "automatic but always springlike kindness," was annoyed by the excessive drinking; Claudel letters, quoted in McDougall, 424, 135; Simone de Beauvoir, preface to Gisèle Freund and V. B. Carleton, JJ in Paris: His Final Years (New York: Harcourt, Brace & World, 1965), viii.

Summer vacations: Josephson, Life among the Surrealists, 367; Fitzgerald to Hemingway, 23 Aug. 1929, Bruccoli, Scott and Ernest, 93; McAlmon and Boyle, Being Geniuses Together, 371–72; Harry Crosby, Shadows of the Sun, 262; Unterecker, Voyager, 596–98; JJ to HW, 16 July 1929, I, 282; SC, 171–72; SB to HBD, 8 Aug. and 5 Oct. 1929; SB to SWB, 5 Sept. 1929; Interview with Helen Eddy, 27 May 1978; JJ to SB, 13 Sept. 1929.

Allen Tate: Tate, Memoirs and Opinions, 59–60; Baker, EH: A Life Story, 205; Interview with Eleanor Oldenberger Herrick, 4 Jan. 1979.

Leon Edel: In 1932 Edel earned the Doctorat-ès-lettres (a ministry of education) degree; Edel to NRF, 20 May 1981; Edel, American Scholar, 482.

The Collapse: SB to HBD, 4 Dec. 1929 and 20 Jan. 1930; Putnam, Paris Was Our Mistress, 116; Morrill Cody agrees that Montparnasse "reached its height in 1925, and its decline in 1929," This Must Be the Place, 185; Hiram Motherwell, "The American Tourist Makes History," Harper's Magazine, December 1929, 73.

Joyce anniversary party: JJ to HW, 19 Oct. 1929, I, 285–86; Ellmann, 639; Nino Frank, in Portraits of the Artist in Exile, 89; Harry Crosby, Shadows of the Sun, 280.

Transition and Jolas: McAlmon and Boyle, Being Geniuses Together, 283; Edmund Wilson, "The Dream of H. C. Earwicker," in JJ: Two Decades of Criticism, 326; Kay Boyle, in Being Geniuses Together, 270–71; Stein's attack on Jolas, in unpublished portion of SC.

Joyce's Sullivan obsession: SC, 186–90; JJ to HW, 22 Nov. 1929, I, 287; Philippe Soupault, "JJ," in Portraits of the Artist in Exile, 113; Ellmann, 621; Gorman, JJ, 346; JJ to HW, 18 Mar. 1930, I, 290–91; Nancy Cunard, "Visits from James Joyce," in Hugh Ford, NC: Brave Poet, Indomitable Rebel (Philadelphia: Chilton, 1968), 82; Edel, American Scholar, 471; SB to HW, 4 Dec. 1929.

Antheil returns: SB to HBD, 4 Dec. 1929 and 23 Mar. 1930; Antheil to SB, letters undated; Baker, EH: A LIFE Story, 207; Antheil, Bad Boy of Music, 237–38.

14. The Flowers of Friendship Fade

1930–1931

Joyce complains: JJ to HW, 18 Mar. 1930, Selected Letters, 346–52; SB to HBD, 23 Mar. and 19 Apr. 1930; Bair, Beckett, 101; Lucia Joyce to AM, 16 Apr. 1930, III, 511.

Léon begins: Ellmann, 630; a year later Joyce complained of Léon, "not having read a word I have written except the piece he revised for [Henry] Babou, has no idea what my book is about or what I want," JJ to HW, 11 Mar. 1931, I, 303.

Kahane, other presses, and little magazines: SC, 132–33; Ford, Published in Paris, 350; Anna Livia poem reprinted in Padraic Colum et al., Homage to JJ, (n.p.: Folcroft Library, 1974), 14.

Joyce's publicity stunt: Ellmann, 624 ("In the

newspaper articles [JJ] contrived to have Sullivan mentioned prominently, and Vogt also").

Marian Willard visits Jung and Paris: Interview with Marian Willard Johnson, 31 Aug. 1980; JJ to HW, 24 June 1921, I, 166.

Sylvia has pneumonia: SB to CB, 9 Dec. 1930; SB to SWB, 24 Aug. and 17 Oct. 1930; SB to HBD, 18 July 1930; JJ to SB, 18 July 1930, III, 512.

Joyce on Lawrence: JJ to HW, 27 Sept. 1930, I, 294; Lawrence, quoted in Dorothy Brett, Lawrence and Brett: A Friendship (Philadelphia: Lippincott, 1933), 81.

Byron's Cain and Sullivan: JJ asked Herbert Gorman to help him prune Byron's text: "the combination

Cain-Byron-Antheil-Sullivan with myself thrown in as scissors-man would be the greatest event in the artistic future," JJ to Antheil, 7 Dec. 1930 and 3 Jan. 1931, I, 296–97; JJ later claimed that Antheil had "missed the chance of a lifetime," JJ to George Joyce, 29 Oct. 1934, III, 327; Interview with Myrsine Moschos, 24 June 1978; SB to SWB, 17 Oct. 1930; JJ to HW, 5 Oct. and 13 Oct. 1930, III, 203–4.

The Beckett-Péron translation of ALP: Bair, *Beckett*, 113.

Gorman: Ellmann, 631.

Economics and first nights: SB to HBD, 2 Dec. 1930; SB to CB, 9 Dec. 1930.

Sinclair Lewis: Wambly Bald, "The Sweet Madness of Montparnasse," in *Left Bank Revisited*, 286; Allen Churchill, *The Literary Decade* (Englewood Cliffs, N.J.: Prentice-Hall, 1971), 319–21.

Contract: SC, 202–4 (facsimile of contract, p. 203), and early drafts; Flanner, "The Infinite Pleasure: Sylvia Beach," in *Janet Flanner's World*, 313.

Joyce tirades against women: Ellmann, 631, 639; Frank Budgen, *James Joyce and the Making of* Ulysses (London: Smith and Haas, 1934), 7; Mary Colum, *Life and Dream* (Garden City, NY: Doubleday, 1947), 394–95, 398; Nutting diary and interviews with Arthur Power and Maria Jolas in Ellmann, 631; Ellmann recently argued that when JJ sat down to write, he put aside his misogyny and "his talent took over," "Joyce and His Women," (London) *Sunday Times*, 7 Feb. 1982, 43; Lidderdale and Nicholson, *Dear Miss Weaver*, 301; Interview with Jane Lidderdale, 18 Mar. 1978; Nora, quoted by Beckett in Ellmann, 629; Ellmann adds that Nora was speaking of JJ the man, not JJ the writer (*Times*, 43).

Joyce spending: Ellmann, 633; bookshop record books; JJ to HW, 22 Dec. 1930, III, 209; JJ to HW, 16 Feb. and 11 Mar. 1931, I, 100, 103; Lidderdale and Nicholson, *Dear Miss Weaver*, 303; Colum, *Life and Dream*, 385.

Edith Sitwell reads: Early drafts of *SC;* SB to HBD, 16 Jan. 1931; Sitwell Reading file, SB Papers; SB to Natalie Barney, 27 Dec. 1954, Jacques Doucet Library; "A lot of doors in Paris [slammed] shut on Edith as a result" of her offending of Stein, claims John Pearson, in *The Sitwells: A Family's Biography* (NY: Harcourt Brace Jovanovich, 1978), 275; Allen, *New Walt Whitman Handbook*, 279.

Stein meets Joyce: SC, 32; Alice B. Toklas to Donald Sutherland, 30 Nov. 1947, *Staying on Alone: Letters of ABT*, ed. Edward Burns (NY: Liveright, 1973), 91–92; Interviewer unnamed, "Samuel Beckett: Tea with Gertrude Stein" (7 April 31), in *Left Bank Revisited*, 141.

Louis Gillet meets Joyce: LG to JJ, 10 Jan. 1931, III, 211; Gillet, *Claybook for JJ*, 29, 88, 49, 91; SB to HBD, 16 Jan. 1931; SB to Natalie Barney, 7 Feb. 1931, Jacques Doucet Library; JJ to HW, 16 Feb. 1931, I, 300; JJ confided to HW, 18 Feb. 1931, I, 300, that "a dinner fund is being subscribed on both sides of the rue de l'Odéon," the actual host not having the necessary funds"; JJ to Frank Budgen, 17 July 1933, I, 337.

JJ on Anna Livia translation: JJ to HW, 4 Mar. 1931, I, 302.

Patrick's party: Paul Léon to Lucie Noël (Léon), 17 Mar. 1931, in *JJ and Paul Léon: The Story of a Friendship* (NY: Gotham, 1950), 47; McAlmon and Boyle, *Being Geniuses Together*, 345–46; Colum, *Life and Dream*, 391; JJ to HW, 16 Feb. and 11 Mar. 1931, I, 100, 103; Soupault describes Joyce's behavior as resembling at times "the sulky unhappiness of a child," in *Portraits of the Artist in Exile*, 114; SB claims that Mary Colum's version of a falling out between JJ and herself this evening is "a whopper," SB to HBD, 2 May 1949.

Anna Livia reading: JJ to HW, 11 Mar. 1931, I,

302; Edel, who knew no one except the two hostesses, has given the fullest account of the evening, in "A Paris Letter," *Canadian Forum*, April 1931, and in "The Genius and the Injustice Collector," *American Scholar* (autumn 1980); Bair, *Beckett*, 129; AM, "Joyce's *Ulysses* and the French Public" (1940), in McDougall, 112–26; Interview with Samuel Beckett, 17 Aug. 1980; Beckett to NRF, 6 Oct. 1980; Bair (to NRF, 11 June 1981) claims that the Beckett-George Reavey correspondence confirms Beckett's memory; Edel claims that the record was played last; JJ to SB, 10 May 1931, I, 304; Lidderdale and Nicholson, *Dear Miss Weaver*, 303; McAlmon to SB, 17 Feb. 1932; Edel to NRF, 20 May 1981; SB to HBD, 4 Apr. 1931; McAlmon and Boyle, *Being Geniuses Together*, 316; Ellmann, 637.

Joyce plans marriage: JJ to HW, 11 Apr. 1931, III, 215; Lidderdale and Nicholson, *Dear Miss Weaver*, 304–6; Ellmann, 639.

Reprinting Pomes Penyeach: SB to SWB, 25 Apr. 1931; Tomlinson to SB, 4 May 1931.

Spring visitors: SB to Hemingway, 21 Apr. 1931, Kennedy Library.

Publishing offers for Joyce: Ben Huebsch to SB, 16 May 1931; Lawrence E. Pollinger's Curtis Brown correspondence with JJ is in Morris Library, Southern Illinois University, Carbondale.

Adrienne's letter to Joyce: AM to JJ, 19 May 31, Berg Collection, NY Public Library; Maria Jolas, "The Joyce I Knew and the Women around Him," *Crane Bag* (Dublin), 4 (1980), 85; Ellmann, 651–52; Mary and Padraic Colum, *Our Friend JJ*, 93–94; *SC*, 202.

Sylvia sets her price: SB to EH, 8 June 1931, Kennedy Library; SB to Lawrence Pollinger, 11 June 1931, Morris Library.

Joyce marriage: Ellmann, 639; SB to HBD, 27 July 1931.

Curtis Brown withdraws: SB to HBD, 18 July 1931; Claude Kendall to L. E. Pollinger, 29 July 1931, Morris Library; From his perspective, Pollinger (1) wanted only U.S. rights, which he did not believe would hamper her European sales, (2) feared high legal and publishing costs, and (3) could not understand why SB did not share the JJ royalties (a plan JJ did not suggest); Boski Antheil to SB, 9 June 1931; SB to SWB, 26 Sept. 1931.

Sylvia rests: SB to HBD, 18 July and 27 July 1931; JJ to HW, 6 Dec. 1931, I, 307.

Viking contract: SB to HBD, 18 July 1931; JJ to SB, 13 July 1931, Lockwood Memorial Library, SUNY, Buffalo; SB to JJ, n.d.; Gilbert, introd. to I, 38; When Joyce had not written more on *Work in Progress* by July of 1932, he offered to return the Faber and Faber advance (they agreed to wait), Paul Léon to Ralph Pinker, 14 July 1932, I, 323.

Zeitung: JJ to SB, 13 Aug. 1931; Ellmann, 640; SB to HBD, 14 Aug. and 12 and 25 Sept. 1931.

Economic difficulties and the Roth piracy: SB to SWB, 16 Oct. 1931; SB to HBD, 12 and 25 Sept. and 23 Oct. 1931; JJ to James Pinker, 19 Oct. 1931, Morris Library.

Joyce to Pinker: JJ to HW, 27 Sept. 1931 (suppressed portion of I, 306); JJ to HW, 1 Oct. 1931 (suppressed portion of III, 230).

SB resists losing Ulysses: SB to HBD, 18 July and 23 Oct. 1931; HW to SB, 6 Nov. 1931; *SC*, 202; JJ to HW, 8 Oct. 1931.

Temporary relief of tensions: JJ to James Pinker, 19 Oct. 1931, Morris Library; JJ to HW, 21 Nov. 1931, III, 233–34; SB to HBD, 1 Dec. 1931; JJ to HW, 27 Nov. 1931, III, 235, and 7 Dec. 1931, I, 308; Arthur Power, *From the Old Waterford House* (London: Mellifont, 1944), 64; Marianne Moore, "How Do Justice," *Mercure*, 13.

Huebsch's offer for Ulysses: JJ to HW, 27 Nov. 1931 (suppressed portion of III, 235), 17 Dec. 1931, I,

309 (and suppressed portion), and 18 Dec. 1931, III, 236; SB to James Pinker, 25 Nov. 1931; Thomas McGreevy to HW, 6 Jan. 1932, British Library; JJ to HW, 22 Dec. 1931.
The break: SC, 204, and several unpublished drafts; JJ informed HW that SB "screamed at him" (17 Jan. 1932, *Selected Letters*, 360); Colum reported to JJ that his pictures were removed from the bookshop walls and that SB had nearly thrown Colum out, JJ to HW, 22

Dec. 1931; She later claimed that if Joyce had asked in person, she "probably would have torn up" the contract; To others, the Colums were critical of Joyce and expressed sympathy for Sylvia, whom they claimed to have defended during this episode (Interviews with Eleanor Oldenberger Herrick, 4 Jan. 1979, with Myrsine Moschos, 22 June 1978, and with Jean Henley, 4 July 1978); Jean Henley to NRF, 23 Apr. 1981.

15. IN THE WAKE
1932-1933

Joyce grieves: JJ to HW, 17 Jan. 1932, I, 312; Ellmann, 645; JJ poem, in Ellmann, 646.
Joyce gives lilacs and challenges: SB to HBD, 3 Feb. 1932; JJ to HW, 1932 (not in Harriet Weaver Papers), quoted in Ellmann, 652; Interview with Jean Henley, 4 July 1978; Lidderdale and Nicholson, *Dear Miss Weaver*, 310.
Léon and the Jolases take over: Paul Léon to SB, 8 Feb. 1932; Léon to HW, 2 Mar. 1932 (all Léon letters to HW are in the HW Papers, British Library); Lucie Noël (Léon), *JJ and Paul Leon*, 46; JJ to HW, 28 Jan. 1933, I, 313.
SB response to break with JJ: Several unpublished drafts and suppressed portions of *SC;* SB to HBD, 26 Apr. and 6 Mar. 1933; *SC*, 205.
JJ response to break with SB: JJ, *Finnegans Wake* (NY: Viking, 1968), 564; SB excused him in part: "I know how desperately he needed the money," *SC*, 205; Colum, *Life and Dream*, 338; JJ to HW, 1 Oct. 1931 (suppressed postscript of III, 230); Mary and Padraic Colum, *Our Friend JJ*, 193; T. S. Eliot to John Quinn,9 May 1921, Quinn Collection, NYPL; Gilbert, introd. to I, 31; Malcolm Cowley, *—And I Worked at the Writer's Trade: Chapters of Literary History, 1918–1978* (NY: Penguin, 1979), 246–66; Edel, *American Scholar*, 486–87; JJ to HW, 13 Mar. 1932; Maria Jolas, *Crane Bag*, 86.
Harriet Weaver visits: Ellmann, 651; Lidderdale and Nicholson, *Dear Miss Weaver*, 312.
Random House contract: Carolyn Reidy (Random House) to NRF, 18 June 1982; Bernard R. Crystal (Columbia University Library) to NRF, 29 June 1982; JJ to T. S. Eliot, 4 Mar. 1932, I, 316; Maria Jolas, *Crane Bag*, 87; Frances Steloff to SB, 10 Mar. 1932; Léon to SB, 9 Mar. 1932; Cerf's colorful version of negotiating the contract at Shakespeare and Company in the presence of both SB and JJ is probably an exaggerated version of a meeting during the fall of 1930, *At Random* (NY: Random House, 1977), 90–93; JJ to Bennett Cerf, 2 Apr. 1932, III, 242; JJ to Stuart Gilbert, 17 Apr. 1932, British Library; As had been prearranged, the copy sent to Random House was seized on 1 May 1932, JJ to HW, 7 May 1932; SB to HBD, 26 Apr. 1932.
SC's financial stability: SB to HBD, 31 Dec. 1931 and 2/3 Feb. and 26 Apr. 1932; SB to SWB, 18 Apr. 1932; Bookshop records.
Jean Henley assists: SB to HBD, 26 Apr. and 2 Sept. 1932; Interview with Henley, 4 July 1978; Henley to NRF, 25 Oct. 1977; Katherine Anne Porter, "Paris: A Little Incident in the Rue de l'Odéon," *Ladies Home Journal*, Aug. 1964, 54; Edward Woodbridge Beach to SB, 14 May 1932 and 20 Mar. 1933; The advice of JJ on SWB's eye operation is in SB to HBD, 12 May 1932; McDougall, 59, 54.
SB refuses Continental edition: Jonathan Cape to SB, 9 Feb. 1932; Lidderdale and Nicholson, *Dear Miss Weaver*, 315; John Lane published *Ulysses* in England in 1936; Darantière to SB, 5 Apr. 1932; *SC*, 205; Henley remembers that SB occasionally devoted whole days to his business, went shopping with him, and stayed with Lucia (Jean Henley to NRF, 23 Apr. 1981); JJ to

HW, 7 May 1932 (this same letter reveals that JJ mistakenly believed that *Ulysses* was SB's only source of income).
Parties and publishing ventures: SB to HBD, 12 May 1932; Bair, *Beckett*, 142.
Joyce visit: JJ to HW, 25 June and 21 July 1932; JJ to HW, 10 July 1932, I, 321; Lidderdale and Nicholson, *Dear Miss Weaver*, 316; Ellmann, 662–63; Ellmann interview with Jung, 679.
Les Déserts: SB to HBD, 21 July 1932; AM to SWB, 12 Aug. 1932.
AM catalog and SB translation: SB to SWB, 26 Aug. 1932; SB to HBD, 3 Sept., 11 Oct., and 6 Dec. 1932; Holly and Fred Dennis were writing articles for popular publications; *SC*, 161; Paul Valéry to SB, n.d., *Mercure*, 151; SB unsuccessfully tried to place the Valéry piece in America, in *Hound and Horn* (SB to Bernard Brandler, 18 Oct. 1932; Lincoln Kirstein to SB, 8 Nov. 1932); SB to SWB, 11 Oct. 1932.
Hemingway attacks Stein: Hemingway, "The Farm," *Cahiers d'Art*, 9 (1934), 28–29; Hemingway turned a more vicious aim at Stein thirty years later in *A Moveable Feast*, 117–19; The Jolases and other former friends answered her in "Testimony against Gertrude Stein," *Transition* supplement (1935).
Antheil and Hemingway flush: Antheil, *Bad Boy of Music*, 226; Baker, *EH: A Life Story*, 229–30.
Exchanging assistants: SB to HBD, 11 Oct. 1932 and 6 Mar. 1933; SB to SWB, 27 June 1933; JJ to HW, 21 Nov. 1932; Interview with Myrsine Moschos, 24 June 1978.
Joyce ill: JJ to HW, 25 Nov. 1932, I, 328; JJ to HW, 7 Jan. 1933, III, 267–68 (date corrected by Lidderdale); JJ to HW, 18 Jan. 1933 (partially published in I, 331–33).
Sylvia improves: SB to HBD, 11 Oct. 1932; SB to Hemingway, 25 Nov. 1932, Kennedy Library; SB's letters contradict JJ's reports to HW of her poor health; JJ to HW, 17 Oct. 1932.
Albatross Press: JJ to HW, 8, 11, and 17 Oct. and 29 Nov. 1932; Interview with Jane Lidderdale, 22 Mar. 1981; JJ, *Finnegans Wake, 337; JJ to HW, 11 Nov. 1932 (unpublished portion of I, 326); SB to HBD, 6 Mar. 1933; SC*, 206; JJ poem, in Ellmann, 654–55; "I am determined not to take up any glove, shoe, hat, or umbrella thrown down," JJ confided to HW (29 Nov. 1932); Léon to HW, 7 Jan. 1933, III, 268.
Entertaining friends: SB to HBD, 30 Nov. and 6 Dec. 1932; Allen Tate, "Memories of Sylvia," *Mercure*, 38; SB to SWB, 28 Dec. 1932 and 17 Jan. 1933.
Katherine Anne Porter: Porter, *Ladies Home Journal*, 54; Porter Papers, Humanities Research Center, University of Texas, Austin; SB to HBD, (?) Feb. and 29 June 1933; SB to MacLeish, 20 Feb. 1933; Porter to SB, 6 Feb. 1956, in *Mercure*, 154; *SC*, 206–7.
Miss Weaver visits: SB to SWB, 17 Feb. 1933; Lidderdale and Nicholson, *Dear Miss Weaver*, 323; Paul Léon to HW, 17 Mar. 1933; Léon to HW, 25 and 27 Apr. and 23 Sept. 1933, III, 277–78, 285 (Nora irrationally bore a grudge against Léon for the broken engagement of Lucia); JJ to HW, 25 Nov. 1932, I, 328; Léon to HW, 23 Mar. 1933, III, 275.

Varied interests for Sylvia: SB to HBD, 14 Mar. 1933; SB to CB, 21 Feb. 1933.

Willa Cather: Two undated notes from Cather to SB speak of two visits to the bookshop, probably in 1933, when she received the Prix Femina Américain.

Vacation: SB to HBD, 12 July and 12, 17, and 29 Aug. 1933.

Short-term visitors: SB to HBD, 27 Sept. 1933.

Farewell to Montparnasse: Wambly Bald, "La Vie" (25 July 1933), in *Left Bank Revisited,* 146–49; Rice, *Left Bank,* 216–18; Putnam, *Paris Was Our Mistress,* 241, 247, 250; Rueckert, *Glenway Wescott,* 88.

Joyce problems: SB to HBD, 14 Sept. 1933; Paul Léon to HW, 23 Sept. 1933, III, 285–87.

Pope blesses Ulysses: SB to HBD, 27 Sept. 1933;

*Dewitt Eldridge to SB, 18 Sept. 1933, Cornell University Library.

Business is terrible: SB to SWB, 27 June 1933; SB to HBD, 14 Oct. and 28 Nov. 1933.

A defensive Hemingway visits: SB to HBD, 27 Oct. 1933; Baker, *EH: A Life Story,* 246, 608; Morrill Cody to NRF, 7 June 1978; Hemingway wrote the preface to James Charters's *This Must Be the Place;* Hemingway to Cody, (11?) Nov. 1933.

An American Ulysses: The preface by Ernst and the decision by Woolsey are published in the Random House edition of *Ulysses* (1934); Ellmann, 666; JJ to Carola Giedion-Welcker, (?) Apr. 1934, III, 312; Leslie Katz, "Meditations on Sylvia," *Mercure,* 84.

16. STORM CLOUDS
1934–1935

Hemingway and the tulips: SB to HBD, 23 Mar. 1934; Typed note on his book damages, 24 Mar. 1934; Early drafts of *SC* and 83; Though Baker says she showed him the article, her several drafts indicate that he found the article himself; Wyndham Lewis, "The Dumb Ox: A Study of EH," *Life and Letters,* 10 (April 1934), 33–45 (reprinted with a shortened title as a chapter in *Men without Art* (NY: Russell & Russell, 1934), a play on the Hemingway title *Men Without Women*); Baker, *EH: A Life Story,* 256–58; SB to HBD, 20 Apr. 1934; Lewis, quoted by Marshall McLuhan, "The Personal Approach," *Renascence,* 13 (autumn 1960), 43; Hemingway, *Moveable Feast,* 109.

Hemingway and Katherine Anne Porter: KAP to SB, 6 Feb. 1956, reprinted in *Mercure,* 155; Porter claims she never saw Hemingway again, *Ladies Home Journal,* 54–55; It is highly unlikely that EH had heard of KAP's views of his writing. In a letter to McAlmon, she had called EH a "fraud" who had not created "one plausible human being," quoted by Kay Boyle, in *Being Geniuses Together,* 114–15; EH confided to Malcolm Cowley that he "just can't read" Porter's fiction, for it "seems so terribly dull," 17 Oct. 1945, *Selected Letters,* 602.

Joyce birthday: Interview with Myrsine Moschos, 24 June 1978; Lidderdale and Nicholson, *Dear Miss Weaver,* 331. A holograph note by HW says she was in Paris from the "end of January to 6 February 1934," HW Papers, British Library.

Bloody Tuesday: Janet Flanner, "Bloody Tuesday," *Paris Was Yesterday,* 111–13; SB to HBD, 8 Feb. 1934.

Women's club: SB to HBD, 9 Jan., 8 Feb., and 23 Mar. 1934.

Joyce: Paul Léon to HW, 11 Mar. 1934; JJ to HW, 21 Oct. 1934, I, 349; Lidderdale and Nicholson, *Dear Miss Weaver,* 336–37.

Rotarians: SB to HBD, 23 Mar., 20 Apr., and 4 and 29 May 1934. Maria Jolas, who opened a bilingual school in Neuilly, was also a member of the women Rotarians.

McAlmon: Ellmann, 674; Joyce believed Lucia's story that McAlmon had proposed to her (JJto HW, 24 Apr. 1934, I, 339) and initially feared she would be mentioned in the book; Pound to McAlmon, 2 Feb. 1934, *Letters to Ezra Pound,* 252; The final chapter of Sanford Smoller's *Adrift among Genuises* is entitled "Journey to Oblivion, 1935–56."

Ulysses sales: JJ to George and Helen Joyce, 1 July 1934, I, 343; Nora Joyce to George and Helen Joyce, 15 June 1934, III, 307; Léon to Ralph Pinker, 25 Sept. 1934, I, 347; Thomson, *Virgil Thomson,* 77; Cerf, *At Random,* 94, 99–102; JJ to HW, 24 Apr. 1934, I, 340; SB to HBD, 4 May 1934; Ellmann, 672;

Pleasure amid crisis: Cyprian to SB, (n.d.) 1934; SB to Jean Wright, 12 July 1934, Princeton; SB to

Frances Steloff, 26 July 1934, Berg Collection, NY Public Library; Morris L. Ernst and Alexander Lindey, *The Censor Marches On: Recent Milestones in the Administration of the Obscenity Law in the United States* (NY: Doubleday Doran, 1940), 285; SB to HBD, 28 May, 13 June, and 14 Aug. 1934; SB to SWB, 8 Sept. 1934, HBD to SB, 9 Oct. 1934.

Financial difficulties: SB to SWB, 10 July 1934; SB to Tom Dunne, 5 Oct. 1934; SB to HBD, 27 Nov. 1934.

Stein: Stein, quoted in James Mellow, *Charmed Circle: Gertrude Stein and Company* (NY: Avon, 1974), 497.

Popper: Edwin Popper to NRF, 9 Mar. 1969.

Assistance to MacLeish and Chamson: MacLeish's *Panic,* a 1935 verse drama, and *Public Speed* (1936) present his dual interest in drama and social issues; MacLeish to SB, 17 Oct. and 20 Dec. 1934, and SB to MacLeish, 10 Nov. 1934, Princeton; SB to HBD, 27 Nov. 1934; "Remarks by André Chamson," *Fitzgerald / Hemingway Annual, 1973,* 72.

Mesures and Michaux: SB to HBD, 30 Apr. 1935; AM, "Number One" (1938), in McDougall, 138; Dorothy Richardson to SB, Dec. 1934, in *Mercure,* 128; *SC,* 175. Joyce never converted Sylvia to the poetry of Yeats.

Alice in Wonderland: AM, "Alice in Wonderland" (1935), in McDougall, 160–64; JJ to SB, 22 May 1928, I, 262.

Sale of rare books and manuscripts: SB to HBD, 18 Jan. 1935; Janet Flanner to SB, n.d. (1935). When Flanner sold the copy of *Ulysses,* in 1950, she gave the $100 to Sylvia.

Strain in relations with Joyce: JJ to George and Helen Joyce, 19 Feb. and 19 Mar. 1935, III, 345, 351, and 5 Feb. 1935, I, 357; JJ to HW, 7 Apr. 1935, I, 362 (the portion in parentheses was suppressed from the published version of the letter); Interview with Richard Ellmann, 16 Mar. 1981; JJ to HW, 1 May 1935, I, 366; Ellmann, 684.

Help from friends: SB to HBD, 18 Jan. and 5 Mar. 1935; In the fifties, when SB wanted advice on the writing of her memoirs, she consulted Bradley's widow, Jenny Serruys Bradley, who had taken over his business; MacLeish to SB, 7 Mar. and 20 May 1935.

Thomas Wolfe: Holograph draft of *SC,* 208; Andrew Turnbull, *Thomas Wolfe* (NY: Scribners, 1967), 209 (there is no record that Wolfe visited Shakespeare and Company in 1930, on his first visit to Paris).

Stein: Leo Stein to Mabel Weeks, *Journey into Self,* ed. Edmund Fuller (NY: Crown, 1950), 134.

Marie Monnier exhibit: SB to HBD, 30 Apr. and 13 June 1935; JJ to Lucia Joyce, 15 May 1935, III, 356.

Sale of MSS: SB to HBD, 5 Mar. 1935; SB to SWB, 14 June 1935; SB to HBD, 13 June 1935; Record book of aid received 1935-1955, Princeton; Carlotta Welles Briggs to SB, 23 July 1935; Fitzgerald to SB, 18 July 1935.

Subsidy rejected: André Gide to SB, 27 Oct. 1935.

Literary politics: SB to HBD, 26 June 1935.

Simone de Beauvoir: De Beauvoir and Sartre, excluded from *SC*, are discussed in its early drafts; Freund and Carleton, *JJ in Paris*, 41; Flanner, *Paris Was Yesterday*, 116; Beauvoir, introd. to Freund and Carleton, *JJ in Paris*, vii.

The Friends of Shakespeare and Company organized: AM, "Readings at Sylvia's" (1936), in McDougall, 134-35; SB to SWB, 12 Dec. 1935; SB to HBD, 18 Jan. 1936.

Political demonstrations: SB to HBD, 29 Nov. 1935; SB to SWB, 12 Dec. 1935; JJ to HW, 1 May 1935, I, 367.

Gisèle Freund: Interview with Freund, 11 Aug. 1969; Interview with Eleanor Oldenberger Herrick, 4 Jan. 1979; Freund and Carleton, *JJ in Paris*, 4.

Bryher's visit: SB to SWB, 12 Dec. 1935; Bryher, *Heart to Artemis*, 275; Bryher claims (209) that she also met Romains, Michaux, Schlumberger, Prévost, and Chamson at No. 18.

Sylvia to cemetery: SB to HBD, 18 Jan. 1936; For nearly twenty years, at the urging of Holly (who needed her complicity), Sylvia had changed the date of her birth.

17. LES AMIS DE SHAKESPEARE AND COMPANY

1936-1937

Gide reading: Interview with François Valéry, 20 June 1978; SB to HBD, 18 Jan. and 5 Feb. 1936; Huddleston, *Paris Salons*, 285; AM, "Readings at Sylvia's" (1936), in McDougall, 135; When Gide's novel, a fictional account of his honeymoon with an Arab boy, was published, in 1937, both Sylvia and Adrienne thought the sexual explicitness in bad taste, interview with Eleanor Oldenberger Herrick, 7 Mar. 1978 and 23 Feb. 1982.

Keeler Faus: Interview with Faus, 20 June 78.

Elizabeth Bishop: Harriet Tompkins later wrote "SB, Ambassadrice des Lettres," *New York Herald Tribune* (Paris), 30 Oct. 1935; Interview with Bishop, 28 June 1978; Later, in New York, at an invitation from Marianne Moore that she could not sway away from, Bishop met the owner of *Life and Letters To-Day,* Bryher, a close friend of Sylvia and Marianne.

François Valéry: *SC,* 161-62; Interview with Valéry, 20 June 1978; Valéry library cards, SB Papers.

Old friends offer help: SB to HBD, 18 Jan. 1936; Huddleston, *Paris Salons,* 286-87; Miss Rogers to Marian Willard, 18 Jan. 1937; SB Papers; Willard to SB, 19 Jan. 1937.

Friends: Regular members—there were forty-eight in 1936—included Natalie Barney, Dr. Fontaine, the Churches, the Gilberts, Desmond Harmsworth, the Joyces, Kahane, Mrs. Massey, Victoria Ocampo, Ambassador and Mrs. Granville-Barker, the Jacques Lemaîtres, Alice Linossier-Ardoin, the Jolases, the Léons, Gisèle Freund, the Bécats, and assistants at both shops.

Valéry reading: Huddleston, *Paris Salons,* 325-26; Interview with Samuel Beckett, 27 Aug. 1980; Interview with François Valéry, 20 June 1978; AM, "Readings at Sylvia's" (1936), in McDougall, 135; Valéry's *The Graveyard by the Sea,* trans. C. Day Lewis, in *Selected Writings of Paul Valéry* (NY: New Directions, 1964), 49; Ellmann, 702; Valéry's *Silhouette of the Serpent,* trans. by David Paul, in *Paul Valéry: An Anthology* (Princeton: Princeton University Press, 1977), 263; Interview with James Briggs (6 July 1978) and François Valéry (20 June 1978).

Sylvia to London: SB to T. S. Eliot, 21 Mar. 1936; SB to SWB, 24 Mar. 1936; SB to HBD, 2 and 29 Apr. 1936; Antiquarians begged for Hemingway first editions—"I could make a Fortune," she told Holly—but expressed no interest in Joyce's books; Lidderdale and Nicholson, *Dear Miss Weaver,* 357.

Schlumberger and Paulhan readings: SB to HBD, 2 Apr. 1936; Interview with Elizabeth Bishop, 28 June 1978; AM, "Readings at Sylvia's" (1936), in McDougall, 135-36; SB to SWB, 12 and 19 May 1936; *SC,* 211.

Joyce attends: Paul Léon to HW, 22 May and 22 Aug. 1936; Ellmann, 687, 690; Lidderdale and Nicholson, *Dear Miss Weaver,* 360-61; JJ to HW, 9 June 1936, III, 386.

Eliot readings: T. S. Eliot to SB, 28 and 30 May 1936; Eliot, "Miss Sylvia Beach," *Mercure,* 9; AM, "Readings at Sylvia's" (1936), in McDougall, 136; Freund and Carleton, *JJ in Paris,* 49; SB to Eliot, 21 Mar. 1936; Probably because of the publicity about the readings, library subscriptions increased from fifty-four members in July to eighty-six in November.

Communism: André Gide et al., *The God that Failed,* ed. Richard Crossman (NY: Bantam, 1965), 157-76; Gide's disillusionment with Soviet communism diminished Sylvia's sympathy for communism, says James Briggs (interview, 6 July 1978); Miss Weaver, even after the Soviet invasion of Hungary in 1956, did not reject communism, Lidderdale and Nicholson, *Dear Miss Weaver,* 347.

U.S. visit after twenty-two years: Boski Antheil to SB, 14 Oct. 1936; SB to HBD, 2 and 6 Oct. and 17 Nov. 1936; "Sylvia's interest, enthusiasm, and energy made me believe in myself," testified Marian Willard Johnson in an interview, 31 Aug. 1980; SB to Frances Steloff, 24 Nov. 1936, Berg Collection, NY Public Library; SB to SWB, 17 Oct. 1936.

Estrangement with Adrienne: Interviews with Eleanor Oldenberger Herrick (8 Mar. 1978) and Gisèle Freund (11 Aug. 1969); SB to SWB, 5 Nov. 1937; SB to HBD, 15 Nov. 1937.

Returning to PEN and the Friends: Jan Parandowski, "Meeting with Joyce," in *Portraits of the Artist in Exile,* 716; Ellmann, 703-4; SB to SWB, 14 Nov. 1936; SB to HBD, 17 Nov. and 11 Dec. 1936; SB to Kay Boyle, 12 Dec. 1936; Aldous Huxley to SB, 18 Dec. [1936].

Miss Weaver's last visit with Joyce: Lidderdale and Nicholson, *Dear Miss Weaver,* 362-65; Léon to HW, 3 and 18 Nov. 1936 (HW destroyed several Léon letters concerning intimate Joyce-family affairs); HW to SB, 9 Nov. 1936 and 25 May 1947.

Skiing and preparing for readings: SB to HBD, 11 Dec. 1936; SB to SWB, 7 Feb. 1937.

Romains reads, Adrienne is honored: Romains's *Men of Good Will* is a twenty-seven-volume novel cycle (1932-1947); SB to HBD, 19 Feb. 1937; SB to SWB, 7 Feb. 1937; As a result of the honor, AM was asked to write the library section for the great, new *Encyclopédie Française;* Cyprian Beach to SB, 30 Mar. 1937.

Spender, Hemingway, and Bryher visit: SB to HBD, 19 Feb. 1937; Baker, *EH: A Life Story,* 305; SB to SWB, 7 Feb. 1937.

Maurois reading: *SC,* 211.

Isherwood and Auden: Christopher Isherwood to SB, 7 Apr. 1937; SB to Isherwood, 8 Apr. 1937.

Hemingway-Spender reading: SB to HBD, 16 and 25 May 1937; Interview with Gisèle Freund, 11 Aug. 1969; Baker, *EH: A Life Story,* 309, 312-13; AM, "Americans in Paris" (1945), in McDougall, 416; Undated French news clippings and Francis Smith, "Hemingway Curses, Kisses, Reads at SB Literary

Session," Paris *Herald Tribune*, 14 Mar. 1937; SB, BBC interview (24 Oct. 1959); A holograph note by SB in her copy of *Winner Take Nothing* gives the date and title and is followed by EH's note at the liberation of Paris: "Lu et approuvé Paris, August 25, 1944" (AM claimed it was the twenty-sixth); Stephen Spender to NRF, 8 July 1977; Spender's "Regum Ultima Ratio" appeared in *New Statesman*, 13 (15 May 1937), 811, and later as "Ultima Ratio Regum" in *Selected Poems* (London: Faber and Faber, 1965), 46; Though newspaper accounts say Spender read five poems, he later listed six titles inside SB's copy of his collected verse; Spender, in *The God That Failed*, 222; Frederick R. Benson,

Writers in Arms: The Literary Impact of the Spanish Civil War (NY: NYU Press, 1967), 4; *SC*, 111.

Trips and movies: Polly Dennis was also the aunt of Holly's husband; SB to HBD, 16 and 25 May 1937; SB to Bryher, 19 May 1937.

Expo 37: SB to SWB, 7 Feb., 30 June, and 6 July 1937; In its December 1937 issue, the *Nouvelle Revue Française* reproduced portions of SB and AM's translations of *Paris 1900*, published in full in 1940; AM, "Our Friend Bryher" (1940), in McDougall, 204–6; Bryher, *Heart to Artemis*, 22–34; *SC*, 212.

Bryher subsidy: SB to SWB, 18 July and 7 Oct. 1937; SB to HBD, 19 and 20 Aug. 1937.

18. HANGING ON
1937–1939

Arrivals, preparations, and politics: Interviews with Eleanor Oldenberger Herrick, 7 and 8 Mar. 1978 and 14 Feb. 1980; Telephone interview with Sylvia Peter Preston, 1 June 1978; SB to SWB, 7 Oct. and 1 Dec. 1937; Samuel Hynes, *The Auden Generation: Literature and Politics in England in the 1930's* (NY: Viking, 1977), 414; HW to SB, 9 July and 22 Dec. 1937 and 30 Dec. 1938.

PEN reception: Nino Frank, "The Shadow That Had Lost Its Man," in *Portraits of the Artist as Exile*, 100–101; SB to HBD, 15 Nov. 1937.

The pace slows: SB to SWB, 5 Nov. 1937; Frank, in *Portraits of the Artist as Exile*, 91–93.

"The Day of the Rabblement": SB to HBD, 15 Nov. 1937.

Friendships broaden, Beckett returns: SB to SWB, 5 Nov. 1937; Interview with Herrick, 7 Mar. 1978; Bair, *Beckett*, 270–73; Interview with Samuel Beckett, 27 Aug. 1980.

Anne Yeats and Tania Whitman: SB to HBD, 5 Feb. 1938.

Inflation and bookselling: SB to SWB, 5 Nov. 1937; SB to James Laughlin, 30 Dec. 1936; Interview with Herrick, 7 Mar. 1978.

Pauline seeks Hemingway: Interview with Herrick, 8 Mar. 1978 and 4 Jan. 1979; Baker, *EH: A Life Story*, 323–24; Some critics, such as John L. Brown ("12, rue de l'Odéon," *Mercure*, 73), who assert that Sylvia did not see Hemingway's dark side, are aware only of her remarks in her memoirs. Though Hemingway (at fifty-four) would tell Bernard Berenson (20–22 March 1953, *Selected Letters*, 810) that love is "not fornication," Sylvia believed that he thought otherwise.

Air raids and overdue books: SB to HBD, 2 Mar. 1938; SB to SWB, 27 Apr. 1938; Interview with François Valéry, 20 June 1978; Interview with Myrsine Moschos, 24 June 1978; SB to Mrs. Tracy Kittredge, 27 Oct. 1938; Ford, *Your Mirror to My Times*, 388.

Adrienne's Gazette: Many of the *Gazette* essays were translated in 1976 by McDougall, in *The Very Rich Hours of Adrienne Monnier*; SB to HBD, 5 Feb. and 22 Mar. 1938; André Gide to AM, 15 Apr. 1938, quoted in McDougall, 470.

Publicity for Work in Progress: Freund and Carleton, *JJ in Paris*, 3–4, 59–63; Bair, *Beckett*, 272; Ellmann, *James Joyce* to HW, 2 Feb. 1938.

Daughter of H.D.: Interview with Perdita Schaffner, 7 July 1978.

Natalie Barney assists: SB to Barney, 9 Jan. 1938, and AM to NB, 19 Jan. 1938, Jacques Doucet Library.

Hemingway interest in drama: Baker, *EH: A Life Story*, 321; Bookshop records and Hemingway library cards, SB Papers; NRF, *Fitzgerald / Hemingway Annual*, 1977, 164, 180.

Henry Miller circle: Miller to SB, 18 Feb. 1938; Alfred Perles to SB, 18 Feb. 1938.

James Farrell: Interview with Herrick, 6 Jan. 1979; James Farrell to SB, 20 Mar. 1937.

E. M. Forster: Freund and Carleton, *JJ in Paris*, 52; Interview with Herrick, 8 Mar. 1978.

Sylvia's relations with the wealthy and the artists: Interview with Herrick, 4 Jan. 1979; SB to Jackson Mathews, 2 July 1959; Barney, "For Sylvia," *Mercure*, 18; SB to HBD, 9 June 1938; David Diamond to NRF, 19 Aug. and 4 Oct. 1977 and 25 Oct. 1980; Records show that on 30 Jan. 1939 SB collected 1,000 francs "for the Spanish cause" from Tania Whitman.

Bird wedding and Hemingway visit: SB to HBD, 23 May 1938; McAlmon's memoirs were largely ignored until the sixties, when they were (in part) reissued: Robert E. Knoll, *McAlmon and the Lost Generation: A Self-Portrait* (1962) and McAlmon and Boyle, *Being Geniuses Together, 1920–1930* (1968).

Norman Douglas visit: Bryher, *Heart to Artemis*, 225; SB to HBD, 7 July 1938; Herrick claims SB did collect toys herself.

Les Déserts: SB to HBD, 7 and 29 July and 26 Sept. 1938; Louise Norledge to SB, 3 Aug. and 27 Sept. 1938; SB to SWB, 13 Sept. and 8 Aug. 1938; Jackson Mathews, *Kenyon Review*, 138.

Eleanor and Priscilla assist: Interviews with Herrick, 7 and 8 Mar. 1978, 4, 6, and 9 Jan. 1979, 14 Feb. 1980, and 23 Feb. 1982; Interview with Priscilla Curtis Barker Veitch, 23 July 1978; SB to HBD, 22 Mar. and 14 June 1938; Priscilla Barker, "Shakespeare and Company," *France / Canada*, 1, No. 4 (Apr.–May 1943), 7.

Legion of Honor: SWB to SB, 15 Oct. 1938; SB to HBD, 22 Mar., 7 July, and 9 Dec. 1938; Henri Hoppenot, "Pendant près d'un Quart de Siècle," *Mercure*, 14; CB to SB, 27 Nov. 1938; SB to CB, 31 July 1919 and 23 Aug. 1938.

Gertrude and Alice return: Barker, *France / Canada*, 7; Interview with Herrick, 8 Mar. 1978; Interview with Veitch, 23 July 1978.

Valéry visit: Barker, *France / Canada*, 7.

Hemingway and Spain: Interview with George Seldes, 23 July 1981; SB to HBD, 12 Oct. 1938; Seldes claims that during a bomb hit, Antoine de Saint-Exupéry hurriedly distributed a box of smuggled oranges he had been hoarding.

Joyce neutral: Paul Léon to HW, 17 Aug. 1938; Carola Giedion-Welcker, "Meetings with JJ," in *Portraits of the Artist in Exile*, 270–71.

Hemingway walks out with books: Interview with Herrick, 7 Mar. 78; SB, who in unpublished drafts of her memoirs mentions incidents of Hemingway's generosity, probably believed he was unaware of her financial plight.

Munich Pact: Louis MacNeice, *Autumn Journal* (London: Faber and Faber, 1939), 30.

Thanksgiving with Americans: Arthur J. Knodel to NRF, 25 Feb. 1981; Interviews with James Briggs (6 July 1978) and Knodel (29 May 1981); Delphine Watteau, "Shakespeare and Company," *Delphian Quarterly,* 21 (Oct. 1938), 47.

Selling Stephen Hero: Interviews with Herrick (4 Jan. 1979) and Marian Willard Johnson (31 Aug. 1980); Herrick to NRF, 21 May 1981 and 19 Nov. 1982; Marian Willard to Herrick, 8 Feb. 1939; Suzanne Currier (Houghton Library) to NRF, 28 Aug. 1981.

19. "HOW IT ENDS?"
1939–1941

Reception of Finnegans Wake: Ellmann, 722; SB to HBD, 15 May 1939; George Andrews to SB, 8 and 12 Nov. 1954.

Moby-Dick translated: a 255-page translation was made in 1928 by Marguerite Gay, but the 1939 translation (552 pages) by Lucien Jacques, Joan Smith, and Jean Giono made *Moby-Dick* an immediate success in France; AM to SB, 12 Aug. 1939; AM, "A Letter to André Gide about the Young" (1942), in McDougall, 410.

Saroyan: William Saroyan, *Letters from 75 Rue Taitbout: or Don't Go, But If You Must, Say Hello to Everybody* (NY: World, 1969), 109–110.

Wilder: Early draft of *SC;* Goldstone, *Thornton Wilder,* 151.

Eleanor and Priscilla: SB to Eleanor Oldenberger, (16?) May and 13 June 1939; Priscilla Curtis to SB, n.d. (Aug. 1939); *SC,* 209; SB to HBD, 15 May 1939.

Gorman biography: the Gorman-JJ correspondence is in Morris Library, Southern Illinois University, Carbondale; Gorman, *JJ,* 286, 285, 321; SB, who lent him photographs, informed HBD (2 May 1949), "Gorman and I are old friends and I like his biography."

Summer of 1939: Janet Flanner, "Gaieté Parisienne," *Paris Was Yesterday,* 220–21; SB to SWB, 7 Aug. 1939; *SC,* 213.

Others flee war: CB to SB, (Nov. or Dec.?) 1939; Interview with James Briggs, 6 July 1978.

Adjusting to war and winter: SB to HBD, 12 Sept. and 10 Dec. 1939 and 9 Jan. 1940; SB to SWB, 4 and 23 Nov. and 30 Dec. 1939.

Joyce in Saint-Gérand-le-Puy: When she expressed sympathy (after having received a detailed letter from JJ concerning Helen), HW was accused by JJ of improper curiosity, Lidderdale and Nicholson, *Dear Miss Weaver,* 377–78 (Miss Weaver destroyed their letters concerning this quarrel); Ellmann, 728.

Bryher and Walter Benjamin: SB to Helen Hoppenot, 2 Mar. 1940; Bryher, *Heart to Artemis,* 289–92, 277; SB to HBD, 6 Mar. 1940.

Surrounded by friends: Jane Van Meter Hineman to SB, 9 Feb. 1940; SB to HBD, 9 Jan. and 6 Mar. 1940; AM to SB, 18 May 1940; SB to Eleanor Oldenberger, 29 Apr. 1940; SB to SWB, 10 May 1940.

Arthur Koestler: Koestler, *The Invisible Writing* (London: Hutchinson, 1969), 512; Koestler, "Un Trèfle à quatre feuilles," (AK to Gisèle Freund, 5 Oct. 1955), *Le Souvenir d'Adrienne Monnier* (Mercure, Apr. 1956), 79–80; AM, "Occupation Journal" (1940), McDougall, 391–93; Koestler to NRF, 24 July 1981.

Walter Benjamin: AM, "Note sur Walter Benjamin" (1952), *Rue de l'Odéon* (Paris: Editions Albin Nickel, 1960), 176–77.

Freund exhibit: SB to HBD, 9 Dec. 1938 and 15 May 1939; AM, "In the Country of Faces" (1939), in McDougall, 231–33.

War approaches: W. H. Auden, "In the Memory of W. B. Yeats," *Collected Poems* (London: Faber and Faber, 1976), 197; SB to SWB, 24 Mar. 1939; CB to SB, 4 Mar. 1939; Carlotta Briggs to SB, 19 Nov. 1939; SB to HBD, 20 Apr. 1939.

Business slows, bombing begins: SB to Bryher, 29 May 1940; Thomson, *Virgil Thomson,* 320; Smoller, *Adrift among Geniuses,* 284; Knoll, *Robert McAlmon,* 351; *SC,* 213–14, and early drafts; AM, "Occupation Journal" (1940) in McDougall, 394–96; Bryher to SB, 11 June 1940; McDougall, 484; Interview with Keeler and Colette Faus, 25 June 1978 and 3 Sept. 1980; AM claims that the Fauses—Colette was an old friend of Marie Monnier Bécat—"lived with us during the first months of the Occupation, then followed the embassy to Vichy, Baden-Baden, to the United States," AM, "Americans in Paris" (1945), in McDougall, 416.

Occupation: AM, "Occupation Journal" (1940), in McDougall, 398–403; *SC,* 215; SB to Adelaide Norledge, 29 Aug. 1940; Eleanor Oldenberger Herrick (interview 4 Jan. 1979) claims that SB was "fiercely pro-Jewish"; Ellmann, 733.

Beach family news: CB to SB, 23 Aug. 1940, and undated (1941) letter; Interview with Helen Eddy, 27 May 1978.

Joyce's end: Leon Edel, *JJ: The Last Journey* (NY: Gotham, 1947), 35; Paul Ruggiero, "JJ's Last Days in Zurich," and Carola Giedion-Welcker, "Meetings with Joyce," in *Portraits of the Artist in Exile,* 285, 278; Ellmann, 734–41; Lord Derwent, "JJ Hail and Farewell," in C[arola] Giedion-Welcker, ed., *In Memoriam JJ* (Zurich: Fretz and Wasmuth, 1941), 15; HW was given total authority in all literary matters relating to the published and unpublished writings of JJ. Her money had helped feed and clothe him, and now it helped bury him. She continued to help support the remaining members of the Joyce family until their deaths (Nora died in 1951, HW in 1961).

Valéry: *SC,* 162, and early drafts; AM, "Lust" (1945), in McDougall, 169–73.

Hoppenot, Bernheim, and the Craigs: SB to MacLeish, 20 Sept. 1940; AM to SB, 31 Dec. 1940 (second letter marked "undeliverable"), Library of Congress; Incidents concerning Violaine Hoppenot, Françoise Bernheim, and the Gordon Craig family were suppressed from *SC* (probably by her editor).

Benoist-Méchin: Interview with Jacques Benoist-Méchin, 10 June 1978.

Saint-John Perse: Perse to AM, 26 Mar. 1948, *SJP Letters* [Alexis Leger], trans. and ed. Arthur J. Knodel (Princeton: Princeton University Press, 1979), 545.

The closing: *SC,* 215–16, and several early drafts; Jackson Mathews, "My Sylvia Beach," *Mercure,* 25; AM, "A Letter to Friends in the Free Zone" (1942), in McDougall, 407; Maurice Saillet to Richard McDougall, 17 July 1975; SB, "Interned," *Mercure,* 136.

20. THE OFFICIAL PERIOD
1942–1962

Epigraph quotation: Recalled by Marcelle Fournier, interview 14 Aug. 1969.

Poulenc opera: AM, "At the Opéra with Francis Poulenc" (1942), in McDougall, 246. In order to affirm his faith in France after her fall, Poulenc dramatized in the opera the seventeenth-century fables of Jean de La Fontaine.

Internment and release: Sarah Watson to Bryher, 9

May 1948, Beinecke Library, Yale; SB, "Interned," *Mercure*, 136–43; Interview with Marcelle Fournier, 14 Aug. 1969; Interview with Jacques Benoist-Méchin, 10 June 1978; *SC*, 216–17, and earlier drafts.

Liberation: SC, 81 (when SB wanted the liberation story cut from her memoirs, her editor, Margaret Marshall, insisted she keep the episode); AM, "Americans in Paris" (1945), in McDougall, 416–17; Interview with Maurice Saillet, 1 Aug. 1969; Saillet to McDougall, 25 Mar. 1975 (kindly summarized by McDougall); NRF, *Fitzgerald/Hemingway Annual, 1977*, 172–74.

Former customers: Leon Edel to NRF, 20 May 1981; Edel, introd. to Glassco, *Memoirs of Montparnasse*, ix; David Scherman to NRF, 16 May 1978; Interview with Keeler Faus, 25 June 1978; Interview with Janet Flanner, 29 July 1977.

Pressure to reopen: Connolly, "Comment," in the "News out of France" issue of *Horizon*, May 1945, 304; Eliot, "Miss Sylvia Beach," *Mercure*, 9; SB to HBD, 17 June 1945; Saillet, "Mots et Locutions de Sylvia," *Mercure*, 9; Art Buchwald, *New York Herald Tribune*, 13 Mar. 1959.

Life in the forties: SB to HBD, 1 Apr. 1947, 17 June 1945, 19 Feb. 1946, and 4 Dec. 1947; SB to Bryher, 22 Nov. 1945 and (?) Apr. 1949; As editor of a new poetry series for the *Mercure*, AM published a volume of Bonnefoy's poetry; Interview with Joseph Barry, 12 June 1978; W. D. Rogers (brought by Stein) later published a book about these and other women of the arts, *Ladies Bountiful* (NY: Harcourt, Brace and World, 1968).

Translating: SB to HBD, 7 May and 10 June 1948; AM, "Return to London" (1953), in McDougall, 328–34; SB to Bryher, 24 June 1948; Eliot to SB, 31 May 1948; SB to HBD, 19 Nov. 1947 and 12 Feb. 1948; Sylvia contacted numerous friends for books on mescaline for Michaux, who wrote two volumes under its influence; Joseph Barry reviewed the Michaux book and the party for the *NY Times Review of Books*, 11 Sept. 1949.

Joyce Business: Flanner, *Paris Journal*, 111–12; The JJ society was organized on 3 Feb. 1947, in the Gotham Book Mart, in NYC; SB to HBD, 21 Jan. 1947; 24 May 1947, and 2 May 1949; When Gilbert's volume of JJ letters appeared, in 1957, SB typed a list of corrections, including her introduction of Larbaud to JJ, on Christmas Eve of 1920, and JJ's invisible pulling of strings, which his letters appear to deny; SB to HBD, 7 June 1949; SB to Archibald MacLeish, n.d. (Miss Weaver rejected all proposals to stage JJ's work); William Robert Rogers collected many impressions from JJ associates (SB insisted that AM be included), SB to HBD, 7 July 1949; SB to W. R. Rogers, 1 Nov. 1949; SB to Jackson Mathews, 22 Apr. 1958; Lidderdale and Nicholson, *Dear Miss Weaver*, 410; After the death of Nora in 1951, HW sent the *Finnegans Wake* manuscript to the British Library.

Cyprian's death: Interview with Helen Eddy, 27 May 1978.

New York and London: Donald Allen to SB, 22 Aug. 1953; AM gave a detailed description of the London trip in "The Coronation of Elizabeth II," *Lettres Nouvelles*, July 1953—*LN* was edited by Saillet—in McDougall, 335–46.

Death of Adrienne: Interview with Helen Eddy, 27 May 1978; SB to Bryher, 20 June 1955; SB to HW, 1 July 1955; Jackson Mathews, *Kenyon Review*, 141; AM's note in McDougall, 64–65; Holograph note in SB Papers; After the burial, SB and Marie Monnier went to visit Bryher and then Carlotta in Bourée—SB dreaded

returning to Paris with AM gone, SB to HW, 15 Dec. 1955; Stephen Longstreet, *We All Went to Paris: Americans in the City of Light, 1776–1971* (NY: Macmillan, 1972), 348.

Joyce scholarship: The collector and bibliographer John Slocum, Prof. Richard M. Kain (who rented a mezzanine room) and Prof. Richard Ellmann were among those who pursued the life and work of JJ in a manner that SB thought worse than stamp collecting. Ellmann, whom she had last seen in uniform after the war, climbed to Les Déserts in the summer of 1953, only to be unceremoniously shooed away; SB to HW, 2 Feb. 1955; Interview with Ellmann, 16 Mar. 1981; On advice from friends (SB believed his "Prescutting" of her JJ material would devalue her collection) she ejected Joseph Prescott, who accused her of ruining his career and secured first priority rights (when the JJ papers were sold) from HW (who controlled the rights); SB to HW, 9 Apr. 1957, and HW to SB, 28 Apr. 1957; When the appraiser Bertram Rota took a number of her books to England to sell, Jackson Mathews immediately took SB and two suitcases to London and collected the books; Interview with Jackson Mathews (May 1969) and Marthiel Mathews (18 July 1978).

Publication of memoirs: SB to Hemingway, 29 Aug. 1956, Kennedy Library; SB to Bryher, 18 May 1959; Bryher to SB, 23 Sept. 1959 (Bryher believed that SB had "idealized" her); Margaret Marshall of Harcourt, Brace organized the sections that SB sent her; Ironically, SB, who had allowed her author numerous proofs on which to change and to add a third of *Ulysses*, paid HB $242.77 for making minor changes; Cyril Connolly, "A Rendezvous for Writers," *Mercure*, 162.

Joyce collection to Buffalo: From 9 Dec. 1959 to 1 Mar. 1960, the University of Buffalo (now SUNY) proudly displayed its valuable Joyce collection; the 450 items (20,000 written pages) are catalogued by Peter Spielberg in *JJ Manuscripts and Letters at the University of Buffalo* (1962).

Twenties exhibit: Though Morrill Cody wished to feature the bistros, music, and Josephine Baker, SB was firm on presenting a literary exhibition; Interviews with Maurice Saillet and Helen Baltrusaitis (1 Aug. 1969) and Darthea Speyer (9 June 1978); SB to HBD, (?) Dec. 1958; SB to Margaret Marshall, 5 Dec. 1958; Thornton Wilder to NRF, 22 May 1969; Janet Flanner, *Paris Journal: 1944–1965*, ed. William Shawn (NY: Atheneum, 1965), 413–16.

Final years: The Sylvia Beach Papers, purchased by Princeton University in 1964 from HBD, were considerable, comprising thousands of letters, pictures, library borrowers' cards, original manuscripts, first editions, rare books, and bookshop records; SB to Justin O'Brien, 7 July 1962, Columbia University; JJ Tower Committee minutes, Frances Steloff Papers, Berg Collection, NY Public Library; John Gale, "Joyce Was so Easily Shocked," *Observer*, 17 June 1962.

Death: Interviews with Keeler and Colette Faus (25 June 1978) and Darthea Speyer (9 June 1978); Faus diary, 13 Oct. 1932; David Schneider to NRF, 30 Apr. 1969; In his memorial to Sylvia (London *Times*, 14 Oct. 1962), Cyril Connolly also recalled her "unquenchable irony and . . . permanent airy chuckle"; McDougall, 65; Rev. Donald M. Meisel to NRF, 4 Nov. 1977; Archibald MacLeish, "What One Remembers . . . ," *Mercure*, 35; "My wife and I," says MacLeish, "walked down the rue de l'Odéon at the time when, as ! subsequently learned, she was lying dead on the floor of her apartment," MacLeish to NRF, 11 Apr. 1969.

INDEX